THE BEST PLAYS OF 1985–1986

THE
BURNS MANTLE
YEARBOOK

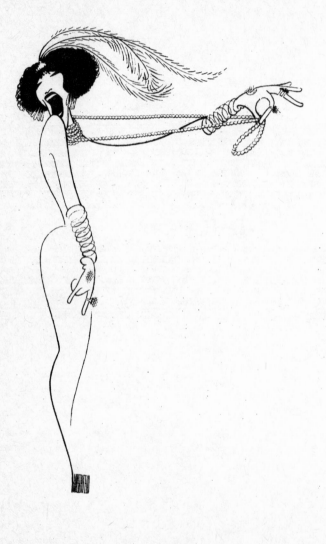

THE
BEST PLAYS
OF 1985-1986

EDITED BY OTIS L. GUERNSEY JR. AND JEFFREY SWEET

*Illustrated with photographs and
with drawings by* HIRSCHFELD

○○○○○○

DODD, MEAD & COMPANY, INC.

NEW YORK

EDITOR'S NOTE

THE FIRST TIME I reviewed a Broadway show was April 29, 1943 for the now-defunct but much regretted New York *Herald Tribune.* The show, *The First Million,* was very short-lived. I was a reporter (not a regularly practicing critic) on special assignment and had no inkling at the time how long my play-reviewing career might run. Now, in 1986, I feel as though I have covered at least my first million Broadway, off-Broadway, off-off-Broadway, regional and foreign stage productions, so the title of that first show was more prophetic than I could know.

The point is, I've had my say; and though I don't promise never again to review a single play or whole New York theater season, I've passed the specific assignment of covering and reviewing the Broadway and off-Broadway theater for *The Best Plays of 1985–86* to a supremely able colleague, Jeffrey Sweet, who has worked with me on many projects (including contributions to the *Best Plays* volumes) over the past 16 years. He is a seasoned reporter (for the *Dramatists Guild Quarterly*), critic (cf., his book on improvisation, *Something Wonderful Right Away*), teacher (of playwrights in New York City and elsewhere), a member of the Tony Awards nominating committee and withal a frequently produced playwright whose *Porch, The Value of Names, Ties* and other works have appeared on New York and regional stages and on TV. I will continue as editor-in-chief of these Best Plays volumes, with continuing input into the choice of the ten Best Plays, but as associate editor, Mr. Sweet will take on most of that responsibility and all of the reportorial and critical function in this volume's Broadway and off-Broadway coverage.

Also in this 1985–86 *Best Plays* yearbook, the order of the contents has been rearranged in a more logical and compact presentation of each area of critical and reference concern. Instead of separating text summaries and factual listing, as in the past, here they are collected in the following order of four principal sections: 1. Broadway and off Broadway (including Jeffrey Sweet's report, Al Hirschfeld's drawings, the Best Plays, listings of casts and credits and Stanley Green's replacements); 2. Off off Broadway (including Mel Gussow's report and selections of outstanding productions, and Camille Croce's listing); 3. Cross-country theater (including the three ATCA citations and Sheridan Sweet's new-play listing); and 4. Facts and figures as before (runs, awards, publications, necrology and past Best Plays).

The 1985–86 *Best Plays* content itself won't change in any way except as it always has: ever widening its grasp. In addition to his annual survey of the off-off-Broadway scene, Mel Gussow has selected outstanding 1985–86 productions for special attention in those pages. Since both the Gussow selections were principally performance rather than scripted works, they are represented with photos instead of excerpts from their scripts. The latter, on the other hand, is the way in which a trio of outstanding cross-country productions, selected by a committee of the American Theater Critics Association under the chairmanship of Lawrence DeVine of the Detroit *Free Press,* is celebrated in these pages. And Camille Croce and Sheridan (Mrs. Jeffrey) Sweet have once again assembled their uniquely comprehensive data on OOB programs and new works in cross-country theaters, respectively, which, together with the Broadway and off-Broadway listings, are the all-important staple of the *Best Plays* annual reference coverage.

Stanley Green's list of major cast replacements in New York, Rue E. Canvin's necrology and publications list, William Schelble's Tony Awards facts, Richard Hummler's New York Drama Critics Circle record of the voting, Best Plays synopses by Sally Dixon Wiener and Jeffrey Sweet, historical footnotes by Thomas T. Foose and research on long-run statistics by Arne Brucker are some of the direct, invaluable contributions to this 67th volume in the series in continuous publication by Dodd, Mead & Company beginning with the 1919–20 season. Equally appreciated are the continuing, indispensable efforts of Jonathan Dodd supervising the publication; the editor's faithful wife painstakingly assisting in preparing the text (which of course couldn't be assembled in the first place without the help of the scores of men and women in the producers' press offices, who are as much the *auteurs* of this project as anyone); and the continuous, informal, consultational help of Henry Hewes, Dorothy Swerdlove, Ralph Newman of the Drama Book Shop, Robert Nahas of the Theater Arts Book Shop and Glenn Young of Applause Books.

The graphics, too, are a special asset for which we are enormously grateful: Al Hirschfeld's incomparable drawings defining as they do each theater season; the sketches of outstanding scene designs by Tony Walton and costume designs by Lindsay W. Davis; and the photos by Martha Swope and her associates (Susan Cook and Carol Rosegg) and Bert Andrews, Stephen Aucoin, Richard Carter, William B. Carter, Peter Cunningham, Carl Davis, Michael F. Donadio, Howard Dratch, Kenn Duncan, T. Charles Erickson, Gerry Goodstein, Henry Grossman, Ken Howard, JWL, Brigitte Lacombe, Joan Marcus, Marion Valentine, Adam Newman, Alan Pappé, Michael Romanos, Norman Seeff, Gary W. Sweetman and Jerry Vezzuso.

And last but first, there are the plays themselves which, contrary to the convictions of some, were *not* created by the actors speaking the lines, but by an act of faith and courage on the part of the playwrights, composers, lyricists and librettists who dared to face up to the challenge of a blank piece of paper and provided us with a New York theater season on, off and off off Broadway, from the Best Plays to the abysmal flops. To them we owe our most profound gratitude for their persistence as well as for their talent in making possible a living theater of new growth in the discouraging economic and artistic environment of the 1980s —and yes, we include in our gratitude those authors who couldn't get a play on in the season of 1985–86 for one reason or another but will surely make it into the stage and thus provide us with yet another season of theater in the twelve months to come.

OTIS L. GUERNSEY Jr.

July 1, 1986

CONTENTS

THE SEASON
ON AND OFF
BROADWAY

AUNT DAN AND LEMON—In the title roles of Wallace Shawn's play are (*above,* in the English cast) Linda Hunt (Aunt Dan) and Kathryn Pogson; and (*below,* in the American cast) Kathy Whitton Baker (*foreground,* Lemon) and Pamela Reed

BROADWAY AND OFF BROADWAY

By Jeffrey Sweet

EVERY YEAR, millions of Americans turn on their televisions to watch the Tony Awards show under the impression that what they are seeing represents the best of New York theater. The awards, of course, represent only Broadway, and Broadway long ago stopped being where most of the theatrical action is.

Certainly one didn't look to Broadway this season for much by way of new plays and musicals. As if uncertain how to engage the present in dramatic terms, in one way or another Broadway repackaged the past. The happy consequences of this were the best of the revivals, including first-rate stagings of *Blood Knot*, *The House of Blue Leaves* and *Hay Fever*. The discouraging aspect was the series of musicals and musical entertainments with recycled scores. *Jerry's Girls*, *Uptown . . . It's Hot!*, *Jerome Kern Goes to Hollywood* and *Singin' in the Rain* all had pleasures to offer, but new songs were not among them. Even *Big Deal*, the so-called new musical conceived and directed by Bob Fosse, featured old songs, albeit in new contexts. Two works from seasons past provided most of the musical theater excitement this season: a slambang revival of the Bob Fosse–Neil Simon–Cy Coleman–Dorothy Fields 1966 collaboration, *Sweet Charity*, and the two-day run at Lincoln Center's Avery Fisher Hall of a concert version of the Stephen Sondheim–James Goldman–Hal Prince–Michael Bennett epic, *Follies*. Organized to produce a new recording of the Sondheim score, the *Follies* concert served as a reminder of the glories Broadway musical theater writing can achieve. A reminder and a reproach, for no new score on Broadway this season came anywhere near the standard Sondheim set in that and many of his other shows. However, a few of the numbers in *The Mystery of Edwin Drood*—easily the best new musical of the Broadway season and a Best Play—indicated that author-lyricist-composer-orchestrator Rupert Holmes may well do fine things in the future. As for new plays, though occasional scenes and themes tantalized (in the cases of Michael Frayn's *Benefactors*, Emily Mann's *Execution of Justice* and Herb Gardner's *I'm Not Rappaport*, sufficiently to merit citations as Best Plays), again Broadway presented little new work of sustained satisfaction.

Owing to the efforts of some talented composers and lyricists (if not book writers), the musical season off Broadway was somewhat better than on, but the best news was the number of provocative straight plays which premiered, about which more below. Off Broadway also hosted a number of revivals; one could quibble with the advisability of some of these projects, but almost always there were performances to savor.

As has come to be expected from seasons past, much of the new material on

New York stages originated elsewhere. As usual, there were a number of British plays: *Benefactors*, *Season's Greetings*, *A Map of the World*, *Corpse!* and *Not About Heroes*. Also plays from Canada (*Quiet in the Land*) and Czechoslovakia (*Largo Desolato*). Quite a few of the new scripts arrived by way of regional theaters; among the companies who got the jump on New York on one or more offerings this season were Long Wharf, the Philadelphia Drama Guild, San Francisco's Eureka Theater, Actors Theater of Louisville, the Arena Stage, the Guthrie, Baltimore's Center Stage, Theater Cornell, Seattle's Empty Space, the San Jose Rep, the Berkeley Rep, the Seattle Rep, the Cleveland Play House, the Williamstown Theater Festival, the New Theater Company of Chicago, Yale Rep, South Coast Rep, the Alliance Theater of Atlanta and the Burt Reynolds Jupiter Theater in Florida. At the Joyce Theater, a house which usually hosts dance troupes, a subscription series of productions from three regional companies was presented under the sponsorship of the American Theater Exchange. Two of these were productions of new American scripts; Adrian Hall and Robert Woodruff's adaptation of Jack Henry Abbott's *In the Belly of the Beast* was from the Mark Taper Forum (other versions had been produced at the Trinity Square Rep in Providence and Chicago's Wisdom Bridge) and Heather McDonald's *Faulkner's Bicycle* hailed from Yale. The third production was the aforementioned *Season's Greetings*, a Best Play by Alan Ayckbourn offered by Houston's Alley Theater. As if to balance the New York premiere of a British play by an American company, off Broadway also saw the New York premiere of an American play originally produced by a British company, Wallace Shawn's *Aunt Dan and Lemon*, which began its life at London's Royal Court before moving to New York's Public Theater.

The Public Theater, under the artistic direction of Joseph Papp, proved to be the most vital and artistically successful producing organization of the season. Three of the season's Best Plays, *Aunt Dan and Lemon*, Vaclav Havel's *Largo Desolato* and Rupert Holmes's aforementioned *The Mystery of Edwin Drood* were given under its sponsorship. In addition there were a remarkable *Hamlet* starring Kevin Kline, two provocative if ultimately unsatisfying plays on political subjects —*A Map of the World* and *Rum and Coke*—the debut of a promising young writer with *Jonin'*, Robert DeNiro's return to the stage in *Cuba and His Teddy Bear* and a *Measure for Measure* in Central Park.

Two companies which had introduced distinguished new plays in the past had disappointing seasons. Neither Circle Rep nor the Negro Ensemble Company found material to match the excellences of their actors. Two of the Circle Rep productions were revisions by resident playwright Lanford Wilson of problematic scripts, *Talley & Son* (previously titled *A Tale Told*) and *The Mound Builders*. (It was left to an off-off-Broadway troupe, the Second Stage, to give Wilson his most satisfying staging of the season, an inspired version of his early play *Lemon Sky* which, heartbreakingly, did not transfer to a commercial run because the cast could not be reassembled.)

The Manhattan Theater Club fared better. A revival of Paul Osborn's *Oliver Oliver* and John Patrick Shanley's *Women of Manhattan* found little favor, but substantial chunks of Richard Nelson's *Principia Scriptoriae* were admired, and Terrence McNally's Best Play *It's Only a Play* and a revival of Joe Orton's black

The 1985–86 Season on Broadway

PLAYS (7)

I'M NOT RAPPAPORT
(transfer)
The Boys of Winter
Execution of Justice
Precious Sons
So Long on Lonely Street
Social Security
The Boys in Autumn

MUSICALS (7)

Singin' in the Rain
Song & Dance
Mayor
(transfer)
The News
**THE MYSTERY OF
EDWIN DROOD**
(transfer)
Wind in the Willows
Big Deal

REVUES (3)

Jerry's Girls
Jerome Kern Goes to
Hollywood
Uptown . . . It's Hot!

FOREIGN PLAYS IN
ENGLISH (3)

BENEFACTORS
Corpse
The Petition

FOREIGN-LANGUAGE
PRODUCTIONS (5)

Italy on Stage:
La Gatta Cenerentola
I Due Sergenti
Pipino Il Breve
Il Campiello
Tango Argentino

REVIVALS (11)

The Odd Couple
(revised version)
Follies
(concert version)
The Iceman Cometh
Circle in the Square:
The Marriage of Figaro
The Caretaker
Blood Knot
Hay Fever
Loot
(transfer)
Sweet Charity
Long Day's Journey
Into Night
The House of Blue Leaves
(transfer)

SPECIALTIES (6)

The Grand Kabuki
(two programs)
*The Search for Signs of
Intelligent Life in the
Universe.*
The Magnificent Christmas
Spectacular
The Robert Klein Show
Lillian
Juggling and Cheap
Theatrics

HOLDOVER WHICH
BECAME A HIT IN
1985–86

Big River

Categorized above are all the new productions listed in the Plays Produced on Broadway section of this volume.
Plays listed in CAPITAL LETTERS have been designated Best Plays of 1985–86.
Plays listed in *italics* were still running after June 1, 1986.
Plays listed in **bold face type** were classified as successes in *Variety*'s annual estimate published June 4, 1986.

farce *Loot* were generally well received (*Loot*, in fact, moved to Broadway). Playwrights Horizons stumbled with an original musical called *Paradise*, an absurdist farce called *Anteroom* and a meditation on contemporary parenting called *Little Footsteps* but scored solidly with one of the true delights of the season, A.R. Gurney Jr.'s Best Play, *The Perfect Party*.

Circle in the Square had limited success this season, beginning with Andrei Serban's staging of Richard Nelson's adaptation of Beaumarchais' *The Marriage of Figaro*, followed by a co-production with Chicago's Steppenwolf troupe of Harold Pinter's *The Caretaker* and the New York premiere of Bernard Sabath's *The Boys in Autumn*. Revivals, as usual, also dominated Roundabout's schedule, most notably productions of *Mrs. Warren's Profession* and *Room Service*.

New York theater's continuing soap opera, the Lincoln Center operation, returned this season with a new leading player, company director Gregory Mosher. Recruited from the directorship of Chicago's Goodman Theater (where, in the 1983–84 season, he originated the productions of Best Plays *Glengarry Glen Ross* and *Hurlyburly* which subsequently flourished on Broadway), Mosher started his administration unprepossessingly downstairs in the Mitzi E. Newhouse Theater by staging a bill of modest one-acts by his longtime collaborator, David Mamet. Things picked up considerably with a smash revival of John Guare's Best Play *The House of Blue Leaves,* which was transferred from the Newhouse to the Vivian Beaumont upstairs. The company also sponsored offerings as so-called sideshows—monologuist Spalding Gray in three full-length pieces and the return of the Flying Karamazov Brothers and their special blend of comedy and juggling.

Who were this season's plays about? There were the usual (and frequently autobiographical) meditations on the state of the American family (e.g., *Precious Sons*, *A Lie of the Mind*, *Little Footsteps*, *So Long on Lonely Street* and *Daughters*). Quite a few plays reflected writers' perennial obsession with writers (among them, *Faulkner's Bicycle*, *It's Only a Play*, *Not About Heroes*, *Lillian*, *The News*, *Rum and Coke*, *Gertrude Stein and a Companion*). Teachers were central to the action in *Aunt Dan and Lemon*, *The Perfect Party* and *Largo Desolato*. Assorted criminals, street people and sleazies populated *Big Deal*, *Drinking in America*, *The Shawl*, *Execution of Justice*, *House of Shadows*, *In the Belly of the Beast*, and *The Search For Signs of Intelligent Life in the Universe* among others. *I'm Not Rappaport*, *The Petition* and *The Boys in Autumn* dealt with pairs of elderly characters trying to sort out their pasts and presents. There were also politicians (*Jonah and the Wonder Dog*, *Map of the World*, *Eyes of the American*), an architect (*Benefactors*), a platoon of soldiers (*The Boys of Winter*) and, inevitably, many actors and other theatrical types. There was also a trend for musicals to feature singing animals among their *dramatis personae*. None of these anthropomorphic efforts—*Just So*, *Hamelin* and *Wind in the Willows*—offered much reason for the trend to continue.

Speaking of trends, live video was featured in four productions this season—*Execution of Justice*, *In the Belly of the Beast*, *The News* and the Circle Rep revival of Camus's *Caligula*—in no case to advantage. The metaphoric nature of the theater didn't mix well with the literalness of TV images. Whenever the monitors blinked on, the stage seemed to shrink. A fifth show, *Cuba and His Teddy Bear* mixed the stage and video in another combination. Because of Robert DeNiro's presence in the cast, the limited engagement sold out quickly. To oblige more of the public, Joseph Papp set up a monitor in another room where those sufficiently desperate could watch a live closed-circuit broadcast for $7. Ah, what memories those theatergoers will have to share with their children! ("I actually saw Robert DeNiro in a play on the stage on TV!")

If the season was less than memorable for new plays, there was no lack of star power. Many well-established names from the worlds of film and television chose to take the challenge of acting in front of live audiences again, among them Ed Harris, Robert DeNiro, Jack Lemmon, George C. Scott, Judd Hirsch, Glenn Close, Sam Waterston, Kevin Kline, Mark Hamill, Lily Tomlin, Christopher Reeve, James Coco, Jason Robards, Stockard Channing, Christopher Walken, Kevin Bacon, Marlo Thomas and Matt Dillon. The season was also graced by such welcome and familiar theatrical faces as Rosemary Harris, Mary Beth Hurt, Joseph Maher, Harvey Keitel, Lindsay Crouse, Judith Ivey, Zoe Caldwell, John Cullum, Elizabeth Wilson, Linda Hunt, Danny Aiello, Zakes Mokae, Milo O'Shea, Keith Baxter, Marcia Rodd, Douglas Turner Ward, George Grizzard, Jan Miner, Marian Seldes, Frances Foster, Charles Kimbrough, Barnard Hughes, Dorothy Loudon, Chita Rivera, Leslie Uggams, Ann Wedgeworth, Ron Silver, George Rose, Betty Buckley, Edward Herrmann and Peter MacNicol, among many others. Some actors found time to be in more than one project, among them Swoosie Kurtz, Zeljko Ivanek, Geraldine Page, Pamela Reed, Harris Yulin, Mark Blum, Joanna Gleason, Mike Nussbaum and Anthony Heald. One actor, Keith Reddin, managed to simultaneously co-star in *Room Service* and participate in the New York premiere of his play *Rum and Coke*. Reddin's role in *Room Service*? The young playwright, of course.

SINGIN' IN THE RAIN—Don Correia and Faye Grant *(center)* as silent film stars in the stage version of the Comden & Green film musical

Several figures this season fulfilled more than one function on their productions. A number of dramatists appeared in their own works—Athol Fugard starring in (and directing) *Blood Knot*, Carol Hall among the ensemble of *To Whom it May Concern*, Eric Bogosian in *Drinking in America*, Spalding Gray in his monologues and Wallace Shawn featured in *Aunt Dan and Lemon*. Fugard was not the only writer to direct his own material; others included Emily Mann of *Execution of Justice*, David Hare of *A Map of the World*, Sam Shepard of *A Lie of the Mind*, Bob Fosse of *Big Deal* and Richard Maltby, Jr., who, in addition to staging Andrew Lloyd Webber's *Song & Dance*, augmented Don Black's original lyrics with new lyrics of his own.

The busiest director in town this season had to be John Tillinger, who staged *Loot* and *It's Only a Play* at the Manhattan Theater Club, *The Perfect Party* at Playwrights Horizons and *Corpse!* on Broadway (in addition to a trim production of Philip Barry's *Paris Bound* at Long Wharf in New Haven, where he is literary manager). Circle Rep's artistic director Marshall W. Mason directed three productions at his theater, the two Lanford Wilson plays and *Caligula*. Several productions were directed by figures also known as actors, notably Brian Murray, Geraldine Fitzgerald, Jerry Zaks, John Malkovich and Dianne Wiest. Some of the best-respected directors in the business had disappointments this season, including Mike Nichols, Bob Fosse, Melvin Bernhardt and Michael Lindsay-Hogg. These disappointments were offset to some degree by the appearance of relatively new directing talent such as Andre Robinson Jr., who did a splendid job of creating disciplined chaos in *Jonin'*, and Paul Lazarus, who, with the gifted choreographer D.J. Giagni, did nimble work on the off-Broadway revue *Personals*.

Not surprisingly, there was not always a correlation between the quality of the scripts and the sets on which they were played. Set designer David Mitchell and lighting designer Pat Collins conjured up an extraordinary vision of hell on earth for John Pielmeier's Vietnam drama *The Boys of Winter*. Michael Merritt's designs of a smoking car at night and a slightly seedy Chicago apartment distinguished the production of the Mamet double bill. David Potts's Connecticut getaway in *The Beach House* (lit by Dennis Parichy and Mal Sturchio) and Tony Walton's evocation of Central Park for *I'm Not Rappaport* (also featuring Pat Collins's lighting) created worlds into which many of the audience would have happily strayed. Walton, in association with lighting designer Paul Gallo, did brilliant work with another New York subject, would-be songwriter Artie Shaughnessy's apartment, and the neighborhood and city that pressed in on it in *The House of Blue Leaves*. John Lee Beatty designed several plays for Circle Rep and the Manhattan Theater Club this year. He and lighting designer Parichy scored a particular success with his adroit use of projections in *The Mound Builders*.

As happy a task as it is to honor other artists of the theater, the Best Plays annual's primary responsibility is the honoring of plays and playwrights. This season the job was complicated by a matter of definition. Where should one draw the line between a play and performance art or dance? This question, at the heart of controversy regarding eligibility for both the Tony Awards and the Pulitzer Prize (discussed below), came to a head in weighing the eligibility of Eric

Bogosian's *Drinking in America* and Spalding Gray's *Terrors of Pleasure*—both of which featured their author-performers in compelling solo works—as Best Plays. After much soul-searching, the editors decided that, for the purposes of this book, *Drinking in America* is a play and *Terrors of Pleasure* is not. The distinction lies between what is metaphor and what is actuality. A play is not the presentation of real actions, it is the representation of actions. Using the actor's art, Bogosian represented a variety of characters, inhabiting the souls of people other than himself. Spalding Gray, on the other hand, presented himself as a person sitting on a stage, directly addressing the audience about his experiences, and that, in fact, was what he was. (This, of course, opens up the question of whether the same material would be a play if performed by somebody else. Interesting question. Can we get back to you on that?)

Regarding the principles under which the Best Plays are chosen, as Otis L. Guernsey, Jr. has noted in past editions, "Each Best Play selection is now made with the script itself as the first consideration, for the reason that the script is the spirit of the theater's physical manifestation. It is not only the quintessence of the present, it is most of what endures into the future. So the Best Plays are the best scripts, with as little weight as humanly possible given to comparative production values. The choice is made without any regard whatever to a play's type— musical, comedy or drama—or origin on or off Broadway, or popularity at the box office, or lack of same.

"We don't take the scripts of bygone eras into consideration for the Best Play citation in this one, whatever their technical status as American or New York 'premieres' which didn't happen to have a previous production of record. We draw the line between adaptations and revivals, the former eligible for Best Play selection but the latter not, on a case-by-case basis. We likewise consider the eligibility of borderline examples of limited-engagement and showcase production case by case, ascertaining whether they're probably 'frozen' in final script version and no longer works in progress before considering them for Best Play citation (and in the case of a late-season arrival the determination may not be possible until the following year).

"If a script influences the character of a season, or by some function of consensus wins the Critics, Pulitzer or Tony Awards, we take into account its future historical as well as present esthetic importance. This is the only special consideration we give, and we don't always tilt in its direction, as the record shows."

The Best Plays of 1985–86 are listed below for visual convenience in the order in which they opened in New York (a plus sign + with the performance numbers signifies that the play was still running after June 1, 1986).

I'm Not Rappaport
(Off B'way, 181 perfs.; B'way, 223 + perfs.)

Season's Greetings
(Off B'way, 20 perfs.)

The Mystery of Edwin Drood
(Off B'way, 24 perfs.; B'way, 208 + perfs.)

Aunt Dan and Lemon
(Off B'way, 191 + perfs.)

Benefactors
(B'way, 185 + perfs.)

It's Only a Play
(Off B'way, 17 perfs.)

Drinking in America
(Off B'way, 94 perfs.)

Execution of Justice
  (B'way, 12 perfs.)

Largo Desolato
  (Off B'way, 40 perfs.)

The Perfect Party
  (Off B'way, 70+ perfs.)

Goblin Market (special citation)
  (Off B'way, 57+ perfs.)

New Plays

A heartening number of the season's new scripts addressed social and political issues. Only a handful of these could be called successful, but the others tended to stumble in fascinating and thought-provoking ways.

Wallace Shawn's *Aunt Dan and Lemon* was one of the season's most controversial works. Lemon, a sickly English girl, has long talks with a family friend nicknamed Aunt Dan, during which Dan inculcates the impressionable child with her values. Dan worships people who are effective, people who have the strength to overcome obstacles—such as the conventions of civilized behavior—and *do* things. The morality of the things they do seems to be of less compelling interest to her. Among the figures who excite her admiration are Henry Kissinger and a prostitute named Mindy, who, in a graphically staged flashback, cheerfully carries out a commission to murder one of her clients. Dan teaches her lesson so

THE PETITION—Jessica Tandy and Hume Cronyn in Brian Clark's play

well that, when she becomes critically ill and consequently is unable to "do" herself, Lemon abandons her. At the end of the play, though Aunt Dan is gone, her influence lives on. Lemon, older but not wiser, addresses a final speech to the audience in which she harnesses her mentor's philosophy in a defense of Nazi genocide.

What made the play unpalatable to many in the audience was the lack of an effective (effective!) rebuttal to Aunt Dan's arguments, a lack which led some to believe that Shawn endorses the values of his title characters. But the days in which a dramatist's own position is necessarily reflected in dialogue are over. There was nobody on the stage in *Aunt Dan and Lemon* to tell the audience, "And the moral of the story is . . ." Rather, Shawn's game was to provoke us to respond with our own arguments. Shawn was stating the outrageous to outrage us, to goad us to rebut. Much as a vaccine introduces a weakened form of a disease into the system so as to stimulate the production of antibodies, Shawn presented Dan's moral disease so as to stimulate the production of our ethical antibodies. This is not to claim that the play was perfect; the horror of some of the arguments was blunted by unnecessary repetition. Still, *Aunt Dan and Lemon* was a bracing experience and clearly one of the genuinely important new plays of the year.

Also political and provocative was *A Map of the World*. Written and directed by David Hare (author and director of the Best Play *Plenty*), it told the story of a run-in between a young left-wing British journalist named Stephen Andrews and a conservative expatriate Indian novelist named Victor Mehta. Both arrive in Bombay for a UNESCO conference on poverty, Andrews to cover it, Mehta to address it. Some of the Third World representatives to the conference, having seen their governments lampooned in the novelist's books, threaten to disrupt the proceedings unless Mehta agrees to precede his speech by a disclaimer they have had drafted. Co-written by Andrews, the disclaimer contends that fiction, being by definition a product of the imagination, bears too little resemblance to the real world to merit serious consideration in geopolitical discussion. Strongly believing that, to the contrary, fiction is a tool in the service of truth, Mehta refuses to read the statement.

At this juncture, a beautiful movie actress named Peggy Whitton (who, conveniently, is in the neighborhood, has a background in philosophy and has attracted the romantic attentions of both the journalist and the novelist) steps forward to suggest that the matter be decided by a debate between Andrews and Mehta to be judged by a black American newswoman. To add spice to the situation, Miss Whitton proposes her favors as a prize for the winner. Though this development is patently contrived, the first act was so tantalizing that one was more than happy to grant Hare suspension of disbelief in exchange for the promised fireworks of the second. Alas, the fireworks failed to materialize. Having frustrated the appetite he whetted for a rigorous contest, Hare then short-circuits his own dramatic device by having Andrews withdraw from the contest. One couldn't help feeling that the dramatist felt compelled to resort to this so as not to have to choose a winner. Hare's production made the most of his script's strengths, however, featuring first-rate performances by Roshan Seth as Mehta, Zeljko Ivanek as Andrews and Ving Rhames as an African politician.

Richard Nelson's *Principia Scriptoriae* bore more than a passing resemblance

The 1985–86 Season Off Broadway

PLAYS (38)

PH 1985:
Fighting International Fat
Raw Youth
I'M NOT RAPPAPORT
In the Belly of the Beast
For Sale
Theater in Limbo:
 *Vampire Lesbians of
 Sodom & Sleeping
 Beauty or Coma*
Times Square Angel
Two Can Play
 (return engagement)
The Custom of the Country
Circle Rep:
 Tomorrow's Monday
 The Beach House
 Alice and Fred
NEC:
 Eyes of the American
 House of Shadows
 Jonah and the Wonder
  Dog
 Louie and Ophelia
Public Theater:
 AUNT DAN AND
  LEMON
 Jonin'
 Rum and Coke
 Cuba and His Teddy Bear

PH 1986:
Anteroom
Little Footsteps
THE PERFECT PARTY
Inside Out
CSC:
 Frankenstein
 A Country Doctor
 A Lie of the Mind
 Prairie du Chien & The
  Shawl
Be Happy for Me
Gertrude Stein and a
 Companion
MTC:
 IT'S ONLY A PLAY
 Principia Scriptoriae
 Women of Manhattan
 Another Paradise
 Daughters
 Orchards
 Smoking Newports, etc.
 A Place Called Heartbreak

MUSICALS (11)

Options
THE MYSTERY OF
 EDWIN DROOD
Paradise!

REVIVALS (36)

Dames at Sea
Measure for Measure
LOOM:
 Sweethearts
 (10 operettas in running
  repertory)
Springtime for Henry
Curse of the Starving Class
Circle Rep:
 Talley & Son
  (revised version)
 The Mound Builders
 Caligula
Roundabout:
 The Waltz of the
  Toreadors
 Mrs. Warren's Profession
 Room Service
 Tatterdemalion
CSC:
 Brand
 A Medieval Mystery
  Cycle
MTC:
 Oliver Oliver
 Loot
 The Importance of Being
  Earnest

Yours, Anne
Hamelin
Just So
Nunsense
To Whom It May Concern
Halala!
Williams & Walker
GOBLIN MARKET

FOREIGN PLAYS IN ENGLISH (7)

Faulkner's Bicycle
SEASON'S GREETINGS
Public Theater:
 A Map of the World
 LARGO DESOLATO
Not About Heroes
Quiet in the Land
Cheapside

SPECIALTIES (7)

DRINKING IN
 AMERICA
Anaïs Nin
Elisabeth Welch
Mummenschanz
Spalding Gray
 (three programs)

Mirror:
 The Time of Your Life
 Children of the Sun
 The Circle
 El Grande de Coca-Cola
 Hamlet
 The House of Blue Leaves
 The Eden Cinema
 Ten by Tennessee
  (two programs)

REVUES (9)

Ladies and Gentlemen,
 Jerome Kern
What's a Nice Country, etc.
 (revised version)
The Golden Land
Personals
Sweet Will
The Alchemedians
Beehive
National Lampoon's Class of
 '86
Professionally Speaking

Categorized above are all the productions listed in the Plays Produced Off Broadway section of this volume. Plays listed in CAPITAL LETTERS have been designated Best Plays of 1985–86. Plays listed in *italics* were still running after June 1, 1986.

to Hare's. Again the two leading characters were writers from different cultures embroiled in Third World politics—in this case an American journalist and a Latin American poet who spend the first act trying to distract themselves with intellectual discussion while facing uncertain futures in the jail of a country not unlike Somoza's Nicaragua. In the second act, most of which takes place 15 years later, the two meet again. The poet is now a functionary in the revolutionary government which has since taken over the country, and the journalist is observing a delegation trying to persuade that government to release a political prisoner. The two who had been comrades now face each other with suspicion. Naturally, we hope to learn what has happened in the intervening years to affect such a change in their relationship. But the confrontation Nelson delivers is curiously perfunctory, almost as if he couldn't be bothered with addressing the dramatic question he's raised. The second act has its considerable consolation, though: the introduction of the poet's superior, the minister of culture (adoitly played by Shawn Elliot), who, in Shavian tradition, has a fine time saying wittily outrageous things at the expense of the delegation's (and presumably the audience's) liberal sympathies.

Dealing with another aspect of political turmoil in Latin America, Keith Reddin's *Rum and Coke* was a satiric account of the Bay of Pigs debacle from the point of view of a Candide-like CIA agent named Jake Seward involved in training the would-be Cuban invaders. The perspective was unique, but, despite a good deal of bright dialogue (winningly played by Peter MacNicol as Jake and Polly Draper as his politically compromised sister), Reddin presented no new insights into how the United States got itself into such a godawful mess. That the C.I.A. was not a bastion of idealism and integrity came as no revelation to audiences that have seen the agency and its employees depicted as villains and fools in countless movies, TV shows and novels. (Perhaps the only thing that would have been genuinely surprising would have been if Reddin had written in the agency's defense.)

Two of this year's Best Plays, *Largo Desolato* by Vaclav Havel (translated by Marie Winn) and *The Perfect Party* by A.R. Gurney Jr., were about professors locking horns with their societies. The differences between the two scripts illuminate the differences between the societies from which they sprang. Havel, a Czech playwright whose work is prohibited production in his own country, created a character in a situation similar to his own. For the crime of having written some offending paragraphs in a philosophical work, Dr. Leopold Kopriva waits in a state of dread anticipation for the day when the police will fulfill their threat to spirit him away as a political prisoner. The waiting imposes its own kind of imprisonment. In the shadow of the approaching incarceration, Kopriva finds himself unable to do anything. The state's psychological terror has all but eroded his sense of self. Almost as bad as the terror inflicted upon him by the state is the terror brought by those who think of themselves as his supporters. They keep urging him to take on a more assertive role as a dissident. But Kopriva is miscast as a hero, and the pressure applied trying to make him act like one does nothing so much as bring him face to face with his own keenly felt shortcomings.

What made Havel's work all the more remarkable was that it was often wildly funny. Many of the critics had serious problems with Richard Foreman's direc-

Sketch by scene designer Tony Walton for his Central Park
setting of tunnel, bridge and benches for *I'm Not Rappaport*

tion, which they believed to be so stylized as to obscure the script. Not ordinarily
being much of a Foreman enthusiast, I was surprised to find myself delighted by
most of the production, from Josef Sommer's *tour de force* performance to the
painstaking choreography of the blocking, which transformed mundane gestures
into elaborate rituals, at once absurdly comic and threatening, and underscored
the rigidity of the system in which the characters were trapped.

One of the characteristics of living in a society with an official culture is that
one knows where one stands in relation to it. Unlike Czechoslovakia, however,
the United States has no official culture. Rather than speaking with one voice,
it speaks with many. What Tony, Gurney's professor, tries to do in throwing *The
Perfect Party* is to create a structure in which those voices will harmonize. If
Kopriva's situation moves him to inertia (to paraphrase comedian Peter Cook),
Tony's drives him to a frenzy. Tony's attempt to create a metaphor which will
contain American culture is doomed to run up against our culture's essential
disorderliness and anarchy. Gurney's protagonist also tempts fate by inviting a
critic from what is obviously intended to be *The New York Times* to review his
party, which leads to a central point of Gurney's satire: We threaten to ruin our
own pleasure when, rather than relishing the vitality and diversity around us, we
vest institutions like the *Times* with the right to determine standards. To do so,
says Gurney, is to rush headlong toward a prison of homogeneity not dissimilar
to the one in which Havel's protagonist suffers.

Miraculously, these weighty thoughts are given form in a farce whose breezi-
ness would rival a tornado. The jokes and epigrams jostle for elbow room with
broad physical comedy and a liberal infusion of raunch. Benefitting from an

immaculate production by director John Tillinger and a sparkling cast headed by John Cunningham as the professor and Charlotte Moore as the critic, *The Perfect Party* is the high point of Gurney's career and was one of the funniest plays of the season.

Another was Terrence McNally's *It's Only a Play*, a farcical account of the opening night party of a Broadway disaster featuring more than a few autobiographical elements. If the script didn't quite have enough plot to sustain a full evening, it did afford the pleasure of hearing said out loud many of the catty things people in the theater say under their breath. James Coco and Christine Baranski were particularly delightful under the direction of John Tillinger (it was his year to stage parties), and Joanna Gleason was featured to considerable advantage as an exuberantly bitchy actress with a weakness for controlled substances.

John Tillinger also directed *Corpse!*, a British thriller by Gerald Moon which didn't amount to much as a play, but offered the fun of watching Keith Baxter dash back and forth in the double role of a pair of vile twins, one intent on doing away with the other.

Two scripts, *Execution of Justice* and *In the Belly of the Beast*, dramatized the failings of the American criminal justice system through recent homicide cases. *Execution of Justice*, a Best Play, dealt with the trial in 1979 of Dan White, a former member of San Francisco's Board of Supervisors who, on November 27, 1978, shot and killed Mayor George Moscone and gay Supervisor Harvey Milk. Charged with two counts of murder, White was convicted instead of two counts of voluntary manslaughter and was paroled from prison less than five years later (he subsequently committed suicide). Drawing on the court transcript and her own investigations, Emily Mann composed a powerful script in which she examined how the social forces which helped create the circumstances behind the crimes also warped the judicial process. Unfortunately, as director, Mann employed so much flash and dazzle—live video, loud music, abrupt lighting transitions—that, despite strong performances by Peter Friedman, Gerry Bamman and John Spencer, the considerable merits of her script were nearly obscured. It seemed odd to employ such theatrical hysteria in mounting a play about the tragic effects of political hysteria. It is to be hoped that the failure of the Broadway production will not prevent the script from having a continued life.

In the Belly of the Beast was an adaptation by Adrian Hall of the autobiographical book by Jack Henry Abbott, augmented by documentary material (which, according to the program, was "further adapted" by director Robert Woodruff). Vivid letters about prison life sent to novelist Norman Mailer by convicted murderer Abbott led to Mailer's successful campaign to secure for their author a parole and a book contract. The book was greeted enthusiastically, but Abbott's freedom was short-lived; a misunderstanding escalated to his killing a young waiter-actor named Richard Adan. Found guilty of first-degree manslaughter, Abbott was returned to the environment in which he has spent most of his life. The story was patently dramatic, the prose from the book has undeniable power, and Andrew Robinson gave a remarkable performance in the central role. Still, the result was unsatisfying as drama. Abbott's prose is so vivid and so complete unto itself that the staging could do little but alternate between illustrating what was self-evident from the text and applying a variety of intense but arbitrary theatrical devices. For example, at one point the two actors who supported Robinson recited a passage in unison from opposite ends of the stage; first one spoke louder, then the other—an interesting choral effect, yes, but a choral effect in the service of what? This, the deafening blasts of a klaxon and (again) the use of TV monitors seemed to be included not for any organic reason but to persuade the audience of the evening's theatricality. Had the material received a less theatrical treatment, it might have been better theater.

At first look, Michael Frayn's second Best Play *Benefactors* would not seem to have much in common with his 1984 Best Play *Noises Off*. *Noises Off* was a romp whose action began with a rehearsal for a cheesy sex farce. *Benefactors* is a drama whose action begins with an architect winning an assignment. Though the tones of these plays are very different, both are about plans which go very awry. The rehearsal in *Noises Off* is a prelude to a dizzying series of personal and theatrical disasters. The architect's assignment in *Benefactors* turns friends into enemies and raises the ill will of the very people it is designed to benefit.

The assignment in question involves designing a housing development in a rundown area in southeast London. David, the architect, is an idealist, and his delight in winning the job arises not only from the prestige the job confers but —as he explains to his wife Jane—the challenge to build exemplary homes for working-class households. Living across the street from David are an old friend —a cynical journalist named Simon—and his beleaguered wife Sheila. Where David sees apples, Simon delights in spotting worms. Simon, in fact, becomes one of the worms in David's project, organizing opposition to prevent the demolition of the tenements David wants to replace with his urban-renewal dream.

Simon's war does not spring from idealism but pique. As a result of Jane's urging, David had given Sheila a job as his assistant. The confidence Sheila gained from succeeding at the job had precipitated Sheila and Simon's break-up. So Simon's actions are by way of retaliation: holding David responsible for pulling down the structure of his marriage, Simon moves to pull down one of David's structures, ultimately having the added satisfaction of winning Jane's ideological sympathy in his battle against her husband.

The audience's sympathies, too, shift. Instead of a cluster of small buildings designed to reinforce the community's identity and cohesion, David finds himself compelled to design huge towers which would inevitably destroy it. So Frayn places us in the uncomfortable position of giving our emotional sympathies to David while reluctantly ceding our intellectual sympathies to the disagreeable Simon.

Curiously, although the prime contest of the play is between David and Simon, in performance the evening belonged to Sheila. There is a certain irony in this as Frayn, like David, appeared to be a victim of his own conscientious architecture. The script is so precisely crafted that onstage there was a kind of airlessness to much of the proceedings. One felt as if the theater had been turned into a laboratory for the purpose of demonstrating Frayn's hypothesis. The articulateness of most of his characters worked to the disadvantage of drama. They were so good at recognizing, analyzing and verbalizing the ironies of their situations that they left little for the audience to figure out. It is precisely because Sheila was the least articulate character that she proved to be the most interesting. Since, unlike the others, she didn't explain herself, we in the audience had the pleasure of speculating about her contradictions and coming to our own conclusions about what made her tick. The New York production had the particular advantage of Mary Beth Hurt in the role, who magically reconciled what would seem to be the character's mutually exclusive strains of timidity and rebelliousness, sentimentality and toughness, to create a portrait of a woman at war with herself.

The season's other Best Play from Britain, presented in a swift and trim production by Pat Brown from Houston's Alley Theater, was Alan Ayckbourn's *Season's Greetings*, an ironically titled comedy about a family and its guests coming to grief on the shoals of a traditional English Christmas. The meat of the play lay in the contrast between the cheer they try to offer each other and the sorrow they unintentionally inflict. A dinner is disastrous in preparation and inedible when served, a puppet show preciptates a fight rather than amusement, the malfunctioning of children's toys thwarts a romance between two lonely people. One of the few images of conviviality occurs when several of the ensemble crowd in front of a television to share the questionable pleasures of a violent movie. Ayckbourn's people are alternately silly and noble, capable one minute of callousness and the next of generosity. That these contradictions give his characters dimension rather than exploding them in implausibility is a measure of his considerable art. He is frequently compared to Neil Simon, but under the guise of a light comedy Ayckbourn has written a wise and rueful play which recalls nobody more than Chekhov.

A Lie of the Mind walked off with a number of awards and was greeted by several critics as one of Sam Shepard's best. I regret that I cannot share their enthusiasm. The play begins strongly. Jake, prone to violent fits of irrational

A LIE OF THE MIND—Harvey Keitel and Geraldine Page as son and mother in the Critics Award–winning play written and directed by Sam Shepard

jealousy, has beaten and left his wife Beth for dead. She has survived, however, and, recuperating in her parents' house, hopes to return to the husband she still loves. Jake, in the meantime, has also been scooped up by a family in whose home, recovering from some unspecified malady, he fevers for the woman he's brutalized.

So far so good; but there are still two acts to go, and they go nowhere slowly. The script is filled with situations and incidents, but a series of situations and incidents does not automatically constitute a plot; a plot requires that these elements be linked coherently. Instead of coherence, Shepard (who also directed) provided arbitrariness, lurching randomly hither and yon, stopping now and again (and again) for extended passages of low-grade semantic quibbling and the unveiling of yet another crop of dog-eared symbols. In the play's home stretch, Shepard finally brings Jake and Beth together for the scene we've been waiting for. This should be the climactic confrontation of the evening, but it fizzles. No, they don't reunite, but the reasons why they don't are so vague as not to register. Despite the script's deficiencies, pleasure was still to be found watching the moment-to-moment work of the strong cast Shepard assembled for its premiere, including Harvey Keitel and Amanda Plummer as Jake and Beth and Geraldine Page, Ann Wedgeworth and Aidan Quinn as beleaguered relations.

The Lucille Lortel Theater housed two plays on literary subjects this season. The first, Stephen MacDonald's *Not About Heroes*, chronicled the friendship between two British poets, Siegfried Sassoon and Wilfred Owen, in the shadow of World War I. The second, the late Win Wells's *Gertrude Stein and a Companion*, dealt with the expatriate American author and her longtime companion Alice B. Toklas. Neither playwright overcame the central dilemma any dramatist writing about writers must face: figuring out how to credibly dramatize a creative process which is by definition internal and therefore not observable by an audience.

Of the two plays, MacDonald's had a bit more dramatic meat; Sassoon and Owen had serious differences over Owen's proper participation in the war both of them thought criminally unnecessary, and this provided some tension. In Wells's play, Stein and Toklas differed about very little except their opinions of Ernest Hemingway; a two-character play in which the two characters get along famously for two acts isn't likely to generate much by way of compelling action, and such was the case here. Though neither play worked particularly well as drama, both offered the consolations of intelligent conversation and affecting performances—Sassoon and Owen played by Edward Herrmann and Dylan Baker, Stein and Toklas by Jan Miner and Marian Seldes.

Another leading light of literature showed up in Heather McDonald's *Faulkner's Bicycle*, the story of a young woman who meets and gets involved with William Faulkner in the last days of the author's life. The central problem with the play was that, aside from the fact that Faulkner spends time with her, there was very little of interest about the young woman. Ms. McDonald clearly meant us to perceive her leading character as special and sensitive, but she didn't succeed in differentiating her from any other groupie who tries to build self-esteem by associating with the famous or talented.

Precious Sons represented a change of pace for playwright George Furth, author of the comedy *Twigs* and the book for the celebrated musical *Company*. A writer known for his light, ironic touch, this time he attempted to do for his family what Williams and O'Neill did for theirs: examine its dynamics with a balance of criticism and love. The most promising character in his story was the mother, a woman whose consuming drive for security paradoxically ends up endangering the welfare of those she's working so hard to protect. Unfortunately, the story got tangled up in Furth's elaborate network of plot strands and such exhausted conventions of the genre as conveniently timed letters and phone calls. Still, sandwiched between the clunky exposition at the beginning and the inevitable heartfelt explanations of things already understood by the audience at the end, there were many bright passages. One had to grateful for a script which gave actors of Judith Ivey and Ed Harris's caliber the opportunity to do such fine work.

Nat, the old Jew who is the hero of *I'm Not Rappaport*, is an expert manipulator, spinning stories out of whole cloth in his attempts to ingratiate himself. The play, too, manipulated to ingratiate, playwright Herb Gardner often resorting to contrivances barely more credible than the whoppers his central character invents. The story deals with the relationship between Nat and his benchmate, an old black janitor named Midge who wants little more than to be left alone. In order to give dramatic expression to these contrasting attitudes, Gardner brings on a parade of other characters. Scenes involving the smooth-talking head of a co-op committee trying to fire Midge and Nat's loving but exasperated daughter are the most dramatically successful interactions between the two leads and the world at large.

But evidently Gardner felt the need to crank up some more story, so he drags in a sadistic hooligan to victimize Nat and Midge and a sadistic drug dealer to victimize a beautiful young artist Nat and Midge befriend. As annoying as the melodrama was, and as self-consciously charming as Nat and his creator were, *I'm Not Rappaport* was for the most part a treat. Gardner played three-card monte with language, misdirecting the audience's eye in order to surprise with sudden flashes of wisdom and humor. If the play was a bit of a con job, the audience was more than happy to be taken. Under Daniel Sullivan's direction, the production boasted virtuoso performances by Judd Hirsch as Nat and Cleavon Little as Midge in an enchanting set by Tony Walton.

As a genre, the play for solo performer has built-in traps, one of the biggest being the tendency of the creators to so identify with their characters that they lose the detachment necessary for an honest, unsentimental presentation. The result is that often the material is not content simply to present the characters but insists on simultaneously editorializing on them. In the audience, one feels coerced into accepting the conclusions of this editorializing rather than being allowed the freedom to come to one's own interpretations. Such a problem plagued *Lillian*, William Luce's portrait of Lillian Hellman. Though Zoe Caldwell gave a vigorous performance, the script, being drawn in the main from Hellman's autobiographic works, presented only that side of the controversial figure that she herself wanted to have seen. This had the effect of reducing a fascinating and complicated woman to a two-dimensional portrait of unrelenting integrity and pluck.

SOLO PERFORMANCES: *Left,* Zoe Caldwell as Lillian Hellman in William Luce's *Lillian; right,* Lily Tomlin in *The Search for Signs of Intelligent Life in the Universe,* written and directed by Jane Wagner

Lily Tomlin's solo performance, *The Search for Signs of Intelligent Life in the Universe* (for which her longtime partner Jane Wagner was credited as director and sole author), shuttled between the exhilarating and the frustrating. What was exhilarating was the high level of the material's intelligence and Tomlin's finely tuned turns as more than a dozen characters of different ages, classes, races and sexes. What was frustrating was that the portraits suffered from a sameness in presentation. Time and again, rather than being dramatized in dynamic situations, the characters were displayed almost as if fixed in amber offering a litany of opinions. As in *Lillian*, the result was that Tomlin and Wagner tended to have the characters explain themselves rather than allow the audience the pleasure of discovering and evaluating them. (Trudy, the philosophical bag lady who served as a kind of Greek chorus throughout the play, was made so relentlessly endearing that she became off-putting.)

The chief exception to this format, and the high point of the show, was a piece which followed the tragicomic fortunes of a circle of women alternately inspired by the promise of the women's movement and dismayed by its real fruit, implying that by broadening opportunities the movement raised expectations and so also broadened the range of potential frustrations and disappointments. This chronicle, covering some 14 years, was structured as a series of dramatic vignettes which, because of their brevity and the speed with which Tomlin went from the one to the next to the next, avoided the dramatic stasis which undercut the effectiveness of much of the rest of the show's material.

The most successful solo dramatic presentation of the season was *Drinking in America*, a Best Play written and performed by Eric Bogosian. Bogosian's presentation consisted of a gallery of characters whose common denominator was addiction. In some cases the addiction was to substances—alcohol, cocaine, heroin; in others, to soul-destroying ways of life. With a *dramatis personnae* which included a belligerent drunk, a self-deluding salesman at a convention, a punk joy-riding through a nightmarish evening on 'ludes, and a solid citizen whose claims to normalcy border on the pathological, few of these characters were sympathetic in a conventional sense. Certainly none was someone with whom one felt cozy. But, without resorting to special pleading or sentimentality, Bogosian presented each as an achingly human reminder of the potential for desperation that lies in every human heart.

Among the new writers represented this season, Sandra Deer, Gerard Brown, John Morgan Evans and Judi Ann Mason compelled attention more for their promise than the fulfillment of that promise. Deer's work in *So Long on Lonely Street* was at its best in those stretches when she relieved her characters of the burden of revealing yet another deep, dark family secret and allowed them to open their hearts to each other. The ease and naturalness of much of the resulting scenes seemed at war with the almost farcical construction of coincidences and ironies in which the characters were imprisoned. (Something must be wrong with a play when the management feels it must include a chart to explain the genealogy of the principals.) Manipulative plotting also hobbled Brown's play, *Jonin'*, a raucous sketch of fraternity life in a black university. Though the construction was shaky, *Jonin'* benefitted from fine ensemble work under the direction of Andre Robinson Jr. and gave ample evidence of its author's considerable talent for pointed dialogue. In *Daughters*, John Morgan Evans gave Marcia Rodd a role full of rich dramatic promise and then proceeded to nearly bury her under a stream of easy jokes and forced epiphanies. Judi Ann Mason's *Jonah and the Wonder Dog* also featured a fascinating central figure who did not reach full potential, a black Senatorial candidate (in a bravura performance by Douglas Turner Ward) torn between his public and private lives. One hopes Miss Mason will give this character another chance by creating a play that deserves him, and so give Mr. Ward a sturdier vehicle in which to show his considerable stuff.

A number of other fine actors were limited by the vehicles they chose this season. Jessica Tandy and Hume Cronyn returned to Broadway with *The Petition*, a two-hander by Brian Clark (author of the Best Play *Whose Life Is It Anyway?*) concerning a longtime married couple who explore their political and personal differences in the shadow of her imminent death. Clark's objective was to draw parallels between their political beliefs and the conduct of their their private lives, but the contrived machinery constructed to produce a new revelation every 15 minutes trivialized the serious subjects invoked. Tandy and Cronyn were, as ever, a joy, though the effect was a bit like watching a pair of classical pianists dig into the subtleties of "Chopsticks." Bernard Sabath's *The Boys in Autumn*, a speculation on how Mark Twain's Huck and Tom might have turned out 50 years later, was another two-hander which pushed a series of dramatic revelations down the chute at regular intervals. Despite the synthetic nature of the material, George C. Scott and John Cullum, under the direction of Theodore Mann, were able to generate some real sparks.

Marlo Thomas received top billing in *Social Security*, but Andrew Bergman's comedy, under Mike Nichols's direction, failed to give the attractive and talented performer much to do. Bergman, making his Broadway debut with this play, has written some of the funnier screenplays of the past few years, and *Social Security* had some well-tooled jokes; but the plot, having to do with the problems a couple face when the wife's widowed mother intrudes on their marriage, suffered in comparison to Neil Simon's light comic classic *Barefoot in the Park*, which Nichols also directed. In *Barefoot*, the mother's presence helped define the couple's differences and paved the way to a reconciliation. In *Social Security*, the mother's presence seems to change the dynamics of the couple's relationship not a whit. But then Bergman doesn't give us much of an opportunity to see what the old lady could do to her daughter's apparently happy marriage, for no sooner has mother come to stay than she improbably captures the heart of a Chagall-like artist who promptly takes her off their hands. With no problem to solve, there was little for the principals to play except the wisecracks. Ron Silver, having been allotted a generous number of these, came off looking good, as did Joanna Gleason and Kenneth Welsh, who managed to instill a condescendingly written couple of suburban squares with some new life.

Robert DeNiro, a movie star and twice an Academy Award–winner, generated so much magnetism in his return to the legitimate stage in Reinaldo Povod's melodrama *Cuba and His Teddy Bear* that Joseph Papp, unable to accommodate the demand for tickets, arranged to have the play closed-circuit televised into a second Public Theater auditorium. Under Bill Hart's direction, DeNiro's role was that of a drug pusher whose teen-aged son falls into bad company and puts himself in danger of acquiring the habit. Popularity aside, some found that it confined the star's powerful personality to a monotone of macho anger, calling upon him to turn the volume of his performance way, way up without a corresponding increase in the emotional voltage. But its evident popularity persuaded Papp to move it up to Broadway after the end of the season.

Several of our leading dramatists accepted the challenge of writing pieces derived from Chekhov stories for the Acting Company on a program entitled *Orchards*. David Mamet pulled off a neat little piece about an unorthodox card game keyed to bureaucratic status, and there were moments of magic in John Guare's offering of mismatched skydivers, but Wendy Wasserstein, Michael Weller, Samm-Art Williams, Maria Irene Fornes and Spalding Gray, all of whom have distinguished themselves on numerous occasions elsewhere, seemed to be at a loss.

Mamet met with less success with *Prairie du Chien* and *The Shawl*, the pair of short plays Gregory Mosher staged as the first presentation of the newest incarnation of the Lincoln Center Theater Company. The Mamet-Mosher team has resulted in several of contemporary theater's most exciting productions, the Broadway staging of Mamet's Pulitzer Prize–winning Best Play *Glengarry Glen Ross* being the most recent. The Lincoln Center bill, despite fine acting by Lindsay Crouse, Mike Nussbaum and Jerry Stiller, was a disappointment. *Prairie du Chien* began its life as a radio play, and, reading the script, it is easy to imagine how effective it must have been with the disembodied voice of a mysterious storyteller on a train telling his tale of murder, madness and suicide to a fellow traveller. But seeing the storyteller adds nothing to the event; rather, it diminishes what was magical and suggestive to literal circumstances.

The second and longer play, *The Shawl* is the story of a medium who may or may not be a fake, his male lover and the woman who may or may not be being victimized by them. Dialogue of an almost clinical sparseness has long been a hallmark of Mamet's style, but here his fascination with idiomatic speech patterns has the curious effect of upstaging rather than revealing the characters. This is particularly frustrating because the script seems to contain the seeds of a larger and compelling play about questions of faith, trust and betrayal.

Other authors of Best Plays of the past had disappointments this season. Samm-Art Williams, author of *Home*, wrote of the evolution of an idealist into a dictator on a Grenada-like island in *Eyes of the American*, doing well by the individual stages of his central character's progress, but not quite bringing off the transitions from stage to stage. Ted Tally, last represented by *Terra Nova*, stumbled with *Little Footsteps*, a comedy about a marriage under the pressure of new parenthood, the leading characters of which seemed to be dragged around by an imposed plot rather than behaving according to their natures. *Nevis Mountain Dew* author Steve Carter missed his usual firm control in *House of Shadows*, a script in which the mock melodramatic story conflicted with the lyricism of the writing, leaving one uncertain as to Carter's intentions.

The season's specialty attractions clustered around poles of highly verbal and non-verbal entertainments. Some highlights of the former have been discussed previously in this report. Among highlights definitely in the non-verbal camp was *The Alchemedians*, a show featuring the talents of Bob Berky and Michael Moschen. Berky's contributions were mainly in the area of clowning, his most engaging moments coming out of a segment in which he selected two audience members as apprentices and attempted with great seriousness to teach them a few lessons in the absurd. Moschen's solo spots concentrated on his ability to manipulate inanimate objects in such a way that they seemed to take on lives of their

PRECIOUS SONS—Judith Ivey and Ed Harris in George Furth's play

own. A twirling white rod, for example, ceased to be merely a rod and became the physical manifestation of a geometric abstraction—a line segment that of its own volition appeared to splinter into several segments which in turn formed a dazzling variety of geometric shapes. The two performers had less success when working as a team. An extended routine that one assumed had something to do with alchemy took a long time to go nowhere, and the fire-juggling routine at the end of the evening, while spectacular, bore no discernible relationship to any other element of the presentation. In sum, a fifty-fifty proposition: one half came close to trying the patience, the other half enchanted.

Something similar could be said about this season's presentation by the Mummenschanz ensemble, called simply *The New Show* to distinguish it from the version that played for three years on Broadway in the late 1970s. The Mummenschanz mimes build their episodes out of the exploration of various costumes and props which obliterate the performers' identities as human beings, turning them into giant microbelike figures and huge disembodied hands and whiplike tentacles. Many of the effects in this edition were ingenious and beguiling, but the program would have benefitted by cutting several redundant sequences.

The Flying Karamazov Brothers, a team of five comedian-jugglers, opened Lincoln Center Theater's Sideshow series. This was in fact their second appearance in a legitimate New York house; they had an unsuccessful run on Broadway in 1983. That engagement, however, had been in the Ritz, the proscenium stage of which had placed a psychological distance between them and their audience. For the Lincoln Center run, a few rows in the Vivian Beaumont were removed to create a large three-quarters round space. This simple change in their spacial relationship with the audience made all the difference. The Beaumont was transformed into a cozy rumpus room, and the jugglers took on the roles of the audience's playmates.

At one point, one of the five bet that he could juggle any three objects of the audience's choosing for a count of ten. If he won the bet, he was entitled to a standing ovation. Losing would net him a pie in the face. The night I attended, many had come prepared for this, bringing a variety of unwieldy stuff, including a large and very ugly fish head and a container filled with white gelatinous glop, the exact constitution of which was left happily undefined. After a valiant series of tries which teetered on the brink of success, the poor man ended up covered with glop and pie; the audience gave him a standing ovation anyway. One would think that there would be a limit to how long jugglers—even jugglers of such charm and proficiency—could maintain an audience's attention. Wherever that limit lies, between the intricate routines and an inexhaustible supply of deliciously low puns, the Karamazovs never reached it.

The broad physical comedy of the Karamazovs was followed by the verbal subtleties of Spalding Gray, who, seated behind a desk and referring occasionally to notes, presented three of his autobiographical monologues in repertory. The matter with which Mr. Gray dealt in *Terrors of Pleasure*—the travails he faced pursuing the urbanite's dream of a place in the country—was not too distant from material one might expect a guest on the "Tonight Show" to explore. But Gray's reference level and use of imagery went beyond the talk show guest's easy observations and self-promotion. *Swimming to Cambodia*, an account of his experiences working as an actor in the film *The Killing Fields*, dealt with darker stuff, juxtaposing show biz anecdotes with the horrors of genocide the film was depicting. In the final third of the piece, Gray strayed from this fascinating double focus to dwell on highjinks on and off the set. As amusing as these stories were, one wished he had maintained to the end of the piece the Pirandellian tension between reality and its dramatization. This must be counted as a minor failing, however, in the face of Gray's larger accomplishment as storyteller.

Here's where we list the Best Plays choices for the outstanding achievements of the season in New York, on and off Broadway. In the acting categories, clear distinction among "starring," "featured" or "supporting" players can't be made on the basis of official billing, which is as much a matter of contracts as of esthetics. Here in these volumes we divide acting into "primary" or "secondary" roles, a primary role being one which might some day cause a star to inspire a revival in order to appear in that character. All others, be they vivid as Mercutio, are classed a secondary. Furthermore, our list of individual standouts makes room for more than a single choice when appropriate. We believe that no useful purpose is served by forcing ourselves into an arbitrary selection of a single best when we come upon multiple examples of equal distinction.

Here, then, are the Best Plays bests of 1985–86:

PLAYS

BEST PLAY: *Aunt Dan and Lemon* by Wallace Shawn; *The Perfect Party* by A.R. Gurney, Jr.

BEST FOREIGN PLAY: *Largo Desolato* by Vaclav Havel; *Season's Greetings* by Alan Ayckbourn

BEST REVIVAL: *Hamlet* by William Shakespeare; *Hay Fever* by Noël Coward; *The House of Blue Leaves* by John Guare

BEST ACTOR IN A PRIMARY ROLE: Ed Harris as Fred Small in *Precious Sons*; Kevin Kline as Hamlet in *Hamlet*; John Mahoney as Artie Shaughnessy in *The House of Blue Leaves*

BEST ACTRESS IN A PRIMARY ROLE: Rosemary Harris as Judith Bliss in *Hay Fever*; Mary Beth Hurt as Sheila in *Benefactors*

SPECIAL CITATION: Spalding Gray in solo performances and the casts of *Hay Fever* and *The House of Blue Leaves* for outstanding ensemble work

BEST ACTOR IN A SECONDARY ROLE: Charles Kimbrough as Richard Greatham in *Hay Fever*; Ving Rhames as M'Bengue in *A Map of the World*

BEST ACTRESS IN A SECONDARY ROLE: Joanna Gleason as Virginia Noyes in *It's Only a Play* and Trudy in *Social Security*; Charlotte Moore as Lois in *The Perfect Party*

BEST DIRECTOR: Liviu Ciulei for *Hamlet*; Brian Murray for *Hay Fever*; Jerry Zaks for *The House of Blue Leaves*

BEST SCENERY: David Mitchell for *The Boys of Winter*; Tony Walton for *The House of Blue Leaves* and *I'm Not Rappaport*

BEST LIGHTING: Pat Collins for *The Boys of Winter* and *I'm Not Rappaport*; Jennifer Tipton for *Hamlet*

BEST COSTUMES: Jennifer Von Mayrhauser for *Hay Fever*

MUSICALS

BEST MUSICAL: *Goblin Market*; *The Mystery of Edwin Drood*

BEST BOOK: Rupert Holmes for *The Mystery of Edwin Drood*

BEST MUSIC: Lance Mulcahy for *Sweet Will*; Polly Pen for *Goblin Market*

BEST LYRICS: David Crane, Seth Friedman and Marta Kaufman for *Personals*

BEST REVIVAL: *Sweet Charity* by Neil Simon, Cy Coleman, Dorothy Fields and Bob Fosse

BEST ACTOR IN A PRIMARY ROLE: Ben Harney as Bert Williams in *Williams & Walker*

BEST ACTRESS IN A PRIMARY ROLE: Chita Rivera in *Jerry's Girls*; Terri Klausner as Laura and Ann Morrison as Lizzie in *Goblin Market*

SPECIAL CITATION: Elisabeth Welch in *Jerome Kern Goes to Hollywood* and *Time to Start Living*

BEST ACTOR IN A SECONDARY ROLE: Howard McGillin as John Jasper and Mr. Clive Paget in *The Mystery of Edwin Drood*; Michael Rupert as Oscar in *Sweet Charity*

BEST ACTRESS IN A SECONDARY ROLE: Faye Grant as Lina Lamont in *Singin' in the Rain*; Bebe Neuwirth as Nickie in *Sweet Charity*; Jana Schneider as Helena Landless and Miss Janet Conover in *The Mystery of Edwin Drood*

BEST DIRECTOR: Wilford Leach for *The Mystery of Edwin Drood*

BEST CHOREOGRAPHY: Bob Fosse for *Big Deal*

BEST SCENERY: Bob Shaw for *The Mystery of Edwin Drood*

BEST LIGHTING: Paul Gallo for *The Mystery of Edwin Drood*

BEST COSTUMES: Lindsay W. Davis for *The Mystery of Edwin Drood*

Musicals

So thoroughly has Stephen Sondheim come to dominate American musical theater that one is tempted to label seasons as Sondheim or non-Sondheim. This season our preeminent composer-lyricist did not produce a new work, and Broadway was the poorer for it.

The season did, however, mark the theatrical debut on Broadway of a signifi-

Sketches by designer Lindsay W. Davis for two of his
costumes for the musical *The Mystery of Edwin Drood*

cant new talent, pop songwriter and singer Rupert Holmes, who wrote the book,
songs, and orchestrations of a Best Play, *The Mystery of Edwin Drood*. The book
from which the show was derived was to have been Charles Dickens's first
mystery, but Dickens died before he finished the manuscript, leaving the solution
to the puzzle he had proposed in doubt. Holmes addressed this circumstance by
leaving certain plot questions to be decided by audience election, including which
of the principals was to break down and confess to murder in the penultimate
number. This was great fun, but before this point the pleasures were of a milder
sort. The piece was structured as a show within a show, the adaptation of
Dickens purportedly being played by an English music hall troupe. Consequently,
the bulk of the score was made up of pastiches of English music-hall songs, many
of which made little pretense of being seriously related to the plot. Every now and
then, though, Mr. Holmes gave clues as to his true musical colors. Two songs in
particular, "Moonfall" and "Perfect Strangers," demonstrated a rare gift for
haunting and passionate melody, a gift one hopes will be given more expression
in his next score for the theater. Under the resourceful direction of Wilford
Leach, the cast was uniformly excellent, made up of both established performers
(George Rose, Betty Buckley, Jerome Dempsey, Joe Grifasi and Cleo Laine) and

a slew of gifted newcomers (most notably Jana Schneider, John Herrera and Howard McGillin). If *Edwin Drood* did not represent a significant advance in the form of the Broadway musical, it at least gave good value as an evening's diversion.

The considerable talents of singer-actress Bernadette Peters and a company of dancers were used to little advantage in Andrew Lloyd Webber's *Song & Dance*. The first act introduced Miss Peters as a British girl named Emma newly arrived in New York. In an hour-long cycle of solo songs, composer Webber and his lyricists, Don Black and Richard Maltby, Jr. (Maltby also directed), took their heroine through a series of affairs, the blossoming of a designing career, disillusion and spiritual regeneration. The form was ambitious, but, for all of their expertise, the creators never came up with a reason for us to care about Emma. From the first she appeared to be self-consumed and in the pursuit of shallow goals. Her final determination to return to her ideals did not impress because there never seemed to be much substance to those ideals in the first place.

After the intermission, the show shifted its focus from a singing protagonist to a dancing one, Emma's sometime boyfriend, Joe, played by Christopher d'Amboise. Choreographed by Peter Martins, the balletic second act described the naive and good-hearted Joe's odyssey through various New York scenes. At the end he too emerged from his adventures spiritually regenerated, making him a fit companion, at last, for Emma. Much of the dancing was exhilarating, but this could not hide the cliched nature of the scenario or offset Webber's music, a set of souped-up variations on Paganini's A-minor *Caprice* which pummelled the audience with overamplified bombast. The frustration of this presentation was heightened by the knowledge that both Webber and Maltby are capable of much better work. As for Miss Peters, she was a joy to watch and will undoubtedly be even more of a joy when she again puts her gifts into the service of a show that deserves them.

The News, a rock opera with music and lyrics by Paul Schierhorn, intended to be a blistering satirical look at exploitative tabloid journalism, but it succeeded only in being as exploitative as that which it intended to skewer. As is so often the case with unsuccessful shows, the company included some very able performers, most notably Anthony Crivello (as a serial killer) and Cheryl Alexander, both of whom had the opportunity to show off extraordinary singing voices.

As noted earlier, several of the offerings this season featured music familiar from elsewhere. Two of these were tributes to Broadway songwriters. *Jerome Kern Goes to Hollywood* was a revue comprised of the composer's songs conceived and directed by David Kernan. In London, the show played in a vest-pocket theater in Covent Garden and featured the talented Mr. Kernan as one of the stars. Here, the theater was the substantially larger Ritz, a far cry from the intimate and clublike atmosphere for which the show had been designed. Another loss was Mr. Kernan's performance; cast instead was a young singer named Scott Holmes. Unfortunately, Mr. Holmes appeared to have been directed to imitate Kernan, the result being that he seemed to be giving a performance of a performance. Elaine Delmar and Liz Robertson did rather better, but the evening belonged to a 77-year-old singer named Elisabeth Welch, whose pure, unadorned performances of "Smoke Gets in Your Eyes" and "I've Told Every Little Star" were the show's highlights. (Not long after the show closed, by popular demand Miss Welch reappeared off Broadway with great success in a production in which she alternated songs and anecdotes called *Time to Start Living*.)

The other composer given the retrospective treatment was Jerry Herman in *Jerry's Girls*. Featuring an all-female cast, the enterprise revealed both Mr. Herman's considerable strengths and weaknesses. There are few composer-lyricists with a stronger sense of how to build a ballad, and Leslie Uggams did full justice to several of his best. On the other hand, there are few composer-lyricists with a shakier sense of how to write a comedy song. Lyric after lyric squeezed supposed humor out of rude comments about aging and declining personal appearance. That expert comedienne Dorothy Loudon was burdened with the bulk of this material, the nadir being a number in which she played a showgirl the sight of whose body leads a hostile audience to demand that she put clothes on. The honors of the evening went to Chita Rivera, whose several dance numbers marked the season's highest expression of old-fashioned Broadway musical comedy pizazz.

Uptown . . . It's Hot!, which featured Maurice Hines as star, director and choreographer, was another retrospective, this time of black popular music from the 1930s to the present day. After getting past a coy introduction set in Heaven, the first act, concentrating on the 1930s and 1940s, was one show-stopping number after another, climaxing with Hines's extraordinary tap number dedicated to the memory of John Bubbles. The second act, however, was a letdown, much of it devoted to nightclub-style impersonations of contemporary performers.

Singin' in the Rain featured not only familiar songs but familiar choreography, being a stage version of the M-G-M musical about the early days of sound movies. The dances were well worth reviving. Routine after routine from the film was welcomed by the audience like an old friend. Choreographer Twyla Tharp was responsible for adapting the exuberant Gene Kelly and Stanley Donen originals to the proscenium as well as creating some witty new dances of her own. Where the show ran into trouble was when the orchestra was at rest. Betty Comden and Adolph Green's screenplay had been tailored for the very specific talents and personalities of the film's stars, Gene Kelly and Donald O'Connor. Unfortunately, the unnamed hands who adapted this material to the stage didn't perform a similar job of tailoring for Don Correia and Peter Slutsker, with the result that these performers seemed as misfitted in their roles as they would have had the management forced them to wear Kelly and O'Connor's unaltered clothes. Mary D'Arcy in the Debbie Reynolds part appeared to better advantage, but most successful in the company was Faye Grant, who played the treacherous silent movie star Lina Lamont with a hilarious trace of Mussolini (or was it Mick Jagger?).

With *Big Deal*, writer-director-choreographer Bob Fosse tried to make old songs serve new purposes. Instead of commissioning an original score, he assembled a collection of standards to ornament his tale of a black Chicago gang of the 1930s and their attempt to pull off a robbery. But rather than illuminate character, the songs were mostly used for quick payloads of easy irony (e.g., a prison gang singing "Ain't We Got Fun"). As a result, the protagonists remained stick figures. If anything, the story, adapted from the Italian film *Big Deal on Madonna Street*, was even sketchier than the characters; in an effort to hide the fact that he had no more tale to tell by the middle of Act II, Fosse padded the evening with four redundant fantasy sequences. Nor did he seem to care much about exploring the era in which he set his story; Fosse's musical associates, Gordon Lowry Harrell and Ralph Burns, were instructed to arrange and orchestrate the songs with a heavy disco beat, which only served to obliterate any trace of the period the numbers were presumably selected to characterize. As one would expect from a Fosse show, there was some spectacular dancing, but this was icing on a half-baked cake.

Off Broadway, too, hosted shows without original scores, including *Beehive* and *Williams & Walker*. *Beehive* was amiable nostalgia for those with a weakness for the girl groups of the 1950s and 1960s. More seriously, *Williams & Walker* was a small-scale biography of black song-and-dance man Bert

BIG DEAL—Valarie Pettiford, Gary Chapman and Barbara Yeager in the "Me and My Shadow" number in the Bob Fosse musical

Williams featuring a number of the songs Williams sang during his career on Broadway and in minstrel shows. One suspects economic reasons led writer Vincent D. Smith and director Shauneille Perry to try to tell their story with only two actors accompanied by a piano and percussion. Whatever the cause, this economy-class treatment precluded a full dramatic realization of Williams's sad battle against the racism of the entertainment world. Though the potential of the material was unrealized, the show gave Ben Harney the opportunity to create a compelling portrait of a man caught in the contradictions of his own character and of the society in which he lived.

Two of the more rewarding off-Broadway musicals of the season leaned heavily on preexistent texts. Lance Mulcahy's cabaret entertainment *Sweet Will* was comprised of Shakespeare's lyrics set to Mulcahy's frequently surprising and uncommonly melodic music. The composer shared the musical honors with musical director Michael Ward, who was responsible for the intricate and inventive arrangements. *Goblin Market*, a musical dramatization by Polly Pen and Peggy Harmon of a Victorian poem by Christina Rossetti, was surely the most unusual musical of the season. The story, concerning two sisters and their dealings with forbidden fruit and the goblins who offer it to them, is a sexual allegory. Pen and Harmon, in collaboration with director Andre Ernotte, took this fragile source and made of it a work that simultaneously conveyed an ironic perspective on the repressive society which gave birth to the poem and summoned up images of enchantment and wonder. The score, mostly by Pen, was the best of the season, and the performances, by Terri Klausner and Ann Morrison, were both musically and dramatically superb, meriting a special Best Play citation for excellence in musical composition, adaptation and performance.

More new musical theater writing talent debuted in the revue *Personals*. David Crane, Seth Friedman and Marta Kaufman collaborated on a remarkably sharp set of lyrics, which were in turn scored by several different composers, most notably Stephen Schwartz and Alan Menken. The same threesome who wrote the lyrics did less well with the sketches, many of which tried to pry humor out of physical deformity and tired jokes about weird sexual habits. One series of scenes, about a shy man learning how to talk to women from a cassette recording, bore an uncomfortably close resemblance to a classic Second City sketch. On balance, though, between the score, the ingratiating cast, and imaginative staging by director Paul Lazarus and choreographer D.J. Giagni, *Personals* was a welcome introduction to some very promising talents.

To Whom It May Concern, with book and score by Carol Hall, the composer-lyricist of *The Best Little Whorehouse in Texas*, was staged in St. Stephen's Church, an appropriate venue, given that the action of the piece takes place during a church service. In a series of songs and dialogues, the service's participants reflect on and debate the place and value of religion in contempoary life. The spoken material was of variable quality; for every passage of wit and feeling there seemed to be another with the insight of a Hallmark card. Miss Hall's score, however, was an almost constant delight, beautifully sung by a cast of 14 under the supervision of musical director–pianist Michael O'Flaherty, who was also responsible for the spirited vocal arrangements.

But off Broadway was as capable as Broadway of coming up with dispiriting musicals. Playwrights Horizons played host to *Paradise!*, in which a vile American family attempted to despoil a tropical island. George C. Wolfe wrote the book and lyrics which betrayed so much contempt for the characters that one wondered how he expected the audience to want to keep company with them. Also off-putting was *Nunsense*, a musical about five nuns presenting a variety show in order to raise money to finish burying the bulk of their order (the victims of food poisoning). Though the performers were plucky and there were occasional bright moments (notably an unlikely ventriloquist act in which the dummy was also, natch, a nun), two acts of jokes about habits and the characters' not-so-hidden obsessions with show business grew wearisome.

Revivals

If Broadway introduced little by way of new drama this season, it couldn't be accused of neglecting the old. Eugene O'Neill, Athol Fugard, John Guare, Noël Coward, Harold Pinter, Joe Orton and Beaumarchais were among the playwrights represented by revivals. O'Neill, in fact, was represented by two productions of the plays many believe to be his greatest works, *The Iceman Cometh* and *Long Day's Journey Into Night*.

There was much controversy over director Jonathan Miller's approach to *Long*

THE HOUSE OF BLUE LEAVES—Julie Hagerty *(at top)*, Swoosie Kurtz, John Mahoney and Stockard Channing in a scene from the Lincoln Center Theater revival of the play by John Guare

Day's Journey, a particular bone of contention being his decision to have the actors interrupt and talk over each other's lines, a choice which rendered some of the dialogue unintelligible and shortened the play's considerable running time. Personally, I had little problem with this. O'Neill had many gifts, but dramatic economy was not one of them. His characters constantly go over the same ground, so the loss of the odd speech did not appreciably damage the sense of the play. Besides, as Miller pointed out, members of a family rarely take polite turns when fighting.

My problem with the production lay in casting. Jack Lemmon can do and indeed frequently has done remarkable work, but Miller's choice of him for James Tyrone undermined much of the play's meaning. As written, Tyrone once had the makings of a great Shakespearean actor but ruined his career by making such a tremendous success in a potboiler that ultimately nobody wanted to see him play anything else. Frustrated by not having fulfilled himself onstage, he is driven to play the part of the tragedian in private life with his family. His conversation, freighted with syntax and vocabulary borrowed from the works he loves and the parts he wishes he'd played, makes him a tempting target for his sons. A measure of how violently they have turned away from his values can be gleaned from their Broadway-drenched slang and the fun they have burlesquing his classical affectations. But the sons' burlesques can mean nothing in performance if the actor playing the father is not a credible Shakespearean. This is where Mr. Lemmon, for all of the intelligence and sensitivity of his work, was lacking. One could admire his unadorned approach to the passage in which Tyrone talks of how he betrayed his potential, but when he spoke of Edmund Booth praising his Othello, it was simply impossible to accept the mental picture of Jack Lemmon as the Moor.

Certainly there are roles in O'Neill for which Lemmon is wonderfully well-suited (for instance, *Hughie* or Sid in *Ah, Wilderness!*), but this is not one of them. (The 1986 Tony nomination committee disagreed with me; Mr. Lemmon was nominated for best actor.) Bethel Leslie made the unusual choice of mining the least sympathetic aspects of Mary Tyrone, and Kevin Spacey and Peter Gallagher did strong work as the sons.

Jason Robards began his association with O'Neill when José Quintero directed him in the 1956 off-Broadway revival of *Iceman*. In the years since, that production has achieved the status of theatrical legend, so the reteaming this season of Quintero and Robards with the play that launched their reputations was one of the year's most eagerly awaited events. Alas, here again the results were something of a disappointment. *Iceman* is most successful in an intimate house where the audience feels it is sitting one table away from the deluded regulars of Harry Hope's bar. This production, however, was booked into the Lunt-Fontanne, a large proscenium theater which usually houses musicals, necessitating performances of a size sufficient to communicate to distant back rows. Unfortunately, the subtleties of the characters were largely lost in this venue. Robards still managed to score with Hickey, particularly in the *tour de force* fourth act monologue, and there was solid work by much of the supporting cast, most notably John Pankow, Roger Robinson, James Greene and Barnard Hughes as Hickey's cronies and Natalia Nogulich, Kristine Nielsen and Caroline Aaron as three hookers. But one emerged from the production wishing it had been staged in a smaller house on a thrust stage.

The key elements of another legendary production were reassembled this season. In 1961, a young white South African playwright named Athol Fugard and a young black South African actor named Zakes Mokae appeared together in Johannesburg in the premiere of Fugard's *The Blood Knot*. A quarter of a century later, Fugard and Mokae revived the play at the John Golden Theater, recreating their original roles as half-brothers, one of whom can pass as white. The plot concerns the circumstances under which, because of the institutionalized racism of South Africa, the two lose sight of their bond as brothers and come to the point of blows because of their differing skin colors. The script is vulnerable to criticism on a number of counts; the exposition is artless and much of the development is schematic. This production, too, was vulnerable; Fugard and Mokae were way too old for their roles. But these criticisms must give way in the face of the passion fueling this presentation. Fugard and Mokae were not merely playing parts, they were bearing witness to the tragedy of the country they call home. Their connection to the material charged the evening with an urgency which compelled attention. At the end of the play, one was left not only with the memory of an extraordinary pair of performances but also with the sad realization that, far from being dated, Mr. Fugard's play speaks even more to the situation in South Africa than it did when first produced.

Down the street at the Music Box, *Hay Fever* was given an immaculate revival under the direction of Brian Murray. Noël Coward's affectionate portrait of a family whose theatrical posturings and cheerful rudeness drive their weekend guests to the verge of hysteria provided a beautifully matched cast the opportunity to demonstrate their extraordinary facility at verbal and physical comedy. In a stunning contrast to her poignantly understated performance as a middle-class housewife in the previous season's *Pack of Lies*, Rosemary Harris played an extravagantly mannered semi-retired West End star, managing to tickle laughs even out of straight lines. Robert Joy, a young American actor who has previously made a specialty of drug dealers and other seedy types, was wonderfully insufferable as the star's spoiled brat of a son. Charles Kimbrough, playing a diplomat whose skills face their severest test in this anarchic household, gave the finest performance of his Broadway career so far; his run-in with a barometer was arguably the funniest moment of the season. This acclaimed (though financially unsuccessful) *Hay Fever* (124 performances) was all the more remarkable because, our corresponding historian Thomas T. Foose notes, "*Hay Fever* has had an unhappy history in New York. There was a minor off-off production at the Provincetown in 1976–77. There was a very unsuccessful Broadway revival at the original Helen Hayes Theater in 1970–71, with Shirley Booth. Before this, there was Equity Library Theater's only staging of this play in 1945–46, a 1931–32 production with Constance Collier (95 performances) and the 1925–26 Broadway original with Laura Hope Crews (49 performances). This play has never been filmed."

Circle in the Square, home to so many distinguished revivals in the past, had less luck this season. John Malkovich directed three of his colleagues from the Tony Award–winning Steppenwolf troupe in Harold Pinter's *The Caretaker*. Jeff

Perry's performance was the standout feature of the production, Perry giving a particularly fine monologue about experiences in a mental hospital, but Alan Wilder and Gary Sinese both have been and undoubtedly will be seen to better advantage in other projects. Prior to this production was an adaptation by Richard Nelson (author of *Principia Scriptoriae*) of Beaumarchais' *The Marriage of Figaro*. An accomplished company, led by Anthony Heald, Mary Elizabeth Mastrantonio and Christopher Reeve, were overwhelmed by director Andrei Serban's preoccupation with irrelevant clevernesses.

Sweet Charity was first assembled in 1966 as a vehicle for the remarkable Gwen Verdon, who was at that time married to director-choreographer Bob Fosse. This season, Fosse, assisted by Miss Verdon, reassembled it as a vehicle for the remarkable Debbie Allen. No, *Charity* is not a first-rate musical. Typical of Fosse projects, the book (by Neil Simon) is light on plot, functioning mainly to provide cues for a series of numbers, some of which bear only the most tenuous connection to the story. But, solidly supported or not, many of the numbers, written by Cy Coleman and the late Dorothy Fields, were welcome for their own sakes, particularly "Big Spender," the wonderfully sleazy come-on of the Fan-Dango Ballroom hostesses as they slither across a railing on display. Ms. Allen's exuberant Charity was supported by a sharp and sassy cast including Alison Williams, Lee Wilkof and Tony winners Michael Rupert and Bebe Neuwirth.

Two revivals began on small stages before being transferred to Broadway houses. When *Loot* was first produced on Broadway in 1968, Joe Orton's black

SWEET CHARITY—Michael Rupert and Debbie Allen in the Tony Award–winning revival of the Cy Coleman–Dorothy Fields–Neil Simon–Bob Fosse musical

farce was something of a shock, what with its blithe attitude toward homosexuality, murder and police corruption and its subversive suggestion that innocence is the first cousin of stupidity. Since then, we have had a fairly steady diet of *Monty Python's Flying Circus* and similar purveyors of cheerful, taste-defying outrageousness with the result that *Loot* now seems quaint and a bit tame. This was in no way the fault of John Tillinger's staging at the Manhattan Theater Club, which was a model of comic precision, featuring particularly fine performances by a stellar cast including Zeljko Ivanek, Kevin Bacon, Joseph Maher and Zoe Wanamaker. The production, with most of its cast intact, was moved to the Music Box hard on the heels of *Hay Fever*'s closing.

If time has blunted the impact of *Loot*, it has enhanced *The House of Blue Leaves*, revealing it to be a pointed meditation on the American tendency to confuse religion and celebrity. The visit of the Pope is treated as a show biz event, a nun refers to the TV set as a shrine, a frustrated no-talent songwriter named Artie Shaughnessy sees his big-time movie producer friend as having the ability to raise him Lazarus-like from his dead life. John Mahoney, a member of the Steppenwolf ensemble, found a nice balance between Artie's sweetness, ambition and savagery. Others in an ensemble without a weak link were Swoosie Kurtz as his deranged wife, Stockard Channing as his girl friend, Ben Stiller as his homicidal son and Julie Hagerty as a deaf starlet. Tony Walton's set reinforced the play's social dimension by placing Artie's apartment within the larger context of the neighborhood he so wishes to escape, the promise of the Manhattan skyline within sight but out of reach. The production, which began its life in the intimate Mitzi Newhouse Theater, met with such enthusiasm that it was swiftly moved upstairs to the larger Vivian Beaumont, making it eligible for several well-deserved Tony nominations.

There were also revivals aplenty outside the borders of the Broadway district. The Roundabout Theater's production of George Bernard Shaw's *Mrs. Warren's Profession* was of special interest because of a glorious piece of miscasting. At one point, Shaw has Vivie, Mrs. Warren's daughter, say of her mother and her mother's friends, "If I thought *I* was like that—that I was going to be a waster, shifting along from one meal to another with no purpose, and no character, and no grit in me, I'd open an artery and bleed to death without one moment's hesitation." The problem is that nobody with eyes and ears could observe Uta Hagen's Mrs. Warren and claim to see no grit in her. Miss Hagen was palpably a tower of grit, which undercut the dramatic point of most of the first half of the play and robbed Mrs. Warren's revelation of her past in prostitution of its surprise and power. Miscast though she may have been, Miss Hagen was never less than compelling, and she was well matched by Pamela Reed's Vivie.

Shaw was followed into the Roundabout by *Room Service*, the John Murray–Allen Boretz farce about a seedy Broadway producer and his entourage. Alan Arkin directed some of the city's best character actors in a production overflowing with immaculately choreographed physical comedy. In a generally excellent ensemble, Andrew Bloch and Keith Reddin were particularly engaging, Bloch as a shambling director and Reddin as a naive young playwright. If Mark Hamill's performance as the producer lacked the rapacious edge that distinguished Ron Leibman's interpretation of the part in a Broadway revival some years back, his nimbleness and timing more than justified his place in this very fast company. If Hamill's intention was to prove proficiency outside the realm of the *Star Wars* series which made his name, it is an intention he has amply realized.

Circle Rep gave over two slots to resident playwright Lanford Wilson's revised versions of *A Tale Told*, retitled *Talley & Son*, and *The Mound Builders*. *Talley & Son*, the third in a series of plays about the Talley family (the first two having been Best Plays *Fifth of July* and *Talley's Folly*), was given the usual proficient Circle Rep production under the direction of Wilson's longtime collaborator, Marshall W. Mason, but even in this revised form was unpersuasive. The revised version of *The Mound Builders*, on the other hand, featured a rich gallery of characters isolated near an archeological dig in downstate Illinois. If the violence which brings the play to its conclusion felt cranked up simply to accomplish just that, there was still the considerable pleasure of watching Tanya Berezin return to her Obie-winning role as one of the few believable novelists ever portrayed onstage. *The Mound Builders* played in repertory with an adaptation of Camus's *Caligula*, a script which has built-in problems. By the end of the first act, Caligula's capacity for arbitrary violence has been so thoroughly explored that the second act's horrors are redundant. Mason tried very hard to make an end run around this flaw by pulling out a variety of dazzling theatrical devices, but ultimately the material proved to be intransigent.

America's greatest playwright, Tennessee Williams, was represented by *Ten by Tennessee*, a two-evening retrospective of his short plays performed by the Acting Company. These one-acts, the majority of which were drawn from his early career, were of interest more for the tantalizing hints of the extraordinary works to come than for their own sakes. The chief exception was *The Unsatisfactory Supper*. The characters in this piece later were the subject of his classic screen play for *Baby Doll*, but in contrast to the dark and rueful comedy of that film, *Supper* presents them as figures in a farcial landscape. Laura Hicks, a young actress who seemed uncomfortable elsewhere in the bills, did wonders with the eccentric, elderly Aunt Rose. Our Mr. Foose comments on the Williams program, "Several of these works are very rare. I could find no prior performances at all for *The Strangest Kind of Romance*. Since the management claimed no premiere, however, one must assume that this 1942 one-act had previously has a professional staging somewhere at some time."

The Village Gate housed a revival of *El Grande de Coca-Cola* by Ron House, Diz White, Alan Shearman and John Neville-Andrews, a comic fantasia on the ineptitude of a Latin American family's obsession with show business conventions. The other significant musical revival off Broadway was a well-received production of *Dames at Sea*, a spoof of old-fashioned movie musicals which played at the Lamb's Theater.

The triumph among off-Broadway's revivals was Kevin Kline's performance in *Hamlet*. His interpretation focussed on Hamlet as a man whose many roles —his father's avenger, his mother's embittered son, Ophelia's lover, Rosencrantz and Guildenstern's friend, etc.—were on such a collision course as to necessitate the creation and assumption of yet another role—madman. Hamlet's restless intellect was given added urgency by Kline's awesome skills as a clown. In the passage in which the prince speaks of the dead being food in their graves, one of

O'NEILL REVIVALS ON BROADWAY: *Above,* Jason Robards *(standing)* with Frederick Neumann and Roger Robinson *(at left table),* Leonardo Cimino *(at right table)* and others in a scene from *The Iceman Cometh; below,* Bethel Leslie as Mary Tyrone and Jack Lemmon as James Tyrone in *Long Day's Journey Into Night*

his fingers transformed into a worm undulating in a hypnotic dance. There was much to admire, too, in Harriet Harris's Ophelia, in Leonardo Cimino's Polonius and in Jeff Weiss's turns as the Ghost, the Player King and Osric. Liviu Ciulei's staging—augmented by Jennifer Tipton's extraordinary lighting and a versatile set by Bob Shaw comprised of mobile columns—was full of bold images and choices.

Some critics complained of Ciulei's setting Ophelia's mad scene in the middle of the funeral supper after Polonius's burial, but this interpolation struck me as entirely consistent with other scenes in which Shakespeare dramatized the spiritual and social disruption of the state by the disruption of social conventions (viz., Claudius halting the players in mid-performance, Hamlet and Laertes leaping into Ophelia's grave, Claudius and Laertes fixing the fencing contest). Too often, attending a *Hamlet* feels like an obligatory visit to a monument. Minor quibbles could be raised about details, but, without sacrificing the richness of the language or its philosophical content, this production reminded one of what a thrilling story Shakespeare had to tell.

Offstage

From a statistical point of view, the news this season was discouraging. The creative malaise that plagued Broadway was echoed by an economic malaise. *Variety* reported that both box office income and attendance shrank. The total box office figure was $190,619,862, representing a decline of about 8 percent from last season's $202,006,181. Attendance fell to 6,527,498 from last season's 7,156,683, a withering of nearly 9 percent. As *Variety*'s Richard Hummler observed, the Broadway audience, having declined by two-fifths in the past five seasons, was the smallest since the early 1970s.

The number of Broadway productions showed an increase to 42 from 35 last year (see the one-page summary accompanying the opening chapter of this report), but the 1985–86 total was inflated with visiting foreign-language offerings, a half dozen specialties and 11 revivals. In the nitty-gritty area of new work, 1985–86 was about level with 1984–85: 7 new plays, 7 new musicals, 3 new foreign plays in English and 3 new revues, a total of 20 which included three transfers. In the important matter of playing weeks (if 10 shows play 10 weeks, that's 100 playing weeks), there was a small drop to 1,049 in 1985–86 from 1,062 in 1984–85. On the road, total receipts from first class productions rose this year to $235,619,902 from the previous year's $225,959,429, earned on 983 playing weeks, ten fewer than last year's total.

Of Broadway's commercial productions, five—*Benefactors, I'm Not Rappaport, The Search for Signs of Intelligent Life in the Universe, Tango Argentino* and a rewritten version of Neil Simon's *The Odd Couple*—made back their investments. Of these, it will be noted that there numbered no mainstream Broadway musical (*Tango Argentino* was a plotless dance show), though *The Mystery of Edwin Drood* and the revival of *Sweet Charity* appeared likely to eventually turn profits, and last season's late entry, *Big River*, moved into the black this year. Revivals of classy plays of the past were generally received with less enthusiasm by the audience than the critics. At season's end, *Blood Knot*, *Hay Fever* and *The Iceman Cometh* had closed in red ink, and *Loot* and *Long Day's Journey Into Night* were doing disappointing business. In contrast, the revival of *The House of Blue Leaves* was doing well at the box office, but it could not be counted as a commercial hit; produced by the Lincoln Center Theater Company, it was one of Broadway's not-for-profit presentations.

Though the lack of a full-tilt smash-hit musical didn't help attendance figures, surely much of the audience resistance could be attributed to the price of theater tickets. One wistfully recalls the mid-1960s when there was considerable debate as to whether the public would be willing to go beyond a $9.60 top; now it's rare to find a $9.60 bottom. This season, an orchestra seat for *Big Deal* ran $47.50 and a similar seat for *Benefactors* ran $37.50. The League of American Theaters and Producers responded to the grumbling by releasing a study to prove what a bargain these prices represent. According to the study, the increase in prices has not kept pace with the escalation of producing costs. A chart in support of the survey made the additional claim that ticket prices for Broadway attractions have steadily declined in terms of real dollars since 1929. Whatever the statistics, however, there was general acknowledgment that, in the age of $3 videotape rentals and $6 first-run movies, $47.50 is likely to be seen as a daunting figure for one evening's entertainment.

One of the keys to stabilizing or lowering ticket prices is to lower or stabilize production expenses, not a small portion of which are labor costs. The grim statistics gave members of the League and other producers potent ammunition in their dealings with unions whose contracts came up for renewal. As part of their new three-year contract, the stagehands union, Local 1, IATSE, agreed to a one-year wage moratorium, the first pay freeze in their history. This set the pattern for other contracts, box office personnel, wardrobe supervisors and hair stylists also agreeing to one-year wage freezes. At season's end, the producers were hoping to win similar concessions in negotiations with press agents and managers and Equity.

Of course, a producer has to raise money to meet even frozen costs, not an easy task when expenses are high and the chance of recouping an investment is low. A few Broadway producers tried new tactics this season in an effort to attract investors to their projects. Both *Benefactors* and *Precious Sons* broke from the traditional 50-50 split of net profits between producers and backers by offering backers 70 percent of the net returns. Seventy percent of a flop is not a significant improvement on 50 percent of a flop, as the investors in *Precious Sons* discovered. But, being a hit, *Benefactors* benefitted its backers handsomely. (In this case, it should be noted that the general partner, James M. Nederlander, was also the largest investor, putting up 44 percent of the show's capitalization.)

As for hard figures, *Benefactors*, featuring a cast of four, was capitalized at $850,000. *I'm Not Rappaport*, with a cast of seven, came to Broadway for $600,-000, opening first off Broadway for $350,000, the additional $250,000 representing the cost to transfer it from the American Place Theater's stage to the Booth Theater. *Hay Fever* was capitalized at $900,000 and lost that and an additional $100,000 before it succumbed. The biggest losers are almost always flop musicals, this season's star entry being *Big Deal*, which had been capitalized for $5,000,000.

The term Broadway refers not only to plays but real estate. This season saw the completion of a new theater, the Marquis, for which James and Harry Nederlander and Terry Allen Kramer signed a 35-year lease, bringing the number of Nederlander-controlled Broadway theaters to ten. At the season's end, plans were afoot for the theater's premiere attraction, *Me and My Girl*, a revival of a prewar British musical which was a major hit in London's West End last season. The Marquis is in the newly opened Marriott Marquis Hotel in Times Square, which also features several conference rooms named for playwrights, including one proclaimed in large golden letters to be the Brecht Room. One can imagine what Brecht himself would have made of this honor.

To make way for the construction of the hotel, the Morosco, the Bijou and the old Helen Hayes Theaters had been torn down, an event which prompted many in the theatrical community to organize to preserve other theaters by having them declared as landmarks. In August, three Broadway houses—the Virginia, the Neil Simon and the Ambassador—were declared as deserving landmark status by New York's Landmark Preservation Commission, status which was subsequently confirmed by the New York City Board of Estimate. As might be expected, theater owners were less than thrilled with the designations and the likelihood that this would lead to other theaters being similarly designated. Under the landmark guidelines, proposed structural alterations must be approved by the Landmarks Commission. This would block the destruction or modification of the buildings in question to clear the way for potentially lucrative construction. The theater owners also feared that this might threaten their ability to cash in on air rights over the buildings. Gerald Schoenfeld, president of the Shubert organization, declared the city's policy regarding midtown zoning in general to be "a tragedy and a farce at the same time." He was quoted as saying that it was time for the city to establish clear priorities regarding the aims of the zoning regulations in the Broadway area. Was the primary objective, he asked, "landmarking the theaters, preserving low density development or preserving the theaters?" In response, Deputy Mayor Robert Esnard acknowledged that the confusion in zoning regulations reflected a lack of clear policy among officials regarding Broadway theaters.

No landmark status as yet protects the Biltmore Theater, which was sold to Murray Hill Investments, a New York real estate development company, for a price *Variety* described as being "in the neighborhood" of $5,000,000. The Murray Hill management was quoted as saying that the air rights were the primary appeal of the property, though they would refurbish the Biltmore in an attempt to keep it alive as a theater. If theatrical income didn't pick up, however, they reportedly were considering the building's demolition.

Moving from one kind of demolition to another, the season gave the lie to the accepted wisdom that a bad notice from the New York *Times* automatically spells a play's doom. As he collected his Tony for *I'm Not Rappaport*, Herb Gardner quipped, "This proves there's life after Frank Rich," Mr. Rich having had little good to say about the play when it opened. If one needed further proof that the *Times* did not have the absolute power to make or break a production, one had only to turn to the example of Sam Shepard's *A Lie of the Mind*. Though it did record business off Broadway at the Promenade Theater in the immediate

The season's foreign visitors included the musical *Tango Argentino* (with Maria and Carlos Rivarola, *above*) fresh from its hit run in Paris.

wake of a glowing review from Mr. Rich (among others), the play had a run which disappointed the expectations of its producers, Lewis Allen and Stephen Graham. Even winning the New York Drama Critics Circle Award for best play of the season didn't help much; it closed a few weeks later.

Similarly, *Sunday in the Park With George*, which opened in the 1983–84 season to a rave notice from Mr. Rich, won the Pulitzer Prize and was supported by a near-constant stream of feature articles in the *Times,* closed this season having lost 25 percent of its $2,300,000 investment. The apparent lesson to be re-learned is that the audience does not have a Pavlovian response to critical opinion; the public will not necessarily salivate whenever the *Times* rings a bell.

To continue on the subject of critics, a letter signed by Harvey Sabinson, executive director of the League of American Theaters and Producers, proposed returning to the custom of having the press write their notices on the basis of opening night performances. In recent years, first-string critics have grown accustomed to attending designated previews. In support of a single press opening performance, Sabinson wrote, "Openings have become pretty drab affairs, especially when a lot of people walk in knowing the critical reaction." The proposed change in policy was designed to restore "excitement and glamour" to opening nights. But excitement and glamour gave way to practicality as critics persuaded the League that more time to write results in better-written and better-considered reviews.

Dramatists working in showcase and regional theaters had cause to celebrate when Actors' Equity Association and the League of Resident Theaters announced the contract they had negotiated. Under the so-called conversion clause in prior contracts, a regional theater producing a play which had premiered as a showcase was compelled to hire, sight unseen, the actors who had originated the parts in the premiere or buy them out with three weeks' salary at LORT rates. According to many members of the Dramatists Guild—the organization devoted to the interests of professional writers for the stage—this obligation all but guaranteed that plays premiered in showcase situations would not receive second productions in regional venues. Rather than risk seeing their scripts placed into this limbo, a number of playwrights announced their intention to withhold works from presentation by showcase theaters. This understandably upset the showcase producers, who need new scripts of quality to attract critical interest in and funding for their companies.

In the meantime, the Guild leadership threatened Equity with legal action if it didn't do something substantive to alter the situation. The result was a readjustment of the conversion clause. Under the new agreement, actors in showcase productions would still be paid off if they weren't hired to recreate their roles, but the payment would come out of a subsidiary rights fund derived from contributions by LORT and showcase theaters. What made this palatable to the LORT theaters was that sums equal to what they paid into this fund would be deducted from the amounts they were required to pay into the Equity pension fund. In effect, this constituted a transfer of monies from the pension fund to the subsidiary rights fund which, as one dramatist wryly observed, meant that, for all intents and purposes, the actors would be paying themselves.

This did not make everybody happy. The showcase producers, always pressed for money, did not appreciate the fact that, without consulting them, Equity and LORT had agreed to require them to contribute money to this fund. In addition, some playwrights, though relieved that this would make second productions likelier, still revolted against the principle underlying the conversion clause, i.e., that the work actors do on a new play in a showcase by definition enhances the script's value to such a degree that they merit compensation. ("If somebody becomes a star because of being seen in a showcase of my work, I don't participate in his future income, even though it was my script that showed him to advantage," commented one writer, "so why should he expect to profit from the future of my play?") Still, it was generally agreed that the new agreement, by removing a blockade between the dramatists and the showcase producers, would be likely to stimulate new play development off off Broadway and in other low-budget arenas. As many Broadway and off-Broadway productions of the past have come from showcase situations, this could in turn mean the stimulation of new-play production in these venues.

Having seen one thorny issue settled, the Dramatists Guild turned its attention to another matter concerning regional theater. For years, the Guild has safeguarded its members' interests on Broadway through a recommended contract guaranteeing royalties, artistic control, etc. Very few new plays originate in the Broadway economy these days, however. Increasingly they first see light of stage in nonprofit theaters around the country. These theaters have a bewildering variety of policies regarding authors' royalties and the theaters' participation in the future income of plays they premiere. Given the importance of this arena in contemporary play development, the leadership of the Guild began investigating the development of a standardized contract for new play production in LORT houses. The Guild started by polling its membership to find out what their contractual experience in this arena has been in the past. Presumably this information will influence the construction of the proposed new contract.

When it came time to honor new plays, the New York Drama Critics Circle (including its new member, William Henry III of *Time*) chose *A Lie of the Mind* as best new play and *Benefactors* as best new foreign play. Details of the voting will be found in the Facts and Figures section of this volume, courtesy of the organization's secretary, Richard Hummler. The Critics declined to give an award in the category of best musical, and award giving was an even bumpier matter elsewhere, as the Pulitzer Prize and the Tony Awards stirred up controversy. For the first time since 1963 (when Edward Albee's *Who's Afraid of Virginia Woolf?* was denied the honor), the board administering the Pulitzers refused to bestow their award for drama on the work recommended by its drama jury. Speculation over the grounds for the refusal centered on a number of possibilities: Only three hours of the projected nine-hour work in question, Robert Wilson's *CIVIL warS, a tree is best measured when it is down*, had actually been presented. Also, though nothing in the present rules specifies where the winning play must have been produced in order to be eligible, all awards in the past have been given in the wake of, if not directly to, New York productions, and the three-hour excerpt had been produced not in Manhattan but in Cambridge, Massachusetts at the American Repertory Theater.

There was also considerable disagreement over whether the piece in question was, in fact, drama in the sense that the Pulitzer board employs the term. An epic "planetary opera" described by critic Robert Coe in *American Theater* as "a series of living tableaux that swept across continents and eons, a masque of humanity from prehistory to beyond the stars," *CIVIL warS* is not a piece the qualities of which could be appreciated from the script. As the Pulitzer is generally understood to honor literary excellence, some observers suggested that the board balked at giving the award to a work in which literary qualities are not a major feature.

The authorship of the piece raised another issue. The award is supposed to go to an American playwright; Wilson is American, but a substantial portion of the text was written by East Berlin playwright Heiner Müller. *New York Times* critic Mel Gussow, who chaired the panel of judges which made the recommendation (the other two judges being Edwin Wilson of the *Wall Street Journal* and Bernard

Weiner of the San Francisco *Chronicle*), subsequently observed that another section of the Wilson piece was scheduled to be produced in New York in the 1986–87 season, and he hoped that future judges would persist in recommending it.

Shortly after the Pulitzer storm broke, the nominations for the Tony Awards became the subject of debate. *The House of Blue Leaves* (off-Broadway premiere: 1971) and *Blood Knot* (off-Broadway premiere: 1964) were nominated in the "best play" category rather than in the category for "best reproduction of a play or musical" because, never having been presented on Broadway before, neither had been eligible for a Tony previously. (According to this logic, as *Times* critic Frank Rich noted, *All's Well That Ends Well*, which received its first Broadway production only a few seasons back, could have been nominated for "best play" in the 1982–83 season.) More controversy surrounded the "best musical" nominations which included the dance recital, *Tango Argentino*, leading some observers to question whether this set a precedent under which future nominations could go to ballet troupes that play Broadway engagements. Ultimately, *Tango Argentino* lost to *The Mystery of Edwin Drood*, and, as noted above, *The House of Blue Leaves* and *Blood Knot* lost to *I'm Not Rappaport*. But *Rappaport*'s win was widely believed not to be a "clean" win. Despite its many qualities, few claimed that it was a better play than the two older plays it had aced. Rather, many believed that Tony voters couldn't in good conscience vote for the Fugard or the Guare as new plays. Clearly, the administration of the Tony Awards will have to reexamine the question of what constitutes eligibility for which categories.

Whatever the quality of the awards, winning the big ones can still translate into substantial box office. The New York *Times* reported that *Drood*'s average daily sales went up from $53,000 to $98,600, $110,252 and $94,660 in the three days following its win. *Rappaport* reportedly went up from $16,000 to $20,000 and then to $50,000.

There was plenty of drama backstage at the Tony Awards. Alexander H. Cohen, who with his wife Hildy Parks has produced the Tony Awards television specials for 20 years, proposed to the board of directors of the American Theater Wing (which owns the Tony trademark) that it break its relationship with the League of American Theaters and Producers. Cohen, who had resigned from the League after the 1985 broadcast, alleged that the agreement between the Wing and the League gave the League too much control over the awards, the League occupying 13 of the 20 seats on the administration committee and Wing designees occupying only three seats. (The other four were occupied by representatives from the playwrights', actors', directors' and designers' professional organizations.) Representatives of the Wing and the League subsequently met, and an agreement was reached under which the administration committee will be reconstituted to give the League and the Wing equal representation. Under the new agreement, the Wing will also net a percentage of the proceeds from Tony shows and broadcasts. Wing president Isabelle Stevenson wanted to keep Cohen as producer of the television show, but the League, irritated at Cohen's lobbying against their interests, vetoed this. In the wake of the 1986 Tony broadcast, the new administration board was assembled and was poised to address, among other questions, who is to replace Cohen. Indeed, the Tonys' future on network TV is still in doubt, no deal between the administration and any network having yet been announced for the 1987 show.

A key question those in the audience face is whether the makeup of the 1986–87 season will be such that the 1987 Tony show will have more genuinely new works in credible contention for the "best play" and "best musical" awards than was the case in the 1985–86 season. The time has long passed when the American theater *was* Broadway, as the number of Best Plays chosen from off Broadway attests, but to see an arena which over the years has presented so much of value become steadily weaker is dismaying. The list of prospects for the new season has been posted, among them projects representing the stage's finest writers, actors and directors. One has good reason to hope that the overview next year will be more upbeat.

A GRAPHIC GLANCE

Mary D'Arcy, Don Correia, Faye Grant and Peter Slusker in *Singin' in the Rain*

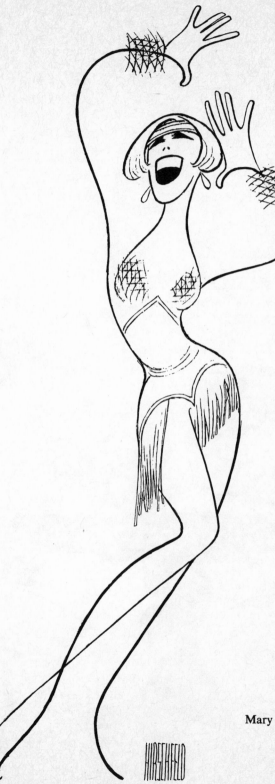

Mary D'Arcy in *Singin' in the Rain*

Kevin Spacey, Peter Gallagher, Bethel Leslie and Jack Lemmon in *Long Day's Journey into Night*

Peter Gallagher in *Long Day's Journey into Night*

Aidan Quinn, Harvey Keitel and Amanda Plummer in *A Lie of the Mind*

Harvey Keitel in *A Lie of the Mind*

Judd Hirsch in *I'm Not Rappaport*

Cleavon Little in *I'm Not Rappaport*

Simon Jones in *Benefactors*

Sam Waterston in *Benefactors*

(Upper left) Marcia Jean Kurtz, Donal Donnelly, John DeVries and Earle Hyman
(directly below) Stanley Tucci *(the cop),* Lisabeth Bartlett *(the witness),* Wesley Snipes

(cigar-smoking nun), Nicholas Kepros (top center) and (left to right) John Spencer,
Gerry Bamman and Peter Friedman in Execution of Justice

(Clockwise from lower left) Patti Cohenour, Howard McGillin, Cleo Laine, Joe Grifasi, John Herrera, Jana Schneider, George N. Martin, Betty Buckley and *(center)* George Rose in *The Mystery of Edwin Drood*

Cleo Laine in *The Mystery of Edwin Drood*

Betty Buckley in *The Mystery of Edwin Drood*

Howard McGillin in *The Mystery of Edwin Drood*

Swoosie Kurtz in *The House of Blue Leaves*

Julie Hagerty, Swoosie Kurtz, John Mahoney and Stockard Channing in
The House of Blue Leaves

Anthony Rapp, Ed Harris, Judith Ivey and William O'Leary in *Precious Sons*

Ed Harris in *Precious Sons*

(*Top*) Matt Dillon and Brian Tarantina
(*center*) Wesley Snipes, Thomas Ikeda,
D.W. Moffett, Tony Plana (*bottom*)
Andrew McCarthy and Ving Rhames
in *The Boys of Winter*

Rita Moreno and Sally Struthers in *The Odd Couple*

Rosemary Harris and Roy Dotrice in *Hay Fever*

Barbara Bryne in *Hay Fever*

Kathryn Pogson, Linda Hunt and Wallace Shawn in *Aunt Dan and Lemon*

(Foreground) Richard Jordan, Mary Elizabeth Mastrantonio, John Getz and Tom Toner *(rear)*, Nathan Lane and Robert Stanton in *Measure for Measure*

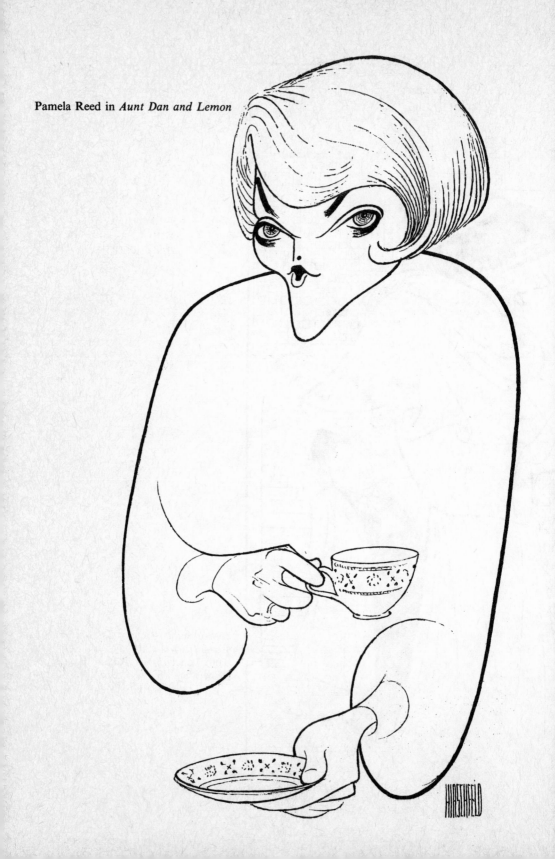

Pamela Reed in *Aunt Dan and Lemon*

John Getz in *Measure for Measure*

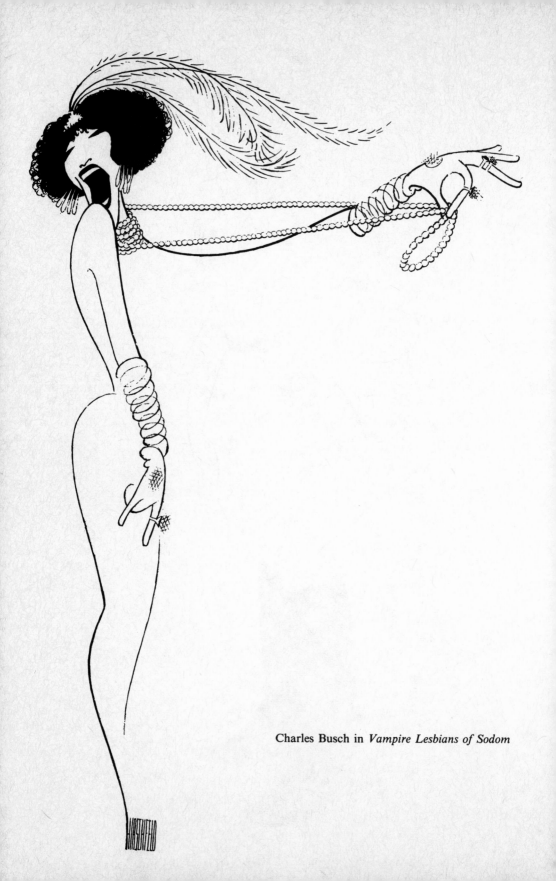

Charles Busch in *Vampire Lesbians of Sodom*

Kathy Bates in *Curse of the Starving Class*

The Grand Kabuki

Sol Frieder in *A Rosen by Any Other Name*

Jeff Perry, Alan Wilder and Gary Sinise in *The Caretaker*

Frances Sternhagen, Timothy Dale and Nancy Marchand in *Oliver Oliver*

Trish Hawkins, Amy Epstein, Robert Macnaughton and Helen Stenborg in
Tomorrow's Monday

Peter MacNichol in *Rum and Coke*

Zoe Wanamaker in *Loot*

Donna Kane in *Dames at Sea*

Terri Klausner in *Goblin Market*

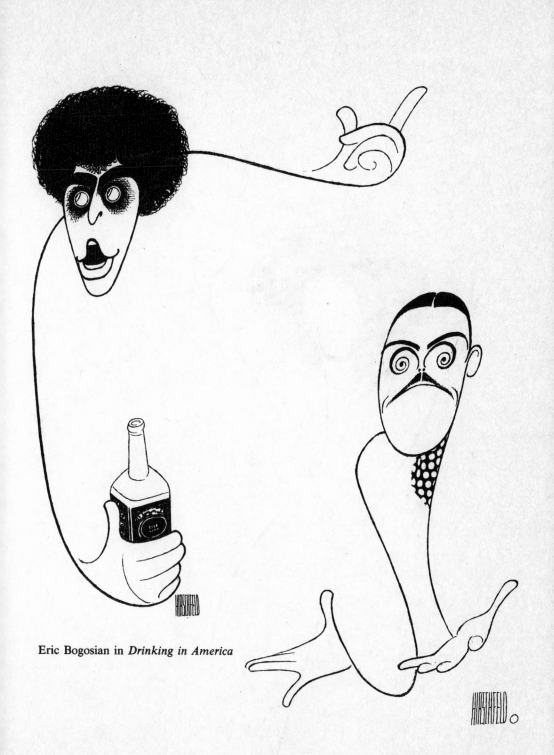

Eric Bogosian in *Drinking in America*

Mark Hamill in *Room Service*

Lily Tomlin in *The Search for Signs of Intelligent Life in the Universe*

Uta Hagen in
Mrs. Warren's Profession

Leonardo Cimino, Kevin Kline, Harris Yulin and
David Pierce in *Hamlet*

Zoe Caldwell in *Lillian*

Naanim Timoyoko in *Tango Argentino*

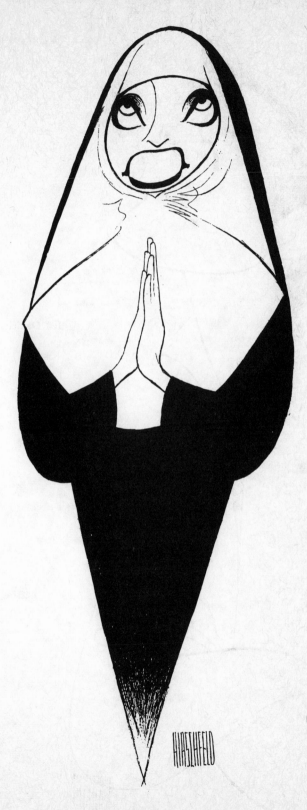

Semina De Laurentis in *Nunsense*

Jeff Daniels in *Lemon Sky*

Charlotte Moore in *The Perfect Party*

(Top) Ron Silver and Marlo Thomas *(bottom)* Joanna Gleason, Kenneth Welsh, Stephen Schnabel and Olympia Dukakis in *Social Security*

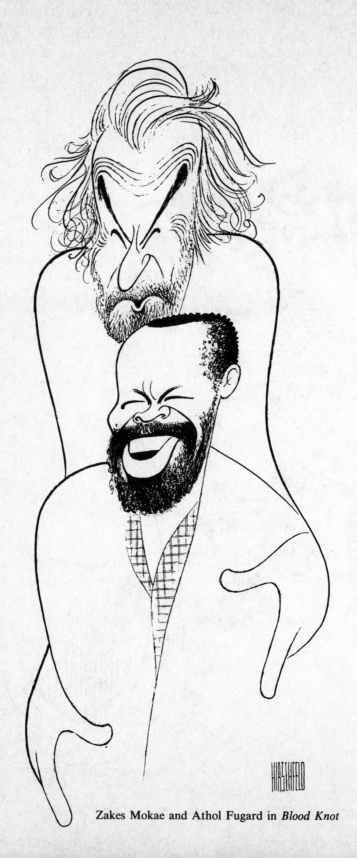

Zakes Mokae and Athol Fugard in *Blood Knot*

Michael Rupert in *Sweet Charity*

Elizabeth McGovern in *A Map of the World*

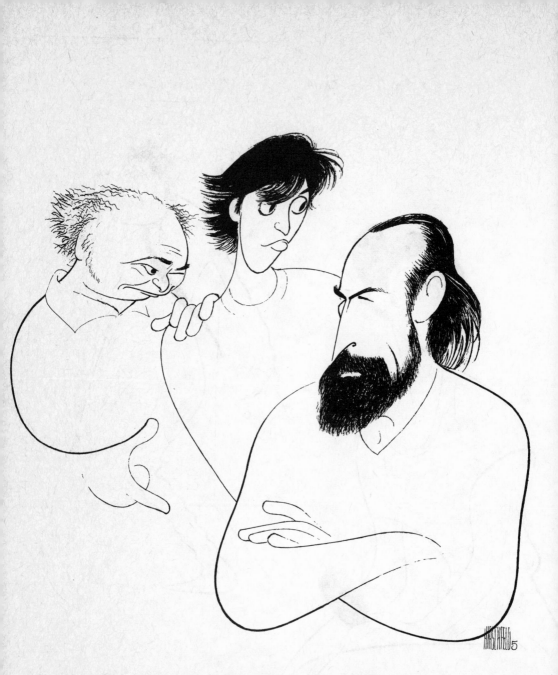

Burt Young, Ralph Macchio and Robert DeNiro in *Cuba and His Teddy Bear*

Chita Rivera, Dorothy Loudon and Leslie Uggams in *Jerry's Girls*

Jessica Tandy and Hume Cronyn in *The Petition*

John Cullum and George C. Scott in *The Boys of Autumn*

(Clockwise from lower left) Frederick Neumann, Allen Swift, John Pankow, James Greene, Bill Moor, Jason Robards, Donald Moffat, Barnard Hughes and Paul McCrane in *The Iceman Cometh*

Alisa Gyse, Marion Ramsey and Maurice Hines in *Uptown . . . It's Hot!*

Daniel Gerroll in *The Second Man*

Farley Granger in *Talley & Son*

Jeff Conaway, Lisa Michaelis and Anthony Crivello in *The News*

Keith Baxter and Milo O'Shea in *Corpse!*

Cleavant Derricks, Loretta Devine and Alan Weeks *(top)* in *Big Deal*

Anthony Heald and Dana Ivey *(center)* surrounded by *(clockwise from bottom left)* Louis Zorich, Caitlin Clarke, Christopher Reeve, Mary Elizabeth Mastrantonio and Carol Teitel in *The Marriage of Figaro*

THE TEN
BEST PLAYS

Here are details of 1985–86's Best Plays—synopses, biographical sketches of authors and other material. By permission of the publishing companies which own the exclusive rights to publish these scripts in full in the United States, most of our continuities include substantial quotations from crucial/pivotal scenes in order to provide a permanent reference to style and quality as well as theme, structure and story line.

In the case of such quotations, scenes and lines of dialogue, stage directions and descriptions appear *exactly* as in the stage version or published script unless (in a very few instances, for technical reasons) an abridgement is indicated by five dots (. . . . .). The appearance of three dots (. . .) is the script's own punctuation to denote the timing of a spoken line.

I'M NOT RAPPAPORT

A Play in Two Acts

BY HERB GARDNER

Cast and credits appear on pages 304 and 326

HERB GARDNER was born in Brooklyn December 28, 1934 and was educated at New York's High School of the Performing Arts (where he wrote his first play, the one-acter The Elevator*), Carnegie Tech (where he studied playwriting along with sculpture) and Antioch. He soon switched visual arts from sculpture to drawing, doing parts of TV commercials and creating the cartoon characters "The Nebbishes," which earned him the wherewithal to concentrate on writing his play* A Thousand Clowns, *based partly on his 1956 short story* The Man Who Thought He Was Winston Churchill *and partly on his own life experiences. It was produced on Broadway April 5, 1962 for 428 performances and was named a Best Play of its season.*

Gardner's subsequent New York productions of record have included The Goodbye People *(Broadway, 1968 and 1979),* Thieves *(Broadway, 1974),* Love and/or Death *(OOB, 1979), the book and lyrics for the musical* One Night Stand *(Broadway, 1980) and his second Best Play, this season's* I'm Not Rappaport, *which was produced off Broadway June 6 for 181 performances before moving to Broadway November 19 for a continuing run and winning the best-play Tony Award. He is also the author of the one-acters* How I Crossed the Street for the First Time All by Myself, The Forever Game *and* I'm With Ya, Duke, *the screenplays of* A Thousand Clowns *(winner of the Screen Writers Guild Award for best screenplay and Academy Award nominee),* Thieves, The Goodbye People *(which he also directed) and* Who Is Harry Kellerman and Why Is He Saying Those Terrible

Things About Me? *(an adaptation of one of his many short stories) and the novel* A Piece of the Action. *Gardner makes his home in New York City.*

Time: *Early October 1982*

Place: *A bench near a path at the edge of the lake in Central Park*

ACT I

SYNOPSIS: At 3 o'clock in the afternoon, Midge (black) and Nat (white), *"both about 80 years old,"* are seated at opposite ends of a bench in front of an arched tunnel running under a Romanesque bridge in New York City's Central Park. While the nearby Carousel is heard playing "The Queen City March" and a jogger runs by on the bridge, Nat is trying to remember an important point he was making to Midge, who *"wears very thick bifocals and an old soft hat; he is reading* The Sporting News. *Nat wears a beret and has a finely trimmed beard"* and keeps nearby a cane with an ivory handle.

Midge is irritated with Nat for telling tall stories and is determined not to listen to him any more. Nat admits that his pretense at being an escaped Cuban terrorist named Hernando is only what he calls a "cover story," implying that he is engaged in some sort of undercover activity. Nat captures Midge's interest with a tale of being approached in the Medicaid office—"They figure an old man, nobody'll pay attention. Could wander through the world like a ghost, pick up

Judd Hirsch as Nat and Cleavon Little as Midge in *I'm Not Rappaport* by Herb Gardner some tid-bits"—and being paid an extra thousand dollars on each Social Security check while he remains in deep cover. Midge even goes so far as to accept a friendly tuna fish sandwich from Nat—but then suddenly Midge realizes he's once more being had.

MIDGE: Bullshit! Lord, you done it to me *again!* You done it!
    Throws the sandwich fiercely to the ground.
Promised myself I wouldn't let ya, and ya done it again! Deep cover! . . . . . You done it again!

NAT *(smiling to himself as he continues eating):* That was nice . . . a nice long story, lasted a long time . . .

MIDGE *(shouting, poking Nat sharply):* That's *it!* That's it, no more conversin'! Conversin' is *over* now, Mister! No more, ain't riffin' *me* no more!

NAT: Please control yourself—

MIDGE: *Move* it, boy; *away* with ya! This here's *my* spot!

NAT: Sir, I was—

MIDGE: This is *my* spot, I come here first!

NAT: I was merely—

MIDGE: Get offa my spot before I lay you out!

NAT: *Your* spot? Who made it *your* spot? Show me the plaque. Where does it say that?

MIDGE: Says right here. . . *(Remains seated, slowly circling his fists in the air like a boxer.)* You read them hands? Study them hands, boy. Them hands were Golden Gloves, summer of Nineteen and Twenty-Four. This here's *my* spot, *been* my spot six months now, my good and peaceful spot till you show up a week ago start playin' Three Card Monte with my head. Want you *gone,* Sonny! *(Continues circling his fists.)* Givin' ya three t'make dust; comin' out on the count o'three. *One*— *(Rises, moving to his corner of the "ring.")*

But Midge can hardly see Nat even through his thick bifocals, let alone hit him with his fist. Lunging at Nat, Midge stumbles against the bench and suffers that bane of old age, a fall. Midge lies still while Nat checks him to make sure he has suffered no serious damage (he hasn't), while regaling Midge with an account of his experience of being dead, according to the doctor, for six full minutes: "You know what it's like? Boring. First thing you float up and stick to the ceiling like a kid's balloon, you look around. Down below on the bed there's a body you wouldn't give a nickel for. It's you. Meanwhile you're up on the ceiling, nobody sees you. Not bad for a while, nice; you meet some other dead guys, everybody smiles, you hear a little music. But mostly boring."

Midge, still on the ground but recovering, doesn't believe this tale either. Nat admits that he sometimes makes "alterations" in the truth, like a tailor, when it doesn't quite fit. But it's true that he had a triple bypass a year ago, and his truth also consists of "a Social Security check that wouldn't pay the rent for a chipmunk; what's true is going to the back door of the Plaza Hotel every morning for yesterday's club rolls. I tell them it's for the pigeons. I'm the pigeon. Six minutes dead is *true.*"

Since his death, Nat has decided to go all out with his "alterations." This morning he told a Walgreen's counterman that he was an American Indian whose grandpa fought the U.S. Cavalry. While Midge picks himself up gingerly and moves to a bench, Nat complains that his daughter Clara wants to put him in an old folks home where all he will do is sit and stare and fall down once in a while.

Midge boasts of his own superior status: "You talkin' to Midge Carter here, boy—super-in-tendant in charge of Three Twenty-One Central Park West; *run* the place, *been* runnin' it forty-two years, July. They got a furnace been there long as *I* have—an ol' Erie City Special, fourteen *tonner,* known to *kill* a man don't show he's boss. Buildin' don't move without that bull and that bull don't move without *me.* Don't have to make up nobody to be when I *am* somebody! . . . . . How you figure I keep my job? Near fifteen years past retirement, how you figure I'm still super there? I ain't mentioned a raise in fifteen years, and they ain't neither. Moved to the night shift three years ago, outa the public eye. Daytime a buncha A-rab supers has come and gone, not Midge. Dozen Spic doormen dressed up like five-star generals, come and gone, not Midge. Mister, you lookin' at the wise old invisible man."

Nat calls Midge "a dead person, a ghost" with no raise in 15 years, but Midge is satisfied with his relatively secure lot (and he pays a young man named Gilley $15 a week to walk him from here back to the apartment house at 5 o'clock every day to protect him from harm in this mugger-infested neighborhood). Nat prefers to make people notice him and feels that Midge's self-effacement gives old age a bad name.

Peter Danforth, *"in his early 40s and wears a newly purchased jogging outfit,"* jogs in, spots Midge and promises to come back to talk to him after he's done a couple more miles. Danforth jogs off, and Midge explains that he's the head of a tenants' committee reorganizing Midge's building to go co-op. Midge is worried, because it's getting around the building that he's too nearsighted to hold his job (he has cataracts in both eyes, and glaucoma, and a tenant saw him walk into the elevator door the other day). Nat also has trouble with his eyes. They compare notes on how much they can and can't see.

Nat promises Midge that he'll take care of his problem with Danforth and the apartment building, in the interests of seeing justice done: "Don't thank me; thank Karl Marx, thank Lenin, thank Gorky, thank Olgin." Nat tells Midge he joined the Communist Party in 1919 and helped Ben Gold organize the fur workers. Nat admits that the Soviet Union screwed up the Communist ideal, but the ideal remains.

NAT: . . . . . The ideas are still fine and beautiful, the ideas go on, they are better than the people who had them. Ben Gold, they hit him with the Taft-Hartley and the fire goes out, but the voice goes on; the conflict goes on like the turning of the stars and we will crush Danforth before supper time.
> *He taps his cane with finality; sits back, crosses his legs, waiting for his adversary. Midge is silent for a moment. Then he turns to Nat, quietly, calmly.*

MIDGE: You done now? You finished talkin'? *(Nat nods, not looking at him.)* O.K., listen to me; Danforth comes, don't want you speakin'. Not a word. Not one word. Don't even want you here. Got it? You open your face once I'm gonna give Gilley ten bucks to nail you permanent. Got that? Am I comin' through clear?

NAT *(turns to Midge, smiling graciously):* Too late. I have no choice. I'm obligated. The conflict between me and Danforth is inevitable. I am obligated to get you off your knees and into the sunlight.

MIDGE: No you ain't. Lettin' you outa that obligation right now. *(Leans toward Nat, urgently.) Please,* it's O.K., I got it all worked out what to say to him. Just gotta hang in till I get my Christmas tips, see—they only got to keep me three more months till Christmas and I'll be—

NAT: Christmas! Compromises! How do you think we lost Poland? Danforth has no right! The man has no right to dismiss you before your time—

MIDGE: Man, I'm eighty-*one*—

NAT: And when we finish with *him,* at five o'clock we'll take care of the hoodlum, Gilley. Together we'll teach *that* punk a lesson.

MIDGE *(looks up at the sky desperately):* Why, Lord? Why are you doing this to me? Lord, I asked you for help and you sent me a weird Commie blind man . . .

NAT: What Lord? Who is this Lord you're talking to? Oh *boy,* I can see I've got a lot of work to do here . . .

A pretty girl, Laurie, *"soft, delicate, innocent, about 25,"* sets herself up with a sketch pad on the bridge above the two men and proceeds to work on a charcoal drawing of the landscape. The men continue arguing until Nat promises to let Midge handle Danforth.

Nat offers Midge a share of a marijuana cigarette legally prescribed for his glaucoma. Midge hesitates (he quit smoking pot at 70 to avoid "goin' foolish" as his father did), but soon they are sharing the joint and looking at Laurie, who seems now to have acquired a gentle glow that reminds them of the girls they remember best from long ago. Their sweetest memories are edged with sadness, and Midge kicks himself for having cheated on all the women he loved.

MIDGE: . . . . . It's a curse. "Don't do it, Midge; don't do it," I kept sayin' while I did it. *Damn* my cheatin' soul.

NAT: No, no, you were *right!* You dared and you did, I yearned and regretted. I *envy* you. You were always what I have only recently become.

MIDGE: A dirty old man.

NAT: A *romanticist!* A man of hope! Listen to me, I was dead once so I know things—it's not the sex, it's the romance. It's all in the head. Now, finally I know this. The schmeckle is out of business, but still the romance remains, the adventure. That's all there *ever* was. The body came along for the ride. Do you understand me, Carter?

MIDGE: I'm thinkin' about it . . .

NAT: Because, frankly, right now I'm in love with this girl here.

MIDGE *(after a moment):* Well, fact is, so am I. I got to admit. *(Peers up at Laurie for a few seconds.)* Son-of-a-gun . . . First time I ever fell in love with a white woman.

NAT: The first? Why the first?

MIDGE: Worked out that way.

NAT: All the others were black? Only black women?

MIDGE: Listen, you ran with a wild, Commie crowd; where *I* come from you stuck with your own. Bein' a black man, I—

NAT: A what?

MIDGE: A black man. Y'see, in my day—

NAT: Wait. Stop. Excuse me.

>*A beat. Then Nat takes his bifocals out of his jacket pocket, puts them on, leans very close to Midge. He studies him for a few moments.*

(*Quietly.*) My God, you're right. You *are* a black man.

>*Silence for a mement. Then Nat bursts into laughter, pointing at Midge.*

MIDGE (*after a moment, catching on to the joke, a burst of laughter*): Sly devil, you sly ol' *devil* . . .

They enjoy Nat's joke perhaps a little more boisteriously than if they hadn't been smoking pot. Midge suddenly drops off to sleep for a few seconds, then wakes up singing "Alabamy Bound," inspiring them both to a soft-shoe dance which receives Laurie's silent approval. For Laurie's benefit, the two men go into a Willie Howard routine in which Midge must reply "I'm not Rappaport" to anything Nat says.

NAT: Hey, Rappaport, what happened to you? You used to be a tall, fat guy; now you're a short, skinny guy.

MIDGE: I'm not Rappaport.

NAT: You used to be a young fellah with a beard, now you're an old guy with a beard! What happened to you?

MIDGE: I'm not Rappaport.

NAT: What happened, Rappaport? You used to dress up nice, now you got old dirty clothes!

MIDGE: I'm not Rappaport.

NAT: And you changed your *name* too!

Nat roars with laughter and Midge, finally getting the joke, laughs too. Their laughter continues even though at this point Danforth shows up on the bridge and goes through his winding-down motions.

Nat agrees to butt out and settles himself on a bench while Midge confronts Danforth who—being a teacher of communication arts—beats all around the bush in telling Midge that the apartment is going co-op and the agency has recommended that they let Midge go in November, with a pension and six weeks' severance pay. Danforth adds, "Time, Midge—we're not dealing with an evil Tenants' Committee or a heartless Managing Agent—the only villain here is time. We're all fighting it." But Midge insists that they're still going to need him.

MIDGE (*leans back calmly*): Got an ol' Erie City boiler down there; heart of the buildin'. Things about that weird machine no livin' man knows, 'cept Midge

Carter. Christmas. Take me till Christmas to train a new man how to handle that devil.

Pats Danforth's knee.

You got it, have the new man set up for ya by Christmas.

DANFORTH: Midge, we're replacing the Erie City. We're installing a fully automatic Rockmill Five Hundred; it requires no maintenance.

Silence for a moment. Midge does not respond.

You see, that Rockmill's just one of many steps in an extensive modernization plan; new electrical system, plumbing arteries, lobby renovation—

MIDGE: Well, *now* you're *really* gonna need me. Pipes, wires, you got forty years of temporary stuff in there, no blueprint's gonna tell you where. Got it all in my head; know what's behind every wall, every stretch of tar.

Clamps his hand on Danforth's shoulder.

O.K., here's the deal. My place in the basement, *I* stay on there free like I been, *you* get all my consultin' free. No *salary,* beauty deal for ya—

DANFORTH: Midge, to begin with, your unit in the basement is being placed on the co-op market as a garden apartment—

MIDGE: Don't you get it, baby? Blueprints, blueprints, I'm a walking treasure-map—

DANFORTH: Please understand, we've had a highly qualified team of building engineers doing a survey for months now—

MIDGE *(suddenly):* Hey, forget it.

DANFORTH: You see, they—

MIDGE: I said forget it. Ain't interested in the job no more. Don't *want* the job. Withdrawin' my offer.

Turns away. Opens his newspaper.

DANFORTH *(moving closer):* Midge, listen to me . . .

MIDGE: Shit, all these years I been livin' in a garden apartment. Wished I knew sooner, woulda had a lot more parties.

DANFORTH: I have some news that I think will please you . . . *(His hand on Midge's arm.)* Two of the older tenants on the Committee, Mrs. Carpenter, Mr. Lehman, have solved your relocation problem. Midge, there's an apartment for you at the Amsterdam. No waiting list for *you,* Mr. Lehman seems to know the right people. Caters especially to low-income senior adults and it's right here in the neighborhood you've grown used to—

MIDGE: Amsterdam's ninety per cent foolish people. Ever been in the lobby there? Ever seen them sittin' there? Only way you can tell the live ones from the dead ones is how old their newspapers are.

DANFORTH: As I understand it from Mr. Lehman—

MIDGE: Amsterdam's the end of the line, boy.

DANFORTH: I'm sorry, I thought—

MIDGE: You ask Mr. Lehman *he* wants to go sit in that lobby; you ask Mrs. Carpenter *she* ready to leave the world. You tell 'em both "no thanks" from Midge, he's lookin' for a garden apartment.

DANFORTH: See, the problem is—

MIDGE: Problem is you givin' me bad guy news, tryin' to look like a good guy doin' it.

Danforth is really ashamed and offers Midge ten weeks' severance pay, promising to shove it through his committee. Midge is ready to accept this offer, resignedly if not happily, when Nat interrupts with the statement "We find that unacceptable" and introduces himself as Ben Reissman of the firm of "Reissman, Rothman, Rifkin and Grady," legal advisers to the "HURTSFOE" unit (Human Rights Strike Force) of Midge's union. Midge must be retained on salary, Nat argues, as a consultant for the one- or two-year duration of the building's reconstruction.

Midge tries to disown Nat, and Danforth tries to ignore him, but Nat presses on: Midge can't be fired without an arbitration hearing at which Danforth will have to come up with four tenants to testify against Midge. "Oh, that will be interesting," Nat continues under a full head of steam. "*Find* them. I want to *see* this, Danforth. Four tenants who want to be responsible—*publicly* responsible—for putting this old man out of his home and profession of forty-two years. *(His hand on Midge's shoulder.)* A man who was name Super of the Year by the *New York Post* in 1968; a man who fought in World War Two, a man who served with the now legendary Black Battalion of Bastogne at the Battle of the Bulge."

And Nat observes that the union he represents will make no contract with the building as long as the hearings on Midge's case can be made to last, which Nat assures Danforth will be a long, long time. Even Midge is now spellbound by Nat's harangue, and Danforth is confused. "Idiot," Nat continues. "you've hit every Human Rights nerve there is. I'm talking old, I'm talking black, I'm talking racial imbalance."

Danforth still tries to argue until Nat threatens not only HURTSFOE agitation leading to a strike but also the use of Danforth's name as an individual symbol of injustice: "*Do* it, Danforth, *fire* him, it's your one shot at immortality!" At this, Danforth blinks and backs off, and Nat presses his advantage: "I'm sorry, the spolight falls on you because it must. Because you are so extraordinarily ordinary, because there are so many of you now . . . . . You collect old furniture, old cars, old pictures, everything old but old people. Bad souvenirs, they talk too much. Even quiet, they tell you too much, they look like the future and you don't want to know. Who *are* these people, these oldies, this strange race, they're not my type, put them with their own *kind,* a building, a town, *put* them some place. *(Leans toward him.)* You idiots, don't you know? One day you *too* will join this weird tribe. Yes, Mr. Chairman, you *will* get old; I hate to break the news. And if you're frightened now, you'll be terrified then. The problem's *not* that life is short but that it's very long; so you better have a policy. Here we are. Look at us. We're the coming attractions. And as long as you're afraid of *it,* you'll be afraid of *us,* you will want to hide us or make us hide from you. You're dangerous. *(Grips his arm urgently.)* You foolish bastards, don't you under*stand?* The old people, they're the *survivors,* they *know* something, they haven't just stayed late to ruin your party. The very old, they are miracles like the just born; close to the end is precious like close to the beginning. What you'd like is for Carter to be nice and cute and quiet and go away. But he won't. I won't let him. Tell him he's slow or stupid—O.K.—but you tell him that he is unnecessary, and that is a sin, that is a sin against life, that is abortion at the other end."

Nat's outburst impresses Danforth, and he resolves to take the whole Midge matter back to his committee for further consideration. This has been, for Danforth, "an important exchange of ideas," he declares as he exits. Nat raises his cane in triumph, but Midge has serious doubts that they'll get away with this. Nat argues, "You're better off than you were twenty minutes ago, right? You still have your job, don't you? A week, a month, by then I'll have a *better* idea, *another* plan." Nat savors the feeling that for a minute there he took on the persona of Ben Gold, the labor leader and hero of his youthful admiration.

Gilley enters on the bridge, causing Laurie to pick up her art supplies and make a hasty exit. Gilley is "*an Irish kid, about 16; an impassive, experienced and almost unreadable face.*" He is dressed in faded jeans and "*has a constant awareness of everything around him, the precision of a pro and the instincts of a street creature.*" Gilley is the young punk who escorts Midge home every day for a $3 fee. Instinctively, Nat makes a move to cope with this new problem, but Midge stops him, forces him to sit and warns him to leave Gilley alone.

MIDGE: . . . . . These kids is crazy; beat up old folks for *exercise,* boy. Sass this kid he stomp us *good*—*(Pointing to the offstage benches.)*—and these folks here, while he's doin' it they gonna keep *score,* gonna watch like it's happenin' on the TV.
> *Gilley appears in the darkened tunnel, some distance behind them. He remains quite still, deep in the tunnel, waiting.*

Toll on this bridge is three dollars and that bridge gonna take me home.
> *Rises, taking his newspaper.*

Call it a *day,* boy. See you some time.
> *Midge starts into the tunnel towards the waiting Gilley. Silence for a moment.*

GILLEY *(flatly):* Who's that?

MIDGE: Friend of mine.

GILLEY: Where's he live?

MIDGE: Dunno. Hangs out here; he—

GILLEY *(moves down behind Nat's bench, leans towards him; quietly):* Where you live?

NAT: First, I'll tell you where I work. I work at the Nineteenth Precinct— *(Turns, holds out his hand.)* Danforth; Captain Pete Danforth, Special Projects, I—

GILLEY *(takes his hand; not shaking it, just holding it, tightly):* Where you live?

NAT: Not far, but I'm—

GILLEY: Walk you home, y'know.

NAT: That won't be necessary, it's—

GILLEY: Cost you three.

NAT: Listen, son, I don't need—

GILLEY: Cost you four. Just went up to four, y'know. *(To both.)* Saw this lady this morning. Dog-walker, y'know. Five, six dogs at a time. Give me an idea. Walk you both home. Terrific idea, huh? *(To Nat.)* Terrific idea, right?
> *Silence for a moment. Gilley tightens his grip on Nat's hand. Nat nods in agreement. Gilley lets go of his hand; pats Nat gently on the head.*

Right. Walk you both. Four each.

MIDGE: But our deal was—
GILLEY: Four.
MIDGE: O.K.

But when Gilley moves out, followed by Midge, Nat just stands there. Midge begs Nat to move, but he doesn't, and Gilley moves over to him threateningly. Nat tries a verbal snow job on Gilley, playing up to Gilley's Irishness and trying to establish a kinship of the underdog: "You're angry. You should be. So am I. But the trouble's at the Top, like always—the Big Boys, the Fat Cats, the String-Pullers, the *Top*—we're down here with you, kid. You, me, Midge, we have the same enemy, we have to stick together or we're finished. It's the only chance we got."

Gilley's response is to raise the fee to $5, payable in advance. Nat admits he has $22 on him but cannot bring himself to pay over any of it in tribute to the hoodlum. When Gilley draws a hunting knife and threatens Nat with it, Nat delivers a painful blow to Gilley's wrist with his cane, making him drop the knife. Gilley reaches for it, and Nat, *"more in fear and frustration than courage,"* strikes Gilley across the back. Leaving the knife, Gilley goes for Nat, easily disarms him and throws him backward against a stone ledge. Nat lies motionless, face down, as Gilley grabs Nat's wallet and moves quickly toward the tunnel.

GILLEY *(shouting over his shoulder at Midge):* Tell your friend the rules! You better tell your friend the rules, man—
> *Gilley stops—looks back at the very still form of Nat—then races quickly off into the darkened tunnel, forgetting his knife, disappearing into the shadows of the park. Midge moves down towards Nat as quickly as possible, kneels next to him.*

MIDGE *(quietly):* Hey . . . hey, Mister? . . .
> *Silence. He touches Nat, gently.*

Come on now, wake up . . . wake up . . .
> *Nat remains quite still. Silence again. Midge rises to his feet, shouting out at the lake.*

Help! . . . Over here! . . .
> *No response. Midge looks out across the lake, a near-blind old man staring into the darkness around him.*

Look what we got here! . . .
> *Silence again; only the sound of the early evening crickets. The park grows darker, Midge's face barely visible now in the lamplight, as the curtain falls.*

ACT II

Scene 1: Three in the afternoon, the next day

The Carousel is playing "We All Scream for Ice Cream"; Laurie is in her place on the bridge, and Midge is seated at left, reading, when Nat comes on very slowly (in a walker) but jauntily, singing "Puttin' on the Ritz." After finishing his song, he jabs the air with his cane and boasts that he frightened off the young punk.

MIDGE *(not looking up from the paper):* Tell me somethin', Rocky; you plannin' to sit here on this bench? 'Cause if you *are* I got to move to another spot.

NAT: I'm sure you were about to inquire about my health. *(Taps his hip.)* Only a slight sprain, no breaks, no dislocations. I am an expert at falling down. I have a gift for it. The emergency room at Roosevelt was twenty dollars. Not a bad price for keeping the bandit at bay.

MIDGE *(folding newspaper):* You movin' or am *I* movin'? Answer me.

NAT: I guarantee he will not return today. He wants the easy money, he doesn't want trouble—

MIDGE *(puts on his hat)*: O.K., leavin' now . . .

NAT: And if by some odd chance he *does* return, I feel we were close to an understanding. We must realize, you and I, that this boy is caught like us in the same dog-eat-dog trap—

MIDGE *(rises):* Goodbye; gonna leave you two dogs to talk it over. Movin' on now.

NAT: Wait, Carter—

MIDGE *(leans close to him):* Can't see your face too good; what I *can* see got Cemetery written all over it. So long for *good,* baby.

NAT: Sir, a friendship like ours is a rare—

MIDGE: Ain't no friendship. Never *was* no friendship. Don't even know your Goddamn *name.*

NAT: Yesterday you helped a fallen comrade—

MIDGE: You was out *cold,* Mister. Waited for the ambulance to come, done my duty same's I would for *any* lame dog. Said to myself, that ain't gonna be *me* lyin' there.

Takes Gilley's leather-sheathed hunting-knife from pocket.
See this item here? Kid run off without his weapon, see. He comin' back for it today sure. I come here to give it back to him, stay on the boy's *good* side. *(Starts down path towards stone ledge at far left.)* O.K., waitin' over here so he sees you and me is no longer *associated*; which we *ain't,* got that? He comes, don't want you *talkin'* to me, *lookin'* at me, contactin' me any way whatever.

NAT: So; the Cossack leaves his sword and you return it.

MIDGE: You bet. *(Settles down on ledge.)*

NAT *(leans toward him):* You have had a taste of revolution and will not be able to return to subjection, to living in an occupied country!

MIDGE: Watch me. *(Closes his eyes, puts his huge handkerchief over his face, curls up on ledge.)*

Nat's daughter Clara *("attractive, early 40s, stylishly Bohemian clothes")* enters and is distressed to see her father bandaged and using a walker. Nat is a fighter, she knows all too well—he made a violent scene at the butcher's last month to protest high prices, and now he has tangled with a mugger. In his various masquerades to promote social justice, Nat usually includes a phone call to Clara

Judd Hirsch and Mercedes Ruehl (Clara) in a scene from *I'm Not Rappaport*

at her office as part of the act. Clara remembers, "In one year I've been the Headquarters for the Eighth Congressional District, CBS News, the Institute for Freudian Studies and the United Consumers Protection Agency," and only this morning Danforth was on the phone to her with a message for HURTSFOE and the lawyer Reissman. Clara has been looking for her father to tell him these charades must stop.

CLARA: Searched this damn park for two hours . . . . . What happened? You're not giving speeches at the Bethesda Fountain any more?
NAT: Why should I? So you can find me there? Shut me up, embarrass me?
CLARA: It's *me,* huh? It's me who embarrasses *you*—
NAT: Exactly; hushing me like I was a babbling child, a—
CLARA: Embarrassment, let's talk about embarrassment, O.K.? Three weeks ago I came back to my office after lunch, they tell me my Parole Officer was looking for me.
NAT *(bangs his cane on the ground):* Necessary retaliation! It was important that you see what it's like to be pursued, watched, guarded . . . *(Turns to her, quietly.)* You *do* frighten me, Mrs. Gelber. You do frighten me, you know. I'm afraid of what you'll do out of what you think is love. Coming to the Fountain once a week—it's not stopping me from talking; that's not so bad. It's the test questions.

CLARA: I don't—

NAT: The test questions to see if I'm too old. *(Taps his head.)* Checking on the arteries. "Do you remember what you did yesterday, Dad?" "Tell me what you had for lunch today, Dad?" One wrong answer you'll wrap me in a deck-chair and mail me to Florida; *two* mistakes you'll put me in a home for the forgettable. I know this. My greatest fear is that some day soon I will wake up silly, that time will take my brain and you will take me. That you will put me in a place, a home —or worse, *your* house. Siberia in Great Neck. Very little frightens me, as you know; just that. Only what you will do.

CLARA: Dad . . .

NAT: I don't answer the door when you come. That's why. I watch through the hole in the door and wait for you to go away. That's why I moved from the Fountain, Clara. And why next week you won't find me *here* either.

CLARA *(after a moment):* You don't understand, I . . . I care . . . Someone has to watch out for you. Jack doesn't care, or Ben, or Carole. They don't even speak to you any more.

NAT: Good; God bless them; lovely children, Lovely, distant children.

CLARA: It isn't fair, Dad; I don't deserve this.

NAT: Dad? Who is this "Dad" you refer to? When did *that* start? I'm a "Pop," a Pop or a Papa, like I always was. You say "Dad" I keep looking around for a gentleman with a pipe.

Nat accuses Clara of losing her passion for social justice, of going into the real estate business and giving up "Marx and Lenin for Bergdorf and Goodman." Nat reproaches his daughter for being false to the memory of her namesake, one Clara Lemlich, who as a teenager inspired a hall full of vacillating shirtwaist makers to strike action, as witnessed by 8-year-old Nat attending the meeting with his father. But to Clara the name has been more of a curse than an inspiration: "Everybody else gets a two-wheeler when they're ten, I got *Das Kapital* in paperback." Clara often found herself without playmates, shunned because of her association with the Cause.

NAT: Unfair! This isn't *fair.* Later you believed in your *own* things and I loved you for it. You gave up on the Party, I respected you. The Civil Rights, the Anti-War; you marched, you demonstrated, you *spoke*—that was *you,* nobody *made* you, you loved it—

CLARA: I *did* love it—

NAT: You *changed*—

CLARA: No, I just noticed that the world didn't.

NAT: Ah, first it was me, then it was the world. It's nice to know who to blame. Ten *years,* what have you done?

CLARA: What have I *done?* I got married and had two children and lived a life. I got smarter and fought in battles I figured I could win. That's what I've done.

NAT: Lovely. And now, at last, everybody on the block plays with you, don't they? Yes, all the kids play with you now. You married Ricky the smiling radiologist; he overcharged his way into a house in Great Neck where your children, as far as I can see, believe firmly in cable television. They'll fight to the death for it! And all the kids play with *them* too. It's the new Utopia: everybody plays with everybody! My enemies, I keep up! My enemies, I don't forget; I cherish them like my friends, so I know what to *do*—

It's all too easy to keep on fighting old wars, Clara argues, and adds, "The battle is *over*, Comrade; didn't you notice? Nothing's *happened*, nothing's changed! And the Masses, have you checked out your beloved Masses lately? They don't *give* a crap." She wants no more part of any revolution, or of demonstrations like the ones she used to participate in as a Columbia student, she just wants to get through the week. Nat gets her smiling again by persuading her to join him in a version of the "I'm Not Rappaport" routine, but soon she returns to her worries about her father. She's afraid he'll get himself killed somehow. She offers him three alternatives: Great Neck, an old folks home or (an experiment she'll try for one month) staying in his apartment but going every day to the West End Senior Center instead of wandering around the city. When Nat rejects all three alternatives, Clara threatens to take legal action to protect him from himself: "I look at that bandage, I . . . You can hardly see, and with that walker you're a sitting duck. I don't want you hurt, I don't want you dead. Please don't force me to go to court. If you fight me, you'll lose. If you run away, I'll find you. I'm prepared to let you hate me for this."

Nat realizes that Clara means what she is saying, and he responds by telling her a tale of the past which he'd intended for her to hear in a letter left after his death. Nat met Clara's mother Ethel during the political turbulence of 1939, married her and fathered Clara two years later and the other children during the subsequent decade. But in 1956, Nat confesses to Clara, he fell head over heels in love with a young woman half his age, Hannah Pearlman, in the second-floor reading room of the Grand Street Library. Four months later, since nothing could come of their affair because Nat was already married, Hannah Pearlman left for Israel, and six months after that came a letter announcing the birth of a child. There were a few other letters over the years. And then only three months ago the child, a beautiful 26-year-old daughter who resembles her mother and is a sergeant in the Israeli army, came to New York to study at the Art Students League and looked up her father.

NAT: Here's the point. She has decided to take care of me; to live with me. That's why I've told you all this, so you'll know. In December, we leave for Israel. This is where I will end my days. You see, there is nothing for you to worry about.
          Silence for a few moments.
    CLARA (*quietly*): This is . . . this is a lot for me to take in, all at once. A lot of information . . .
    NAT: Not easy, but I'm glad I told you. Better you know now.
    CLARA: I want to meet her.
    NAT: You shall.
    CLARA: When?
    NAT: In two days. Friday. At the Socialists' Club, in the dining room, Friday at lunch time. I'll bring sandwiches.
    CLARA: Good. (*After a moment, softly.*) She'll . . . she'll take care of you.

NAT: That's the point.

CLARA *(letting it all sink in):* Israel . . .

NAT: Yes, Clara.

> *She turns away, trying to cover her emotion. He touches her arm, gently.*

Clara, don't be upset, I'll be fine. It's for the best, Clara . . .

CLARA: Well, at last you've got a daughter who's a soldier.

NAT: Sit. Where are you going?

CLARA *(checks watch):* My train. You know, the Siberian Express.

NAT *(holds out his hand to her):* They got them every half hour. Sit a minute.

CLARA: Got to go. See you Friday. *(She moves quickly toward the stone steps; near tears.)*

NAT: Wait a minute—*(She goes quickly up the steps.)* Hey, Rappaport! Hello, Rappaport! *(She exits.)* Rappaport, what happened to you? You used to be a tall, fat guy, now you're a—*(She is gone. He shouts.)* Rappaport! *(Silence for a moment. He speaks quietly.)* Hey, Rappaport . . . *(Silence again. Nat remains quite still on the bench. He strokes his beard nervously, sadly.)*

Midge has overheard the whole conversation and knows perfectly well that Nat invented the story about the Israeli daughter. Midge feels it was a dirty trick to play on a loving daughter like Clara and tries to make Nat see how upset she will be when she goes to the club to meet Nat and finds that he doesn't show up and has disappeared with no explanation.

They hear someone coming on the bridge, but it isn't Gilley as Midge fears, it's the Cowboy (*"A tall, genial-looking tourist, about 35, he wears an immaculate white Stetson, finely tailored buckskin jacket and polished boots"*). The Cowboy approaches Laurie and compliments her on her work.

LAURIE *(not looking at him):* Fuck off, Cowboy.

COWBOY *(cordially, tipping his Stetson as though returning her greeting):* Afternoon, M'am.

LAURIE: How did you find me?

COWBOY: Natural born hunter, Miss Laurie. 'Specially rabbits.

LAURIE: Ever tell you how much I hate that bullshit drawl? *(Turns to him.)* What is this, Halloween? You haven't been west of Jersey City.

COWBOY: Pure accident of birth, M'am. My soul's in Montana where the air is better.

LAURIE *(abruptly hands him bank envelope):* See ya later, Cowboy. *(She starts briskly, calmly, across the bridge.)*

COWBOY: Well, thank-you, M'am. *(Opens envelope, starts counting bills inside . . . . . Quietly.)* Three hundred and twenty . . . ?

> *Laurie quickens her pace across the bridge, almost running.*

Three hundred and twenty outa two *thousand*—

> *Laurie races toward the stone steps at right. The Cowboy darts up left, disappearing. Midge quickly grabs Nat, breaking into his reverie, pulling him to his feet.*

MIDGE: Come on now—

Moves Nat into the safety of the shadows at the left of the bridge.
(Whispering.) Bad business . . . bad park business here.

Laurie races breathlessly down the stone steps towards the tunnel, an escape—but the Cowboy suddenly emerges from the tunnel, blocking her path.

COWBOY *(calmly, evenly):* See the rabbit run. Dirty little rabbit.

Grips her arms, thrusts her forward towards the bench; she bumps against the bench, dropping her sketch-pad. He remains a few steps away.

(Continuing quietly, evenly.) I live in a bad city. What's *happenin'* to this city? City fulla dirty little rabbits. Park fulla junkies; *un*reliable, *dis*honorable junkies . . .

LAURIE: That's all I could—

COWBOY *(holding up the envelope):* Kept your nose filled and your head happy for a year and a half and look what you do. Look what you do.

It's all the money she has, Laurie pleads, but the Cowboy slaps her and throws the envelope onto the ground. He warns her that she must come up with the rest by 6 P.M. the next day. He hits her again, sharply, before exiting.

The two men come out of concealment and try to comfort Laurie, though they now know she is not the radiant innocent they had thought her. She can't raise the rest of what she owes the Cowboy, and Midge advises her to flee the city—but she knows they'd catch up with her wherever she went. Nat is reassuring her that things will work out, as the scene blacks out.

Scene 2: Five in the afternoon, the next day

Both men are dressed a little better than usual—Midge in a suit jacket and Nat in sunglasses, white scarf and homburg, carrying a cane (his walker is folded and hidden). The Carousel is playing "The Sidewalks of New York." The men run over the details of Nat's plan: Nat is pretending to be a big-time mobster called Tony "the Cane" Donatto, while Midge is Missouri Jack, a henchman. They hope to give the Cowboy the impression that they have a whole organization behind them.

The Cowboy comes in and sits, waiting for Laurie. What he gets is Midge as Missouri Jack delivering the message that his boss, Donatto, wants to speak to him. But the Cowboy refuses to budge until Nat calls to him peremptorily. Midge, sensing defeat, prepares to make good his escape from the area.

NAT: Hey, Tom Mix. *(The Cowboy turns. Nat pats the bench.)* You, Roy Rogers; over here.

COWBOY: What do *you* want?

NAT: I want not to shout. Come here. *(No response. Midge quickens his pace up the steps.)* Laurie Douglas, two thousand dollars.

COWBOY: What—

NAT: You know the name? You know the sum? *(Pats bench.)* Here. We'll talk.

The Cowboy starts toward him. Midge stops in the shadows halfway up the steps, turns, curious, watching them at a safe distance. Nat will remain aloof behind his sunglasses, seldom facing the Cowboy, never raising his voice.

COWBOY *(approaching bench):* What *about* Laurie Douglas? Who are you?

NAT: I am Donatto. Sit.

COWBOY: Look, if that junkie bimbo thinks she can—

NAT: The junkie bimbo is my daughter. Sit.

COWBOY: She's got a father, huh? *(Sits.)* Thought things like her just accumulated.

NAT *(taking old silver case from jacket, removing small cigar):* Not that kind of father. Another kind of father. I have many daughters, many sons. In my family there are many children. I am Donatto.

He lights the cigar. The Cowboy studies him.

COWBOY: I never heard of—

NAT: On your level, probably not. *(Patting the Cowboy's knee.)* A lot of you new boys don't know . . . . .

Nat explains the he and Midge take their orders from Los Angeles and New Orleans and are called "The Travel Agents" because they arrange for certain one-way trips. Nat pretends that he will book the Cowboy for departure if he doesn't leave Laurie alone; but the ruse collapses because the Cowboy noticed Nat and Midge here in the park the day before and knows they aren't gangsters, but helpless old men. Wanting to know where Laurie is, the Cowboy tightens Nat's scarf around his neck and tries to shake the information out of him.

Midge had been edging away but sees that Nat is in serious trouble. He draws Gilley's knife and advances on the Cowboy, threateningly. The Cowboy retreats into the tunnel, Midge following him, brandishing the knife. But Midge can't see that the Cowboy is hiding in the tunnel's shadows, and when Midge moves triumphantly after him into the tunnel, *"The Cowboy moves suddenly out of the shadows behind Midge. We see the sharp, violent thrust of the Cowboy's hand as he grabs Midge's shoulder. Blackout."*

Scene 3: Twelve days later, 11 a.m.

The Carousel is playing "The Queen City March" on a cloudy autumn morning. Nat is seated, wrapped in a thick scarf and wearing his winter coat. Midge works his way through the tunnel, leaning heavily on a special cane with four rubber-tipped aluminum legs.

Nat welcomes Midge, who is just out of the hospital (he wouldn't permit Nat to visit him there, for fear he might tell some outlandish story and try to horn in on the treatment). "I have retired my mouth," Nat promises, having taken pity on his daughter Clara that Friday at lunch and admitted that he has no Israeli daughter. Midge is glad to hear it; because of Nat's mouth he has lost his job, with no severance pay—the lawyer for the tenants discovered that there was no HURTSFOE behind Midge. Furthermore, Gilley has returned and now charges $5.50, and Laurie doesn't dare come back to this place. "Seems to me you pretty much came up 0 for five on the whole series here," Midge observes.

Nat likens Midge's bravery in defiance of the Cowboy to General Custer's, but Midge rejects the comparison: Custer was wiped out. Midge had the Cowboy on the ropes until he landed "a lucky left jab." Midge remembers proudly the fear in the Cowboy's eyes when he saw Midge's knife; and he flaunts a piece of the Cowboy's buckskin fringe which Midge tore off and will keep as a souvenir of near-triumph.

Nat has to leave—he is due at the Senior Center, and Clara checks up on him. He stands up in his walker, preparing to make his way off. But before he goes, he owes Midge an apology—and, for once, the truth. His real name is Nat Moyer; he did serve briefly with the Fur Workers' Union, but for the past 41 years he has been a waiter in a dairy restaurant on West Houston Street. "I was, and am now, no one. No one at all," Nat finishes and turns to go.

MIDGE (quietly, shaking his head): Shit, man, you still can't tell the truth.
NAT (continues moving away): That was the truth.
MIDGE: Damn it, tell me the truth.
NAT: I told you the truth. That's what I was, that's all—
MIDGE (angrily, slapping the bench): No, you wasn't a waiter. What was you really?
NAT: I was a waiter . . .
MIDGE (shouting, angrily): You wasn't just a waiter, you was more than that. Tell me the truth, damn it . . .
NAT (stops on the path, shouts): I was a waiter, that's it! (Silence for a moment. Then, quietly.) Except, of course, for a brief time in the motion picture industry.
MIDGE: You mean the movies?
NAT: Well, you call it the movies; we call it the motion picture industry.
MIDGE: What kinda job you have there?
NAT: A job? What I did you couldn't call a job. You see, I was, briefly, a mogul.
MIDGE: Mogul; yeah, I hearda that. Ain't that some kinda rabbi or somethin'?
NAT: In a manner of speaking, yes. (Moving towards bench.) A sort of motion picture rabbi, you might say. One who leads, instructs, inspires; that's a mogul. (Sitting on bench.) It's the early Fifties, blacklisting, the Red scare, terror reigns, the industry is frozen. Nobody can make a move. It's colleague against colleague, brother against brother. I had written a few articles for the papers, some theories on the subject. Suddenly, they call me, they fly me there—boom, I'm a mogul. The industry needs answers. What should I do?
MIDGE (leans toward him, intently): What did you do?
NAT: Well, that's a long story . . . a long and complicated story . . .
> He crosses his legs, leans back on the bench, about to launch into his story, the carousel music building loudly, as the curtain falls.

SEASON'S GREETINGS

A Play in Two Acts

BY ALAN AYCKBOURN

Cast and credits appear on pages 324-25

ALAN AYCKBOURN was born in London April 12, 1939. His father was a member of the London Symphony Orchestra, his stepfather a bank manager and his mother a writer. He grew up in Sussex, was educated at Haileybury and went straight into the theater after leaving school in 1957, working as an actor and stage manager with touring and repertory companies (including Donald Wolfit's) at Edinburgh, Worthing, Leatherhead and Oxford. He joined Stephen Joseph's company at Scarborough in 1962 as an actor and there began writing plays, encouraged by Joseph, the son of the actress Hermione Gingold. He moved with the company to Stoke-on-Trent and finally left to join the BBC at Leeds as a radio drama producer from 1964 to 1970. In 1971 he became director of productions at Scarborough's Library Theater (later the Stephen Joseph Theater in the Round), where many of his playscripts have received their premiere production.

Ayckbourn achieved his first West End production with Mr. Whatnot *at the Arts Theater in 1964. His second was the highly successful* Relatively Speaking *(twice produced in New York OOB in the 1980s), and his short play* Countdown *was part of a program about marriage at the Comedy Theater in 1969. The first Ayckbourn play to reach Broadway was* How the Other Half Loves, *produced in the West End in 1970 and on Broadway in 1971 with Phil Silvers for 73 performances. His* Absurd Person Singular *opened in London in July 1973 and on Broadway in October 1974 (eventually playing 592 performances) and was still running in both places at the time of the opening of his* The Norman Conquests *in London in 1974 and on Broadway in 1975. This interlocking trilogy of full-length comedies—*Table

Manners, Living Together *and* Round and Round the Garden—*was Ayckbourn's first Best Play, ran for 76 performances of each play and was later presented in a British TV version on the American Public Service network.*

Ayckbourn's Absent Friends, *produced in London in 1975, appeared on tour in America in 1977 but never made it to New York. His* Bedroom Farce *did, however, following productions in Scarborough in 1975 and at England's National Theater in London in 1977, opening in New York in March 1979, playing 73 performances and becoming its author's second Best Play. His third Best Play,* Season's Greetings, *had its American premiere at the Alley Theater in Houston last season and was brought to New York July 6, 1985 for a special off-Broadway engagement in the Joyce Theater Foundation's American Theater Exchange program.*

Ayckbourn's plays have been translated into 24 languages and produced worldwide. His canon includes Standing Room Only *(1962),* The Sparrow *(1967),* The Story So Far *(1970),* Time and Time Again *(1971),* Confusions *(1975),* Just Between Ourselves *(1976),* Ten Times Table *(1977),* Family Circles *and* Joking Apart *(1978),* Sisterly Feelings *(1979) and* Way Upstream *(1982, also produced at the Alley), plus the children's play* Ernie's Incredible Illucinations *(1969) and the book and lyrics for* Jeeves *(1975). This season in England he has been directing the National Theater production of his* A Chorus of Disapproval *in London, while his* Woman in Mind *was being prepared for its world premiere in Scarborough. He is married and lives in London.*

The following synopsis of Season's Greetings *was prepared by Jeffrey Sweet.*

Time: *The present*

Place: *The home of Neville and Belinda Bunker*

ACT I

Scene 1: Christmas Eve, 7:30 p.m.

SYNOPSIS: We see the front hallway of Neville and Belinda Bunker's home in a London suburb and, downstage from it, the sitting room and dining room (we see neither the doors nor the walls separating these two rooms from the hallway, though the actors play as if they are indeed there). The hallway also leads to a passageway to the unseen kitchen, and a staircase leads up to the second floor. At the foot of the staircase is a half-decorated Christmas tree of substantial size.

Harvey Bunker is in the sitting room relishing the action-packed adventure movie he is watching on TV. Harvey is in his 60s *"with cropped hair and a slightly military appearance."* Dr. Bernard Longstaff descends the stairs carrying wrapped presents. Hearing Harvey's laugh, he looks into the sitting room, where Harvey extols the virtues of the film. They note the fact that most of the players in the picture are long gone. "Damn fine film though," says Harvey. "Even if they are all dead."

Belinda, attractive and in her early 30s, comes downstairs, also carrying gifts. She has just finished getting her children to bed. She and Bernard put presents under the tree, and she heads for the kitchen. Harvey, calling from the other room, tells Bernard that the kids should come down and watch the film with him. It's full of terrific fights, would help prepare them for the real world. This is calculated to disturb the mild-natured Bernard, and it does. He protests that introducing children to images of violence only encourages imitation. Harvey continues jibing: "I'll tell you what I've given them all for Christmas, and I'm not ashamed to say so. I've given them all a gun. All except Gary who's got a crossbow because he had a gun last year. But Lydia, Katie, Flora and Zoe, they're not getting any of your wee-weeing dollies and nurses' uniforms from me. They've all got guns, so there." Bernard resists being drawn further into what is evidently an annual set-to on this subject.

Belinda returns from the kitchen with a stepladder. She informs Bernard that his wife Phyllis wants to see him in the kitchen, where she is attempting to cook Christmas Eve dinner. During the course of the scene, one gets the idea that Phyllis has a bit of a drinking problem and consequently her competence in this area (and indeed most areas) is questionable. Bernard heads for the kitchen. Belinda sticks her head into the sitting room long enough to determine that Harvey could use a small ginger wine.

Pattie, seven months pregnant and in her thirties, appears at the top of the stairs. Pattie is looking for her husband Eddie. Their son won't go to sleep without seeing him. Belinda tells Pattie that she doesn't know where either of their husbands is. Pattie wafts back upstairs before Belinda can determine what Pattie wants to drink.

Bernard returns from the kitchen, white with the flour Phyllis dropped during a dizzy spell. Bernard assures Belinda that all is under control in the kitchen. He begins to lay place mats on the table while Belinda goes to the sideboard for the promised drinks. Belinda gently suggests taking over from Phyllis in the kitchen, but Bernard insists that this cooking is good for Phyllis.

Belinda's husband, Neville, and Pattie's husband, Eddie, appear from the back of the house. Neville is self-assured and in his late 30s. Eddie, a friend and former employee, is insecure, apparently with good cause. Neville and Eddie are discussing electronic gear, one of Neville's passions. Belinda tries to cut through to Neville, reminding him he still hasn't made the drinks he promised to make a half hour ago and asking him if there is any more ginger wine. Neville promises to take care of everything and leaves for the back shed where the extra ginger wine is stored. In the meantime, Eddie assumes the obligation of assembling drinks in the dining room, pouring two scotches and a ginger ale while Belinda trims the tree.

Harvey calls out that whoever is in hearing distance is missing "a first-rate shark fight." Pattie appears at the top of the stairs, and Belinda relays to Eddie Pattie's request that he come up and help her deal with the children. Eddie promises to come up in a minute. Pattie again wafts off before Belinda can find out what she wants to drink.

Eddie comes to the dining room doorway to chat a bit with Belinda. He is lost in admiration for the workshop Neville has constructed in the back. Belinda, on the other hand, is not enamored with it.

EDDIE: . . . . . Man's got to have a hobby, hasn't he?
BELINDA: Why?
EDDIE: Well . . . *(He is momentarily floored.)* He just does. He's got to get away, hasn't he?
BELINDA: Away from what?
EDDIE: Well. Everything.
BELINDA: Me?
EDDIE: I didn't say that.
BELINDA: Obviously me. What else? Me and the kids.
EDDIE: Well, I'm saying nothing. You take that up with Nev.
BELINDA: I would. Except I never see him. He's always in his bloody shed.

Eddie decides not to pursue this any further and returns to the dining room to finish making the drinks. Bernard reappears from the kitchen, carrying plates and seeking information on the number of guests expected. Rachel, Belinda's sister, has invited someone named Clive Morris to spend holidays with them and is at the train station now, waiting for her guest to arrive. In the meantime, Bernard casually informs Belinda that Phyllis is recovering from a not-very-serious nosebleed, the result of yet another accident in the kitchen. Belinda continues decorating the tree. Bernard returns to chores in the dining room, where Eddie broaches the subject of the puppet show Bernard presents to the children every Christmas. Eddie advises Bernard that he might do well to make this year's presentation a bit zippier than the ones of years past. Bernard takes offense.

BERNARD *(icily):* Has Harvey put you up to this?
EDDIE: No, no.
BERNARD: I will continue to do my puppet plays as I wish to do them and as I know children enjoy them. I think you know that I will always accept help with the manipulation but I will not have people interfering with the content of my plays. I refuse to pander. I will not include gratuitous violence or sex. Not for anyone. I will not do that. I'm sorry.
EDDIE: Who's talking about sex? I didn't mention sex.
BERNARD: I know what you're talking about, don't worry.
EDDIE: I don't know why you bring sex into it.
BERNARD: I thought as a parent you might have been a little more responsible.
EDDIE: All right. All right. *(He walks into the hall with the ginger ale.)* I did not speak. I never spoke.

Bernard exits into the kitchen as Eddie and Belinda talk further about the puppet show. It seems Bernard's productions are generally a combination of tedium and ineptitude, and he's much mistaken in his belief that the kids enjoy them. Nobody has quite had the heart to tell him, but the kids may not be so tolerant with Uncle Bernard this year.

Eddie goes into the sitting room and gives Harvey a drink. Meanwhile, Neville enters the hallway from the kitchen with the news that Phyllis is "lying stretched out on the kitchen table with three yards of kitchen towel stuck up her nose." They guess that she's downed the red wine that was supposed to go into the gravy. Eddie watches a bit of the movie with Harvey and would watch more except Harvey sips the drink Eddie brought and chokes. Instead of ginger wine he's been brought a ginger ale. Eddie promises to bring the correct drink shortly.

Bernard emerges from the kitchen into the dining room, upset and rambling about how hard he tries. Neville, in the dining room for an errand, doesn't know what he means. We gather from what Bernard replies that Phyllis's condition has deteriorated further, to Bernard's embarrassment and dismay. Sympathetically,

Michael Alan Gregory as Clive and Lillian Evans as Phyllis in *Season's Greetings* by Alan Ayckbourn

Neville tells him, "You don't have to explain to us, Bernard, we know. We all know. We've seen what you've . . ." Bernard replies, "I have to explain to someone. Sometimes. I need to." He returns to the kitchen.

Belinda and Neville are concerned that Bernard's agitation will continue for the rest of the holiday. Eddie, who has overheard some of this, believes his mentioning the puppet show triggered this. The news that there will be another puppet show doesn't cheer Neville. "I'm not sitting through another one of those, I'm sorry. Ali Baba last year was my lot. Forty thieves and they all came on with ten-minute intervals between them." Belinda tries to get Neville to reconsider, but he is adamant.

NEVILLE: No way. *(He toasts Eddie.)* Cheers.
EDDIE *(responding):* Cheers.
NEVILLE: Happy Christmas.
EDDIE: Yes.
BELINDA: Thanks very much. I don't get one, then?
EDDIE: Oh.
NEVILLE: Didn't know you wanted one.
BELINDA: Probably because you didn't ask me. . . . . .
NEVILLE: My darling, I'm not psychic. If you'd said something . . .
BELINDA: My darling, you only had to ask me.
NEVILLE: All right, I'm asking you now.
BELINDA: You just have to ask, that's all. "Darling, would you like a drink?"
NEVILLE: Darling, would you like a drink? I'm asking you—
BELINDA: —then you'd find out, wouldn't you?
NEVILLE: Would you like a drink, darling? I'm asking you now. Would you like a bloody drink? Yes or no?
BELINDA: Yes, please. I'll have a gin.
NEVILLE: Thank you so, so much.
EDDIE *(carrying the ginger wine):* I'll get it.
NEVILLE: Thank you, Eddie.
BELINDA: No, you won't. He'll get it.
NEVILLE: I'll get it. What's the difference?
BELINDA: The difference is you are getting me something for a change. That's the difference.
NEVILLE: All right.
EDDIE *(cheerfully, as he crosses the hall to the sitting room):* Now, we don't want to start Christmas like this, do we?
    Pattie appears at the top of the stairs.
PATTIE: Eddie, are you coming up or aren't you?
EDDIE *(savagely):* In a minute. In a minute.
PATTIE *(hurt):* All right.
    Pattie goes back.

Eddie looks apologetically at the people who've witnessed this exchange. "I'm doing this, aren't I?" he says, indicating the ginger wine for Harvey, and goes into the sitting room. Neville leaves a drink for Belinda, and Harvey takes his drink from Eddie. These errands done, Neville reminds Eddie that he wanted to show him the new contraption he's built.

As they are about to get into it, Belinda's sister Rachel returns from the train station. Her guest Clive Morris failed to show up. Rachel pretends not to be upset, but she fools nobody. She hurries upstairs. In the conversation that follows between Belinda, Eddie and Neville, we learn that the missing man is an author. Neville tells Eddie that Rachel lent them a copy of his book if Eddie's interested in reading it. It seems that neither Belinda nor Neville has gotten around to it. Neville can't recall the last time he read a book. "I can," says Belinda wryly. "You read a quarter of one soft-porn novel shortly after we were married and that's your lot. We've been to the theater twice, and you fell asleep both times, and we've been to one open-air jazz festival when we left early because it rained." "We've been to the cinema," Neville insists. "Oh yes, I beg your pardon," says Belinda. "I mustn't forget that visit."

Neville changes the subject to the remote control gadget he's built. With a touch of a button, the Christmas tree lights go on, nearly startling Belinda off the ladder. Neville presses another button, which triggers a cassette recorder concealed at the base of the tree. *A loud Christmas song blares out.* " Belinda tells him to turn it off; there are kids trying to sleep upstairs. In the meantime, Harvey is annoyed to see that somehow the channel on the TV has jumped from the action movie to the Russian ballet. Neville turns the TV back to the proper channel and returns to his remote control device to try to figure out what went awry. He presses a button again, and again the music blares. Belinda again demands he turn it off. Neville explains that it's a present for the kids. Belinda tells him to wrap it up and save it till Boxing Day (December 26), at which time most of the major presents are scheduled to be opened.

In the middle of this discussion, Pattie reappears at the top of the stairs and tells Eddie that their son is now convinced Daddy's dead. Would Eddie kindly finally make his promised appearance upstairs? Eddie begins to complain that perhaps if Pattie were to get a little firmer with their son . . . Pattie gets dangerously quiet. "If I got a little what? Firm? Did you say firm, by any chance? Don't try to be funny. Please." Embarrassed, Eddie heads upstairs as Pattie, for the first time, gets downstairs.

Bernard enters looking for the first-aid kit (Phyllis has somehow managed to cut herself on a saucepan). Neville follows Bernard into the kitchen, giving Pattie and Belinda a moment alone. Pattie is a bit numb from an overdose of children's literature. Rachel comes downstairs, very depressed. Belinda suggests her Clive may be arriving by the next train, and perhaps Rachel should go meet it. Rachel affects indifference and wanders into the sitting room where Harvey also quizzes her on the subject of Clive, observing that he's likely to miss his dinner (which, considering Phyllis is doing the cooking, may be a stroke of luck for Clive). Bernard returns to the dining room to set the table.

Pattie, alone again with Belinda, confides in her. She doesn't really want to have the baby she's carrying. This will be the fifth child, and she's convinced that Eddie doesn't really want it. To come down to the bitter truth, she's convinced that Eddie wishes he didn't have a wife and children at all, that he looks upon them as hindrances to his career. We gather that Eddie's fortunes began their decline when he left working for Neville to start what has turned out to be an unsuccessful business on his own. Pattie is a little surprised that Eddie and Neville are still friends, given the circumstances. "Oh well, you'll never break that up," says Belinda.

In the meantime, Harvey is now talking to Rachel about his enthusiasm for the movie he's watching on TV and how much he'd like to meet the fellow who wrote it.

RACHEL: Oh. You think somebody actually wrote this?
HARVEY: Of course somebody wrote it.
RACHEL: Oh, you amaze me.
HARVEY: What a damned stupid thing to say. How utterly damned stupid. They'd hardly make this up as they went along, would they? They'd hardly invent the dialogue, would they?
RACHEL: I don't know what dialogue you mean. Nobody's said anything for ten minutes. Nobody's talking at all.
HARVEY: Well, of course, they're not talking. Not at the moment. They're punching each other.
RACHEL: Oh yes.
HARVEY: They can't talk while they're fighting, can they?
RACHEL: No. True.
HARVEY: Damn stupid thing to say then, wasn't it? Oh now, this is good. This bit's marvellous. You watch this fellow on the left.

Bernard briefly sticks his head into the hallway to apologize to Belinda for anything intemperate he may have said earlier, then returns to the dining room. Pattie is dismayed to learn from Belinda that he's planning on another of his puppet shows. With sudden determination, Rachel stands up and marches out of the sitting room. She's decided to meet the 8:05 in case Clive is on it, though she's prepared for the likelihood that he won't be. "Thirty-eight-year-old woman behaving like a teenager, aren't I? Well, if he's not on this train, bugger him, that's what I say." And she leaves. In the meantime, Pattie has been drawn in by the film Harvey's watching and is now sitting cheering the exciting parts with him.

Neville appears with some wine for dinner and tells Belinda that the meal allegedly will be ready in ten minutes, though it's his opinion that the leg of lamb is looking fresher than its cook. Belinda talks of her memories of Christmas as a child. Neville's memories are of his sister Phyllis crying in terror at the fear that Father Christmas might barge into her room. "Santaphobia" is his term for it.

BELINDA: I don't even get any surprises these days. I know what I've got. I went out and bought them myself. I brought them home and wrapped them up. I even paid for them out of the joint account.
NEVILLE: Oh, come on.
BELINDA: You could at least have written the labels, Nev.
NEVILLE: Darling, it's Christmas time.
BELINDA: Happy Christmas, Belinda or something. To my dear wife, whose face seems faintly familiar or something . . .

NEVILLE: It is Christmas time.

BELINDA: That's what I'm saying.

NEVILLE: I don't have to tell you about Christmas time, do I?

BELINDA: No. You don't have to tell me about Christmas time.

NEVILLE: Like it or not, darling, you married a retailer. But if you would like me to tell you about Christmas time . . .

BELINDA (over this): Oh, dear God, he is now going to tell me about Christmas time . . .

NEVILLE: Because if you would—

BELINDA: Forget it.

NEVILLE: —I'd be quite happy . . .

BELINDA: Thank you.

NEVILLE: Just say the word.

BELINDA: Shut up.

Bernard emerges to say that everybody should sit at the table and begins delivering food to the dining room. Belinda goes to the sitting room to tell Harvey and Pattie about the imminence of dinner. "Just a minute, just a minute," says Harvey. "This is a fight to the death." Belinda stays to watch this part with them. Eddie comes downstairs and also gets hooked on the film. Neville, sent by Bernard to bid the others to dinner, goes to the sitting room and sees them transfixed.

NEVILLE (craning to see through them): What are you all watching?

BELINDA (making room for him slightly): Look.

NEVILLE: Oh, this thing. It's not on again, is it?

PATTIE: Ooh.

EDDIE: Whoops.

HARVEY: Ha-ha . . .

NEVILLE: Look out.

BELINDA: There he goes.

HARVEY: Not quite.

 Bernard comes back to the dining room doorway.

BERNARD: What are you all doing? Come on.

BELINDA: Sorry, Bernard, coming. *(Back to the television.)* Oh no.

BERNARD (joining them): What are you all . . . *(Seeing the screen.)* Oh good gracious. He's going to fall off that, isn't he?

ALL: Shhh.

 Phyllis enters along the kitchen passageway, a woman in her late 30s. She is a woman exhausted and slightly drunk: a martyr to cooking. She totters into the hall.

NEVILLE: He's going.

PATTIE: There he goes.

HARVEY: He's gone. Bravo. *(He claps.)*

 They all join in. Phyllis, arriving at this precise moment, assumes their applause is for her and acknowledges it with a modest curtsy.

PHYLLIS: Thank you, thank you. *(Realizing her mistake.)* Oh.

BERNARD *(applauding her):* Well done, Phyllis, well done.
BELINDA: Oh, yes, well done, Phyllis. God, I'm starving.

The spell of the movie broken, the bulk of the assemblage drifts into the dining room. Belinda is turning off unnecessary lights when the doorbell rings. She goes to the door. It's Clive. Somehow Rachel has missed him at the station. Belinda helps Clive with his coat. As they stand looking at each other in the glow of the Christmas tree lights, there is a moment between them . . . *Curtain.*

Scene 2: Christmas Day, noon

Eddie is in the dining room eating cornflakes and reading a comic book. Belinda, carrying a tray, appears in the kitchen passageway and encounters Bernard, who is descending the stairs. It's been a bad night for Phyllis and, consequently, a bad night for Bernard. At least there's the comfort of knowing that, with the dinner over, Phyllis has no other responsibilities for the rest of the visit.

Belinda and Bernard enter the dining room. Eddie remarks to them that the comic book (intended as a present for his son) is quite good. Bernard tells them he's about to unload his puppet paraphernalia. Recalling the endless procession of thieves in last year's show, Eddie is relieved to learn that this year's is *The Three Little Pigs.* "Just the three of them, is it?" says Eddie. "Well, and their wives and families, of course," Bernard replies. Bernard goes upstairs with a cup of coffee for Phyllis.

Pattie appears from the back part of the hallway, cautioning her offstage children to wait in the kitchen while she fetches Daddy. Belinda, on her way to the kitchen with dirty dishes from the dining room, tips Pattie off as to Eddie's whereabouts. Pattie reminds Eddie he promised to go on a walk with her and the children. He's changed his mind and wants to be left alone. Pattie grabs the comic book. Eddie tells her that if she doesn't put the comic down he is liable to "do something I will really regret in a minute." "It won't be the first time, will it?" says Pattie.

At this point, Belinda enters the dining room. She senses she's walked in on something and walks right out again, disappearing up the kitchen passageway. *"Pattie puts the book quietly back on the table and leaves the dining room. She stands in the hall for a minute, staring fixedly at the Christmas tree, trying to compose herself."* Bernard comes downstairs and, on his way out the front door, tells her he is going out to get the puppet works from the car. Pattie gives no indication of having heard.

Neville emerges from the kitchen with silverware to put away. He tells Pattie that her children are asking for her, then joins Eddie in the dining room. Neville and Eddie note that both Clive and Rachel are absent, leading them to speculate about the possibility that Rachel might have spent the night with her guest. They dismiss this as unlikely. As far as they know, Rachel is and has always been celibate.

Pattie, in the meantime, has picked up a package from under the tree. It is one of the toys for their son Gary. She coolly reminds Eddie that it doesn't work and that he should either fix it or get rid of it, "Because if Gary opens it tomorrow and it doesn't work, it'll break his heart." Eddie says he'll see to it, and Pattie exits.

Neville suggests that he and Eddie pop down to the village pub when it opens. He characterizes this action as getting "out of their way." In the meantime, they will deal with the problem of the toy, *"a battery-operated vehicle."*

Bernard enters carrying the first of several loads of his puppet paraphernalia —a small stage, string-controlled puppets, handmade scenery. *"Hours of love have gone into the creation of it all, though it remains, sadly, rather inept."* He stores the stuff in the sitting room and ducks into the dining room to tell Neville that he's getting ready for a go at *The Three Little Pigs.* "Just the three of them, is it?" asks Neville. Bernard replies with an irritated "Yes," and leaves to bring in another load.

Neville tells Eddie that he's planning on opening a third shop. He knows that Eddie left to try working on his own, but they have to acknowledge that hasn't worked out so well. Neville's going to need a new manager and a full staff for the new store. Is Eddie interested? Eddie is overwhelmed. Neville tells him to think about it a bit and give him an answer by New Year. For the moment, Neville will take the toy into his shed, see if he can get it to function. "You know me, I like a challenge." Neville disappears as Bernard brings another load into the sitting room and leaves again through the front door.

Now Belinda returns. She is irked by the kids' candies stuck to the floor and by Bernard's leaving the front door open. In fact, she is irked generally. She looks into the dining room and sees that half of the silverware Neville was supposed to put away is still out. She turns to Eddie, who has picked up the comic again, and demands, "Has he just left this half done and walked away?" She explodes. One bloody thing she asks him to do for the whole bloody holiday, and he can't even do that. Eddie moves as if to finish the job, but Belinda forbids it. It's Neville's job, and nobody is to do it but him. Is that understood? Eddie, not about to challenge her in this temper, says yes.

In the meantime, Clive has descended the stairs carrying a couple of presents; so, when Belinda sweeps out of the dining room, she is practically on top of Clive. Her manner changes. A moment or two of pleasantries, and she's off to get him a cup of coffee. Clive briefly says hello through the dining room doorway to Eddie, who volunteers that if he's ever stuck for ideas for another book he'll be happy to give him a few. Clive says thanks and retreats back into the hallway, where he encounters Bernard hauling in some more of his stuff. A few words, and Bernard takes this new lot into the sitting room.

Now Harvey appears in the front door, fresh from church. He tells Clive he goes once a year, just to "keep the options open." Bernard edges past Harvey back outside for another load. After Bernard is gone, Harvey tells Clive that if he's ever in need of a doctor, he should avoid Bernard's practice like the plague.

HARVEY: He's the worst doctor in the world.
CLIVE: Is he?
HARVEY: Total washout. He's sent people to their graves, convinced they were critically ill when in fact they were perfectly fit. He's pronounced people A-One,

and they've dropped dead in his waiting room on the way out. Very poor doctor with a second-class brain. Don't go near him, he's lethal. You've seen his wife?

CLIVE: Phyllis?

HARVEY: My niece. See what he's done to her. She always was peculiar, mind you. Now she's completely loopy. She drinks like a fish, too. He ought to be struck off before he does any more damage.

Bernard returns through the front door, with more stuff.

BERNARD: Excuse me, please.

HARVEY: What's all that?

BERNARD: Just my theater.

HARVEY: Oh Gawd.

Bernard goes into the sitting room.

(*To Clive, confidentially.*) Dozy little sod. Wait till he see what I've got him for Christmas.

CLIVE: What's that?

HARVEY: Something to wake his ideas up. (*Removing his coat.*) The biggest alarm clock you've ever seen. Alarm like a fire bell. Got it second-hand. Slightly faulty. Goes off without the slightest warning. Always find something. Last year I gave him a box of maroons. Set one off in his bedroom. I ran back from church, would you believe that?

CLIVE: Ran?

HARVEY: I still keep fit. Thirty-seven years with a security firm, you see.

CLIVE: Were you?

HARVEY: Fighting the bastards on the streets most of the time. Clubs, ammonia, pick-axe handles, pepper, socks full of sand . . .

BERNARD (*squeezing past them again*): Excuse me.

Bernard goes out.

HARVEY: Not that you could ever stop it. Not on your own. It's an irreversible process. It's all coming apart, you know. The whole fabric. Ripping like tissue paper. One day, we'll wake up—if we wake up at all, that is—and our so-called civilization will have vanished overnight. And you can put that in your book . . . . .

Harvey insists he's prepared. Physically fit and armed. If someone gives him trouble, there's a six-inch knife strapped in a sheath to the side of his leg, ready for business. Not to mention the gun upstairs. Harvey speaks with enthusiasm of the havoc he is capable of wreaking. Clive makes an effort at being pleasant, but it's obvious Harvey is making him uneasy. Having made his points, Harvey goes to the sitting room to watch another movie on TV. Within minutes, he's fallen asleep. Bernard, in the meantime, loaded with more stuff, returns and, in passing, warns Clive that Harvey is "completely mad."

Belinda enters with Clive's coffee, which gives Clive the opportunity to give her the presents he's brought by way of a thank you for having him as a guest. They sit on a bench in the hallway for a chat. Belinda confesses embarrassment at not being familiar with his writing, but then it's hard to keep track of all the new authors. "I mean, there's so many of you, aren't there? Names to watch, I mean. Every week there's another dozen. The most exciting since, the best since, the most promising since so-and-so and occasionally, it's really awful because I've never even heard of so-and-so." Clive tells her that his novel, which apparently has been well-reviewed and is selling nicely, is a fictionalized treatment of his failed marriage. They end up sitting quite close together. Something is beginning to happen between them. They both know it and they know each other knows it. It's a little awkward but not unpleasant.

Rachel comes downstairs, and Belinda takes Clive's empty cup and disappears into the kitchen. Rachel has arranged to take Clive on a walk. With an air of determined perkiness she talks to Clive about a number of things of no particular consequence, but she can sense something new is in the air. "I have a feeling I should have got up a bit earlier this morning for some reason," she says. Seeing that Clive doesn't have the appropriate footwear to go for a walk in the country, she excuses herself to go upstairs to find something. A few seconds after she leaves, Belinda appears with boots. Clive has just put these on when Rachel appears with the boots she's found. She sees that Belinda has beaten her to it.

BELINDA: I've just lent him Nev's.
CLIVE: Sorry.
RACHEL: Oh. Well. Wasted journey, wasn't it?
    (She drops the boots over the banisters.)
BELINDA: God knows whose those are. Probably belonged to the builders. I'll take them out back.
    Clive stands up. Rachel comes downstairs.
Are those OK for you?
CLIVE: They're fine. Perfect fit.
RACHEL *(pulling on her coat):* Off we go then.
CLIVE *(following her):* OK.
BELINDA: Oh wait. Here. *(She holds out her scarf.)*
CLIVE: Ah. *(He goes to take it.)*
RACHEL: What's that?
BELINDA: It's a scarf for Clive.
RACHEL: He doesn't need a scarf.
BELINDA: Yes, he does. It's cold.
RACHEL: That's your scarf.
BELINDA: Yes, I know it is, but I'm not going out, am I?
RACHEL: He can't wear that.
BELINDA: Why not?
RACHEL: It's a woman's scarf. He can't wear a woman's scarf.
BELINDA: It's not a woman's scarf. It's just a scarf.
RACHEL: He'd look extraordinary.
BELINDA: Oh Rachel, don't be idiotic.
RACHEL: I'm not being idiotic. I just refuse to be seen going out with a man dressed in a woman's scarf. I'm sorry.
BELINDA: Rachel, for God's sake.
CLIVE: It's all right, really. I don't need a scarf. I've gone off the whole idea of a scarf. Thanks all the same.
BELINDA: OK. Suit yourself.

RACHEL *(irritably, thrusting Clive's coat at him):* Oh, do come on, if you're coming.
> *Rachel goes out by the front door.*
CLIVE: Goodbye, then.
BELINDA: Goodbye. I'll see you later.
CLIVE: Yes.
BELINDA: Keep warm, won't you?
CLIVE: I will.
> *Clive goes out the front door after Rachel.*

Neville now appears, still fiddling with the toy. He tells Belinda that he and Eddie are going out for a pint down at the pub. While Neville continues to monkey with the toy, Belinda talks brightly about what a happy couple they are. That they're still in love, right? Neville nods and mumbles agreement, but his focus is still the toy. Belinda keeps at it, about how, apart from everything else, they're also friends. She says she believes that men and women can truly be friends: "Maybe not friends like you and, say, Eddie or between me and some—woman friend. I don't think a man and a woman could ever get that close. No. Not as friends." "No," Neville echoes distractedly.

BELINDA: But we still definitely have something, don't we? Apart from sharing the same house. And the same children. We must have.
NEVILLE *(after a pause):* Yes, I'd say that was—very true, yes.
BELINDA: What is?
NEVILLE: What you said. *(He rises.)* Look, I'd better go and get that drink in. You be all right, will you?
BELINDA: Yes—yes . . .
NEVILLE *(ruffling her hair):* Cheer up, then. Love me?
BELINDA: Yes.
NEVILLE: That's what I like to hear.

Neville calls to Eddie in the dining room that he's close to fixing the toy and that it's time they were on their way. Neville disappears into the kitchen. Eddie, following after Neville, explains to Belinda that they're off to the pub. "Oh super, super," says Belinda *"savagely."* Eddie doesn't understand her reaction and doesn't want to stick around to try. He leaves. Belinda stands alone, *"desolate"* in the hallway, holding her scarf and the boots Rachel brought down.

Bernard enters with the last of his stuff. He shows Belinda one of his puppets —the Big Bad Wolf. "Better be careful or he'll huff and he'll puff and he'll blow your house down, eh?" Laughing, he goes to the sitting room. After a moment, Belinda drifts back to the kitchen.

Scene 3: Christmas Day, midnight

In the sitting room, Eddie is asleep in an armchair. Rachel is sitting immobile in the dark on the window seat, holding what's left of a drink. Across the stage, in the dining room, Neville, Clive, Bernard and Phyllis are playing one of the board games intended for the children. From the way they play, one gathers a fair amount of wine has been consumed. Bernard, who is keeping an apprehensive eye on Phyllis, seems to be the only one not enjoying this. It doesn't help matters that he's losing badly.

Pattie enters to collect whatever needs to be washed. It seems that, while these four have been playing, she and Belinda have been cleaning up after the dinner. Phyllis makes a gratuitous comment about having already done her work by cooking dinner the previous night, which brings out the fact that Pattie cleaned up Phyllis's mess, too. Bernard diplomatically rises to help Pattie by taking the dirty glasses into the kitchen.

Pattie finds Eddie asleep in the sitting room. She tries to rouse him, not an easy thing to do given the amount he's consumed. She is startled to realize that Rachel is in the room, too. Pattie tells Rachel that her Clive is very nice. Rachel replies that Clive isn't hers. They've had dinner together a few times, at her instigation. In a grimly honest vein, she says the only reason Clive hasn't told her to get lost is because he's too polite. "I'm sure he's wondering how on earth he came to be here," says Rachel. She knows he's happy he did come, but she doesn't flatter herself to think that it has anything to do with her.

Pattie tries to advise Rachel that if one wants something badly one should fight for it. "I had to fight for this," says Pattie, referring to Eddie. She was one of four after Eddie, and look where it got her, she observes ironically. Eddie wakes up a little. As Pattie guides him upstairs, he tells her that Neville's going to make him the manager of a new shop.

A cry of triumph: Phyllis has won the game. In high spirits, she and Clive and Neville indulge in some fairly drunken banter. Neville toddles off to the kitchen to check on Belinda. Bernard reappears with hot water bottles and suggests to Phyllis that they go to bed. But Phyllis would rather stay and talk to Clive, whom she declares to be witty and charming, so Bernard heads upstairs on his own.

Phyllis tells Clive that his next book should be about her and Bernard's relationship, the story of a brilliant doctor who sacrifices his career in an effort to cure his wife. Neville emerges from the kitchen, says goodnight to Phyllis and Clive and staggers upstairs. Phyllis continues to show her interest in Clive. She wants to know where his books come from. "Are you a homosexual, for instance?" No, says Clive.

Belinda, finally emerging from the kitchen, bids them good night and goes up. Clive suggests to Phyllis that perhaps they, too, should retire for the night, but Phyllis wants to show him something. He follows her to the Christmas tree, where she looks through the packages till she finds the gift she and Bernard are giving to one of the girls. She unwraps it, a battery-operated model of a bear with a drum. Phyllis places it in the middle of the hall floor and switches it on. The bear begins to drum up a storm. *"In the silence of the night, the noise seems quite deafening."* Phyllis is delighted by it; Clive is not. He moves to turn it off as Harvey, who has been roused from his sleep, comes downstairs to investigate. Hearing Harvey approach, Phyllis has hidden behind the tree, and, as Harvey upbraids Clive, she echoes the old man mockingly. Harvey registers her presence, then goes back to bed.

"Lord! What do you think he thought we were doing?" says Phyllis. This is not a subject on which Clive wants to dwell. He manages, finally, to propel Phyllis up the stairs and is rewrapping the present when he is startled by Rachel, who only now emerges from the black of the sitting room.

She has something to say to him, and she seems about to when Belinda appears on the stairs, dressed in night things. Belinda makes some lame excuse about having possibly left the oven on. She comes downstairs, goes to the kitchen, then trots out again and back up the stairs. And now Rachel unburdens herself. What she's looking for out of a relationship—serious companionship without sex—is different than, say, what Belinda or most women look for. She is realistic enough to understand that the possibility of such an arrangement enduring is slim. She figures that even if she and Clive were to succeed platonically, a woman with an interest in a sexual relationship would probably come along and mess things up between them.

CLIVE: What you're saying is you want one but not the other.

RACHEL: Well, I've managed without the other extremely well for thirty-eight years. More or less. And I haven't honestly missed it and—well, I feel about it a bit like smoking—it would be stupid to take it up at my age and possibly damage my health when I've done so well so far. I hesitate to say all this to you because men usually take this terribly personally and feel hurt and hit back and accuse me of being frigid or a lesbian. Neither of which is true, as it happens. I do feel some things very passionately quite often. And I don't fancy a woman cluttering up my bed any more than a man. Still, that's it. I realize I can't have only half, so I'm handing you all back. I'm a bit drunk, or I'd never have said this. I hope it makes sense. If I have hurt you, I'm sorry because I wouldn't want to do that. Not for the world.

CLIVE: I'm sorry too. We could—this all sounds very corny but I hope we can carry on in some sense. I really do value your friendship, you know.

RACHEL: Oh? Thank you.

CLIVE (awkwardly): All I'm saying is, I wouldn't want to lose that. That's all.

RACHEL: No. Good. That's good.

> Rachel suddenly caves in and start to cry. Clive, for a moment, is transfixed with surprise.

CLIVE (recovering): Rachel . . . Now, Rachel, come on, now.

RACHEL (between sobs): I'm sorry—I really am sorry. I never usually behave like this.

CLIVE (beside her): That's all right.

RACHEL: I really don't. You must believe me.

CLIVE: No, no, I realize.

RACHEL: Oh, why does sex go and spoil everything? (She sniffs.) God, I'm revolting. Have you got a . . .?

CLIVE: No, I'm afraid . . .

RACHEL: No, you never do have one, do you? That little brown parcel there. (She points to the base of the tree.) There's some in there, I think. Could you pass me one of those?

CLIVE (getting them): Right. (Holding up the the parcel.) This one?

RACHEL: Yes, I think so.

CLIVE *(tearing it open):* Yes, right first time. *(He pulls a handkerchief from the gift pack and hands it to Rachel. Rachel blows her nose.)* Better?

RACHEL: Thank you.

CLIVE: I'll wrap these up again. Nobody'll know the difference. Whose are they?

RACHEL *(starting to cry again):* They were my present to you.

CLIVE: Oh, I see.

RACHEL: I had them embroidered specially because I knew you never had any. *(Wailing.)* Now, you haven't got anything from me at all now.

CLIVE: It's all right, Rachel. Look, I'm wrapping them up again. See?

RACHEL *(getting louder):* Oh God, I'm such a mess, aren't I?

CLIVE *(as to a child):* Look, you see. *(By now he's wrapped them up again.)* Now I've forgotten. Forgotten what it is. Good heavens, what's this? No idea. Rachel, Rachel, please.

> He breaks off. Harvey is back at the top of the stairs. Rachel turns, sees him, and quietens down.

HARVEY: What the hell is going on?

CLIVE: Sorry.

HARVEY: One-thirty.

CLIVE: Yes.

HARVEY: A.M.

CLIVE: Yes. We were just wrapping presents.

> A sob from Rachel.

HARVEY: Who is that? Is that Rachel?

RACHEL *(getting up, handkerchief clasped to her face):* Yes.

> She goes upstairs past Harvey.

CLIVE: Rachel . . .

RACHEL: Good-night.

HARVEY: Good-night.

CLIVE: Good-night.

> Rachel goes off upstairs.

HARVEY: I don't know what you're up to down there, Morris, but I'll say this, I can't say I've liked what I've seen. You take my tip, you'll buzz off to bed this minute.

Harvey returns to bed, and Clive returns to rewrapping the gift. Now Belinda comes downstairs again, this time allegedly to check whether she left the deep-freeze open. After a look into the kitchen, she returns to the hall.

A few words are exchanged between Clive and Belinda about the events of the night. Then Belinda says, "Oh God, I want you." The feeling is very definitely mutual. They embrace. They decide to make love right now. Where? No, not in the sitting room, Belinda insists. Clinging to each other, they make their way to the dining room, but that doesn't seem appropriate either. So Clive begins to guide them toward the kitchen. Belinda objects. "I'm not making love in a bloody kitchen. I'm too old for that." By default, it will be in the hallway, under the Christmas tree.

But as they are about to begin, Belinda inadvertently bumps a box causing the little drumming bear to begin hammering away again. Trying to find the box, Belinda jostles Harvey's present to Bernard. It's the defective alarm clock, and the jostle is all it needs to start clanging. In the meantime, Clive has run afoul of Neville's remote control device, and the cassette of the Christmas carols blares out. The rest of the family, dressed in their night clothes, assemble at the top of the stairs and look down on them. Belinda and Clive finally manage to muzzle the various gadgets. They look up at the others. Belinda finally volunteers, "Sorry. We—just couldn't wait to open our surprises." *"The others look distinctly unconvinced"* as the act ends.

ACT II

Scene 1: Boxing Day

In mid-afternoon, the children and some of their friends will be returning to the house soon, and most of the adults are involved in various plans to amuse them. First the kids are to see Bernard's puppet show; then Clive, dressed up as Father Christmas, is to distribute gifts to them; then they are to have tea in the dining room. Phyllis and Belinda would like to get the dining room in order, but Neville and Eddie are currently occupying the table, attempting to fix the drumming bear that got damaged the night before. In the meantime, Clive is upstairs trying on the costume, and Bernard, with the reluctant help of Pattie, is in the sitting room readying his gear for a run-through of the show.

While Bernard prepares, Harvey wanders into the dining room. Neville asks what the kids will be returning from, and Harvey tells him that he sent the kids off to play with their guns. Neville comments that Harvey is "extremely bloodthirsty." "Why not?" Harvey responds. "They've got to learn. There's going to come the time when any housewife who steps out of her front door without a loaded revolver in her basket will just be asking for trouble."

Harvey confides in Neville and Eddie his doubts about Clive and the events of the previous evening. Neville doesn't want to dwell on the subject. "I trust my wife," he says staunchly. The sexual aspect hadn't occurred to Harvey. What he's concerned about is "the looting." Every time he came downstairs last night, Harvey saw Clive ripping open presents. He suspects that this writing business is simply a cover, that Clive is really nothing but a thief. Harvey's been in security for years, he knows what he's talking about.

Harvey also repeats Phyllis's suspicion that Clive is homosexual. Neville and Eddie don't take this at all seriously. Harvey goes into the hall, picks up the bag of presents Clive will be carrying as Father Christmas and starts to count the gifts, presumably to make sure that the number Clive distributes is the same as what's there.

Belinda comes out of the kitchen and tries to get Neville to move his stuff. She also chides Phyllis for setting out the children's treat, frozen mousse, way before proper time. Phyllis's feelings are hurt, and she retreats into the kitchen.

Bernard tells Pattie they'll be ready to start soon. "Oh, hooray," says Pattie, who goes into the hallway and tells Harvey (who's just finishing his counting) that

Michael Alan Gregory and Robert Cornthwaite
(Harvey) in a scene from *Season's Greetings*

Bernard's rehearsal is imminent. Harvey goes into the kitchen to see if Phyllis wants to subject herself to Bernard's creation.

Pattie and Belinda have a moment alone in the hallway. Pattie's a bit more upbeat than she was the night before. She tells Belinda how excited Eddie is to have been offered the managership of Neville's new store. Something about what Pattie says surprises Belinda, but before she can pursue it, Harvey emerges from the kitchen where he has just encountered a tearful Phyllis mumbling something about mousse.

Belinda goes to the kitchen. Neville and Eddie continue to tinker in the dining room, so it's only Harvey and Pattie in the sitting room with Bernard. "I'm your only audience," says Harvey. "So get on with it. Entertain me." Bernard tells Pattie that he will be calling on her to hand him puppets and pieces of scenery at certain moments, so she must hold herself in a state of readiness. To begin with, he wants her to pass him the puppets of the postman and the pig. She passes him two puppets. Bernard is irritated; she's passed him the second pig and he wants the first pig. "These pigs all look the same," she observes. Harvey reminds them that the kids will be arriving in 27 minutes. Bernard tells Harvey to shut up and cues Pattie to raise the curtain.

And so begins the rehearsal. And Lord, is this show dreadful! The first scene is about the postman's encounter with the three pigs, one at a time. It is done with a complete lack of grace, accompanied by Bernard's tedious dialogue and Pattie's confusion as to which pigs are which. Harvey, standing in for the kids, makes his usual rude comments.

The first scene finally over, Pattie rings the curtain down. Harvey applauds. It's certainly an improvement over last year's, he says. Bernard informs him that this was just the first of 17 scenes. Harvey tells him he'd better pick it up a bit; the kids are due in another 22 minutes. While Bernard and Pattie wrestle with puppets and scenery, Harvey decides to step out into the hallway. There he encounters Clive, dressed in his costume, trying the sack of presents on for size. "I thought you'd like to know I've counted every one of those presents in that sack," says Harvey darkly. Clive, of course, has no idea what Harvey means.

Harvey returns to the sitting room and Clive goes into the dining room. Eddie makes a joke about the costume, but Neville, concentrating on his repair job, doesn't bother to look up. Clive returns to the hall where he encounters Rachel. He tries to start a conversation with her, but Rachel, affecting cheerfulness, evades him by going to the kitchen.

In the meantime, Bernard and Pattie have launched another scene of the puppet show involving some business between the wolf and a dog. Bernard calls it comic relief. Harvey calls it boring. If he were running the show, he'd have the wolf eat the dog as an appetizer.

Phyllis emerges from the kitchen, evidently having been told that her assistance there is unnecessary. She coolly asks Clive if he's sobered up, then goes into the sitting room. Now Belinda emerges from the kitchen, offers Clive a brisk hello and goes into the dining room where she is finally successful in getting Neville to pack up his stuff and leave. She is annoyed to see that Eddie has consumed a number of the sandwiches that had been made for the children. Eddie, gathering into a box the stuff that Neville hadn't managed to collect, slips out of the dining room.

Bernard is having terrible problems with his scenery. Pattie, at her wits' end, manages to grab her husband to come help. Before joining Pattie in the sitting room, Eddie hands his load of stuff to Neville, who has just reappeared in the hallway. With everyone else either in the sitting room or the kitchen, Neville and Clive are alone in the hall. Neville, is looking through the box Eddie handed him as Clive approaches.

CLIVE: Look—Neville . . .
NEVILLE: Santa? What can I do for you?
CLIVE: Something has to be said about last night.
NEVILLE: No need.
CLIVE: I think there is.
NEVILLE: We were all drunk. You were drunk, she was drunk. So was I. Forget it.

CLIVE: Look, we really weren't that drunk.

NEVILLE: I think I'd prefer it if you were.

CLIVE: Sorry?

NEVILLE (quietly and pleasantly): Let's put it this way. If I thought for one moment that you'd been down there on the floor in my hall under my Christmas tree, trying to screw my wife while you were both stone-cold sober, that would put a very different complexion on things. Because in that case, I promise you I would start to take you to pieces bit by bit. And as for her, she'd find herself back on Social Security before she had time to pull her knickers up. OK, Santa? (He winks at Clive.) Good lad.

> Neville pats Clive on the shoulder and goes out along the kitchen passageway. Clive stands bemused. Belinda comes back in view in the dining room, having rearranged the table. She now leaves the room and moves past Clive to the kitchen.

CLIVE: Er . . .

BELINDA (turning): Yes?

CLIVE: Nothing.

BELINDA: No. Right.

> Belinda goes back to the kitchen. Clive sits on the bench in the hall.

In the sitting room, Bernard, Pattie and Eddie get into a terrible fight as they try to work together on the puppet show. Pattie's pregnant tummy keeps knocking over scenery and she keeps misunderstanding Bernard's not-very-clear instructions. Harvey adds fuel to the fire by making nasty cracks and regularly announcing how little time they have left before the kids arrive. Bernard explodes, calling Pattie a "silly, stupid woman." Phyllis attempts to calm Bernard down, but tempers escalate. Bernard bellows at Pattie, Eddie comes to her defense, Pattie runs out of the room in tears, Bernard yells at Phyllis and Eddie decides he's had enough and leaves. For a moment in the hallway, it looks as though Eddie will do something concrete to comfort his wife, but when he actually opens his mouth it's to say that, if she wants him, he'll be with Neville. Eddie exits. A despondent Pattie sits down on the stairs.

Harvey tells Bernard that he has three minutes left in which to rehearse. Bernard snaps that there's no way to finish the play off in three minutes. Oh yes there is, says Harvey, who grabs the puppets.

HARVEY: Here's your ending. Har-har-har-hallo, Mr. Pig. I've come to eat you. Really, Mr. Wolf? Well, take that. Bash, bam, wallop, biff, whack.

> Harvey crashes the puppets together with great savagery, simulating a fight. This culminates with him hurling the wolf high in the air so that it lands some distance away in the corner of the room, a tangle of limbs and strings. Harvey kicks the scenery in the theater over for good measure, then stands triumphant.

End of wolf. Good enough for you?

> A silence.

PHYLLIS (crying): He took so much care making those.

BERNARD (in a deep rage now, his voice low and controlled): You are a loathesome man, Harvey, you really are. You're almost totally negative, do you know that? And that's such an easy thing to be, isn't it? So long as you stay negative, you're absolutely safe from laughter or criticism because you've never made anything or done anything that people can criticize. All they can really say about you is that you're a snob, a bigot, a racist, a chauvinist, an ignorant, insensitive, narrow-minded, intolerant, humorless wart.

HARVEY *(having digested this):* Very well. We shall see. We'll see who's negative. Ha!

> *Harvey goes out into the hall. Rachel comes along from the kitchen with a cup of coffee. She stops as she sees Harvey.*

We'll see. *(Speaking to the house in general.)* You'll all be glad of me sometime. Laugh now but you'll see.

> *Harvey goes out by the front door.*

Clive, in a scene that begins in the hallway and moves into the dining room, tries to be honest with Rachel. First, he wants her to understand he wasn't drunk last night. Second, she shouldn't blame herself at all. "You've been feeling guilty because you felt you'd been holding back on me—failing to give me what you felt I needed from you." Rachel acknowledges this. Clive goes on to say that she shouldn't feel bad about it because he was never interested in her in that way. If he gave her another impression, he's sorry. Rachel absorbs and accepts this. Clive says that as soon as he's finished playing Father Christmas as he promised, he'd like to go to the railway station and remove himself. Rachel says that the only problem is that the next train isn't until about 6 o'clock in the morning, and nobody takes that. Clive is determined that he will. Rachel volunteers to drive him to the station, but Clive says he'd prefer to take care of it by himself. Rachel offers to lend him an alarm clock. Clive tells her that she's been marvelous and that everything that's gone wrong has been his fault. "This is always happening to me," says Rachel. "The more I try and apologize for me, the more other people accuse me of making them feel guilty." She moves away from him to the dining room table. Clive returns to the hallway, berating himself and pacing.

Belinda now appears in the hallway with the news that the kids have arrived. Is everybody ready? Hearing no objection from Pattie (still sitting on the stairs) or Clive (glum in his costume), she goes into the kitchen to bring them in.

In the sitting room, Phyllis asks Bernard what he's going to do. Bernard rises and begins to straighten his theater saying, "The show must go on." The lights fade.

Scene 2: December 27, 5:15 a.m.

Harvey, in his dressing gown, is in a chair in the dining room angled so that he would have a view of the hall and front door—if he were awake. A fully dressed Bernard comes quietly downstairs. After noting that it has begun snowing, he goes to the sitting room, where he sits and looks wistfully at his disassembled puppet theater. Now another figure appears, this time from the kitchen: Rachel, dressed for the outdoors. They become aware of each other's presence. Rachel has risen early to run Clive to the station in time for the early train. For his part,

Bernard explains that he was awakened by the malfunctioning of the alarm clock Harvey gave to him. Phyllis slept through it, but Bernard thought, as long as he was up, he might as well get a jump on loading the puppet works into the car —except that he's discovered it's snowing very hard, so he's decided not to attempt it until later.

BERNARD: . . . . . You know, it just occurred to me, maybe because it's so early in the morning, I really am a dreadful failure, you know.
RACHEL: Oh no.
BERNARD: Yes. Really and truly.
RACHEL: Is it because of the show yesterday?
BERNARD: Maybe partly that. I mean, let's face it. The poor little blighters were utterly bored to tears, weren't they? I hate to say it, but Harvey was right. Absolutely right. He has a thoroughly unpleasant way of putting things but he was right. I really mustn't do any more of them. Enough's enough.
RACHEL: Perhaps you could do something else.
BERNARD: No, no. You get out of touch with children, you see. If you don't have any yourself. Phyllis and I really should have had some but she's so very weak physically, you see. Maybe I should have done something about that, but I'm not a very good doctor either. I don't think I've killed anyone, mind you. Not to my knowledge. I hope not. But I honestly don't think I've cured many people either. Just left things very much as they were. Oh well.

Clive comes downstairs. Bernard says goodnight and returns to his bed. Rachel tells Clive, in spite of what he said, she decided to get up and take him to the station. And a good thing, too, given the snow. She's also made him sandwiches to tide him over on the long, slow train back to London. And she's brought him a balacalva to help him keep warm. "Are you sure you don't mind? I mean, it is a woman's balaclava," says Clive. "It's OK," says Rachel, smiling. "It's this woman's."
Rachel has something else she wants to bring up: her lack of willingness to sleep with him. He had replied that it was O.K. because it wasn't something he wanted anyway. She tells him she believes he said that so as to make things easier for her. But the fact is, she's decided she really does "want to give it" if he wants it. "You see, I think I only said I didn't want to give it because I felt you didn't want it," she explains.
Clive is nonplussed. He explodes in frustration with himself about the mess he's made of his life. "Look at me. I'm a writer, for God's sake, a writer. Every time something of value comes along, I . . ." This triggers another crying fit from Rachel. Looking for the handkerchiefs Rachel gave him, he realizes he's left them in his room. Rachel tells him not to worry about them, but Clive refuses to go without them. He puts his suitcase down by the Christmas tree and heads upstairs. Rachel goes outside to warm up the car. The noise she makes as she exits wakes up Harvey.
For the first time we can see that Harvey is holding a revolver. He hears the sound of Clive on the stairs and hides. Clive now appears carrying the box containing his handkerchiefs. Harvey pops out, turns a flashlight on Clive and

orders him not to move. Clive panics, leaping for his suitcase. *"Harvey fires a warning shot in the direction of the Christmas tree. There is a clang as it hits the tub, then the Christmas tree lights come full on and there is a brisk burst of a children's Christmas song which finishes in a few seconds with a shrill shriek as the tape snaps, evidently damaged by the shot. During this, Clive grabs his case, holds it up in front of him like a shield and backs a little way to the door."* Clive tells Harvey not to shoot, but Harvey does indeed fire, and, with a cry, Clive falls at the foot of the glowing Christmas tree.

Belinda, Neville, Pattie and Eddie appear to investigate the noise. Neville shouts at Harvey, "You stupid old loony. Where did you get that gun?" Belinda tells Neville that if he weren't so oblivious he would have known, as did everybody else, that Harvey is "a walking arsenal." Neville orders Eddie to take a hysterical Pattie back to bed. Rachel returns, absorbs what's happened and grills Harvey, who, in his defense, insists that Clive was looting.

Bernard appears with his bag to determine Clive's condition. After examining Clive, he stands up and gravely announces that he is dead. A silence falls on the group; a silence that is broken by Clive moaning. Rachel and Belinda kneel beside Clive. He's alive! Bernard, *"standing alone in agony"* mutters, "Dear God, what a failure. I can't even get that right."

Upon closer examination, Clive seems to have been hit in the arm or shoulder. Rachel proposes they take him to the hospital. They'll use Bernard's station wagon. Bernard is agreeable as long as they don't expect him to be able to manage driving. As they are about to take him outside, Clive begins to come to. They hush up to hear what he has to say.

CLIVE *(suddenly quite clearly):* I want you. I need you so much. Belinda. Belinda.
    A silence.
BELINDA: He's delirious.
RACHEL: Yes.
BELINDA: He means you. He's got us muddled up. He's saying my name but it's definitely you he wants.
RACHEL *(flatly):* Yes. Well, it really doesn't matter to me one way or the other.
NEVILLE: Come on, then. Let's get him in the car.

Rachel, Bernard, Belinda and Neville take Clive out to the car while Harvey, not entirely cognizant of what's going on, drifts upstairs. Neville and Belinda return. Belinda notices that Clive's suitcase has been left behind. Picking it up, she sees that a bullet has gone through it. "Probably saved his life but ruined his laundry," Neville remarks. He's got to call the police, of course.

NEVILLE: . . . . . If I don't, the hospital will. You can't go around shooting your guests, you know, whatever you might think of them. He can put that in his book anyway.
BELINDA: I'm going to make some tea. *(She moves to the kitchen.)*
NEVILLE: Fine. No, you see, the bullet went through the case and . . . *(Something at the base of the Christmas tree catches his attention.)* Hallo.

BELINDA: What?

NEVILLE *(examining the tub):* It's gone straight through here, see.

BELINDA: Oh yes.

NEVILLE: Oh, no. He's hit this. *(He pulls out the cassette player hidden in the tub.)*

BELINDA: What's that?

NEVILLE: The kids' Christmas cassette player. The one I rigged for them. *(Opening the lid.)* Oh, look at this. *(He puts the machine on the table and pulls away handfuls of loose tape.)* What a mess. Looks as if he hit the capstan.

BELINDA: Nev . . .

NEVILLE: So long as he's missed the motor.

BELINDA: Nev—you going to phone?

NEVILLE *(absorbed again):* In a sec. In a sec.

BELINDA: Hey. About Eddie.

NEVILLE: Yes.

BELINDA: Did you offer him the job with you?

NEVILLE: Yes, why?

BELINDA: Pattie said you'd offered him manager.

NEVILLE: Manager?

BELINDA: Of the new branch.

NEVILLE: You're joking.

BELINDA: You haven't?

NEVILLE: Not a hope.

BELINDA: She said he swore you had.

NEVILLE: No. I'd never offer him manager. Not Eddie. He couldn't cope with all that. I told him I was opening a new branch and I'd need staff, that's all.

BELINDA: Oh, that's all right then. I was going to say . . . *(Moving to the kitchen again)* Hope he's all right.

NEVILLE: Who?

BELINDA: Clive. I hope he's all right.

NEVILLE: Yes, he'll be all right. He's got Rachel, hasn't he?

BELINDA: Yes. He's got Rachel.

> *Belinda goes into the kitchen. Neville continues to tinker with the cassette, as the lights fade and the curtain falls.*

THE MYSTERY OF EDWIN DROOD

A Musical in Two Acts

BOOK, MUSIC AND LYRICS BY RUPERT HOLMES

SUGGESTED BY THE NOVEL BY CHARLES DICKENS

Cast and credits appear on pages 304 and 330

RUPERT HOLMES (book, music, lyrics) was born in 1947 in Cheshire, England, where his American father and British mother were living during his father's service in the U.S. Army. The family moved to Nyack, N.Y. in 1950, and Holmes (an American now entitled to dual citizenship) was educated there, through high school. He grew up with music as a major interest—his father was a jazz saxophonist and a conductor for NBC radio—and in 1965 he entered Manhattan School of Music to study composing and theory. At the same time, he was making recordings on his own, and he left school in 1968 when the very teachers evaluating his work as a student were playing his work as a recording artist in the classroom.

As long as he can remember, Holmes loved making up stories as well as writing music, so that his songs—such as "Escape" ("The Piña Colada Song"), which reached the top of all the charts—tend to have definite story lines. This is true of most of the 70 numbers written, produced and performed by their author in seven albums of recordings. It was natural for him, therefore, to take on the librettist's as well as the songwriter's function in the authorship of The Mystery of Edwin Drood. *He had always been fascinated with the unfinished Dickens novel, which had musical elements in the story itself—a choirmaster and a delicate soprano among the characters. Setting it as a play-within-a-play (as a British music hall company is introduced to the audience by their chairman, played by George Rose, then settles into a performance of the* Drood *characters) permitted him to make "quantum leaps" in the story line and in the introduction of musical numbers. After consultations with Joseph Papp and his wife, Gail Merrifield, New York Shakespeare Festival's dramaturg, Holmes resolved to take the "frightening gamble" of writing for the theater. The gratifying result, a Best Play, was produced by Papp at the Delacorte in Central Park August 4 and moved to Broadway December 2, where it still reigns as of our press date, and where it won the Tony Award for best musical and three Drama Desk Awards (let alone a fourth for best musical) for his personal achievement: best book, best score and best orchestrations, of which latter, requiring 600 pages of music manuscript, he is especially proud.*

Holmes continues to produce recordings of his own songs sung by himself and other major performing artists, and his latest movie score is Columbia's No Small Affair. *He lives in Tenafly, N.J., with his wife, who is an attorney.*

The Mystery of Edwin Drood
is forever dedicated to the lovely memory of

WENDY ISOBEL HOLMES

(1976-1986)

ACT I: THE SITUATION

Prologue: The Music Hall Royale

SYNOPSIS: The Chairman of the acting company, Mr. William Cartwright, welcomes the audience to the Music Hall Royale's premiere presentation of the drama *The Mystery of Edwin Drood* in the song "There You Are."

CHAIRMAN *(sings):*
. . . . . It matters not to me what part of town you've come from,
We but cheer you've made it here at all
Here within this garish parish called the Music Hall.
CHAIRMAN and COMPANY *(sing):*
And there you are!
CHAIRMAN:
How very glad we are
CHAIRMAN and COMPANY:
That there you are!
CHAIRMAN:
It isn't who you are but
CHAIRMAN and COMPANY:
Where you are,

And there you are,
And grateful are we to see
CHAIRMAN:
How fine and
CHAIRMAN and COMPANY:
Fair you are!
There you are!

Members of the company mingle jovially with the audience as the song continues. Chairman Cartwright introduces the show as "a musicale with dramatic interludes" and explains that the company will enact Charles Dickens's *The Mystery of Edwin Drood* which, unfortunately, its author didn't live to finish. Therefore, the Chairman tells the audience, "I shall be asking you to vote upon key questions regarding the outcome of our plot." After the audience has voted, the company will make the story come out the way the audience wants it to.

The Chairman further advises the audience that the ingenues are willing to provide companionship for anyone who desires it during the show and beyond, provided that "All goods are returned tomorrow morning None the Worse for Wear."

Having said as much, the Chairman raps his gavel and the play begins.

Scene 1: The Home of John Jasper at Minor Canon Corner in the cathedral city of Cloisterham

On a morning in late December, church music is heard as the curtains reveal a fireplace with a portrait of Rosa Bud hanging above it in the home of John Jasper, choirmaster of the cathedral in Cloisterham. The actor (Mr. Clive Paget) playing the character (Jasper) grins at the audience as the orchestra gives him a brassy fanfare, then steps back into his brooding character in the song "A Man Could Go Quite Mad."

JASPER *(sings)*:
Another trifling day,
One more soul-stifling day
Of blinding pain:
Boredom grinds my brain
Down to the grain.

A man could go quite mad
And not be all that bad
Consider each superb, disturbing urge you've ever had,
To curse aloud in church
Or choke each bloke who throws a smile your way . . .
Be that as it may . . . . .

I hide myself in thought
Where one cannot be caught

And feed on dreams that contradict each edict I've been taught.
And if some day I lose my way and mind, you'll find me glad—
A man could go quite, man could go quite,
Man could go quite mad!

The Chairman introduces Mr. Cedric Moncrieffe playing the Rev. Septimus Crisparkle. The latter, in character, enters Jasper's house and comments that Jasper looks "a little worn." Jasper is expecting a visit from his young nephew, Edwin Drood, and the Rev. Crisparkle departs as Drood arrives. Drood is played by Miss Alice Nutting; the Chairman explains that "Devotees of male impersonation are more used to seeing Miss Nutting in top hat and tails, when she does her inimitable rendition of 'Aren't I Half a Toff?' But this evening, she hides her distinctive form beneath the garb of young Edwin Drood."

Uncle and nephew greet each other affectionately, as equals (there is only a half dozen years' difference in their ages). They toast the subject of the portrait, Rosa Bud, who is betrothed to Drood. A cathedral wedding followed by a honeymoon in Egypt are imminent. Drood, it seems, is the author of the portrait. He doesn't consider it worthy of the important place it holds in Jasper's room. Jasper keeps it there, he says, because it reminds him of his nephew "and of the happiness I wish you and Rosa."

DROOD *(moodily):* Oh, I'm sure we'll be quite happy . . . though our courtship suffers from an unavoidable flatness, owing to the fact that *my* dead and gone father and *her* dead and gone father had as good as married us at birth. Why the devil couldn't they have left us alone?

JASPER: Tut, tut, dear boy—

DROOD: Tut, tut? Yes, Jack, it's all very well for *you.* You have the freedom to love whomsoever you choose.
    Drood stops himself, alarmed by something he sees in Jasper's face.

JASPER: Don't stop, dear fellow, do go on.

DROOD: Have I hurt your feelings, John?

JASPER: How could you have hurt my feelings?
    He immediately staggers back against whatever furniture will support him.

DROOD: Good heavens, Jack, you look frightfully ill! There's a strange film come over your eyes!

JASPER *(forcing a smile and straightening himself):* I—I have been taking— medicine for a pain—an agony that overcomes me. I've been forced of late to seek —treatment in London for my condition. Fear not, the effects will soon be gone. Then take it as a warning! And Ned . . . Edwin . . . this is a confidence between us.

DROOD: It shall be sacredly preserved, John.

They clasp hands and sing of their mutual devotion in "Two Kinsmen"—"Two kinsmen, more than brothers/We know no next of kin/And yet we know no others/Closer 'neath the skin."

Betty Buckley as Miss Alice Nutting playing Edwin Drood, Patti Cohenour as Miss Deirdre Peregrine playing Rosa Bud, John Herrera as Mr. Victor Grinstead playing Neville Landless and Jana Schneider as Miss Janet Conover playing Helena Landless, taking bows in the play-within-the-play format of the Rupert Holmes musical *The Mystery of Edwin Drood*

Scene 2: The conservatory of the Nun's House, a seminary for young women, in Cloisterham

Later that morning: the conservatory is furnished with a piano near some French windows and occupied by a group of young ladies. One of them—Miss Deirdre Peregrine who is to play the role of Rosa Bud—comes forward for a special bow before taking on her character.

Jasper comes in and wishes Rosa a happy birthday (and the other girls exit, giggling). As a birthday present, Jasper has written a song for her, "Moonfall." Rosa is reluctant to sing it, but Jasper prevails upon her, and she does so in a state of emotional agitation.

ROSA *(sings):*
 Between the very dead of night and day,
 Upon a steely sheet of light, I'll lay,
 And in the moonfall, I'll give myself to you.
 I'll bathe in moonfall and dress myself in dew . . . . .

 . . . . . Moonfall.
 I feel its fingers.
 Lingers the veil of nightshade,
 Light made from stars that all-too-soon fall,
 Moonfall that pours from you.

 Betwixt our hearts, let nothing intervene.
 Between our eyes, the only sight I've seen
 Is lust'rous moonfall as it blinds my view,
 So that soon I only see but you.

Rosa is shaken by the emotion implied in these words, but Jasper asks her to sing the song again. As he begins the introduction on the piano, the Landlesses —Helena and Neville, twin brother and sister (played by Miss Janet Conover and Mr. Victor Grinstead)—enter with the Rev. Crisparkle. They watch Rosa collapse from emotion as she tries to sing the song (they attribute this to stage fright and fear of Jasper, her instructor).

Crisparkle introduces the Landlesses as having "both arrived from Ceylon, where they no longer have any family," with Neville now in the Reverend's care and Helena planning to live at the Nun's House. Their parents died young, and now that their hated (by Neville) stepfather, who was a brute, has died too, they have come to make a new life here in Cloisterham.

Neville, dazzled by Rosa, asks about her and learns that she is betrothed to Drood. He comments, "I should like to meet this . . . Drood . . . and see what sort of man is worthy of the affection of Miss Bud." Jasper goes off to choir practice and the men also exit, leaving the two women alone.

HELENA: You are feeling better now, aren't you?

ROSA: Oh much, thank you.

HELENA: These surroundings, which may seem very secure to you, are new and unsettling to me. You will be my friend, won't you?

ROSA: I will be as good a friend as such a mite of a thing can be to such a womanly and handsome creature as you.

They kiss in sisterly fashion.

HELENA: Who is Mr. Jasper?

ROSA *(turning away)*: My Edwin's uncle, and my music . . . master.

HELENA: You know that he loves you?

ROSA *(fearfully)*: Oh don't! Don't! He terrifies me. I feel I am never safe from him. He has made a slave of me with his looks . . . forced me to keep silent without his uttering a single threat.

They reprise the ominous "Moonfall," joined by the other women of the company.

Scene 3: Cloisterham High Street, outside the residence of Mayor Thomas Sapsea

That afternoon (after Chairman Cartwright introduces "the Clown Prince of the Music Hall Royale" who is to play Durdles, a tipsy codger who knows his way around the cathedral tombs). This same Durdles, his Deputy and a crowd of villagers await the return of Mayor Thomas Sapsea. When the actor playing Sapsea fails to make his entrance on cue, the Chairman steps into the role.

Sapsea is greeted by Durdles, who complains of "tombatism"—an ache acquired in preparing the late Mrs. Sapsea's resting place beneath the cathedral. The Deputy declares that he saw to the lock on the crypt himself, "And it'll be my pleasure to unlock the door and slide your old woman right in there tomorrow." Durdles adds, "That crypt is a national treasure, if I may make so bold, your grace; just a while ago Mr. Jasper asked if I'd take him down into the crypts to see it." (The Chairman steps out of Sapsea's character and points out to the audience that they'd better take note of this, as it might be a Clue.)

Scene 4: The opium den of the Princess Puffer in the East End of London

At dawn the next day, ominous Oriental music, lighting and smoke pervade the den operated by Princess Puffer (played by Miss Angela Prysock), who is sipping gin and filling pipes for her many comatose clients lying around the room, which the Chairman identifies as "Below the street and beneath contempt." The Princess bemoans the fact that "The Wages of Sin" are generally very inadequate.

PRINCESS PUFFER *(sings):*
"Crime don't pay!" That's wot I tells 'em.
If it did, would I be here?
Mixing pipes, wot then I sells 'em
For a pint of rotten beer.
Throats you cut to pocket thruppence,
Or you slut to cop some sleep.
Bash a face for bleedin' tuppence . . .
Pure disgrace to work so cheap.

So I say, don't be a sinner
For the price of London gin.
You can't pay for one square dinner
With the wages of sin.
Sell my soul? 'Cor love, come off it!
Who would buy this sack of skin?
On the whole, there ain't much profit
In the wages of sin, in the wages of sin.
In the wages of sin!

The man in Bed 11 is Jasper, who sits up and calls for laudanum wine so that he will be free to enjoy his dreams of Rosa Bud (made manifest with the dance number "Jasper's Vision"). There is a scuffle ending in murder near Jasper, but he takes little notice of it and cries out for more laudanum to make his vision last. All at once, Jasper snaps out of his dream, pays the Princess Puffer what she asks for her services and exits en route to the railway station, his senses restored.

Scene 5: Cloisterham High Street

That afternoon, Rev. Crisparkle, strolling with Drood and Rosa, meets the Landlesses and introduces Drood, who tells them of his impending trip to Egypt with his betrothed. Drood has a grand plan to take over his family's engineering company in Cairo and build a road to Alexandria with stone taken from the pyramids. The very idea of such desecration of ancient monuments angers Neville, who blurts out, "This is English blasphemy! Is it not enough that you take our delicate brew of tea leaves and likewise improve *it* by pouring cow's milk into the—"

But Crisparkle pours oil on these conversational waters before they can become overly troubled. Drood's plans mingle with the Landlesses' sentimental memories of Ceylon, and the company joins them, in the number "Ceylon." Helena and Neville sing the Eastern place names fondly recalled and now so far away.

DROOD (sings):

It's perfectly fine for them
To speak of their minor gem,
But there is a role for me,
A goal I intend to see,
A vision that's in my sight--
A scene that's clean and
Bright before me!
You cannot ignore me

I will soon be
Shaping, molding
Holding fortune
In my hand and
I'll improve and
Shake and move and
Change the lay and
Nature of the land!

COMPANY (sings):

Ceylon,
Ceylon,
'Cross the Injun seas!
T'wards the
Fjords of
Thornaby-on-Tees

HELENA AND NEVILLE (sing):

Monsoons
Typhoons
Break upon the
Coast of Malabar
Quaking!
Shaking!
Change the way you are, hey!

ENSEMBLE, NEVILLE, HELENA, ROSA (sing):

Ceylon, Ceylon,
By the Bengal Bay.
East of Jaipur,
West of Mandalay . . .

HELENA:

How warm are the winds of our golden isle,

NEVILLE:

How cool are their winds and how cold is their smile:

HELENA AND NEVILLE:

They wish us gone!
We'll be back someday
Ceylon!

ALL: Sail on, to Ceylon!

ENSEMBLE:

They've become a threat
Straight from
Ceylon!

The others exit as Jasper and Sapsea enter, with Jasper warning the mayor of the hostility that has arisen between Drood and Neville Landless. Jasper remarks on the duality of human nature, saying of his nephew, "There is something of the tiger in his blood," and beneath the surface of Neville's English manners, "There is a heathen Landless, a tribesman Landless, a half-blooded, half-bred half-caste who would kill as easily as he combs his sleek hair."

Jasper confesses that he himself has sometimes suffered from a kind of duality (and Chairman Cartwright admits he's having trouble distinguishing between his

dual role as m.c. of the company and Mayor Sapsea in the drama). They develop
this notion in "Both Sides of the Coin."

JASPER *(sings):*
    I am not myself these days.
    For all I know, I might be you
    There's more than room enough for two inside my mind!
SAPSEA *(sings):*
    I am likewise in a haze
    Of who I am from scene to scene;
    What's more, we two, (we *four,* I mean), are in a bind!
JASPER:
    For is it I, or is it me?
SAPSEA:
    And if I'm him *and* if I'm he,
    Each one of us might not agree on what to do.
JASPER:
    And if I take opposing sides
    Within myself, then who divides
    Up what is right or wrong?
SAPSEA:
    I'll go along with you.
BOTH:
    Ha'penny, one penny, tupenny, thrupenny,
    Twelve to a shilling, twice that to a florin,
    And would you not fancy the currency foreign
    To find the same face on both sides of the coin?
    Bob is your uncle from pennies to guineas,
    The two-sided mint is the rule, not exception,
    And would you not feel quite the fool of deception
    To find the same face on both sides of the coin?

SAPSEA:	JASPER:
Odds or evens,	Heads or tails,
It's high or low,	Or black or white,
It's up or down,	Or left or right,
Or night.	Or day!

Following the song, Sapsea promises to keep an eye on the duplicitous Neville
Landless.

Scene 6: The crypts of Cloisterham cathedral

Late that night, light from the vault labeled "Mrs. Thomas Sapsea" illuminates
the underground chamber and passageways. Jasper emerges from it with a lantern
and, from the supine form of Durdles lying nearby, takes a ring of keys and
removes one of them.

Durdles's Deputy comes down a staircase looking for his master, causing

Jasper to feel that he's being spied upon. Furious, Jasper attacks Deputy, who goes limp just as Durdles stirs, observes what is going on and cries "Murder!" At this, Jasper's raging manner and behavior changes to benign concern, as though someone had flicked a switch. Jasper bends over Deputy who, playing possum, kicks Jasper in the stomach as soon as he gets close enough. Jasper can't understand why Deputy would want to attack him. Deputy picks himself up and runs off, commenting, "You're ripe for the asylum, Mr. Jasper."

Durdles is coming out of his wine-induced daze, as the cathedral clock tower tolls 3 A.M.

DURDLES: . . . . . Well, that was excellent wine you gave me, Mr. Jasper. More potent than I'm accustomed. Did you get to look inside Mrs. Sapsea's crypt while I was asleep?

JASPER: No, I seem to have gotten . . . lost.

DURDLES: Oh, well, I was lost myself in a fitful dream, Mr. Jasper. I imagined someone touched me and took something from me. *(He sees the key ring on the floor.)* And here's what it was—fell from me, did you? Mayor Sapsea wouldn't like me leaving the key to his wife's crypt laying about here right in front of her tomb—and now that very same key is missing. What do you think, Mr. Jasper?

JASPER: I think that your world down here still remains somewhat of a mystery to me. Come along, Durdles. *(He mounts the stairs.)*

DURDLES *(to audience):* Not so great a mystery as you are to me. Mr. John Jasper.

> Nods ominously. Curtain.

Scene 7: The ruins of Cloisterham

On Christmas Eve, strolling near the ruins, Edwin and Rosa finally articulate their real feelings.

DROOD: No, Rosa, we are not legally bound to marriage.

ROSA: Then, Eddie dearest, let us change to brother and sister from this day forth.

DROOD: Never be husband and wife?

ROSA: Never.

DROOD: I am honor-bound to confess that this thought does not originate with you alone, Rosa.

ROSA: I know, dear one. You have not been truly happy with our engagement. Nor have I.

DROOD: I'm sorry, Rosa.

ROSA: And I for you, poor boy.

DROOD: . . . if only our marriage had not been assured since birth . . . perhaps then we would know how we truly feel towards each other.

Drood and Rosa confirm their feelings with the song "Perfect Strangers."

DROOD *(sings):*
. . . . . If we were perfect strangers,
I'd find my way with ease.
ROSA *(sings):*
I'd see the path before me,
The forest from the trees.
DROOD:
Could life be real without you?
You're always there.
ROSA:
How do I feel about you?
DROOD:
I care . . .
ROSA:
. . . Too near to touch you.
My dearest Ned, how much you mean to me . . .
DROOD:
But are we lovers, how would we know it?
How could we feel it? How would we show it?
ROSA:
How much you've been to me . . .

Rosa gives Drood an heirloom, a clasp of her mother's, symbolizing their enduring friendship. Drood believes that this breaking-off of their engagement will come as a shock to his Uncle Jasper. Rosa and Drood agree to keep it from him for the time being.

Scene 8: *The home of John Jasper*

A short time later, a thunderstorm is approaching and dinner is being prepared at Jasper's with Neville, Helena and the Rev. Crisparkle as guests. Crisparkle, it seems, was once engaged to Rosa's mother but proved "a bit too Anglican, a bit too Angular for her taste." She drowned during a party by the sea a few months after giving birth to Rosa.

Drood and Rosa enter, remarking on the special effort of hospitality Jasper has made to entertain his guests (it's in honor of Rosa's presence, Jasper indicates). Neville and Drood begin to clash, but Jasper distracts them from their hostility with glasses of mulled wine, made from a recipe he "acquired on a recent trip to London." The two pledge to cease their ill will toward each other. But when Neville speaks to Rosa about her planned trip to Egypt, Drood gives him offense by suggesting he accompany them to carry their luggage. Neville replies in song, "No Good Can Come From Bad."

NEVILLE *(sings):*
Sir, I don't much like your tone,
That supercilious sneer you wear!
Clear, you wear a finer cut
Than mine, ah but

A waistcoat worn
Can soon be torn,
And faggots, too,
'Till maggots feed on you!
ROSA (turns to audience, sings aside):
Something in this speech seems ominous to me!
HELENA:
Twin, don't overreach, pray promise this to me!
CRISPARKLE (standing to offer grace, sings):
Praise to him divine, for this we should be glad . . .
JASPER:
Won't you try some wine?
ALL:
No good can come from bad!

Drood continues the song, characterizing Neville as a man of impure blood, with a half-caste in his ancestry. This chilling development is glossed over (still in song) by Jasper offering a toast to the soon-to-be-newlyweds and the arrival of the roast goose. Invited to carve, Drood grabs the knife and Neville the fork, expressing their antagonism almost in the manner of crossed swords—and in song.

NEVILLE AND DROOD (sing):
Glances cut like blade through bone,
With daggers drawn I glare at you,
There at you who dare presume
To stare at whom
I'd make my wife
And share my life—
I'd see you dead
Before sweet Rosa wed.

All are alarmed at this open display of hostility, repeating "No good can come from bad!" as the last line of the song. But the two are persuaded to shake hands. As Jasper pours more wine, (and the rivals are already inebriated), the thunder rises. Drood decides to stroll down by the River Weir to observe the storm. Neville will come too, but the Rev. Crisparkle will escort the ladies home (and they exit, Helena warning Neville, "Be careful how you tread"). Jasper declines to join in the walk but lends Drood his caped coat. "Come, Edwin, destiny awaits!" cries Neville, and Drood replies, "Then goodbye, Uncle! Goodbye all!" The sky erupts as the two youths depart.

The next day, Christmas, the storm has disappeared, and so has Edwin Drood—there has been no sign of him since he went out walking with Neville the previous evening. Rosa fears that something may have happened to him. The Rev. Crisparkle sends his assistant, Bazzard, to see if there is any news, but there is none. As Rosa prays for Drood's safety, Crisparkle notices how much she resembles her drowned mother, whom he loved.

Scene 9: Minor Canon Corner

That evening, Rosa and the Rev. Crisparkle are strolling toward the cathedral for evensong. Jasper and Sapsea enter discussing the situation: Neville Landless "was last seen fleeing the district," and Drood has disappeared. They believe murder has been done and resolve to find and seize Landless.

There are sounds of a pursuit, following which Deputy comes in to tell Jasper they've found Neville. He runs off as Bazzard comes in.

BAZZARD: Oh, Mr. Jasper. Look what I've discovered!
    He shows something in his hand, and Jasper angrily grabs it.
JASPER: Why, it's my coat, the one I gave to Edwin last night! It's been torn to ribbons . . . and blood, oh God, there's his blood on it! Where did you find this?
BAZZARD: Under a rock by the River Weir!
JASPER *(without hope):* My dear boy is murdered. I take this oath before you, Bazzard! Record it in your memory: that I will fasten the crime of murder upon the murderer, and that I devote myself to his destruction. *(He exits, sustained only by a mission.)*
BAZZARD *(for the benefit of the third balcony):* I shall remember your words, Mr. John Jasper!

Phillip Bax (Bazzard) and William Cartwright (Sapsea) step out of their *Edwin Drood* roles momentarily, to discuss the inferior grade of roles Mr. Bax has been assigned to recently. The Chairman, in fact, wonders why Dickens wrote in the role of Bazzard at all unless he intended something significant for Crisparkle's assistant later in the plot. Mr. Bax—who, like the character of Bazzard he portrays, has aspirations as an author—has written a song, "Never the Luck," which the Chairman now permits him to perform in front of the audience.

BAX *(sings):*
    Never the luck,
    And never the lead,
    And "Never you mind," they say.
    In time we all taste
    The lime in the light
    And I'll have my night someday.

Bax continues imagining, in song, that if he keeps on practicing his singing and dancing, he will be called upon in an emergency and "I'll leap center-stage/The music will play/I'll waltz my way into your heart!" His sympathetic fellow cast members join him at the end of his song. During the applause which follows, Neville Landless is dragged onstage by Horace, an acting constable, and other angry citizens who handle Neville roughly until the Rev. Crisparkle enters and —with surprising strength—breaks up the fight.

DEPUTY: There's your murderer, sir!

NEVILLE: Reverend Crisparkle. What have I done?

CRISPARKLE: Nothing, I'm certain, lad. I'm sure there is some—

HORACE: Landless!! Where is Edwin Drood?

> *Jasper, who is now wearing a black arm-band, views the proceedings.*

NEVILLE: Where is . . . Why do you ask me that way?

JASPER: Because you were the last person in his company, and he is nowhere to be found!

HORACE: Mayor Sapsea, do you wish to question him?

SAPSEA *(prodded by Jasper):* Ehm—you left the river with Edwin Drood at what time?

NEVILLE: I—in all honesty I cannot recall anything of what transpired once Edwin and I reached the river. That was indeed potent wine you poured for us last night, Mr. Jasper!

SAPSEA: What are those bloodstains upon your shirt-front . . . and upon your walking stick, Mr. Landless?

NEVILLE: I acquired these bloodstains sir, just now . . . when these men of yours dragged me forcibly back from the countryside where I had been walking.

HORACE: Neville Landless, as acting constable for the district, I place you under arrest.

Helena enters, sizes up the situation and, a Portia in defense of her brother, points out that they cannot make an accusation of murder without a *corpus delicti.* All agree that she is right, and Neville is released.

As the townspeople and others gossip, Jasper encounters Rosa and stares at her until *"She is as alone and as frozen as a cobra's intended victim."* She summons up the resolve to tell Jasper that she will no longer take musical instruction from him.

> *Jasper smiles and takes her arm, twisting it between her body and his,*
> *so that his actions can't be seen by those nearby.*

JASPER: I do not forget how many eyes command a view of us. But you shall still hear me, even against your wishes. Dearest Rosa.

> *Additional unseen pressure. She suppresses a cry of pain.*

Charming Rosa. Even when my dear boy was engaged to you, I loved you madly. I hid my—our secret loyally, did I not?

ROSA: You were as false to him, sir, daily and hourly, as you are now. You know that you made me afraid to open his kind eyes to the truth . . . that you are a bad, bad man!

JASPER: How beautiful you are! You are even more beautiful in anger than repose! I don't ask for your love . . . give me yourself and your hatred, that pretty rage, that enchanting scorn! It will be enough for me.

> *She starts to pull away, but he snaps her back.*

I warn you sweet witch, rare charmer, you must stay or do more harm than can be undone.

ROSA: You're mad!

JASPER: I mean to show you how mad my love is—

ROSA *(bitterly):* Love!! You dare to use that word!

Jasper and Rosa reprise "The Name of Love" and "Moonfall," as a blood-red moon emerges from the clouds and Rosa is gripped in fascinated terror of Jasper.

ROSA *(sings):*
..... You call it love
I call it rude
I call it lust
I call it lewd
I call it cruel
I cannot bear
To call it love
I think it foul
I think it vile
No more I'll take
Of cunning guile
You're worse than bad
You give to sin
The name of love .....

JASPER *(sings):*
..... I call it love
You call it rude
You think me just
A bit too crude.
And I the fool,
Yet still I dare
To call it love.
I see you scowl,
You see me smile
'Tis you I'll break!
I've no denial
My words are mad:
I speak them in
The name of love .....

ROSA and JASPER:
    Beneath these skies one night unknown would he/she dare?
    Between our eyes one sight alone we share
    The sight of moonfall
    As it comes into view . . .

ROSA:
So that
Soon I
Only
See but
You!
See but you!
            Curtain.

JASPER:
So I promise that you shall be
Soon a golden idol whom I
Own and love and lead into a
Sea of light! Tis but the falling
Moon!
Falling moon!

ACT II: THE SLEUTHS

Prologue: The Music Hall Royale

Without any sign that the intermission has ended except that the orchestra has begun to play, the Chairman comes out and watches the audience taking its seats. He sums up the situation in Cloisterham: six months have passed, and there has been no sign of Edwin Drood. A mysterious bearded detective named Dick Datchery and the Princess Puffer are about to arrive in Cloisterham by train.

Scene 1: Cloisterham Station and Cloisterham High Street

John Jasper, dressed in mourning and *"back from another treatment in London"* gets off the same train as Datchery and the Princess. Datchery is *"a ragged bundle of a man with long platinum hair and beard.*" He and the Princess are here "Settling Up the Score," which apparently involves solving the mystery of Edwin Drood's disappearance, as they sing: "I've come to town my ear at every door/Did Edwin drown or was he washed ashore?/I'm bearing down to settle up the score/Red herring on a briny beach."

At the High Street, Rev. Crisparkle encounters Mayor Sapsea, provides the information that his assistant Bazzard is away from town on business and exits as Durdles and Deputy come in. Durdles, noting the presence of a stranger (Datchery), approaches him in the guise of an official greeter and finds that Datchery is looking for lodging near the cathedral. Sapsea, overhearing, mentions the rooms upstairs in Jasper's house. Datchery indicates that he knows Jasper is Drood's uncle. At the mention of Drood's name the Princess Puffer pricks up her ears. Datchery exits, limping pronouncedly, in search of lodging. All, even the Princess, feel that there is something suspicious about him. The Chairman warns against jumping to conclusions and leads the company into their anthem song, "Off to the Races," which echoes his advice.

ALL *(sing):*
. . . . . And the race is won by the tardy,
Not the foolhardy fools that we be.
Don't unlace your madcap abandon
Do and you'll land undone.
Not me!

So we call upon you all to hold your horse's reins
Before you solve this dickens of a crime
Sometimes having patience is as good as having brains
So take your bloody time . . .
Pour out the spirits, the end is near, it's only a length or so
Don't begin to beat your tar off, for the finish isn't far off.
To the races!
Off to the race we go . . . Tally-ho!

Rosa and Helena enter, and at the sight of Rosa the Princess Puffer, "*stunned, gasps for breath.*" Apparently she now has some of the information for which she came to Cloisterham, and she's determined to remain until she gets the rest of it, as she sings in "Don't Quit While You're Ahead"—"In life, we start the same as when we're done:/If you lose, you're just where you've begun/If you've won, don't quit while you're ahead/Just press your blessed luck instead"—and she is joined by the other principals and the company, as the song is reprised.

ALL *(sing):*
And now at last, we see the slightest glimm'ring of light
Quite shimm'ring in the dim, dull of night.
So long have we been blind,
But fin'lly we unwind the plot.
The truth is this: we find that what we—

Their voices and the music abruptly cease. Puffer and Datchery look around anxiously; we hear the orchestra members frantically thumbing through their music looking for the next page of score. Jasper/Paget steps out of character and peers in the direction of the Chairman as if to ask what is going on. The orchestra conductor likewise steps inquiringly towards the Chairman, wondering what happens next. The audience may get the uncomfortable feeling that someone has forgotten a line, that Something Has Gone Wrong . . . the play collapses.

CHAIRMAN *(at last, and with great sadness):* Ladies and gentlemen. It was at this point in our story that Mr. Charles Dickens laid down his pen forever. And so, my dear friends, this is all we shall ever know for sure about the mystery of Edwin Drood. Tonight, however, at least within the confines of this humble theater, we shall together solve, resolve and conclude: *(Gavel once.)* The mystery . . . *(Gavel twice.)*

ALL: Of Edwin Drooood! *(Final gavel.)*

The Chairman further explains that many have believed that ~~Datchery~~ is in fact *John*
one of the characters in disguise. At this performance the role has been played ~~(he tells the audience as he strips off Datchery's whiskers)~~ by the same ~~Alice~~ Nutting who portrayed Edwin Drood—but this doesn't mean that Drood is necessarily alive.

George Rose as Mr. William Cartwright playing Mayor Thomas Sapsea *(right foreground)* and the cast of *The Mystery of Edwin Drood*

CHAIRMAN: . . . . . Which brings us to our first key question: Is Edwin Drood dead . . . or alive? Mr. Charles Dickens experimented with many different titles for our story, for example:

NUTTING/DROOD: The Loss of Edwin Drood.

CONOVER/HELENA: The Flight of Edwin Drood.

GRINSTEAD/NEVILLE: The Disappearance of Edwin Drood.

CHAIRMAN: But nowhere the Death or Murder of Edwin Drood. On the other hand, many would say that a Mystery without a Murder is no mystery at all. Tonight, ladies and gentlemen, our questions shall be answered primarily by you . . . . .

But the cast will vote first, the Chairman says, and they unanimously vote that Drood is dead—except for Alice Nutting, who maintains that Drood is alive, disguised as Datchery, and exits the stage (and eventually the theater itself) in a huff. The next question is, who is Datchery? Helena disguised as a boy (a trick she was fond of working in her youth)? Bazzard playing a role? Neville trying to clear his name? Crisparkle, responsible for Neville, trying to clear his ward's name? Even Rosa?—the Chairman cites intriguing hints in the text which point to each of these characters as a possible Datchery. Which is the clue and which are red herrings? "This much I do know for certain," the Chairman asserts, "Datchery is not John Jasper, the Princess Puffer, Durdles, Deputy or even Mayor Sapsea . . . for in our play and in Mr. Dickens's novel, they all appear in scenes with him."

The Chairman calls for a vote by audience applause as to which of the remaining possibilities is posing as Datchery. According to the outcome of this vote, the character in question leaves the stage to change costume into Datchery's disguise.

The next question is, who is the murderer? Is it John Jasper, the Chairman inquires; could it be that "the obvious villain of the piece did indeed kill his nephew in a hopeless attempt to win the love of the fair Miss Rosa Bud. Ladies and gentlemen, where then the mystery? That's taken the wind out of your sails, Big Mouths, hasn't it? Eh? Where then the mystery? Where indeed?"

The suspects step forward one by one.

HELENA: Helena Landless. Did I, in trying to save my brother, bring harm to Edwin Drood?

BAZZARD: Bazzard. My need for attention has made me quite mad. Someone stop me before I sing again!

ROSA: Rosa Bud. Why on earth should someone as innocent and pure as myself murder my own true Ned?

NEVILLE: Neville Landless. In all honesty I cannot recall anything of what transpired once Edwin and I reached the river.

PRINCESS PUFFER: Who am I? And what am I?

CRISPARKLE: The Reverend Crisparkle. Have I in some way confused my mission here on earth?

JASPER: John Jasper. I have stood in the cold shade of suspicion since our story began.

As the Chairman and suspects reprise "Settling Up the Score," a vote is taken in the audience as to who is the murderer. As the votes are being counted the house lights dim and the Chairman heralds the finale of *The Mystery of Edwin Drood.*

THE CONCLUSION

It is dawn as the curtain rises on the streets of Cloisterham, with Princess Puffer asleep in a corner of the cathedral and Rosa Bud dressed for a journey and hurrying along. The Princess stops Rosa and confesses that she has known her in her infancy; she was Rosa's nanny. Since those days, the Princess has been on "The Garden Path to Hell," as she sings, "Marriage in me 'ead/What I got instead/Was a bed in Camden town . . . and then to me, 'e said/'Should I send around a friend, be nice to him, this swell/Stroll him down your garden path to hell.' " It was only a few short steps to prostitution and drugs, the Princess Puffer tells Rosa in song.

There immediately follows "Puffer's Confession," a song explaining why she is here in Cloisterham, sung to Rosa Bud (except that if Rosa Bud has been selected as Datchery she will be offstage changing into the costume and the Princess will be singing to herself). She tells of how, one evening, a client ordered laudanum wine, crying out "Rosa Bud!"

PUFFER *(sings):*
. . . . . We are both made from God's most wretched clay and mud . . .
But how comes this man to cry out "Rosa Bud!"
I can't see too clear but I followed him here.
Finding out who was, who I've come back a time or two.
Then last night, tracking me, was this Mister Datchery
    Datchery enters.
So I follow his tracks to *his* lodgings in the backs
Tho I hate to confess, well, I watched this man undress
And I saw suddenwise without his bold disguise.

Depending upon who has been voted to be Datchery in disguise, Bazzard, Crisparkle, Helena, Neville or Rosa sings a couplet admitting to be Datchery, pulls off his/her beard and wig and launches into the song "Out on a Limerick." The lyrics to this song differ in each case and explain the character's motivation for impersonating a detective (Bazzard yearning for the limelight, Crisparkle, Helena, Neville and Rosa to clear Neville's name, with the latter also seeking vengeance). All the different versions have the same lyric ending, however, approximately as follows:

So I crept in the lodgings of Jasper—
Dressed in this wig, what a sight!
There I found Rosa Bud's clasp, her
Mother's she gave Drood that night.

Jasper took it from Ned after hurling him dead
Towards the Weir riverbed, I suppose.

Tell him that Datchery knows!
And the proof is quite clear,
Let us bring Jasper here
To be tried and then tied up and strung!
And from this limerick, let him be hung!

Jasper is dragged from his house by Horace and other citizens. An expression of *"maniacal joy"* comes over him, as he sings in "Jasper's Confession" about having a split personality, one of whose personae is the totally evil opium-smoker who now takes possession of him. He dreamed of killing Drood, and when it came to it (he sings), "The deed was much too easily done." But if Jasper has *not* been voted the murder by the audience, Durdles then steps forward.

DURDLES: No, I can't let it happen! *(To Jasper.)* You placed the coat that young Drood wore that night down at the River Weir to throw suspicion on Neville Landless. You're a bad one, Jasper, when the evil one is inside you! But you're not a murderer! You didn't kill Edwin Drood!
SAPSEA: Durdles . . . let me understand—are you saying that John Jasper did not kill his newphew?
DURDLES: Exactly, your lordship, sir. It was a wild night that Christmas Eve, as you'll remember, squire, and I'd sought shelter near Mr. Jasper's door. That's when I saw One Amongst You throttle Edwin Drood, and in a convenient flash of lightning—I Saw Who It Was! . . . . . Suddenly I see Mr. Jasper stagger out of his own home under the influence of Potent Medicine. Suddenly he collapses and picks up young Drood, carrying him to the cathedral and down into the crypt, depositing the body— *(He suppresses a laugh.)* —in your wife's tomb, Mr. Sapsea.
SAPSEA: What?
DURDLES: Yes, I told you there was plenty of room in there—
SAPSEA: But now you must tell us, Durdles: Who Did It?
DURDLES *(savoring the moment, he regards the candidates):* Lord love me . . . It was—

It was Bazzard, the Rev. Crisparkle, Helena Landless, Neville Landless, the Princess Puffer or Rosa Bud, Durdles reveals, according to the way the audience voted. Five different versions of the song "Murderer's Confession" are then available, one of them to be sung according to the identity of the murderer, as follows:

BAZZARD *(sings):*
I saw the chance to be a legend in my time,
For all in town thought Neville might do violent crime.
To solve a myst'ry would pluck me from off my shelf
So I insured the crime by killing Drood myself!
Reprises of "A Man Could Go Quite Mad" and "Never the Luck."

CRISPARKLE *(sings):*
 In saving sinners, there's a chance you'll sin sometime!
 In saving criminals, one might commit a crime!
 And to protect the harmless lambs within my fold,
 I had to kill the wolf—your culprit you behold!
  Reprises of "A Man Could Go Quite Mad" and "No Good Can Come
  from Bad."

Crisparkle killed Drood, mistaking him for Jasper because he was wearing Jasper's cloak. He wanted to drive Satan out of Jasper—and, he confesses, he was forced to drown Rosa's mother, his erstwhile beloved, for the same reason.

HELENA *(sings):*
 You know the fury and the fire I can vent!
  Turns on Jasper.
 Thought you I'd idly wait while Neville you torment?
 With this, his one, his only chance to start anew . . .
 You surely know by now I meant to murder *you.*
  Reprises of "A Man Could Go Quite Mad" and "No Good Can Come
  From Bad."
NEVILLE *(sings):*
 I was the likeliest of suspects you could find—
 So qualified, you ruled me out of sight and mind.
 Of *course* I killed our Master Ned! Could I forego
 The chance to gain my pride *and* Rosa with one blow?
  Reprises of "A Man Could Go Quite Mad" and "No Good Can Come
  From Bad."
PUFFER *(sings):*
 May God have mercy, your forgiveness do I need!
 My string of sins ends here with this most dreadful deed!
 I only meant to save my Rosa Bud, it's true . . .
 You bastard Jasper! Christ, I meant to murder *you!*
  Reprise of "The Wages of Sin."
ROSA BUD *(sings):*
 Were you so blind you could not see I killed him?
 Yes!
 And it was wonderful to do, I do confess.
 To have it done, to do him in, to see it through . . .
  Whirling on Jasper.
 You surely know by now I meant to murder *you!*
  Reprises of "A Man Could Go Quite Mad" and "No Good Can Come
  From Bad."

Rosa, if guilty, then collapses, beating the ground with her fist, crying, "Jasper! Damn your existence and your fraudulent love! Damn Cloisterham that looked the other way when you looked at me in your way! Damn—you—all!"

After whichever of these cases of "Murderer's Confession" is applicable, the

Chairman steps forward and stresses the need for a happy ending. To achieve this, he must pair a couple of lovers, and again he asks the audience to vote its preference as to which of the women is to be paired off with which of the men (including not only Neville and Jasper but also Crisparkle, Bazzard, Durdles, Sapsea and Deputy) to live happily ever after. Depending on the audience's choice, there is a brief scene to go with each possible pairing, with emotional reactions ranging from "hopeful, vulnerable" (Rosa and Crisparkle) through "chummily" (Princes Puffer and Durdles) to "in horror" (the Landless twins, Helena and Neville).

After the lucky couple reprises "Perfect Strangers," the Chairman wonders what Edwin Drood might say of all this if he could speak from beyond the grave. *"There is an ominous rumbling beneath the ground, aided by a similar rumbling from the orchestra. Suddenly, wonderfully, the crypt of Mrs. Sapsea rises from the earth below, breaking through the floor of the stage as it pushes stone and dusty earth aside. From its doorway emerges a cheery Edwin Drood."* Drood declares "I'm alive!! Halloo all!" and sings, in "The Writing on the Wall," that "When I struck my head against the street" he was stunned and then woke up to find himself fighting for every breath down in the crypt. He managed to escape and didn't return to Cloisterham until he could discover who wanted to kill him.

DROOD *(sings):*
>I have read the writing on the wall,
>And the greatest myst'ry
>Is not the hist'ry
>Of Jasper, Drood, and one and all!

>I have met my maker and returned!
>What advice I'm giving
>To all those living
>Is just to learn what I have learned . . .

>Life is dear.
>There can be no vict'ry in defeat
>If outnumbered, beat a fast retreat
>To the nearest shelter and dig in . . .
>When you live, then you win!

>. . . . . I have read the writing on the wall
>Try to live forever
>And give up never
>The fight—you'll need the wherewithal!
>Can't you read the writing,
>As I plead,
>Inciting you to read the writing on the wall!

All join hands and take their bows, acknowledging the orchestra and reprising "Don't Quit While You're Ahead."

ALL *(sing):*
    Ta-rah-ta-ree!
    Boom!
    Bang it, bash it, Glory be!
    Boom!
    Clang it, clash it, oo-lah-dee-dee!
    Don't quit while you're ahead!
    Sing out, "There's more in store for me."
        Curtain.

AUNT DAN AND LEMON

A Full-Length Play in One Act

BY WALLACE SHAWN

Cast and credits appear on page 339

WALLACE SHAWN was born November 12, 1943 in New York City, the son of The New Yorker *editor William Shawn. He attended the Dalton School, then continued his education at the Putney, Vt. School, Harvard (B.A. 1965) and Oxford (M.A. 1967). It was during his Oxford years that he made his first serious effort at playwriting (it was not produced) and has persisted in following this gleam while at the same time establishing himself in a stage and screen acting career in such films as* My Dinner With Andre *(which he co-authored with Andre Gregory),* Manhattan, The Hotel New Hampshire *and his own plays in New York and London.*

Shawn's first New York stage production, Our Late Night, *was developed OOB at Gregory's The Manhattan Project and formally presented January 9, 1975 for 38 performances by New York Shakespeare Festival, winning an Obie Award for distinguished playwriting. In the 1977–78 season, New York Shakespeare Festival staged his translation of Niccolo Machiavelli's* The Mandrake, *while the Ensemble Studio Theater put on his* The Family Play. *Again on February 3, 1980 New York Shakespeare Festival produced his* Marie and Bruce *for 47 performances. OOB two seasons later, LaMama put on his* The Hotel Play.

Shawn's first Best Play, Aunt Dan and Lemon, *was first produced by the Royal Court Theater in London, where the play's action is set, in the summer of 1985. It opened off Broadway October 28, 1985 at New York Shakespeare Festival as part of that group's ongoing exchange with the the British organization.*

Time: Now

Place: A room in London

SYNOPSIS: In a darkened room, *"A woman named Lemon, born in 1960 . . . . . sits in an armchair, weak and sick."* Within her reach are numerous bottles of fruit and vegetable juice (lime and celery are her favorite) which, with bread, is all that sustains her now. Lemon expects to die young, like her parents before her, but this does not bother her (she informs the audience in an opening monologue). Reading is her principal diversion, and recently she has been reading about the Nazi death camp Treblinka where women and children were stripped naked, then herded into an outdoor passageway ("the Road to Heaven") where guards drove them into the gas chambers.

LEMON: . . . . . Apparently the Nazis had learned that it was possible to keep everyone calm and orderly when they were inside the sheds, but that as soon as they found themselves outside, naked, in that narrow passageway, they instinctively knew what was happening to them, and so guards were stationed there with whips to reduce the confusion to a sort of minimum. The strategy was to deal with them politely for as long as possible, and to use whips when politeness no longer sufficed. Today, of course, the Nazis are considered dunces, because they lost the war, but it has to be said that they managed to accomplish a great deal of what they wanted to do. They were certainly successful against the Jews.

Lemon's own life has narrowed pretty much to this room, avoiding the daily shocks of current events and living with her memories—not of her own experiences, which have been limited, but of what she was told by others and absorbed, especially in childhood. "So I may not have done very much in my life," Lemon concludes, "and yet I really feel I've had a *great* life, because of what I've learned from the people I knew."

Lemon retains vivid first-hand memories of her mother and father and their friend, Aunt Dan, and second-hand memories ("They're mine now. They're my memories.") of people she's been told about, including Raimondo *("a Hispanic man in his 40s")*, Mindy *("an English woman in her 20s")*, June *("an English woman in her 20s")*, Jasper *("an American man in his 40s")* and Andy *("an American man in his early 30s")*, memories which she will share with us later. But first she introduces her father, an American who loved England so much he settled there, married an English girl and got a job in an auto parts factory. In monologue, Lemon's father tells of the intense demands his work (which his former Oxford friends don't seem to appreciate) places upon him. There is unrelenting pressure on him to *perform*, pressure that would soon exhaust his academic friends in his place.

FATHER: . . . . . Because the amazing thing about the work *I* do is that you don't just do your work and then say to yourself, "Well done, my boy. That was very well done!" You see, that's what scholars do. That's what writers do. And if you're a scholar or a writer—great—fine—no one in the world can say, "No, no, but your work was bad." Or they can say it, maybe, but then *you* can say, "Oh no, you're wrong, it really was good." But in *my* work there's an actual test, a very simple test which tells you without any doubt or question or debate at all whether your work was in fact "good," or whether it was, in fact, very, very "bad" —and the test is, how did your product do in the market? Did people buy it? Well, your work was good. What? They didn't? Well, I'm very, very sorry, your work was *bad.* It was *very bad.* You did a *bad job.* You see, it's no good saying, "But the public doesn't understand me, in twenty years they'll know I was right." Because in twenty years the product won't be on the shelves, you see, so it will be perfectly irrelevant in twenty years. In twenty years that product will be out of date—it will be worthless garbage."

And there's no relaxing at the executive level, because the penalty for "bad" work, even for a single day's lapse, is harsh: You lose your job.

At the family dinner table, Lemon refuses to eat and is excused. Father reproaches Mother for allowing her anxiety to exacerbate the child's obvious neurosis. Father is afraid that Lemon may be turned into a very sick child. Lemon explains to the audience that she perceived the stress in her parents' voices,

Kathryn Pogson (Lemon), Linda Hunt (Aunt Dan), Larry Pine (Andy), Lynsey Baxter (Mindy), Linda Bassett (June) and Wallace Shawn (Jasper) in the English cast of the latter's play *Aunt Dan and Lemon*

though she didn't grasp exactly what they were saying. She thought of her father as a caged and untended animal gradually deteriorating—"His fur was falling out"—his condition ignored by her saintly mother who herself sickened and died at the age of 50. Lemon remembers her mother talking to her about how much she enjoyed Oxford, savoring its dawns and taking walks in a meadow at the edge of town. One day, another woman, also enjoying a stroll, came up to her and introduced herself.

MOTHER: She marched up with a sort of mischievous grin, extended her hand, and announced in a forthright American accent, "My name's Danielle." And you know, Dan in those days used to wear these delicate white Victorian blouses and these rough nineteenth-century men's caps, and I'd never met anyone quite like her in my life. So we walked together for a little while, and then I said to her, "Well why don't you come back to my room for tea?" And so we went back, and we talked for a very long time, and we drank a lot of tea and got very excited, and we drank some sherry that I'd put away somewhere, and I told her things I hadn't told people whom I'd known for years . . . . .

After that, they saw a good deal of each other. One day Dan brought around an American friend, Lemon's future father (Lemon was named Leonora and got her nickname from Dan). Lemon remembers how close the association continued between "Aunt Dan" and her parents, spending long summer evenings in the garden of their house near London, talking, playing charade games, reading poetry aloud. Over the years the games and the poetry readings were discontinued, but in the meantime Lemon had moved her bed and belongings into a little house her father had originally planned as a study. It was there that Aunt Dan would visit Lemon for an evening talk every time she came to see her parents.

LEMON: . . . . . When I look back on my childhood, it was those talks which I remember more than anything else that ever happened to me. And particularly the talks we had the summer I was eleven years old, which was the last time my parents and Aunt Dan were friends, and Aunt Dan stayed with us for the whole summer, and she came to visit me every night. And in a way it was an amazing thing that a person like Aunt Dan would spend all that time talking to an eleven-year-old child who wasn't even that bright, talking about every complicated subject in the world, but listening to Aunt Dan was the best, the happiest, the most important experience I'd ever had . . . . . My mother and father had other friends, and they had their own lives, and they had me. But I had only Aunt Dan . . . . .

When Aunt Dan came to visit, she and Lemon's parents would no longer spend the evenings in the garden talking and playing games. Instead, she would visit Lemon—in pajamas and tucked in under the covers, eagerly awaiting Aunt Dan —in the little house, where the older woman regaled the child with detailed accounts and evaluations of adult experiences like her love affair with a professor when she was a student; manners and mores ("*I never, ever, shout at a waiter,*" Aunt Dan declared emphatically, because waiters are as important as presidents to a society which would self-destruct if workers lost the pride and incentive to perform their indispensable tasks); entertainments and adventures in the company of college companions; the character and characteristics of her friends like Mindy, who thought bodies were funny and indulged herself in playful, promiscuous sex; and, repeatedly, her obsessive admiration of Henry Kissinger.

AUNT DAN: You see, I don't *care* if he's vain or boastful—maybe he is! I don't *care* if he goes out with beautiful girls or likes to ride around on a yacht with millionaires and sheikhs. All right—he enjoys life! Is that a bad thing? If he enjoys life, maybe he'll be even more inspired to do his job of *preserving* life, to help us all lead the life we want! I mean, you can hardly call him a frivolous man. Look at his face! Look at that face! He can stay up night after night after night having a wonderful time with beautiful girls, but he will always have that look on his face, my Lemon, that look of *melancholy*—that look that can't be erased, because he has seen the power of evil in the world.

Aunt Dan pursues the subject, commenting on small, poor countries whose people (she judges) nevertheless "are very happy" with what they have, including their leaders, until intellectuals who've "studied economics at the Sorbonne or Berkeley" stir up rebellion which results in all manner of oppression, including murder. As the press sees it, if Kissinger supports the rebels he betrays leaders who have been friends; if he supports the leaders, he's a bully. "Hypocrisy," Aunt Dan calls it.

Aunt Dan explains Kissinger's complicated political chess game with the Russians and Chinese over Vietnam and tells Lemon a story about going to a Washington club for lunch and seeing Kissinger seated across the room studying a paper while he, like Aunt Dan, was waiting for a luncheon partner.

AUNT DAN: . . . . . The most striking thing was that, seated in an uncomfortable position in this uncomfortable chair, Kissinger was utterly immobile. Each time I looked over, his position was exactly the same as it had been before. His pose was more or less determined by what he was doing—he was reading the manuscript held in his lap—but to me the downward-looking angle of his entire head, so characteristic of Kissinger, expressed something more—my feeling was that it expressed the habitual humility of a man whose attitude to life was, actually, prayerful, a man, I felt, who was living in fear of an all-knowing God. The boastful exuberance of the public Kissinger was nowhere to be seen in this private moment.

Instead, Aunt Dan observed, Kissinger seemed to be engrossed in a problem and saddened by the thought that he might not find the right solution for it. But when his friend arrived for lunch, Kissinger's mood changed to one of extreme cordiality, for which Aunt Dan much admired him.

Lemon dreamed of going to live with Aunt Dan in London and imagined that Kissinger would call on them often—Lemon would have been happy to become his slave. But Lemon noticed that tension arose between her mother and Aunt Dan when they discussed Kissinger, because her mother didn't like him at all, feeling that preconceptions might dangerously influence his decisions. This tension spoiled the garden conversations and made Aunt Dan's evening visits to Lemon in the little house seem "nicer and nicer," as the adult disagreement over Kissinger and government loomed larger and larger.

AUNT DAN: . . . . . The whole purpose of government is to use force. So we don't have to. So if I move into your house and refuse to leave, you don't have to kick me or punch me, you don't have to find some acid to throw in my face —you just nicely have to pick up the phone and call the police! And if some other country attacks our friends in Southeast Asia, you and I don't have to go over there and fight them with rifles—we just get Kissinger to fight them for us.

MOTHER: But Dan—

AUNT DAN: These *other* people use force, so we can sit here in this garden and be incredibly nice. Otherwise we'd be going around covered with scars and bruises and our hair all torn out, like stray cats.

MOTHER: But are you saying that governments can do anything, or Kissinger can do anything, and somehow it's never proper for us to say, "Well we don't like this, we think this is wrong"? Do you mean to say that we don't have the right to criticize this person's decisions? That no one has the right to criticize them?

AUNT DAN: No, I don't say that. Go right ahead. Criticize his decisions all you like. I don't know. Go ahead and criticize everything he does.

MOTHER: I don't—

AUNT DAN: Particularly if you have no idea what you would do in his place.

MOTHER: Dan, I'm not . . . *(Silence.)*

While the ordinary citizen can sit and chat and criticize, Aunt Dan continues, leaders "do what they *have* to do" and accept the responsibility for their actions and for the defense of others. Probably Kissinger devoutly wishes he were merely an ordinary citizen free to do as he pleases instead of what he must. Aunt Dan berates the press—"these filthy, slimy worms, the little journalists"—for its small-minded treatment of her hero. She works herself up into a fantasy of cowardly reporters "screaming and bleeding and shitting in their pants," unable to confront the armed enemy, let alone come to decisions on what to do about him.

Mother still questions whether Kissinger has the heart to arrive at correctly compassionate conclusions. Aunt Dan scoffs at the image of him weeping and sobbing at his desk: "The heart just responds to the present moment—it just sees these people in a village who've been hit by a bomb, and they're wounded and dying, and it's terribly sad. But the mind—the mind sees the story through to the end. It sees that yes, there are people who are wounded and dying in that village. But if we *hadn't* bombed it, some of those same people would have been marching tomorrow toward the *next* village with the grenades and machine guns they'd stored in that pretty little church we blew up . . . . ." Mother just hopes that Kissinger approaches his decisions "with scrupulous honesty"—and yes, she'd like to think of him as weeping at his desk.

Andy is conjured at Lemon's bedside to talk about Mindy—who was always short of money and would do anything to get it. Late one night she turned up at his flat with a visiting Chicagoan named Jasper who had in his pocket 100,000 pounds he'd just won at a gambling casino. June and Aunt Dan (age 30) were present, as Mindy set out to get as much of the money as she could from Jasper, whom Mindy considered a worthless, expendable person no one would miss. As for Jasper, he was strongly attracted to Mindy.

JASPER: God, you're pretty—you know, I really like you.

MINDY: I told you, Jasper—I have a serious boyfriend, you're not allowed to think of me like that—don't look at me like that, I'm telling you, Jasper, or I'm just going to send you home in a cab.

ANDY: She's serious, Jasper—it's hopeless, my friend, I've tried for years.

JASPER: Years? What? You don't really have a boyfriend, do you, you weasel? I mean, what is this "years"? If it's been all these years, then where's the boyfriend? He's just an excuse. He doesn't exist. Does he, Andy?

ANDY: Well, I must admit, *I've* never met him. But she's sure been faithful to the guy, I'll say that much.

JASPER: But is there really a guy, or are you just a tease?

MINDY: What is this, Jasper, are you calling me a liar?

JASPER: Yes, I am. You know you'll have me if I give you money.

MINDY: Hey, wow—now don't insult me.

JASPER: Well, I'd love to have you without the money, but you told me no. So now I'm asking you *with* the money.

MINDY: Is that what you're saying? And you think I would?

JASPER: For a thousand pounds, no. That would be too cheap—just prostitution. But *ten* thousand pounds, that's more like marriage. That would be like an intensely serious, permanent relationship, except it wouldn't last beyond tomorrow morning.

MINDY: No, Jasper.

JASPER: What is this no? Are you totally nuts?

MINDY: Give me all of it!

JASPER: Get lost!

JUNE: I think this discussion is going in circles.

ANDY: Friends, please! Let's try to approach our problems sensibly, all right? Now, Jasper, you're asking very little of Mindy, in my opinion. You merely want to strip her clothes off for a few hours and probably fuck her twice at the most, and for this you are offering her ten thousand pounds. Mindy, *my* opinion is, the exchange would be worth it. June, don't you think so? Tell us your opinion.

JUNE: Jasper seems to me an attractive man. He's extremely polite, he's extremely friendly. I'd be very surprised if he had any diseases—diseases, Jasper?

JASPER: Absolutely not. Do you think this kind of thing is my normal life? I *never* do this. I'm on vacation. Now here's the situation: I'm going back home tomorrow morning, and I'm going to put this money in the bank, and right now I'd like to spend some—ten thousand pounds.

JUNE: I think it's a good idea.

MINDY: For ten thousand pounds you can see my tits.

Linda Bassett, Linda Hunt and Wallace
Shawn in a scene from *Aunt Dan and Lemon*

As the evening progressed, Mindy managed to extract 60,000 pounds from Jasper. Jasper finally passed out, while Mindy sat there, naked, confiding stories about her life to Aunt Dan. She recounted in detail the events of one particular evening when she and her American friend Freddie contrived a plan to meet a certain Raimondo Lopez in a night club as if by chance. At the night club, Mindy was introduced to Raimondo as "Rosa Gatti," and Raimondo was increasingly attracted to her. When it came time to leave, Raimondo arranged to take "Rosa" home to her apartment. There she allowed him to start undressing her, removing her shoes and stockings. She poured him a glass of brandy, and it soon became obvious that the drink was drugged, as Raimondo collapsed onto the bed.

> *Mindy is standing by the bed, dressed in a robe, looking down at Raimondo, who is out cold. She shakes him roughly, and he groans slightly but doesn't wake up. Then she opens a drawer, pulls on a pair of jeans, takes out some pieces of rope and loops them around the knobs at the head of the bed and the knobs at the foot. She slips the nooses around Raimondo's wrists and ankles. She picks up the pair of stockings, and he suddenly speaks. His voice is indistinct.*

RAIMONDO: Rosa? Rosa?

> *She freezes. After a moment, he feels the ropes, then speaks again, a bit louder.*

What are you doing? Rosa?

> *She steps onto the bed behind him.*

Rosa! Please! No! No!

> *She puts her feet on his shoulders, leans back against the headboard,*

puts the stockings around his neck and starts to strangle him. She looks straight ahead of her, not at his face, as he struggles and gags.

AUNT DAN *(to Lemon):* She had to put the guy in this plastic sack, kick him down her back stairs, haul him outside and stick him into the trunk of a car that was parked in an alley. Apparently he'd been working with the police for some time against her friend Freddie.

A silence.

Well. My teeth were chattering as I listened to the words of this naked goddess, whose lipstick was the dreamiest, loveliest shade of rose. Then she fell silent for a long time, and we just looked at each other. And then she sort of winked at me, I think you would call it, and I wanted to touch that lipstick with my fingers, so I did. And she sort of grabbed my hand and gave it a big kiss, and my hand was all red. And then we just sat there for another long time. And then, to the music of Jasper snoring on the couch, I started to kiss her beautiful neck. I was incredibly in love. She kissed me back. I felt as if stars were flying through my head. She was gorgeous, perfect. We spent the rest of the night on the couch, and then we went out and had a great breakfast, and we spent a wonderful week together.

Pause.

LEMON *(to Aunt Dan):* Why only a week?

AUNT DAN: Huh?

LEMON: Why only a week?

Pause.

AUNT DAN: Lemon, you know, it's because . . . *(Pause.)* Because love always cries out to be somehow expressed. *(Pause.)* But the expression of love leads somehow—nowhere . . . . .

The expression of love, Aunt Dan continues, brings you into activities unrelated to the beauty which attracted you in the first place, "extremely fascinating for as long as you can stand it, but it has nothing to do with the love you originally felt."

After that summer when Lemon was 11, Aunt Dan's friendship with her parents faded away, and she never came for a visit again. Lemon would occasionally go up to London to see Aunt Dan and perhaps have dinner in some fine restaurant. Lemon was always aware of strong mutual attraction between them, but she never gave in to the impulse to lean over and kiss Aunt Dan—they never touched each other. Finally, when Lemon was 19 and paying her last visit at the bedside of a dying Aunt Dan, she realized that the spell was broken: "I feel no need now ever to see her again." Aunt Dan's final communication to Lemon was about the nurse who was devotedly caring for her, and how they would sit in this room, silently, listening to everything going on around them: "The insects, the wind, the water in the pipes. Sharing these things. Literally *every*thing. The whole world."

Back in her own darkened room, as at the beginning of the play, Lemon drinks her lime and celery juice and returns to the subject of the Nazis, about whom she has recently been reading. She explains to the audience that the Nazis "were trying to create a certain way of life for themselves," in the belief that their society's troubles were being caused by the intrusion of non-Germanic people into their tribal circle. They therefore began ruthlessly to eliminate the intruders, which horrified the rest of the civilized world—"But," Lemon contends, "the mere fact of killing human beings in order to create a certain way of life is not something that exactly distinguishes the Nazis from everybody else. That's just absurd. When any people feels that its hopes for a desirable future are threatened by some other group, they always do the very same thing."

Lemon goes on to say that if criminals or Communists became strong enough to threaten her society's way of life, they would be killed, just as the Europeans killed off the North American Indians in order to establish their own way of life in the Indians' territory, "So it becomes absurd to talk about the Nazis as if the Nazis were unique. That's a kind of hypocrisy. Because the fact is, no society has ever considered the taking of life an unpardonable crime or ever, really, a major tragedy. It's something that's done when it has to be done, and it's as simple as that."

Lemon's analogy is an infestation of cockroaches. Those who hate to kill anything might put up with a few cockroaches here and there, but even they would be driven to kill if there were insects all over the place, disturbing their way of life. "It is very unpleasant to kill another creature—let's admit it," Lemon declares, recalling in detail her disgust at having to squash a particularly large cockroach and watching its feeble attempts to stay alive. And the bigger a living creature is, the more difficult and unpleasant it is to kill it.

LEMON: We know it takes at least ten minutes to hang a person. Even if you shoot them in the head, it's not instantaneous—they still make those squirming movements at least for a moment. And people in gas chambers rush to the doors they know very well are firmly locked. They fight each other to get to the doors. So killing is always very unpleasant. Now when people say, "Oh the Nazis were different from anyone, the Nazis were different from anyone," well, perhaps that's true in at least one way, which is that they observed themselves extremely frankly in the act of killing, and they admitted frankly how they really felt about the whole process. Yes, of course, they admitted, it's very unpleasant, and if we didn't have to do it in order to create a way of life that we want for ourselves, we would never be involved in killing at all. But since we have to do it, why not be truthful about it, and why not admit that yes, yes, there's something inside us that likes to kill. Some part of us. There's something inside us that likes to do it. Why shouldn't that be so? Our human nature is derived from the nature of different animals, and of course there's a part of animal nature that likes to kill. If killing were totally repugnant to animals, they couldn't survive. So an enjoyment of killing is somewhere inside us, somewhere in our nature. In polite society, people don't discuss it, but the fact is that it's enjoyable—it's enjoyable—to make plans for killing, and it's enjoyable to learn about killing that is done by other people, and it's enjoyable to think about killing, and it's enjoyable to read about killing, and it's even enjoyable actually to kill, although when we ourselves are actually killing, an element of unpleasantness always comes in. But even there, one has to say, even though there's an unpleasant side at first to watching people die, we have to admit that after watching for a while—maybe after watching for a day or maybe for a week or a year—it's still in a way unpleasant to watch, but on the other hand we have to admit that after we've watched it for all that time— well, we don't really actually care anymore. We have to admit that we don't really care. And I think that that last admission is what really makes people go mad about the Nazis, because in our own society we have this kind of cult built up around what people call the feeling of "compassion" . . . . .

Lemon admits that she rather admires the Nazis and enjoys reading about them because they "had the nerve to say, 'Well, what *is* this compassion?' " Lemon doesn't know what it is, though her mother kept insisting she must feel it for other people (she gets a whiff of it from a play or novel but not in life). She's rather relieved to hear about others who don't seem to understand what it is either.

LEMON: . . . . . It was unpleasant to watch that pitiful roach scuttling around on my floor dying, but I can't say I really felt *sad* about it. I felt revolted or sickened, I guess I would say, but I can't say that I really felt sorry for the roach. And plenty of people have cried in my presence or seemed to be suffering, and I remember wishing they'd *stop* suffering and *stop* crying and leave me alone, but I don't remember, frankly, that I actually cared. So you have to say finally, well, fine, if there are all these people like my mother who want to go around talking about compassion all day, well, fine, that's their right. But it's sort of refreshing to admit every once in a while that they're talking about something that possibly doesn't exist. And it's sort of an ambition of mine to go around some day and ask each person I meet, "Well, here is something you've heard about to the point of nausea all of your life, but do you personally, actually remember feeling it, and if you really do, could you please describe the particular circumstances in which you felt it and what it actually felt *like?*" Because if there's one thing I learned from Aunt Dan, I suppose you could say it was a kind of honesty. It's easy to say we should all be loving and sweet, but meanwhile we're enjoying a certain way of life—and we're actually *living*—due to the existence of certain other people who are willing to take the job of killing on their own backs, and it's not a bad thing every once in a while to admit that that's the way we're living, and even to give to those certain people a tiny, fractional crumb of thanks. You can be very sure that it's more than they expect, but I think they'd be grateful, all the same.

The lights fade as she sits and drinks. Curtain.

BENEFACTORS

A Play in Two Acts

BY MICHAEL FRAYN

Cast and credits appear on page 309

MICHAEL FRAYN was born August 9, 1925 in northwest London, the son of a sales representative. He attended Kingston Grammar School but left in 1952 and went into the Army, which assigned him to train for the job of interpreter studying Russian at Cambridge and in Moscow. He received a commission as an intelligence officer before his discharge in 1954, when he returned to Cambridge to study philosophy and—in 1957—to co-author a college-produced musical comedy, Zounds!.

Frayn worked for the Manchester Guardian *as reporter and satirical columnist until 1962, and for the London* Observer *until 1968, the year in which his first dramatic work,* Jamie on a Flying Visit, *was televised on the BBC. His London stage debut took place in 1970 at the Garrick Theater with* The Two of Us, *a program of four short works:* Black and Silver, The New Quixote, Mr. Foot *and* Chinamen. *There followed* The Sandboy *(1971 at the Greenwich Theater);* Alphabetical Order *(1975 in London and later in the U.S.A. at the Long Wharf Theater);* Donkeys' Years *(1976);* Clouds *(1976);* Balmoral *(1979), revised as* Liberty Hall *(1980); and* Make and Break *(1980). Frayn's first Best Play,* Noises Off, *had its premiere at the Lyric Theater, Hammersmith, February 11, 1982 and soon transferred to the Savoy Theater in the heart of London, where it continued as a long-run hit while its American production was being staged on Broadway December 11, 1983 for 553 performances. His second Best Play,* Benefactors, *opened at the Vaudeville Theater in London April 4, 1984 and was presented on Broadway December 22 after receiving multiple London best-play awards (his* Alphabetical Order, Donkeys' Years, Make and Break *and* Noises Off *were also best-play award winners in London).*

Frayn's stage credits also include an adaptation of Jean Anouilh's Le Numbril, *retitled* Number One; *and translations of Tolstoy's* The Fruits of Enlightment, *Chekhov's* The Cherry Orchard *and an adaptation of Chekhov's earliest, untitled play (as* Wild Honey*), the latter three produced by England's National Theater. His published works include collections of his newspaper writings, a volume of philosophy* (Constructions) *and the novels* The Tin Men, The Russian Interpreter *(for which he won the Hawthornden Prize),* Towards the End of the Morning, A Very Private Life *and* Sweet Dreams. *Among his numerous TV productions have been documentaries on Berlin, Vienna, Australia, Jerusalem and the London suburbs. Frayn is married, with three daughters, and lives near Blackheath.*

The following synopsis of Benefactors *was prepared by Sally Dixon Weiner.*

ACT I

SYNOPSIS: The preponderance of the play's action takes place in a middle-class London family's kitchen, at right. There are the usual appliances, children's drawings and open shelves displaying pottery plates. There are chairs along each side and at each end of a rectangular wooden dining table that, when not being used at meals, is also utilized as a desk or work surface. There is a door to the rest of the house at right. A door upstage right is the entrance from the outside. A third doorway, upstage left, is sometimes the entrance to the house across the way and at other times is one of a number of different doorways or areas elsewhere in the vicinity. A chair downstage from this third doorway is sometimes changed from one type to another to indicate different locales. The open area, downstage left, is a limbo area, in contradistinction to the more realistic kitchen.

The action of the play takes place over 15 years, slipping back and forth between the present and memories of the past. The action is very fluid. The four characters, as they play out the scenes, alternately and sometimes even contiguously, discourse on their remembrances of their reactions to each other and to the past events that shaped their lives.

The play begins with David—tall, dark, charismatic, wearing a brown corduroy suit with a blue shirt and knit tie—in the kitchen with Jane, a warm, self-confident, handsome woman in brown slacks, a silk shirt and sweater vest.

DAVID: Basuto Road. I love the name!

JANE: Basuto Road. How I hate those sour grey words!

DAVID: Basuto Road, SE15. And at once you know when it was built and what it looks like. You can practically smell the grey lace curtains in those little bay windows. Don't you think?

JANE: You look back in life and there's a great chain of cloudshadows moving over the earth behind you. All the sharp bright landscape you've just travelled through has gone grey and graceless.

DAVID: Basuto Road. But when you think how fresh and hopeful that must have sounded once, back in 1890! There's the whole history of ideas in that one name.

JANE: There it is, on the box-files all along the shelf—Basuto Road, Basuto

Sam Waterston as David and Glenn Close as Jane in *Benefactors* by Michael Frayn

Road, Basuto Road. Grey-faced reproachful words, shuffling towards you out of the shadows. I look away—and there they are again, running downwards on the chest where he keeps his old drawings—Basuto Road, Basuto Road, Basuto Road.

DAVID: Also Bechuana Road and Matebele Road and Mashona Road and Barotse Road.

JANE: Then ten years, fifteen years away behind you the land's out in sunlight again. You can see everything small and shining in the distance—so clear you feel you could reach out and touch it.

DAVID: Plus Maud Road, Daisy Road, Frances Road, and Phoebe Road. I suppose they were the builder's daughters. Rather sad—it's all coming down. About fifteen acres. What do you think?

JANE: Basuto Road. It started in the sunlight. He was happy then. Yes! He was! He was happy! He came back in the middle of the day to tell me about the job, and he was like a child with a new bicycle. Ten years ago? No, twelve or more. But that day, at any rate—that's out in the sunlight again.

DAVID: It's probably an impossible site. It's jammed between a railway line and a main road. What do you think?

JANE: He couldn't sit still. He couldn't stop talking about it.

DAVID: It's zoned at 150 to the acre. I bet it's more like 200. I'll need you to check that for me.

JANE: We were both still children. Middle-aged children.

DAVID: But that would mean housing for three thousand people. It's probably not possible. What do you think? If it's possible the council wouldn't be asking me—they'd be doing it themselves. It would be a huge job—I'd have to double the size of the office. But that's where the work is, Jane, in local authority housing. That's where the real architecture's being done. So what do you think?

Jane asks herself what she did think. She can't remember, but imagines she was probably not in favor of it, that usually whatever David was for, she was against. But she admits, as David hurries off, that then, really, whatever David was in favor of, she was also—though she wouldn't have told him so. He knew it anyway.

But shortly thereafter, she remarks, she had to take David's side on the project because of Colin. Colin has come on, in khakis and shirt, none too amiable. If David was for it, then Colin was against it. "It was like the start of a game," Jane explains. "King opposite king. Queen on her color." Colin, sardonically as is his wont, gathers that David has got a big slum clearance job, that he'll change the face of London and is on the way to bettering himself professionally. She points out to Colin that it's not slum clearance—the area is a "twilight area," which Colin thinks sounds beautiful.

David comes on, as does Sheila (a shortish, shambling, not-so-much shy as watchful ugly duckling with cropped hair, muted plaid skirt, flat shoes and huge round glasses). David picks up the defense of his project as they all sit down to wine and supper. David and Colin, in his tongue-in-cheek manner, argue about the project. Colin frequently and in a patronizing manner speaks for Sheila, saying that anyway *she* takes David seriously.

"Nice little semis with nice little gardens" unfortunately won't show a net housing gain, David explains.

DAVID: Work it out for yourself. You were Senior Whatsit.

COLIN: Was I?

DAVID: I thought you were Senior Whatsit? At Eton, or wherever it was?

COLIN: Senior Classical Whatsit. Not Senior Town Planning Whatsit, like you.

DAVID: Difficult to rise above Senior Milk Monitor at my school.

COLIN: Wake up, Sheila. It's the barefoot boyhood again.

DAVID: Sheila's all right. Sheila's awake.

COLIN: She's not saying very much. Are you, my pet?

DAVID: She's talking more sense than some people.

COLIN: If only we could find out what Sheila wanted we'd know what everyone wanted.

JANE: Over dinner, this would be. The children out of the way. Occasional clicks and whimpers on the baby-alarm from their two across the street. Colin and Sheila—I don't know—they seemed to live round here. She'd leave the children here at some point in the day. That's what usually happened. Then when she came to collect them she'd sit down for a cup of coffee, and sooner or later she'd be saying, "This is awful—I haven't done anything about the children's tea." And I'd say, "That's all right—they can have something here." And then next thing I knew it would be, "This is terrible—I haven't done anything about getting a meal for Colin." And I'd say, "Give him a ring—we've got plenty." And she'd say, "This is awful—we seem to live round here."

DAVID: They're not here *again?*
JANE: Your friends, not mine.
DAVID: Sheila's *your* friend.
JANE: Sheila's *not* my friend.
DAVID: They seem to live round here!
JANE: You were the one who told them that house was coming up.
DAVID: *That* house! Not *this* house!
JANE: Anyway, I thought we were supposed to be helping them?
DAVID: I've been helping people all day. I've been helping two hundred people to the acre. I don't want to help people all evening.

Sheila and Colin are in David and Jane's kitchen again, Colin asking about "Basutoland." David doesn't feel like talking about it after the problems he's encountered during the day, which he then proceeds to describe at some length —access problems, lift sizes, etc. He doesn't want to build high but needs the high-rise subsidy to meet the Yardstick: HCY 1. Housing Cost Yardstick 1. But he'll fight, and compromises will be reached, and waivers will be gotten. He's not going to build towers: "No one wants to live in a tower." The game again, Jane opines later, for Colin tells David he would like to. "At the top. Surrounded by silence." Despite Jane's warning that the lifts would break down, and David's pointing out that he'd never meet the neighbors, Colin calls it a paradise.

We did like them, Jane goes on—well, him. David did. But Colin actually urged David to build towers. Colin would always get to David, she would try to keep the conversation balanced, and the Dormouse, Sheila, would just sit, saying nothing. That year must have been 1969 or 1970, Jane thinks.

Sheila remembers that it was 1968 when David started on the Basuto Road project, in April. Sheila would go popping over to the warmth and friendliness of their kitchen, envious of Jane's boundless energy, basking in the feeling of being made welcome. She admits to crying when she thinks about it now.

Sheila, with her little disasters, a blocked lavatory, a child sick, would call out "Hoo-hoo," and you knew she was there, Jane recounts. David suggests locking the door, but Jane says they can't—and Sheila's there again. She's due at the hospital for a child's appointment, and Jane says she will take them. Sheila doesn't drive. Jane says David could teach her and then, even though Sheila knows Colin wouldn't buy a car, Sheila could use theirs.

Colin accuses Sheila of being in love with Jane when Sheila calls to say they've been invited for supper again. Sheila did invite David and Jane for supper on occasion also, but David would protest—"It'll be all cold and dark brown." And David and Jane's children would protest when Sheila and Colin and their children were included in family outings.

Sheila recalls David taking them all to see the Basuto Road site. David is contemplating a courtyard—two vast slab blocks that, while sacrificing light, will keep road and railway noise away. Sheila remarks that it sounds like David's college. He's pleased that Sheila gets the point, the feeling of community that a building with its back turned on the world gives.

A testy remark of Jane's sets Jane and David to snapping at each other, much to Colin's delight; but he claims that Sheila has withdrawn and feels excluded.

SHEILA: No, I'm not. I'm very interested.

DAVID: Come here, Sheila. My favourite pupil.

SHEILA: No, I was just thinking, it must be wonderful to change things. It must be magical to look at some new thing that wasn't there before and think, *I* did that!

DAVID: No, it's not, Sheila. It's heartbreaking. It's always just warped windows and condensation problems. It was going to be so new and amazing, and it never is, it's always just like everything else. I'll tell you what's wonderful, Sheila . . . I'm not talking to you two . . . I'll tell you what's really magical. A bare building site. Something still quickens in me when I smell that raw damp smell of green brickwork and wet cement. When I feel the loose hardcore shift and grind under my shoes. I love those huge holes in the ground when people are going to go really high. Amazing emptiness, like the emptiness of a conjuror's hat, because you know that marvels will come out of it. I love looking at the site when it's like this, even—all other houses, all clutter waiting to be cleared.

COLIN: Some elegant new concrete block in the East End blew up last week.

DAVID: One flat blew up. There was a gas escape.

COLIN: The whole lot came down like a pack of cards.

DAVID: One side came down.

COLIN: Progressive collapse.

DAVID: Because it was system-built. The walls were holding up the floors. I shall use a steel frame.

JANE: Come on. The children will be screaming with hunger.

COLIN: The words will outlast the building, even so.

DAVID: What words?

COLIN: Wonderful words. "Progressive collapse."

Jane speaks of her discouragement, walking the streets with her clipboard, surveying the housing requirements in the project district because of David's fear that the council's density figure—and the mix, too—are not right. Ringing the bells, no one answering, or eyes looking through the letter-box, people suspicious of or not understanding what she's after, or taking advantage of her to help with their own problems. And the morning's gone.

Sheila admires Jane, how good she is at helping people. She ought to be, Jane comments, because all she ever does is to help David and the children, but she's not sure she likes people—all she's doing on Basuto Road is attempting to count people. Sheila would like to be someone who helps other people (she was a nurse), but now she feels *she's* other people. David interrupts their chat, Sheila rushes off to fetch her child. David and Jane discuss Colin and Sheila's relationship, living together in secret until long after she became pregnant.

DAVID: . . . . . I sometimes think he only married her because we happened to meet her.

JANE: We didn't *happen* to meet her. She came knocking on the door, saying Colin was in Durham and she was in labor.

DAVID: My first sight of *him* was saying grace in Hall. Very grave and unsmiling. Collar and tie, yellow flower in his buttonhole, scholar's gown; no shoes or socks. It was our first term. I can still remember the shock. The world wasn't really serious after all!

JANE: Imagine being married to him, though.

DAVID: Imagine being married to Sheila. Where did he pick her up?

JANE: Outside Lugano railway station.

DAVID: Thirty, and he was giving English lessons.

JANE: She'd had her rucksack stolen.

DAVID: Senior Classical Whatever-it-was, and he was giving English lessons in Lugano.

JANE: He's got a perfectly good job now.

    Enter Colin.

There's no need to feel sorry for him.

DAVID: Working on a women's magazine?

JANE: Yes, but then he's got that encyclopedia thing he does in his spare time. He's the editor of that.

Sheila enters and suggests that she do the Femininity section for the encyclopedia, but Colin thinks Jane could do it. David banters a bit about the encyclopedia, but concedes to Colin that many people will find it to be of help. Colin retorts that David could benefit himself if he looks up "D for Domination . . . . . Symbols of male potency; towers, high-rise, getting the thing up . . . . ."

Later, Colin and Sheila's discussion turns into a nasty diatribe on Colin's part accusing her of being smutty, imitating him and having no sense of humor, telling her she's "deaf to all shades of relation and meaning." He sends her off to bed, saying that she disgusts him.

David is frantic with problems about the site. There are drains under the playground area, plus problems with wire, pipes and sewers. Sheila keeps saying, "Poor David," but Jane assures her that he's in his element. It seems Sheila has problems of her own, however. She's in a bad state and petrified at the thought of what she'll do if Colin leaves her. She's worried about money and couldn't go back to nursing because she has to get Lizzie at three each afternoon. It isn't anything Colin has said, she just knows he thinks she is hopeless, and she's sure she's "held him back somehow." Jane assures her that Colin loves her, but Sheila's convinced she should have had that baby on her own. She would have coped—she wasn't always like she is now. Colin has pulled her down. And maybe she wants Colin to go.

Sheila asks Jane if she is happy, but Jane refuses to answer her directly. Nobody ever says it, Sheila comments. She's not sure whether they're frightened to say it or whether the fact is that no one is happy. Jane proposes that Sheila is "going a bit mad over there," what she needs is a job. Jane suggests that Sheila could come to work for David two or three hours a day, freeing Jane to spend more time attending to problems at Basuto Road.

DAVID: There's less and less you can do there now.

JANE: There's more and more! There's that woman who's being evicted. There's that couple I promised to take down to Ashford to see their son. They'll never go if I don't drive them.

DAVID: No good asking you to help me. You go off and help everyone else in the world instead.

JANE: I don't want to help anyone. I hate helping people. I want to study them. I'm an anthropologist, not a social worker.

DAVID: You'll have to learn to pass by on the other side occasionally.

JANE: You pass by on the other side, and there's someone in that gutter.

DAVID: Jane, I'm really under pressure.

JANE: Yes, you need more help.

DAVID: Don't you want to help me?

JANE: Not forever. I've always said that. I'm not a secretary.

DAVID: *She's* not a secretary. She's a nurse.

JANE: You need a nurse.

DAVID: Oh, Jane. You know what I love? I love dropping in at the house in the middle of the day, and there you are.

JANE: I hear your step in the hall, and my heart leaps.

DAVID: When I worked at home—that was the best time. When we both worked in the same room all day, because there wasn't anywhere else. Or anyone else. That was the best time of all.

JANE: Things have to change, though, love.

DAVID: Do they?

JANE: That's your profession, isn't it, changing things?

DAVID: My absurd and foolish profession.

JANE: And when you think about poor Colin and Sheila . . .

DAVID: I suppose we still live in one room, by comparison.

JANE: Anyway, it'll only be for a couple of hours a day. You'll hardly see her.

DAVID: Do we have to?

JANE: That's what the children always ask.

DAVID: And do we?

JANE: Yes, we do.

DAVID: What the children always ask then is, Why do we have to?

JANE: And what we always answer is, Because you do.

Sheila at first demurs about coming to work for David. It seems she's frightened of him and used to be frightened of Jane. And what will Colin think? Colin wants to know how much David will pay her—if he's going to pay her. Sheila supposes he is. Colin tells her to try the job, but only if she's not doing it out of charity, only if she's not just enabling Jane to get out "because he's so beastly to her," and Colin will expect her to return home daily with "David-and-Jane stories."

Sheila begins the job with great trepidation, left on her own as David goes rushing off, leaving the vaguest of instructions about letters, filing and paying the milkman. Jane comes in to find Sheila struggling with phone calls and offers to make lists of people who may call, including all their relatives, David having failed to do so.

David comes to realize Sheila's a quick learner. She manages the job so well and becomes so indispensable that Jane begins to wonder how they ever survived without her. Sheila was happy then, she remembers.

SHEILA: And after I'd collected Lizzie at three I'd come back and give the children their tea. All five of them—Matt and Lizzie as well—all round the table together. And I wouldn't just get a packet of fish fingers out of the freezer. I'd make them toad-in-the-hole, or I'd fry up all the leftovers into some great concoction of my own. And little Poppy's eyes would light up, and even Jake once said, "That was great, Sheila." And I'd sit there at the head of the table, being Mum, making them wash their hands and lay and clear, and I'd feel so pleased with myself. Isn't it . . . I don't know . . . pathetic, I suppose.

    Enter Colin.

Then I'd have to go back and cook dinner for Colin.

COLIN: I must say, that steak and kidney pie was a triumph. Even with the crust beginning to char, the center was still frozen. Steak and kidney Alaska.

SHEILA: I'm sorry—I couldn't get back any earlier. David came home from this meeting, and he was in a great state about it. You know how he gets. Apparently the planning department are being absolutely rigid about daylight angles.

COLIN: What was that girl in Ibsen called?

SHEILA: What?

COLIN: The one who made the old boy climb up the scaffolding?

SHEILA: No, but it means he can't put a five-story slab along the railway.

COLIN: Inspired by her youth and vitality, he climbed to the top of his new high-rise.

SHEILA: No, but that means he can't meet the Yardstick with the point blocks at eighteen stories.

COLIN: And fell off and broke his neck.

SHEILA: I'm not going to give it up, you know. I'm not. You've taken everything else away from me. You've laughed me out of everything I ever had. But not this! I'll fight you about this! I will, Colin! I'll fight you! I'll fight you!

David is at the kitchen table struggling over his sketch pad and talking to himself, when Sheila appears. She's on her way to get Lizzie. David, frustrated by his work problems, decides to go along. This was their first walk together, Sheila recalls. Later they walked to the park a few times, sometimes to the woods, David perhaps talking about his work, other times just going along in silence. She remembers one time catching a falling leaf on her hand: "A year's happiness."

Jane comes into the kitchen, complaining of the long wait at the hospital with someone's child, and is surprised to see Colin, who announces that he's fed the children and that they are watching television upstairs. He doesn't know where Sheila is. The school called him a half hour after it ended to report that Lizzie was still waiting by the gate. David's office believes he's at home, so Jane supposes David and Sheila have been taking a walk as they sometimes do, that perhaps they've taken shelter from the rain. She doesn't know.

Colin asks Jane if she knows that Sheila's in love with David. He can't believe it's news to her. Jane says it is, and, angry at Colin, observes, "David wants everyone to love him," whereas Colin wants everyone to hate him—or perhaps to love him despite his hatefulness. Colin doesn't imagine that David loves Sheila, though, any more than Jane did when Sheila was in love with her. Jane accuses

Colin of wanting to pull Sheila down, making her insecure. Colin wants to know if Sheila has said to her that she thinks he will desert her.

JANE: *Are* you going to leave her?

COLIN: Jane, I have a quiet laugh sometimes when I think about you going down there to Basutoland and helping people. In fact we both have a quiet laugh about it. I can still make her laugh, you know. About you and David, at any rate. You and David are a great force in keeping us together. Because I can't imagine what you make of the Basutos. You don't seem to understand the plain, everyday folk across the street. You haven't grasped one basic general principle—that other people's lives are at least as complicated as your own. At least as dense and extraordinary. And just as unlike your life as your life is unlike theirs.

JANE: You haven't answered my question.

COLIN: I am answering it. Sheila and I have been through all this business before, you see. The falling in love. The running across the road. The "Help me, help me." The "I'm going mad." The "Oh, God, he's going to leave me." Last time it was a couple of music teachers. This is when we were living in that flat, before you kindly found us the house. She started with Mrs., got Mrs. driving her everywhere, giving her meals, looking after the baby. Then she announced that she wanted to take up singing. Mrs. taught singing. Give her an interest, take her out of herself. So for six months she had singing lessons. Practised, too. An hour a day, without fail. Have you heard Sheila singing . . . ? Then she said she wanted to learn the oboe. Mr. taught the oboe. And she would have done it, too, Jane! She would have practised the oboe!

JANE: Poor Sheila.

COLIN: She's tone deaf.

JANE: So you stopped her?

COLIN: I had a word with Mrs.; life goes round like a wheel, Jane. What we've done once we do again. Round and round. We don't change. We never escape.

JANE: She may not be good at music, but she's good at helping David and me. So that's a change from last time.

COLIN: Good, is she? What, efficient? Well-organized?

JANE: I don't know what we'd do without her.

COLIN: I can believe that, as a matter of fact. How absurd things are.

JANE: I hope she'll go on working here. So that's another change from last time. And *are* you going to leave her?

COLIN: She used to be frightened of me once, of course. She used to be in love with me. I've got to have one stick left in the rack.

When David and Sheila come in, Sheila asks where the children are. Assured that they are upstairs, Lizzie included, she explains that she had called the school and asked them to tell Lizzie to go home with Matt. It seems Sheila and David were caught in the rain, spent a long time in a teashop, and then got caught in the rush hour. Sheila goes up to the children, but Colin leaves without answering when David asks him if they will stay for supper.

Lizzie didn't get the message because Sheila didn't really ring the school. She forgot about Lizzie, "truly awful." And when she saw Colin and Jane together in the kitchen, she was sure of what he'd been telling Jane. She was not in love with the oboe teacher, or his wife, but, yes, she was with David. Not that he was in love with her. Nobody was ever in love with her, Sheila admits, excepting Colin —three months in Switzerland and one month after that in London.

Jane isn't sure, she recalls, that David knew Sheila was in love with him. Maybe he did. And he did like to have somebody there to talk to about his "big idea" for Basuto Road. Skyscrapers are the answer, David is telling Sheila, the only solution. There will be 150 low-rise walk-ups, for families with young children, and "two socking great skyscrapers," 50 stories high—"highest residential buildings in Europe"—with 600 units for the others. It can be done, he's found out, and he will do it.

David euphorically describes his feelings about the towers, seeing them in his mind, how they will sometimes be higher than the clouds, and how it will be possible to see from them, in good weather, all of the North Downs, and the Thames Valley one direction, the Thames Estuary the other; "a hazard to aircraft"; "half of London" in the rain-shadow; the whole climate changed—he's joking, he tells Sheila. But he's envisioning standing on the Chilterns and seeing his skyscrapers over Hampstead Heath.

David is shocked when the evening paper reports that residents in the area are speaking out against the plans to use skyscrapers in the redevelopment scheme. A pensioner is quoted as saying that they haven't been consulted, and David is bewildered. There are no plans as yet. He hasn't even outlined the proposals. The article reports the skyscrapers might be a "hazard to aircraft" and might possibly affect the South London weather. Jane asks David if he told Sheila, and he admits to doing so. Jane insists he'll have to let her go, but David defends Sheila. She wouldn't have called the newspapers. That would have been Colin, Jane points out. It is his profession, she says. He's jealous of David, and Sheila's in collusion with Colin.

Their discussion is interrupted by Sheila's arrival, bag and baggage, with her children. She has left Colin, and she can't stop talking about how she's let David down.

A newspaperman had telephoned asking to talk to David about a report that David was planning skyscrapers that would be in the path of aircraft. Sheila had panicked. All she could think of was that Colin had done this to her, and Colin realized she knew it. She went back to get dinner for him. He was sitting looking at her. She took the leftover stew she'd taken out of the refrigerator and threw it at Colin. "There was this foul brown stuff all over everything," and she was crying, she tells them.

JANE: David, we did everything we could to help them. We did. Both of us. We truly and sincerely did.

DAVID: Yes. If we *hadn't* tried to help them they'd still be together. Perhaps I should go round. What do you think?

JANE: We rang him in the morning. There was no reply. We rang him in the evening. We rang him next day, and the next. Then his office rang us; he hadn't been in all week. He'd vanished! So in the end I went to look for him.

Enter Sheila.

I didn't say anything to Sheila. I just quietly took their spare key out of the tin on the refrigerator and went across the road. It was a kind of brown twilight inside their house. The curtains were still drawn; they'd been drawn all week. There were children's toys underfoot, and overturned cardboard boxes. I opened the living-room door, and there was the life they'd shared, abandoned at one muddled arbitrary moment in time. Clothes waiting to be mended; more toys; open newspapers; two unwashed nursery mugs. Everything gone cold and still . . . I opened the kitchen door . . . I can feel even now that sudden wave of cold spreading up from my stomach, shrinking the skin on my face, then the scalp over my head. Because there it was—the unmistakeable stench of putrefying flesh . . . Funny, when I look back on it. I'd worked out what it was by the time I managed to see anything. It was just like Sheila had said—foul and brown and everywhere. But it *was* me who found him in the end. In a derelict house in Frances Road, in the middle of David's redevelopment area. The council had just started to move people out. I saw this front door standing ajar, and I pushed it open. I don't know why. I suppose I thought there might be something bad inside. And there he was.

Enter Colin.

COLIN: Come in. Welcome to the battlefront.

Curtain.

ACT II

DAVID: Basuto Road. Those sour stale words. You look up from your work, and there they are along the files. Or you're going down some other path in your mind altogether—and suddenly they're coming towards you. The same shabby sad-eyed pair. And before you know what you're doing you've turned and crossed the street to avoid them. Why? What could they say that hasn't been said?

Enter Jane and Sheila.

SHEILA: In Basuto Road?

JANE: In Frances Road, to be precise.

DAVID: After all, the Basuto Road scheme included our very successful redevelopment of Colin and Sheila. We should have had awards for our work on them, we should have had bronze plaques to put up.

SHEILA: "Welcome to the battlefront"? What battlefront?

JANE: He's going to stop the scheme.

DAVID: I mean that. Jane used to say that when she opened the front door in Frances Road she didn't recognize him for a moment. He seemed taller. His eyes were fully open. He was alive. And I say, good for him.

SHEILA: And he's *living* there? He's got himself a flat on David's site?

JANE: It's a squat.

SHEILA: A *squat?*

JANE: The council have started clearing the houses. As the tenants move out so the squatters move in.

DAVID: And I wouldn't have recognized Sheila when she heard the news. All of a sudden she was—well, yes, she was *alive.* And I say, good for her.

SHEILA: What sort of squatters?
JANE: I don't know. Young people.
SHEILA: Colin hates young people.
JANE: Rather tired old young people, so far as I could see.
SHEILA: He hates old people. He hates everyone.
JANE: They've got electricity and water, and one or two bits of furniture. It's not too bad.

Sheila can't believe Colin is capable of organizing a campaign to stop the scheme, since he isn't even capable of organizing the children or himself. She warns Jane that Colin is an evil person, that he will destroy them as he destroyed her. When she is told that Colin has quit his job, she is worried about what she and the children will live on. David tells her she can work full time for him.

Jane comments to David when they are alone on the irony of David supporting Sheila so that Colin can set about ruining David's livelihood. David doesn't feel that Colin can do much damage, but Jane isn't so sure. Furthermore, David is concerned about Colin and wants to know if anything should be done for him —if they help Sheila, shouldn't they help him, so as not to "take sides"?

Jane tries to convince David that Colin is not a friend, that he is the enemy, that the sides have already been drawn, but David persists, in what she refers to as his "moral blindness," that perhaps he should go see Colin, or that Jane should. She refuses. Her reaction to Colin is like Sheila's. She hopes he will starve.

David, looking back, recalls that he "felt like a bemused neutral observer" as the Basuto Wars began. "They all took it so personally," he remembers. He didn't understand Colin—he never had—and he believed that Colin was not on a personal vendetta against any of them, but really was against the scheme.

Glenn Close, Mary Beth Hurt (Sheila), Sam Waterston
and Simon Jones (Colin) in a scene from *Benefactors*

Colin continues living in the squat on Frances Road, enjoying "a lightness, a physical lightness" in his bare surroundings, though he admits to having cried sometimes, for the children, with their colds and coughs, their "hot muddled aching heads" on his chest. And he smugly expects that eventually David will turn up, all concerned about Sheila, but more so about him, and maybe concerned to some degree about the scheme as well. Why had Colin done it? David would ask. Colin doesn't know exactly why.

But it's Jane that finally comes, bringing his mail and asking the question. She also wants to know why he was so cruel as to have married Sheila. Colin doesn't reply and instead asks Jane if she will fold some of his leaflets. She tells Colin that Sheila says he may see the children on Saturday. Colin suggests that Jane drive them to Frances Road, as he has no car, he's out of work, he's just one of her Basutos.

JANE: A squat. So this is what you want, is it, Colin?

COLIN: What do you think I've been living in for the last ten years? Actually it reminds me of school. Bare boards and cold water and smelly feet.

JANE: And a lot of admiring fourth-formers.

COLIN: Yes, and something serious to do.

JANE: Folding leaflets?

COLIN: Another house to beat for the house shield. Someone to defeat. And you want to know why I married Sheila? Out of kindness, Jane. Out of the kindness of my heart. My one crime.

JANE: Colin, can I tell you something I've never told you before? Something I've never said to anyone, ever.

COLIN: A secret.

JANE: Yes, a secret.

COLIN: This is why you've come to see me, is it?

JANE: Possibly.

COLIN: You're in love with me.

JANE: More secret than that. I don't like you.

COLIN: Oh, Jane.

JANE: I never have liked you.

COLIN: Jane, Jane, Jane.

JANE: So now I've said it.

COLIN: After twenty years. Does David know?

JANE: He does now. And what a stupid farce it was, pretending I did like you! Because now you don't even like David! You hate him!

COLIN: I like you, Jane.

JANE: No, you don't.

COLIN: Oh, yes. I like you because I see in you a little of the blackness I have in me. That's why you don't like me. Because you know I can see it.

JANE: Yes. Well.

COLIN: Anyway, you have more hot soup to distribute. I'll tell you another secret, though, Jane. You're the expert on helping the Basutos, and you know the scheme's not going to help them. You loathe it as much as I do. You won't tell

David that, of course. Don't worry—*I* won't tell him. That really *is* a secret
. . . Or do you mean it was even a secret from yourself?
JANE: Saturday—I'll leave the children at the door.

Sheila and David are in the kitchen. David is at work finishing the elevations
due at the Borough Architect's office the next morning. He's exhausted but in a
light-hearted frame of mind as he amuses himself putting people in the design.
Jane comes in, and David wants to know what she thinks of the work. Rather
offhandedly, she says it's good. David doesn't think Colin's activities are anything
to worry about. The full design will be ready for the council by winter, and only
then will the Basutos know of it, when the big scale model is displayed at the
Town Hall.

Jane, obviously distracted, is not really listening. She finally blurts out that
she's been offered a job by the housing trust in Wandsworth but hasn't decided
whether or not to accept it. David, put out, remarks that if housing is her interest,
he is doing that. The trust in Wandsworth, however, doesn't build houses, it does
rehabilitation, she explains, adding that her thinking cannot always be the same
as his. And he agrees that she should think what she likes and do as she chooses.

Colin and David take turn and turn about reminiscing about the Basuto Wars
as they went on and on. Colin was delighted to discover, he relates, that something from his classical education proved useful to him. Knowing how to write
Greek hexameters enabled him to write political slogans that fit on a cardboard:
"Don't scrape the skies—just sweep the streets."

David was disturbed because some Housing Committee members regarded the
water garden in his scheme as dangerous and were afraid people would become
dizzy looking down from such high balconies. "Been got at by someone," he
supposed. Colin and his supporters, he says, even took to writing on lavatory
walls—high-rise slogans like "Living in the sky is strictly for the birds," low-rise
slogans like "Hands off our homes! Save our streets!", and some "lower still," like
"Skyscrapers = SS." David recalls "the sheer labour of it"—the foundation
problems, the diversion of the megavolt cable, and out there people working to
make things more difficult—whereas Colin recalls "the sheer pleasure of it!"—
spraying walls, shouting down council meetings, the liberation of having nothing
so that they could do anything. David remembers feeling sad for Colin, and Colin
remembers laughing as he thought of David and his scheme that would never be
built. David had wished he'd had Jane's help. Colin claimed he did do "one fair
and tidy thing" when he suggested Jane as a field worker to the Wandsworth
people.

David is doing a rehabilitation job on Sheila's house. Jane wonders why he
doesn't raze it and rebuild it, and why he didn't pull theirs down.

SHEILA: Jane, there are lots of people who haven't got homes at all. We've got
to build them *something*. I know you worry about it, Jane, but it's got to be done.
You know it has.
JANE: It's like a bonfire, isn't it. Faith, I mean. It flares up here—it dies down
there. You never know where or when.
SHEILA: Jane, perhaps I shouldn't say this, but I see you and David every day,

and I know you don't really agree with what he's doing, and I can't help worrying about it. Because I know what you think. You think we ought to ask people more what they actually want. But, Jane, it's no good asking people what they want, because they don't know what they want until they've got it. No one asked them if they wanted Basuto Road the way it is now. Probably in the first place they didn't! It may have been years before they realized they wanted it like that! People aren't all as clever as you, Jane! *I'm* not! I didn't want to work for David. You made me. And you were right, and I'll be grateful until the day I die!

JANE: This is what David's been telling you?

SHEILA: David doesn't know what people want, but I do, because I know what *I* want. I don't want David to ask me what color my kitchen should be. I want him to tell me. I don't want him to ask me whether I want the house redesigned. I just want him to do it. And when I say I feel awful about it and he shouldn't be doing it I don't want him *not* to do it! That's what people are like, Jane! That's what most people are like. Colin doesn't know what he wants! I know you feel sorry for him and you take his part—but he doesn't know what he wants any more than I do! Or he didn't, until he saw somebody else who did, and then he knew he wanted to stop it and smash it. Because it's all part of the same old battle between good and evil, the same old war between light and dark. I know you won't like my saying that. But it is, Jane, and you mustn't let him win you over!

It's a dark November morning. Colin wonders why he should bother to get up. What does it matter about some grey houses and grey people? If David wants to "pursue the meaningless," why shouldn't that be his reward? Jane arrives with Colin's overcoat and other winter clothing and comments on how badly he looks. He's not ill, he tells her, it is "loss of appetite." He inquires about David, but Jane isn't talking about him. Colin says he knows what David thinks—that he's life and Colin is death, but it isn't Colin building "gigantic monumental tombstones." Jane supposes she ought to thank him for her job and says she'll bring Matt and Lizzie Saturday.

David wonders about going on with the whole scheme. In his discouragement he tells Sheila he knows how it will be, the concrete spalling, ceilings cracking, the people living in it hating it and hating him. He'll feel differently the next day, Sheila reassures him, and he supposes he will. If he can just get those two towers up, they'll stay the same, not moving around each other, not leaning on each other, not knocking each other down. And he has no choice but to go on—it's his livelihood and his life.

Sheila is sure Jane would do nothing to hurt him. Sheila loves them both and could not bear it if something happened to the two of them. David wonders if Colin ever has doubts.

David asks Jane if she would stop the scheme, if she could and if he'd never know. She hedges, telling him she thinks public opinion is different since the collapse of an East End block, that is all she's saying. David supposes she needn't say any more because she "*is*" public opinion.

When it was spring again, David recalls, their spirits returned. Because a General Election was called, he was working hard to complete the design before there might be policy changes at the Ministry. And then Colin was everywhere, in the papers and on television.

Sheila comes in to tell David that "Colin is standing now! In the election!"—an Independent candidate in jeans and a T-shirt with *Get 'em down!* on it. He's reported to have given up his career in journalism and is warning that a progressive collapse of the planned skyscrapers would send concrete down on several acres. People are cheering when he discusses architects interested in building monuments to themselves, "monstrous tombstones." Colin hates David, he actually does, David thinks.

Sheila greets Jane as she comes in with the news that Colin is standing for Parliament, but Jane shrugs it off, saying that he won't make it. David suspects Jane must have known about it. He is hurt that she hadn't told him. Jane has had a hard day, doesn't want to get into an argument with David and turns on Sheila, claiming Sheila's always running off when she comes in, leaving "a row behind her." She's started one now, and she may as well stay for it. David urges Sheila to go, but Jane is insistent.

JANE: I said she can stay! So, all right, I didn't tell you Colin was standing. I'm sorry. It didn't seem of any great moment. He won't get in. He'll get sixty-five votes. I'm sorry, though. All right? I've apologized. What else? Is that all? May I sit down now and eat my supper? I've got work to do afterwards.

DAVID: Where's he getting the money from?

JANE: What money?

DAVID: For the Election. Posters, halls, deposit. He's living on social security.

JANE: How should I know?

DAVID: He's not getting it from you? You're not giving him money? It's not our money?

JANE: Is that what you're worrying about?

DAVID: *Is* it our money?

JANE: No!

DAVID: Is he getting it from the people you work for?

JANE: He's getting a little from the Trust.

DAVID: So you do know, then?

JANE: It's not *my* idea! In fact I've consistently opposed it!

DAVID: You said you didn't know. But you do know. Why did you say you didn't know?

JANE: David, I'm not going to be cross-examined like this.

SHEILA: Please!

DAVID: That's the first time you've ever lied to me.

SHEILA: Please! Please!

JANE: Listen, David. Not once, not once have I ever done or said anything that could possibly be disloyal! Not once! I mean, it's ridiculous! I hate the man! I've always hated him! That's all I ever concealed from you!

DAVID: You hate the scheme, too.

JANE: All right, I'll tell you what I think about the scheme. I've never said it to anyone, and I'll never say it again. But if you want to know, I'll tell you. I think those towers of yours are two giant tombstones.

DAVID: Tombstones?

JANE: One for each of us. Anyway, now I've said it.

DAVID: Now you've said it.

JANE: So now you're happy. And don't start snivelling now, Sheila! The row's over.

> *Exit Sheila.*

DAVID: Tombstones. It was a coincidence, of course. She'd never heard him use the phrase. She was certain of that. All the same, she wouldn't go and see him again.

On Saturday Colin telephones because Jane has failed to appear with the children. Jane tells him she's sorry, but he must make other arrangements about them with Sheila. Colin also jubilantly reports on the previous evening's torch-light procession—tell David, he says—thousands of people on Basuto Road singing.

Jane ought to have told Colin she wasn't bringing the children, David thinks. Jane exits, leaving David musing over the possibility of going and seeing Colin himself, and what understanding comments he might make to him. Colin enters, having come to see his children, and when Jane comes back she is furious at finding Colin with David. She berates David for letting him in. The children are upstairs with Sheila, who's in a state. Jane wants David to put Colin out, she won't have him in the house. David says he can't—"He's not a cat"—and Jane goes up to Sheila.

David tells Colin he is sorry but admits that Jane is right. He tries to make peace with Colin, struggling to let him know that he understands Colin's resent-ment of him, but that he won't apologize for things having gone well for himself. David is ambivalent—he says he's worked hard for his luck, that he likes his work; and then he claims he doesn't like most of it, because most of his work is fighting. Colin's a fighter, but David isn't.

Jane returns, saying that Sheila won't come downstairs until Colin leaves. David says Colin won't leave until arrangements about the children have been made. Jane accuses David of taking Colin's side. David flares up at her, claiming he didn't pay Colin to ruin his work or go sneaking off for talks with him.

Sheila finally comes downstairs to tell David and Jane to stop fighting each other, to fight Colin, "sitting there grinning." Jane tells Sheila to get out of the kitchen, and David tells Jane to let Sheila alone. He's incredulous when Jane says that Sheila is "the cause of it all." When Colin tells David that Sheila is in love with him, Sheila *picks up a steaming saucepan* and throws it in Colin's face. Jane and David get cold water and a towel, and Jane takes Colin off to get medical assistance.

David is appalled at what Sheila has done, but Sheila insists Colin should not have said what he did. David supposes Jane must have known, but he hadn't. Sheila is apologetic and is about to get the children and leave, but David says it isn't necessary. It doesn't change things. They will go on working as usual, but he can't believe she could have done such a thing. "I don't know anything about anyone," he muses.

Colin recalls that it was good for some votes, however—the bandages, the stories in the newspapers. "Ban-the-towers Colin in mystery attack." In the end, he got a mere 173 votes.

David has taken to visiting Colin and tells Sheila not to worry about him or the children—children know people fight—and that he and Jane are going together for a short trip. Since the vote is in, it won't hurt if the development scheme is a little later getting in. And Colin recalls David at the door with the children, all smiling concern, "like a dog wanting to be taken in and loved." But that all ended when the scheme was stopped.

SHEILA: *Stopped?*

JANE: They rang him this morning. Didn't he tell you?

SHEILA: I knew it! I knew it! This was the Housing Committee last night?

JANE: Apparently the Ministry had rejected the revised estimates. I thought you'd know all about it.

SHEILA: David was sure the council would fight them!

JANE: Apparently not.

SHEILA: Oh, Jane, it's all my fault! I held him up! If he'd got the drawings finished a month earlier . . . A week earlier, even . . . !
    Enter David, with keys.
Oh, David! It was me, wasn't it? It was me!

DAVID: No, no. It's all in here. " 'We Did It!' says Giantkiller Colin."

SHEILA: Colin? Colin did it?

DAVID: " 'I always knew we'd wear them down in the end,' grinned lone campaigner Colin Molyneux today."

SHEILA: Colin?

JANE: I thought it was the electricity people? I thought they said it was going to cost another half-million pounds to divert the cable?

DAVID: Yes, or else it was the Ministry, because they wouldn't pay the Generating Board. Or the council, because they wouldn't fight the Ministry. Or that block in the East End. No, it was Colin. Among others. Why wouldn't the Ministry pay? Why wouldn't the council fight them? Because no one believes in going high any more. Because public opinion has changed.

SHEILA: Not *my* opinion, David.

DAVID: No, not your opinion.

JANE: I'm going to put dinner on the table. I've got to work afterwards.

SHEILA: I shall always blame myself.

DAVID: I was too late, that's all. A week, a year—who knows?

SHEILA: It was me.

DAVID: It was people. That's what wrecks all our plans—people.

The Basuto Road area was rehabilitated instead of razed, Jane recalls. Sheila, looking back, wonders what would have happened to David if Jane hadn't had her own work. David's practice declined. It took seven years for him to get a tower built, she remembers—private offices, not housing, and it won a prize, but then it was the recession. And Colin supposes Jane's influence got him his job writing about rehabilitation schemes, to rehabilitate him. David didn't want to build high, but you had to, David remembers, and then he didn't want "to come down to earth again," but he had to. If no one changes, nothing in the world would ever happen.

DAVID: We all change. Everything changes. I'm rather proud of some of those rehab schemes I've done for Jane. I'm happy enough, anyway. We're happy enough . . . Look, I can't keep the meal hot indefinitely.

JANE: Just coming.

SHEILA: I see David's building sometimes when I'm on my way to my sessions with Dr Medtner. It makes me think of . . . I don't know—summer coming, the feeling that things are going to change.

DAVID: The only one who never changed was Sheila. She went on believing to the end, like some old Stalinist. Still does, for all I know. She moved away when they divorced. I couldn't keep her on, of course—I couldn't keep anyone on. It was best for her, anyway—she'd got completely dependent on us. It was pulling her down—it was part of her depression. I think Jane found her a job somewhere.

COLIN: Even Sheila's being rehabilitated. Or so I gather from Lizzie. Lizzie's nineteen, now. She says Sheila goes to see some woman of Central European extraction in Hampstead.

SHEILA: Dr Medtner says I can learn to change. I have the capacity for happiness, she says . . . . .

DAVID: I drove down Basuto Road the other day. The sun was shining, and some woman was standing in a doorway with her children and laughing, and it all looked quite bright and cheerful.

SHEILA: Basuto Road. Yes, and at once it's summer, and everything is about to change.

COLIN: I did one good thing in this world, anyway. I helped poor old David. I saved him from a lifetime of public execration.

JANE: Basuto Road? It's strange; the cloud moves on, and there's the landscape out in sunshine again.

DAVID: Basuto Road. There's the whole history of human ideas in that one name.

JANE: And yes! I was! I was happy!

DAVID: Laughing and laughing. But what she was laughing about I never discovered.

    Curtain.

IT'S ONLY A PLAY

A Play in Two Acts

BY TERRENCE McNALLY

Cast and credits appear on page 348

TERRENCE McNALLY was born in St. Petersburg, Fla., November 3, 1939 and grew up in Corpus Christi, Texas. He received his B.A. in English at Columbia where in his senior year he wrote the varsity show. After graduation he was awarded the Harry Evans Travelling Fellowship in creative writing. He made his professional stage debut with The Lady of the Camellias, *an adaptation of the Dumas story produced on Broadway in 1963. His first original full-length play,* And Things That Go Bump in the Night, *was produced on Broadway in 1965 following a production at the Tyrone Guthrie Theater in Minneapolis.*

McNally's short play Tour *was produced off Broadway in 1968 as part of the* Collision Course *program. In the next season, 1968–69, his one-acters were produced all over town:* Cuba Si! *off Broadway in the ANTA Matinee series;* Noon *on the Broadway program* Morning, Noon and Night; Sweet Eros *and* Witness *off Broadway that fall, and in early winter* Next *with Elaine May's* Adaptation *on an off-Broadway bill that was named a Best Play of its season.*

McNally's second Best Play, Where Has Tommy Flowers Gone?, *had its world premiere at the Yale Repertory Theater before opening off Broadway in 1971. His third,* Bad Habits, *was produced OOB in 1973 by New York Theater Strategy, directed then and in its off-Broadway and Broadway phases in the 1973–74 season by Robert Drivas. His fourth,* The Ritz, *played the Yale Repertory Theater as* The Tubs *before opening on Broadway January 20, 1975 for a run of 400 performances. His fifth,* It's Only a Play, *was produced in a pre-Broadway tryout under the title*

Broadway, Broadway *in 1978 and OOB under its present title by Manhattan Punch Line in 1982. It finally arrived in the full regalia of an off-Broadway production—and Best Play designation—this season January 12 for 17 performances on Manhattan Theater Club's schedule.*

Other McNally presentations in one of the most active and successful playwriting careers in his generation have included Whiskey *(1973, OOB) the book for the John Kander–Fred Ebb musical* The Rink *(1984 on Broadway) and* The Lisbon Traviata *(1985, OOB). He also adapted his own* The Ritz *for the movies and is the author of a number of TV plays. He has been the recipient of Obie and Hull-Warriner Awards (for* Bad Habits*), a CBS, a Rockefeller and two Guggenheim Foundation fellowships and a citation from the American Academy of Arts and Letters. McNally lives in Manhattan and has served as vice president of the Dramatists Guild, the organization of playwrights, composers, lyricists and librettists, since 1981.*

Time: Now

Place: Julia Budder's townhouse

ACT I

SYNOPSIS: An opening night party is heard noisily in progress downstairs in the producer's, Julia Budder's, New York townhouse. Upstairs at curtain rise the spacious bedroom is empty, but the king-sized bed is gradually being covered by mink and other overcoats belonging to the guests and being piled there by Gus Washington, *"black, cool and street smart,"* an attendant dressed in a dinner jacket. At right is a desk with several phones, and the furnishings also include a chaise longue, a spinet, a TV set, a bookcase and several armchairs. The door to the hall leading to stairs and the party is up center, and the bathroom door is at left.

Gus enters with an armful of coats and dumps them on the bed. He is soon followed by James Wicker, *"pleasant, open features and a personality of great charm,"* a middle-aged actor who has detached himself from the noisy, celebrity-laden revelry downstairs looking for a quite place to talk to his agent in California on the phone. Gus (who has taken acting lessons and would like to be in show business himself) recognizes James as someone he has seen perform but can't place him until James identifies himself as an actor in the California-based TV series *Out on a Limb.*

While James is on hold at the phone, he hears sounds made by an angry dog locked in the bathroom—the Budders' dog Torch who bit Arlene Francis this evening, seriously enough so that she was taken to the hospital along with Mr. Budder, who was mugged earlier. James waves his empty champagne glass at Gus, who goes to get a refill. James's agent comes on the phone, curious to know how the new play went tonight. "A thirty-five pound Butterball," James says and settles himself comfortably for a long conversation.

JAMES: . . . . . Bob Fosse asked me what I thought at intermission, and all I said was, "Gobble, gobble," and he wet himself. Of course I don't want you to give that to Liz Smith. Are you crazy? I may want to work with these people. How was Jack Nimble? He was terrible, just terrible. But tell me this and tell me no more: when was he ever any good? All of my mannerisms and none of my warmth. Of course I would have been wonderful in it. It was written for me. And you want to hear the killer? I wasn't even mentioned in Peter's biography in the *Playbill.* I mean, let's face it. I did create the lead in his one and only hit, but do you think I got so much as even a mention in his bio tonight? Well, that's a best friend for you. I fly in three thousand miles on the goddamn Red Eye for his opening, and I'm not even mentioned in the goddamn *Playbill.* The egos in this business! What about Virginia Noyes? Terrible, just terrible. I haven't seen a performance like that since her last one. Well of course she wanted to come back to Broadway. After her last couple of pictures, she had to go somewhere. Terrible direction, just terrible. Boy wonder he may well be; the new Trevor Nunn he's not. He's not even the old Mike Nichols. Frank something. He's out of Chicago. Aren't they all? Sets? What sets? It took place on a goddamn tilted disc. Give me scenery or count me out. Hideous costumes. Darling, I would have made my first entrance in a leather codpiece and sort of antlers. I kid you not. There but for the grace of ABC went I! Darling, Arnold Schwarzenegger couldn't have held this one up. Oh, and guess who was sitting next to me at the theater? Rita Moreno in a Day-Glo turban. She was with Calvin Klein. I wish you could have seen her face when he introduced her to Jean Kennedy as Chita Rivera! Who? Rita or Chita? Terrible, just terrible. But listen, darling, what do I know? What do any of us old gypsies know? I liked *The Rink.*

Virginia Noyes, *"high cheekbones, throaty voice, a firecracker,"* drifts through, looking for the bathroom and disappears into it, apparently without activating the dog Torch. James remarks to his agent, Sue, that Virginia is "washed up at 37" and then continues with his own concerns—he doesn't like his TV show's new time slot.

As the phone conversation ends, Gus comes back with a bottle of champagne and a message from the hostess to James—she wants a word with him and will be right up. Meanwhile, Virginia comes out of the bathroom, comments, "There is a dog in there when you get right up close to it," sits and prepares to dose herself from her liberal and varied supply of recreational drugs. She can't place James Wicker immediately any more than Gus could, but she finally realizes that they once did a film together.

VIRGINIA: When they sent me Peter's play, they told me you were doing Jack's part.
JAMES: There was some talk about it, they wanted me desperately, as a matter of fact, but with my series . . .
VIRGINIA: You got a series?

JAMES: For five years now.

VIRGINIA: I'm sorry. I do a lot of self-destructive things but I draw the line at television. I don't watch it and I won't do it.

JAMES: I take the money and run.

VIRGINIA: Yeah. But are you happy?

JAMES: Relatively. Are you?

VIRGINIA: Fan-fucking-tastic.

JAMES: Speaking of Peter.

VIRGINIA: Peter? I wrote the book. Oh, that Peter!

JAMES: Where is he?

VIRGINIA: Beats me. Maybe he's just hiding until the reviews are out. Speaking of which, have you heard anything?

JAMES: You're home free with this one.

VIRGINIA: You really think so?

JAMES: Darling, I could phone these raves in.

VIRGINIA: I hope so. Living in L.A. so long, you forget what being on a real stage is like. My only mistake was going out there in the first place. I guess I just wanted to see myself forty feet tall.

JAMES: We all do.

VIRGINIA: I wanted to see what they'd do with my tits.

JAMES: Me. too.

VIRGINIA: I don't see the crime in that.

JAMES: It's the American Dream.

Virginia leaves, and James turns on the TV to catch the first reviews. Frank Finger *("seething, dark, intense")*—who directed the play—comes in and casually pockets a small antique box worth several hundred dollars, putting James in the awkward position of not knowing quite what he should do about this.

Though James is aching to know what the critics think of tonight's play, Frank turns the TV sound off, commenting, "Watching only encourages them," so James can't hear what Stewart Klein has to say. James begs Frank to turn the volume back up, which he does just in time to hear Stewart Klein comment, ". . . . . perfect staging by Frank Finger, the brilliant young director . . . . ." A burst of applause is heard from the party guests downstairs, who are also listening to the TV reviews.

Julia Budder—the *"attractive and genuinely pleasant"* young producer and hostess of this opening night party—comes in just as Frank leaves. She is elated by the review just heard, convinced she has a hit. She goes to the bathroom to pat Torch and asks James to bring her his dog yummies in the silver box (not knowing what they were, James has been munching them himself and reacts accordingly, but brings her the box).

Having attended to Torch, who remains in the bathroom, Julia admits she's worried about the author of the play, Peter Austin, who isn't at the party but sent her this note she promised not to open until the reviews are in. James made no promises, though, and he takes Peter's note from Julia, opens it and reads it aloud. In it, Peter tells Julia how grateful he is that she produced his play, and he hopes for the best. He even wishes Frank luck.

JULIA: You should've heard some of the names Frank called him during rehearsal. Failure. Has-been. Hack.

JAMES: No!

JULIA: Loser. Fake. Phony. Written out.

JAMES: I get the picture.

JULIA: He said I was just an amateur, dilettante, rich bitch.

JAMES: Why did you stand for it?

JULIA: I didn't. My husband said, "You can't speak to my wife like that," and he punched him right in the mouth.

JAMES: Good for Elliott.

JULIA: You don't understand. Frank punched Elliott. He knocked him out and then barred him from the theater.

JAMES: As the producer, you should have done something.

JULIA: I'd already been barred from the theater.

JAMES: This play sounds like a total nightmare for you from the first day of rehearsal right up until tonight.

JULIA: It's been bliss. Sheer creative bliss.

James continues to read the note, in which Peter absolves Julia of all blame if the show doesn't succeed and wishes her luck with the new Lanford Wilson script she's optioned. Gus comes in with another batch of coats, as James comes to a P.S. on Peter's note: "The play never really had a chance without James Wicker in it. Of course he was a son of a bitch not to have done it, and I wish him and his fucking series a sudden and violent death."

Downstairs at the party Lena Horne is singing "Stormy Weather," and Gus wishes he could get a chance to sing, to show off his ability. Julia sees no reason why he shouldn't and sits at the piano to accompany him. The audition is interrupted by the ringing of Julia's private phone, so James ushers Gus out while Julia answers it—it's her husband, Elliott, and they discuss some of their nontheatrical business ventures while James scans a pile of playscripts on the coffee table and reads one of the titles aloud: "*Bluestocking* by Caroline Comstock."

Ira Drew, a critic, "*wears glasses, very sure of himself,*" comes into the room, putting James on guard—but James makes sure that Ira knows who he is (Drew remembers that he reviewed James once as Mercutio). Drew is so controversial that the producers have taken him off the press list, and he buys his tickets. When Julia gets off the phone, Ira advises her that a script she has been sent—*Bluestocking* by his protegée, Caroline Comstock—is "the best American play I've come across in a long time," and what's more (James learns to his astonishment) it was written with James Wicker in mind for the lead. Ira backs out as though leaving the presence of royalty and is heard falling down the stairs.

James comments that he hopes Ira doesn't run into Peter Austin at the party, because Ira wrote cruelly of Peter's last play, "The American theater would be a better place today if Peter Austin's parents had smothered him in his crib." At this moment Peter Austin enters, dressed in evening clothes. He is warmly welcomed by Julia and in turn warmly greets his friend James, whose presence at the opening he greatly appreciates.

Julia wonders where Peter has been; "I've been out there growing up," he replies. He spent the seemingly interminable first act of his play in a bar across the street from the theater.

PETER: Thank God for Dolores Guber. She was in the original production of *Panama Hattie.* I told her I had a play opening. That play. "Welcome to the theater, kid," she said. I told her I was already in the theater. You know, off Broadway, off-off. "They ain't theater," she said and nodded towards the Barrymore, "That's theater." And then it was intermission. I saw you, Jimmy, talking to Bob Fosse. He was bent over double. God, you are a funny man. I wanted to cross the street and join you. Instead I threw up. I walked over to St. Patrick's but it was closed, so I just walked around the theater district. So many theaters dark. Marquees left up because nothing new has come in. It's scary. I felt such a responsibility. I saw that goddamn new hotel.

JAMES: Terrible, just terrible.

PETER: They tore down three theaters for that? *Streetcar* opened at the same theater we did tonight. December third, 1947. My birthday. How could you tear that down? By now it was after the play and everyone was gone. Our marquee was still lit. I think that was the first time I really saw it. Before that I was always too nervous. *"The Golden Egg,* a new play by Peter Austin." It's a beautiful marquee, Julia. Downtown we never had that. Don't believe anyone who says it isn't nice. And then someone inside turned the lights off, and we went dark. It was like we never existed. It's only a play. I grabbed the first cab I saw, it was a lulu! Asked them to drop me off here, then go to the *Times* and wait for the revi .w. This is where I want to be and the people I most want to be with, if not for the rest of my life, at least until the *Times* is out.

JULIA: Next play I promise you that turntable.

PETER: Next play I'm going to want two turntables.

JULIA: Done! That's the Peter I like to see.

JAMES: Are you grown up? Can we go down now?

Julia signals James to make much of Peter (though James is somewhat irritated at the praise for Jack, the actor who played the role intended for James), then Julia tactfully retires into the bathroom. All Broadway is downstairs at the party waiting to congratulate Peter. James also wishes "the best possible success" to Peter, who, James admits, "put us both on the map" with his first play, *Flashes.*

JAMES: . . . . . I was a middle-aged, not Robert Redford-looking character actor, one of thousands in this city. I would have gone on having ten lines in each act in New York and forty lines in stock for the rest of my life. Maybe once, just once, I would have played Willy Loman or Falstaff in a city my friends and agent wouldn't mind coming to. And I would have gone on thinking I was lucky. Then you sent me *Flashes.* Make no mistake! I knew I was very, very lucky.

PETER: Then I'm glad I saw you do those ten lines in that awful play at the Cherry Lane.

JAMES: So am I. And it was fourteen lines. I was on a roll that season.

PETER: Jack was O.K. tonight?

JAMES: Jack was fine.

Julia comes back into the room, as Virginia enters and greets Peter, who calls her performance tonight "fantastic" but reminds her that she dropped a bottle ("It fucking slipped," Virginia argues) and changed a line in the second act, for which Virginia finally apologizes. Peter hugs her, and they exit.

James and Julia are preparing to join the party, but Frank comes in complaining about being called a genius too many times. He *is* a genius, Julia declares, that's why she hired him—and he always gets good reviews, and he's from Chicago. James notices that Frank has purloined his cigarette lighter, a gift from Carol Burnett, and he manages to get Frank to give it back to him. Before they go downstairs, Frank wants them to realize that he is in despair.

FRANK: The emperor isn't wearing any clothes!
JAMES *(anticipating/mimicking Julia):* What emperor, darling?
JULIA: What emperor, darling?
FRANK: This emperor. I'm a fake. My work's a fake. I can't go on like this— the critics' darling—knowing that it's all a fake.
JULIA: Try to hold on just one more time.
FRANK: I've had fourteen hits in a row off Broadway and thirty-seven Obies. I want a flop. I need a flop. Somebody, tell me please: when is it my turn? I'm no good. You've got to believe me. I'm no good.
JAMES: We believe you. Julia, now can we go down—?
FRANK: Hold me.
JULIA: We can't leave him like this.
FRANK: Do you know the only flops I've ever had? At drama school. Nobody liked my production of anything. My art deco *Three Sisters.* My spoken *Aida.* My gay *Godot.* But what got me expelled was my *Titus Andronicus.* I did the whole thing in mime. No dialogue. No poetry. No Shakespeare.
JULIA: What did it have?
FRANK: Blood bags. Every time somebody walked on stage: splat! They got hit with a big blood bag. God, it was gross!
JULIA: It sounds interesting.
FRANK: It was terrible. But at least everyone said it was terrible. I'm pulling the same stunts in New York, and everybody says it's brilliant.
JULIA: It is brilliant.
FRANK: I hate it! God I miss Yale.

Remorsefully, Frank empties his pockets of various things he has compulsively picked up including a pepper shaker of Julia's and a cigarette case inscribed "Mary. You are the Sound of Music. All our love. Dick and Oscar."

Virginia enters, hopping mad over a TV review on Channel 7 which reported "Virginia Noyes stinks" but called *The Golden Egg* "good solid theater," the same words Stewart Klein used in his review. Peter comes in and calls their press agent, Buzz, to see if he's heard anything yet about the *Times* review. Buzz has heard it's a rave and expects all the reviews to be good. Peter is both elated and apprehensive: "If we have a smash hit on our hands, I hope I can handle it."

James turns up the TV sound with the remote control device so they can hear the Channel 2 review. A substitute critic filling in for the first stringer says, "It was quite a kick for me to cover a big-time Broadway opening. I was sitting next to award-winning director Bob Fosse. I asked him what he thought. 'Forget what I thought,' Mr. Fosse laughed, 'Let me tell you what—' " James turns off the volume, pretending he did it by mistake. By the time he gets it back on, the TV critic is saying, "—'Gobble, gobble!' Anyway, for what it's worth, I thought Peter Austin's play was the kind of good, old-fashioned play nobody writes any more except Peter Austin. But what do I know?"

Not a very good notice, they all agree—but then the phone rings, and Peter answers it. It's Buzz the press agent again with review quotes that Peter repeats aloud aloud as he hears them over the phone.

PETER: . . . . . Hats off and hallelujah. Peter Austin has written the best American play since *The Man Who Had Three Arms.* Virginia Noyes lights up Broadway.

VIRGINIA: You bet your fucking A I do!

PETER: Frank Finger's direction is superb, taut and just plain perfect.

FRANK: That's it?

PETER: Along with David Mamet, Sam Shepard, Michael Weller, Albert Innaurato, David Rabe, John Guare, Wendy Wasserstein, Tina Howe, Christopher Durang, Ted Tally, David Henry Hwang, Beth Henley, Lanford Wilson, Marsha Norman, A.R. Gurney Jr., Wallace Shawn, Ntozake Shange and Hugh Golden . . .

OTHERS: Who?

PETER: . . . Peter Austin is in that small handful of our promising young American dramatists.

JULIA: Amen.

PETER: The Newark *News.* Thanks, Buzz. How much longer before we get Rich? Very funny. Another half hour?

He hangs up.

We're a smash in Newark.

They turn the TV back on to Channel 7 just in time to hear, "I'd call this the best American play of the season hands down," but it turns out it's not *The Golden Egg* the critic is reviewing, but a workshop production. "Thank God we know the *Times* is a rave," Peter observes, and he suggests that someone go downstairs and ask Walter Kerr what he thought of the play.

The sound of a pane of glass breaking behind the drapes interrupts them—the cast of *Annie* is throwing snowballs. Downstairs there is a commotion that sounds like a brawl, and soon Ira Drew rushes in, handerchief held to mouth, and goes to the bathroom where immediately the sound of Torch attacking him is heard. Then there is the sound of a gunshot, and Ira comes out, pants legs in shreds, carrying a pistol and still holding the handkerchief to his mouth. At the sight of the pistol, Julia screams—but Ira assures her that Torch is O.K., the pistol is loaded with blanks. Noticing the others, Ira tells Virginia he enjoyed her performance and "I liked your work too, Mr. Finger, but then I always do. *Titus Andronicus.* SPLAT."

It seems that it was Peter who punched Ira, but Ira assures Julia that "Just because I think someone's a little shit doesn't mean I'm going to give him a bad review." Virginia wonders what Ira thought of the play. Julia points out that it's rude to ask a critic what he thinks before he's written his review.

IRA: Besides, waiting for the *Times,* that's what tonight's all about. Who cares what a nonentity like me thinks.

JULIA: You're not a nonentity, and you're very well thought of.

IRA: Not well enough, apparently, for a performance scheduled to begin this evening at 6:45 sharp to begin at 6:45 sharp because the critic from the *Times* wasn't in his seat.

JULIA: Well, with this blizzard . . .

IRA: It snows for all of us, Mrs. Budder. Then, just as I'm lighting another cigarette and wondering whether John Simon minds being so unpopular, a stretch cab pulls up, the *Times* pops out and there's a stampede towards the theater. By the time I get to my seat, the play's already begun. I don't want Mr. Rich's job. I just want to finish my cigarette. I am sounding petty.

JULIA: Nonsense. It's good for a producer to hear these things—!

IRA: All right! I am sick and tired of half the audience, every time there is a laugh line, turning around in their seats to see if he is laughing. I have been reviewing plays for eighteen years, and no one has ever, not once, turned around in their seat to see if I were laughing.

JULIA: That's the saddest thing I ever heard.

IRA: I saw you peeping at him through the side exit curtains tonight, Mrs. Budder.

JULIA: I wasn't peeping at him, Mr. Drew. I swear to God, I wasn't peeping.

IRA: Don't deny it, Mrs. Budder.

JULIA: All right, yes, I was!

IRA: What am I? The Invisible Man?

VIRGINIA: You're one of the most vicious critics in New York.

Ira denies this, but Virginia accuses him of writing, cruelly, "She reminds me of nothing so much as a female impersonator in search of a female to impersonate" years ago about an obscure young actress who, it seems, was Virginia; and after the review she changed both her name and her appearance. Ira apologizes. Peter comes in with Frank, apologizes to Ira for hitting him. Ira comments that they both have the right to free expression, Peter to write plays, Ira to criticize them.

Peter drops to his knees with "Hear a playwright's prayer, Oh Lord," and calls a blessing upon all those concerned with the production of *The Golden Egg.* When James enters, he asks a blessing for James and "James's series which is rumored to be going off the air" (James is shattered to hear this, but he kneels beside Peter like everybody else except Ira). He asks a blessing for Ira (who is now putting on his yarmulke) "for writing the one and only pan of my first play *Flashes* which all the other critics loved and made me rich and famous, which made him look something of a fool and which is why I hit him" but adds that Ira is his "newest friend." And Peter goes on: "Bless all critics who mean well and are only trying to uphold the standards of the theater without knowing how

Mark Blum as Peter Austin and Paul Benedict as
Ira Drew in *It's Only a Play* by Terrence McNally

truly hard it is to write a play. Shower them with the same mercy they deny others. And bless the theater in which we all serve. Bless this ancient art which is so superior to the movies."

Gus enters to get Lauren Bacall's coat but is persuaded to kneel with the others, as Peter blesses the taxi driver who is going to bring them the *Times* review; and, finally, he prays for a hit.

The phone rings; James answers it and learns that his series has indeed been cancelled. Meanwhile, Ira has made another disparaging remark to Peter, who immediately tries to strangle Ira, while Virginia and Frank are calmly dosing themselves with cocaine. At this point Emma, a taxi driver "*wearing a leather jacket, jeans and a cloth cap,*" enters and surveys the turbulent scene: Peter choking Ira, Virginia and Frank sniffing, James in shock.

> *Emma puts two fingers in her mouth and whistles. It is a loud whistle.*
> *Everyone stops what they are doing and looks at her.*

EMMA: Hey you!

PETER: What?

EMMA: You know that paper you're waiting on?

ALL *(except James):* Yes!

EMMA: The one with the review?

ALL: Yes!!

EMMA: The *New York Times?*

ALL: Yes!!!

EMMA: They got it down there.

> *Total chaos. Emma is knocked over in their surge to get downstairs and*
> *get that paper.*

What's wrong with these people? It's only a play!

> *The curtain is falling, James looks like something out of the Last Judgment. All the phones on Julia's desk have started ringing. Torch is barking and tearing at the bathroom door. Curtain.*

ACT II

A few moments later, Gus is still looking for Lauren Bacall's coat, Emma is still wondering at the behavior of celebrities and James is still desperately trying to figure out what he's going to do, now that his series has been cancelled.

Peter, Julia, Virginia, Frank and Ira come rushing back, each trying to grab the section of the *Times* containing the review. James gets ahold of the TV page reporting that "ABC Announces Four Cancellations; *Out on a Limb* Among Them" and takes it aside to read it. Frank finds an announcement, "For reasons of space, Frank Rich's review of last night's opening at the Barrymore appears today on page seventy-six under 'Dogs, Cats and Other Pets.'" Julia finds the right page, but Peter snatches it away. James goes to the phone to call ABC pretending to be a spokesman for a large group protesting the cancellation, but Peter breaks the connection and insists that everybody now pay attention. It's his moment, and he's going to read the review. But he can't; he can hardly get past the subtitle "Actor scores brilliant triumph." He hands the paper first to Emma and then to Gus, who have nothing at stake, but they can't read it aloud properly, so Peter finally tackles it.

PETER: . . . . . "Peter Austin makes his eagerly awaited Broadway debut. Would that he hadn't." *(He looks up.)* It's going to be mixed. *(He resumes.)* "This is the kind of play that gives playwriting a bad name and deals the theater, already a somewhat endangered species, something very close to a death blow." *(He looks up.)* I don't think he liked it.

VIRGINIA: Peter.

PETER: I'm O.K., Ginny, I'm O.K. *(Resumes.)* "It tarnishes the reputation of everyone connected with it, not permanently perhaps, but certainly within their lifetime."

The review includes even the cloakroom attendants in the above. The *Times* critic didn't like the title, and he hated the play—Peter can read no more. Ira takes up the newspaper and continues reading that "Ira Drew, who I generally find the least perceptive and most prejudiced of the New York critics . . . . . (was) a prophet crying in the wilderness" when he alone panned Peter's first play, *Flashes.* Though he is still described in the review as the most "physically unappetizing and generally creepy drama critic in New York," Ira manages to continue reading and gets to the part about the acting.

IRA: "I can be more cheerful about the acting . . ."

VIRGINIA: I should hope so.

IRA: ". . . but not much. Only Jack Nimble, as the unlucky Tamburini, a role that was clearly tailored for James Wacker . . ."

JAMES: Wicker!

IRA: It says Wacker. *(He resumes.)* ". . . emerges with distinction. If there is any justice in our theater—and I am becoming less and less convinced that there is; how can there be when plays like this get produced? . . ."

PETER: Leave me alone, goddamnit!

IRA: ". . .—then Mr. Nimble is a shoo-in for this season's Best Actor Tony Award."

JAMES: A what?

IRA: "As for Mr. Wicker . . ."

JAMES: What did I do?

IRA: They got it right this time. *(He resumes.)* ". . . who is chiefly remembered hereabouts for his somewhat overpraised performance in Mr. Austin's *Flashes* . . ."

JAMES: For my what?

IRA: Somewhat overpraised performance. *(He resumes.)* "Certainly I preferred his replacement, Charles Nelson Reilly, who brought a more masculine presence and yet strangely cutting sensitivity to the role . . ."

JAMES: A more what?

JULIA *(always helpful):* A more masculine presence and—

JAMES: Shut up, Julia. I heard what he said.

IRA: ". . . he should count himself lucky to be out of this turkey due to his commitments to his enormously popular television series (I must admit I'm mad for it, but don't tell my colleagues) *Out on a Lamb.*"

JAMES: *Limb,* dammit, *Limb.*

James snatches the paper and reads that Virginia "wears out her welcome on her first speech"; that Julia, instead of producing this play, "should have done something worthwhile: such as open a mental hospital in which to have her head examined . . . . . or produced a Lanford Wilson . . . . . or a Hugh Golden"; that Frank has directed a "stunning production . . . . . This is a man who can do no wrong" (Frank calls this "bullshit"), and that they must already be striking the scenery at the Barrymore.

JAMES: ". . . Unless, of course, it hasn't already collapsed out of sheer embarrassment. Oh well, onwards and upwards with the arts." *(Short pause.)* That's it.

> He lets the review drop to the floor and sits. No one moves. There is a long, gloomy pause now.

PETER: I think it's important that we all love one another very, very much right now.

VIRGINIA: He didn't even say I was pretty. I always got pretty at least before.

JAMES *(he will never really get over this):* Charles Nelson Reilly?

As a critic, Ira perceives their pain, but they don't want his sympathy. Peter tries to convince himself and the others that they'll get word-of-mouth praise and run. Virginia isn't so sure, and she fears she may have let them all down, but Peter reassures her. Emma and Gus drift out. Peter orders James to go find out what Walter Kerr thought, and he goes on this errand. Peter starts putting all the telephone receivers back on the hooks (they were removed to stop them ringing), but they all start ringing again (one of them is Lanford Wilson, worried that Julia might cancel the production of his play).

Emma comes back with a plate of food. James comes back with the information that Walter Kerr is returning the mass card Peter had sent him before the show, but they got another "good solid theater" from the *Wall Street Journal.* On the phone, Julia encourages the unknown playwright named Hugh Golden to send her his script. She puts off other callers, but then she takes a call from Joseph Papp. It seems to Peter as though the very existence of his play is being washed away by all the other concerns bubbling up.

JULIA: How large a donation were you thinking of, Mr. Papp? Of course I'll support an Offenbach in the Park festival next summer. Don't bite my head off. I just didn't expect you to ask me to put my money where my mouth is tonight.

IRA: That's the kind of behavior which has gotten him where he is today, which is almost everywhere.

JULIA *(hanging up):* I can never say no to that man. He wants thirty thousand dollars. Who is Offenbach?

> *Julia rips a check out of her ledger-sized checkbook.*

PETER: A dead French composer. I am a living American playwright. Why don't you give me thirty thousand dollars?

JULIA: I'm trying to give you a hit.

PETER: Do you have to do that now?

JULIA: It's just money. Besides, he's on his way over for it.

PETER: How? On his dog sled! All the reviews aren't in yet, Julia.

JULIA: How many p's in Papp?

PETER: Four. I'm still here, people. My play isn't over. I sense an avalanche. I feel an abandonment. I smell a stampede.

No one is paying any attention to Peter. Ira is trying to bring up the subject of his protegée's play *Bluestocking.* Emma is looking for the vacuum cleaner to do a job on this room. James has been in and out of the bathroom and somehow has managed to dominate Torch in doing so. Julia, Ira and Emma go in search of the vacuum while Peter dials a number on the phone.

PETER: . . . . . Hello! Did I wake you? Good. This is James Wicker.

JAMES: What are you doing?

PETER: I just read your review of the new Peter Austin play, and I think you're full of shit.

> *He hangs up.*
I guess that's telling him.

JAMES: Who was that?

PETER: Frank Rich.

JAMES: Frank Rich?

PETER: You see what they're driving me to?

JAMES: Frank Rich??

PETER: You're not listening to me.

JAMES: Frank Rich. You listen to me. You call him right back and tell him that wasn't me.

PETER: I love you. You're my best friend. I don't want to do these things.

JAMES: I love you, too, and I don't want you doing them. Dial.

PETER: It means that much to you!

JAMES: Of course it means that much to me.

> *Peter is looking up the number again. Emma appears pushing the vacuum cleaner.*

EMMA: It was right across the hall.

PETER: Where's your famous sense of humor?

JAMES: I never had one. Ever. It was all a lie. Hurry up. Before he reviews me again. What are you doing with his number, anyway?

PETER: I have all the critics' numbers.

JAMES: And they have yours! *(To Emma.)* He called Frank Rich and said it was me!

EMMA: You see an outlet?

PETER *(into phone):* Hello, Mr. Rich? That wasn't James Wicker who just woke you up and said you were full of shit.

JAMES: Thank you, God. It was Charles Nelson Reilly.

PETER: It was Lanford Wilson.

> *He hangs up.*

If I weren't a playwright, I'd be a very nice person.

JAMES: Grow up, Peter. Face facts. Your play is a flop.

James has finally said it out loud. Peter resents it, of course, and James reminds his friend that the note hoping his series would die wasn't exactly encouraging. Their bickering about who has done what to and for whom in the theater gets more and more intense, in front of Emma, who has turned off the vacuum cleaner to listen and comments sarcastically, "Grown men!"

The men agree that "this is a wrap for our friendship," as Julia and Ira return with Gus. The Shubert office calls to inform Julia that the unions at the Barrymore aren't likely to take salary cuts just to keep *The Golden Egg* open, even though Peter, as the author, is expected to waive his royalties for this purpose. If she closes the show, Julia tells the others after hanging up the phone, the Barrymore will book a Dutch porno film, *Leather Maidens of Amsterdam*.

If she can get just one magnetic critical quote, Julia declares, "I'll run this play forever," but it is not to be. Buzz the press agent (whose sources deceived him re the *Times* review) phones in the *Daily News* and *Post* reviews, which are at best merely encouraging and at worst ("Mr. Finger is one emperor who isn't wearing any clothes"—Clive Barnes) send Frank into a tantrum, after which he feels better and empties his pockets of purloined objects. It looks as though there won't be any magazine reviews, because Julia, weeping, sees that she's going to have to close the show.

PETER: I'll tell you one thing, Mr. Drew. God punishes people who get their plays done on Broadway. He punishes them good.

IRA: That's why He invented regional theater.

PETER: Don't give me regional theater. I'll tell you what regional theater is: plays that couldn't get produced in New York with actors who couldn't get a job in New York performed for audiences who wish they still lived in New York. This is my regional theater. Right here.

JULIA: Peter!

PETER: I still wish I was dead.

EMMA: I just hope all you nice people have the good sense not to brood over this and get on with the next one. You heard him: onwards and upwards.

JULIA: Thank you, Emma.

EMMA: See, if this was nuclear physics I'd keep my big mouth shut, but I know something about show business. The original Harvey was a giraffe. Making him a rabbit happened in my cab.

JULIA: I can't deal with a remark like that.

Gus has gone out to check the party and returns to report that it is breaking up. The phone rings again—it's Peter's father calling from Ohio, and when Peter puts the phone down he's weeping. Pretty soon, all of them except Ira but including Emma (her father wanted to see Finland once more but died before he could get there) are weeping, each for his own reason—even Torch in the bathroom joins in with a whine. Soon they are trying to comfort each other, but Julia is inconsolable: "The thought of that beautiful theater dark even one night, or a pornographic film place, or worse, demolished!"

Finally even Ira breaks down and sobs as he confesses that he is really Caroline Comstock, author of *Bluestocking,* which he describes through his tears as a one-set masterpiece with only two characters, a man and a woman. James and Virginia are immediately curious about the roles, and Ira describes them as a kind of Everyman and Everywoman, the former "extremely virile," the latter "very vital." They would be ideal, Ira insists, for James and Virginia, and the play could be staged on the disc being used as a set for Peter's play right now.

James is getting to like the idea of stepping from a sinking TV series into a Broadway lead, and Virginia is getting to like the idea of stepping from one role into another.

FRANK *(suddenly):* He's right! It could be done on our set.

JULIA: But the Shuberts will want us out of there long before we could be ready to open this one.

FRANK: Wrong again. We could preview tomorrow.

VIRGINIA: Tomorrow? You know me and lines, Frank.

FRANK: Dig this for a concept: two actors, a bare disc.

JULIA: I'm getting goosebumps. Go on.

FRANK: That's it.

JULIA: I like it.

FRANK: Somebody . . .

    Gus enters.

GUS: That's it.

FRANK: . . . a black mute—puts a script in their hands and pushes them on. Instant theater.

VIRGINIA: I buy it.

JAMES: I love it.

JULIA: It's brilliant, Frank. What do you think, Emma?

EMMA: That sounds interesting.

IRA: But that's exactly the idea behind *Bluestocking*. The play is set in a rehearsal situation. The two actors are meant to be carrying their scripts. It's part of my concept.

FRANK: Your concept? Who's directing this show anyway? Let him direct it for you, Julia.

JULIA: Mr. Drew didn't mean it like that. *(To Frank.)* Frank, we could preview tomorrow, you say?

FRANK: Preview?! *(Their spirits all collapse.)* We could open. No rehearsals, no rewrites, no previews. *(There is a great renewal of the spirit.)* The whole risk with a project like this, Julia, is the actors getting stale.

JAMES: I don't get stale. I ripen.

PETER: What the hell is going on here?

GUS: Don't say nothing, but I think we're doing another play.

JULIA: All I'm thinking, Peter, is that with *Bluestocking,* Virginia, Frank and now James will be right back to work, Gus will get to Broadway, and the Ethel Barrymore will be blazing anew with us tomorrow night at eight.

FRANK: We need more scripts.

IRA: They're right downstairs.

He dashes out of the room.

Peter hates to see his play go down the drain, but the others' rising enthusiasm for the new project overwhelms him. They encourage him to get started on a new play, but in the meantime . . . Ira comes back with the scripts, and the Shubert Office is on the phone again, wanting a decision from Julia. Seeing that the others are ready to go, she makes up her mind and says to the phone, "Tell your Leather Maidens they can't have the Barrymore. We're staying. We're holding back the night. We're putting our fingers in the dike. Budder's back in business," then she hangs up. She clutches to her bosom a script just delivered by Hugh Golden, which she is going to read while the others rehearse Ira's script.

Frank makes it official, declaring "I am in rehearsal." Virginia decides, "I'm going to wear my hair in little jump curls," and James muses, "I see this guy in a plaid jumpsuit," Frank declares, "People, we have an opening," and Julia sums it all up: "This is exciting." Frank consults Ira's script.

FRANK: "At rise, nothing." *(To cast.)* Let's make that something.

IRA: But—! It has to be nothing . . .

FRANK: If he keeps this up, I'm gonna want him barred, Julia.

EMMA: I thought of something else people want in a play. Life! Lots and lots of life.

PETER: Thanks, I'll try to remember that.

FRANK: What do all these dots mean?

IRA: Hesitations, pauses.

JAMES: I don't do hesitations.

IRA: Pinter uses dots.

FRANK: Fuck Pinter.

> *He rips pages from Ira's script. James, Virginia and Gus follow suit.*
> *Ira agonizes.*

JULIA: I hope you're taking this all in, Emma, it's the real thing.

EMMA: I never knew it was like this.

JULIA: Wait! It gets better.

PETER *(he sees his next marquee):* "*It's Only a Play,* a new play by Peter Austin."

FRANK: Lights up. "A woman screams in the distance."

> *Virginia screams.*

"Or is it a woman?"

> *James screams.*

"An ineffable sound."

GUS: Me?

FRANK: No—Julia.

> *Julia screams.*

Yes, you.

> *Gus screams. A star is born!*

Where have you been all my life?

> *He gives Gus a big kiss.*

VIRGINIA *(to James, low):* We got our hands full with this one.

EMMA *(to Julia):* The kid's good.

GUS: Thank you.

FRANK: May we continue? Virginia, you'll be downstage right in a spot. James, downstage left.

> *The lights begin to fade on the grouping as they continue to rehearse.*

PETER *(beginning to create):* "The curtain rises. An opening night party is in progress."

> *The lights are beginning to fade on him, too. The lights fade to black.*
> *The first curtain call is taken by Torch. He comes out of the bathroom.*
> *He is an adorable beagle. Curtain.*

DRINKING IN AMERICA

A Play in 14 Scenes

BY ERIC BOGOSIAN

Cast and credits appear on page 357

ERIC BOGOSIAN was born in Boston April 24, 1953, the son of an accountant. His college years were equally divided between the University of Chicago and Oberlin, to which he transferred after two years and from which he received his B.A. in theater in 1976. A year later, in New York City, he founded the dance program known as The Kitchen, which he ran until 1981. He had always wanted to write, however, and he kept at it with stage vehicles for his own performance. In July 1982 New York Shakespeare Festival workshopped his Men Inside *and* Voices of America, *solo pieces which he performed and which were repeated in September of that year. A collection of mostly sinister characterizations written and acted by Bogosian and entitled* Fun House *was put on by New York Shakespeare Festival in workshop and then moved to full off-Broadway production September 29, 1983 for 70 performances.*

Bogosian's first Best Play, also a writing-and-solo-acting presentation, is Drinking in America, *which began its run January 19 at American Place. He has received grants from the National Endowment and the New York State arts council. He is married, lives in New York City and hopes "to continue writing, for people besides myself."*

Our method of representing Drinking in America *here differs from that of the other Best Plays. Instead of trying to précis all 14 of the distinct characterizations in this one-man show, we note 11 of them briefly and present three in their entirety as prime examples of the style and quality of this Best Play.*

1. Journal

April 11, 1971 *("introduced casually as an old diary entry rediscovered, read out loud"):* A college student takes "acid," and, under the drug's influence, feels omnipotently "messianic" and all-seeing and decides to drop out and enjoy his new-found power over all the rest of the world.

2. American Dreamer

Wino imagines that he has it all: innumerable women, cars and other luxuries. He enjoys them in his imagination, until he passes out.

3. Wired

Hollywood agent awakens groggily to a phone call from a New York producer who wants to consult him on casting. After a snort of cocaine and a belt of Jack Daniels, the agent is ready to wheel and deal in verbose fashion, West Coast style, on his two phone lines.

4. Yuppie in Bed

Young man blurts out excuses to his girl friend about his inability to perform sexually—and about his own integrity and others' conspiracy preventing him from getting ahead at the office.

5. Texas Ceramic Salesman

> *Standing with arms outstretched, a champagne bottle in one hand, speaking to an unseen woman, Texas dialect.*

TEXAS CERAMIC SALESMAN: Whoooeeee! I'm feelin' good tonight, I'm feelin' fine tonight . . . Come here, come here, come here, come to Daddy, give me a kiss . . . give me a kiss . . . *(Mime kiss.)* Do you love me: Do ya love me? Sure ya do . . . Come on, ya have to have some more champagne, now, have some more champagne!

> *Offers bottle.*

YEAH? WHO IS IT? COME ON IN, DOOR'S OPEN . . . YEH, FINE, JUST PUT IT OVER THERE BY THE BED. GREAT. THANK YOU. PUT IT ON MY TAB AND GIVE YOURSELF FIVE BUCKS. YEAH, THANK YOU TOO. I WILL. LOCK THE DOOR ON YOUR WAY OUT. THANK YOU. GOOD NIGHT. Where were we? Oh, yeah, you gotta drink some because I just can't drink it all myself! I drink it all myself, I'm gonna throw up all over your pretty little party dress there. Whoooeeeee!!!! I'm feelin' good tonight! *(Stomps his foot.)* I'm feelin' fine tonight! *(To himself.)* Shit!

> *Stumbles back into his chair.*

Michelle? Michelle . . . Michelle! Turn around for me a second, darlin', let me take a look at you . . . *(Appraising.)* You are one hell of a good lookin' girl, you know that? You are. You're just about the most beautiful girl I seen in the last twenty-four hours. You have beautiful breasts, you know that? And you have a beautiful behind too. *(Contemplating her.)* You got everything right where it belongs and plenty of it. You can stop turning around now.

    Starts to sip from his bottle.

How old did you say you were? Uh-huh . . . Just a babe out of the woods, eh? . . . Guess . . . Go ahead, guess. Forty-seven years old. My wife says I look like I'm sixty. She says being on the road all the time makes you get old. She thinks I enjoy being on the road. I hate being on the road. I get lonely on the road. I'll tell you a secret, tomorrow's my daughter's fourteenth birthday, and I can't be there. And you wanna know why? Because I have to be here at this damn convention. Because I am an industrial ceramic tile salesman. And when you are an industrial ceramic tile salesman you gotta do one thing, you gotta sell industrial ceramic tile. And I do . . . I sell tile, and I sell a lot of it. I sell it all the way from Tampa to San Diego, I sell tile. I hustle. Because it's a dog-eat-dog world out there, Michelle, and I'm out there biting. Biting hard. Working my ass off . . . we all have to work, you got your job, I got mine. Everybody's got to work in this world . . . everybody except my wife . . . She thinks money grows on check books. She thinks her job is spending the money I earn. She thinks I enjoy being a million miles from home.

    Interrupts himself.

Forget my wife, let's stop talking about her. What do you do when you're not doing this, Michelle? Uh-huh. Good. You keep going to school. It's important to go to school. No future in this escort business, I'll tell you that. You keep going to school, Michelle, because . . . I want you to. You're a beautiful, sensitive girl, and I wanna see good things happen to you, so you keep going to . . . What's that look? What's that look? I know, I know, I know what you're thinking . . . you're looking at me, and you're thinking: here's another middle-aged, overweight, half-drunk . . . ceramic tile salesman . . . I know, I know . . . well, let me tell you something, little girl, I may be middle-aged, and I may be a little round at the edges, and I may be feeling pretty good tonight . . . but I'm very different than the rest of these idiots you see here at this convention . . . and I'll tell you why . . . because I, you're looking at, the number one ceramic tile salesman in the United States of America. Numero Uno. The man sitting before you sells more tile than anybody else, more than all these other characters together. I'm good, I'm the best, I'm special. And I'm special . . . because I care about people. And I care about you, Michelle. I do . . . no, I do . . . You know, tonight, when I came into the hotel, I thought to myself, I'm just gonna have a couple of drinks, go up to my room and pass out. But I saw you standing in the lobby, and I thought to myself, there is a beautiful, sensitive, intelligent, sophisticated girl . . . a beautiful girl with beautiful blue eyes . . . *(Steals a glance, corrects himself.)* . . . green eyes, beautiful green eyes . . . there's a girl I could talk to tonight. That's what I thought to myself. Because I'll be honest with you, Michelle, I just need a little companionship. I'm just a lonely guy.

    Hurt puppy look.

You know, you get on the road and every room looks like the next one, and you get up in the morning with the alarm clock ringing, I open my eyes and the first thing I see is the toilet, next thing I see is the luggage on the floor, the maid's knocking on the door, I got a headache and a hangover and I don't know where the hell I am! Now if I don't know where I am, how the hell is anybody else supposed to know where I am? I feel like I'm the last man on the face of the earth . . . and I get lonely, Michelle . . . You sure you don't want any more champagne? The last drop? Shit, I'm high. I'm high and I need a big hug. Come here and hug me for just a minute, babe. Yeah, that feels good. Yeah, rub my neck like that, it feels good. That's nice. That's nice. Whoa . . . I think I just might pass out on you any minute. Listen, honey . . . uh, Michelle . . . it was nice talking to you and everything, but, uh, just so that hundred bucks isn't a total waste, you think you could do a little something for me, just so your boss knows you're working? They tell you what I like downstairs? Think you could do some of that? A nice quick one? A nice slow, quick one? That's it, you got the idea . . . there you go, you got it . . . ummmmm . . . yeah, I feel one hundred percent better already.

6. Commercial

An actor taping a beer commercial strives to combine macho and warmth in delivering a reverential tribute to the product.

7. Melting Pot

Greek short-order cook is training a new assistant to make French fries, while declaring his determination to blend into the American scene the American way, by working incessantly to earn enough money to buy a house.

8. Our Gang

Music is playing loudly. Richie walks out and pops open a can of beer. He's shouting to someone out past the audience. He speaks in some sort of Northeastern urban accent, punctuating often with a leering laugh. He uses his body when he tells the story.

RICHIE: Hey, Jimmy, Jimmy! Jimmy! Shut that shit off, huh? Shut it off! I got a hangover! It's givin' me a headache.

Music ends.

Thank God! Listen, Tony, you goin' to the store? Get me a pack of cigarettes, will ya? Marlboro . . . Hard pack. And a Ring-Ding. I'm hungry. And uh, get me a Diet Pepsi, I didn't have no breakfast . . . Come on man, I got a hangover, I'm disabled . . . thanks, I'll pay you later!

Sips his beer, speaking to someone standing to his left.

I'm alright . . . so Joe, where were you last night? It was great. Listen, I'll tell you where my car is . . . Frankie had 'ludes, so me and Frankie and Sally and Joanie are all doin' 'ludes, so I figure let's take my car, go up to the highway, drive around, good place to do 'ludes, right? Get mellow. So we're drivin' around and I'm not gettin' off on the 'ludes, so I turns to Frankie and I says, "Frankie, I'm not gettin' off on the 'ludes." Frankie just turns to me and says, "Don't worry, man, you will . . ." You know, with that wisdom Frankie's got? So, I'm drivin', and I looks down, and I sees I got this piece of dirt on my shoe, and you know

Eric Bogosian in a monologue from his *Drinking in America*

me, I hate gettin' anything on my clothes, so I'm bendin' down, scratchin' off this dirt . . . I got my hand on the wheel, I'm drivin' the car, Joe, I swear, out of nowhere this guardrail comes up BOOM up the front of the car! The car starts turnin' around, and the chicks is screamin', and the cars are honking their horns. Bang we go over the guardrail, and we're on the other side of the highway. Now cars is like blinking their headlights at us and shit . . . like I don't know we're on the wrong side of the road, right? People can be so stupid . . . So anyway, we finally go right off the road into this like, you know, gully-thing . . . and the car stops . . . So I get out of the car and Frankie gets out of the car and Joanie gets out of the car and Sally gets out of the car. Everybody gets outta the car . . . nobody's hurt. Right? Great! But the car, Joe . . .

  Looking at the imaginary car and laughing.

. . . the car is like totaled. The whole outside is gone, the headlights and the bumpers is torn off, and the windshield wipers is gone, and even the gas tank lid is ripped off. The car's like one big scrape. It looks like E.T. or something . . . Frankie comes up to the car and says, "Fuck the fuckin' car, man, the fuckin' car's fucked!" What a wit. Just thinks these things up. So we figure, let's get out of here before the cops come, Frankie's got the 'ludes and everything, so we start hitching on the highway . . . So we're hitchin' and this van comes along, it's like a hippie van with a big peace sign on the side and flowers and stuff painted on it, like something outta prehistoric times. The door opens up, and the guy drivin' the van he's got hair down to his butt, he's wearin' a headband, there's incense burnin', Grateful Dead music on the stereo. A complete jerk, right? So we decide, what the hell, take a ride with him. Joanie gets in the front, and the rest of us gets in the back. Joe, we start drivin' along, and this guy starts rollin' joints, they're the size of your dick, huge. The size of my dick.

> *Laughs at his joke.*

Made outta some kind of strange super-grass, Taiwan or somethin'. So we start smokin' these joints, and we're gettin' totally totally totaled, right? Meltin' into the upholstery. It's oxygen tent time! The 'ludes kick in, and we're like . . . blahhhhhhhh . . . beautiful! Truckin' with the fuckin' doo-dah man. So we're drivin' along, and all of a sudden the guy reaches out his hand and puts it on Joanie's leg. So Frankie says, "Like man, take ya hand off my girlfriend's leg," right? And the guy turns to Frankie and says . . . *(Give the finger.)* . . . "Fuck you!" And Frankie just like whips out this knife, right, and says, "No, man, fuck you!" And then the guy, he reaches into his glove compartment and pulls out this handgun and points it at Frankie and says, "No, MAN, FUCK YOU!" Right? And I'm like shittin' my pants . . . because you do not, you know, you do not fuckin' fuck with Frankie! Frankie's sittin' in the seat just like vibratin' with the knife in his hand. The guy turns back to look at the road for a second, and Frankie goes like zip, bing, and touches the guy right behind the ear with the knife. Just a little cut. Nothing. The guy gets pissed off! He pulls the car over to the side of the road and says, "OK, get out of the van." And Frankie, he just went after the guy. Hittin' 'im.

> *Mime.*

Bam. Bam. Bam. Takes the gun off the guy, kicks him outta his own van, right? Guy doesn't even know what's happenin'. We leave him by the side of the road, lookin' like the hippie revolution or something . . . So Frankie's drivin' the van, and he gets off the highway, in case a cops, and we're drivin' through the woods. And he's goin' around sixty, bouncin' over rocks and into trees and shit. Just drivin' in the dark. "Oh, there's a tree." BANG! "Oh, there's another tree!" BANG! "There's a rock." Bang, we break the axle. We all get outta the van, we're in the middle of nowhere, Frankie says, "Don't worry, man, I can fix it," and he goes back to the van and takes out this can of gasoline and starts pourin' it all over the inside of the van. I figure out what he'd doing! Frankie's so cool. And then he steps back, lights a cigarette real slow, and then . . .

> *Mimes flicking the lit cigarette at the van.*

BOOM. It was fuckin' great, Joe. You shoulda seen it. Flames ten, fifteen feet high, colors. It was beautiful Lightin' up all the trees, the stars overhead, quiet in the middle of the woods, just the van burning. It was like . . . spiritual. And we're watchin' the flames, and Frankie puts his hand out . . .

> *Mime handing off a small object.*

. . . here man, take this. And I says, "No man, listen, I'm already wasted." He says, "Take it, it will wake you up." I says, "What is it?" He says, "Trust me

. . ." So I take it and the chicks take it. Figure it's speed or pep pills or crystal or something, right? It's triple-strength acid. So we're tripping our brains out walking through the woods like Alice in Wonderland or something, and I'm tellin' you, Joe, this is woods, right? Like with trees and bushes and rocks and scary shit like that! And Frankie's still got the gun, and he's shooting into the sky, wants to see how high the bullet goes.

> *Mime.*

To make a long story short, we come to this clearin', right, and in the middle of it is this like old farmhouse. Nice farmhouse. The kind of place the Pepperidge Farm guy would live in . . . And there's a light on. So Frankie says, "Watch this" . . . He goes up to the front door of the farmhouse and rings the doorbell . . . and this old lady comes to the door, right? And Frankie pulls out the guy's gun, he still had it, he pulls it out and says to the lady: "Helter skelter, run for shelter. You gotta let us in." Frankie's so fuckin' funny . . . So the old lady lets us in, and this old guy is comin' down the stairs puttin' on his bathrobe, right, and goin' like, "What is all this commotion down here?"

> *Mime pointing the gun aggressively.*

And Frankie just goes up to the guy, and he's not gonna hurt the guy or nothing, points the gun at his head and says: "One more word outta you, Granpa, and your brains is gonna be all over the wallpaper!" The guy's so funny, what an imagination . . . he just thinks this shit up! So we get the old lady and the old man on the floor, and we cut the phone and tie 'em up with the wire like on *Kojak,* and Frankie's standin' over 'em saying like, "We're the Charles Manson gang, and if you tell anybody about us we're gonna come back and burn your house down . . ." And we're goin' like, "Come on, Frankie, time to go. Don't want to give these people the wrong impression." So we borrow their car and some a their booze. And it's like four in the morning, and we go to Frankie's house. His father's never home, you know, he's probably in a gutter somewhere at that time of day. And we're all pretty wasted playin' the music up loud, and Frankie and me are dancing around, and Joanie's in the bathroom pukin' as usual, and suddenly Sally's comin' on to me. Yeah! Right. Like I've been tryin' to make this chick for three months, and there she is in front of me: "Richie, Richie, I really want to go home with you. Take me home, I love you." Right? And I'm thinkin', here's this chick, she's beautiful, she's wasted, she doesn't know what the fuck she's sayin', her eyes aren't even open . . . so I figure what the hell, and I take the car keys to drive her home. And I'm drivin' her home, and she's hot, she's got her hands down my pants, she's got her tongue in my ear, she's makin' me hotter than a locomotive. I'm driving as fast as I can. At least ten miles an hour. I can't see nothing but shapes and colors . . . Anyway, I finally gets in front of her house, and I park out front, and I look over at her, and she's passed out! She's all curled up in a ball down on the floor where you, you know, put your feet! Under the glove compartment. So I says to myself, "Fuck this!", and I drag her outta the car, up to her parents' door, and her parents they got like a regular door and a screen door, so I opens the screen door, and I push her up between the two doors, lock it, ring the doorbell, get the fuck outta there! Pretty good, huh?

Mime pissing on wall, still talking.

So anyway, Joe, we're going out again tonight, it should be fun. You should come too. Frankie likes you and everything. I just gotta ask you one question: You got a car???

9. No Problems

Man comes out onstage, casual, speaks with no particular accent . . . an average guy.

MAN: I have no problems. I'm happy with life. Things are just fine, as far as I'm concerned. I know other people have problems, some have quite a few. But fortunately, I have none. First of all, I'm in good health. I've just had a complete physical and the doctor says I'm in A-1 condition. No high blood pressure. No odd lumps. My weight is good. My heart sounds good, as do my lungs. Everything's fine. He even checked my teeth. No cavities. I have a good job that I like. It's a semi-creative job with very little pressure to perform. I get paid well for what I do, get weekends off and three weeks paid vacation in the summer. I like it. I love my wife. We've been married fifteen years. I find her very attractive and loving. We have very good sex. I don't fool around. I think it was Paul Newman who said why go out for hamburger when you can have steak at home? I subscribe to that theory. Our daughter just turned ten last month. She's a very pretty, precocious little girl. Does very well in school, high grades, has lots of friends. After school she, um, studies modern dance and, um, the violin. She's a lovely little girl and very smart, and we love her very much . . . Our parents are alive on both sides. They're all healthy and happy. We all get along very well. They are totally self-sufficient. They worked hard and saved during their working years and now have time to enjoy a golden harvest. Our friends are all happy and healthy. We usually see them once a week or so. Sometimes they come over for dinner, sometimes we go to their house. Or we might go see a movie, or a show . . . or bowling . . . we've had a lot of good times together. Our neighborhood is safe and clean. We have an excellent town council. Activist school committee. The police and fire departments are both top-rated . . . the house is in good shape, just had the roof repaired last year . . . and the Volvo's running smoothly. I have to admit that at times I am concerned when I read about all the trouble in the rest of the world. But then I realize that there's always been trouble, and I should just be thankful for all the good things I have in my life. Anyway, the future looks good. We'll have the house paid off in ten years, and we're buying a little cottage down by the ocean as a sort of vacation/investment . . . Like I said, I have no problems. None. I'm happy. Things look good for the future. I'm healthy and I like my job. I love my wife and my kid . . . That's what it's all about, I guess.

10. Godhead

A junkie, who has nothing and expects nothing from the world or from the powers that be, just wants to be left alone to enjoy his daily heroin rush—and if the drug finally destroys him, well, life itself is a heavy burden to him.

11. The Law

A neo-Fascist, racist preacher urges his congregation to rise up against the Sodoms and Gomorrahs of today and use force if necessary to destroy the Satanic enemy: abortionists, homosexuals, urban blacks, heathens, etc.

12. Master of Ceremonies

Disc jockey sings the praises of such rock combos as "The Molesters," "Satan Teens" and "Cerebral Hemorrhage," inspiring his audience to get into the mood for their sado-masochistic frenzies.

13. Now

Pantomime of the frenetic activities of a rock performer named Heavy Metal in the full, abandoned cry of a performance, ending up lying on the floor of the stage, spent.

14. New Wino

The man lying on the floor rises slowly and, a garrulous drunk, approaches someone in the first row of the audience and explains that he's like a fried egg, being flipped this way and that by life, never knowing which side is going to turn up—but he is just as necessary to the scheme of things as the affluent person he's speaking to, he argues, because there cannot be a top unless there is also a bottom.

○○○
○○○
○○○
○○○
○○○
○○○
○○○ # EXECUTION OF JUSTICE

A Play in Two Acts

BY EMILY MANN

Cast and credits appear on page 312

EMILY MANN was born April 12, 1952 in Boston but went to school in Northampton, Mass. when her father, a professor of American history, moved there to teach at Smith College. Her high school was the University of Chicago Laboratory, and she received her B.A. from Harvard-Radcliffe in 1974 and her M.F.A. in theater two years later on a Bush Fellowship at the University of Missouri, which provided that she spend her second year of study at the Guthrie Theater as a director-in-residence. Directing was her preoccupation in the theater, but she had been writing fiction on the side. She started to put together an oral history of the Holocaust, but she found herself developing the first taped interview into a one-character play, Annulla, Autobiography of a Survivor, *produced at the Guthrie in 1978 and later on "Earplay" and at the Goodman Theater in Chicago, and still later at the Repertory Theater at St. Louis, in 1985, in a revised version entitled* Annulla, an Autobiography.

Miss Mann's second play, Still Life, *was first produced in 1980 at the Goodman and received an Obie in an off-Broadway production the following year.* Execution of Justice *is her third play, her first Best Play and her Broadway writing and directing debut. A docudrama of the trial of Dan White for the 1978 double murder of George Moscone, mayor of San Francisco, and Harvey Milk, a supervisor, it was commissioned by the Eureka Theater of San Francisco in 1982 and first produced by the Actors Theater of Louisville in 1984, a co-winner of that group's Great American Play Contest. It was produced on Broadway under its author's direction (and with her husband, Gerry Bamman, in the cast) on March 13, 1986 for a mere 12 performances but has had a long run of productions elsewhere including Center Stage in Baltimore, Theater Cornell, The Empty Space in Seattle, the Arena Stage, the Alley Theater, Berkeley Rep, San Jose Rep and the Guthrie.*

Miss Mann's numerous accolades have included Guggenheim, NEA Playwrights, NEA Artistic Associates and McKnight Fellowships, a CAPS grant, the Rosamond Gilder Award for outstanding achievement and the Dramatists Guild Committee for Women's annual award for "dramatizing issues of conscience." She is a member of New Dramatists and lives in Rockland County with her husband and son, Nicholas.

Because Execution of Justice *dramatizes real events which are a matter of public record, the events themselves—the "plot"—are of less artistic consequence than the author's treatment of them. Therefore, we forego a detailed synopsis in our presentation of this fine script and instead offer the fullest possible representation of its style and creative thrust in a few extended excerpts selected as the heart of the play's matter and the core of its conscience.*

Time: 1978 to the present

Place: San Francisco

ACT I: MURDER

SYNOPSIS: The play begins on a bare stage with a screen overhead for the projection of photographic images, now showing San Francisco scenes and personalities. It is November 27, 1978. Dianne Feinstein, president of the San Francisco Board of Supervisors announces that Mayor George Moscone and Supervisor Harvey Milk have been shot dead in their City Hall offices, probably by ex-Supervisor Dan White, who has been arrested and is in custody.

Dan White, his wife, the Court and others enter onstage. The trial of the People v. Dan White for first degree murder begins and is the frame of the action—but with many digressions—which follows. A policemen articulates the atmosphere in which the killings occurred and the trial is now occurring.

COP *(quiet):* Yeah, I'm wearing a "Free Dan White" t-shirt. You haven't seen what I've seen—my nose shoved into what I think stinks. Against everything I believe in. There was a time in San Francisco when you knew a guy by his parish.

> *Sister Boom Boom enters in nun drag, white face, heavily made up, spike heels.*

Sometimes I sit in church and I think of those disgusting drag queens dressed up as nuns, and I'm a cop, and I'm thinkin' there's gotta be a law, you know, because they're making me think things I don't want to think and I gotta keep my mouth shut.

Boom Boom puts out cigarette.

Take a guy out of his sling—fist fucked to death—they say it's mutual consent, it ain't murder, and I pull this disgusting mess down, take him to the morgue, I mean, my wife asks me, "Hey, how was your day?" I can't even tell her. I wash my hands before I can even look at my kids.

    The Cop and Sister Boom Boom are very aware of each other but possibly never make eye contact.

BOOM BOOM: God bless you one. God bless you all.

COP: See, Danny knew—he believes in the rights of minorities. Ya know, he just knew—we are a minority, too.

BOOM BOOM: I would like to open with a reading from the book of Dan. *(Opens book.)*

COP: We been workin' this job three generations—my father was a cop—and then they put—Moscone, Jesus, Moscone put this N-negro-lovin', faggot-lovin' Chief tellin' us what to do—he doesn't even come from the neighborhood, he doesn't even come from this city! He's tellin' us what to do in a force that knows what to do. He makes us paint our cop cars faggot blue—he called it "lavender gloves" for the queers, handle 'em, treat 'em with "lavender gloves," he called it. He's cuttin' off our balls. The city is stinkin' with degenerates—I mean, I'm worried about my kids, I worry about my wife, I worry about me and how I'm feelin' mad all the time. You gotta understand that I'm not alone—it's real confusion.

BOOM BOOM *(reads):* "As Dan came to his day of reckoning, he feared not, for he went unto the lawyers and the doctors and the jurors, and they said, 'Take heart, for in this you will receive not life but three to seven with time off for good behavior.'"

    Closes book reverently.

COP: Take a walk with me sometime. See what I see every day . . . Like I'm supposed to smile when I see two bald-headed, shaved-head men with those tight pants and muscles, chains everywhere, french-kissin' on the street, putting their

Peter Friedman as Douglas Schmidt, Nicholas Kepros as The Court and Gerry Bamman as Thomas F. Norman in *Execution of Justice* by Emily Mann

hands all over each other's asses, I'm supposed to smile, walk by, act as if this is RIGHT???!!

BOOM BOOM: As gay people and as people of color and as women, we all know the cycle of brutality and ignorance which pervades our culture.

COP: I got nothin' against people doin' what they want, if I don't see it.

BOOM BOOM: And we all know that brutality only begets more brutality.

COP: I mean, I'm not makin' some woman on the streets for everyone to see.

BOOM BOOM: Violence only sows the seed for more violence.

COP: I'm not . . .

BOOM BOOM: And I hope Dan White knows that.

COP: I can't explain it any better.

BOOM BOOM: Because the greatest, most efficient information gathering and dispersal network is the Great Gay Grapevine.

COP: Just take my word for it—

BOOM BOOM: And when Dan White gets out of jail, no matter where Dan White goes, someone will recognize him. All over the world, the word will go out. And we will know where Dan White is.

COP: The point is: Dan White showed you could fight City Hall.
    Pause.

BOOM BOOM: Now we are all aware, as I said, of this cycle of brutality and murder. And the only way we can break that horrible cycle is with love, understanding and forgiveness. And there are those who were before me here today—gay brothers and sisters—who said that we must somehow learn to love, understand and forgive the sins that have been committed against us and the sins of violence. And it sort of grieves me that some of us are not understanding and loving and forgiving of Dan White. And after he gets out, after we find out where he is . . . I mean, not, y'know, with any malice or planning . . . You know, you get so depressed and your blood sugar goes up and you'd be capable of just about *ANYTHING!* And some angry faggot or dyke who is not understanding, loving and forgiving is going to perform a horrible act of violence and brutality against Dan White. And if we can't break the cycle before somebody gets Dan White—somebody will *get Dan White*—and when they do, I beg you all to love, understand and *for-give. (Laughs.)*

The trial of Dan White begins with the defense lawyer, Douglas Schmidt, and the prosecuting attorney, Thomas F. Norman, quickly selecting a jury. The case is presented: Dan White, a husband, father, war veteran, hero fireman and ex-policeman, had been a conscientious member of the Board of Supervisors but resigned because of outside financial pressures. Then, when he wanted to withdraw his resignation and return to that post, Mayor Moscone and Supervisor Milk made difficulties, the mayor observing, after investigating the voters of White's district, "The only one in favor of the appointment of Dan White is Dan White himself."

On November 27, the day that the appointment was to be announced, White went to City Hall carrying his police .38, entered by a window to avoid the metal detector at the main entrance and gained access to Mayor Moscone's office. After learning that he wasn't going to be appointed, White put four bullets into Moscone (two into his head after he was lying prone), then went to Supervisor Milk's office and, reloading, shot Milk five or six times. White then phoned his wife, Mary Ann, and arranged to meet her at the cathedral, from where he proceeded to the police station to give himself up.

In his political speeches, White had made it clear that he believed that "malignancies," a blight on beautiful San Francisco, were causing an exodus of good people from the city, and that those who remained should try to "transcend the apathy which has caused us to lock our doors while the tumult rages unchecked through our streets." At the Northern Police Station, White tried to explain his actions to homicide Inspectors Frank Falzon and Edward Erdelatz, who treated ex-policeman Dan White as a colleague, with sympathy and respect. White, with an occasional sob in a highly emotional state, explained that he only wanted to serve his city, but "it came out that Supervisor Milk and some others were working against me." He was going to see the mayor about this, and on the way out of his house he happened to pick up his service revolver and ammunition and take them with him, for no special reason. White's description to the inspectors of the ensuing events at City Hall was taped and is later played back at his trial.

FALZON: You went directly from your residence to the Mayor's office this morning?

WHITE: Yes, my aide picked me up but she didn't have any idea ah . . . you know, that I had a gun on me or, you know, and I went in to see him an, an he told me he wasn't going to reappoint me and he wasn't intending to tell me about it. Then ah . . . I got kind of fuzzy and then just my head didn't feel right and I . . .

FALZON: Was this before any threats on your part, Dan?

WHITE: I, I never made any threats.

FALZON: There were no threats at all?

WHITE: I, I . . . oh no.

FALZON: When were you, how, what was the conversation, can you explain to Inspector Erdelatz and myself the conversation that existed between the two of you at this time?

WHITE: It was pretty much just, you know, I asked, was I going to be reappointed. He said, no I am not, no you're not. And I said, why, and he told me, it's a political decision and that's the end of it, and that's it and then he could obviously see, see I was obviously distraught an then he said, let's have a drink an I, I'm not even a drinker, you know I don't, once in a while, but I'm not even a drinker. But I just kinda stumbled in the back and he was all, he was all smiles —he was talking an nothing was getting through to me. It was just like a roaring in my ears an, an then . . . it just came to me, you know, he. . . .

FALZON: You couldn't hear what he was saying, Dan?

WHITE: Just small talk that, you know, it just wasn't registering. What I was going to do now, you know, and how this would affect my family, you know, an, an just, just all the time knowing he's going to go out an, an lie to the press an, an tell 'em, you know, that I, I wasn't a good supervisor and that people didn't want me an then that was it. Then I, I just shot him, that was it, it was over.

FALZON: What happened after you left there, Dan?

WHITE: Well, I, I left his office by one of the back doors an, I was going to go down the stairs, and then I saw Harvey Milk's aide across the hall at the supervisors' an then it struck me about what Harvey had tried to do an I said, well I'll go talk to him. He didn't know I had, I had heard his conversation and he was all smiles and stuff and I went in and, you know, I, I didn't agree with him on a lot of things but I was always honest, you know, and here they were devious. And then he started kinda smirking, 'cause he knew, he knew I wasn't going to be reappointed. And ah . . . I started to say you know how hard I worked for it and what it meant to me and my family and then my reputation as, as a hard worker, good honest person and he just kind of smirked at me as if to say, too bad an then, an then, I just got all flushed an, an hot, and I shot him.

FALZON: This occurred inside your room, Dan?

WHITE: Yeah, in my office, yeah.

FALZON: And when you left there did you go back home?

WHITE: No, no, no I drove to the, the Doggie Diner on, on Van Ness and I called my wife and she, she didn't know, she . . .

FALZON: Did you tell her, Dan?

WHITE (sobbing): I called up, I didn't tell her on the phone. I just said she was working. I just told her to meet me at the cathedral . . . . .

ERDELATZ: Dan, right now are you under a doctor's care?

WHITE: No.

ERDELATZ: Are you under any medication at all?

WHITE: No.

ERDELATZ: When is the last time you had your gun with you prior to today?

WHITE: I guess it was a few months ago. I, I was afraid of some of the threats that were made in, I, I, just wanted to make sure to protect myself you know this, this city isn't safe you know and there's a lot of people running around an well I don't have to tell you fellows, you guys know that.

ERDELATZ: When you left home this morning, Dan, was it your intention to confront the mayor, Supervisor Milk or anyone else with that gun?

WHITE: No, I, I, what I wanted to do was just, talk to him, you know, I, I ah, I didn't even know if I was going to be reappointed or not be reappointed. *Why do we do things, you know, why did I, I don't know. No, I,* I just wanted to talk to him that's all an at least have him be honest with me and tell me why he was doing it, not because I was a bad supervisor or anything but, you know, I never killed anybody before, I never shot anybody . . .

ERDELATZ: Why did . . .

WHITE: . . . I didn't even, I didn't even know if I wanted to kill him. I just shot him, I don't know.

ERDELATZ: What type of gun is that you were carrying, Dan?

WHITE: It's a .38, a two-inch .38.

ERDELATZ: And do you know how many shots you fired?

WHITE: Uh . . . no I don't, I don't. I, I out of instinct when I, I reloaded the gun ah . . . you know, it's just the training I guess I had, you know.

ERDELATZ: Where did you reload?

WHITE: I reloaded in my office, when I was . . . I couldn't out in the hall.
    Pause.

ERDELATZ: When you say you reloaded, are you speaking of following the shooting in the Mayor's office?
WHITE: Yeah.
ERDELATZ: Inspector Falzon?
FALZON: No questions. Is there anything you'd like to add, Dan, before we close this statement?
WHITE: Yes. Just that I've been honest and worked hard, never cheated anybody, and I wanted to do a good job, I'm trying to do a good job and I saw this city as it's going, kind of downhill, and I was always just a lonely vote on the board. I was trying to do a good job for the city.

After hearing the above statement, the Court at the trial of Dan White takes a recess. *Curtain.*

ACT II: IN DEFENSE OF MURDER

The trial continues with defense lawyer Schmidt examining Inspector Falzon, who, having known Dan White for many years, serves as a character witness for him. Others testify to White's abilities and distinguished career, as a friend of Harvey Milk comments, "What galled me most was the picture of Dan White as the All American Boy . . . . . Maybe as a gay man, I understand the tyranny of the All American Boy."
In an interlude alone in an empty courtroom, former District Attorney Joseph Freitas Jr. declares, "I was voted out of office" and goes on to consider various other aspects and effects of the White murders and trial.

FREITAS: Well, I'm out of politics, and I don't know whether I'll get back into politics, because it certainly did set back my personal ah . . . aspirations as a public figure dramatically. I don't know. You know, there was an attempt not to allow our office to prosecute the case because I was close to Moscone myself. And we fought against that. I was confident— *(Laughs.)* I chose Tom Norman because he was the senior homicide prosecutor for fifteen years, and he was quite successful at it. I don't know . . .
There was a great division in the city then, you know. The city was divided all during that period. It divided on emerging constituencies like the gay constituency. That's the one that was used to cause the most divisive emotions more than any other, so the divisiveness in the city was there.
I mean, that was the whole point of this political fight between Dan White and Moscone and Milk: The fight was over who controlled the city.
The Right couldn't afford to lose Dan. He was their saving vote on the Board of Supervisors. He blocked the Milk/Moscone agenda. Obviously Harvey Milk didn't want Dan White on the Board.
So, it was political, the murders.
Maybe I should have, again in hindsight, possibly Tom, even though his attempts to do that may have been ruled inadmissible, possibly Tom should have been a little stronger in that area. But again, at the time . . . I mean, even the press was shocked at the outcome . . .

But—well, I think that what the jury had already bought was White's background—no, now, that's what was really on trial. Dan White sat there and waved his little American flag, and they acquitted him. They convicted George and Harvey. Now, if this had been a poor Black or a poor Chicano or a poor white janitor who'd been fired, or the husband of an alleged girlfriend of Moscone's, I don't think they would have bought the diminished capacity defense. But whereas they have a guy who was a member of a county Board of Supervisors who left the police department, who had served in the army, who was a fireman, who played baseball—I think that's what they were caught up in—that kind of person *must* have been crazy to do this. I would have interpreted it differently. Not to be held to a higher standard, but uh . . . that he had all the tools to be responsible.

One of the things people said was: "Why didn't you talk more about George's background, his family life, etcetera?" Well . . . one of the reasons is that Tom Norman did know that, had he opened up that area, they were prepared, yeah —they were prepared to smear George—to bring up the incident in Sacramento. With the woman—(and other things). It would be at best a wash, so why get into it? If you know they're going to bring out things that aren't positive. We wanted to let the city heal. We—and after Jonestown . . . Well—it would have been the city on trial.

If the jury had stuck to the facts alone, I mean, the confession alone was enough to convict him . . . I mean, look at this kid that shot Reagan, it was the same thing.

And then about White being anti-gay, well . . . White inside himself may have been anti-gay, but that Milk was his target . . . As I say—malice was there. Milk led the fight to keep White off the Board, which makes the murder all the more rational. I know the gay community thinks the murder was anti-gay: political in that sense. But I think they're wrong. Ya know, some people—in the gay community—ah—even said I threw the trial. Before this, I was considered a great friend to the gay community. Why would I want to throw the trial—this trial in an election year?

Oh, there were accusations you wouldn't believe . . . At the trial, a woman . . . it may have been one of the jurors—I can't remember . . . actually said, "But what would Mary Ann White do without her husband?" And I remember my outrage. She never thought, "What will Gina Moscone do without George?"

I must tell you that it's hard for me to talk about a lot of these things, all of this is just the—just the tip of the iceberg . . .

We thought—Tommy and I—Tom Norman and I—we thought it was an open and shut case of first degree murder.

The defense brings on several psychiatrists to testify as to the defendant's state of mind. The first, Dr. Jones, is questioned by the defense attorney.

SCHMIDT: Now, there is another legal term we deal with in the courtroom, and that is variously called "malice" or "malice aforethought" . . . And this must be present in order to convict for murder in the first degree.

JONES: O.K., let me preface this by saying I am not sure how malice is defined. I'll give you what my understanding is. In order to have malice, you would have to be able to do certain things: to be able to be intent to kill somebody unlawfully. You would have to be able to do something for a base and anti-social purpose. You would have to be aware of the duty imposed on you not to do that, not to unlawfully kill somebody or do something for a base, anti-social purpose, that involved a risk of death, and you would have to be able to act, despite having that awareness of that, that you are not supposed to do that, and so you would have to know that you were not supposed to do it, and then also act despite—keeping in mind that you are not supposed to do it. Is that your answer—your question?

SCHMIDT: I think so.

JONES *(laughs):* I felt that he had the capacity to do the first three: that he had the capacity to intend to kill, but that doesn't take much, you know, to try to kill somebody, it's not a high-falutin' mental state. I think he had the capacity to do something for a base and anti-social purpose. I think he had the capacity to know that there was a duty imposed on him not to do that, but *I don't think he had the capacity to hold that notion in his mind while he was acting;* so that I think that the depression, plus the moment, the tremendous emotion of the moment, with the depression, reduced his capacity for conforming conduct.

As ridiculous as this sounds, even to the point of instituting to kill the mayor, what he describes is more simply—is striking out, not intending to kill.

In cross-examining Jones, the prosecuting attorney, Norman, makes the point that "It's a fact that Dan White shot George Moscone twice in the body, and that when George Moscone fell to the floor disabled, he shot twice more into the right side of George Moscone's head at a distance of between twelve and eighteen inches."

Another psychiatrist, Dr. Blinder, testifies that White became increasingly frustrated by what he perceived to be self-serving, corrupt behavior at City Hall.

BLINDER: . . . . . In addition to these stresses, there were attacks by the press and there were threats of literal attacks on supervisors. He told me a number of

Gerry Bamman and Lisabeth Bartlett in *Execution of Justice*

supervisors like himself carried a gun to scheduled meetings. Never any relief from these tensions.

Whenever he felt things were not going right, he would abandon his usual program of exercise and good nutrition and start gorging himself on junk foods . . . . .

Additionally stressed by rumors about his non-reappointment (Blinder continues to testify), White decided to go see the mayor, picking up his gun and ammunition. The mayor then told White he was not going to be reappointed.

BLINDER: . . . . . The mayor puts his arm around him saying, "Let's have a drink. What are you going to do now, Dan? Can you get back into the Fire Department? What about your family? Can your wife get her job back? What's going to happen to them now?"

Somehow this inquiry directed to his family struck a nerve. The Mayor's voice started to fade out, and Mr. White felt "As if I were in a dream." He started to leave and then inexplicably turned around and like a reflex drew his revolver. He had no idea how many shots he fired. The similar event occurred in Supervisor Milk's office. He remembers being shocked by the sound of the gun going off for the second time like a cannon. He tells me that he was aware that he engaged in a lethal act, but tells me he gave no thought to its wrongfulness. As he put it to me: "I had no chance to even think about it."

Answering a question from Schmidt, Blinder tells the jury that "There is a substantial body of evidence that in susceptible individuals, large quantities of what we call junk food, high sugar content food with lots of preservatives, can precipitate anti-social and even violent behavior."

Other witnesses include a psychiatrist testifying for the prosecution to Dan White's undiminished capacity to know what he was doing. Both sides rest their cases, which the lawyers now sum up, Schmidt for the defense and Norman for the prosecution.

SCHMIDT: Lord God! I don't say to you to forgive Dan White. I don't say to you just let Dan White walk out of here a free man. He is guilty. But, the degree of responsibility is the issue here. The state of mind is the issue here. It's not who was killed, it's why. It's not who killed them, but why. The state of mind is the issue here.

. . . . . We played these tapes he made directly after he turned himself in at Northern Station. My God, that was not a person that was calm and collected and cool and able to weigh things out. It just wasn't. The tape just totally fogged me up the first time I heard it. It was a man that was, as Frank Falzon said, broken. Shattered. This was not the Dan White that everybody had known.

Something happened to him and he snapped. That's the word I used in my opening statement. Something snapped here. The pot had boiled over here, and people that boil over in that fashion, they tell the truth . . . . .

If the District Attorney concedes that what is on that tape is truthful, and I believe that's the insinuation we have here, then, by golly, there is voluntary manslaughter, nothing more and nothing less. I say this to you in all honesty. And if you have any doubts, our law tells you, you have to judge in favor of Dan White . . . . .

You can make up a picture of a dead man, or two of them for that matter, and you can wave them around and say somebody is going to pay for this, and somebody *is* going to pay for this. Dan White is going to pay for this. But it is not an emotional type thing. I get emotional about it, but *you* can't because you have to be objective about the facts.

But please, please, just justice. That's all. Just justice here . . . . .

NORMAN: Ladies and gentlemen, I listened very carefully to the summation just given you. It appears to me, members of the jury, to be a very facile explanation and rationalization as to premeditation and deliberation. The evidence that has been laid before you *screams* for murder in the first degree.

What counsel for the defense has done is suggest to you to *excuse* this kind of conduct and call it something that it isn't, to call it voluntary manslaughter . . . . .

To reduce the charge of murder to something less—to reduce it to voluntary manslaughter—means you are saying that this was not murder. That this was an intentional killing of a human being upon a quarrel, or heat of passion. But ladies and gentlemen, that quarrel must have been so extreme at the time that the defendant could not—was incapable of forming those qualities of thought which are malice, premeditation and deliberation. But the evidence in this case doesn't suggest that at all. Not at all.

If the defendant had picked up a vase or something that happened to be in the Mayor's office and hit the Mayor over the head and killed him, you know, you know that argument for voluntary manslaughter might be one which you could say the evidence admits a reasonable doubt. But—

Norman reviews the facts of the case—the gun brought in by White, the deliberate avoidance of the metal detector, the reloading of the weapon after the first killing, the extra shots deliberately fired, commenting "Deliberation is premeditation. It has malice. I feel stultified to even bring this up. This is the *definition* of murder . . . . . Ladies and gentlemen, the quality of your service is reflected in your verdict."

The Court analyzes the evidence for the jury, whose Foreman then delivers the verdict that "The jury finds the defendant Daniel James White guilty of violating Section 192.1 of the penal code."

> *Mary Ann White gasps. Dan White puts head in hands. Explosion. Riot police enter.*

GWENN *(a Black lesbian leader):* The police came into the Castro and assaulted gays. They stormed the Elephant Walk Bar. One kid had an epileptic seizure and was almost killed for it. A cop drove a motorcycle up against a phone booth where a lesbian woman was on the phone, blocked her exit and began beating her up.

COURT: Is this a unanimous verdict of the jury?

FOREMAN: Yes, it is, Judge.

GWENN: I want to talk about when people are pushed to the wall.

COURT: Will each juror say "yea" or "nay"?

YOUNG MOTHER: What about the children?

MOSCONE'S FRIEND: I know who George offended. I know who Harvey offended.

JURORS *(on tape):* Yea, yea, yea, yea, yea, yea.

MOSCONE'S FRIEND: I understand the offense.

YOUNG MOTHER: What do I tell my kids?

GWENN: Were the ones who are responsible seeing these things?

YOUNG MOTHER: That in this country you serve more time for robbing a bank than for killing two people?

JURORS *(on tape):* Yea, yea, yea, yea, yea, yea.

GWENN: Hearing these things?

MILK'S FRIEND: I understand the offense.

GWENN: Do they understand about people being pushed to the wall?

YOUNG MOTHER: Accountability?

"Yea's" end.

MILK'S FRIEND: Assassination. I've grown up with it. I forget it hasn't always been this way.

YOUNG MOTHER: What do I say? That two lives are worth seven years and eight months in jail?

MILK'S FRIEND: I remember coming home from school in second grade—JFK was killed—five years later, Martin Luther King. It's a frame of reference.

Explosion.

COURT: Will the Foreman please read the verdict for the second count?

DENMAN *(ex-Undersheriff):* It's a divided city.

FOREMAN: The jury finds the defendant Daniel James White guilty of violating Section 192.1 of the penal code, voluntary manslaughter, in the slaying of Supervisor Harvey Milk.

Dan White gasps. Mary Ann White sobs. Norman, flushed, head in hands. Explosions. Violence ends. Riot police do terror control.

BRITT *(Harvey Milk's successor; on camera):* No—I'm optimistic about San Francisco.

COURT: Is this a unanimous decision by the jury?

FOREMAN: Yes, Your Honor.

BRITT: I'm Harry Britt. I was Harvey Milk's successor.

NOTHENBERG *(Deputy Mayor):* If he'd just killed George, he'd be in jail for life.

BRITT: Now, this is an example I don't often use, because people will misunderstand it, but when a prophet is killed, it's up to those who are left to build the community or the church.

NOTHENBERG: Dan White believed in the death penalty . . .

YOUNG MOTHER: To this jury Dan White was their son.

NOTHENBERG: He should have gotten the death penalty.

YOUNG MOTHER: What are we teaching our sons?

BRITT: But I have hope.

MILK'S FRIEND: It was an effective assassination.

BRITT: I have hope. And as Harvey said, "You can't live without hope."

MILK'S FRIEND: They always are.

BRITT: "And you, and you, and you—we gotta give 'em hope."

JOANNA *(TV reporter, on video):* Dan White was examined by the psychiatrist at the state prison. They decided against therapy. Dan White had no apparent signs of mental disorder . . . Dan White's parole date was January 6, 1984. When Dan White left Soledad Prison on January 6, 1984, it was five years, one month and eight days since he turned himself in at Northern Station after the assassinations of Mayor George Moscone and Supervisor Harvey Milk. Mayor Dianne Feinstein, the current Mayor of San Francisco, has tried to keep Dan White out of San Francisco during his parole for fear he will be killed.

The Cop enters. Sister Boom Boom enters.

BOOM BOOM: Dan White! It's 1984 and Big Sister is watching you.

JOANNA: Dan White reportedly plans to move to Ireland after his release.

MOSCONE'S FRIEND: What do you do with your feelings of revenge? With your need for retribution?

BRITT: We will never forget.

On screen: riot images freeze . . . . . A shaft of light from church window.

BOOM BOOM: I would like to close with a reading from the Book of Dan.

Opens book.

Take of this and eat, for this is my defense.

Eats Twinkie. Exits.

JOANNA: Dan White was found dead of carbon monoxide poisoning on October 21, 1985, at his wife's home in San Francisco, California.

Lights change. Dan White faces the Court.

COURT: Mr. White, you are sentenced to seven years and eight months, the maximum sentence for these two counts of voluntary manslaughter. The Court feels that these sentences for the taking of life is completely inappropriate but that was the decision of the legislature. Again, let me repeat for the record: Seven years and eight months is the maximum sentence for voluntary manslaughter, and this is the law.

Gavel. Long pause.

WHITE *(turns to the audience/jury):* I was always just a lonely vote on the Board. I was just trying to do a good job for the city.

Long pause. Audio: hyperreal sounds of a woman's high heels on marble. Mumbled Hail Marys. Rustle of an embrace. Sister Boom Boom enters and taunts police. Police raise riot shields. Gavel echoes. Curtain.

LARGO DESOLATO

A Play in Two Acts

BY VACLAV HAVEL

TRANSLATION BY MARIE WINN

Cast and credits appear on page 340

VACLAV HAVEL was born into a well-to-do family in Prague, Czechoslovakia in 1936. His family's property was confiscated by the government (his uncle had owned the Barrandov Film Studios, still the nucleus of the nationalized Czech film industry), and under the regulations he was ineligible for formal higher education, regardless of ability. As a worker in the chemical industry, however, he found time for classes in the evening, completing his studies in 1956. Following military service and various jobs in Prague theaters including that of stagehand, he found a place in the avant-garde Balustrade Theater as dramaturg and playwright-in-residence and was even accepted as a student of dramaturgy at the Academy of Dramatic Arts.

Havel remained in this position until the Soviet takeover of Czechoslovakia in 1968. "Ever since then," a biographical note in the New York program of Largo Desolato *states, "he has been harassed by the secret police, persecuted by the authorities, twice held in prison—first as one of the appointed spokesmen for Charter 77, a Czech human rights movement, next as a leading member of the Czech Committee for the Defense of the Unjustly Prosecuted. Last spring (1985) he was temporarily released from the completion of his sentence (four and a half years) for reasons of his health."*

Havel's international reputation as a playwright was established in 1963 by his first play, The Garden Party, *produced in Austria, Switzerland, Sweden, Finland, Hungary, Yugoslavia and 18 West German theaters after its Prague premiere. His second play,* The Memorandum *in 1965, was even more popular and was produced off Broadway by Joseph Papp's New York Shakespeare Festival May 5, 1968 for 49 performances, receiving the Obie Award for best foreign play. Havel's third full-length play,* The Increased Difficulty of Concentration, *won the same Obie in off-Broadway production by the Repertory Theater of Lincoln Center December 4, 1969 for 28 performances. Joseph Papp produced a program of three Havel one-acts—*Interview, A Private View *and* Protest—*at New York Shakespeare Festival November 20, 1983 for 95 performances, as well as Havel's first Best Play,* Largo Desolato, *March 25, 1986 for 40 off-Broadway performances. Though celebrated throughout the international theater community (Samuel Beckett's one-acter* Catastrophe, *produced off Broadway in 1963, was written in Havel's honor), his work has been banned in Czechoslovakia since 1969.*

MARIE WINN (translation) was born in Prague, Czechoslovakia, the daughter of a neurologist and psychiatrist, but came to New York City as a small child and was educated at the public school, the Bronx High School of Science, Radcliffe in Cambridge, Mass., and Columbia, where she received her B.A. Her translations have included four of the 18 short stories in Best Soviet Short Stories, *the novel* Summer in Prague *and operas by Janacek and Smetana. In addition, as a free-lance writer specializing in social comment focussing on children and childhood, she is a regular contributor to the* New York Times Magazine *and the author of 11 books including* The Plug-in-Drug *and* Children Without Childhood. *In 1985 she became the first American to win the International Janusz Corczak Grand Prize in the category of books about children.*

Vaclav Havel's Largo Desolato *is Ms. Winn's first translation for the legitimate stage. She is married, with two children, and lives in New York City.*

Time and Place: *A 36-hour period in Leopold Kopriva's spacious apartment in contemporary Prague*

ACT I

Scene 1

SYNOPSIS: The available wall space is packed with books in the large living room of Leopold Kopriva, a middle-aged philosopher whose last name means "nettle." The front door is down left, and from left to right across the upstage wall are the doors to Zuzana's (his roommate's) bedroom, glass doors beyond which the kitchen is visible and the door to Leopold's bedroom. At right are doors to a balcony and the bathroom. A sofa and coffee table—with a bottle of rum gradually consumed by Leopold and his visitors—hold stage center, and *"Although the apartment is somewhat old and solidly middle-class, the furnishings reveal that it is inhabited by an intellectual."*

Symphonic music, which will be heard from time to time during the play, rises and then fades as the curtain rises. Kopriva gets up from the sofa where he has been sitting staring apprehensively at the front door. He goes to it, looks through the peephole, puts his ear to the door, sees and hears nothing—*"Then the curtain falls abruptly."*

Scene 2

The curtain rises and falls on the above action, which is exactly repeated.

Scene 3

The curtain rises on the above action, repeated—but this time Leopold hears something and is startled. Then the doorbell makes a strident demand. Timidly,

Below, the cast of the New York Shakespeare Festival production of *Largo Desolato* by Vaclav Havel: Matthew Locricchio (Man I), Joseph Wiseman (Olbram), Tom Mardirosian (Olda), Jodi Thelen (Marketa), Edward Zang (Fellow I), Richard Russell Ramos (Fellow II), Josef Sommer (Kopriva), Diane Venora (Lucy), Larry Block (Lada I), Burke Pearson (Lada II), Michael Guido (Man II), Sally Kirkland (Zuzana)

Leopold opens the door and is relieved to find that his visitor is his friend Olda, who perceives Leopold's tension. Olda opens the balcony door to counteract the obvious stuffiness and asks about Leopold's health.

LEOPOLD: At first glance it might appear that there's nothing to complain about today. But still I'd be lying if I claimed I'm my usual self—

OLDA: Are you nervous?

LEOPOLD: I'm always nervous—

OLDA: But what about the internal shivering you had yesterday—is it gone?

LEOPOLD: Unfortunately, no. In fact, it's so intense that one might almost call it a fever. *(Stops suddenly.)* Is somebody coming?

They both listen quietly.

OLDA: It's nothing—

LEOPOLD: Moreover, it goes along with some other things, slight dizziness, for instance, a sort of mild queasiness in the stomach, tingling in the joints, a distracted feeling, loss of appetite and actually even constipation.

OLDA: You didn't go this morning?

LEOPOLD: No—

OLDA: And it's not a hangover?

LEOPOLD: My condition has something in common with a hangover, but it's not a hangover. If for no other reason than the fact that I had almost nothing to drink yesterday—

OLDA: Maybe you're coming down with something—

LEOPOLD: I'm afraid not—

OLDA: But that's good, isn't it?

LEOPOLD: I'd rather be sick than healthy like this! If only I could be sure they weren't coming today—

OLDA: They can't come any more today—

LEOPOLD: You think not? But they can come any time—

Just then, a key is heard in the lock. Leopold is startled. Zuzana enters at the front door, carrying a full shopping bag.

Relieved that it is only Zuzana, his roommate—a chic, attractive blonde—Leopold takes the bag of groceries to the kitchen and returns to tell Zuzana that he hasn't felt well enough to work but has spent the day doing a few housekeeping chores. He suggests that a dinner party tonight with Olda would help ease the tension, but Zuzana declines—she has tickets to the movies—and exits into her bedroom.

Olda suggests that Leopold should get out more often, go for walks, but Leopold would be afraid of what might be happening back in the apartment. The doorbell sounds its strident command again, and, reluctantly, Leopold goes to the door and opens it. He has two visitors, both named Lada, in workmen's clothes (they are employed at the paper mill). They came here to consult Leopold two years ago, but he doesn't remember them.

Zuzana enters, sizes up the situation and takes Olda off into the kitchen, leaving Leopold alone with his two callers.

LADA I: Oh, by the by, we have a lot of interesting material from the paper mill, minutes of meetings and things like that. It would certainly be of interest to you—

LEOPOLD: I'm sure—

LADA II: We'll bring it to you—

>   *A pause.*

LADA I: We know everything—

LEOPOLD: Everything about what?

LADA I: About your situation—

LEOPOLD: I see—

LADA II: Lada meant to say that we're your fans—and we're not alone.

LEOPOLD: Thank you—

LADA I: You're the support and hope of a great many people—

LEOPOLD: Thank you—

LADA II: We believe that everything will turn out all right for you in the end—

LEOPOLD: I'm not so sure—

LADA I: The main thing is not to back down. We believe in you, and we need you, we need somebody like you—

LEOPOLD: Thank you—

A lot more could be done than is being done, Lada I asserts, without going into specifics, though Leopold wishes he knew exactly what they are talking about. Leopold is a respected philosopher, the Ladas insist, while they are mere nobodies, but they will back any efforts to "start the ball rolling again." The Ladas repeat their obviously embarrassing (to Leopold) encouragements until finally the doorbell buzzes again—it's Leopold's girl friend Lucy who enters, is introduced to the Ladas and takes a seat on the sofa.

Leopold offers Lucy a drink of rum, but she refuses it. The Ladas sit there, making no move to depart, even though Leopold starts hinting that he has some work to do. Zuzana and Olda come in from the kitchen, Zuzana greeting Lucy warmly and then disappearing into her room to prepare for her trip to the movies. The Ladas finally decide to go, promising to bring Leopold the information they spoke of and exhorting him, "We're with you! Keep up the good fight! So long!"

Zuzana and Olda also leave. Alone with Leopold, Lucy complains that he never tells her he loves her until she asks.

LEOPOLD: Phenemenology has taught me to be constantly on guard against overstepping the bounds of provable experience through my statements. I'd rather express less than I feel than risk a manifestation of something I don't feel—

LUCY: Don't you consider your love for me to be a provable experience?

LEOPOLD: That depends on how we understand the concept of love. Maybe the word has a slightly different and possibly more extreme meaning for me than it has for you. Just a minute!

>   *Leopold steps away from Lucy, walks to the front door and looks out the peephole.*

LUCY: What's the matter?

LEOPOLD: I thought I heard someone coming—

LUCY: I don't hear anything—

Leopold steps away from the door and turns to Lucy.

LEOPOLD: I'm sorry, Lucy, but is it really necessary for our relationship to consist of nothing but a constant discussion and analysis of it?

LUCY: It's no wonder when you're so unusually evasive—

LEOPOLD: I realize that you crave certainty just as all women do, but don't forget that what's certainty for you is transcendence for a man—

LUCY: It's just my luck to have an especially transcendent lover—

LEOPOLD: Ugh!

LUCY: What's the matter?

LEOPOLD: Please don't use the word lover! At least not in connection with me—

LUCY: Why not?

LEOPOLD: It's lewd—

LUCY: How come?

LEOPOLD: It conjures up a certain image of an eternally naked proprietor of a cock.

Leopold pours them some wine and explains that he didn't feel like writing today. Lucy tells him everyone is waiting for his new essay, but Leopold's thoughts just seem to go around in circles. Lucy feels that lovemaking can revitalize him and proceeds to shower impassive Leopold with affection as the music rises and the curtain falls.

Scene 4

Leopold, with a bathrobe covering his nakedness, is being assured by a friend, Olbram, that "We all love you," even though there are rumors that Leopold is no longer dependable, doesn't answer letters, hasn't read the journal Olbram left for him. Olbram is also curious about Leopold's relationships with Lucy (who keeps calling to him from offstage) and Zuzana, but Leopold isn't forthcoming. Olbram goes on, while Leopold shivers in his bathrobe.

OLBRAM: It's obviously terrible to live with such nervewracking uncertainty— we're all aware of that—none of us knows how we'd stand it ourselves—but for that reason many people are worried about you—I'm sure you understand—

LEOPOLD: I understand—

OLBRAM: I'm not just speaking for myself, I'm actually sort of speaking for everyone—

LEOPOLD: Who's everyone?

OLBRAM: Your friends—

LEOPOLD: You've been delegated?

OLBRAM: If you want to put it like that—

LEOPOLD: And just exactly what are you all worried about?

OLBRAM: How can I say it? I'd hate to be hard and hurt you in any way—but on the other hand I'd be a bad friend and absolutely no help to you at all if I covered up or held back anything—

LEOPOLD: And just exactly what are you all worried about?

OLBRAM: How can I say it? It's not just a matter of the common interest but above all it's a matter of you as a—

LEOPOLD: And just exactly what are you all worried about? . . . . .

OLBRAM: How can I say it? There simply seems to be a growing number of indications that lead to certain probabilities—

LEOPOLD: What indications and what probabilities?

OLBRAM: Your friends—and why beat around the bush, I as well—it's simply as if all of us at a certain point—if only our fears were groundless!—it's simply as if all of us at a certain point began to stop feeling sure that you could stand it—that you'd be up to the demands people make of you based on all your previous achievements—that you'd fulfill the expectations which, I'm sorry to say, people rightfully have of you—in short, that you'd be equal to your mission, that you'd do justice to that great commitment to truth, to the world, and to all those for whom you are a model and a source of hope, hope which you yourself, I'm sorry to say, provided through your work. We're simply beginning to be a little afraid that you might disappoint us somehow, and by doing so also bring upon yourself—and because you are so sensitive, I'm sorry to say, it would certainly turn out that way—untold suffering.

    A short pause.

You're not angry at me for speaking so openly?

LEOPOLD: No, quite the contrary—

With Lucy still calling and Leopold still shivering, Olbram goes on about how worried people are that Leopold won't be able to stand up under "nervewracking uncertainty." Leopold tells Olbram of the visit from the two Ladas from the paper factory. Olbram warns him that he must not change from "being a natural consequence of your beliefs and your work, into merely being their substitute; and though it's had an autonomous and self-sustaining momentum of its own for a long time, that you don't find yourself clinging to it as the one and only proof of your moral existence, so that you end up placing your whole human identity into the casual hands of some uninformed paper-mill workers."

Olbram restates the misgivings of Leopold's supporters that he might not be able to stand the continuous pressure. He senses some crucial support function within Leopold's personality is beginning to crumble. Leopold seems disorganized and vague in his personal relationships and at the mercy of events rather than in command of them: "You're changing from a self-confident subject of your own life into nothing more than a passive object of it." Olbram fears for Leopold, and for those who need his inspiration, and he urges his friend, "Pull yourself together! . . . . . I'm begging you to be that marvelous Leopold Kopriva once again that we all thought so highly of!"

Lucy enters in her bathrobe and maneuvers Olbram into leaving. Lucy wants to talk to Leopold about their relationship and fetches a blanket for him, sitting on the sofa, to wrap himself in. Leopold has obviously had a problem making love this evening, and Lucy tells him, "You're simply all blocked up . . . . . finally you end up feeling duty instead of pleasure." Lucy wants the two of them to admit before all the world that they love each other, but Leopold continues furtive about their affair: "That tireless effort of yours to define our relationship" merely arouses Leopold's defensive reflexes.

Lucy knows that he loves her and believes that if he admitted it—"Only through others, after all, do we discover our true identity," he once wrote—both his life and his work would be vastly enhanced. Leopold admits to her that something inside him is indeed crumbling—"I'm only playing myself rather than actually being myself," he declares, echoing Olbram's worries. His will and emotions have been stifled: "I'm a broken, crippled person, I'll never be different, and the best thing would be if they finally came for me and took me there, where I wouldn't be spreading further misery and causing further disappointment."

Lucy is now reduced to tears, seeing Leopold as just another liar who has become tired of their affair and is using other stresses as an excuse to break it off. As Leopold tries to embrace Lucy, the doorbell sounds. Looking through the peephole, Leopold sees that finally it is "them," the persons he feared, come to take him "there," wherever that may be. Lucy insists on staying with him as he flings open the door to admit two men.

> *Fellow I and Fellow II enter.*
> FELLOW I: Good evening, Professor—
> LEOPOLD: Good evening—
> FELLOW I: I assume that you know who we are—
> LEOPOLD: I have a pretty good idea—
> FELLOW II: You weren't expecting us any more today, were you?
> LEOPOLD: I know you can come at any time—
> FELLOW I: We apologize for disturbing you. *(Glances at Lucy.)* You obviously had other plans for the remainder of the day—
> *Fellow I and Fellow II laugh suggestively.*
> LEOPOLD: That's my business, the sort of plans I had—
> FELLOW II: Maybe we won't keep you long—that depends on you—
> FELLOW I: We're glad to meet you. Our colleagues told us that you're a sensible person, so maybe there's a chance that we'll come to a quick understanding—
> LEOPOLD: I don't know what we could come to an understanding about. My things are all ready. All I need is a little time to get dressed—
> FELLOW II: What's the big hurry?—You don't have to assume the worst ending right at the start.
> FELLOW I: Of course we have to ask this lady to please leave—

Lucy refuses to go, so the Fellows summon two men who drag her, struggling, out of the door, while the Fellows assure Leopold that no harm will come to her; she'll be taken home later. The Fellows inquire idly about Leopold's eating (mostly vitamins), drinking ("the same as everybody else") and work habits. They've come to avoid a confrontation, to make Leopold an offer.

> FELLOW I: . . . . . We've been delegated to inform you that under certain conditions the whole thing you're facing could be dropped—

Diane Venora and Josef Sommer in a scene from *Largo Desolato*

LEOPOLD: How do you mean—dropped?

FELLOW II: The whole thing could be declared invalid—

LEOPOLD: Under what conditions?

FELLOW I: As you know, that thing that's supposed to happen to you is supposed to happen to you because you wrote a certain composition under the name Leopold Kopriva.

FELLOW II: An essay, as you call it—

FELLOW I: Which you don't deny, and by not doing so you actually made things turn out the way they did—it was really through your own doing that the perpetrator became known—

FELLOW II: As a well-informed person you're certainly aware of the fact that if the perpetrator is unknown, we can't proceed, thanks to the so-called principle of perpetrator identity—

FELLOW I: In short, if you sign us a brief declaration saying that you aren't Doctor Leopold Kopriva, the author of the composition in question, the whole thing will be considered invalid and all previous charges will be dropped.

LEOPOLD: If I understand you correctly, you want me to declare that I am not I—

FELLOW I: That may be a suitable interpretation for a philosopher; still, it's legally absurd. It's not, for goodness sake, a matter of you declaring that you aren't you, but a matter of you declaring that you're not identical to the author of the thing—basically it's a formality—

FELLOW II: One name's as good as another—

FELLOW I: Or do you consider the name Kopriva to be so beautiful that you simply couldn't give it up? Look in the phone book and see how many equally nice names—

FELLOW II: Most of them even nicer!

LEOPOLD: Does this mean that I'm suppose to change my name?

FELLOW II: Not at all! You can have any name you want, that's your business after all—that—at least in this connection—doesn't interest anybody. The only important thing here is whether you are or aren't that Leopold Kopriva who wrote the thing—

There are three Leopold Koprivas in the phone book now, the Fellows point out, but it might be "tidier" if he changed his name altogether. Obviously, they're interested in solving their problem with as little fuss as possible, but they can't force Leopold to accept their offer; they can only suggest that unexpected things might lie ahead for Leopold if he doesn't, and that others in the same situation have accepted such an offer, so that "everybody would understand why you did it."

Leopold asks for time to think over the proposition.

FELLOW II (suddenly shouts out): Listen, don't be crazy! To get rid of the heavy load of your past and all its garbage in one fell swoop and get off to a fresh start —a chance like that comes once in a lifetime! What wouldn't I give for such an offer!

> A short pause. Leopold is visibly shivering, either from nerves or from the cold.

LEOPOLD (quietly): Let's see it—

> Fellow I quickly begins rummaging through all his pockets until he finally finds a small, soiled and crumpled piece of paper in one of his back pockets. He places it on the table and quickly smoothes it out with the back of his hand. Then he hands it to Leopold, who holds it for a long time in his trembling hand and carefully reads it. After a while he slowly puts it down on the table and bundles up even more in his blanket. A pause.

FELLOW I: So how about it?

> The music swells. The curtain falls.

ACT II

Scene 5

Leopold is alone, pacing around and around his living room, following the walls, like a prisoner in a cell. In passing, he looks through the peephole in the front door; pops some pills from a box on one of his bookshelves; goes into the bathroom to rinse his face; takes some more pills after listening again at the front door; rinses his face again, groaning, and continues pacing until there is the sound of a key in the lock and Zuzana enters.

Leopold tells Zuzana that the expected happened: "they" came in the night. Since he's still here, Zuzana assumes he must have conceded them something. Leopold tells her of his conversation with Olbram, his "little disagreement" with Lucy and the proposition made to him by the Fellows.

ZUZANA: Boy, they'd like that! For you to renounce your own self and spit on your own work!

LEOPOLD: They're not demanding any major decision from me—they just need a formal reason for declaring the whole thing to be invalid—

ZUZANA: Tsss!

LEOPOLD: They're obviously afraid that if I were there, it would increase the respect I command.

ZUZANA: Whereas if you renounced your work you'd lose every bit of respect! Obviously that would be the best thing for them! I hope you sent them packing—

LEOPOLD: I asked for time to think it over—

ZUZANA: What?

LEOPOLD: But there's nothing wrong with that—

ZUZANA: Have you lost your mind? For God's sake, what do you want to think over? Don't you see that only makes it clear to them that they've broken you— and that now they'll press you that much harder! I knew right away that you got yourself into a mess somehow! You're a chicken!

LEOPOLD: It's easy for you to talk—

ZUZANA: If you're so afraid of it, then you shouldn't have started anything—

Zuzana turns and goes off to her room, Leopold resumes his pacing, pill-popping and face-rinsing. The doorbell rings: it's Olda, wearing a tuxedo. Lucy has been to see him; she's very upset, but Leopold can't leave the apartment right now to go see how she's getting along.

Leopold harangues Olda with his wishes that people would just leave him alone to prowl the bookstores peacefully, as he used to do. The idea of changing his name and taking on a new, obscure existence appeals to him. But he is interrupted by the ringing of the doorbell again. He flees to the bathroom, leaving Olda to go to the door and open it, reluctantly. It is only the Ladas carrying a large suitcase apiece.

The sound of running water in the bathroom finally stops, and Leopold emerges, his hair smoothly combed, to greet the Ladas and watch them extract a great amount of paper from the suitcases—half of it fresh stationery supplies as a present for the professor ("We're already looking forward to everything that will be written on it.")—and half of it records from the factory ("Use it as you see fit . . . . . If you work it up somehow, it will certainly be a bombshell."). Leopold is impressed with its volume, though he has no idea what it contains.

Again and again, the Ladas assure Leopold of their support and that of "a great many people." Leopold plies Lada I with rum, while Zuzana enters wearing an evening gown. She goes into the kitchen with Olda, who has been standing in the background.

Lada I empties his glass of rum again and again but finally puts it down and refuses a refill with "Somebody's got to have some sense." Nervously and surreptitiously, Leopold pops another pill while the Ladas resume their cryptic urging of Leopold to "start the ball rolling again," never specifying what ball or in what direction, but always acknowledging Leopold's leadership role. Leopold escapes into the bathroom to rinse his face again, groaning, but the Ladas are still on the subject when he returns.

LADA I: The things you've written—even though we don't understand them completely—

LADA II: We're ordinary people—

LADA I: And the fact that you stand behind them—

LADA II: Regardless of the consequences—

LADA I: These things directly raise hope that you'll take the last remaining step—

LEOPOLD: What last remaining step?

LADA II: I'm not so good at expressing myself, but I'd say it like this: simply, that you'll take the things you write and somehow or other change them into something that will really take hold—

LADA I: Simply that you'll put the right dot at the end of your philosophy—

LEOPOLD: The trouble is that everybody has a different idea about that dot.

LADA II: You'll find the right form yourself—

LADA I: Who else is there to start the ball rolling again besides you?

LADA II: I'd say it's out-and-out expected of you—

LEOPOLD: Expected by whom?

LADA I: By everyone—

LEOPOLD: That's a bit of an exaggeration, wouldn't you say?

LADA II: Sorry, but you probably aren't quite aware—

LEOPOLD: Aware of what?

LADA I: Your responsibility—

LEOPOLD: For what?

LADA II: For everything—

Nervously, Leopold escapes to the kitchen, from which he returns bringing and eating a plate of onions and almonds. The Ladas irritate him by suggesting that he write a general manifesto about "all the basic things." He still fails to understand exactly what it is he's supposed to do for them.

Zuzana enters with Olda. Leopold appeals to her for advice, but they are on their way to a dance and exit. The Ladas see Leopold's failure to understand their message as a sort of reproach to them for being inarticulate "ordinary people," not philosophers, and they are somewhat hurt.

Leopold's confusion is visualized as a sort of hallucination in which other characters suddenly appear and restate their positions and opinions: Olbram at the bathroom door, Olda at the kitchen door, Zuzana at the door to her room, Lucy at the balcony door, with the Ladas chiming in.

*The pace of these retorts is progressively faster; Leopold keeps turning
in confusion from one to another.*

LEOPOLD *(suddenly cries out):* Enough!
*For a moment there is a deathly silence, then the doorbell rings. Leo-
pold dashes to the bathroom; Olbram steps out of his way; Leopold
disappears into the bathroom, and soon the sound of running water is
heard. All the characters quietly disappear into the doorways where they
first appeared. Ladas I and II vanish through the front door with their
suitcases. Everyone is gone, and all the doors except the door to the
bathroom close up. The sound of running water is heard, to which is
added the sound of Leopold's groaning. The doorbell rings again. The
music swells, the curtain falls.*

Scene 6

The music fades at curtain rise, and Leopold makes his way to the front door
to admit Marketa, a young, attractive female philosophy student, come to consult
the professor. Leopold asks her in and presses a drink of rum on her as she sits
on the sofa. He has just taken a shower and has appeared wet, with nothing but
a towel wrapped around him, but now he goes back to the bathroom for his
bathrobe.

Marketa has read all Leopold's books—"The Phenomenology of Responsibility," "Love and Nothingness" and "The Ontology of the Human Ego."

MARKETA: I've heard that you've had some trouble on account of "The On-
tology of the Human Ego"—
LEOPOLD: I'm supposed to go there on account of it.
MARKETA: What? Actually there? How come?
LEOPOLD: Paragraph 511—intellectual disturbance of the peace.
MARKETA: That's terrible!
LEOPOLD: That's the kind of world we live in now—
MARKETA: For such beautiful ideas!
LEOPOLD: Obviously, somebody doesn't think they're so beautiful—
MARKETA: But is it definite yet?
LEOPOLD: I could avoid it if I denied that I wrote the thing—

It was his essays, Marketa assures Leopold, that got her interested in the study
of philosophy. Leopold refills her rum glass and assures her he's working on a
new idea, something about "love as the existential dimension of being." Marketa
keeps on drinking rum and confides to Leopold that life itself now seems strangely
stifling to her—blank faces on the bus, turmoil on the streets, TV-absorbed
parents, classmates too superficial for meaningful relationships.

Leopold in his turn confides that he himself is having a "meaning-of-life crisis"
and is stimulated by this consultation with one of his readers. He refers to his
complicated thoughts about life's meaning being an "an elusive spiritual state"
possibly defined by "a certain non-verbal area of interexistentiality"—and is
pleased that she seems to grasp his meanings and share his form of malaise.

Leopold tells Marketa—whom he perceives as both beautiful and intelligent—that he's in a very bad way, crumbling inside: "Gone is my former perspective—my humor—my diligence and endurance—the sharpness of my expression." Marketa, continuing to drink rum, assures the professor that self-knowledge, even of disintegration, is an asset in itself. Perhaps, Leopold muses, punishment would provide him with a cleansing atonement for all his misdoings. No, Marketa argues, to imagine benefit from it is to capitulate to it: "You're clinging to it as if it were some way of escaping your own life . . . . . Don't you understand that you didn't do anything wrong and that you don't have anything to atone for? Why, you're innocent!"

Marketa offers Leopold her love, which might help him restore purpose to his life. As he kisses her and she responds, the doorbell rings. Leopold conceals Marketa on the balcony and goes into the bathroom where he puts on his suit and overcoat and emerges carrying a suitcase, ready to go "there" with the Fellows, who enter when Leopold opens the front door. But the Fellows don't seem ready to take Leopold away; and though they summon Marketa in from the balcony, they don't treat her with hostility.

LEOPOLD: . . . . . As you've obviously figured out by now, I'm not going to sign that paper for you. I'd rather die than give up my own self! My human identity is all I have!

FELLOW II: But why such strong words, Professor? You're not going anywhere—

LEOPOLD: What do you mean? Didn't I clearly tell you that I'm not signing anything? I'm innocent!

FELLOW I: But you don't have to sign anything, either! You have an indefinite postponement—

FELLOW II: Even without the signature!

LEOPOLD: What? A postponement?

FELLOW I: You heard correctly: a postponement!

LEOPOLD: You mean neither a signature, nor there—

FELLOW II: For now, I beg you to remember, for now—

LEOPOLD: I don't understand what this means—why don't you want my signature any more?

FELLOW I: Why bother with such formalities? Even without them, after all, it's now clear that the decision in your case was probably invalid—

LEOPOLD: You're trying to say that I am no longer I, aren't you?

FELLOW II: Those are your words, not ours—

    A short pause. Leopold stares wildly at Fellows I and II.

LEOPOLD (*shouts*): I don't want any postponement! I want to go there!

    Leopold abruptly falls to his knees before Fellows I and II and begins to sob.

Please, please, take me away, I beg of you—I can't live like this any longer—

FELLOW I: But obviously you'll have to—

MARKETA: Leopold, get up! How can you beg like that!

LEOPOLD (*shouts at Marketa*): Leave me alone! Everybody leave me alone!

    Leopold collapses to the ground and pounds his fist against the floor. The music swells, the curtain falls.

Scene 7

Leopold is alone, repeating his apprehensive behavior as in Scene 1, staring at the front door, going to it and looking out the peephole and bending over, listening intently.

> *Suddenly the lights go on in the auditorium and the music swells. Leopold quickly straightens up, goes to the footlights and bows to the audience. At the same moment the other characters enter through all the doors onstage and take their bows. Curtain.*

THE PERFECT PARTY

A Play in Two Acts

BY A.R. GURNEY JR.

Cast and credits appear on page 338

A.R. GURNEY JR. was born November 1, 1930 in Buffalo, N.Y., the son of a realtor. He was educated at St. Paul's School and Williams College where he received his B.A. in 1952. After a stint in the Navy, he entered Yale Drama School in 1956 and emerged with an M.F.A. degree after studying playwriting in seminars conducted by Lemist Esler, Robert Penn Warren and John Gassner. His first production, the musical Love in Buffalo, *took place at Yale in 1958.*

Gurney's first New York production of record was the short-lived The David Show *off Broadway in 1968, repeated in an off-Broadway program with his* The Golden Fleece *the following season. His* Scenes From American Life *premiered at Studio Arena Theater in Buffalo in 1970, then was produced by Repertory Theater of Lincoln Center for 30 performances in 1971, winning its author Drama Desk and Variety poll citations as a most promising playwright and achieving many subsequent productions at home and abroad.*

Gurney next made the off-Broadway scene with Who Killed Richard Corey? *for 31 performances at Circle Repertory in 1976, the same year that his* Children *premiered in Richmond, Va. and his* The Rape of Bunny Stunte *was done OOB. The next year,* Children *appeared at Manhattan Theater Club,* The Love Course *was produced OOB and* The Middle Ages *had its premiere at the Mark Taper Forum in Los Angeles. Gurney's* The Problem *and* The Wayside Motor Inn *were done OOB in the 1977–78 season. In 1981–82* The Middle Ages *came to New York OOB and Circle Rep workshopped* What I Did Last Summer.

In that same season Gurney's first Best Play, The Dining Room, *began a*

511-performance run at Playwrights Horizons on February 24. His second Best Play is The Perfect Party, *also at Playwrights Horizons, this season beginning April 2. In the intervening years, New York has seen his* What I Did Last Summer *for 31 performances in full production at Circle Rep,* The Middle Ages *for 110 performances, both in 1983, and Gurney's only Broadway production to date,* The Golden Age, *suggested by Henry James's* The Aspern Papers, *April 12, 1984 for 29 performances.*

Gurney is also the author of the novels The Gospel According to Joe, Entertaining Strangers *and* The Snow Ball, *and the PBS-TV adaptation of John Cheever's* O Youth and Beauty. *He has been a recipient of Rockefeller and National Endowment grants. He is married, with four children, and lives in New York City.*

The following synopsis of The Perfect Party *was prepared by Sally Dixon Wiener.*

Place: Tony's study

ACT I

SYNOPSIS: The set is a middle-class conventional study with desk, filing cabinet, bookshelves, television, beige couch and armchairs. There are a few plants and some undistinguished prints and the usual family photographs. A videocassette recorder is downstage left on a small table. A lamp table upstage right holds a tray with wine bottle and glasses, and there are bottles and mixers on the desk. There is a door upstage which opens into the study from a hallway that leads to the other rooms of the downstairs of the house. The walls are beige, too, and despite a hand-crocheted afghan that is thrown over the couch and an Oriental rug on the floor, there is a beige-ness to the whole room that seems to have accumulated over the years rather than having been part of some long-forgotten decorating scheme.

> *Tony and Lois enter from the hall. Tony is a good-looking, middle-aged man dressed in a tuxedo. Lois is good-looking and wears an elegant black dress.*

LOIS: I understand you plan to make this a perfect party.

TONY: I certainly plan to try.

> *He goes to a bar which has been set up on top of his desk and begins fixing her a Perrier.*

LOIS: No, no. I'm serious. You announced it as such. You sent out invitations. I brought mine along.

> *She produces an elegant invitation from her purse.*

"Come," you say here, "to a perfect party."

TONY: Did I write that?

LOIS: I believe you did. Unless someone is sending out invitations under your name.

TONY: No, no. I'll admit it. I wrote it. It's just that hearing it read aloud, on the eve of battle, so to speak, makes me a little nervous.
LOIS: I should imagine.
TONY: Washington before Yorktown.
LOIS: Yes.
TONY: Custer before the Little Big Horn.
LOIS: Now, now.
TONY: Well, there are bound to be doubts.
LOIS: But you're still committed, aren't you? You still plan to give it a go?
TONY: Oh yes. Absolutely. All the way.
LOIS: Good. Otherwise I'm wasting my time. And possibly yours.

Tony would like to bring her something stronger than Perrier, but Lois wants to keep her head clear in order to decide whether or not to write about Tony and his party. (Also, because she is from a big New York paper, drinking on the job would go "against the very grain" of her profession.) Tony, however, feels the need of mixing himself a martini. He explains to Lois that the reason the party is Black Tie is that he believes people appear and behave best when wearing evening clothes. Lois is curious to know more about his study. He explains that it once served as a family room, but now the children are grown up.

TONY: Finally, when my wife went to work, and my children left home, I moved my books in here, and turned it totally into my study.
LOIS (sitting on the couch, taking notes from time to time): All that says a great deal about American marriage, and the diminishing role of the male within it.
TONY: I may be diminished, but I'm still indispensable. Here's where I pay a good part of the bills. And here's where I prepare courses on American history and literature, which I teach at a local university.
LOIS: Hence your earlier references to American battles.
TONY: Exactly. (Indicates books in bookcase.) And these are some of the authors I teach: Hawthorne, James, Fitzgerald, Cheever, Updike . . .
LOIS: Of course. I've already noticed some of their themes and rhythms, even in your casual discourse.
TONY: Yes, but I have other strings to my bow. Note over here I also have the complete works of Oscar Wilde, bound in leather.
LOIS: Oscar Wilde?
TONY: I inherited him from my grandmother.
LOIS: The source is immaterial. I'd be careful of Wilde. He's not American, and tends to undermine everything that is.

Lois questions Tony as to whether or not a public relations person mailed the invitation to her office, but Tony assures her he sent it himself, believing it to be newsworthy.

TONY: A perfect party. Well. I think everyone in the world secretly wants to give one. It's at the heart of the social impulse. The caveman calling his fellow tribesman to the fire, the astrophysicist cupping his electronic ear to space—

Above, the cast of *The Perfect Party* by A.R. Gurney Jr.: Debra Mooney as Sally, David Margulies as Wes, Charlotte Moore as Lois, Kate McGregor-Stewart as Wilma and John Cunningham as Tony

we all have this yearning to connect in some ultimate way with our fellow man.

LOIS: Or woman?

TONY: Of course. Sorry.

LOIS: Then would you define a perfect party?

TONY: A perfect party has a perfect shape. It starts, it builds, it crests, it explodes, and when it finally subsides, everyone involved—he who gives it, she who attends—is bathed in the pleasant afterglow of sweet remembrance.

LOIS: You make it sound vaguely sexual.

TONY: Do I? I hope I don't offend.

LOIS: No, no. I like sex, coming as I do from New York. But now I must ask you what we call colloquially the Passover question: namely, why now? Why is this night different from all other nights?

TONY: Well, I'm not getting any younger. I hear the clock ticking away. I've lived a complicated life in a complicated country, and I feel the compulsion to pull it all together in some sort of pattern, some sort of shape, just once, at least for an evening, before I die.

Lois is somewhat affected by Tony's little speech, but whether or not she'll write him up will be determined by the guest list. He hands it to her in an elegant leather folder, which again impresses her. She peruses the different headings: friends from school, from college, from the Navy, from academe—"An awful lot of male bonding," she remarks, but Tony urges her to continue the list which includes old girl friends, young students, recreational friends, sex partners and members of the family. There's also a miscellaneous category that includes a waiter from Buffalo. She's interested in whether he's done ethnic or demographic breakdowns of his guest list. Tony doesn't believe in the quota system, but he has tried, racially and regionally, for a full range of diversity, and included also some guests who are unconventionally sexually oriented, a few who are handicapped in one way or another and two registered Republicans.

Lois sees it as a microcosm of the country in the last years of this century and is sufficiently attuned to Tony's thinking to believe that, if the party is a success, then the American sociopolitical experiment could be said to have been a success. What we're talking about is not a party, it's "Whether this nation, or any other nation so constituted, can long endure," she points out to him.

Not only is she going to write him up, she has decided to review him. On the morning following the party, he will have a full-length review, perhaps even a picture as well, in the New York paper. Tony is relieved—he was worried it might be just an announcement, like a wedding or funeral announcement.

Lois confesses to Tony that the arrival of his invitation on her desk gave her an immediate and strong physical reaction because she realized this could be her opportunity to write a perfect review. Her editor told her she would have to write it on spec, however; and because she was paying for her own transportation, she economized by taking Peoples Express. Tony is appreciative of her sacrifice, but Lois believes it was worth it—they were meant to meet and are as dependent on each other as Ahab and the whale in their mutually ambitious pursuits.

A knock on the door interrupts their conversation and Sally, Tony's attractive wife, comes in wearing a becoming blue evening dress and bearing an hors d'oeuvres plate.

SALLY: I was getting bored hanging around in the hall, fussing with flowers, coping with caterers.

TONY (going to greet her): Enter my wife Sally, powdered and perfumed from her bath! Gosh, Sally, you look just about as lovely as a woman of your age and general configuration can possibly look.
    He kisses her.
Darling, this is Lois, who has come all the way from New York to check us out, and write us up.

SALLY: And possibly to put us down, am I right, Lois?

LOIS: Not unless you hurt, confuse, or bore me, Sally.

They shake hands.

SALLY: I'll try to do none of those things. I do hope, however, that somewhere along the line, I'll get a change to express my true feelings.

TONY: Uh-oh.

LOIS: Your true *feelings?* Do you mean to say, Sally, that your true feelings are not in tune with this party, and you are actually, in this day and age, trying to cover them *up?*

SALLY: I'll say no more, though you'll notice how difficult it is for me to maintain eye contact.

Although her ethics forbid her to come between a man and his wife, Lois makes an exception if she senses a story, and she wants Sally to be honest about the party. Sally blandly passes the hors d'oeuvres and says she feels the party is perfect. Lois keeps digging away at it, though, indicating it might affect what she writes. Tony hastily tells Sally that the party could not be "perfect" if she couldn't express her feelings.

It seems Sally doesn't like the party. She hates it, actually—and the mousse, and the Chivas Regal, and also the dress she bought on sale at the shopping mall. The money it cost could have fed some hungry people, bought part of a CAT-scanner or reclaimed some wetlands. Tony is startled at the vehemence of her feelings. Lois feels she might be to blame, as people sometimes overdo a performance for a critic, and suggests that she may leave them and review the mousse, but both Tony and Sally urge her not to go. Sally feels that Lois gives her "a vague sense of sisterhood." Tony says the party couldn't be a perfect one if only the food were reviewed.

SALLY: Shit! There's that expression again. "A perfect party!" What if it isn't perfect, Tony? What if two of your buddy-pals get into a boring argument about batting averages? What if someone spills a drink, or loses his teeth, or puts a cigarette out in a dessert plate?

LOIS: What if someone even *smokes,* for that matter?

SALLY: *Exactly,* Lois. Or what if someone, totally accidentally, farts?

TONY: Good Lord.

SALLY: What if that happens? Does that mean the party is no longer perfect, Tony? Does Lois here go back to New York and tell the world we produced a disaster?

LOIS: Oh well, let's cross that bridge when we come to it.

TONY: I'm sure that Lois will leave some margin for error.

LOIS: Not really. I might if I were from Boston or Saint Louis, but since I'm from New York, I'm compelled to be brutal.

SALLY *(to Tony):* You see? We're setting ourselves up here! I may not be a la-de-da college professor, but I know hubris when I see it. When people start wandering around the house talking about perfect parties, and inviting New York newspapers to write them up, then I get a primitive Sophoclean shudder. We are challenging the gods here tonight, Tony, and I don't like it one iota!

TONY *(to Lois):* Sally majored in Classy Civ at Vassar.
SALLY: Yes, but I got my Master's in Social Responsibility at a Community College.

Tony is urging Sally to have a drink. She refuses, but finally says she will have a Box Car. It's a Depression drink, she explains to Tony, seeming surprised that he wouldn't know how to make one or wouldn't have the right ingredients if he's a "perfect host." Tony slams out, assuring Sally she'll have her perfect drink.

Sally admits to Lois that she doesn't want that drink, she wanted Tony to leave the room, which Lois surmised. Lois agrees to have some wine with Sally. Sally needs to talk to a woman about Tony's obsession, and Lois encourages her. Tony's unreal expectations about parties and his inevitable disappointments have been making life hell. Their marriage is in jeopardy, and Tony's given up his tenured teaching job, even though he was regarded until recently as a good teacher.

LOIS: What happened recently?
SALLY: He tried to turn every class into a perfect class. The students rebelled, of course, and switched into Abnormal Psychology. That's when he quit, so he could turn his total attention to this party.
LOIS: But how does he expect to live, when the party's over?
SALLY: He expects to become a consultant.
LOIS: A consultant?
SALLY: On parties! That's why he brought you into the picture. He desperately wants a review. Because he desperately wants to become a celebrity.
LOIS: But that's what *I* want to be! And there's only room for a few of us at the top!
SALLY: I can't help it. That's what he wants. He says he comes from what was once the ruling class, and if he can no longer lead this nation toward a more perfect union, he can at least show it how to entertain!
LOIS: Yes, but a consultant!
SALLY: I know. He sees himself travelling around the country giving lectures and seminars and workshops on parties in America, and how to give them. The other night he dreamed he was on the Merv Griffin Show.

Sally asks Lois if Tony showed her his list of guests. Sally means his secret list —the people he is hoping will turn up, Abba Eban, for one. Ginger Rogers is another, with whom he might, should she appear, dance to "Follow the Fleet," for which purpose he has purchased the record. Lois sympathizes with Sally for what she's been going through, but Sally's more worried about Tony and his attempt to bridge the gap between how he'd like people to act and how they really do.

Lois tells her that she's glad Sally has told her about these things—woman to woman—but is not pleased when Sally asks her to give Tony a good review. Sally doesn't mean a rave, just something complimentary so he'll have a few quotes to show. Lois refuses, because even though she admits to having affection for Sally, her own future depends on what she writes. Anything that smacks of sham, and she'll be "doomed to cover church suppers and bowling tournaments" even beyond the commuting area. It's the age of narcissism, and she must think of herself.

Sally is getting desperate as Tony returns with the Box Car, a darkish drink with a radish garnish. Sally sips at the drink, then sets it down, insisting that it hasn't agreed with her and that Tony must cancel the party. She must go to bed, and Tony should get a sign on the door that the party has been called off. He should pay off the caterers and call a taxi for Lois and then bring her up some scrambled eggs. Neither Tony nor Lois believe her, so Sally finally gives up and agrees to stand by Tony.

The doorbell rings offstage, even though it's still a bit early for company to arrive. It's Wes and Wilma Wellman, friends and neighbors. *"Wes and Wilma enter awkwardly in old bathrobes. Wilma wears a bandana around her hair."* Wilma is plumpish, and Wes, who is stocky and short, has thinning dark hair. They have come, they explain, to say they can't attend the party. Tony urges them, as they start to leave, to wait to say hello to Lois. Wes and Wilma and Lois exchange the obligatory hellos, and Wilma again starts off, taking Wes by the arm.

WES *(staring at Lois):* Hold it. I know this woman from somewhere.

LOIS: I've slept with a number of men, but I don't think you were one of them.

WES *(moving toward her):* No, this was prior to puberty . . .
    He thinks.
Kindergarten.
    He remembers.
P. S. 101. Brooklyn.

LOIS: You seem to have touched on my educational beginnings, though I like to think I've grown beyond them.

TONY *(hastily):* I'm sure you have, Lois.

WES: You were a strange little girl. You sent out bitter, vindictive valentines to the whole class. And when it came time for the school play—the Teddy Bear's Picnic, I think it was—you sat on the sidelines and loudly complained about the lighting.

TONY: Lois is a critic, Wes. How good to hear that her talents emerged as such an early age.

WILMA: I'm finding it difficult to contribute to the conversation, because I went to private school in the suburbs of Cleveland.

TONY: That's all right, Wilma. Lois is here from New York to write up the party.

LOIS: I am indeed. And I'm already impatient with these sentimental reminiscences. What we were, or did, when we were young is of interest only to our parents and our psychiatrists. What interests *me* is why you two have arrived embarrassingly early and strangely underdressed. This is the time when most people are still in the shower, or poking around in their clothes closets, deciding what to wear and who to be.

WES: That's exactly where we were, five minutes ago.

LOIS: In the shower? Or in the closet?

WILMA *(taking Wes's arm):* In the shower, actually. Both of us. Celebrating the physical side of our marriage.

WES: That's not the point, honey. We have to go.

Tony wants to know the reason they're not coming to the party. Wes and Wilma claim their daughter is having a dance recital and that Wes has a political meeting also. Tony and Sally realize from something Wilma has told them previously that their daughter is not having a dance recital, so Tony believes there's some other reason they're not coming. Wes and Wilma confess that the whole idea of his party has scared them off and they're going to the movies.

WES: We're just simple suburban people, Tony. All right, maybe I'm a urologist with a prestigious appointment at a major medical school . . .

WILMA: And maybe I'm a speech therapist in the local school system, with a strong side interest in ceramics . . .

WES: But still, we're just an ordinary middle-class couple, Tony. And glad to be so.

TONY: No, goddammit! I don't accept that! You guys are easily capable of giving the suburbs a good name!

WES: Oh, hey . . .

TONY: I'm serious. In some ways, you stand for the full flowering of the American dream.

WILMA: Oh now . . .

TONY *(sitting on the arm of the couch):* You do! Your rich ethnic roots, your pleasant home throbbing with the hum of working appliances, your weedless lawn with its well-placed shrubs, your over-educated children—well hell, you folks embody the best of that particular lifestyle, that's all.

Tony is sure Wes and Wilma can rise to the occasion, but they're not sure, even though they've been to their family therapist who has explained to them that their nervousness was caused by their deep-down desperation to be the hit of the party. At the DeVita's party at Christmas, Tony reminds them, they came through. They admit they did. Wilma thinks that maybe if the DeVitas are going to be at Tony's party it might be of some help, but Tony explains that the DeVitas, and another couple, have been asked and decided not to come as they were only to be allowed to stay in a bedroom watching TV and not to try to participate in any discussions. This makes Wilma feel even more pressured.

WES: She's sensitive on these things, Tony. So am I.

TONY: Which is another good reason why I want you guys here! You bring with you a sensitivity which comes from five thousand years of Jewish anxiety.
    A stunned moment.

WILMA: Jewish? You invited us because we were Jewish?

WES: I have a problem with that, Tony.

LOIS: So do I!

SALLY: Yes, Tony! Honestly!
    They all begin to protest noisily.

TONY *(shouting them down):* All I meant was . . . *(They quiet down.)* All I meant was that Wes and Wilma are like the cellos in a Verdi ensemble. They provide a lovely, consistent, melancholy sound under the lighter, more eccentric melodies sung by some of our superficial guests. *(To Wes and Wilma.)* The very fact that you came over here just now, in obvious disarray, to express your concern, says something about your Jewish sense of social responsibility.

The protesting begins again. All talk simultaneously.

SALLY: Worse and worse.

WES: Now I'm feeling vaguely stereotyped.

WILMA: Yes, I'm still having trouble with that, Tony.

LOIS: I'm particularly sensitive, coming as I do from New York . . .

TONY *(shouting them down):* All right, all right! Skip it! But can I count on you two tonight? Will you both go home and change into what I'm sure are particularly fashionable clothes, since you must obviously have relatives in the garment industry.

The loudest protests yet.

Sorry! Really! I'm flailing around here simply because I don't want my cello section to walk out on me right before the opera begins! Now what say, folks? Are you with me or not?

As Wes and Wilma go into private consultation, Tony remarks to Lois that he'll be lost if they go. Lois agrees. Wes and Wilma decide they will come to the party if Tony will allow them not to feel they have to be perfect every minute. Tony accepts their terms. He does add two things to the deal, though—Wilma is not to talk about her children, and Wes is not to talk about Israel. Sally goes off with Wilma and Wes to see them out.

Tony, alone in the study with Lois, comments that she took very little part in the preceding conversation. Something is bothering her, she admits to Tony. It isn't that she doesn't admire what he's attempting, but in between mouthfuls of the hors d'oeuvres he has passed her she tells him she is not going to write about the party after all. She is sorry and tries to explain to herself as well as to Tony her reasoning. It's that there is something missing. There is no "sense of danger."

TONY: Danger?

LOIS: Danger. Every good party has, underneath it, a fundamental sense of danger. And this party has none.

TONY: But I'll have to go back to teaching if it doesn't work.

LOIS: That's frightening, Tony, but it's not frightening enough. If you want this party reviewed, then it's got to be much scarier. Think, for example, of the great parties of history: the revels of Nero during the burning of Rome. The soirées at Versailles under the lengthening shadow of the guillotine. The last frantic dance on the deck of the *Titanic.* Those were dangerous parties, and I'm afraid this can't equal them.

TONY: You're asking for too much, Lois.

LOIS: Maybe I am, but so are you. Oh look, my friend, we're very much alike, you and I. We are born perfectionists. I have struggled out of the polyglot mire of a Brooklyn kindergarten toward the cool, clear vision of some social ideal. You, on the other hand, carry with you the memory of a civilized past gleaned from your corrupt and decadent ancestors. I am moving up. You are moving down.

We have gravitated toward one another all our lives, like two lost planets in search of a sun. There's a tremendous magnetism between us, and if you weren't happily married, I think I'd initiate an affair with you immediately. But there's no danger here, Tony. None. Even a simple birthday party is infused with the sadness of passing time. A wedding is fraught with the perils of sex. A funeral throbs with the ache of last things. Behind the best human gathering is a sense of its own precariousness. We should dance on the edge of the abyss. And that's what I don't sense here, Tony. What is the threat? Where is the pain? It's all cozy and comfortable and polite. In fact, it's so polite, Tony, that you've let me make much too long a speech without interrupting me. It's symptomatic of the whole problem.

TONY: I'll interrupt you now!

LOIS: Yes, but you don't like doing it. You're a nice man with a pretty wife, and from all reports, several fine children. You were born with money, and you married more of it, and you've lived easily all your life. The gods have been good to you, Tony, and it shows . . . . .

To stop Lois as she begins to leave, Tony suggests that he can add some danger, for instance by inviting a neo-Nazi or an escaped convict to the party, or by putting a nuclear device in the basement, but Lois doesn't buy any of this—it would be too contrived, and she would be obliged to say so in the review. As a last-ditch defense, he tells her he has invited his twin brother, Tod, whose nickname is Toad. "German for . . ." Lois says. Yes, Tony tells her, "Death." He describes him as a killer, not a murderer, but a killer of moments, moods. Tony was born first and was a smiling baby. As his parents were celebrating in the recovery room with champagne and getting a telegram off to Yale, his mother gave a shriek, spilling her champagne, and Tod appeared, kicking and screaming.

LOIS: Do you look alike, you and Tod?

TONY: Almost exactly. He, of course, wears a mustache, while I, as you may have noticed, don't. After his birth, he struggled so much against his mother's embrace that she inadvertently dropped him. The infant broke his right leg, which was improperly reset, because he irritated the doctor. The result is that he has a pronounced limp, which gives him a certain Byronic appeal, but makes him a consistently disappointing tennis partner.

LOIS: How sad.

TONY: Yes. He was such an unhappy child that my mother sent him to Sunny Italy for Junior High School. He returned with a book on the Borgias and the permanent speech patterns of a Neapolitan pickpocket.

LOIS: Any other distinguishing characteristics?

TONY: Just one.

LOIS: And what is that?

TONY: He has—(He stops.) Never mind. It's not important. The point is that my brother is, or can be, an ultimately destructive human being. He is in constant competition with me, and everyone else. He has hacked his way through life's dark wood leaving a long, bloody spoor of victims behind him. He has been married at least four times, and divorced only twice. He was expelled from the

THE PERFECT PARTY 275

Teamsters Union and reprimanded by the C.I.A. His conversation is designed to make you thoroughly uncomfortable, and even while he's doing it, you feel he's glancing over your shoulder, seeking out someone else to irritate even more. In short, he is probably the most dangerous person I have ever known, and already I'm having strong second thoughts about inviting him to this party.

LOIS: You said there was another characteristic which distinguished Tod from you.

TONY: Oh well. It's not important, really.

LOIS: Tell me. It might prove to be helpful, later on.

TONY: I thought you were leaving.

LOIS: Frankly, now I'm on the fence. The notion of twins has always had a primitive appeal. It might just work at a party. I'm also intrigued by the mustache and the limp, and the Italian connection is unsettling. So tell me: what else does he have that you don't?

TONY: Well, to put it frankly, Lois, he has a considerably larger penis.
    Long pause.

LOIS: I've decided to stay at this party.

There are offstage party sounds, and Tony must greet his guests. Lois will go with him to look them over and to find out if his brother is there. Tony warns her he might not be coming. Lois asks why and Tony explains, because he was invited. If he were told not to come, he would come. Lois wants very much to meet him. She leaves the room and Tony follows her, simultaneously relieved and dismayed. *Curtain.*

ACT II

The door is open to the empty study, with party sounds offstage. Wes, in a tuxedo, and Wilma, in a long dress, come in. Wes is complaining about Wilma's performance at the party, and she is defending her actions. He closes the door as they continue to argue. Wes feels Wilma was not being responsible when talking to some man at the bar. He was talking about his dog, and Wilma segued into a discussion of their cat, she tells Wes, who is horrified. (Their relationship with their cat is a very private one, it seems.) He berates her for a bad shift in gears onto the subject of urban renewal, but Wilma doesn't think Wes was doing so well at the party, either—slouched on a couch with a Rhode Island man she claims had ravaged his cleaning woman. The mutual recriminations go on until Wes has grabbed Wilma's arm and is twisting it as Sally comes in. They separate, assuring her they were only sparring.

SALLY: Oh God, this party. It doesn't seem to be jelling at all. Everywhere I go, middle-class married couples are bickering irritably over trivial issues. Our younger friends have gone upstairs slamming the door to the guest room, where they smoke dope and listen to loud, shrieking songs, with lyrics which are virtually incomprehensible. To avoid the din, the older folks have congealed in a gloomy corner, where they reminisce about Lawrence Welk and accuse each other of having Alzheimer's disease. Our Black and Hispanic friends, once so full of life, are huddled in sullen groups, discussing social inequities in a vaguely revolutionary tone. The gays and born-agains eye the goings-on with some contempt, depressed with our condition and their own. Even the caterers are losing interest. The bartender plies his trade with cynical abandon, confusing gin with vodka, spilling the bourbon, and stinting on the ice. The miserable maids prowl around the room, offering stale hors d'oeuvres and then snatching them away, before you've even had a chance to grab one. From off in the kitchen come sounds of an angry clatter, and unnecessary breakage, which, I am sure, we will be overcharged for later.

By now, she has collapsed on the couch in despair.

WES: It sounds like an image of America itself.

SALLY: Whatever it is, it is hardly a party, much less a perfect one. And to make things worse, I can't find Tony anywhere. I'm terrified he's doing something desperate.

WILMA: I think I saw him going into the bathroom.

WES: You're not supposed to notice things like that at a party.

WILMA *(furiously to Wes):* Well I *did! (Then to Sally.)* I also noticed that he had with him a small tin of black shoe polish.

Sally stops their bickering and reminds them they are all supposed to be helping Tony, not arguing in the study with that critic poking around out there "like a dental hygienist in a ceaseless search for cavities." Her mood shifts, and she says she's giving up. It's as she's been telling Tony—the only possibility for a social life that is civilized in this country is a few friends and one's family. Wes and Wilma try to comfort Sally, Wes assuring her that almost all parties hit a snag at some point. You can't push or poke a party, it needs stroking.

Sally is also upset because she doesn't know where Tony is, and this is his party.

John Cunningham and Charlotte Moore in a scene from *The Perfect Party*

They remind her that men always are wandering away at parties. Sally gets up from the couch and suggests they all go out and try again. As she opens the door, however, Lois falls in, obviously having been listening, but claiming not to have heard anything. Well, she did hear someone comparing a critic to a dental hygienist. Sally, Wes and Wilma tell Lois they've just been talking about how well the party is going. Wilma asks Lois if she's having fun too, but Lois doesn't choose to pass judgment until all the evidence is in. Sally goes out with Wes and Wilma, and again we hear the party sounds.

> *Lois remains onstage. She takes a compact out of her purse and begins to comb her hair, using the mirror to glance behind her. After a moment, Tod comes in. He wears a tuxedo and looks just like Tony, except that he has a black mustache, slicked-back hair and a pronounced limp. Lois watches him in the mirror as he closes the study door behind him. The party sounds die out.*

TOD (*speaking throughout in a corny Italian accent*): You Lois?

LOIS: I try to be, at least during daylight hours.

TOD: How about at night?

LOIS: Oh well, then I'm the Queen of Rumania.

> *Tod comes farther into the room; he drags his foot behind him in an exaggerated limp.*

A good bit of double and not-double-entendre banter goes on between Lois and Tod before Lois finally tells him that she's on to him and knows that he is at the party to ruin it for his brother. Tod insists he's there to save it, by giving her "such a fucking good time in bed" that she will end up writing a rave review. He plans to do this by first giving her a drink called a Cardinal Sin, which he begins to mix. Then he will sit beside her, caressing her, while one of her hands is holding the drink and the other would be otherwise occupied. He asks her if she gets the picture.

LOIS: I'm afraid I don't, Tod. I mean, here we are in the middle of a party. People are bursting through that door every other minute.

TOD: That's why I'd maneuver you immediately to the master bedroom, under the pretext of showing you pictures of children and dogs.

LOIS: But still, people would come in and out. Visiting the bathroom. Combing their hair. Getting their coats, if the party continues to degenerate.

TOD: We'd solve that problem with Vaseline.

LOIS: Vaseline? Don't be foolish. Vaseline solves many problems, but not that one.

TOD: We'll put it on the doorknob, Lois, rendering it virtually unturnable.

> *He moves toward her again.*

LOIS: You have an answer for everything, don't you?

TOD: I believe I do. Yes.

LOIS: Well I'm still not sure I'd like such a situation, with people banging on the door and rattling the doorknob. I think I'd be distracted.

TOD (*sitting behind her on the back of the couch*): You wouldn't hear a thing,

Lois. And I'll tell you why. Because by that time you would be writhing naked on the bed, among the furs and Burberrys, emitting a series of wild exuberant love cries, ending in a veritable Vesuvian eruption of delight. People will be running for cover, Lois. You'll be scattering red hot lava over a relatively large area. And then, while you're still smouldering, maybe smoking occasionally but temporarily inactive, I'm going to take you into the bathroom, and give you a bath, and anoint your erogenous zones with Oil of Olay. And then dial your editor in New York, and hand you the telephone, and you're going to say into that phone, "Truly this was a perfect party, and I'm mighty glad I came."

There is a pause before Lois opines that Tod thinks she can be bought (he does). She thinks, however, that he's been talking this way to try to shock her, that he wants her to turn down the drink, resist his advances, leave the room and give the party a bad review, but it's not going to work out that way. She orders him to give her the drink at once. (It's a strange-looking bubbly red concoction that's giving off smoke, the Cardinal Sin, and she drinks it down without stopping.) She gets up, ready for action, and wants him to understand she will still be judging the evening with a clear eye. As he takes hold of her and is kissing her, Sally comes in. Sally apologizes, saying she thought he was her husband. Tod says he's Tony's twin brother, and Sally leaves.

After a brief interchange, Lois leaves, and Tony, first finishing the drink that's left in the cocktail shaker, follows after her, remembering to limp.

A moment or so later, Wes comes into the room with Wilma and is kissing her after he's closed the door. Wes tells Wilma she has been fantastic at the party. She praises his efforts also, hugging him and telling him she is eager to share the experience with their children. Wes has a different idea. He is all for going home and getting their cat to show to everyone at the party. Wilma feels she must veto this on the grounds that it could provide only a brief conversational interlude, as it doesn't talk. "Thank God," Wes says, and they are both laughing over this as Sally comes in again. The party sounds are heard once more before she hurriedly closes the door in a state of excitement. It's cresting, she tells them.

SALLY: It's amazing. Everything is suddenly coming together. It's as if somewhere someone had pulled a switch, and a huge gravitational force had come into play. It's like the beginning of civilization itself, if I remember my courses at Vassar correctly. First, there was this man, I don't even remember who he was, who sat down at the piano and started idly fiddling with the keys. Then others began to gather around. A chord was sounded. A tune emerged. Someone began to sing. And then, as if out of nowhere, people produced other musical instruments. Harps . . . xylophones . . . Moog Synthesizers . . . And now!—Well, let's listen, and see how far they've come:
> She opens the door. From offstage we hear the huge sounds of the Mormon Tabernacle Choir—full orchestra and chorus—singing the "Battle Hymn of the Republic." A rich romantic light and an exotic fog spill into the study as the three stagger back, amazed.
VOICES (off): ". . . His Truth is marching on! Glory, Glory Halleluia! Glory, Glory Halleluia! Glory, Glory Halleluia! His Truth is marching on!"

Sally, Wes and Wilma pick up glasses, trays, ice buckets as cymbals, triangles and drums. They march around the room, ending in a wild display of sympathetic enthusiasm. Finally, Sally closes the door and the sounds stop.

SALLY: See?

WILMA *(wet-eyed, hugging her):* It's a good party, Sally.

WES: A very good party indeed.

Remarking that the party is unlikely to top this musical happening and thus will probably end soon, Sally exits, closing the door. Wes wonders if he should get their coats, but Wilma supposes Tony will want them to stay for a post-mortem discussion of the party. They cuddle up on the couch comfortably and have their own post-mortem. Wes isn't sure they didn't need to trim their lines a bit at the party, for instance while he was discussing the urethra's function. Wilma thought his discussion lyrical, but Wes may rework it for another party; and, by the way, he thinks Wilma might think about the joke about her mother. She refuses to consider changing it, claiming you can ruin a thing if you tinker with it.

Lois comes in, and before she closes the door the offstage sounds give every indication that people are leaving the party. Lois is looking for her purse and has the marks of a black mustache on her upper lip. Wilma is surprised to see her, having assumed she had left some time ago, but Lois says she was upstairs.

Lois seats herself, rather carefully, to powder her nose, she notes the mustache marks and powders them up. She is not one to leave before the bitter end, she says, and Wes hopes that expression doesn't indicate any feelings of hers about the party. She answers in an oblique fashion, which doesn't give them any clue to her reactions.

Lois is saying goodnight to Wes and Wilma—"You were interesting minor characters"—as Tony enters. Lois is taken aback as he speaks, then composes herself, saying she thought he was someone else (his twin brother, Tony assumes). Lois says she did meet him. Wilma is surprised to hear that Tony has a twin, but Tony tosses that off, saying that he doesn't broadcast it.

Lois is curious as to whether or not Tony's brother is still at the party, but Tony saw him going off. Lois seems relieved and doesn't want to see Tony's brother again. And she must leave, because of her deadline. She refuses Tony's offer to see her to the door. Sally will be there, she's sure, but she does ask Tony to tell his brother, should he see him, to read the review.

When Sally returns, the guests having all departed, Tony is worrying. He asks her if Lois had anything to say as she left, and Sally reports that she had a furrowed brow but "a Mona Lisa smile." And she'd also told Sally that she had been asked to do a capsule review on local television at 11:27. It's almost that time, and they turn the set on.

TONY: Oh God! She'll say it was terrible! She'll say the food was bad, and the drinks were worse, and the company impossible!

SALLY: Ssshh.

They all watch the screen intently.

TV ANNOUNCER'S VOICE: And now Lois Lumkin, our guest entertainment critic from New York, will tell us where she's been and what she thought of it.
> *The lights come up on Lois's actual face, framed in the TV.*

LOIS (*brightly*): Thanks, Bruce . . . Tonight's party causes me to feel emotions as mixed as its guest list. The basic idea—that someone would set out to give a perfect party—is far-fetched but engaging.
> *Everyone reacts enthusiastically.*

The execution is something else again. It sputters where it should sparkle, and fizzles where it should dazzle.
> *Everyone looks glum.*

Perhaps I'll elaborate on these thoughts tomorrow in a major New York newspaper. Meanwhile, let me simply assign it a Seven . . .

SALLY: Seven's not bad . . .

LOIS: On a scale of seventeen . . .

TONY: Oh Good Lord . . .

LOIS: And I had serious reservations about the lighting.

TONY: The *lighting?*

TV ANNOUNCER'S VOICE: Seen one party, seen 'em all, right, Lois?
> *Lois laughs charmingly.*

SALLY: Turn that thing off.
> *Tony slams shut the cabinet cutting off Lois in mid-laugh.*

All three try to comfort Tony, who believes the whole world is going to know shortly that his party was a flop. It would be even worse, though, if Lois didn't review it at all. That would be being ignored!

Wes and Wilma decide to leave them to deal with their humiliation. Sally begins to clean up as Tony rants on and on (Sally saying nothing) about critics, about probably having to go back to teaching at some high school, and about this affecting Sally also. He imagines she'll lose her hospital job and have to end up selling software in a shopping center. Sally disposes of the guest list in the waste basket, and Tony urges her repeatedly to say he deserves this, but she won't. He wonders if she'll leave him. She might, Sally says, depending on how he answers a question—"Namely, where is thy brother?"

Sally won't believe Tony has a brother. She points out the obvious, that Tony made him up in desperation to try to save the party—with a shoe-polish mustache, a limp and an accent. She has another question for him, too.

SALLY: This is simply a corollary to the first. Namely: did you or did you not copulate with that critic?

TONY: I . . .

SALLY: Yes or no.

TONY: I copulated.

SALLY: Thought so. You left your guests, you went upstairs, you put Vaseline on the doorknob, which was an old trick we used when the children were younger, and then you proceeded to have sexual relations with a woman who writes for the Arts and Leisure section of one of the finest newspapers in the entire free world.

TONY: That's all true.

SALLY: Jesus, Tony! How hungry you must have been for success!

TONY: I was. And I suppose it's no excuse to say that all Americans are.

LOIS: None at all.

TONY: I didn't think so.

SALLY: One final question.

TONY: Sally . . .

SALLY: Now this is a crucial question, and I have to put it carefully. When Lois, on television, implied that this party was disappointing, was she also referring to your sexual performance?

     Long pause.

TONY: Yes.

SALLY: I thought so.

Again Tony wants to know if Sally plans to leave him, and if so, is she planning to take the VCR? She tells him not to jump the gun, possibly one of his problems when he was upstairs with Lois.

Sally is thinking, trying to put it together, but finds concentrating difficult, juggling the things that have happened during the evening. She starts to find a pattern in it all. She would like to explore it with Tony before she decides whether or not to stay married to him. Tony agrees to do so.

SALLY: Now bear with me, love. It seems to me that your attempt to achieve social perfection in the living room is echoed in your attempt to achieve sexual perfection in the bedroom.

TONY: Hmmm.

SALLY: But that's just the tip of the iceberg. This impulse to control, to shape, to achieve perfection permeates the fabric of this country. For example, I think it's indicative of what's wrong with American theater.

TONY: American theater?

SALLY: And American sports. And American foreign policy, where we are attempting to impose some ideal shape on the Middle East, Central America, and Southeast Asia.

TONY: Good God, that's true.

SALLY: I think it is. In other words, you could, in a sense, say that America itself, in its middle age, is trying to give a perfect party, at home and abroad.

TONY: I never looked at things that way before.

SALLY: Well, look at them that way now. Because what we're really talking about is sexual, social, cultural and political *imperialism,* on a large and general scale!

TONY: Good Lord.

SALLY: And it doesn't *work,* Tony. It doesn't work in the bedroom, and it doesn't work outside. That's why Lois walked out of here so bitterly disappointed. And why our embassies are being attacked all over the world. And why the Yankees can't seem to win the pennant.

TONY: So in other words, all I've done tonight is take American idealism and reveal it for the dark, destructive dream it really is.

SALLY: I'm afraid that's the long and the short of it, darling.

TONY: What a grim vision, Sally. You've opened up an abyss. It seems that a party is just a power trip.

SALLY: At least your kind of party is, my love.

Tony is imagining that Sally could be going away with a Third World emissary, taking up alternative theater or going in for ambivalent sexuality, all of which and more she says she's considered but decided against. He knows now that he is a middle-aged fool, he concedes, loaded with "18th century ideals, 19th century impulses and 20th century despair," a wife-betrayer who has embarrassed the family and annoyed the critics. What will happen to him now that he has lost his illusions? he wonders.

The doorbell rings, and Sally tells him that is his answer. His friends are coming back, she explains, only this party will be hers.

SALLY: There will be no attempt to make this party perfect. There will be no shaping or judging or interrupting unless someone gets physically violent or is obviously misinformed. You will simply go among your friends and take them for what they are. There won't even be a caterer. Everyone is bring over various ethnic dishes and has promised to help clean up afterwards.

       Tony crosses to door, opens it, looks out. We hear the sounds of noisy chatter and rock music: "Burning Down the House" by the Talking Heads.

TONY: It could turn into chaos, out there.

SALLY: That's the chance you'll have to take.

TONY: Do you mean to tell me that in that random and noisy disorder lies the future of America?

SALLY: I suppose you could say that.

       Tony closes the door and returns to her.

TONY: I'm not sure I can live with that much ambiguity.

SALLY: You'll have to try.

TONY: But what about our personal life, Sally? Will you ever forgive me?

SALLY: Tony: you've done some terrible things tonight. You've compromised your marriage by fornicating with a first-string reviewer. You've compromised your esthetic sensibilities by putting foul language into the mouth of a fake twin brother. Furthermore, by inventing this brother, you went against everyone's advice and imitated Oscar Wilde. There are many wives, I'm sure, who would be thoroughly fed up. But I'm not, Tony. Through all your foolishness, I somehow sense a fundamental yearning to create a vital human community in this impossible land of ours. And so I forgive you.

Tony kisses Sally and thanks her. Wes and Wilma come into the study, calling to them to come. Even Lois appears, with a big container of fried chicken, ready to re-review everything from a new perspective. There is cheering, and the party sounds grow louder as they go in. *Curtain.*

Special Citation

○○○
○○○
○○○
○○○
○○○
○○○ **GOBLIN MARKET**

A Full-Length Musical in One Act

ADAPTED FROM THE POEM BY **CHRISTINA ROSSETTI** BY **PEGGY HARMON AND POLLY PEN**

MUSIC BY **POLLY PEN**

Cast and credits appear on page 362

PEGGY HARMON (co-adaptor) is the daughter of an Episcopal minister. She was born in Boston in 1953, attended high school in Rochester, N.Y. after her family moved there and graduated B.A. from Brown University in 1975. Her career in the theater has been principally as a performer (she has been playing Susan Wilkes and other roles in the Broadway musical Big River *since its opening last season), and* Goblin Market *is her authorship debut. With her collaborator Polly Pen she adapted it from the narrative poem* Goblin Market *by Christina Rossetti (with excerpts from other works by Rossetti, Theodore Baker, Christopher Morgenstern and John Gay) "as a performance piece, to create something exciting for myself." But when it came time to put it on the stage—first OOB at the Vineyard Theater and then off Broadway April 13, 1986, a specially cited Best Play, directed by Andre Ernotte—she felt it advisable to retain her objectivity in production and not take one of the roles herself. Mrs. Harmon lives in New York City with her husband*

283

Richard, a scenery and lighting designer, and their two-year-old daughter Amanda, and she continues in the cast of Big River.

POLLY PEN (composer, co-adaptor) was born in Chicago March 11, 1954, an artist's daughter educated in Chicago schools and at Ithaca College, graduating in 1976 with a B.A. in English. From the age of ten, however, she had demonstrated a practical interest in music, both composing and giving piano performances, and she "sort of minored" in music at college. She has since been occupied as a musical director, musician (on the piano and other instruments), performer (notably as Skitzy in Charlotte Sweet *and the White Rabbit in* Once on a Summer's Day) *on Broadway, off Broadway and in numerous regional and repertory theaters.* Goblin Market *is her first Best Play but not her first composition for the theater. Her original scores and arrangements have included* The Gilded Cage *for the Production Company and the Denver Center for the Arts,* Out of Our Father's House *at the Michael Bennett Workshop Theater,* Incidents *for the Johanna Boyce Dance Company,* A Winter's Tale *for Theater-at-Monmouth and* The Lady's Not for Burning *for Equity Library Theater. Miss Pen's* Goblin Market *score interpolates excerpts from works of Antonio Lotti, Johannes Brahms and Charles Ives. She lives in New York City.*

*As the musical dramatization of a poem—setting lines of poetry to music, together with original material—*Goblin Market *doesn't fit any ordinary category of stage literature. Therefore we recognize its exceptional achievement with a special citation for excellence in musical composition, adaptation and performance (which latter doesn't usually enter into our consideration for Best Play selection). Unfortunately, we can't represent the sound of the show's music here in these pages, but we pay tribute to the text and performances with three excerpts from the script (selected by the authors) and a Carol Rosegg photo of the two actresses in a scene from the musical.*

GOBLIN MARKET: The story is of two sisters, Laura and Lizzie, who, as adults, return to their childhood nursery. Through the strength of their memories they go back in time to the imaginary world they created in adolescence. It is a shadowy world filled with goblin men who are alternately seductive and threatening. While Laura eagerly embraces the excitement and tastes the fruits that the goblins offer, Lizzie, more beset by fears, resists them. The conflicts that arise from their differing attitudes are ultimately resolved, and the sisters are reunited.

★ ★ ★

LIZZIE:
>   Evening by evening
>   Among the brookside rushes,
>   Laura bowed her head to hear
>   The call of goblin men;

LAURA:

    Lizzie veiled her blushes:
    Crouching close together
    In the cooling weather,

LIZZIE:

    With clasping arms and cautioning lips,
    With tingling cheeks and finger tips.
       Pause. They listen to the wind.

LAURA:

    Lizzie covered up her eyes,
    Covered close lest they should look;

LIZZIE:

    Laura reared her glossy head,
    And whispered like the restless brook:

LAURA:

    Look, Lizzie, look, Lizzie,
    Down the glen tramp little men.

★ ★ ★

LAURA:

    Oh, Lizzie, I cannot hear the goblins—

LIZZIE:

    But Laura, I hear their fruit call,
    Though I dare not look:
    You should not loiter long at this brook:
    Come with me home.

LAURA:

    No! I cannot see the goblins
    Racing, whisking, tumbling, hobbling;
    Nor hear the herds
    That used to tramp along the glen,
    In groups or single,
    Of brisk fruit-merchant men.
    Have I gone deaf and blind?

LIZZIE:

    The stars rise, the moon bends her arc,
    Each glowworm winks her spark,
    Let us get home before the night grows dark.

LAURA:

    Melons, icy cold.
    Plums on their mother twigs,
    Peaches with a velvet nap,
    Cherries, worth getting,
    Figs . . .
    Will I never again buy such wond'rous fruit?

LIZZIE *(to audience):*

    Laura turned cold as stone

Terri Klausner as Laura and Ann Morrison as Lizzie in the
musical *Goblin Market* by Peggy Harmon and Polly Penn

To find I heard that cry alone,
That goblin cry,
"Come buy our fruits, come buy."

★ ★ ★

LIZZIE and LAURA *(sing "Passing Away"):*
Passing away, saith the world,
Passing away:
Chances, beauty and youth
Sapped day by day:
Passing away, saith the world,
Passing away:
Thy life never continueth in one stay.
Is the eye waxen dim,
Is the dark hair changing to grey?
I shall clothe myself in spring
And bud in May.
Passing away.

> *Another morning, Laura is sitting motionless. Lizzie is trying to do her
> daily chores. She's clearly anxious about Laura.*

LAURA:
>   Tender Lizzie could not bear
>   To watch my sad and cankerous care
>   Yet not to share.
>   She night and morning
>   Caught the goblins' cry:
>   "Come buy our orchard fruits,
>   Come buy, come buy:"—
>   Beside the brook, along the glen
>   Lizzie heard the tramp of goblin men,
>   The voice and stir
>   That I so strained to hear;
>   She longed to buy the fruit I craved
>   But feared to pay too dear.
>   She thought of Jeanie in her grave,
>   Who should have been a bride;
>   But who for joys brides hope to have
>   Fell sick and died
>   In her gay prime,
>   In earliest winter time,
>   With the first snow-fall of crisp
>   Winter time.
>
>   Seeing how I dwindled
>   Nearly knocking at Death's door:
>   Lizzie pondered no more;
>   But put a silver penny in her purse,
>   Kissed me, crossed the heath with clumps of furze
>   At twilight, halted by the brook:

LIZZIE:
>   And for the first time in my life,
>   I began to listen and to look.

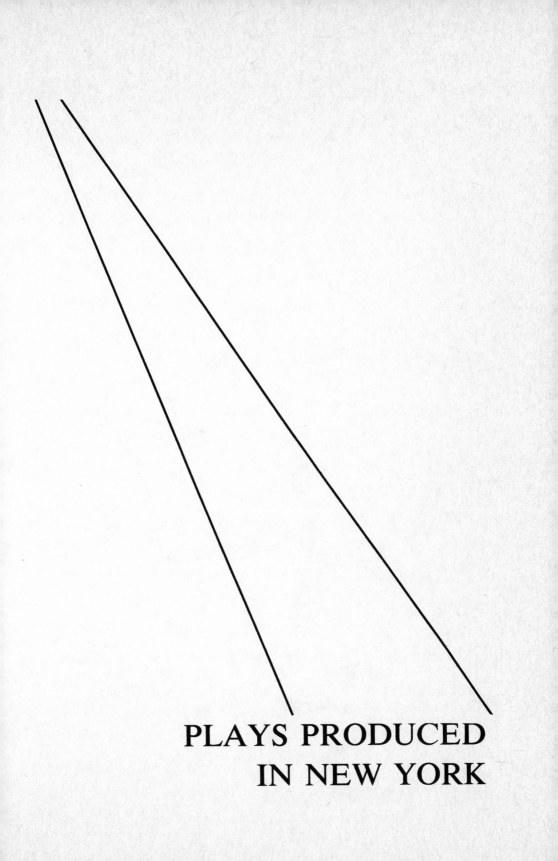

PLAYS PRODUCED
IN NEW YORK

PLAYS PRODUCED ON BROADWAY

Figures in parentheses following a play's title give number of performances. These figures are acquired directly from the production offices and do not include previews or extra nonprofit performances. In the case of a transfer, the off-Broadway run is noted but not added to the figure in parentheses.

Plays marked with an asterisk (*) were still running on June 2, 1986. Their number of performances is figured through June 1, 1986.

In a listing of a show's numbers—dances, sketches, musical scenes, etc.—the titles of songs are identified wherever possible by their appearance in quotation marks (").

HOLDOVERS FROM PREVIOUS SEASONS

Plays which were running on June 1, 1985 are listed below. More detailed information about them appears in previous *Best Plays* volumes of appropriate years. Important cast changes since opening night are recorded in the Cast Replacements section of this volume.

*A Chorus Line (4,504; longest run in Broadway history). Musical conceived by Michael Bennett; book by James Kirkwood and Nicholas Dante; music by Marvin Hamlisch; lyrics by Edward Kleban. Opened April 15, 1975 off Broadway where it played 101 performances through July 13, 1975; transferred to Broadway July 25, 1975.

*Oh! Calcutta! (4,248). Revival of the musical devised by Kenneth Tynan; with contributions (in this version) by Jules Feiffer, Dan Greenberg, Lenore Kandel, John Lennon, Jacques Levy, Leonard Melfi, David Newman & Robert Benton, Sam Shepard, Clovis Trouille, Kenneth Tynan and Sherman Yellen; music and lyrics (in this version) by Robert Dennis, Peter Schickele and Stanley Walden; additional music by Stanley Walden and Jacques Levy. Opened September 24, 1976 in alternating performances with *Me and Bessie* through December 7, 1976, continuing alone thereafter.

*42nd Street (2,405). Musical based on the novel by Bradford Ropes; book by Michael Stewart and Mark Bramble; music and lyrics by Harry Warren and Al Dubin; other lyrics by Johnny Mercer and Mort Dixon. Opened August 25, 1980.

Dreamgirls (1,522). Musical with book and lyrics by Tom Eyen; music by Henry Krieger. Opened December 20, 1981. (Closed August 11, 1985)

*Cats (1,521). Musical based on *Old Possum's Book of Practical Cats* by T.S. Eliot; music by Andrew Lloyd Webber; additional lyrics by Trevor Nunn and Richard Stilgoe. Opened October 7, 1982.

Brighton Beach Memoirs (1,530). By Neil Simon. Opened March 27, 1983. (Closed May 11, 1986)

*La Cage aux Folles (1,161). Musical based on the play *La Cage aux Folles* by Jean Poiret; book by Harvey Fierstein; music and lyrics by Jerry Herman. Opened August 21, 1983.

The Tap Dance Kid (669). Musical based on the novel *Nobody's Family Is Going to Change* by Louise Fitzhugh; book by Charles Blackwell; music by Henry Krieger; lyrics by Robert Lorick. Opened December 21, 1983. (Closed August 11, 1985)

Sunday in the Park With George (604). Musical with book by James Lapine; music and lyrics by Stephen Sondheim. Opened May 2, 1984. (Closed October 13, 1985)

Hurlyburly (343). By David Rabe. Opened June 21, 1984 off Broadway where it played 45 performances through July 29, 1984; transferred to Broadway August 7, 1984. (Closed June 2, 1985)

Ma Rainey's Black Bottom (275). By August Wilson. Opened October 11, 1984. (Closed June 9, 1985)

The King and I (191). Revival of the musical based on the novel *Anna and the King of Siam* by Margaret Landon; book and lyrics by Oscar Hammerstein II; music by Richard Rodgers. Opened January 7, 1985. (Closed June 30, 1985)

Joe Egg (102). Revival of the play by Peter Nichols. Opened January 6, 1985 off Broadway where it played 34 performances through February 3, 1985; transferred to Broadway March 27, 1985. (Closed June 23, 1985)

*Biloxi Blues (492). By Neil Simon. Opened March 28, 1985.

Leader of the Pack (120). Musical with music and lyrics by Ellie Greenwich and others; liner notes by Anne Beatts; additional material by Jack Heifner; based on an original concept by Melanie Mintz. Opened April 8, 1985. (Closed July 21, 1985)

Grind (79). Musical with book by Fay Kanin; music by Larry Grossman; lyrics by Ellen Fitzhugh. Opened April 16, 1985. (Closed June 22, 1985)

*Big River: The Adventures of Huckleberry Finn (474). Musical based on the novel by Mark Twain; book by William Hauptman; music and lyrics by Roger Miller. Opened April 25, 1985.

Aren't We All? (96). Revival of the play by Frederick Lonsdale. Opened April 29, 1985. (Closed July 21, 1985)

As Is (285). By William M. Hoffman. Opened March 10, 1985 off Broadway for 49 performances through April 21, 1985; transferred to Broadway May 1, 1985. (Closed January 4, 1986)

Doubles (277). By David Wiltse. Opened May 8, 1985. (Closed January 4, 1986)

Arms and the Man (109). Revival of the play by George Bernard Shaw. Opened May 30, 1985. (Closed September 1, 1985)

PLAYS PRODUCED JUNE 1, 1985—MAY 31, 1986

The Odd Couple (295). New version of the play by Neil Simon. Produced by Emanuel Azenberg, Wayne M. Rogers and The Shubert Organization at the Broadhurst Theater. Opened June 11, 1985. (Closed February 23, 1986)

THE ODD COUPLE—Rita Moreno and Sally Struthers in a scene from a new version of the comedy by Neil Simon

Sylvie	Jenny O'Hara	Olive Madison	Rita Moreno
Mickey	Mary Louise Wilson	Florence Ungar	Sally Struthers
Renee	Kathleen Doyle	Manolo Costazuela	Lewis J. Stadlen
Vera	Marilyn Cooper	Jesus Costazuela	Tony Shalhoub

Standbys: Misses Struthers, O'Hara, Cooper, Wilson, Moreno—Audrie Neenan; Messrs. Stadlen, Shalhoub—David Ardao; Misses Doyle, Cooper, O'Hara, Wilson, Struthers—Lola Powers.

Directed by Gene Saks; scenery, David Mitchell; costumes, Ann Roth; lighting, Tharon Musser; production stage manager, Martin Gold; stage manager, Bonnie Panson; press, Bill Evans & Associates, Sandra Manley, Jim Baldassare.

Time: The present. Place: Olive Madison's Riverside Drive apartment. Act I: A hot summer's night. Act II, Scene 1: Two weeks later, about 11 P.M. Scene 2: A few days later, about 8 P.M. Scene 3: The next evening, about 7:30 P.M.

Revision of *The Odd Couple* to accommodate two women instead of two men in the leading roles. The comedy's original version was first produced on Broadway 3/10/65 for 964 performances and was named a Best Play of its season. This is its first major New York revival.

Jenny O'Hara replaced Rita Moreno 8/18/85; Rita Moreno replaced Jenny O'Hara 9/8/85; Brenda Vaccaro replaced Rita Moreno 11/19/85.

Singin' in the Rain (367). Musical based on the M-G-M film; screenplay and adaptation by Betty Comden and Adolph Green; songs by Nacio Herb Brown and Arthur Freed. Produced by Maurice Rosenfield, Lois F. Rosenfield and Cindy Pritzker, Inc. at the Gershwin Theater. Opened July 2, 1985. (Closed May 18, 1986)

Dora Bailey	Melinda Gilb	Roscoe Dexter	Richard Fancy
Cosmo Brown	Peter Slutsker	Rod	Robert Radford
Lina Lamont	Faye Grant	Kathy Selden	Mary D'Arcy
Don Lockwood	Don Correia	Sid Phillips;	
R.F. Simpson	Hansford Rowe	Ticket Taker	Martin Van Treuren

Phoebe Dinsmore .... Jacque Dean   Sound Engineer .... John Spalla
Diction Coach;   Zelda Zanders .... Mary Ann Kellogg
A Warner Brother .... Austin Colyer

Cast in film sequences *The Royal Rascal:* Philippe, Pierre (Don Lockwood)—Don Correia; Jeanette, Yvonne (Lina Lamont)—Faye Grant; Enemies of the King ("Talking Picture Demonstration") —Ray Benson, Craig Frawley, Gene Sager, Martin Van Treuren; Man on Screen ("The Duelling Cavalier," "The Dancing Cavalier")—John Spalla; Lady in Waiting—Cynthia Thole; Ladies of the Court—Diane Duncan, Alison Mann, Barbara Moroz; Manservant—Gene Sager; Villain—Martin Van Treuren.

Ensemble: Ray Benson, Richard Colton, Austin Colyer, Jacque Dean, Diane Duncan, Yvonne Dutton, Craig Frawley, Mark Frawley, Melinda Gilb, Katie Glasner, Barbara Hoon, David-Michael Johnson, Mary Ann Kellogg, Raymond Kurshals, Alison Mann, Barbara Moroz, Kevin O'Day, Robert Radford, Tom Rawe, Gene Sager, John Spalla, Amy Spencer, Cynthia Thole, Martin Van Treuren, Shelley Washington, Laurie Williamson.

Swing Performers: David Askler, Cheri Butcher, Brad Moranz, Christina Saffran.

Understudies: Mr. Correia—Ray Benson; Miss D'Arcy—Christina Saffran, Cynthia Thole; Mr. Slutsker—Brad Moranz; Miss Grant—Barbara Moroz; Mr. Rowe—Austin Colyer; Mr. Fancy—John Spalla.

Directed and choreographed by Twyla Tharp; original choreography by Gene Kelly and Stanley Donen; musical direction, Robert Billig; scenery, Santo Loquasto; costumes, Ann Roth; lighting, Jennifer Tipton; sound, Sound Associates; film sequences, Gordon Willis; music supervision and arrangements, Stanley Lebowsky; orchestrations, Larry Wilcox; associate producer, Eugene V. Wolsk; production stage manager, Steven Zweigbaum; stage manager, Arturo E. Porazzi; press, Shirley Herz Associates, Peter Cromarty, Pete Sanders.

Stage version of the 1952 movie about Hollywood in the 1920s in transition from silents to talking pictures, previously produced at the Palladium in London 7/1/83 for 894 performances.

ACT I

Part I: The premiere of *The Royal Rascal*
  Scene 1: Grauman's Chinese Theater at the Premiere, September 1927
  Scene 2: Altoona, Pa.—a vaudeville theater, ten years earlier
    "Fit as a Fiddle"... Don, Cosmo
  Scene 3: Grauman's Chinese Theater, onstage and backstage, at the premiere
  Scene 4: Hollywood Boulevard, later that evening
    "Beautiful Girl" .... Don, Fans
  Scene 5: The Coconut Grove party after the premiere
    "I've Got a Feelin' You're Foolin' "................ Kathy, Coconut Grove Coquettes
Part II: The studios of Monumental Pictures
  Scene 6: Silent stage, Oct. 7, 1927
    "Make 'Em Laugh" .... Cosmo
    "Hub Bub": Cosmo, Studio Stage Hands (Richard Colton, Mark Frawley, Raymond Kurshals, Kevin O'Day, Robert Radford, Tom Rawe; music by Stanley Lebowsky)
  Scene 7: Shooting *The Duelling Cavalier,* a silent film
  Scene 8: An empty sound stage
    "You Stepped Out of a Dream" .... Kathy
      (lyric by Gus Kahn)
    "You Are My Lucky Star" .... Don, Kathy
  Scene 9: Diction lessons
    "Moses Supposes"... Don, Cosmo
      (music by Roger Edens, lyric by Betty Comden and Adolph Green)
  Scene 10: Shooting *The Duelling Cavalier* as a talking picture
Part III: Conversion of *The Duelling Cavalier* to a musical
  Scene 11: The Glendale Theater, sneak preview of *The Duelling Cavalier* as a talking picture, January 1928
  Scene 12: Don's house, later that evening
    "Good Mornin' " .... Don, Kathy, Cosmo

Scene 13: A street near Kathy's house
"Singin' in the Rain" .... Don

ACT II

Scene 1: Filming musical numbers at Warner Brothers Studio
"Wedding of the Painted Doll": Diane Duncan, Yvonne Dutton, Katie Glasner, Kevin
        O'Day, Amy Spencer, Cynthia Thole
"Rag Doll": Richard Colton, Barbara Hoon, Raymond Kurshals
"Temptation": Singer—Melinda Gilb; Dancers—Mary Ann Kellogg, Robert Radford, Shelley
        Washington
"Takin' Miss Mary to the Ball": Singers—Ray Benson, Alison Mann; Dancing Horse—Mark
        Frawley, Tom Rawe (lyric by Edward Heymann)
"Love Is Where You Find It" .... Ensemble
    (lyric by Gus Kahn)
Scene 2: Monumental Pictures' recording studio (a) the next day (b) later that week
"Would You?" .... Kathy
Scene 3: Title production number in *The Dancing Cavalier*
"Broadway Rhythm" .... Company
"Blue Prelude" .... Company
    (music by Al Bishop; lyric by Gordon Jenkins)
Court at Frolic: Ray Benson, Richard Colton, Katie Glasner, Mark Frawley, Barbara Hoon,
        Mary Ann Kellogg, Raymond Kurshals, Robert Radford, Tom Rawe, Amy
        Spencer, Cynthia Thole, Shelley Washington
Apache Dancers: Richard Colton, Yvonne Dutton, Katie Glasner, Barbara Hoon, Mary Ann
        Kellogg, Raymond Kurshals, Kevin O'Day, Tom Rawe, Amy Spencer
Peasants: Austin Colyer, Jacque Dean, Craig Frawley, Melinda Gilb, David-Michael John-
        son, John Spalla
Ladies of the Court: Diane Duncan, Alison Mann, Barbara Moroz
Savate Fighters: Ray Benson, Raymond Kurshals
Other Characters: Pierre—Don Lockwood; Manservant—Gene Sager; Villain—Martin Van
        Treuren; Chanteuse—Laurie Williamson; Danseuse—Shelley Washington
Scene 4: Grauman's Chinese Theater, the premiere of *The Dancing Cavalier*
"Would You" (Reprise) .... Kathy
"You Are My Lucky Star" (Reprise) .... Don, Kathy, Company
"Singin' in the Rain" (Reprise) .... Company

The Grand Kabuki. Repertory of two Kabuki programs in the Japanese language. **Shibaraku** (Just a Moment), **Tachi Nusu-bito** (The Sword Thief), **Kojo** (Name-Taking Ceremony) and **Kasane** (7). Opened July 8, 1985. **Sakura-hime Azuma Bunsho** (The Scarlet Princess of Edo) and **Tsuchi-gumo** (The Earth Spider) (7). Opened July 12, 1985. Produced by the Metropolitan Opera Association in association with Mazda in the Grand Kabuki productions, Onoe Shoroku II artistic director, Takeomi Nagayama chairman of the Grand Kabuki tour, at the Metropolitan Opera. (Repertory closed July 20, 1985)

Principal Actors: Onoe Shoroku II (Living National Treasure), Ichikawa Danjuro XII, Kataoka Takao, Bando Yasosuke V, Ichikawa Ginnosuke, Kataoka Kamezo IV, Onoe Sakon, Onoe Tatsunosuke, Bando Tamasaburo V, Ichikawa Sadanji IV, Nakamura Shibajaku VII, Ichikawa Unosuke III, Kataoka Juzo VI, Kataoka Takataro.
Actors: Nakamura Mannojo, Onoe Karoku, Onoe Juko, Onoe Rokusaburo, Bando Yakichi, Onoe Rokuya, Kataoka Kojiro, Kataoka Matsusaburo, Ichikawa Sasho, Ishikawa Masuju, Kataoka Matsunosuke, Ichikawa Masusuke, Onoe Tatsuo, Bando Minomushi, Ichikawa Shinji, Bando Tamayuki, Onoe Senroku, Ichikawa Riko, Onoe Matsutaro, Bando Moriwaka, Onoe Kotatsu, Ichikawa Omejiro, Kataoka Tosho.
Technical director, Shunichiro Kanai; lighting, Kiyotsune Soma; deputy chairman of the Grand Kabuki tour, Morio Horiuchi; associate artistic director, Onoe Kuroemon II; stage managers

(Kabuki) Takeshiba Ryoji, Takeshiba Joji, (Metropolitan) Thomas Connell; press, Mark Goldstaub.

Musicians: Kiyomoto Shizutayu (Living National Treasure). Kiyomoto Ensemble: Reciters, Kiyomoto Shisaotayu, Kiyomoto Shizukotayu; Shamisen, Kiyomoto Eizaburo, Kiyomoto Shonosuke, Kiyomoto Kikusuke.

Nagauta Ensemble: Singers, Matsushima Shozaburo, Kashiwa Ichiro, Matsushima Eizaburo, Wakayama Tomitaro, Kineya Rokushichiro; Shamisen, Kineya Mitaro, Kashiwa Yojiro, Kineya Mikichi, Kineya Rokuo, Imafuji Chonosuke.

Narimono Ensemble: Mochizuki Tasasuke, Tanaka Denbei, Tanaka Denzo, Mochizuki Tasaji, Tanaka Chojuro, Mochizuki Takishiro.

Kabuki is a traditional Japanese theater form combining performance, design, music and dance and dating from 1697, when it was founded by Ichikawa Danjuro I, ancestor of principal actor in the present cast.

On the first program, *Shibaraku* is an *aragoto* play going back to the beginnings of Kabuki with the drama of a sword-wielding hero rescuing the helpless from a band of villains; *Tachi Nusubito* (choreography, Fujima Kansai; text, Okamura Shiko) is an adaptation of a Kyogen comedy about a city-bred thief who steals a countryman-samurai's sword; *Kojo* is a real and solemn Kabuki ceremony never before performed outside Japan in which Ichikawa Ebizo X received the honor of assuming the name Ichikawa Danjuro XII, as billed among the Principal Actors above; *Kasane* (text, Tsuruya Namboku IV; choreography, Fujima Kanjuro) is a love-death dance duet.

On the second program, *Sakura-hime Azuma Bunsho* is a 19th century character drama of a princess (played by Bando Tamasaburo) who displays many facets of her personality as she sinks into a life of degradation; *Tsuchi-gumo* is an adaptation of a Noh play, a tale of a nobleman in the power of an evil magician who turns himself into a spider.

Follies (2). Concert version of the musical with book by James Goldman; music and lyrics by Stephen Sondheim. Produced by Thomas Z. Shepard at Avery Fisher Hall. Opened September 6, 1985. (Closed September 7, 1985)

Dimitri Weissman	Andre Gregory	Young Sally	Liz Callaway
Roscoe	Arthur Rubin	Emily Whitman	Betty Comden
Sally Durant Plummer	Barbara Cook	Theodore Whitman	Adolph Green
Benjamin Stone	George Hearn	Solange LaFitte	Liliane Montevecchi
Buddy Plummer	Mandy Patinkin	Hattie Walker	Elaine Stritch
Phyllis Rogers Stone	Lee Remick	Stella Deems	Phyllis Newman
Young Buddy	Jim Walton	Carlotta Campion	Carol Burnett
Young Ben	Howard McGillin	Heidi Schiller	Licia Albanese
Young Phyllis	Daisy Prince	Young Heidi	Erie Mills

Chorus: Ronn Carroll, Susan Cella, Robert Henderson, Frank Kopyc, Marti Morris, Ted Sperling, Susan Terry, Sandra Wheeler.

Dancers: Karen Fraction, Linda von Germer, Jamie M. Pisano, Elvera Sciarra.

Directed by Herbert Ross; orchestrations, Jonathan Tunick; dance music, John Berkman; press, Fred Nathan, Bert Fink.

The New York Philharmonic–Symphony Orchestra conducted by Paul Gemigagni and performers presenting the complete Sondheim score of *Follies*, with narrative transitions spoken by Andre Gregory, in a concert recorded for RCA Red Seal Records. *Follies* was originally produced on Broadway 4/4/71 for 521 performances and was named a Best Play of its season.

The list of musical numbers in *Follies* appears on page 311 of *The Best Plays of 1970–71*.

*Song & Dance (292). Musical with lyrics by Don Black; music by Andrew Lloyd Webber; American adaptation and additional lyrics by Richard Maltby, Jr.. Produced by Cameron Mackintosh, Inc., The Shubert Organization and F.W.M. Producing Group by arrangement with The Really Useful Company, Ltd. at the Royale Theater. Opened September 18, 1985.

CAST, ACT I: Emma—Bernadette Peters. ACT II: Joe: Christopher d'Amboise.

Act II Women: Charlotte d'Amboise, Denise Faye, Cynthia Onrubia, Mary Ellen Stuart. Act II Men: Gregg Burge, Gen Horiuchi, Gregory Mitchell, Scott Wise. Act II, Scene 3: Woman in Gold —Mary Ellen Stuart; Her Two Escorts—Scott Wise, Gregory Mitchell. Act II, Scene 5: Woman in Blue—Charlotte d'Amboise; Tourist—Gen Horiuchi; His Two Pick-Ups—Cynthia Onrubia, Denise Faye. Act II, Scene 6: A Man From the Streets—Gregg Burge. Act II, Scene 7: Woman in Grey Flannel—Cynthia Onrubia.

Standby: Miss Peters—Maureen Moore. Understudies: Mr. d'Amboise—Bruce Falco; Misses Stuart, Faye, d'Amboise—Valerie Wright; Miss Onrubia—Mary Ann Lamb, Denise Faye; Mr. Burge —Bruce Anthony Davis; Messrs. Wise, Mitchell—Kenneth Ard; Mr. Horiuchi—Ramon Galindo.

Directed by Richard Maltby, Jr.; choreography, Peter Martins; entire production supervised by Richard Maltby, Jr. and Peter Martins; musical supervision and direction, John Mauceri; scenery, Robin Wagner; costumes, Willa Kim; lighting, Jules Fisher; orchestrations, Andrew Lloyd Webber, David Cullen; production music advisor, David Caddick; executive producers, R. Tyler Gatchell Jr., Peter Neufeld; associate tap choreographer, Gregg Burge; sound, Martin Levan; production stage manager, Sam Stickler; stage manager, Richard Jay-Alexander; press, The Fred Nathan Company, Inc., Anne Abrams.

Time: The present. Place: New York and Los Angeles.

Act I of *Song & Dance* is all singing, with Bernadette Peters singing all the Webber-Black songs in the role of an English girl who has moved to New York City. Act II is all dancing, with music adapted from various classical and modern sources. A foreign play previously produced in London.

Victor Barbee replaced Christopher d'Amboise 1/6/86; Christopher d'Amboise replaced Victor Barbee 3/31/86.

MUSICAL NUMBERS, ACT I: "Take That Look Off Your Face," "Let Me Finish," "So Much to Do in New York," "First Letter Home," "English Girls," "Capped Teeth and Caesar Salad," "You Made Me Think You Were in Love," "Capped Teeth and Caesar Salad" (Reprise), "So Much to Do in New York II," "Second Letter Home," "Unexpected Song," "Come Back With the Same Look in Your Eyes," "Take That Look Off Your Face" (Reprise), "Tell Me on a Sunday," "I Love New York," "So Much to Do in New York III," "Married Man," "Third Letter Home," "Nothing Like You've Ever Known," "Let Me Finish" (Reprise), "What Have I Done?", Finale—"Take That Look Off Your Face."

SCENES, ACT II: Scene 1: A New York subway station. Scene 2: The city. Scene 3: A street outside a disco. Scene 4: Billboards. Scene 5: A bar. Scene 6: A city street. Scene 7: Wall Street. Scene 8: A park. Scene 9: Fifth Avenue. Scene 10: A department store fashion show. Scene 11: New York.

*The Search for Signs of Intelligent Life in the Universe (267). One-woman performance by Lily Tomlin; written by Jane Wagner. Produced by Tomlin and Wagner Theatricalz at the Plymouth Theater. Opened September 26, 1985.

Directed by Jane Wagner; produced by Lily Tomlin; production supervised by Charles Bowden; scenery and lighting, Neil Peter Jampolis; sound, Otts Munderloh; associate producer, Cheryl Swannack; production stage manager, Janet Beroza; stage manager, Pamela J. Young; press, Cheryl Dolby, Domino Media, Inc.

Satire of modern American life and times, in the form of a play in which Miss Tomlin portrays all the roles, each of them identified by a character name in the scene-by-scene listing below.

ACT I: Lily (The Plymouth Theater, New York City); Agnus Angst (The Un-Club, Indianapolis); Trudy (49th Street and Broadway, New York City); Judith Beasley (A public access TV station, Chicago); Trudy (49th Street and Broadway, New York City); Chrissy (A health club, Los Angeles); Vince (A health club, Los Angeles); Kate (A beauty salon, New York City); Trudy (A pocket park, New York City); Agnus (International House of Pancakes, Indianapolis); Lud and Marie (Suburban home, Greenwood, Indiana); Tina (A pocket park, New York City); Lud and Marie (Suburban home, Greenwood, Indiana); Agnus (The Un-Club, Indianapolis).

ACT II: Trudy (A pocket park, New York City); Brandy and Tina (49th Street and Broadway, New York City); Trudy (Howard Johnson's, 49th Street and Broadway); Lynn (A backyard, California); Edie and Marge (Lynn's reminiscence); Trudy (Outside Carnegie Hall, New York City); Kate (A cocktail lounge, New York City); Trudy (Outside the Plymouth Theater).

The Iceman Cometh (55). Revival of the play by Eugene O'Neill. Produced by Lewis Allen, James M. Nederlander, Stephen Graham and Ben Edwards in the American National Theater production, Peter Sellars director, at the Lunt-Fontanne Theater. Opened September 29, 1985. (Closed December 1, 1985)

Rocky Pioggi	John Pankow	Pat McGloin	Pat McNamara
Larry Slade	Donald Moffat	Ed Mosher	Allen Swift
Hugo Kalmar	Leonardo Cimino	Margie	Natalia Nogulich
Willie Oban	John Christopher Jones	Pearl	Kristine Nielsen
Harry Hope	Barnard Hughes	Cora	Caroline Aaron
Joe Mott	Roger Robinson	Chuck Morello	Harris Laskawy
Don Parritt	Paul McCrane	Theodore Hickman	Jason Robards
Cecil Lewis	Bill Moor	Moran	Paul Austin
Piet Wetjoen	Frederick Neumann	Lieb	Walter Flanagan
James Cameron	James Greene		

Understudies: Mr. Hughes—James Greene; Messrs. Swift, McNamara, Neumann—Walter Flanagan; Messrs. Jones, Laskawy, Austin—Christopher McHale; Messrs. Robinson, Flanagan—Thomas Martell Brimm; Messrs. Moor, Greene, Cimino, Moffat—Paul Austin; Messrs. Pankow, McCrane—Stanley Tucci; Misses Nielsen, Aaron, Nogulich—Maggie Baird.

Directed by José Quintero; scenery, Ben Edwards; costumes, Jane Greenwood; lighting, Thomas R. Skelton; production stage manager, Mitchell Erickson; stage manager, John Handy; press, David Powers, Leo Stern.

Place: Harry Hope's bar. Act I: Early morning in the summer of 1912. Act II: Around midnight of the same day. Act III: Morning of the following day. Act IV: Around 1:30 A.M. the next day.

The last major New York revival of *The Iceman Cometh* took place on Broadway 12/13/73 for 85 performances. The 1985 revival was previously produced by American National Theater at Kennedy Center in Washington, D.C.

Italy on Stage. Schedule of American premiere performances by visiting troupes in the Italian language with English subtitles. **La Gatta Cenerentola** (Cinderella the Cat) (2). Musical based on the sixth fable of Giovan Basile's *Pentamerone*; adapted by Roberto de Simone. Opened October 19, 1985. **I Due Sergenti** (The Two Sergeants) (2). Adapted from an 1823 melodrama by Attilio Corsini and Roberto Ripamonte. Opened October 21, 1985. **Pipino il Breve** (Pippin the Short) (2). Puppet musical by Tony Cucchiara. Opened October 25, 1985. **Il Campiello** (2). Revival of the play by Carlo Goldoni. Opened October 30, 1985. Produced by the Italian Government with special assistance from the America-Italy Society in celebration of the City of New York's Italian Cultural Month at the Vivian Beaumont Theater. (Repertory, including concert and other programs, closed October 31, 1985)

LA GATTA CENERENTOLA

Performed by Ente Teatro Cronaca of Naples: Valeria Baiano, Luciano Catapano, Antonella D'Agostino, Isa Danieli, Giuseppe De Vittorio, Lello Giulivo, Anna Incoronato, Gianni Lamagna, Rino Marcelli, Adria Mortari, Anna G. Spagnuolo, Patrizia Spinosi, Virgilio Villani.

Directed by Roberto de Simone; scenery, Mauro Carosi; costumes, Odette Nicoletti; conductor, Renato Piemontese; assistant conductor, Rosario Del Duca; press, Mark Goldstaub Public Relations.

Self-described "musical fable" based on the Cinderella tale and presented in three acts in its American premiere. A foreign play previously produced in Naples.

I DUE SERGENTI

Performed by Actors & Technicians Company of Rome: Gerolamo Alchieri, Stefanco Altieri, Franco Bergesio, Eleonora Cosmo, Sandro De Paoli, Ruggero Dondi, Anna Lisa Di Nola, Roberto Ivan Orano, Silvestro Pontani, Viviana Toniolo.

Directed by Attilio Corsini; choreography, Hasel Moore; scenery and costumes, Uberto Bertacca; music, Giovanna Marini.

Play-within-a-play, with music, about a troupe of actors touring the world with a play called *The Two Sergeants,* presented in its American premiere. A foreign play previously produced in Italy.

PIPINO IL BREVE

Performed by Teatro Stabile di Catania of Sicily; directed by Giuseppe Di Martino; music, Tony Cucchiara.

Life-sized puppets depicting the marriage of King Pippin of France with Berta of Hungary.

IL CAMPIELLO

Performed by Veneto Teatro of Venice; directed by Sandro Sequi.

Comedy about the 18th century working-class residents of the Campiello.

Tango Argentino (198). Musical revue in the Spanish language conceived by Claudio Segovia and Hector Orezzoli. Produced by Mel Howard and Donald K. Donald at the Mark Hellinger Theater. Opened October 9, 1985. (Closed March 30, 1986)

Dancers: Juan Carlos Copes and Maria Nieves, the Dinzels, Gloria and Eduardo, Mayoral and Elsa Maria, Nelida and Nelson, Maria and Carlos Rivarola, Virulazo and Elvira.

Soloist: Naanim Timoyko.

Singers: Raul Lavie, Jovita Luna, Elba Beron, Alba Solis.

Musicians: Sexteto Mayor—Jose Libertella, Luis Stazo bandoneon; Mario Abramovich, Eduardo Walczak violin; Oscar Palermo piano; Osvaldo Aulicino bass. Also Osvaldo Berlingieri piano; Oscar Ruben Gonzalez bandoneon, flute; Rodolfo Fernandez, Juan Schiaffino violin; Dino Carlos Quarlieri violoncello; Lisandro Androver bandoneon.

Directed by Claudio Segovia and Hector Orezzoli; choreography, Juan Carlos Copes; musical direction, Jose Libertella, Luis Stazo, Osvaldo Berlingieri; scenery and costumes, Hector Orezzoli, Claudio Segovia; stage manager, Otto von Breuning; press, Marilynn LeVine, Meg Gordean.

The tango interpreted in song, story and dance by Argentinian artists in a foreign production previously produced in Buenos Aires and Paris.

PART I: Quejas de Bandoneon—Orchestra; El Apache Argentino—Ballet; El Esquinazo—Ballet; Milonga del Tiempo Heroico—Juan Carlos Copes, Maria Nieves; La Punalada—Osvaldo Berlingieri, Orchestra; La Morocha—Gloria and Maria Rivarola; "El Choclo"—Elba Beron; La Cumparsita—Maria and Carlos Rivarola; "Mi Noche Triste"—Raul Lavie; Orgullo Criollo—Virulazo and Elvira; "De Mi Barrio"—Jovita Luna; Bandoneones—Jose Libertella, Luis Stazo, Lisandro Androver, Oscar Ruben Gonzalez.

Also Milonguita: Milonguita—Naanim Timoyko; Ruffian—Juan Carlos Copes; Ruffian's Accomplice—Nelida; Bridegroom—Nelson; Cabaret's Customers—Eduardo, Mayoral, Carlos Rivarola; Prostitutes—Gloria, Elsa Maria, Gloria Dinzel, Maria Rivarola.

Also Nostalgias—Sexteto Mayor; "Cuesta Abajo"—Raul Lavie; El Enterriano—Dinzels; Canaro en Paris—Osvaldo Berlingieri, Orchestra; Taquito Militar—Juan Carlos Copes, Maria Nieves, Nelida and Nelson, Gloria and Eduardo.

PART II: Milongueando en El 40—Gloria and Eduardo; "Uno"—Alba Solis; "La Ultima Curda" —Alba Solis; La Yumba—Mayoral, Elsa Maria; "Nunca Tuvo Novio"—Raul Lavie, Osvaldo Berlingieri, Orchestra; Jealousy—Nelida and Nelson; "Desencuentro"—Elba Beron; Tanguera—Orchestra; Verano Porteno—Juan Carlos Copes, Maria Nieves; "Balada Para Mi Muerte"—Jovita Luna; Adios Nonino—Sexteto Mayor; Danzarin and Quejas de Bandoneon—Ballet.

THE BOYS IN AUTUMN—George C. Scott as Huckleberry Finn and John Cullum as Tom Sawyer, 50 years after their boyhood escapades, in Bernard Sabath's play

*Circle in the Square. Schedule of four programs. **The Marriage of Figaro** (77). Revival of the play by Pierre Augustin Beaumarchais; adapted and translated by Richard Nelson; music by Richard Peaslee. Opened October 10, 1985. (Closed December 15, 1985) **The Robert Klein Show** (16). One-man performance conceived, written by and with Robert Klein. Opened December 20, 1985. (Closed January 4, 1986) **The Caretaker** (45). Revival of the play by Harold Pinter in the Steppenwolf Theater Company production. Opened January 30, 1986. (Closed March 9, 1986) ***The Boys in Autumn** (38). By Bernard Sabath. Opened April 30, 1986. Produced by Circle in the Square, Theodore Mann artistic director, Paul Libin managing director, at Circle in the Square Theater.

THE MARRIAGE OF FIGARO

Figaro....................	Anthony Heald	Countess......................	Dana Ivey
Suzanne .... Mary Elizabeth Mastrantonio		Fanchette..................	Debbie Merrill
Dr. Bartholo	Louis Zorich	Antonio	William Duell
Marceline....................	Carol Teitel	Pedrille...................	Daniel D. Scott,
Cherubino..................	Caitlin Clarke		Scott Lindsay Johnson
Count Almaviva	Christopher Reeve	Gripe-Soleil	Dan Nutu
Bazile	James Cahill		

Peasants: Robertson Carricart, Francine Forbes, David Giella, Paula Redinger, Connie Roderick, Luke Sickle. Shepherd Children: Edna Harris, Piper Lawrence, Carol-Ann Planté.

Musicians: Jill Jaffe violin, Richard Cohen reeds, William Uttley percussion.

Understudies: Mr. Heald—Dennis Bailey; Miss Ivey—Paula Redinger; Mr. Reeve—Robertson Carricart; Messrs. Duell, Zorich, Cahill—Luke Sickle; Misses Clarke, Merrill—Francine Forbes; Miss Teitel—Connie Roderick; Mr. Nutu—David Giella.

Directed by Andrei Serban; musical direction, Donald York; production design, Beni Montresor; assistant director, Charles Otte; skate choreography, Debbie Merrill; stage manager, Michael F. Ritchie; press, Merle Debuskey, William Schelble.

This version of the 1784 comedy, previously produced in 1982 in regional theater in Minneapolis, was presented in two parts. The only previous New York production of record was in French by Théâtre de France 2/25/64 for 5 performances.

THE ROBERT KLEIN SHOW

CAST: Robert Klein. Special Guest Star: Kenny Rankin. Singers: Betsy Bircher, Catherine Russell.

Musicians: Zev Katz bass, Dave Rataczjak drums, Bob Rose guitar.

Musical direction, Bob Stein; production stage manager, Michael F. Richie.

Standup comedy on various contemporary subjects, embellished with a collection of songs by the guest star. The show was presented in two parts.

THE CARETAKER

Mick....................... Gary Sinise   Davies..................... Alan Wilder
Aston .... Jeff Perry

Standbys: Mr. Wilder—Stephen Daley; Messrs. Perry, Sinise—Tom Zanarini.

Directed by John Malkovich; scenery and lighting, Kevin Rigdon; costumes, John Malkovich; production stage manager, Teri McClure; stage manager, Carol Klein.

Place: A house in West London. Act I: A night in winter. Act II: A few seconds later. Act III: Two weeks later.

The last major New York revival of *The Caretaker* was by Roundabout Theater Company off Broadway 1/21/82 for 69 performances. This 1986 production originated in Chicago, presented there by Steppenwolf 9/22/85–11/10/85.

Tom Zanarini replaced Gary Sinise 3/1/86.

THE BOYS IN AUTUMN

Henry Finnegan .... George C. Scott
Thomas Gray .... John Cullum

Understudies: Mr. Scott—William Cain; Mr. Cullum—William Hardy.

Directed by Theodore Mann; scenery, Michael Miller; costumes, Jennifer Von Mayrhauser; lighting, Richard Nelson; incidental music, Bob Israel, Paul Epstein; production stage manager, Michael F. Ritchie; stage manager, Carol Klein.

Time: The early 1920s. Place: The yard and front porch of a house on a bluff overlooking the river outside the town of Hannibal, Mo. Act I: A sunny September afternoon. Act II: That evening.

Reunion after 50 years of Tom Sawyer and Huck Finn in their old age. Previously produced in regional theater in San Francisco.

Mayor (70). Transfer from off Broadway of the musical based on *Mayor* by Edward I. Koch; book by Warren Leight; music and lyrics by Charles Strouse. Produced by Martin Richards, Jerry Kravat, Mary Lea Johnson with The New York Music Company at the Latin Quarter. Opened October 23, 1985. (Closed January 5, 1986)

Mayor .... Lenny Wolpe

Douglas Bernstein   Ilene Kristen
Marion J. Caffey   Kathryn McAteer
Nancy Giles   John Sloman
Ken Jennings

Musicians: Michael Kosarin conductor, piano; Gordon Twist synthesizer; Michael Keller drums; Bruce Samuels bass; Raymond Beckenstein woodwinds.

Understudy: Mr. Wolpe—Scott Robertson; Swing—Krista Neumann.

Directed by Jeffrey B. Moss; choreography, Barbara Siman; musical direction and arrangements, Michael Kosarin; scenery and costumes, Randy Barcelo; lighting, Richard Winkler; orchestrations,

Christopher Bankey; associate producer, Sam Crothers; production stage manager, Marc Schlackman; press, Henry Luhrman Associates, Bruce Cohen, Kathleen von Schmid.

The cabaret musical *Mayor* was originally produced off Broadway at Top of the Gate for 185 performances 5/13/85–10/21/85.

The list of musical numbers and sketches in *Mayor* appears on pages 387–388 of *The Best Plays of 1984–85.*

The News (4). Musical with book by Paul Schierhorn, David Rotenberg and R. Vincent Park; music and lyrics by Paul Schierhorn. Produced by Zev Bufman, Kathleen Lindsey, Nicholas Neubauer and R. Vincent Park with Martin and Janice Barandes at the Helen Hayes Theater. Opened November 7, 1985. (Closed November 9, 1985)

Reporter	Cheryl Alexander	Reporter	Patrick Jude
Circulation Editor	Frank Baier	Girl	Lisa Michaelis
Executive Editor	Jeff Conaway	Reporter	Charles Pistone
Killer	Anthony Crivello	Sports Editor	John Rinehimer
City Editor	Michael Duff	Style Editor	Peter Valentine
Feature Editor	Jonathan S. Gerber	Managing Editor	Billy Ward
Talk Show Host	Anthony Hoylen		

Standbys: Mr. Crivello—Patrick Jude; Messrs. Jude, Pistone—Anthony Hoylen; Mr. Hoylen—Jay Adler; Misses Michaelis, Alexander—Julie Newdow.

Directed by David Rotenberg; choreography, Wesley Fata; conductor, John Rinehimer; scenery, Jane Musky; costumes, Richard Hornung; lighting, Norman Coates; sound, Gary Scott Peck/ Ati; arrangements, John Rinehimer, Paul Schierhorn; supervisor orchestrator, John Rinehimer; associate producers, Patricia Bayer, Annette R. McDonald, Quentin H. McDonald; production stage manager, Robert I. Cohen; stage manager, K.R. Williams; press, Jeffrey Richards Associates, Susan Lee.

Time: The present. Place: The city room of a large metropolitan newspaper, the bedroom of a 15-year-old girl, a one-room apartment and a city street. The play was presented without intermission.

Rock musical (31 songs, only 9 minutes of dialogue) about sensational journalism, previously produced in regional theater in Florida and Connecticut.

MUSICAL NUMBERS

"I Am the News"	Executive Editor, Company
"They Write the News"	Executive Editor
"Mirror, Mirror"	Girl
"Front Page Exposé"	Executive Editor, Reporters
"Hot Flashes (I)"	Reporters
"Dad"	Girl
"She's on File"	Executive Editor
"Super Singo"	Executive Editor, Reporters
"Dear Felicia"	Executive Editor, Circulation Editor
"Horoscope"	Cheryl, Patrick, Charles, Band
"Hot Flashes (II)"	Band, Reporters
"Classifieds/Personals"	Band, Reporters, Girl, Killer
"Wonderman"	Girl
"Shooting Stars"	Killer
"What's the Angle"	Executive Editor, Reporters
"The Contest"	Executive Editor, Reporters, Feature Editor, Band
"Dear Editor"	Killer
"Editorial"	Executive Editor, Reporters, Killer, Band
"Hot Flashes (Financial)"	Band
"Talk to Me"	Killer, Girl
"Pyramid Lead"	Executive Editor, Reporters
"Beautiful People"	Cheryl, Peter, Executive Editor, Killer, Reporters, Band

"Hot Flashes (III)" .... Reporters, Band
"Open Letter".. Executive Editor, Killer, Company
"Mirror, Mirror" (Reprise).. Girl
"Ordinary, Extraordinary Day" .... Killer, Girl
"What's the Angle" (Reprise).. Reporters, Band
"Violent Crime"..................................... Executive Editor, Girl, Reporters
"What in the World"... Patrick, Reporters, Band
"Acts of God (Births, Deaths and the Weather)" .... Company

The Magnificent Christmas Spectacular (120). Holiday revue conceived by Robert F. Jani. Produced by Robert F. Jani at Radio City Music Hall. Opened November 15, 1985. (Closed January 9, 1986)

Scrooge; Santa..........	Thomas Ruisinger	Belinda.....................	Roie Ward
Mr. Cratchit..............	Edward Prostak	Martha..................	Gillian Hemstead
Mrs. Cratchit.............	Ann-Marie Blake	Coachman	Marty McDonough
Sarah Cratchit; Princess......	Stacy Latham	Poultry Man	Tony Cobb
Tiny Tim Cratchit.........	Bradley Latham	Mrs. Claus.................	Nancy Meyer
Peter Cratchit;		Skaters	Laurie Welch, Greg Welch
Drummer Boy.............	Demetri Callas	Narrator..................	David Chaney

The Rockettes: Carol Beatty, Catherine Beatty, Dottie Belle, Susan Boron, Katy Braff, Linda Deacon Burrington, Elizabeth Chanin, Barbara Ann Cittadino, Eileen M. Collins, Susanne Doris, Alexis Ficks, Deniene Fenn, Carol Harbich, Ginny Hounsell, Connie House, Cynthia Hughes, Stephanie James, Joan Peer Kelleher, Dee Dee Knapp, Kim Leslie, Judy Little, Setsuko Maruhashi, Agnes McConlogue, Mary McNamara, Laraine Memola, Barbara Ann Moore, Kerri Pearsall, Gerri Presky, Linda Riley, Mary Six Rupert, Jereme Sheehan, Terry Spano, Maureen Stevens, Susan Theobald, Carol Toman, Patricia Tully, Pauline A. Tzikas, Darlene Wendy, Rose Anne Woolsey.

The New Yorkers: Gina Biancardi, Ann-Marie Blake, Tony Cobb, Peter Fitzgerald, Tom Garrett, Miranda Lind, Nancy Meyer, Steven Edward Moore, Patrice Pickering, Edward Prostak, Wes Skelley, Laurie Stephenson, Susan Streater, Ray Walker.

The Dancers: Paul Abrahamson, Brian Arsenault, Leigh Catlett, M. Dale Cook, Gillian Hemstead, Edward Henkel, Kirsten Iiams, Marty McDonough, Michael L. Mitchell, Laura Streets, Roie Ward, Greg Welch, Laurie Welch, Travis Wright.

Elves: Wiggle—John Edward Allen; Squiggle—Melinda C. Keel; Giggle—Timothy Loomis; Jiggle —Scott Seidman; Bruce—David Steinberg.

Orchestra: Bo Ayers conductor; Don Smith assistant conductor; Louann Montesi concertmaster; Gilbert Bauer, Carmine Deleo, Howard Kaye, Joseph Kowalewski, Julius H. Kunstler, Nannette Levi, Samuel Marder, Holly Ovenden violin; Morris J. Sutow, Barbara Harrison viola; Frank Levi, Pamela Frame cello; Dean Crandall bass; Kenneth Emery flute; Gerard J. Niewood, Edward Lucas, Joseph Camilleri, Joshua Siegel, Kenneth Arzberger reeds; George Bartlett, Nancy Freimanis, French horn; Richard Raffio, Zachary Shnek, Norman Beatty trumpet; John Schnupp, David Jett, Donald Wittekind trombone; John Bartlett tuba; Thomas J. Oldakowski drums; Mari DeCiutiis, Randall Max percussion; Anthony Cesarano guitar; Susanna Nason, Don Smith piano; Jeanne Maier harp; Robert MacDonald organ.

Directed by Robert F. Jani; staging and choreography, Violet Holmes, Linda Lemac, Marilyn Magness; musical direction, Bo Ayers; scenery, Charles Lisanby; costumes, Frank Spencer; lighting, Ken Billington; choral director, Sheldon Disrud; orchestrations, Elman Anderson, Robert M. Freedman, Michael Gibson, Don Harper, Arthur Harris, Bob Krogstad, Philip J. Lang; production stage manager, Howard Kolins; stage managers, Susan Green, Peter Muste, Tony Berk, Peter Taylor; press, Ellen Schiebelhuth, Helene Greece.

Original music: "T'was the Night Before Christmas" by Tom Bahler; "They Can't Start Christmas Without Us" music by Stan Lebowsky, lyrics by Fred Tobias; "My First Real Christmas" music by Don Pippin, lyrics by Nan Mason. Arrangements: "Silent Night," Percy Faith; "The Twelve Days of Christmas," Tom Bahler, Don Dorsey.

Updated version of the Music Hall's annual Christmas show. Overture: The Music Hall Orchestra.

Scene 1: The Nutcracker. Scene 2: A Christmas Carol. Scene 3: It's Christmas in New York. Scene 4: The Twelve Days of Christmas. Scene 5: They Can't Start Christmas Without Us. Scene 6: The Rockettes, The Parade of the Wooden Soldiers. Scene 7: The Night Before Christmas. Scene 8: The Rockette Christmas Carousel. Scene 9: The Living Nativity.

*I'm Not Rappaport (223). Transfer from off Broadway of the play by Herb Gardner. Produced by James Walsh, Lewis Allen and Martin Heinfling at the Booth Theater. Opened November 19, 1985.

Nat	Judd Hirsch	Gilley	Jace Alexander
Midge	Cleavon Little	Clara	Mercedes Ruehl
Danforth	Gregg Almquist	Cowboy	Ray Baker
Laurie	Liann Pattison		

Understudies: Mr. Hirsch—Salem Ludwig; Mr. Little—William Hall Jr.; Misses Ruehl, Pattison—Elaine Brooks; Mr. Alexander—Josh Pais; Messrs. Almquist, Baker—Howard Sherman.

Directed by Daniel Sullivan; scenery, Tony Walton; costumes, Robert Morgan; lighting, Pat Collins; production stage manager, Thomas A. Kelly; stage manager, Charles Kindl; press, Jeffrey Richards Associates, C. George Willard.

Time: Early October 1982. Place: A bench near a path at the edge of the lake in Central Park. Act I: Three in the afternoon. Act II, Scene 1: Three in the afternoon, the next day. Scene 2: Five in the afternoon, the next day. Scene 3: Twelve days later, 11 A.M.

The aging process as comedy, viewed in the friendship of two old men, one white and the other black. Previously produced off Broadway 6/6/85–11/10/85 for 181 performances; see its entry in the Plays Produced Off Broadway section of this volume.

A Best Play; see page 113.

The Boys of Winter (9). By John Pielmeier. Produced by Ivan Bloch, Alan Levin and Bernie Sofronski in association with Elle Shushan at the Biltmore Theater. Opened December 1, 1985. (Closed December 8, 1985)

Bonney	D.W. Moffett	L.B.	Wesley Snipes
Ho	Thomas Ikeda	Monsoon	Matt Dillon
Sarge	Tony Plana	Doc	Ving Rhames
Prick	Brian Tarantina	Radio Voices	Wendell Pierce,
Flem	Andrew McCarthy		Mariye Onouye

Understudies: Messrs. Tarantina, McCarthy—Rob Morrow; Messrs. Rhames, Snipes—Wendell Pierce; Messrs. Moffett, Plana—Nestor Serrano; Mr. Dillon—Grant Show; Mr. Ikeda—Alvin Lum.

Directed by Michael Lindsay-Hogg; scenery, David Mitchell; costumes, Carrie Robbins; lighting, Pat Collins; fights, B.H. Barry; sound, Jan Nebozenko; production stage manager, Herb Vogler; stage manager, Jay B. Jacobson; press, The Jacksina Company, Inc., Judy Jacksina, Marcy Granata, Kevin Boyle.

Time: December 22–26, 1968; before and after. Place: A hilltop in Quang Tri Province, South Vietnam, near the Laotian border and the DMZ. The play was presented without intermission.

Marines on a dangerous mission in the Vietnam War during Christmas week.

*The Mystery of Edwin Drood (208). Transfer from off Broadway of the musical by Rupert Holmes; suggested by the unfinished novel by Charles Dickens. Produced by Joseph Papp in the New York Shakespeare Festival production at the Imperial Theater. Opened December 2, 1985.

Mayor Thomas Sapsea; *Your Chairman, William Cartwright*	George Rose
Stage Manager, Barkeep, Harold; *James Throttle*	Peter McRobbie
John Jasper; *Clive Paget*	Howard McGillin
Rev. Mr. Crisparkle; *Cedric Moncrieffe*	George N. Martin

Edwin Drood; *Alice Nutting* .... Betty Buckley
Rosa Bud; *Deirdre Peregrine* .... Patti Cohenour
Alice; *Isabel Yearsley* .... Judy Kuhn
Beatrice; *Florence Gill* .... Donna Murphy
Helena Landless; *Janet Conover* .... Jana Schneider
Neville Landless; *Victor Grinstead* .... John Herrera
Durdles; *Nick Cricker* .... Jerome Dempsey
Deputy, Statue; *Master Nick Cricker* .... Stephen Glavin
Princess Puffer; *Angela Prysock* .... Cleo Laine
Shade of Jasper; *Harry Sayle* .... Nicholas Gunn
Shade of Drood; *Montague Pruitt* .... Brad Miskell
Clients of Princess Puffer; *Alan Eliot, Christopher Lyon* .... Herndon Lackey, Rob Marshall
Horace; *Brian Pankhurst* .... Charles Goff
Bazzard; *Phillip Bax* .... Joe Grifasi
Dick Datchery .... George Spelvin

Succubae *(Gwendolen Pynn, Sarah Cook, Florence Gill, Isabel Yearsley):* Francine Landes, Karen Giombetti, Donna Murphy, Judy Kuhn. Servants *(Phillip Bax, Violet Balfour, Gwendolen Pynn):* Joe Grifasi, Susan Goodman, Francine Landes.

Citizens of Cloisterham: Karen Giombetti, Charles Goff, Susan Goodman, Nichols Gunn, Judy Kuhn, Herndon Lackey, Francine Landes, Rob Marshall, Peter McRobbie, Brad Miskell, Donna Murphy.

Orchestra: Ronald Oakland, Alvin E. Rogers, Katsuko Esaki, Marshall Coid, Gayle Dixon, Sandra Billingslea violin; Peter Prosser, Laura Blustein, Jeanne LeBlanc cello; David Weiss, Richard Heckman, Lester Cantor, Seymour Red Press reeds; Wilmer Wise, Phil Granger trumpet; Santo Russo, Earl P. McIntyre trombone; Russell Rizner, R. Allen Spanjer horns; James Koval, Edward Strauss (assistant conductor), Donald Rebic keyboards; Melanie L. Punter bass; Skip Reed percussion; Glenn Rhian drums.

Understudies: Misses Buckley, Cohenour—Judy Kuhn; Messrs. McGillin, Herrera—Herndon Lackey; Messrs. Rose, Martin—Peter McRobbie; Mr. Glavin—Brad Miskell; Misses Schneider, Laine—Donna Murphy; Swings—Laurent Giroux, Michele Pigliavento.

Directed by Wilford Leach; choreography, Graciela Daniele; musical direction, Michael Starobin; scenery, Bob Shaw; costumes, Lindsay W. Davis; lighting, Paul Gallo; sound, Tom Morse; magic lantern projections, James Cochrane; orchestrations, Rupert Holmes; associate producer, Jason Steven Cohen; production stage manager, James Harker; stage manager, Robin Herskowitz; press, Merle Debuskey, Richard Kornberg, Bruce Campbell, Barbara Carroll, William Schelble, Don Anthony Summa.

Play-within-a-play adaptation of the Dickens murder mystery, performing both the roles in the Edwin Drood tale and the "performers" (names in italics above) in the "troupe" that is "presenting" it, and with the denouement varied according to the wishes of the audience, polled at each performance. Previously produced off Broadway by New York Shakespeare Festival at the Delacorte Theater in Central Park 8/4/85 for 24 performances; see its entry in the Plays Produced Off Broadway section of this volume.

A Best Play; see page 156.

ACT I: THE SITUATION

"There You Are" .... Chairman, Company
Scene 1: The home of John Jasper at Minor Canon Corner in the cathedral city of Cloisterham, a morning in late December
  "A Man Could Go Quite Mad" .... Jasper
  "Two Kinsmen" .... Drood, Jasper
Scene 2: The conservatory at the Nun's House, a seminary for young women in Cloisterham High Street, later that morning
  "Moonfall" .... Rosa
  "Moonfall" (Reprise) .... Rosa & Helena, Alice & Beatrice
Scene 3: Cloisterham High Street, outside the residence of Mayor Thomas Sapsea, the following afternoon

Scene 4: The opium den of Princess Puffer in the East End of London, dawn the next day
　"The Wages of Sin" .... Puffer
　"Jasper's Vision" .... Shades of Jasper & Drood, Succubae, Satyr
Scene 5: Cloisterham High Street, that afternoon
　"Ceylon" .... Drood, Rosa, Helena, Neville, Ensemble
　"Both Sides of the Coin" .... Jasper, Chairman, Ensemble
Scene 6: The crypts of Cloisterham Cathedral, late that night
Scene 7: The ruins of Cloisterham, Christmas Eve
　"Perfect Strangers" .... Drood, Rosa
Scene 8: The home of John Jasper, a short time later
　"No Good Can Come From Bad" . Neville, Drood, Rosa, Helena, Crisparkle, Jasper, Bazzard
Scene 9: Minor Canon Corner, Christmas Day and Night
　"The Name of Love" and "Moonfall" (Reprise) .... Rosa, Jasper, Ensemble

ACT II: THE SLEUTHS

Scene 1: Cloisterham Station, six months later
　"Settling Up the Score" .... Datchery, Puffer, Ensemble
Scene 2: Cloisterham High Street
　"Off to the Races" .... Chairman, Durdles, Deputy, Ensemble
　"Don't Quit While You're Ahead" .... Puffer, Company
The Voting
　"The Garden Path to Hell" .... Puffer
The Solution

Blood Knot (96). Revival of the play by Athol Fugard. Produced by James B. Freydberg, Max Weitzenhoffer, Lucille Lortel and Estrin Rose Berman Productions in association with F.W.M. Producing Group, in the Yale Repertory Theater production, Lloyd Richards artistic director, at the John Golden Theater. Opened December 10, 1985. (Closed March 2, 1986)

Zachariah .... Zakes Mokae
Morris .... Athol Fugard

　Standbys: Mr. Mokae—Paul Benjamin; Mr. Fugard—David Little.
　Directed by Athol Fugard; scenery, Rusty Smith; costumes, Susan Hilferty; lighting, William B. Warfel; executive producer, Fremont Associates, Inc.; associate producer, Christopher Hart; production stage manager, Neal Ann Stephens; stage manager, Chan Chandler; press, Bill Evans & Associates, Sandra Manley, Jim Baldassare.
　Place: A one-room shack in the non-white location of Korsten, near Port Elizabeth, South Africa. Scene 1: Late afternoon. Scene 2: The next evening; Scene 3: A few days later. Scene 4: An evening later. Scene 5: The next day. Scene 6: Night. Scene 7: The next evening. The play was presented in two parts with the intermission following Scene 3.
　Originally produced in Johannesburg in 1961, *Blood Knot* made its American debut (as *The Blood Knot*) off Broadway 3/1/64 for 102 performances. It was revived off Broadway by Roundabout 3/23/80 for 25 performances. The present Broadway revival originated at Yale Repertory Theater in New Haven, Conn.

Hay Fever (124). Revival of the play by Noel Coward. Produced by Roger Peters in association with MBS Company at the Music Box. Opened December 12, 1985. (Closed March 29, 1986)

Sorel Bliss	Mia Dillon	Sandy Tyrell	Campbell Scott
Simon Bliss	Robert Joy	Myra Arundel	Carolyn Seymour
Clara......................	Barbara Bryne	Richard Greatham	Charles Kimbrough
Judith Bliss	Rosemary Harris	Jackie Coryton.............	Deborah Rush
David Bliss.................	Roy Dotrice		

HAY FEVER—Mia Dillon, Roy Dotrice, Barbara Bryne, Rosemary
Harris and Robert Joy in the revival of Noel Coward's comedy

Understudies: Miss Harris—Angela Thornton; Messrs. Dotrice, Kimbrough—Richard Clarke;
Misses Dillon, Rush—Ashley Gardner; Messrs. Joy, Scott—Thomas Gibson.
Directed by Brian Murray; scenery, Michael H. Yeargan; costumes, Jennifer Von Mayrhauser;
lighting, Arden Fingerhut; "No, My Heart" by John Kander and Fred Ebb; associate producers,
Robert Kamlot, Richard Berg; production stage manager, Martin Gold; stage manager, John
Vivian; press, Bill Evans & Associates, Sandra Manley, Jim Baldassare.
Time: June, 1925. Place: David Bliss's country house in Cookham, outside London. Act I: A
Saturday afternoon. Act II, Scene 1: That evening after dinner. Scene 2: The following morning.
The last major New York revival of *Hay Fever* took place off Broadway 7/30/76 for 14 perfor-
mances.

Jerry's Girls (139). Musical revue with the music and lyrics of Jerry Herman; concepts
by Larry Alford, Wayne Cilento and Jerry Herman. Produced by Zev Bufman and
Kenneth-John Productions at the St. James Theater. Opened December 18, 1985. (Closed
April 20, 1986)

Ellyn Arons
Kirsten Childs
Kim Crosby
Anita Ehrler
Terri Homberg
Robin Kersey

Dorothy Loudon
Joni Masella
Deborah Phelan
Chita Rivera
Leslie Uggams

Onstage Pianist: Sue Anderson. Swing: Jacquey Maltby.
Directed by Larry Alford; choreography, Wayne Cilento; musical direction, Janet Glazener; sce-
nery, Hal Tiné; costumes, Florence Klotz; lighting, Tharon Musser; sound, Peter Fitzgerald; dance
arrangements, Mark Hummel; musical supervision, Donald Pippin; orchestrations, Christopher
Bankey, Joseph Gianono, Jim Tyler; assistant choreographer, Sarah Miles; production stage manager,
Patrick Horrigan; stage managers, Larry Bussard, Brenna Krupa Holden, Barbara Schneider; press,
Shirley Herz Associates, Peter Cromarty.

Compendium of Jerry Herman songs from stage musicals, movies and other sources, previously produced in other versions off off Broadway and on tour.

Members of the company—Ellyn Arons, Kirsten Childs, Kim Crosby, Anita Ehrler, Terri Homberg, Joni Masella and Deborah Phelan—replaced Chita Rivera for one performance 4/8/86.

MUSICAL NUMBERS, ACT I: "It Takes a Woman" (from *Hello, Dolly!*)—Ellyn Arons, Kirsten Childs, Kim Crosby, Anita Ehrler, Terri Homberg, Robin Kersey, Joni Masella, Deborah Phelan; "It Takes a Woman" (Reprise)—Ensemble; "Just Leave Everything to Me" (from *Hello, Dolly!* film)—Dorothy Loudon; "Put on Your Sunday Clothes" (from *Hello, Dolly!*)—Loudon, Ensemble; "It Only Takes a Moment" (from *Hello, Dolly!*)—Leslie Uggams; "Wherever He Ain't" (from *Mack and Mabel*)—Chita Rivera; "We Need a Little Christmas" (from *Mame*)—Arons, Childs, Crosby, Ehrler, Phelan; "Tap Your Troubles Away" (from *Mack and Mabel*)—Loudon, Rivera, Uggams, Ensemble; "I Won't Send Roses" (from *Mack and Mabel*)—Uggams.

Also Vaudeville Medley: "Two-a-Day" (from *Parade*)—Loudon; "Bosom Buddies" (from *Mame*)—Rivera, Uggams; "The Man in the Moon" (from *Mame*)—Loudon; "So Long Dearie" (from *Hello, Dolly!*)—Rivera; "Take It All Off" (written for *Jerry's Girls*)—Crosby, Homberg, Kersey, Masella, Loudon; "Two-a-Day" (Reprise)—Loudon, Uggams, Rivera, Ensemble; "Shalom" (from *Milk and Honey*)—Uggams; "Milk and Honey"—Uggams, Arons, Childs, Crosby, Homberg, Kersey, Phelan; "Before the Parade Passes By" (from *Hello, Dolly!*)—Rivera; "Have a Nice Day" (from *La Cage aux Folles*)—Loudon, Arons, Childs, Crosby, Kersey, Masella; "Showtime" (from *Parade*)—Rivera, Ensemble; "If He Walked Into My Life" (from *Mame*)—Uggams; "Hello, Dolly!"—Loudon, Uggams, Rivera, Ensemble.

ACT II: Entr'acte; Movies Medley: "Just Go to the Movies" (from *A Day in Hollywood*)—Arons, Childs, Crosby, Homberg, Phelan; "Movies Were Movies" (from *Mack and Mabel*)—Uggams; "Look What Happened to Mabel" (from *Mack and Mabel*)—Rivera; "Nelson" (from *A Day in Hollywood*)—Loudon; and "Just Go to the Movies"—Reprise; "I Don't Want to Know" (from *Dear World*)—Rivera; "It's Today" (from *Mame*)—Uggams, Arons, Crosby, Ehrler, Homberg, Kersey, Masella, Phelan; "Mame"—Loudon, Arons, Crosby, Ehrler, Homberg, Kersey, Masella, Phelan; "Kiss Her Now" (from *Dear World*)—Uggams, Childs.

Also The Tea Party (from *Dear World*): "Dickie"—Loudon; "Voices"—Uggams; "Thoughts"—Rivera; "Time Heals Everything" *(from Mack and Mabel)*—Loudon; "That's How Young I Feel" (from *Mame*)—Rivera, Ehrler, Masella; "My Type" (from *Nightcap*)—Loudon; *La Cage aux Folles* Medley: "La Cage"—Rivera, Childs, Ehrler, Homberg, Kersey, Masella, Phelan; "Song on the Sand"—Loudon, Childs, Homberg, Kersey, Phelan; "I Am What I Am"—Uggams; "The Best of Times"—Loudon, Rivera, Uggams, Ensemble.

Wind in the Willows (4). Musical adapted from the book by Kenneth Grahame; book by Jane Iredale; music by William Perry; lyrics by Roger McGough and William Perry. Produced by RLM Productions, Inc. and Liniva Productions, Inc. at the Nederlander Theater. Opened December 19, 1985. (Closed December 22, 1985)

Mole . . . . Vicki Lewis	Badger . . . . Irving Barnes
Mother Rabbit;	Chief Weasel . . . . P.J. Benjamin
Jailer's Daughter . . . . Nora Mae Lyng	Wayfarer Rat . . . . Jackie Lowe
Father Rabbit; Judge . . . . John Jellison	Police Sergeant . . . . Scott Waara
Rat . . . . David Carroll	Court Clerk . . . . Kenston Ames
Toad . . . . Nathan Lane	Prosecutor; Jailer. . . . . Michael Byers
Chief Stoat . . . . Donna Drake	

Ensemble: Kenston Ames, Shell M. Benjamin, Michael Byers, Jackie Lowe, Marguerite Lowell, Nora Mae Lyng, Mary C. Robare, Jamie Rocco, Ray Roderick, Scott Waara. Swings: Teresa Payne-Rohan, Kevin Winkler.

Understudies: Miss Lewis—Donna Drake; Mr. Carroll—Scott Waara; Mr. Lane—Michael Byers; Mr. Barnes—John Jellison; Miss Drake—Shell M. Benjamin; P.J. Benjamin—Jamie Rocco.

Directed by Tony Stevens; choreography, Margery Beddow; musical direction and vocal arrangements, Robert Rogers; scenery, Sam Kirkpatrick; costumes, Freddy Wittop; lighting, Craig

Miller; sound, Jack Mann; musical supervision, Jonathan Tunick; orchestrations, William D. Brohn; dance and incidental music, David Krane; fights, Conal O'Brien; assistant choreographer, James Brennan; production supervisor, Steven Zweigbaum; production stage manager, Jim Woolley; stage manager, Ellen Raphael; press, The Fred Nathan Company, Inc., Glenna Freedman, Merle Frimark.

Adaptation of the imaginative tale of the adventures of Mole, Rat and Badger (Mole is a female in this version). Previously produced at the Folger Theater, Washington, D.C.

ACT I

Scene 1: A meadow in spring
"The World Is Waiting for Me"... Mole
Scene 2: The river
"When Springtime Comes to My River".. Rat
"Messing About in Boats".. Rat, Mole
Scene 3: The wild wood
"Evil Weasel" .... Chief Weasel, Chief Stoat, Weasels, Stoats
Scene 4: The lawns of Toad Hall
"That's What Friends Are For"........................... Toad, Rat, Mole, Rabbits
Scene 5: Rat's dock in summer
Scene 6: The wild wood
"Follow Your Instinct"................................ Mole, Rabbits, Weasels, Stoats
Scene 7: The car park at the Red Lion Inn
"The Gasoline Can-Can"... Toad, Rabbits
"You'll Love It in Jail"...................... Chief Weasel, Chief Stoat, Toad, Policeman
Scene 8: A meadow in autumn
"Mediterranean"... Wayfarer Rat
"The Day You Came Into My Life".. Mole

ACT II

Scene 1: The courtroom
"S-S-Something Comes Over Me" .... Toad
Scene 2: Rat's dock in autumn
"I'd Be Attracted"... Mole, Rat
"When Springtime Comes to My River" (Reprise)............................ Rat
"The Day You Came Into My Life" (Reprise)................................. Mole
Scene 3: Toad Hall
"Moving Up in the World"................... Chief Weasel, Chief Stoat, Weasels, Stoats
Scene 4: A jail cell
"Brief Encounter"... Toad, Jailer's Daughter
Scene 5: The woods
"Where Am I Now?.. Toad
"The Wind in the Willows" .... Company
Scene 6: Rat's dock
"That's What Friends Are For" (Reprise).................. Toad, Rat, Badger, Rabbits
Scene 7: The grand dining room at Toad Hall
"Come What May" .... Company

Benefactors (185). By Michael Frayn. Produced by James M. Nederlander, Robert Fryer, Douglas Urbanski and Michael Codron in association with MTM Enterprises, Inc. and CBS Productions at the Brooks Atkinson Theater. Opened December 22, 1985.

David	Sam Waterston	Colin	Simon Jones
Jane	Glenn Close	Sheila	Mary Beth Hurt

Standbys: Messrs. Waterston, Jones—Lewis Arlt; Misses Close, Hurt—Dale Hodges.
Directed by Michael Blakemore; scenery, Michael Annals; costumes, John Dunn; lighting, Martin

Aronstein; production stage manager, Susie Cordon; stage manager, Laura DeBuys; press, The Fred Nathan Company, Inc., Marc P. Thibodeau.

Personal (marriage, friendship) and public (a housing project for a slum neighborhood) matters go awry in an architect's home and career, presented in two parts. A foreign play previously produced in London.

A Best Play; see page 190.

Corpse! (121). By Gerald Moon. Produced by Martin Markinson, Gary Leaverton and Robert Fox at the Helen Hayes Theater. Opened January 5, 1986. (Closed April 20, 1986)

Evelyn Farrant;	Maj. Walter Powell............ Milo O'Shea
Rupert Farrant.............. Keith Baxter	Hawkins................... Scott LaFeber
Mrs. McGee.............. Pauline Flanagan	

Standbys: Mr. Baxter—Paul Vincent; Messrs. O'Shea, LaFeber—Bernard Frawley; Ms. Flanagan —Paddy Croft.

Directed by John Tillinger; scenery, Alan Tagg; costumes, Lowell Detweiler; lighting, Richard Winkler; production stage manager, Franklin Keysar; stage manager, R. Nelson Barbee; press, Max Eisen, Maria Somma, Madelon Rosen, Barbara Glenn.

Time: London, December 11, 1936. Place: Evelyn Farrant's basement flat in Soho and Rupert Farrant's house in Regent's Park. The play was presented in two parts.

Self-described as "a comedy thriller," an actor hires a killer to eliminate his wealthy twin brother, with Keith Baxter in the dual twin role. A foreign play previously produced in London and on tour in the U.S.A.

Lillian (45). By William Luce; based on the autobiographical works of Lillian Hellman. Produced by Ann Shanks, The Kennedy Center and Ronald S. Lee at the Ethel Barrymore Theater. Opened January 16, 1986. (Closed February 23, 1986)

Lillian .... Zoe Caldwell

Voices at HUAC Meeting: Committee Chairman—Dudley Swetland; Committee Counsel—Allen Leatherman; Joseph Rauh—John Buck Jr.; Reporter—William Rhys.

Directed by Robert Whitehead; scenery, Ben Edwards; costumes, Jane Greenwood; lighting, Thomas Skelton; music and sound, David Gooding; co-producers, Bob Shanks, Kenneth Feld; production stage manager, Dianne Trulock; press, David Powers, Leo Stern.

Time: January 10, 1961. Place: A hospital in New York. The play was presented in two parts.

Zoe Caldwell as Lillian Hellman at the hospital where Dashiell Hammett is dying, with biographical material from Miss Hellman's *An Unfinished Woman*, *Pentimento* and *Scoundrel Time* and from *Profile: Lillian Hellman* courtesy of KERA-TV in Dallas-Fort Worth. Originally produced in regional theater at the Cleveland Play House.

Jerome Kern Goes to Hollywood (13). Musical revue conceived by David Kernan; written by Dick Vosburgh; music by Jerome Kern. Produced by Arthur Cantor and Bonnie Nelson Schwartz by arrangement with Peter Wilson and Showpeople at the Ritz Theater. Opened January 23, 1986. (Closed February 2, 1986)

Elaine Delmar	Scott Holmes
Liz Robertson	Elisabeth Welch

Musicians: Arnold Gross synthesizer, Bruce Samuels bass, Tony Tedesco drums, Steve Usher guitar, Les Scott clarinet, flute.

Standbys: Jeanne Lehman, Michael Maguire.

Directed by David Kernan; musical direction, Peter Howard; scenery, Colin Pigott; costumes, Christine Robinson; lighting, Ken Billington; sound, Tony Meola; associate producer, Harvey Elliott; musical consultant, Clive Chapin; producing associate, Eric Friedheim; production stage manager, Robert Schear; stage manager, Kenneth L. Peck; press, Arthur Cantor Associates, Ken Mandelbaum.

Collection of Kern numbers from his movies of the 1930s and 1940s, presented in two parts. A foreign play previously produced in London as a cabaret musical.

MUSICAL NUMBERS, ACT I: "The Song Is You" and "I've Told Every Little Star" (from *Music in the Air,* lyric by Oscar Hammerstein II)—Ensemble; "Let's Begin" (from *Roberta,* lyric by Otto Harbach)—Liz Robertson; "I Won't Dance" (from *Roberta,* lyric by Otto Harbach, Dorothy Fields and Jimmy McHugh)—Robertson; "Californ-i-ay" (from *Can't Help Singing,* lyric by E.Y. Harburg)—Elaine Delmar, Scott Holmes, Robertson; "I'll Be Hard to Handle" (from *Roberta,* lyric by Bernard Dougall)—Robertson; "Smoke Gets in Your Eyes" (from *Roberta,* lyric by Otto Harbach)—Elisabeth Welch; "Yesterdays" (from *Roberta,* lyric by Otto Harbach)—Holmes, Welch; "Bojangles of Harlem" (from *Swing Time,* lyric by Dorothy Fields)—Delmar, Holmes, Robertson; "I'm Old Fashioned" (from *You Were Never Lovelier,* lyric by Johnny Mercer)—Delmar; "Dearly Beloved" (from *You Were Never Lovelier,* lyric by Johnny Mercer)—Robertson.

Also "Make Believe" (from *Show Boat*, lyric by Oscar Hammerstein II)—Robertson; "Here Comes the Showboat!" (from *Show Boat,* music by Maceo Pinkard, lyric by Billy Rose)—Delmar, Holmes, Robertson; "Why Do I Love You?" (from *Show Boat,* lyric by Oscar Hammerstein II)—Robertson; "I Have the Room Above Her" (from *Show Boat,* lyric by Oscar Hammerstein II)—Holmes; "I Still Suits Me" (from *Show Boat,* lyric by Oscar Hammerstein II)—Holmes, Welch; "Daydreaming" (from *You Were Never Lovelier,* lyric by Gus Kahn), "I Dream Too Much" (from *I Dream Too Much,* lyric by Dorothy Fields), "Can I Forget You?" (from *High, Wide and Handsome,* lyric by Oscar Hammerstein II)—Delmar, Holmes, Robertson; "Pick Yourself Up" (from *Swing Time,* lyric by Dorothy Fields)—Delmar, Robertson; "She Didn't Say Yes" (from *The Cat and the Fiddle,* lyric by Otto Harbach)—Welch; "The Folks Who Live on the Hill" (from *High, Wide and Handsome,* lyric by Oscar Hammerstein II)—Holmes; "Long Ago and Far Away" (from *Cover Girl,* lyric by Ira Gershwin)—Ensemble.

ACT II: "The Show Must Go On" (from *Cover Girl,* lyric by Ira Gershwin)—Ensemble; "Don't Ask Me Not to Sing" (from *Roberta,* lyric by Otto Harbach)—Holmes; "The Way You Look Tonight" (from *Swing Time,* lyric by Dorothy Fields)—Holmes; "A Fine Romance" (from *Swing Time,* lyric by Dorothy Fields)—Delmar, Holmes; "Lovely to Look At" (from *Roberta,* lyric by Dorothy Fields and Jimmy McHugh)—Welch; "Just Let Me Look at You" (from *Joy of Living,* lyric by Dorothy Fields)—Robertson; "Who?" (from *Sunny,* lyric by Oscar Hammerstein II and Otto Harbach)—Ensemble. "Remind Me" (from *One Night in the Tropics,* lyric by Dorothy Fields)—Delmar, Holmes; "The Last Time I Saw Paris" (from *Lady Be Good,* lyric by Oscar Hammerstein II)—Holmes.

Also "Ol' Man River" (from *Show Boat,* lyric by Oscar Hammerstein II)—Delmar, Holmes, Robertson; "Why Was I Born?" (from *Sweet Adeline,* lyric by Oscar Hammerstein II)—Welch; "Bill" (from *Show Boat,* lyric by Oscar Hammerstein II and P.G. Wodehouse)—Robertson; "Can't Help Lovin' Dat Man" (from *Show Boat,* lyric by Oscar Hammerstein II)—Delmar; "All the Things You Are" (from *Till the Clouds Roll By,* lyric by Oscar Hammerstein II)—Delmar, Holmes, Robertson; "I've Told Every Little Star" (from *Music in the Air,* lyric by Oscar Hammerstein II)—Welch; "They Didn't Believe Me" (from *Till the Clouds Roll By,* lyric by Herbert Reynolds) and "Till the Clouds Roll By" (lyric by P.G. Wodehouse)—Ensemble; "Look for the Silver Lining" (from *Sally,* lyric by B.G. deSylva)—Ensemble; "Make Way for Tomorrow" (from *Cover Girl,* lyric by E.Y. Harburg and Ira Gershwin)—Ensemble.

Uptown . . . It's Hot! (24). Musical revue conceived by Maurice Hines. Produced by Allen Spivak and Larry Magid at the Lunt-Fontanne Theater. Opened January 29, 1986. (Closed February 16, 1986)

Alisa Gyse	Tommi Johnson
Lawrence Hamilton	Marion Ramsey
Maurice Hines	Jeffery V. Thompson

Ensemble: Sheila D. Barker, Toni-Maria Chalmers, Leon Evans, Michael Franks, Robert H. Fowler, Lovette George, Ruthanna Graves, Yolanda Graves, Emera Hunt, Leslie Williams-Jenkins, Lisa Ann Mallory, Delphine T. Mantz, Gerry McIntyre, Christopher T. Moore, Elise Neal,

Leesa M. Osborn, Marishka Shanice Phillips, R. LaChanze Sapp, Cheryl Ann Scott, Darius Keith Williams.

Understudies: Misses Ramsey, Gyse—Yolanda Graves; Mr. Thompson—Gerry McIntyre; Mr. Hamilton—Robert Fowler, Michael Franks; Mr. Johnson—Leon Evans.

Directed and choreographed by Maurice Hines; musical direction and supervision, Frank Owens; scenery, Tom McPhillips; costumes, Ellen Lee; lighting, Marc B. Weiss; narrations written by Jeffery V. Thompson, Marion Ramsey; dance arrangements, Frank Owens, Thom Bridwell; assistant choreographer, Mercedes Ellington; associate producer, Stanley Kay; production supervisor, Beverley Randolph; production stage manager, Gwendolyn M. Gilliam; stage manager, Jerry Cleveland; press, Michael Alpert, Ruth Jaffe.

Revue of American popular music from the 1930s to the 1980s, previously produced in Atlantic City, N.J. and Washington, D.C.

ACT I: Overture—Orchestra; Prologue—Jeffery V. Thompson, Alisa Gyse, Lawrence Hamilton, Tommi Johnson, Marion Ramsey, Maurice Hines, Ensemble Men.

The 1930s: Swing That Music—Ramsey; Cotton Club Stomp—Ramsey, Ensemble; Three Gents ("Daybreak Express," "Tap Along With Me," "Dinah")—Hamilton, Christopher T. Moore, Robert H. Fowler; "That Shot Got 'Em!" (adapted by Marion Ramsey and Jeffery V. Thompson)—Thompson, Ramsey, Johnson, Fowler; Stormy Weather Medley ("When Your Lover Has Gone," "Ill Wind," "Body & Soul," "Stormy Weather")—Hines, Gyse; Diga Diga Doo—Ramsey, Gerry McIntyre, Delphine T. Mantz, Ensemble; Lady Be Good—Hines; Cab Calloway and the Nicholas Brothers ("Jim Jam Jumpin' ")—Johnson, Leon Evans, Darius Keith Williams.

The 1940s: Big Band Tribute; Chick Webb Theme Song—Let's Get Together—Orchestra; A-Tisket A-Tasket—Alisa Gyse; Jitterbuggin'! Jumpin' at the Woodside—Hines, Ramsey, Thompson, Hamilton, Mantz, Sheila D. Barker, Ensemble.

ACT II, The 1950s and 1960s: Doo Woppers ("Why Do Fools Fall in Love")—Gyse, Hamilton, Johnson; The Apollo, Master of Ceremonies—Jeffery V. Thompson; The Gospel Caravan ("His Eye Is on the Sparrow"—Hamilton; "Amazing Grace"—Gyse, "Just a Closer Walk With Thee"—Johnson, "Old Landmark"—Hamilton, Gyse, Johnson, R. LaChanze Sapp, Ensemble); Good Mornin' Judge (Judge Pigmeat—Thompson, DeDistrict Attorney—Ramsey, Defendant—Gyse, Sonny Rayburn—Hines, adaptations by Jeffery V. Thompson); Rock & Roll Medley ("You Send Me"—Johnson, "Blueberry Hill"—Thompson, "Tutti Frutti"—McIntyre, "Johnny B. Goode"—Hamilton, Ensemble Men); Battle of the Groups: "Will You Still Love Me Tomorrow"—Toni-Maria Chalmers, Leslie Williams-Jenkins, Mantz, Cheryl Ann Scott, "Be My Baby"—Gyse, Barker, Elise Neal, "Don't Mess With Bill"—Sapp, Lisa Ann Mallory, Leesa M. Osborn, "Dancin' in the Streets" —Yolanda Graves, Lovette George, Emera Hunt, "Stop in the Name of Love"—Ramsey, Ruthanna Graves, Marishka Shanice Phillips, "Ain't Too Proud to Beg"—Hamilton, Williams, Evans, Johnson, McIntyre, "Proud Mary"—Ramsey, Ruthanna Graves, Phillips, Scott.

The 1970s: Station WHOT—Thompson; Stevie Wonder Medley ("Superstition, Keep on Running," "Higher Ground," "Do I Do"), Stevie Wonder—Evans, Devil—Hines, Victim—Gyse, Angel —Hamilton, Ensemble Dancers.

The 1980s: Radio Playoffs—Ramsey, Hamilton, Sapp, Evans, McIntyre, Hines; Express—Ramsey, Thompson, Ensemble Dancers; Rappers ("1999")—Hamilton, Thompson, Company.

Execution of Justice (12). By Emily Mann. Produced by Lester and Marjorie Osterman, Mortimer Caplin and Richard C. Norton & Christopher Stark at the Virginia Theater. Opened March 13, 1986. (Closed March 22, 1986)

Dan White	John Spencer	Harry Britt	Donal Donnelly
Mary Ann White	Mary McDonnell	Joseph Freitas;	
Cop	Stanley Tucci	Mourner	Nicholas Hormann
Sister Boom Boom	Wesley Snipes	Trial Characters:	
Chorus of Uncalled Witnesses:		The Court	Nicholas Kepros
Jim Denman	Christopher McHale	Court Clerk	Lisabeth Bartlett
Young Mother	Lisabeth Bartlett	Douglas Schmidt	Peter Friedman
Milk's Friend	Adam Redfield	Thomas F. Norman	Gerry Bamman
Gwenn Craig	Isabell Monk	Joanna Lu	Freda Foh Shen

Prospective
Jurors. . . . . John Clark, Suzy Hunt
Juror #3/Foreman . . . . Gary Reineke
Bailiff. . . . . Jeremy O. Caplin
Witnesses for the People:
Coroner Stephens . . . . Donal Donnelly
Rudy Nothenberg. . . . . Earle Hyman
Barbara Taylor . . . . Marcia Jean Kurtz
Officer Byrne. . . . . Isabell Monk
William Melia. . . . . Richard Riehle
Cyr Copertini . . . . Suzy Hunt
Carl Henry
Carlson . . . . Nicholas Hormann
Richard Pabich. . . . . Wesley Snipes
Frank Falzon . . . . Jon DeVries
Edward Erdelatz. . . . . Stanley Tucci

Witnesses for the Defense:
Denise Apcar . . . . Lisabeth Bartlett
Sherratt; Dr. Lunde . . . . Gary Reineke
Frediani. . . . . Jeremy O. Caplin
Sullivan . . . . Stanley Tucci
Lee Dolson . . . . Richard Riehle
Dr. Jones. . . . . Earle Hyman
Dr. Solomon . . . . Marcia Jean Kurtz
Dr. Blinder . . . . Donal Donnelly
Dr. Delman. . . . . Jon DeVries
In Rebuttal for the People:
Carol Ruth Silver. . . . . . . Marcia Jean Kurtz
Dr. Levy . . . . Gary Reineke
Action Cameraman . . . . . . Richard Howard
Riot Police: Jeremy O. Caplin, Josh Clark, Jon
DeVries, Richard Riehle, Stanley Tucci.

Understudies: Mr. Tucci—Wesley Snipes, Richard Riehle; Miss Kurtz—Elise Warner; Messrs. DeVries, Caplin, Spencer—Christopher McHale; Misses McDonnell, Hunt, Monk, Shen, Bartlett—Carlotta Schoch; Messrs. Snipes, Redfield, Friedman—Josh Clark; Miss Kurtz—Suzy Hunt; Mr. Hormann—Gary Reineke; Mr. McHale—Jeremy O. Caplin; Messrs. Donnelly, Kepros, Riehle, Hyman, Reineke—Richard Poe.

Directed by Emily Mann; scenery, Ming Cho Lee; costumes, Jennifer Von Mayrhauser; lighting, Pat Collins; sound, Tom Morse; film sequences excerpted from *The Times of Harvey Milk* by Robert Epstein and Richard Schmiechen; production stage manager, Frank Marino; stage manager, Fredric Hanson; press, Betty Lee Hunt, Maria Cristina Pucci.

Time: 1978 to the present. Place: San Francisco. The play was presented in two parts.

Docudrama of the trial of Dan White for the double murder of the mayor of San Francisco, George Moscone, and a city supervisor, Harvey Milk, with text taken from the trial transcripts, reportage and interviews. Previously produced at Arena Stage, Washington, D.C. and other regional theaters.

A Best Play; see page 236.

Precious Sons (60). By George Furth. Produced by Roger Berlind and Marty Bell at the Longacre Theater. Opened March 20, 1986. (Closed May 10, 1986)

Art . . . . William O'Leary
Freddy . . . . Anthony Rapp
Bea . . . . Judith Ivey

Fred . . . . Ed Harris
Sandra . . . . Anne Marie Bobby

Standbys: Miss Ivey—Kelly Bishop; Mr. Harris—George Bamford. Understudies: Messrs. O'Leary, Rapp—Christopher Gartin; Miss Bobby—Mary B. Ward.

Directed by Norman René; scenery, Andrew Jackness; costumes, Joseph G. Aulisi; lighting, Richard Nelson; sound, Tom Morse; associate producer, Michael Sanders; production stage manager, Steven Beckler; stage manager, Phil DiMaggio; press, Solters/Roskin/Friedman, Inc., Joshua Ellis, James Sapp, Cindy Valk.

Time: June 3, 1949. Place: The South Side of Chicago. Act I, Scene 1: Early morning. Scene 2: Dusk the same day. Act II, Scene 1: The following evening. Scene 2: 10 o'clock the following morning.

Crisis in a family, a wife forces her laborer husband to give up his dreams and opportunities of advancement, for the good of their younger son.

*Lincoln Center Theater. Schedule of two programs. **Juggling and Cheap Theatrics** (40). Variety revue devised by the performers known as The Flying Karamazov Brothers. Opened April 1, 1986; transferred to the Mitzi E. Newhouse Theater April 23, 1986. (Closed May 4, 1986) ***The House of Blue Leaves** (40). Transfer from off Broadway of the revival of the play by John Guare. Opened April 29, 1986. Produced by Lincoln Center Theater, Gregory Mosher director, Bernard Gersten executive producer, at the Vivian Beaumont Theater.

JUGGLING AND CHEAP THEATRICS

The Flying Karamazov Brothers:

Fyodor.............	Timothy Daniel Furst	Alyosha..................	Randy Nelson
Dmitri................	Paul David Magid	Ivan	Howard Jay Patterson
		Smerdyakov................	Sam Williams

Press: Merle Debuskey, Robert Larkin.

Juggling, comedy and other antics created by this team of acrobatic performers. Previous versions of this show, presented in two parts, appeared at the Brooklyn Academy of Music in 1982 and on Broadway 5/10/83 for 25 performances.

THE HOUSE OF BLUE LEAVES

Artie Shaughnessy...........	John Mahoney	2d Nun.......................	Jane Cecil
Ronnie Shaughnessy.............	Ben Stiller	Little Nun	Ann Talman
Bunny Flingus..........	Stockard Channing	M.P.; El Dorado Bartender	Ian Blackman
Bananas Shaughnessy........	Swoosie Kurtz	White Man;	
Corrinne Stroller.............	Julie Hagerty	El Dorado Bartender.....	Peter J. Downing
Head Nun	Patricia Falkenhain	Billy Einhorn................	Danny Aiello

Understudies: Mr. Stiller—Ian Blackman; Miss Falkenhain—Jane Cecil; Messrs. Mahoney, Aiello—Brian Evers; Misses Kurtz, Talman—Kathleen McKiernan; Misses Channing, Hagerty—Melodie Somers.

Directed by Jerry Zaks; scenery, Tony Walton; costumes, Ann Roth; lighting, Paul Gallo; sound, Aural Fixation; stage manager, Kate Stewart.

Time: October 4. 1965. Place: The El Dorado Bar and Grill and in an apartment in Sunnyside, Queens.

Transfer from off Broadway (Lincoln Center's Mitzi E. Newhouse Theater) where *The House of Blue Leaves* played 38 performances 3/19/86–4/20/86 to Broadway (Lincoln Center's Vivian Beaumont Theater); see its entry in the Plays Produced Off Broadway section of this volume.

So Long on Lonely Street (53). By Sandra Deer. Produced by Cheryl Crawford, Paul B. Berkowsky and Robert Franz in association with Maxine and Stanford Makover and J. Arnold Nickerson by special arrangement with the Alliance Theater Company at the Jack Lawrence Theater. Opened April 3, 1986. (Closed May 18, 1986)

SO LONG ON LONELY STREET—Pat Nesbit, Ray Dooley and Stephen Root in the comedy by Sandra Deer

Raymond Brown	Ray Dooley	King Vaughnum 3d	Stephen Root
Annabel Lee	Lizan Mitchell	Clarice Vaughnum	Jane Murray
Ruth Brown	Pat Nesbit	Bobby Stack	Fritz Sperberg

Directed by Kent Stephens; original music, Hal Lanier; scenery, Mark Morton; costumes, Jane Greenwood; lighting, Allen Lee Hughes; production supervisor, Roger Shea; press, Jeffrey Richards Associates, Ben Morse.

Time: Late August. Place: Honeysuckle Hill, a few miles outside a small Southern town. The play was presented in two parts.

Southern family gathers at the old homestead for the reading of a will. The play was presented in two parts. Previously produced in regional theater at the Alliance Theater, Atlanta.

*Loot (64). Transfer from off Broadway of the revival of the play by Joe Orton. Produced by The David Merrick Arts Foundation, Charles P. Kopelman and Mark Simon at the Music Box. Opened April 7, 1986.

McLeavy	Charles Keating	Dennis	Alec Baldwin
Fay	Zoë Wanamaker	Truscott	Joseph Maher
Hal	Zeljko Ivanek	Meadows	Nick Ullett

Standbys: Messrs. Keating, Maher—Nick Ullett; Miss Wanamaker—Selena Carey-Jones; Messrs. Ivanek, Baldwin, Ullett—Steven Weber.

Directed by John Tillinger; scenery, John Lee Beatty; costumes, Bill Walker; lighting, Richard Nelson; production stage manager, Peggy Peterson; stage manager, Jon Nakagawa; press, Solters/ Roskin/Friedman, Inc., Joshua Ellis, Cindy Valk.

Time: Afternoon. Place: A room in McLeavy's house. The play was presented in two parts.

This production was produced off Broadway by Manhattan Theater Club for 32 performances 2/18/86–3/15/86 before transferring to Broadway. The American premiere of *Loot* took place on Broadway 3/18/68 for 22 performances. This is its first major New York revival.

*Big Deal (62). Musical based on the film *Big Deal on Madonna Street*; book by Bob Fosse; music by various authors (see musical numbers listing). Produced by The Shubert Organization, Roger Berlind and Jerome Minskoff in association with Jonathan Farkas at the Broadway Theater. Opened April 10, 1986.

Lilly	Loretta Devine	Slick	Larry Marshall
1st Narrator	Wayne Cilento	Sunnyboy	Mel Johnson Jr.
2d Narrator	Bruce Anthony Davis	Willie	Alan Weeks
Kokomo; Dancin' Dan	Gary Chapman	Judge; Bandleader	Bernard J. Marsh
Otis	Alde Lewis Jr.	Phoebe	Desiree Coleman
Charley	Cleavant Derricks	2d Shadow	Barbara Yeager
Pearl; Band Singer;		Little Willie	Roumel Reaux
1st Shadow	Valarie Pettiford	Announcer	Candace Tovar

Dancers: Ciscoe Bruton II, Lloyd Culbreath, Kim Darwin, Cady Huffman, Amelia Marshall, Frank Mastrocola, Stephanie Pope, Roumel Reaux, George Russell, Candace Tovar. Dance Alternates: Bryant Baldwin, Diana Laurenson, Vince Cole.

Onstage Band: Brian Brake drums, Leonard Oxley piano, William Shadel clarinet, Joe Mosello trumpet, Earl May bass, Britt Woodman trombone.

Standbys: Messrs. Derricks, Marshall—Byron Utley; Messrs. Johnson, Marsh—James Stovall. Understudies: Miss Devine—Stephanie Pope; Mr. Weeks—Lloyd Culbreath; Mr. Cilento—Frank Mastrocola; Mr. Davis—Bryant Baldwin; Mr. Chapman (Kokomo)—Kenneth Hanson; Mr. Lewis —Roumel Reaux; Miss Coleman—Amelia Marshall; Mr. Chapman (Dancin' Dan)—Roumel Reaux, Ciscoe Bruton II; Misses Pettiford, Yeager (Shadows)—Stephanie Pope, Kim Darwin; Miss Pettiford (Pearl)—Cady Huffman.

Directed and choreographed by Bob Fosse; scenery, Peter Larkin; costumes, Patricia Zipprodt; lighting, Jules Fisher; orchestrations, Ralph Burns; sound, Abe Jacob; associate choreographer, Christopher Chadman; music arranged and conducted by Gordon Lowry Harrell; executive producer,

Jules Fisher; assistant to the choreographer, Linda Haberman; production stage manager, Phil Friedman; stage managers, Perry Cline, Barry Kearsley; press, The Fred Nathan Company, Inc., Bert Fink.

Time: The 1930s. Place: The South Side of Chicago.

Stage musicalization of the 1960 Italian film about a bungled robbery (a story also presented in a 1984 American film version).

ACT I

Prologue

"Life Is Just a Bowl of Cherries".. Lilly
    (by Lew Brown and Ray Henderson)

"For No Good Reason at All"... Narrators
    (by Abel Baer, Samuel W. Lewis and Joseph Young)

Locker room and fight area

"Charley My Boy"... Charley
    (by Gus Kahn and Ted Fiorito)

The Judge's chambers

"I've Got a Feelin' You're Foolin' " .... Kokomo, Charley, Judge, Narrators
    (by Nacio Herb Brown and Arthur Fried)

Prison yard

"Ain't We Got Fun" .... Prisoners
    (music, Richard Whiting; words, Gus Kahn and Raymond Egan)

Gem Theater

"For No Good Reason at All" (Reprise)........................... Narrators, Dancers

The men's room at the Gem Theater

A camera store

Cottage Grove Avenue

"Chicago" .... Narrators
    (by Fred Fisher)

Pool Hall

"Pick Yourself Up" .... Charley, Willie, Slick, Sunnyboy, Otis
    (music, Jerome Kern; words, Dorothy Fields)

Cottage Grove Avenue

"I'm Just Wild About Harry"... Lilly
    (by Eubie Blake and Noble Sissel)

Paradise Ballroom

"Beat Me Daddy Eight to the Bar"........................... Bandleader, Band, Dancers
    (by Don Raye, Hughie Prince and Eleanor Sheehy)

"The Music Goes 'Round and 'Round"............................... Bandleader, Band
    (by Edward Farley, Red Hodgson and Michael Riley)

Alley outside dancehall

"Life Is Just a Bowl of Cherries" (Reprise)....................................... Lilly

ACT II

Prologue

"Now's the Time to Fall in Love".............................. Narrators, Dancers
    (by Al Sherman and Al Lewis)

Slick's apartment

"Ain't She Sweet" .... Sunnyboy, Phoebe, Narrators, Dancers
    (music, Milton Agar; words, Jack Yellen)

Willie's house

"Everybody Loves My Baby"....................................... Willie, Narrators
    (by Jack Palmer and Spencer Williams)

"Me and My Shadow"....................................... Dancin' Dan, Shadows
    (music, Al Jolson and Dave Dreyer, words, Billy Rose)

A Pawnshop

Slick's apartment
  "Love Is Just Around the Corner"...Narrators
      (by Leo Robin and Lewis E. Gensler)
Charley's room
Lilly's rented room
  "Just a Gigolo"..Bandleader, Charley
      (music, Leonello Casucci; original words, Julius Brammer; English words, Irving Caesar)
  "Who's Your Little Who-zis?"..............................Bandleader, Bandsinger
      (music, Hal Goering and Ben Bernie; words, Walter Hirsch)
Refreshment stand of Gem Theater
Lilly's rented room
  "Yes Sir, That's My Baby"...Charley
      (music, Walter Donaldson; words, Gus Kahn)
  "Button Up Your Overcoat"...Lilly
      (by B.G. DeSylva, Lew Brown and Ray Henderson)
The Robbery
The Fantasies
  "Daddy, You've Been a Mother to Me" ....Willie, Little Willie
      (by Fred Fisher)
  "Hold Tight, Hold Tight"..Otis, Ladies
      (by Leonard Ware, Willie Spottswood, Ed Robinson, Ben Smith and Sidney Bechet)
  "Happy Days Are Here Again" ....Slick, Phoebe, Sunnyboy, Company
      (music, Milton Agar; words, Jack Yellen)
  "I'm Sitting on Top of the World" ....Charley, Company
      (by Samuel M. Lewis, Joseph Young and Ray Henderson)
A Street
"Life Is Just a Bowl of Cherries" (Reprise) ....Lilly

*Social Security (52). By Andrew Bergman. Produced by David Geffen and The Shubert Organization at the Ethel Barrymore Theater. Opened April 17, 1986.

David Kahn....................	Ron Silver	Martin Heyman.............	Kenneth Welsh
Barbara Kahn	Marlo Thomas	Sophie Greengrass.........	Olympia Dukakis
Trudy Heyman	Joanna Gleason	Maurice Koenig............	Stefan Schnabel

Standbys: Misses Thomas, Gleason—Caroline Aaron; Messrs. Silver, Welsh—John Rothman; Miss Dukakis—Ruth Vool; Mr. Schnabel—Joseph Leon.

Directed by Mike Nichols; scenery, Tony Walton; costumes, Ann Roth; lighting, Marilyn Rennagel; sound, Otts Munderloh; associate producer, Susan McNair; production stage manager, Peter Lawrence; stage manager, Jim Woolley; press, Bill Evans & Associates, Sandra Manley, Jim Baldassare.

Act I: New York—the East Side apartment of Barbara and David Kahn, evening. Act II, Scene 1: Two weeks later, evening. Scene 2: Sunday afternoon, one week later.

Comedy, the aged mother in an art dealer's family gears up for a last fling with a famous artist.

*The Petition (46). By Brian Clark. Produced by Robert Whitehead, Roger L. Stevens and The Shubert Organization at the John Golden Theater. Opened April 24, 1986.

Lady Elizabeth Milne...Jessica Tandy
General Sir Edmund Milne...Hume Cronyn

Directed by Peter Hall; production designed by John Bury; production stage manager, William Dodds; stage manager, Amy Pell; press, The Fred Nathan Company, Inc., Merle Frimark.

Time: Between 10 A.M. and 12 noon. Place: An apartment in Belgravia, London.

Wife signing a peace petition precipitates a review of the 50-year marriage between herself and her husband, a retired general. A foreign (British) play in its world premiere in this production.

SOCIAL SECURITY—Stefan Schnabel and Olympia Dukakis *(foreground)* and Ron Silver and Marlo Thomas *(in rear, standing)* in the comedy by Andrew Bergman, directed by Mike Nichols

*Sweet Charity (39). Revival of the musical originally conceived, directed and choreographed by Bob Fosse; based on an original screen play by Federico Fellini, Tullio Pinelli and Ennia Flaiano; book by Neil Simon; music by Cy Coleman; lyrics by Dorothy Fields. Produced by Jerome Minskoff, James M. Nederlander, Arthur Rubin and Joseph Harris at the Minskoff Theater. Opened April 27, 1986.

Charity	Debbie Allen	Mimi	Mimi Quillin
Dark Glasses	David Warren Gibson	Herman	Lee Wilkof
Married Couple	Quinn Baird, Jan Horvath	Doorman; Waiter	Tom Wierney
1st Young Man	Jeff Shade	Ursala	Carrie Nygren
Woman With Hat;		Vittorio Vidal	Mark Jacoby
Panhandler; Receptionist;		Manfred	Fred C. Mann III
Good Fairy	Celia Tackaberry	Old Maid	Jan Horvath
Ice Cream Vendor	Kelly Patterson	Oscar	Michael Rupert
Young Spanish Man	Adrian Rosario	Daddy Johann	
Cop; Brother Harold	Tanis Michaels	Sebastian Brubeck	Irving Allen Lee
Helene	Allison Williams	Brother Ray	Stanley Wesley Perryman
Nickie	Bebe Neuwirth	Rosie	Dana Moore

Singers and Dancers of Times Square: Quinn Baird, Christine Colby, Alice Everett Cox, David Warren Gibson, Kim Morgan Greene, Jan Horvath, Jane Lanier, Fred C. Mann III, Allison Reneé Manson, Tanis Michaels, Dana Moore, Michelle O'Steen, Kelly Patterson, Stanley Wesley Perryman, Mimi Quillin, Adrian Rosario, Jeff Shade, Tom Wierney. Alternates: Michelle O'Steen, Chet Walker.

Standby: Miss Allen—Bebe Neuwirth. Understudies: Mr. Rupert—David Warren Gibson, Michael Licata; Mr. Jacoby—Michael Licata, Kelly Patterson; Miss Neuwirth—Dana Moore; Miss Williams —Kirsten Childs; Mr. Lee—Tanis Michaels; Mr. Wilkof—Tom Wierney; Miss Nygren—Christine Colby; Miss Tackaberry—Jan Horvath. Alternate Understudy: Miss Allen—Kim Morgan Greene.

Directed and choreographed by Bob Fosse; musical direction, Fred Werner; scenery and lighting, Robert Randolph; costumes, Patricia Zipprodt; orchestrations, Ralph Burns; sound, Otts Munderloh; assistant to Mr. Fosse, Gwen Verdon; production stage manager, Craig Jacobs; stage manager, Lani Ball; press, Jeffrey Richards Associates, C. George Willard.

Time: Mid-1960s. Place: New York.

Sweet Charity was originally produced on Broadway 1/29/66 for 608 performances. This is its first major New York revival.

The list of scenes and musical numbers in *Sweet Charity* appears on pages 395–6 of *The Best Plays of 1965–66.*

*Long Day's Journey Into Night (30). Revival of the play by Eugene O'Neill. Produced by Emanuel Azenberg, The Shubert Organization, Roger Peters, Roger Berlind and Pace Theatrical Group, Inc. at the Broadhurst Theater. Opened April 28, 1986.

Mary Tyrone	Bethel Leslie	Edmund Tyrone	Peter Gallagher
James Tyrone	Jack Lemmon	Cathleen	Jodie Lynne McClintock
James Tyrone Jr.	Kevin Spacey		

Understudies: Miss Leslie—Patricia Fraser; Messrs. Spacey, Gallagher—Michael Hammond; Miss McClintock—Laura MacDermott.

Directed by Jonathan Miller; scenery, Tony Straiges; costumes, Willa Kim; lighting, Richard Nelson; associate producer, Mona Schlachter; stage managers, Martin Herzer, Barbara-Mae Phillips; press, Bill Evans & Associates, Sandra Manley, Jim Baldassare.

Place: Living room of the Tyrones' summer home. Act I: 8:30 A.M. of a day in August. Act II, Scene 1: Around 12:45. Scene 2: About a half hour later. Act III: Around 6:30 that evening. Act IV: Around midnight. The play was presented in two parts with the intermission following Act II.

The last major New York revival of *Long Day's Journey Into Night* took place off Broadway 3/18/81 for 87 performances.

PLAYS WHICH CLOSED
PRIOR TO BROADWAY OPENING

Productions which were organized by New York producers for Broadway presentation but which closed during their production and tryout period are listed below.

Sing, Mahalia, Sing. Musical with book by George Faison; original music and lyrics by Richard Smallwood, George Faison and Wayne Davis. Produced by Edgewood Productions, Inc. (Louis G. Bond, Tadd Schnugg and Marty Bronson) in a national tour. Opened at the Warner Theater, Washington, D.C., March 26, 1985. (Closed at the Paramount Theater, Oakland, Calif., Sept. 1, 1985)

CAST: Mahalia Jackson—Jennifer Holliday (Esther Marrow alternating twice weekly); The Richard Smallwood Singers; Lynette Hawkins; Glen Jones.

Directed by George Faison; choreography, George Faison; musical supervision, Timothy Graphenreed; scenery, Tom McPhillips; costumes, Nancy Potts; lighting, Thomas Skelton; sound, Christopher Bond; conductor, Michael Powell.

The career of Mahalia Jackson portrayed in a stage musical.

Babes in Arms. Revival of the musical based on an original book by Lorenz Hart and Richard Rodgers; book by George Oppenheimer; music by Richard Rodgers; lyrics by Lorenz Hart. Produced by Kennedy Lipton Productions (Robert Kennedy and Michael C. Lipton) at the Music Hall, Tarrytown, N.Y. Opened June 26, 1985. (Closed August 9, 1985)

Matt McClusky . . . . Michael O'Steen	Bunny . . . . Donna Theodore
Libby Appleton . . . . Kim Morgan	Seymour Fleming . . . . John Granger
Barney Flanagan . . . . Jack Doyle	Lee Calhoun . . . . Todd Patterson
Terry Thompson . . . . Michele Franks	Jennifer Owen . . . . Lisa Donovan
Gus Field . . . . James Brennan	Phyllis Owen . . . . Joy Hodges
Valentine White . . . . Randall Skinner	Steve Edwards . . . . Michael Williams
Susie Ward . . . . Karen Ziemba	

Directed by Ginger Rogers; choreography, Randall Skinner; musical direction, arrangements and orchestrations, Bruce Pomahac; scenery, Linda E. Hacker; costumes, Sam Fleming; lighting, Clarke Thornton; musical conductor, Stephen Bates; dance assistant, Debra Ann Draper; production stage manager, Charles Collins; press, Fred Hoot.

The April 14, 1937 Rodgers & Hart musical presented in two acts, with the addition of the musical numbers "Manhattan" and "Mountain Greenery." The only major New York revival of *Babes in Arms* took place off Broadway in the 1950–51 season.

Leave It to Jane. Revival of the musical based on the play *The College Widow* by George Ade; book and lyrics by Guy Bolton and P.G. Wodehouse; music by Jerome Kern. Produced by Goodspeed Opera House, Michael P. Price, producer. Opened at Goodspeed Opera House, East Haddam, Conn., October 2, 1985. (Closed at the Royal Poinciana Playhouse, Palm Beach, Fla., January 18, 1986)

Ollie Mitchell . . . . Jack Doyle	Copernicus Talbot . . . . Michael Waldron
Matty McGowan . . . . Dale O'Brien	Jane Witherspoon . . . . Rebecca Luker
Stub Talmadge . . . . Michael O'Steen	Hiram Bolton . . . . Tom Batten
Silent Murphy . . . . Patrick McCord	Billy Bolton . . . . David Staller
Peter Witherspoon . . . . Robert Nichols	Elan Hicks . . . . Gary Gage
Bessie Tanner . . . . Iris Revson	Bub Hicks . . . . Nick Corley
Flora Wiggins . . . . Faith Prince	

Ensemble: Patricia Forestier, Donna M. Pompei, Mercedes Perez, Lisa Pompa, Keith Savage, Marc Hunter, Paul Cira.

Directed by Thomas Gruenewald; choreography, Walter Painter; musical direction, Lynn Crigler; scenery, James Leonard Joy; costumes, John Carver Sullivan; lighting, Craig Miller; additional orchestrations, Donald Jonston, Lynn Crigler; dance arrangements, D'Vaughn Pershing, Lynn Crigler; assistant musical director, Patrick Vaccariello; music research consultant, Alfred Simon; associate producer, Warren Pincus; producing associate, Sue Frost; stage manager, Michael Brunner; press, Max Eisen.

Leave It to Jane was originally produced on Broadway 8/28/17 for 167 performances and was revived off Broadway in the season of 1959–60.

MUSICAL NUMBERS, ACT I: Overture, "Good Old Atwater," "Wait Till Tomorrow," "Just You Watch Your Step," "Leave It to Jane," "Sirens' Song," College Medley, "There It Is Again," "Cleopaterer," "The Crickets Are Calling," Finaletto.

ACT II: Entr'acte, "Football Song," "Sir Galahad," "Football Song/Leave It to Jane" (Reprise), "The Sun Shines Brighter," "I Am Going to Find a Girl," "It's a Great Big Land," Finale.

The Night of the Iguana. Revival of the play by Tennessee Williams. Produced by Fred Walker, Michael J. Lonergan and Jacqueline de la Chaume at the Mechanic Theater, Baltimore. Opened October 15, 1985. (Closed November 9, 1985)

Directed by Arthur Sherman; scenery, Oliver Smith; costumes, Lucinda Ballard; lighting, Feder; sound, Jack Mann; press, Solters/Roskin/Friedman, Inc., Josh Ellis, Keith Sherman. With Jeanne Moreau, Michael Moriarty, Eileen Brennan, Roy Dotrice, Penelope Allen, Sam J. Coppola, M'el Dowd, Marita Garaghty, Kevin Gray, Martin Shakar, Brad Greenquist, Julian Reyes.

The Night of the Iguana was originally produced on Broadway 12/28/61 for 316 performances and was named a Best Play of its season and won the New York Drama Critics Award for best American play.

Citizen Tom Paine. By Howard Fast; based on his novel. Produced by Don Gregory and Kenneth F. Martell at the Nederlander Theater. (Closed in rehearsal February 24, 1986)

CAST: Tom Paine—Richard Thomas; Leilani Jones, Tom Toner, Robert Gerringer, Robert Molnar, Robert Aberdeen, Steven Haworth, Rand Bridges, Zach Grenier, Carole Monferdini, Michael Sgouros, James Hurdle.

Directed by James Simpson; scenery, John Arnone; costumes, Dunja Ramicova; lighting, Richard Riddell; press, John Springer.

The life and times of Tom Paine, previously produced in Williamstown, Mass.

PLAYS PRODUCED
OFF BROADWAY

Some distinctions between off-Broadway and Broadway productions at one end of the scale and off-off-Broadway productions at the other were blurred in the New York theater of the 1970s and 1980s. For the purposes of this *Best Plays* listing the term "off Broadway" is used to distinguish a professional from a showcase (off-off-Broadway) production and signifies a show which opened for general audiences in a mid-Manhattan theater seating 499 or fewer and 1) employed an Equity cast, 2) planned a regular schedule of 8 performances a week in an open-ended run and 3) offered itself to public comment by critics at a designated opening performance.

Occasional exceptions of inclusion (never of exclusion) are made to take in visiting troupes, borderline cases and nonqualifying productions which readers might expect to find in this list because they appear under an off-Broadway heading in other major sources of record.

Figures in parentheses following a play's title give number of performances. These figures do not include previews or extra nonprofit performances.

Plays marked with an asterisk (*) were still running on June 2, 1986. Their number of performances is figured from opening night through June 1, 1986.

Certain programs of off-Broadway companies are exceptions to our rule of counting the number of performances from the date of the press coverage. When the official opening takes place late in the run of a play's regularly priced public or subscription performances (after previews), we count the first performance of record, not the press date, as opening night—and in each such case in the listing we note the variance and give the press date.

In a listing of a show's numbers—dances, sketches, musical scenes, etc.—the titles of songs are identified wherever possible by their appearance in quotation marks (").

Most entries of off-Broadway productions which ran fewer than 20 performances or scheduled fewer than 8 performances a week are somewhat abbreviated, as are entries on running repertory programs repeated from previous years.

HOLDOVERS FROM PREVIOUS SEASONS

Plays which were running on June 1, 1985 are listed below. More detailed information about them appears in previous *Best Plays* volumes of appropriate date. Important cast changes since opening night are recorded in a section of this volume.

*The Fantasticks (10,856; longest continuous run of record in the American theater). Musical suggested by the play *Les Romanesques* by Edmond Rostand; book and lyrics by Tom Jones; music by Harvey Schmidt. Opened May 3, 1960.

*Forbidden Broadway (1,816). Cabaret revue with concept and lyrics by Gerard Alessandrini. Opened May 4, 1982. Revised (1984) version opened October 27, 1983. Revised (1985) version opened January 29, 1985. Revised (1986) version opened June 11, 1986.

*Little Shop of Horrors (1,603). Musical based on the film by Roger Corman; book and lyrics by Howard Ashman; music by Alan Menken. Opened July 27, 1982.

Fool for Love (1,000). By Sam Shepard. Opened May 26, 1983. (Closed September 29, 1985)

Isn't It Romantic (733). Revised version of the play by Wendy Wasserstein. Opened December 15, 1983. (Closed September 1, 1985)

*The Foreigner (678). By Larry Shue. Opened November 1, 1984.

New York Shakespeare Festival. Tracers (186). Conceived by John DiFusco; written by Vincent Caristi, Richard Chaves, John DiFusco, Eric E. Emerson; Rick Gallavan, Merlin Marston and Harry Stephens with Sheldon Lettich. Opened January 21, 1985. (Closed July 7, 1985) The Normal Heart (294). By Larry Kramer. Opened April 21, 1985. (Closed January 5, 1986) The Marriage of Bette and Boo (86). By Christopher Durang. Opened May 16, 1985. (Closed July 28, 1985) Rat in the Skull (39). By Ron Hutchinson. Opened May 21, 1985. (Closed June 23, 1985)

3 Guys Naked From the Waist Down (160). Musical with book and lyrics by Jerry Colker; music by Michael Rupert. Opened February 5, 1985. (Closed June 30, 1985)

Hannah Senesh (161). By David Schechter; developed in collaboration with Lori Wilner; based on diaries and poems of Hannah Senesh, with English translation by Marta Cohn and Peter Hay; originally developed by Dafna Soltes. Opened April 10, 1985. (Closed August 18, 1985)

*Penn & Teller (434). Magic show with Penn Jillette and Teller. Opened April 18, 1985.

Lies & Legends: The Musical Stories of Harry Chapin (79). Musical revue by Harry Chapin; original concept by Joseph Stern. Opened April 24, 1985. (Closed June 30, 1985)

Orphans (285). By Lyle Kessler. Opened May 7, 1985. (Closed January 5, 1986)

Mayor (185). Musical based on *Mayor* by Edward I. Koch; book by Warren Leight; music and lyrics by Charles Strouse. Opened May 13, 1985. (Closed October 21, 1985 and transferred to Broadway; see its entry in the Plays Produced on Broadway section of this volume)

Ceremonies in Dark Old Men (62). Revival of the play by Lonne Elder III. Opened May 15, 1985. (Closed June 30, 1985)

Man Enough (33). By Patty Gideon Sloan. Opened May 19, 1985. (Closed June 16, 1985)

The Return of Herbert Bracewell (57). By Andrew Johns. Opened May 20, 1985. (Closed July 7, 1985)

The Voice of the Turtle (56). Revival of the play by John van Druten. Opened May 22, 1985. (Closed July 7, 1985)

For No Good Reason by Nathalie Sarraute and **Childhood** adapted by Simone Benmussa from the book by Nathalie Sarraute (38). Opened May 29, 1985. (Closed June 30, 1985)

PLAYS PRODUCED JUNE 1, 1985–MAY 31, 1986

Playwrights Horizons. 1984–85 schedule included **Fighting International Fat** (15). By Jonathan Reynolds. Opened June 5, 1985. (Closed June 16, 1985) **Raw Youth** (15). By Neal Bell. Opened July 10, 1985. (Closed July 21, 1985) Produced by Playwrights Horizons, Andre Bishop artistic director, Paul S. Daniels managing director, at Playwrights Horisons (*Fighting International Fat* on the Mainstage, *Raw Youth* at the Studio). Press, Bob Ullman.

FIGHTING INTERNATIONAL FAT

Directed by David Trainer; scenery, Tony Straiges; costumes, Rita Ryack; lighting, Frances Aronson; sound, Scott Lehrer; production stage manager, M.A. Howard; with Jessica Walter, Ann McDonough, Ruth Jaroslow, B. Constance Barry, Stephen Ahern, John Gabriel, Lisa Banes.

Simultaneous comic treatments of TV talk shows and weight-loss schemes.

RAW YOUTH

Directed by Amy Saltz; scenery, Thomas Lynch; costumes, Kurt Wilhelm; lighting, Ann G. Wrightson; sound, Scott Lehrer, Lia Vollack; production stage manager, J.R. MacDonald; with Ben Siegler, John Seitz, James Ray.

Father and son help the F.B.I. to set a trap for a Congressman.

American Theater Exchange. Schedule of three programs. **Faulkner's Bicycle** (28). By Heather McDonald. Opened June 6, 1985. (Closed June 22, 1985). **Season's Greetings** (20). By Alan Ayckbourn. Opened July 11, 1985. (Closed July 27, 1985) **In the Belly of the Beast** (20). By Jack Henry Abbott; adapted by Adrian Hall; further adapted by Robert Woodruff. Opened August 15, 1985. (Closed August 31, 1985) Produced by the Joyce Theater Foundation, Inc., Cora Cahan executive director, *Faulkner's Bicycle* with the Yale Repertory Theater, *Season's Greetings* with the Alley Theater, Inc. and *In the Belly of the Beast* with the Center Theater Group/Mark Taper Forum, Gordon Davidson artistic director and producer, at the Joyce Theater.

FAULKNER'S BICYCLE

Mama	Kim Hunter	Jett	Tessie Hogan
Claire	Cara Duff-MacCormick	Faulkner	Addison Powell

Directed by Julian Webber; scenery, Pamela Peterson; costumes, Scott Bradley; lighting, Mary Louise Geiger; sound, Ken Lewis; projections, William B. Warfel; production stage manager, Patrice Thomas; press, Shirley Herz, Pete Sanders.

The first in this American Theater Exchange series of three offerings by visiting resident companies, *Faulkner's Bicycle*, is about a struggling writer returning to her home town (which happens to be Oxford, Miss. in the last year of William Faulkner's life) to renew her artistic strength. A foreign (Canadian) play previously produced by Yale Repertory Theater and presented in their production without intermission.

SEASON'S GREETINGS

Harvey Bunker	Robert Cornthwaite	Belinda	Robin Moseley
Dr. Bernard Longstaff	Dale Helward	Pattie	Cynthia Lammel

DAMES AT SEA—Donna Kane in the off-Broadway revival of the musical

Neville . . . . Richard Poe		Phyllis. Lillian Evans	
Eddie . . . . Charles Sanders		Clive . . . . Michael Alan Gregory	
Rachel . . . . Lawr Means			

Understudies: Messrs. Sanders, Gregory—Joe Barrett; Messrs. Cornthwaite, Helward, Poe—K. Lype O'Dell. Misses Moseley, Lammel, Means, Evans—Susan Pellegrino.

Directed by Pat Brown; scenery, Michael Holt; costumes, Fotini Dimou; lighting, Richard W. Jeter; sound, Jan Cole; assistant to the director, Beth Sanford; stage manager, Glenn Bruner.

Time: The present. Place: The home of Neville and Belinda Bunker. Act I, Scene 1: Christmas Eve, 7:30 P.M. Scene 2: Christmas Day, noon. Scene 3: Christmas Day, midnight. Act II, Scene 1: Boxing Day. Scene 2: December 27, 5:15 A.M.

A family's Christmas reunion and disruptions. A foreign play previously produced in London and in its American premiere last season in this Alley Theater, Houston, production.

A Best Play; see page 131.

IN THE BELLY OF THE BEAST

Jack Henry Abbott .... Andrew Robinson   Reader 2............ William Allen Young
Reader 1.................... Andy Wood

Directed by Robert Woodruff; scenery, John Ivo Gilles; costumes, Carol Brolaski; lighting, Paulie Jenkins; music, Douglas Wieselman; sound, Stephen Shaffer; video, Chip Lord, Branda Miller; associate producer, Madeline Puzo; produced in association with Seymour Morgenstern; stage manager, Al Franklin.

Understudies: Messrs. Wood, Young—Michael Tulin; Mr. Robinson—Andy Wood.

Mark Taper Forum production dramatizing material from a convicted killer's book of letters, plus trial transcripts and various interviews surrounding the play's events. The play was presented without intermission.

I'm Not Rappaport (181). By Herb Gardner. Produced by James Walsh, Lewis Allen and Martin Heinfling at American Place Theater. Opened June 6, 1985. (Closed November 10, 1985 and transferred to Broadway; see its entry in the Plays Produced on Broadway section of this volume)

Nat .... Judd Hirsch   Gilley .... Jace Alexander
Midge..................... Cleavon Little   Clara..................... Cheryl Giannini
Danforth................. Michael Tucker   Cowboy .... Ray Baker
Laurie.................... Liann Pattison

Understudies: Mr. Hirsch—Salem Ludwig; Mr. Little—William Hall Jr.; Misses Giannini, Pattison —Elaine Bromka; Mr. Alexander—Josh Pais; Messrs. Tucker, Baker—Howard Sherman.

Directed by Daniel Sullivan; scenery, Tony Walton; costumes, Robert Morgan; lighting, Pat Collins; production stage manager, Thomas A. Kelly; stage manager, Charles Kindl; press, Jeffrey Richards Associates, Ben Morse.

Time: Early October 1982. Place: A bench near a path at the edge of the lake in Central Park. Act I: Three in the afternoon. Act II, Scene 1: Three in the afternoon, the next day. Scene 2: Five in the afternoon, the next day. Scene 3: Twelve days later, 11 A.M.

The aging process as comedy, viewed in the friendship of two old men, one white and the other black.

A Best Play; see page 113.

Ladies and Gentlemen, Jerome Kern (22). Musical revue conceived by William E. Hunt; music by Jerome Kern. Produced by West Dobson at the Harold Clurman Theater. Opened June 10, 1985. (Closed June 30, 1985)

Michael Howell Deane   Michele Pigliavento
Louise Edeiken   John Scherer
Milton B. Grayson Jr.   Toba Sherwood
Delores Hall   Frank Torren

Musicians: Janet Glazener piano, conductor; T.O. Sterrett synthesizer; Ellen Geiss drums.

Directed by William E. Hunt; choreography, Valarie Pettiford; musical direction, Hank Levy; scenery, James Wolk; costumes, David P. Pearson; lighting, Dan Kotlowitz; production stage manager, Donald Christy; press, Henry Luhrman Associates, David Mayhew, Terry M. Lilly, Andrew P. Shearer.

Collection of Kern songs from stage and screen, 1905–1946, presented in two parts.

ACT I, Songs From the Stage: "How'd You Like to Spoon With Me?" (from *The Earl and the Girl*)—Ensemble; "They Didn't Believe Me" (from *The Girl From Utah*)—Milton B. Grayson Jr.; "Till the Clouds Roll By" (from *Oh, Boy*)—Ensemble; "Go Little Boat" (from *Miss 1917*)— Louise Edeiken; "Who?" (from *Sunny*)—Men; "Sunny" (from *Sunny*)—Ensemble (danced by Michele Pigliavento); "Can't Help Lovin' That Man" (from *Show Boat*)—Toba Sherwood; "Ol' Man River" (from *Show Boat*)—Grayson; "Life Upon the Wicked Stage" (from *Show Boat*)—John Scherer, Delores Hall, Sherwood, Edeiken.

Also "Don't Ever Leave Me" and "Why Was I Born" (from *Sweet Adeline*)—Hall; "She Didn't Say Yes" (from *The Cat and the Fiddle*)—Ensemble; "The Night Was Made for Love" (from *The Cat and the Fiddle*)—Michael Howell Deane, Edeiken; "I've Told Every Little Star" (from *Music in the Air*)—Pigliavento; "Let's Begin" (from *Roberta*)—Ensemble; "Yesterdays" (from *Roberta*)— Frank Torren; "Smoke Gets in Your Eyes" (from *Roberta*)—Hall; "All the Things You Are" (from *Very Warm for May*)—Ensemble.

ACT II, Songs From the Movies: "I Won't Dance" (from *Roberta*)—Hall, Scherer; "Lovely to Look At" (from *Roberta*)—Pigliavento, Deane; "Pick Yourself Up" (from *Swing Time*)—Ensemble; "The Way You Look Tonight" (from *Swing Time*)—Torren; "This Is a Fine Romance" (from *Swing Time*)—Ensemble; "The Folks Who Live on the Hill" (from *High, Wide and Handsome*)—Edeiken, Scherer; "Remind Me" (from *One Night in the Tropics*)—Sherwood; "The Last Time I Saw Paris" (from *Lady Be Good*)—Ensemble; "Sure Thing" (from *Cover Girl*)—Ensemble; "Long Ago and Far Away" (from *Cover Girl*)—Grayson; "Can't Help Singing" (from *Can't Help Singing*)—Ensemble; "In Love in Vain" (from *Centennial Summer*)—Hall; "All Through the Day" (from *Centennial Summer*)—Ensemble; "You Couldn't Be Cuter" (from *Joy of Living*)—Ensemble (curtain call).

Dames at Sea (278). Revival of the musical with book and lyrics by George Haimsohn and Robin Miller; music by Jim Wise. Produced by Jordan Hott and Jack Millstein in association with the Asolo State Theater of Florida at the Lamb's Theater. Opened June 12, 1985. (Closed February 9, 1986)

Mona Kent	Susan Elizabeth Scott	Ruby	Donna Kane
Hennesey; Captain	Richard Sabellico	Dick	George Dvorsky
Joan	Dorothy Stanley	Lucky	Dirk Lumbard

Musicians: Jane Aycock, Steve Flaherty pianists; Jim LeBlanc percussionist.
Standbys: Mana Allen, John Scherer.
Directed and choreographed by Neal Kenyon; musical direction and additional dance arrangements, Janet Aycock; scenery and costumes, Peter Harvey; lighting, Roger Morgan; associate choreographer and tap sequences, Dirk Lumbard; production stage manager, Dan Carter; press, The Jacksina Company, Inc., Ted Killmer.
Time: The early 1930s. Act I: Any 42d Street theater. Act II: On the battleship.
Dames at Sea was produced off Broadway 12/20/68 for 575 performances, following an OOB production the previous season under the title *Golddiggers Afloat*. It was revived in cabaret 9/23/70 for 170 performances. This version was previously produced 4/6/85 in regional theater in Sarasota, Fla.
The list of musical numbers in *Dames at Sea* appears on page 442 of *The Best Plays of 1968–69*. Lyrics for "The Sailor of My Dreams," "Singapore Sue," "Good Times Are Here to Stay" and "The Echo Waltz" are by George Haimsohn; all others are by George Haimsohn and Robin Miller.
Robert Fitch replaced Richard Sabellico 1/21/85.

For Sale (8). By Jeffrey Gurkoff. Produced by Beacon Street Productions in association with Jerry Goralnick at Playhouse 91. Opened June 18, 1985. (Closed June 23, 1985)

Directed by Andrew Cadiff; scenery, John Culbert; costumes, Tom McKinley; lighting, Arden Fingerhut; sound, Bruce Ellman; production stage manager, Bill McComb; with Katherine Cortez, Ron Parady, Craig Wasson, Inness-Fergus McDade, Josh Blake, Richard Grusin, Wayne Tippit, Judith Barcroft, John P. Connolly, Stephen C. Prutting, Dave Florek, Jerry Mayer.
Marriage crumbles when a couple loses their home.

*Theater in Limbo. Repertory of two programs. ***Vampire Lesbians of Sodom** and ***Sleeping Beauty or Coma** (363). Program of two plays by Charles Busch. Opened June 19, 1985. **Times Square Angel** (23). By Charles Busch. Opened December 11, 1985. (Closed February 9, 1986) Produced by Theater in Limbo, Kenneth Elliott artistic director, and Gerald A. Davis at the Provincetown Playhouse.

VAMPIRE LESBIANS OF SODOM—Robert Carey, Arnie Kolodner and Charles Busch in a scene from Mr. Busch's long-running camp comedy

PERFORMER	"SLEEPING BEAUTY OR COMA"	"VAMPIRE LESBIANS OF SODOM"	"TIMES SQUARE ANGEL"
Tom Aulino	Ian McKenzie	Oatsie Carewe	Reporter; Mrs. Paine; Milton Keisler; Agnes
Michael Belanger			Dexter Paine III
Ralph Buckley			Duke O'Flanagan; Chick LaFountain
Charles Busch	Fauna Alexander	Virgin Sacrifice; Madeleine Astarte	Irish O'Flanagan
James Cahill			Voice of the Lord
Robert Carey	Barry Posner	Ali; P.J.	Johnny the Noodle; Georgie
Kenneth Elliott	Sebastian Lore	King Carlisle	
Andy Halliday	Miss Thick	Etienne; Danny	Eddie
Julie Halston			Mrs. Tooley; Stella
Arnie Kolodner	Craig Prince	Hujar; Zack	Abe Kesselman; Albert
Theresa Marlowe	Anthea Arlo	Renee Vain; Tracy	Cookie Gibbs; Valerie Waverly
Meghan Robinson	Enid Wetwhistle	La Condesa; Succubus	Miss Ellerbe; Olive Sanborn; Old Mag
Yvonne Singh			Peona

Understudies, *Vampire Lesbians of Sodom*: Michael Belanger. *Times Square Angel*: Messrs. Halliday, Carey, Aulino, Kolodner, Buckley—Michael Belanger; Misses Marlowe, Robinson, Singh. Mr. Busch—Julie Halston.

Directed by Kenneth Elliott; choreography, Jeff Veazey; scenery, B.T. Whitehill; *Vampire Lesbians of Sodom* costumes, John Glaser; *Times Square Angel* costumes, Debra Tennenbaum; lighting, Vivian Leone; production stage manager, Elizabeth Katherine Carr; press, Shirley Herz Associates, Pete Sanders.

Sleeping Beauty or Coma time, the 1960s; place, in and around London. *Vampire Lesbians of Sodom*, Scene 1: Sodom in the days of old, the entrance to a forbidding cave. Scene 2: Hollywood, 1920, La Condesa's mansion. Scene 3: Las Vegas today, a rehearsal hall. *Times Square Angel* time, from 1938 to 1948; place, New York City and in heaven.

Camp comedies satirizing fairy and horror tales. The one-act curtain-raiser *Sleeping Beauty or Coma* takes place in the mod fashion world. *Vampire Lesbians of Sodom* makes fun of multitudinous depravities, Subtitled, "A Hard-Boiled Christmas Fantasy," *Times Square Angel* portrays the adventures of a night club queen accompanied by a guardian angel.

New York Shakespeare Festival. Summer schedule of two outdoor programs. **Measure for Measure** (25). Revival of the play by William Shakespeare. Opened June 30, 1985; see note. (Closed July 21, 1985) **The Mystery of Edwin Drood** (24). Musical by Rupert Holmes; suggested by the unfinished novel by Charles Dickens. Opened August 4, 1985; see note. (Closed September 1, 1985 and transferred to Broadway; see its entry in the Plays Produced on Broadway section of this volume) Produced by New York Shakespeare Festival, Joseph Papp producer, with the cooperation of the City of New York, Edward I. Koch mayor, Bess Myerson commissioner of cultural affairs, Henry Stern commissioner of parks and recreation, in association with New York Telephone at the Delacorte Theater in Central Park.

BOTH PLAYS: Costumes, Lindsay W. Davis; associate producer, Jason Steven Cohen; press, Merle Debuskey, Richard Kornberg, Bruce Campbell, Don Anthony Summa.

MEASURE FOR MEASURE

Vincentio	John Getz	Elbow	Tom Toner
Escalus	Joseph Warren	Froth	Robert Stanton
Angelo	Richard Jordan	Justice	Steven Dawn
Lucio	Gregory Salata	Angelo's Servant	Mark Zeisler
Gentleman #1	Reg E. Cathey	Juliet	Elizabeth Perkins
Gentleman #2	John N. Cutler	Mariana	Laura MacDermott
Mistress Overdone	Rosemary DeAngelis	Abhorson	Antonio Fargas
Pompey	Nathan Lane	Barnardine	William Duff-Griffin
Claudio	Joe Urla	Friar Peter	Eldon Bullock
Provost	Tom Mardirosian	Varrius	Ralph Zito
Friar Thomas	John Wylie	Young Friar	Howard Samuelsohn
Isabella	Mary Elizabeth Mastrantonio	Townswoman	Erika Gregory
Francisca	Gretchen Taylor	Nun; Midwife	Teri Tirapelli

Officers: Kevin Dwyer, Ken Forman, Joseph Gargiulo, Rick Parks.

Understudies: Mr. Getz—John N. Cutler; Mr. Jordan—Tom Mardirosian; Mr. Warren—John Wylie; Mr. Urla—Mark Zeisler; Mr. Salata—Antonio Fargas; Messrs. Cathey, Cutler—Rick Parks; Mr. Zito—Steven Dawn; Messrs. Mardirosian, Bullock—Kevin Dwyer; Mr. Dawn—Ken Forman; Messrs. Wylie, Toner—Ralph Zito; Mr. Lane—Howard Samuelsohn; Messrs. Fargas, Duff-Griffin—Joseph Gargiulo; Miss Mastrantonio—Elizabeth Perkins; Misses MacDermott, DeAngelis —Gretchen Taylor; Miss Perkins—Erika Gregory; Miss Taylor—Teri Tirapelli.

Directed by Joseph Papp; scenery, Robin Wagner; lighting, Richard Nelson; music, Allen Shawn; production stage manager, James Bernardi; stage manager, Tracy B. Cohen.

Time: 1910. Place: Vienna. The play was presented in two parts.

Shakespeare's play staged in the Viennese waltz era. The last major New York revival of *Measure for Measure* was by New York Shakespeare Festival at the Delacorte 7/29/76 for 27 performances.

THE MYSTERY OF EDWIN DROOD

Mayor Thomas Sapsea; *Your Chairman, William Cartwright*	George Rose
John Jasper; *Clive Paget*	Howard McGillin
Rev. Mr. Crisparkle; *Wilfred Barking-Smythe*	Larry Shue
Edwin Drood; *Alice Nutting*	Betty Buckley
Rosa Bud; *Deirdre Peregrine*	Patti Cohenour
Alice; *Isabel Yearsley*	Judy Kuhn
Beatrice; *Florence Gill*	Donna Murphy
Helena Landless; *Janet Conover*	Jana Schneider
Neville Landless; *Victor Grinstead*	John Herrera
Durdles; *Nick Cricker*	Jerome Dempsey
Deputy; *Robert Bascomb*	Don Kehr
Princess Puffer; *Angela Prysock*	Cleo Laine
Statue; *Christopher Lyon*	Stephen Glavin
Portrait; *Brian Pankhurst*	Charles Goff
Harold; *James Throttle*	Robert Grossman
Julian; *Alan Eliot*	Herndon Lackey
Horace; *Brian Pankhurst*	Charles Goff
Bazzard; *Phillip Bax*	Joe Grifasi
Dick Datchery	George Spelvin

Clients of Princess Puffer *(Harry Sayle, Montague Pruitt, James Throttle, Alan Eliot):* Nicholas Gunn, Brad Miskell, Robert Grossman, Herndon Lackey. Succubae *(Gwendolen Pynn, Sarah Cook, Florence Gill, Isabel Yearsley):* Francine Landes, Karen Giombetti, Donna Murphy, Judy Kuhn.

Citizens of Cloisterham: Karen Giombetti, Stephen Glavin, Charles Goff, Nicholas Gunn, Robert Grossman, Judy Kuhn, Herndon Lackey, Francine Landes, Brad Miskell, Donna Murphy.

Musicians: David Weiss, Richard Heckman, Lester Cantor reeds; Wilmer Wise, Phil Granger trumpets; Santo Russo trombone, baritone horn; Earl M. McIntyre bass trombone, tuba; Russell Rizner French horn; Peter Prosser cello; James Kowal, Edward Strauss (assistant conductor), Donald Rebic keyboards; Melanie L. Punter bass; Skip Reed percussion; Glenn Rhian drums.

Understudies: Messrs. Grifasi, Shue—Charles Goff; Messrs. Rose, Dempsey—Robert Grossman; Misses Buckley, Cohenour—Judy Kuhn; Messrs. McGillin, Herrera—Herndon Lackey; Mr. Kehr—Brad Miskell; Misses Schneider, Laine—Donna Murphy.

Directed by Wilford Leach; choreography, Graciela Daniele; musical direction, Michael Starobin, Edward Strauss; conductor, Michael Starobin; scenery, Bob Shaw; lighting, Paul Gallo; sound, Otts Munderloh; production stage manager, James Harker; stage manager, Robin Herskowitz.

Play-within-a-play adaptation of the Dickens murder mystery, with dual roles in the Edwin Drood tale and the "performers" (names in *italics* above) in the "*troupe*" that is presenting it, and with the denouement varied according to the wishes of the audience, polled at each performance.

A Best Play; see page 156.

Note: Press date for *Measure for Measure* was 7/10/85, for *The Mystery of Edwin Drood* was 8/21/85.

Options (2). Musical with book and lyrics by Walter Willison; music by Jeffrey Silverman. Produced by Jeffrey Betancourt Productions, Inc. and Marck Adrian Fedor at Circle Repertory Theater. Opened July 11, 1985. (Closed July 12, 1985)

Directed by Michael Shawn; scenery, Ron Placzek; costumes, Dona Granata; lighting, Tom Hennes; sound, Rob Gorton; production stage manager, Nancy Harrington; with Jeffrey Silverman, Walter Willison, Julie Budd, Jo Anna Rush.

A songwriting team creates a musical.

Roundabout Theater Company. 1984–85 schedule included **Springtime for Henry** (55). Revival of the play by Benn W. Levy. Opened July 17, 1985; see note. (Closed September 1, 1985) Produced by Roundabout Theater Company, Gene Feist artistic director, Todd Haimes managing director, at the Christian C. Yegen Theater.

Mr. Dewlip	Peter Evans	Mrs. Jelliwell	Tovah Feldshuh
Mr. Jelliwell	George N. Martin	Miss Smith	Jodi Thelen

Directed by Tony Tanner; scenery, Holmes Easley; costumes, Robert Pusilo; lighting, Barry Arnold; sound, Philip Campanella; production stage manager. K. Siobhan Phelan; press, Solters/Roskin/Friedman, Inc., Adrian Bryan-Brown, Jackie Green.

Time: 1932. Place: The sitting room of Mr. Dewlip's flat. Act I: Spring. Act II: Evening, three months later. Act III: The next morning.

The last major New York revival of *Springtime for Henry* took place on Broadway 3/14/51 for 53 performances.

Note: Press date for *Springtime for Henry* was 8/1/85.

The Negro Ensemble Company. 1984–85 schedule included **Two Can Play** (86). Return engagement of the play by Trevor Rhone. Produced by The Negro Ensemble Company, Douglas Turner Ward artistic director, Leon B. Denmark managing director, at Theater Four. Opened July 18, 1985. (Closed September 29, 1985)

Gloria... Hazel J. Medina
Jim... Sullivan H. Walker

Directed by Clinton Turner Davis; scenery, Llewellyn Harrison; costumes, Julian Asion; lighting, Sylvester Weaver; sound, Bernard Hall; production supervisor, Llewellyn Harrison; production stage manager, Jerry Cleveland; press, Burnham-Callaghan Associates, David Lotz.

Time: The late 1970s. Place: The home of Jim and Gloria Thomas, Kingston, Jamaica, West Indies. Act I, Scene 1: Late night. Scene 2: Evening, three days later. Scene 3: One week later. Scene 4: Three weeks later. Scene 5: Two months later. Act II, Scene 1: Three weeks later. Scene 2: Next day. Scene 3: Later that evening. Scene 4: Noon next day.

Victory over male chauvinism in a two-character farce previously produced by NEC 4/11/85 for 30 performances.

Curse of the Starving Class (267). Transfer from off off Broadway of the revival of the play by Sam Shepard. Produced by Patricia Daily and Arthur Master Productions, Inc. at the Promenade Theater. Opened July 30, 1985. (Closed February 16, 1986)

Wesley	Bradley Whitford	Weston	Eddie Jones
Ella	Kathy Bates	Ellis	Jude Ciccolella
Emma	Karen Tull	Malcolm; Slater	Stephen Bradbury
Taylor	James Gleason	Emerson	Dan Patrick Brady

Understudies: Mr. Jones—Jude Ciccolella; Mr. Whitford—Dan Patrick Brady; Mr. Gleason—Stephen Bradbury; Messrs. Ciccolella, Brady, Bradbury—Rick Dean; Misses Tull, Bates—Carlotta Schoch.

Directed by Robin Lynn Smith; scenery, Brian Martin; costumes, Frances Nelson; lighting, Mark W. Stanley; production stage manager, Penny Marks; stage manager, Richard Dean; press, Burnham-Callaghan Associates, Gary Murphy.

Place: Southeast California. Act I: Late morning, Act II: The next morning. Act III: The next day.

Curse of the Starving Class was produced off Broadway by New York Shakespeare Festival 2/14/78 for 62 performances, following an Obie-winning OOB production the previous season. This revival was first produced in an OOB showcase at the Image Theater.

What's a Nice Country Like You . . . Doing in a State Like This? (252). Revised version of the revue with music by Cary Hoffman; lyrics by Ira Gasman. Produced by Alice

Kopreski and Bick Goss at Actors' Playhouse. Opened July 31, 1985. (Closed February 9, 1986)

Missy Baldino   Hugh Panaro
Jane Brucker   Rob Resnick
Steve Mulch

Understudies: Females—Susan Peahl; Males—Jay Bodin.

Directed and choreographed by Suzanne Astor Hoffman; based on the original staging by Miriam Fond; musical direction and additional arrangements, Dean Johnson; scenery, Charles Plummer; costumes, Henrietta Louise Howard; stage manager, Stephanie Klapper; press, Francine L. Trevens.

The original version of this revue was first produced off Broadway April 19, 1973 for 543 performances including a 1974 revision. The present revision was first presented last season in an OOB production at American Place.

Patty Granau replaced Jane Brucker 9/3/85.

MUSICAL NUMBERS, ACT I: "Get Out of Here"—Company: "Church and State"—Steve Mulch, Rob Resnick; "What the Hell"—Jane Brucker "I'm in Love With"—Missy Baldino; "Terrorist Trio"—Hugh Panaro, Resnick, Mulch; "Hard To Be a Liberal"—Panaro; "I'm in Love With" (Reprise)—Baldino; "Male Chauvinist Pig of Myself"—Panaro; "Liberation Tango"—Brucker; "Changing Partners"—Baldino, Mulch, Brucker; "The Last One of the Boys"—Mulch; "I'm in Love With" (Reprise)—Baldino.

Also "Runaway Suite"—Company (A. "Runaways"—Mulch, Baldino, Company; B. "It's Getting Better"—Mulch; C. "I Like Me"—Baldino); "I'm in Love With" (Reprise)—Baldino; "Update"—Company; "I Just Pressed Button A"—Resnick; "Nuclear Winter"—Baldino, Panaro; "New York Suite"—Company (A. "But I Love New York"—Company; B. "Girl of My Dreams"—Panaro; C. "A Mugger's Work Is Never Done"—Resnick; D. "How'm I Doing?"—Mulch).

ACT II: Entr'acte—Dean Johnson; "Why Do I Keep Going to the Theater?"—Company; "Carlos, Juan & Miguel"—Mulch, Panaro, Resnick; "Nicaragua"—Brucker; "I'm Not Myself Anymore"—Resnick; "I'm in Love With" (Reprise)—Baldino; "Keeping the Peace"—Company; "I'm in Love With" (Reprise)—Baldino; "America, You're Looking Good"—Panaro; "They Aren't There"—Baldino, Mulch; "Farewell"—Company.

Also "Fill-er Up"—Baldino; "Porcupine Suite"—Company (A. "People Are Like Porcupines"—Company; B. "I'm Not Taking a Chance on Love"—Baldino, Panaro; C. "Threesome"—Mulch, Brucker, Resnick; D. "Scale of 1 to 10"—Panaro, Baldino; "People are Like Porcupines"—Company); "Everybody Ought to Have a Gun"—Resnick, Company; "Hallelujah"—Mulch, Company; "Johannesburg"—Mulch; "I'm in Love With" (Reprise)—Baldino; "Take Us Back, King George" —Brucker, Panaro, Resnick, Mulch; "Come On, Daisy"—Baldino, Company; Finale—Company.

The Custom of the Country (17). Adapted by Jane Stanton Hitchcock from the novel by Edith Wharton. Produced by the William and Mary Greve Foundation, Tony Kaiser producer, at Second Stage. Opened September 22, 1985. (Closed October 6, 1985)

Directed by Daniel Gerroll; scenery, Kate Edmunds; costumes, David Murin; lighting, Anne G. Wrightson; with Valerie Mahaffey, Trey Wilson, Nesbitt Blaisdaell, Michael Countryman, Karen MacDonald, Jane Murray, Gloria Cromwell, David Rasche, John C. Vennema, Carl Wallnau.

The turn-of-the-century adventures of a social-climbing divorcée.

Circle Repertory Company. Schedule of six programs. **Talley & Son** (42), revival of the play by Lanford Wilson previously entitled *A Tale Told*, opened September 24, 1985, see note; and **Tomorrow's Monday** (27), by Paul Osborn, opened October 4, 1985, see note. Repertory of two programs (repertory closed December 1, 1985). **The Beach House** (56). By Nancy Donohue. Opened December 19, 1985. (Closed February 2, 1986) **The Mound Builders** (19), by Lanford Wilson, opened January 30, 1986; **Caligula** (16), revival of the play by Albert Camus, adapted by Marshall W. Mason and Harry Newman from a translation by Stuart Gilbert, opened February 2, 1986; and **Quiet in the Land** (17), by

THE MOUND BUILDERS—Jake Dengel and Bruce McCarty in
a scene from the Circle Repertory revival of Lanford Wilson's play

Anne Chislett, opened March 16, 1986. Repertory of three programs. (Repertory closed
April 13, 1986) Produced by Circle Repertory Company, Marshall W. Mason artistic
director, *Talley & Son*, *A Tale Told* and *The Beach House* at Circle Repertory, *The Mound
Builders*, *Caligula* and *Quiet in the Land* at The Triplex (Theater II).

ALL PLAYS: Associate artistic director, B. Rodney Marriott; sound, Chuck London Media/
Stewart Werner; press, Reva Cooper.

PERFORMER	"TOMORROW'S MONDAY"	"TALLEY & SON"
Richard Backus	Richard Allen	Harley Campbell
Julie Bargeron		Avalaine Platt
Joyce Reehling Christopher		Lottie
Steve Decker		Emmet Young
Lisa Emery		Viola Platt
Amy Epstein	Mary Davis	
Farley Granger		Eldon
Trish Hawkins	Esther Allen	Sally
Laura Hughes		Olive
Robert Macnaughton	John Allen	Timmy
Lindsey Richardson		Buddy
Edward Seamon	Dr. Nichols	Mr. Talley
Helen Stenborg	Mrs. Allen	Netta
Diane Venora	Lora Allen	

BOTH PLAYS: Scenery, John Lee Beatty; lighting, Dennis Parichy; production stage manager,
Leslie Loeb; stage manager, Richard Costabile.
TOMORROW'S MONDAY: Directed by Kent Paul; costumes, Jennifer Von Mayrhauser.
Time: Sometime in the mid-1930s. Place: Somewhere in the Midwest Act I: A Saturday afternoon
in October. Act II: The next afternoon, Sunday. Act III: Later that night.
1936 play of progressive ideas impacting upon a conservative Midwestern family, in its first New
York production.

TALLEY & SON: Directed by Marshall W. Mason; costumes, Laura Crow.

Time: Independence Day, 1944. Place: The front parlor of the Talley Place, a farm near Lebanon, Mo. The play was presented in two parts.

Revival—in somewhat revised form—of the third in the series of Talley family plays, previously produced off Broadway under the title *A Tale Told* 6/11/81 for 30 performances.

THE BEACH HOUSE

Chris.................... Robert Leonard		Art .... Paul Chalakani	
John .... George Grizzard		Dan........................ Angelo Tiffe	
Annie .... Swoosie Kurtz			

Directed by Melvin Bernhardt; scenery, David Potts; costumes, Jennifer Von Mayrhauser; lighting, Dennis Parichy, Mal Sturchio; production stage manager, Ginny Martino.

Time: The present. Place: A beach house in Connecticut. The play was presented in three parts.

A stabilizing female presence is introduced into a chaotic father-son household. Previously produced in a different version at the Long Wharf Theater, New Haven, Conn.

PERFORMER	"THE MOUND BUILDERS"	"CALIGULA"	"QUIET IN THE LAND"
Margaret Barker		(Claudia-Claudius; Mereia)	Hannah Bauman
Tanya Berezin	D.K. (Delia) Eriksen	(Cherea)	(Lydie Brubacher)
Paul Butler		(Claudia-Claudius)	(Bishop Eli Frey; Recruitment Officer)
Kelly Connell		(Mucius)	(Menno Miller; Bishop Eli Frey)
Jake Dengel	(Prof. August Howe)	(Octavia-Octavius; Lucia-Lucius)	(Christy Bauman)
Stephanie Gordon	Cynthia Howe	Caesonia	(Lydie Brubacher)
Trish Hawkins	(Dr. Jean Loggins)	(Octavia-Octavius; Lepida-Lepidus)	
Alice King		(Mucius's Wife)	Esther Miller
Zane Lasky		(Intendant; Cassius)	Zepp Brubacher
Abby Levin		(Metella-Metellus)	Martha Brubacher
Ken Marshall	(Dr. Dan Loggins)	Caligula	Mr. O'Rourke
Paul Martell		(Metella-Metellus; Scipio)	(Paddy O'Rourke; Menno Miller)
Bruce McCarty	(Chad Jasker)	(Scipio; Mucius)	Yock Bauman
James McDaniel	(Chad Jasker)	(Cassius; Helicon)	
Randy Noojin			(Paddy O'Rourke)
Jay Patterson	(Dr. Dan Loggins)	(Helicon; Cherea)	(Levi Miller)
Scott Phelps		Patricius	(Recruitment Officer)
Jane Sanders			Nancy Brubacher
Sharon Schlarth	(Dr. Jean Loggins)	(Mucius's Wife; Lucia-Lucius)	Katie Brubacher
Edward Seamon	(Prof. August Howe)	(Lepida-Lepidus; Mereia)	(Levi Miller; Christy Bauman)

(Parentheses indicate roles in which the performers alternated)

ALL PLAYS: Scenery, John Lee Beatty; costumes, Jennifer Von Mayrhauser; lighting, Dennis Parichy; production stage manager, Fred Reinglas; stage manager, Leslie Loeb.

THE MOUND BUILDERS: Directed by Marshall W. Mason; original music, Jonathan Hogan.

Time and place: February, Champaign-Urbana; the previous summer in Blue Shoals, Ill. The play was presented in two parts.

The Mound Builders, about an archaeological site and the persons exploring it, was previously produced off off Broadway by Circle Repertory Theater Company Feb. 1, 1975 and received an

Obie Award for distinguished playwriting. This is its first major New York production of record.

CALIGULA: Directed by Marshall W. Mason. Guards, Aides, Wives, Poets: Jay Corcoran, Alice King, Abby Levin, Tom Miller, Randy Noojin, Michael Quarry, Jane Sanders, Michael Swain.

Time: The present. The play was presented in two parts.

Modern-dress *Caligula*, with male and female performers alternating in some of the parts. The Camus play was originally presented on Broadway 2/16/60 in the Justin O'Brien adaptation for 38 performances and was named a Best Play of its season. This is its first major New York revival.

QUIET IN THE LAND: Directed by Daniel Irvine. Other Members of the Congregation: Nicole Acarino, Jay Corcoran, Tom Miller, Kristina Oster, Michael Swain.

Place: An Amish farming community near Kitchener in Ontario, Canada. Act I: Early to late fall of 1917. Act II: Early summer to winter of 1918.

Amish family life in Canada during World War I. A foreign play previously produced at the Winnipeg, Manitoba Theater Center.

Note: Press date for *Tomorrow's Monday* was 10/20/85, for *Talley & Son* was 10/22/85.

Roundabout Theater Company. Schedule of five programs. **The Waltz of the Toreadors** (54). Revival of the play by Jean Anouilh; translated by Lucienne Hill. Opened September 25, 1985; see note. (Closed November 9, 1985). **Mrs. Warren's Profession** (93). Revival of the play by George Bernard Shaw. Opened November 27, 1985; see note. (Closed February 9, 1986) **Room Service** (64). Revival of the play by John Murray and Allen Boretz. Opened January 29, 1986; see note. (Closed March 23, 1986). **Cheapside** (56). By David Allen. Opened March 29, 1986; see note. (Closed May 11, 1986) and *Master Class* by David Pownall, press opening scheduled for 6/5/86. Produced by Roundabout Theater Company, Gene Feist artistic director, Todd Haimes executive director (*Cheapside* in association with the White Barn Theater Foundation, Lucille Lortel founder and artistic director). at the Christian C. Yegen Theater.

THE WALTZ OF THE TOREADORS

Mme. St. Pé.	Tammy Grimes	Eugenie.	Elizabeth Owens
Gen. St. Pé.	Lee Richardson	Mlle. de Ste.-Euverte.	Carole Shelley
Gaston	Eric Swanson	Mme. Dupon-Fredaine	Elizabeth Owens
Sidonie	Jane Jones	Father Ambrose.	Wyman Pendleton
Estelle.	Amanda Carlin	Pamela	Whitney Reis
Dr. Bonfant	Alvin Epstein		

Directed by Richard Russell Ramos; scenery, Kate Edmunds; costumes, Robert Pusilo; lighting, Barry Arnold; sound, Philip Campanella; production stage manager, Kathy J. Faul; stage manager, K. Siobhan Phelan; press, Solters/Roskin/Friedman, Inc., Joshua Ellis, Adrian Bryan-Brown.

Place: The study of Gen. St. Pé and in his wife's adjoining bedroom. Act I, Scene 1: The study, a spring morning. Scene 2: The study, that afternoon. Act II, Scene 1: The study, a few minutes later; Scene 2: The bedroom, immediately following. Act III: The study, early evening.

The last major New York revival of *The Waltz of the Toreadors* was by Circle in the Square on Broadway 9/13/73 for 85 performances.

MRS. WARREN'S PROFESSION

Vivie Warren	Pamela Reed	Sir George Crofts	Harris Yulin
Praed	George Morfogen	Frank Gardner	William Converse-Roberts
Mrs. Kitty Warren	Uta Hagen	Rev. Samuel Gardner	Gordon Sterne

Directed by John Madden; scenery, Andrew Jackness; costumes, Nan Cibula; lighting, Frances Aronson; sound, Philip Campanella; production stage manager, K. Siobhan Phelan.

Act I: The garden of a rented cottage near Haselmere, Surrey, late afternoon. Act II: Inside the cottage, later that evening. Act III: The Rectory garden, the following morning. Act IV: Honoria Fraser's chambers in Chauncery Lane, London, some days later. The play was presented in two parts with the intermission following Act II.

The last major New York revival of *Mrs. Warren's Profession* was by New York Shakespeare Festival at Lincoln Center 2/18/76 for 55 performances.

ROOM SERVICE

Sasha Smirnoff.............	Pierre Epstein	Leo Davis.................	Keith Reddin
Gordon Miller.............	Mark Hamill	Hilda Manney..............	Barbara Dana
Joseph Gribble..........	Eugene Troobnick	Simon Jenkins;	
Harry Binion..............	Andrew Bloch	Timothy Hogarth.......	MacIntyre Dixon
Faker Englund.............	Lonny Price	Dr. Glass; Sen. Blake......	Timothy Jerome
Christine Marlowe........	Ann McDonough	Bank Messenger............	Anthony Arkin

Directed by Alan Arkin; scenery, Daniel Ettinger; costumes, A. Christina Giannini; lighting, Barry Arnold; production stage manager, Kathy J. Faul.

Time: 1937. Place: Gordon Miller's room in the White Way Hotel. Act I: A Friday afternoon in spring. Act II: The following day. Act III: Five days later.

The last major New York revival of *Room Service* took place off Broadway 5/12/70 for 71 performances.

CHEAPSIDE

Robert Greene.............	Daniel Gerroll	Cutting Ball..................	Joe Morton
William Shakespeare........	Robert Stanton	Alice........................	Susan Cash
Christopher Marlowe.....	Dennis Boutsikaris	Mary Frith................	Robin Bartlett

Directed by Carey Perloff; scenery, Adrianne Lobel; costumes, Susan Hilferty; lighting, James F. Ingalls; sound, Philip Campanella; production stage manager, Matthew T. Mundinger.

Political and artistic tensions beset the poet and playwright Robert Greene and friends in a squalid section of 16th century London. The play was presented in two parts. A foreign (Australian) play previously produced there, in London and at the White Barn Theater, Westport, Conn.

Note: *Cheapside* held no formal opening but closed after a series of subscription previews. For the record, we are including it in this listing with its first preview date as opening date.

Note: Press date for *The Waltz of the Toreadors* was 10/16/85, for *Mrs. Warren's Profession* was 12/15/85, for *Room Service* was 2/13/86.

*Playwrights Horizons. Schedule of five programs. **Paradise!** (14). Musical with book and lyrics by George C. Wolfe. Music by Robert Forrest. Opened September 28, 1985. (Closed October 14, 1985) **Anteroom** (22). By Harry Kondoleon. Opened November 20, 1985. (Closed December 8, 1985) **Little Footsteps** (22). By Ted Tally. Opened February 27, 1986. (Closed March 16, 1986) ***The Perfect Party** (70). By A.R. Gurney Jr. Opened April 2, 1986. And *The Nice and the Nasty* scheduled to open 6/5/86. Produced by Playwrights Horizons, Andre Bishop artistic director, Paul S. Daniels executive director, James F. Priebe managing director, at Playwrights Horizons.

PARADISE!

The Coupes:		Toddie.....................	Ben Wright
Grace....................	Janice Lynde	The Mahaneyheyans:	
Dan	Jerry Lanning	Heath....................	Tommy Hollis
Caddy	Danielle Ferland	Local	Charlaine Woodard

Directed and choreographed by Theodore Pappas; musical direction, David Loud; scenery, James Noone; costumes, David C. Woolard; lighting, Frances Aronson; sound, Paul Garrity; special effects, Jauchem & Meeh, Inc.; orchestrations and additional arrangements, John McKinney; production stage manager, M.A. Howard; press, Bob Ullman.

Time: This weekend. Place: An ocean and an island. The play was presented in two parts.

An Atlanta family finds itself shipwrecked on a paradise isle. Previously produced in regional theater in Cincinnati.

REVIVED AT THE ROUNDABOUT THIS SEASON: *Above,* Uta Hagen in the title role and Pamela Reed as Vivie in George Bernard Shaw's *Mrs. Warren's Profession*; *below,* Andrew Bloch, Mark Hamill and Keith Reddin in a scene from Alan Arkin's staging of the John Murray–Allen Boretz farce *Room Service*

ANTEROOM

Parker....................	Albert Macklin	Craig........................	Colin Fox
Wilson	Mitchell Lichtenstein	Joy	Janet Hubert
Fay....................	Elizabeth Wilson	Barbara.....................	Crystal Field
Maya.......................	Susan Cash		

Directed by Garland Wright; scenery, Adrianne Lobel; costumes, Rita Ryack; lighting, James F. Ingalls; sound, Scott Lehrer; production stage manager, Robin Rumpf.

Time: Summer, the present. Place: Southampton, L.I. The play was presented in two parts.

Comedy of the crumbling social structure in the affluent Long Island summer colony.

LITTLE FOOTSTEPS

Ben	Mark Blum	Charlotte	Jo Henderson
Joanie	Anne Lange	Gil......................	Thomas Toner

Directed by Gary Pearle; scenery, Thomas Lynch; costumes, Ann Hould-Ward; lighting, Nancy Schertler; sound, Scott Lehrer; music, John McKinney; fights, B.H. Barry; production stage manager, M.A. Howard.

Place: Ben and Joanie's apartment. Act I: A Sunday afternoon in late autumn. Act II: A Sunday afternoon in early spring.

A New York City couple on the threshold of parenthood.

THE PERFECT PARTY

Tony...................	John Cunningham	Wes......................	David Margulies
Lois....................	Charlotte Moore	Wilma.............	Kate McGregor-Stewart
Sally	Debra Mooney		

Directed by John Tillinger; scenery, Steven Rubin; costumes, Jane Greenwood; lighting, Dan Kotlowitz; sound, Gary Harris; production stage manager, Suzanne Fry.

Place: Tony's study. The play was presented in two parts.

Comedy, a professor sets out to give the perfect party, under the close and critical scrutiny of a newspaper columnist.

A Best Play; see page 264.

*New York Shakespeare Festival. Schedule of eight programs. **A Map of the World** (63). By David Hare. Opened October 1, 1985. (Closed November 24, 1985) *Aunt Dan and Lemon** (191). By Wallace Shawn; a New York Shakespeare Festival/Royal Court Theater production. Opened October 28, 1985. (Closed January 26, 1986 after 82 performances) Reopened after recasting March 23, 1986. **Jonin'** (46). By Gerard Brown. Opened December 17, 1985. (Closed January 26, 1986) **Rum and Coke** (64). By Keith Reddin. Opened January 27, 1986. (Closed March 23, 1986) **Hamlet** (70). Revival of the play by William Shakespeare. Opened March 9, 1986. (Closed May 11, 1986)

Also **Largo Desolato** (40). By Vaclav Havel; translated by Marie Winn. Opened March 25, 1986. (Closed April 27, 1986) *Cuba and His Teddy Bear** (14). By Reinaldo Povod. Opened May 18, 1986. And *Vienna: Lusthaus* (transfer from off off Broadway) scheduled to open 6/4/86. Produced by New York Shakespeare Festival, Joseph Papp producer, Jason Steven Cohen associate producer, at the Public Theater (see note).

A MAP OF THE WORLD

Stephen Andrews.............	Zeljko Ivanek	3d Waiter; Crew	N. Erick Avari
Elaine Le Fanu	Alfre Woodard	Peggy Whitton.........	Elizabeth McGovern
Victor Mehta................	Roshan Seth	Camera Man; Senior Diplomat ..	Tom Klunis
1st Waiter; Crew	Ravinder Kumar	Script Girl	Erika Gregory
2d Waiter; Crew	Homi Hormashji	Angelis...................	Joseph Hindy

Sleeping Man; Diplomat......... Joe Costa
Sound Man;
  Man With Feathers .... Herb Downer
Clapper Boy;
  Man With Flowers........... Mike Starr

Makeup Girl .... Judith Moreland
Paul; Diplomat; Crew...... Thomas Gibson
Martinson................ Richard Venture
M'Bengue.................. Ving Rhames

Understudies: Mr. Seth—N. Erick Avari; Mr. Hindy—Joe Costa; Mr. Rhames—Herb Downer; Mr. Ivanek—Thomas Gibson; Miss McGovern—Erika Gregory; Mr. Venture—Tom Klunis; Miss Woodard—Judith Moreland.

Directed by David Hare; scenery, Hayden Griffin; costumes, Jane Greenwood; lighting, Rory Dempster; music, Nick Bicāt; production stage manager, William Chance; stage manager, Karen Armstrong; press, Merle Debuskey, Richard Kornberg, Bruce Campbell, Don Anthony Summa.

Time: 1978 and the present. Place: Bombay, India. The play was presented in two parts.

Personal hostilities and world problems at a UNESCO conference on hunger. A foreign play previously produced at the Adelaide Festival (which commissioned it) and the National Theater, London.

AUNT DAN AND LEMON

Lemon .... Kathryn Pogson
Mother; June; Flora .... Linda Bassett
Father; Freddie; Jasper....... Wallace Shawn
Aunt Dan.................... Linda Hunt

Mindy..................... Lynsey Baxter
Andy; Marty .... Larry Pine
Raimondo............... Mario Arrambide

Directed by Max Stafford-Clark; scenery, Peter Hartwell; costumes, Jennifer Cook; lighting, Christopher Toulmin, Gerard P. Bourcier; sound, John del Nero, Andy Pink; production stage manager, Bethe Ward; stage manager, Janet P. Callahan.

Time: Now. Place: A room in London. The play was presented without intermission.

A study of civilized society's potential lapses into political and personal atrocity. A New York Shakespeare Festival/Royal Court Theater production previously produced at the Royal Court Theater, London. The London cast played 82 performances; the American cast (see below) played 109 performances.

A Best Play; see page 179.

Second cast as of 3/23/86:
Lemon .... Kathy Whitton Baker
Mother; June; Flora .... Ellen Parker
Father; Freddie; Jasper........... Paul Perri

Aunt Dan.................... Pamela Reed
Andy; Marty .... Larry Pine
Mindy................. Margaret Whitton
Ray...................... Kenneth Ryan

Understudies: Misses Baker, Whitton—Laura Hicks; Misses Parker, Reed—Annalee Jeffries; Messrs. Perri, Pine—Kenneth Ryan; Mr. Ryan—Joe Espinosa.

Associate director—Simon Curtis; stage manager, Frank DiFilia.

Laura Hicks replaced Kathy Whitton Baker 4/20/86; Christina Moore replaced Laura Hicks 4/22/86; Pippa Pearthree replaced Christina Moore 5/10/86.

JONIN'

Steve................... Timothy Simonson
Fred .... Jerome Preston Bates
Constance.................. Mark Vaughn
Duffy .... John Canada Terrell
Eddie .... Eric A. Payne

Greg .... Gregory Holtz Sr.
QT .... Jaime Perry
Willie .... Eriq LaSalle
Sheila .... Carla Brothers

Understudies: Messrs. Bates, Holtz, LaSalle—Kent Gash; Messrs. Vaughn, Simonson, Payne—Victor Love; Messrs. Terrell, Perry—Scot Robinson; Miss Brothers—Toni Ann Johnson.

Directed by Andre Robinson Jr.; scenery, Wynn P. Thomas; costumes, Karen Perry; lighting, Ric Rogers; music supervision, Bill Toles; production stage manager, Dwight T.B. Cook; stage manager, Sheryl Nieren.

The pranks of black college fraternity brothers eventually have unhappy consequences. The play was presented in two parts.

Music: "The Hymn" (music and lyrics by Noble Lee Lester); "Foreign Eyes" (music and lyrics by Michael Raye and Ralph Piper Jr.); "Dreams (Follow Your Dreams)" (music by Kenneth Taylor, lyrics by Tonya Wynne); "Dreams" (music and lyrics by Sheldon Becton); "Party With Me" (music and lyrics by Bill Toles); "Dreams" (Reprise); "The Hymn" (Reprise); additional music, Bill Toles; fraternal lyrics, Jerome Preston Bates.

RUM AND COKE

Jake Seward............... Peter MacNicol
Rodger Potter; Ramon......... Michael Ayr
Tod Cartmell; Fidel Castro; Cmdr.
  Tyler............... John Bedford-Lloyd
Bar Patron; Richard M. Nixon;
  Grandmother........... Frank Maraden
Bar Waiter;
  Felix Duque......... Jose Ramon Rosario

Linda Seward................ Polly Draper
Tom Tanner; Larry Peters... Larry Bryggman
Bob Stanton; New York Waiter;
  Child #2; Soldier #1...... Robert Stanton
Jorge; Child #1................ Jose Fong
Miguel....................... Tony Plana

Understudy: Mr. Plana—Jose Fong.

Directed by Les Waters; scenery, John Arnone; costumes, Kurt Wilhelm; lighting, Stephen Strawbridge; projections, Wendall K. Harrington; production stage manager, Janet P. Callahan; stage manager, David Lansky.

Time: Between 1959 and 1961. Place: Various locations. The play was presented in two parts.

Idealistic young bureaucrat is disillusioned by Washington's hardball politics in the Bay of Pigs era. Earlier versions were produced in regional theater at Yale Repertory in New Haven and South Coast Repertory, Costa Mesa, Calif.

HAMLET

Bernardo;
  2d Sailor........ Richard Michael Hughes
Francisco; Fortinbras.......... Peter Crook
Marcellus............... Mario Arrambide
Horatio.................... Richard Frank
Ghost; Player King; Osric........ Jeff Weiss
Claudius.................... Harris Yulin
Voltemand;
  4th Player (Lucianus)......... Ron Faber
Cornelius.................... Garry Kemp
Laertes..................... David Pierce
Polonius................. Leonardo Cimino
Hamlet.................... Kevin Kline
Gertrude.................. Priscilla Smith
Ophelia.................... Harriet Harris
Reynaldo; 2d Valet............ Paul Walker

Rosencrantz................. Randle Mell
Guildenstern.............. David Cromwell
Player Queen; Lady-in-Waiting.. Lynn Cohen
3d Player (Prologue); 1st Gravedigger;
  Gentleman.............. Peter Van Norden
5th Player; 2d Gravedigger; Old
  Gentleman................ William Duell
Musician (flute);
  Lady-in-Waiting.............. Mary Barto
Musician (cello); Gentleman..... Garo Yellin
Norwegian Captain;
  Danish General........... David Adamson
Valet........................ Dan Nutu
1st Sailor; Danish Officer..... Marco St. John
Priest; Minister of Finance.... Joseph Warren
Ladies-in-Waiting.............. Kate Falk,
                               Sharon Laughlin

Directed by Liviu Ciulei; scenery, Bob Shaw; costumes, William Ivey Long; lighting, Jennifer Tipton; fight direction, B.H. Barry; vocal and text consultant, Elizabeth Smith; production stage manager, Alan Traynor; stage manager, Pat Sosnow.

The last major New York revival of *Hamlet* was by City Stage Company off Broadway 12/15/83 for 41 performances. In this 1986 production, the play was presented in two parts.

LARGO DESOLATO

Dr. Leopold Kopriva......... Josef Sommer
Olda.................... Tom Mardirosian
Zuzana.................... Sally Kirkland
Lada I...................... Larry Block
Lada II.................... Burke Pearson
Lucy...................... Diane Venora

Olbram................... Joseph Wiseman
Fellow I.................... Edward Zang
Fellow II.......... Richard Russell Ramos
Man I................. Matthew Locricchio
Man II.................... Michael Guido
Marketa.................... Jodi Thelen

Directed by Richard Foreman; scenery, Richard Foreman, Nancy Winters; costumes, Lindsay W. Davis; lighting, Heather Carson; production stage manager, Karen Armstrong; stage manager, Chris Fielder.

Time: The present, a 36-hour period. Place: Leopold Kopriva's spacious apartment in contemporary Prague. The play was presented in two parts.

Semi-autobiographical black comedy about a professor's growing fear of being arrested and locked up by the secret police. A foreign (Czechoslovakian) play in its American premiere.

A Best Play: see page 249.

CUBA AND HIS TEDDY BEAR

Cuba	Robert DeNiro	Lourdes	Wanda DeJesus
Teddy	Ralph Macchio	Che	Michael Carmine
Jackie	Burt Young	Dealer	Paul Calderon
Redlights	Nestor Serrano		

Directed by Bill Hart; scenery, Donald Eastman; costumes, Gabriel Berry; lighting, Anne E. Militello; production stage manager, Ruth Kreshka; stage manager, Joel Elins.

Macho drug pusher is alarmed when his teen-aged son falls into bad company and experiments with drug-taking. The play was presented in two parts.

Note: In Joseph Papp's Public Theater there are many auditoria. *A Map of the World* and *Hamlet* played the Estelle R. Newman Theater; *Aunt Dan and Lemon* played Martinson Hall; *Jonin'* and *Largo Desolato* played LuEsther Hall; *Rum and Coke* and *Cuba and His Teddy Bear* played the Susan Stein Shiva Theater.

Yours, Anne (57). Musical based on *Anne Frank: The Diary of a Young Girl* and the play by Frances Goodrich and Albert Hackett; libretto by Enid Futterman; music by Michael Cohen. Produced by John Flaxman at Playhouse 91. Opened October 13, 1985. (Closed December 1, 1985)

Mrs. Van Daan	Betty Aberlin	Mr. Frank	George Guidall
Anne Frank	Trini Alvarado	Mr. Dussel	Hal Robinson
Peter Van Daan	David Cady	Margot Frank	Ann Talman
Mr. Van Daan	Merwin Goldsmith	Mrs. Frank	Dana Zeller-Alexis

Musicians: Al Rogers violin; Bob Keller flute, clarinet; Ann Yarborough French horn; Mark Lipman, Anne Callahan piano; Dan Strickland synthesizer, celeste.

Standby: Misses Zeller-Alexis, Aberlin—Karen Gibson. Understudy: Mr. Cady—Joseph Fuqua.

Directed by Arthur Masella; musical direction, Dan Strickland; scenery, Franco Colavecchia; costumes, Judith Dolan; lighting, Beverly Emmons; orchestrations, James Stenborg; movement, Helena Andreyko; sound, Jack Mann; associate producer, Arlene Caruso; production stage manager, Beverley Randolph; press, Becky Flora.

Time: June 12, 1942—August 4, 1944. Place: Amsterdam, Holland.

Musicalization of the famous diary of a young victim of the Holocaust and of the play based upon it.

ACT I

"Prologue" ... Company
"Dear Kitty: I Am Thirteen Years Old" ... Anne
"Dear Kitty: It's a Dangerous Adventure" ... Anne
"An Ordinary Day" ... Company
"Schlaf" ... Mrs. Frank
"She Doesn't Understand Me" ... Mrs. Frank, Anne
"Dear Kitty: In the Night" ... Anne
"They Don't Have To" ... Company
"Hollywood" ... Anne

"Dear Kitty: I Have a Nicer Side" .... Anne
"We Live With Fear" .... Company
"A Writer" .... Mr. Frank, Anne
"I'm Not a Jew".. Peter, Anne
"The First Chanukah Night" .... Company

ACT II

"Dear Kitty: It's a New Year/We're Here" .... Anne, Company
"Dear Kitty: My Sweet Secret" .... Anne
"My Wife" .... Van Daans, Mr. Frank, Dussel
"Dear Kitty: I Am Longing" .... Anne
"I Remember" .... Company
"I Think Myself Out" .... Anne, Peter
"Nightmare".. Anne
"For the Children".. Mr. & Mrs. Frank
"Something to Get Up For" .... Margot
"Dear Kitty: I Am a Woman"... Anne
"When We Are Free" .... Company
"Dear Kitty: I Still Believe" .... Anne

Not About Heroes (24). By Stephen MacDonald. Produced by Luther Davis and Arthur W. Cohen by special arrangement with Lucille Lortel at the Lucille Lortel Theater. Opened October 21, 1985. (Closed November 10, 1985)

Siegfried Sassoon.. Edward Herrmann
Wilfred Owen .... Dylan Baker

Standbys: Mr. Herrmann—John Jubak; Mr. Baker—Jack Koenig.
Directed by Dianne Wiest; scenery, Phillip Baldwin; costumes, Linda Fisher; lighting, Ronald Wallace; sound, Robert Kerzman; produced in association with Ray Larsen and by arrangement with the Williamstown Theater Festival, Nikos Psacharopoulos artistic director; production stage manager, Trey Hunt; stage manager, Patricia O'Halloran; press, Jeffrey Richards Associates, Ben Morse.
The friendship of two noted English poets, developed in a World War I military hospital. The play was presented in two parts. A foreign (British) play previously produced at the Edinburgh Festival and in Williamstown, Mass.

Alice and Fred (14). By Dan Ellentuck. Produced by the Rolfe Company, Mickey Rolfe producer, and Joel Key Rice at the Cherry Lane Theater. Opened October 23, 1985. (Closed November 3, 1985)

Directed by Gloria Muzio; scenery and lighting, Dale F. Jordan; costumes, Lloyd K. Waiwaiole; music, George Andoniadis; sound, George Andoniadis; produced in association with Billy Livingston; production stage manager, Kit Liset; press, Howard and Barbara Atlee; with J. Smith-Cameron, Greg Germann, Bruce Tracy, Victor Slezak, Laura Innes.
Drama of a 19th century tomboy lesbian, based on a true story and previously produced in regional theater in Albany, N.Y.

*The Negro Ensemble Company. Schedule of four programs. **Eyes of the American** (77). By Samm-Art Williams. Opened October 25, 1985. (Closed December 29, 1985) **House of Shadows** (29). By Steve Carter. Opened January 24, 1986. (Closed February 16, 1986) **Jonah and the Wonder Dog** (37). By Judi Ann Mason. Opened February 28, 1986. (Closed March 30, 1986) ***Louie and Ophelia** (21). By Gus Edwards. Opened May 16, 1986. Produced by The Negro Ensemble Company, Douglas Turner Ward artistic director, Leon B. Denmark managing director, at Theater Four. All plays: Production supervisor, John Harris.

EYES OF THE AMERICAN

James Horsford Ottley III .... Glynn Turman   Roberta Ottley; Velda.......... Seret Scott
Benny Parker;
  Cheddy Boswell .... Graham Brown

Directed by Walter Dallas; scenery, Llewellyn Harrison; costumes, Julian Asion; lighting, Sylvester N. Weaver Jr.; sound, Bernard Hall; production stage manager, Lisa L. Watson; press, Irene Gandy, Misani Gayle.

Time: The present, midnight to dawn. Place: An island in the independent West Indies. The play was presented without intermission.

Political unrest and chicanery in a Caribbean nation.

Eugene Lee replaced Glynn Turman 12/3/85.

HOUSE OF SHADOWS

Eric....................... Teddy Abner   Hector .... Raymond Rosario
Cassie..................... Frances Foster   Mary........................ Joan Grant
Aaron..................... Daniel Barton   Majeski.................. Victor Steinbach

Directed by Clinton Turner Davis; scenery, Daniel M. Proett; costumes, Julian Asion; lighting, Sylvester N. Weaver Jr.; original music, Grenoldo; sound, Bernard Hall; production stage manager, Lisa L. Watson.

Time: Now and then. Place: Chicago. The play was presented without intermission.

Horror drama taking place in a haunted house.

JONAH AND THE WONDER DOG

Nick... Kevin Hooks
Jonah Howard.. Douglas Turner Ward

Directed by Douglas Turner Ward; assistant director, LaTanya Richardson; scenery, Charles H. McClennahan; costumes, Judy Dearing; lighting, Sylvester N. Weaver Jr.; sound, Bernard Hall; production stage manager, Lisa L. Watson.

LOUIE AND OPHELIA—Douglas Turner Ward (who also directed) and Elain Graham in the title roles of the play by Gus Edwards

Time: The present. Place: Jonah Howard's study, Reno, Nev. The play was presented in two parts. Confrontation between a self-made politician and his Harvard-educated son.

LOUIE AND OPHELIA

Ophelia .... Elain Graham
Louie .... Douglas Turner Ward

Directed by Douglas Turner Ward; scenery, Charles H. McClennahan; costumes, Judy Dearing; lighting, Sylvester N. Weaver Jr.; sound, Dennis Ogburn; production stage manager, Lisa L. Watson.
Troubled romance of an ill-matched couple.

Tatterdemalion (25). Revival of the musical with book, music and lyrics by Judd Woldin; freely based on Israel Zangwill's novel *The King of Schnorrers*. Produced by Eric Krebs at the Douglas Fairbanks Theater. Opened October 27, 1985. (Closed November 17, 1985)

Sadie; Mrs. Mendoza ..... Annie McGreevey	David .... Stuart Zagnit
Isaac; Wilkinson; Cosmetician;	Mendoza..................... K.C. Wilson
Furtado .... Robert Blumenfeld	Da Costa .... Jack Sevier
Herschel; Belasco .... Ron Wisniski	Deborah .... Tia Speros
Rivka; Housekeeper .... Suzanne Briar	

Understudies: Mr. Sevier—Ron Winiski; Misses Speros, McGreevey—Suzanne Briar; Messrs. Blumenfeld, Wisniski, Zagnit—John Barone.
Directed by Eric Krebs; musical direction, Edward G. Robinson; scenery, Ed Wittstein; costumes, Patricia Adshead; lighting, Whitney Quesenbery; music supervision and arrangements, Peter Howard; musical staging, Mary Jane Houdina; orchestrations, Robert M. Freedman, Judd Woldin; additional lyrics, Susan Birkenhead; production stage manager, Patricia Flynn; press, Bruce Cohen, Kathleen von Schmid.
Time: 1791. Act I, Scene 1: A street market in the East End of London. Scene 2: The dining room in Mendoza's mansion. Scene 3: Morning in the Da Costa home. Scene 4: David Ben Yonkel's cabinetmaking shop. Scene 5: The street at Da Costa's post. Scene 6: The villa of Luis Belasco. Scene 7: The street outside Da Costa's home. Scene 8: Inside Da Costa's home. Scene 9: Outside Da Costa's home.
Act II, Scene 1: The street. Scene 2: Outside Furtado's home. Scene 3: Furtado's dining room. Scene 4: The street. Scene 5: Deborah's window. Scene 6: David's shop. Scene 7: Chamber of the Sephardic Council. Scene 8: The street.
This musical about a a gifted "schnorrer," or beggar, was originally produced in regional theater in New Brunswick, N.J. under the title *Petticoat Lane* and was previously produced off Broadway 10/9/79 for 30 performances under the title *King of Schnorrers*. In this version, the score has been revised.

ACT I

"Petticoat Lane".. Peddlers
"Ours"... Da Costa
"Chutzpah"... Mr. and Mrs. Mendoza
"Tell Me" .... Deborah
(lyrics by Susan Birkenhead and Judd Woldin)
"Born to Schnorr" .... Peddlers
"I Have Not Lived in Vain"... Belasco
"A Man Is Meant to Reason" .... Da Costa
(lyrics by Susan Birkenhead and Judd Woldin)
"Blood Lines".. Peddlers
"Leave the Thinking to Men"....................................... David, Deborah
(lyrics by Susan Birkenhead)

"It's Over" .... Sadie, Peddlers
    (lyrics by Herb Martin)

ACT II

"Murder" .... Sadie
"Dead" .... David, Furtado
"A Man Is Meant to Reason" (Reprise) .... Da Costa, David
"I'm Only a Woman" .... Deborah
    (lyrics by Susan Birkenhead)
"An Ordinary Man" .... David
    (lyrics by Susan Birkenhead)
"Tell Me" (Reprise).. Deborah, David
"Well Done, Da Costa".. Da Costa
    (lyrics by Susan Birkenhead)
"Each of Us" .... Company

City Stage Company (CSC). Schedule of four programs. In repertory: **Brand** (32), revival
of the play by Henrik Ibsen, translated by Michael Meyer, opened November 3, 1985;
Frankenstein (23), adapted by Laurence Maslon from Mary Shelley's novel, opened December 1, 1985; **A Medieval Mystery Cycle** (6), program of medieval mystery plays,
opened December 18, 1985. (Repertory closed January 7, 1986) **A Country Doctor** (34).
By Len Jenkin; based on a story by Franz Kafka. Opened April 13, 1986. (Closed May
11, 1986) Repertory produced by City Stage Company, Craig D. Kinzer artistic director,
Will Maitland Weiss managing director; *A Country Doctor* produced by CSC Repertory,
Ltd., Craig D. Kinzer artistic director, Carol Ostrow managing director, in association
with River Arts Repertory, Lawrence Sacharow artistic director, at CSC Repertory.

PERFORMER	"BRAND"	"FRANKENSTEIN"
Mike Atkin		Gendarme
Paul Behar		William
Susan Bruce	Gerd	Elizabeth Lavenza
Sally Chamberlin	Brand's Mother	
Frank Dwyer	Doctor; Schoolmaster	Prof. Waldman
Patrick Egan	Sexton	The Creature
David Friedlander	Guide's Son; 4th Man	
Jeffrey Havenga	Ejnar	
Richard Johnson	2d Man	
Kathryn Klvana	Gypsy Woman	
Katherine Marie Loague	Headlands Woman	
Michael McGuinness	1st Man	Son
John Ryker O'Hara	3d Man	
Erika Peterson	Agnes	Justine
Michael Rothhaar		Henry Clerval
David Sennett		Boy
Tom Spackman	Guide; Provost	Victor Frankenstein
Robert Stattel	Brand	
Patrick Tull	Mayor	Man in Forest

A MEDIEVAL MYSTERY CYCLE

Procession .... Company
The Nativity
  God .... Frank Dwyer
  Gabriel.............. Michael McGuinness
  Angel................. Kathryn Klvana

Mary .... Susan Keller
Elizabeth .... Sally Chamberlin
Joseph .... Richard Johnson
The Second Shepherd's Play
  1st Shepherd .... Mike Atkin

2d Shepherd . . . . John Ryker O'Hara
3d Shepherd . . . . Mark Ballora
Mak . . . . David Sherrick
Gill. . . . . Sandra McAllister
Lamb . . . . Kia Heath
Angel . . . . Dierdre Ryan
Mary . . . . Susan Keller
Joseph . . . . Richard Johnson
Herod the Great
Messenger . . . . Nicola Glick
Herod. Patrick Tull
1st Knight . . . . Richard Renzaneth
2d Knight . . . . David Sennett
3d Knight . . . . David Friedlander
Counsellors: Lisa Shea, Janet Geist. Demons:
John Ryker O'Hara, Renette Zimmerly.
The Flight Into Egypt
Angel . . . . Kathryn Klvana
Joseph . . . . Richard Johnson
Mary . . . . Susan Keller

Slaughter of the Innocents
Messenger . . . . Nicola Glick
Herod. Patrick Tull
1st Knight . . . . Richard Renzaneth
2d Knight . . . . David Sennett
3d Knight . . . . David Friedlander
1st Mother . . . . Maria Lee Wallace
2d Mother . . . . Katherine Marie Loague
3d Mother . . . . Sally Chamberlin
Counsellors: Lisa Shea, Janet Geist. Demons:
John Ryker O'Hara, David Sherrick, Renette
Zimmerly.
Saint George and the Dragon
Father Christmas . . . . Frank Dwyer
Prince George . . . . Michael McGuinness
Dragon . . . . David Friedlander, John
                                      Ryker O'Hara
Dragon's Voice . . . . David Sennett
Doctor . . . . Maria Lee Wallace
Turk. . . . . Mike Atkin
Egypt . . . . Mark Ballora
Sabra . . . . Kia Heath

BRAND: Villagers—Mark Ballora, David Friedlander, Richard Johnson, Christina Heath, Sandra McAllister, Michael McGuinness, John Ryker O'Hara, Dierdre Ryan.

Directed by Craig D. Kinzer; scenery, Rick Butler; costumes, Catherine Zuber; lighting, Stephen Strawbridge; sound, Tom Gould; dramaturg, Laurence Maslon; stage manager, Bonnie L. Becker; press, Bruce Allardice.

Time: The middle of the 19th century. Place: In and around a fjord township on the west coast of Norway. The play was presented in two parts.

The only previous New York *Brand* revivals of record in this century were in repertory 3/14/10 (the fourth act only) and OOB in the 1971 and 1979 seasons.

FRANKENSTEIN: Directed by Craig D. Kinzer; scenery, Rick Butler; costumes, Catherine Zuber; lighting, Whitney Quesenbery; sound, Tom Gould; production stage manager, Bonnie L. Becker.

Time: The dawn of the 19th century. Place: Geneva. Ingolstadt and its environs. The play was presented in two parts.

The Creature (not a monster) as Mary Shelley conceived him, more sinned against than sinning in this latest adaptation of the fanciful tale.

A MEDIEVAL MYSTERY CYCLE: Directed by John Camera; scenery, Gerry Lantaigne; costumes, Sue Jane Stoker; dramaturg, Laurence Maslon; choreographer, Tina Kronis; lighting, Whitney Quesenbery; incidental music, Mark Ballora; stage manager, Tonia Payne.

Musicians: Mark Ballora, Renette Zimmerly recorder; Michael McGuinness flute; Katherine Marie Loague, Dierdre Ryan, Lisa Shea drums.

Program of mystery plays "culled from the best plays of the Nativity sections in all four major cycles" which comprised scores of short plays created for celebrations in the 14th–17th centuries.

A COUNTRY DOCTOR

CAST: Nurse, Doctor, Housemaid, Maxine—Jayne Haynes; Patient, Rose, Woman in the "Blind Pig"—Laura Innes; Kafka, Doctor, Groom—Olek Krupa; Wedding Guest, Doctor—Stephen Mellor; Pitchman, Father, Doctor, Charlie, Man at Literary Gathering—Richard Merrell; Mother, Doctor, Woman in 7-11—Rocky Rochelle Parker; Doctor, Liveliner, Truckdriver, Exhibitor, Man in the "Blind Pig"—Rocco Sisto; Villagers—Laurence Gleason, Holli Harms, Kia Heath, Anna Lank.

Directed by Lawrence Sacharow; scenery, Marjorie Bradley Kellogg; costumes, Marianne Powell-Parker; lighting, Arden Fingerhut; sound, Tom Gould; original music, Peter Gordon; associate set designer, Rick Butler; stage manager, Rickie Grosberg.

Metaphor of inner decay as a physician is summoned to treat a strange patient, based on a Kafka short story. The play was presented without intermission.

Hamelin: A Musical Tale From Rats to Riches (33). Musical with book by Richard Jarboe, Harvey Shield and Matthew Wells; music by Richard Jarboe and Harvey Shield. Produced by Craig Anderson at Circle in the Square Downtown. Opened November 10, 1985. (Closed December 8, 1985)

Lech	Scott Fless	Jigger; Otto	Andrew Kraus
Piper	Patrick Hamilton	Gilda	Liz Larsen
Mayor	G. Wayne Hoffman	Gertrude	Jodi Mitchel
Rudolph	Steven Jacob	Chigger; Utta	Erica L. Paulson

Musicians: Madelyn Rubinstein synthesizer, conductor; Barry Harwood synthesizers; Jon Kaufman drums.

Standby: Messrs. Fless, Hamilton, Hoffman, Kraus—Stephen Terrell.

Directed by Ron Nash; choreography, Jerry Yoder; scenery, Steven Rubin; costumes, Mark Bridges; lighting, Rick Belzer; musical supervision and routining, Ronald Melrose; synthesizer programming and design, Steven Oirich; associate producers, Jan Jalenak, Golden Rose Productions; production stage manager, Michael A. Clarke; press, Becky Flora, Mary Bryant, Glen Gary.

Time: The afternoon of June 26, 1284. Place: A street in Hamelin.

The Pied Piper tale as a rock musical. Previously produced off off Broadway at Musical Theater Works.

ACT I

"We're Rats"	Lech, Company
"The Mayor Doesn't Care"	Rudolph, Gilda, Rats
"Doing My Job"	Mayor, Gertrude
"Rat Trap"	Company
"Easy for Me"	Piper, Company
"What a Day"	Piper, Kids
"Paradise"	Piper, Gilda, Rudolph
"Charismatic"	Lech, Mayor, Gertrude
"Better Keep Your Promise"	Mayor, Gertrude, Lech, Rats
"Follow the Music Man"	Piper, Company

ACT II

"Feel the Beat"	Piper, Kids
"Serving the People"	Mayor, Gertrude, Gilda, Rudolph
"Mother"	Gilda
"Gold"	Mayor, Gertrude, Company
"I'll Remember"	Piper, Gilda, Rudolph
"You've Outstayed Your Welcome"	Company
"Follow the Music Man" (Reprise)	Piper
"Paradise" (Reprise)	Company

*The Golden Land (229). Musical revue in the Yiddish and English languages, created by Zalmen Mlotek and Moishe Rosenfeld. Produced by Sherwin M. Goldman, Moishe Rosenfeld and Westport Productions, Inc. at the Second Avenue Theater. Opened November 11, 1985.

Bruce Adler	Avi Hoffman
Phyllis Berk	Marc Krause
Joanne Borts	Neva Small

Voice of the Grandmother—Sonia Hagalili. Standbys: Jacob Ehrenreich, Ellen Gould.

Golden Land Klezmer Orchestra: Zalmen Mlotek conductor; Michael Larsen assistant conductor, piano; Sandra Schipior violin; Ed Covi woodwinds; Edward R. Kalny trumpet; Paul Bernardi trombone; Steve Alcott bass; Don Mulvaney drums.

Directed by Jacques Levy; musical staging, Donald Saddler; musical direction and arrangements, Zalmen Mlotek; scenery, Lindsey Decker; costumes, Natasha Landau; lighting, John McLain; sound, Jack Weisberg; orchestrations, Peter Sokolow; associate producer, William Twohill; production stage manager, Deborah Clelland; stage manager, Craig Butler; press, Milly Schoenbaum, Kevin Patterson.

The Jewish immigration experience from Ellis Island days through World War II, recalled in songs and scenes of Yiddish theater, presented in two parts. Previously produced off off Broadway and in regional theater.

*Manhattan Theater Club. Schedule of six programs. **Oliver Oliver** (24). Revival of the play by Paul Osborn. Opened November 12, 1985. (Closed December 1, 1985) **It's Only a Play** (17). By Terrence McNally. Opened January 12, 1986. (Closed January 26, 1986) **Loot** (32). Revival of the play by Joe Orton. Opened February 18, 1986. (Closed March 15, 1986 and transferred to Broadway; see its entry in the Plays Produced on Broadway section of this volume) **Principia Scriptoriae** (22). By Richard Nelson. Opened April 10, 1986. (Closed April 27, 1986) ***Women of Manhattan** (7). By John Patrick Shanley. Opened May 25, 1986. Produced by Manhattan Theater Club, Lynne Meadow artistic director, Barry Grove managing director, at City Center Theater.

OLIVER OLIVER

Gertrude	Joan Inwood	Judith Tiverton	Nancy Marchand
Constance Oakshot	Frances Sternhagen	Phyllis Tiverton	Patricia Clarkson
Carl Bridgewater	Nicholas Kaledin	Oliver Oliver	Timothy Daly
Williamson	Alexander Reed	Justin Stock	Kurt Knudson

Directed by Vivian Matalon; scenery, Tom Schwinn; costumes, Albert Wolsky; lighting, Richard Nelson; production stage manager, Don Walters; press, Virginia P. Louloudes.

Place: A room in Constance's Country House. The play was presented in three acts.

Oliver Oliver was first produced on Broadway 1/5/34 for 11 performances. This is its first major New York revival of record.

IT'S ONLY A PLAY

Gus Washington	Jihmi Kennedy	Julia Budder	Christine Baranski
James Wicker	James Coco	Ira Drew	Paul Benedict
Virginia Noyes	Joanna Gleason	Peter Austin	Mark Blum
Frank Finger	David Garrison	Emma	Florence Stanley

Standbys: Messrs. Kennedy, Garrison, Blum—Steven Culp; Messrs. Coco, Benedict—Scott Robertson.

Directed by John Tillinger; scenery, John Lee Beatty; costumes, Rita Ryack; lighting, Pat Collins; sound, Stan Metelits; production stage manager, Tracy B. Cohen; stage manager, Anne Marie Kuehling; press, Virginia P. Louloudes, Charles M. Gomes.

Time: Now. Place: Julia Budder's townhouse. The play was presented in two parts.

Comedy of show biz characters at a producer's party after a Broadway opening night, reacting to the reviews and each other. Previously produced in 1978 in Philadelphia in a pre-Broadway tryout under the title *Broadway, Broadway* and OOB in 1982 at Manhattan Punch Line.

A Best Play; see page 210.

LOOT

McLeavy	Charles Keating	Dennis	Kevin Bacon
Fay	Zoë Wanamaker	Truscott	Joseph Maher
Hal	Zeljko Ivanek	Meadows	Nick Ullett

Directed by John Tillinger; scenery, John Lee Beatty; costumes, Bill Walker, lighting, Richard Nelson; production stage manager, Peggy Peterson, press, Virginia P. Louloudes, Claudia Jacobs.

Loot was produced on Broadway 3/18/68 for 22 performances. This is its first major New York revival, presented in two parts.

PRINCIPIA SCRIPTORIAE

Bill Howell...............	Anthony Heald	Alberto Fava.............	George Morfogen
Ernesto Pico....................	Joe Urla	Norton Quinn.............	Steven Gilborn
Man in Prison; Soldier.....	Erneste Gonzalez	Hans Einhorn.............	Mike Nussbaum
Julio Montero..............	Shawn Elliott		

Directed by Lynne Meadow; scenery, John Lee Beatty; costumes, William Ivey Long; lighting, Jennifer Tipton; sound, Scott Lehrer; production stage manager, Don Walters; stage manager, Steve Wappel.

Act I: 1970, Latin America. Act II: The same country, 15 years later. Coda: 1970, Latin America. Two writers, former prisoners, at odds 15 years later over differing forms of political tyranny.

WOMEN OF MANHATTAN

Billie......................	Nancy Mette	Bob....................	Keith Szarabajka
Rhonda................	J. Smith-Cameron	Duke.......................	Tom Wright
Judy	Jayne Haynes		

Standbys: Mr. Wright—Michael Genet; Mr. Szarabajka—Peter Mackenzie.

Directed by Ron Lagomarsino; scenery, Adrianne Lobel; costumes, Ann Emonts; lighting, James F. Ingalls; sound, Stan Metelits; production stage manager, Tom Aberger.

Comedy, three women seek romance in the upper strata of Manhattan society. The play was presented without intermission.

The Importance of Being Earnest (73). Revival of the play by Oscar Wilde. Produced by The Harold Clurman Theater, Jack Garfein artistic director, and Halcyon Produc-

LOOT—Joseph Maher, Zeljko Ivanek, Charles Keating and Zoë Wanamaker in a scene from the revival of the black comedy by Joe Orton

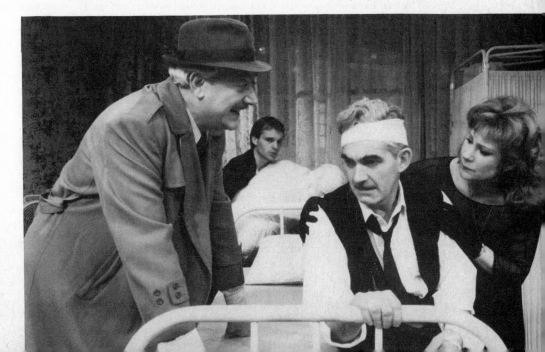

tions at the Samuel Beckett Theater. Opened November 13, 1985. (Closed January 19, 1986)

Lane .... A.D. Cover	Miss Prism .... Carmella Ross
Algernon Moncrieff .... Anthony Fusco	Cecily Cardew .... Cherry Jones
John Worthing .... Samuel Maupin	Rev. Canon Chasuble .... William Dennis
Lady Bracknell .... Dina Merrill	Merriman .... Robert North
Hon. Gwendolyn Fairfax ..... Cynthia Dozier	

Understudy: Kelli Kruger.

Directed by Philip Campanella; scenery, David R. Ballous; costumes, Peggy Farrell; lighting, Jackie Manassee; production stage manager, Lee Bloomrosen; press, Henry Lurhman Associates, Terry M. Lilly, David Mayhew, Andrew P. Shearer.

Time: 1895. Act I: Algernon Moncrieff's flat in Half-Moon Street, W. Act II: The garden at the Manor House, Woolton. Act III: Drawing-room at the Manor House, Woolton.

The last major New York revival of *The Importance of Being Earnest* was by Circle in the Square on Broadway 6/16/77 for 108 performances.

Peg Small replaced Dina Merrill 1/7/86.

*Personals (217). Musical revue with words and lyrics by David Crane, Seth Friedman and Marta Kauffman; music by William Dreskin, Joel Phillip Friedman, Seth Friedman, Alan Menken, Stephen Schwartz and Michael Skloff. Produced by John-Edward Hill, Arthur MacKenzie and Jon D. Silverman in association with Fujisankei Communications Group at the Minetta Lane Theater. Opened November 24, 1985.

Louis; Others .... Jason Alexander	Sam; Others .... Jeff Keller
Kim; Others .... Laura Dean	Louise; Others .... Nancy Opel
Claire; Others .... Dee Hoty	Typesetter; Others .... Trey Wilson

Understudies: Misses Dean, Hoty, Opel—Kathryn Morath; Messrs. Alexander, Keller, Wilson—Stephen McNaughton.

Orchestra: Michael Skloff conductor, piano, synthesizer; Gregory Utzig guitars; William Harris reeds; Bruce Doctor percussion; Wayne Abravanel synthesizers.

Directed by Paul Lazarus; choreography, D.J. Giagni; musical direction and vocal arrangements, Michael Skloff; scenery, Loren Sherman; costumes, Ann Hould-Ward; lighting, Richard Nelson; sound, Otts Munderloh; orchestrations, Steven Oirich; production stage manager, Tom Aberger; stage manager, Lauren Class Schneider; press, The Fred Nathan Company, Inc., Glenna Freedman, Merle Frimark.

Classified lonelyhearts ads as a springboard for comic treatment of our life and times.

MUSICAL NUMBERS, ACT I: "Nothing to Do With Love" (music by Stephen Schwartz)—Company; "After School Special" (music by William Dreskin)—Jason Alexander, Company; "Mama's Boys" (music by Seth Friedman and Joel Phillip Friedman)—Dee Hoty, Laura Dean, Trey Wilson, Company; "A Night Alone" (music by Michael Skloff)—Jeff Keller, Alexander, Wilson, Company; "I Think You Should Know" (music by Seth Friedman and Joel Phillip Friedman)—Dean, Keller; "Second Grade" (music by Michael Skloff)—Keller, Alexander, Wilson, Company; "Imagine My Surprise" (music by William Dreskin)—Hoty; "I'd Rather Dance Alone" (music by Alan Menken)—Company.

ACT II: "Moving in With Linda" (music by Stephen Schwartz)—Keller, Company; "A Little Happiness" (music by Seth Friedman and Joel Phillip Friedman)—Wilson; "I Could Always Go to You" (music by Alan Menken)—Hoty, Nancy Opel; "The Guy I Love" (music by William Dreskin)—Opel, Alexander; "Michael" (music by William Dreskin)—Dean; "Picking Up the Pieces" (music by Seth Friedman and Joel Phillip Friedman)—Alexander, Wilson; "Some Things Don't End" (music by Stephen Schwartz)—Company (lyrics to all songs by David Crane, Seth Friedman and Marta Kauffman).

Inside Out (23) by James Van Lare. Produced by Robert Mansdorf at the Players Theater. Opened November 26, 1985. (Closed December 15, 1985.

Neil........................ John Kudan	Alice..................... Jo Anna Rush
Rich .... Adam Oliensis	

Standby: Miss Rush—Sharon Talbot.

Directed by James Van Lare; scenery, Donald Jensen; lighting, John Michael Deegan; costumes, Shell Walker; associate producer, Michael J. Kay; production stage manager, John Hodge; press, The Jacksina Company, Inc., Kevin Boyle, Darrel Joseph.

Place: Neil's apartment, New York City. Scene 1: Saturday evening, 9 o'clock. Scene 2: Later that evening. Scene 3: Sunday morning. The play was presented without intermission.

Dramatic triangle: husband, wife, young male homosexual.

Just So (6). Musical based on Rudyard Kipling's *Just So Stories*; book by Mark St. Germain; music by Doug Katsaros; lyrics by David Zippel. Produced by Ivan Bloch, Joanne L. Zippel, New Day Productions and Mary Fisher Productions at the Jack Lawrence Theater. Opened December 3, 1985. (Closed December 8, 1985)

Eldest Magician.......... Andre De Shields	Elephant's Child .... Tina Johnson
Giraffe .... Keith Curran	Leopard .... Tico Wells
Camel.................... Teresa Burrell	Man .... Jason Graae
Rhino .... Tom Robbins	

Understudy: Misses Burrell, Johnson—Rene Rodriguez.

Musicians: David Friedman conductor, keyboards; Albin Konopa keyboard II; Jamie Lamm bass, guitar; James Harrington drums, percussion.

Conceived and directed by Julianne Boyd; choreography, David Storey; musical supervision and direction, David Friedman; scenery, Atkin Pace; costumes, Ann Hould-Ward; lighting, Craig Miller; vocal and dance arrangements and orchestrations, Doug Katsaros; sound, Tom Gould; production stage manager, Renee Lutz; stage manager, Richard Hester; press, the Jacksina Company, Kevin Boyle.

Time: The world's first day.

Kipling animal stories set to a rock score. Previously produced in regional theater in Allentown, Pa.

ACT I

"Just So"... Eldest Magician, Animals	
"The Whole World Revolves	
Around You".......................... Eldest Magician, Animals, Man	
"Arm in Arm in Harmony" .... Man, Animals	
"Chill Out!" .... Djiin, Man	
"Camel's Blues"... Camel	
"Eat, Eat, Eat"................................ Rhino, Man, Animals	
"Desert Dessert"............................... Parsee Man, Animals	
"Itch, Itch, Itch" .... Rhino	
"Everything Under the Sun".......................... Man	
"The Gospel According to the Leopard"........................ Leopard, Man, Animals	

ACT II

"My First Mistake" .... Eldest Magician	
"Shadowy Forest of Garadufi Dance" .... Leopard, Animals	
"Giraffe's Reprise"....................................... Giraffe	
"The Answer Song".................................. Kolokolo Bird, Elephant Child	
"I've Got to Know".. Elephant Child	
"I Have Changed" .... Eldest Magician, Animals	
"Lullaby" .... Eldest Magician	

A Lie of the Mind (186). By Sam Shepard. Produced by Lewis Allen and Stephen Graham at the Promenade Theater. Opened December 5, 1985. (Closed June 1, 1986)

Jake	Harvey Keitel	Lorraine	Geraldine Page
Frankie	Aidan Quinn	Sally	Karen Young
Beth	Amanda Plummer	Baylor	James Gammon
Mike	Will Patton	Meg	Ann Wedgeworth

Musicians: The Red Clay Ramblers—Clay Buckner fiddle, harmonica; Mike Craver piano, melodeon; Jack Herrick guitar, bass, bazouki, whistles, cello, trumpet; Tommy Thompson banjo, bass; Jim Watson mandolin, guitar, bass.

Understudies: Mr. Gammon—Beeson Carroll; Misses Wedgeworth, Page—Georgine Hall; Misses. Plummer, Young—Deirdre O'Connell; Mr. Keitel—Bill Raymond; Messrs. Quinn, Patton—John Griesemer.

Directed by Sam Shepard; scenery, Andy Stacklin; costumes, Rita Ryack; lighting, Anne E. Militello; sound, Janet Kalas; associate producer, Guadalupe/Hudson Productions; production stage manager, Ruth Kreshka; stage manager, Jane Grey; press, David Powers, Leo Stern.

Two Western families are torn by emotional agonies but bound together by a violence-wracked marriage in which the husband has attempted, nearly successfully, to kill the wife. Incidental music —consisting of traditional numbers and songs by Jack Herrick and Tommy Thompson, Lefty Frizzell, Mike Craver and Stephen Foster—comments on the dramatic events. The play was presented in three parts.

Salome Jens replaced Geraldine Page 2/4/86; David Strathairn replaced Harvey Keitel and Don Harvey replaced Aidan Quinn 3/5/86; Sally Gracie replaced Salome Jens 3/11/86; Louise Latham replaced Ann Wedgeworth 3/19/86; Deirdre O'Connell replaced Amanda Plummer, John Griesemer replaced Will Patton, Betsy Aidem replaced Karen Young and Beeson Carroll replaced James Gammon 3/25/86.

*Nunsense (197). Musical with book, music and lyrics by Dan Goggin. Produced by The Nunsense Theatrical Company in association with Joseph Hoesl and Bill Crowder at the Cherry Lane Theater. Opened December 12, 1985.

Sister Mary Cardelia	Marilyn Farina	Sister Mary Amnesia	Semina De Laurentis
Sister Mary Hubert	Vicki Belmonte	Mister Mary Leo	Suzi Winson
Sister Robert Anne	Christine Anderson		

Musicians: Michael Rice conductor, piano; Sande Campbell synthesizer; David Henderson woodwinds; Grace Milan drums, percussion.

Understudy: Susan Gordon-Clark.

Directed by Dan Goggin; musical staging and choreography, Felton Smith; Musical direction, Michael Rice; scenery, Barry Axtell; lighting, Susan A. White; production stage manager, Trey Hunt; press, Shirley Herz Associates, Pete Sanders.

Time: The present. Place: Mt. Saint Helen's School Auditorium in Hoboken.

Five nuns assemble a talent show to raise funds. Previously produced OOB at the Baldwin Theater.

ACT I

Welcome	Sr. Mary Cardelia
"Nunsense Is Habit-Forming"	Company
Opening Remarks	Srs. Cardelia, Mary Hubert
"A Difficult Transition"	Company
The Quiz	Sr. Mary Amnesia
"Benedicite"	Sr. Mary Leo
"The Biggest Ain't the Best"	Srs. Leo, Hubert
"Playing Second Fiddle"	Sr. Robert Anne
Taking Responsibility	Sr. Cardelia
"So You Want To Be a Nun"	Sr. Amnesia
A Brilliant Idea	Company

A Word From the Reverend Mother.. Sr. Cardelia
"Turn Up the Spotlight"... Sr. Cardelia
"Lilacs Bring Back Memories"....................... Srs. Cardelia, Hubert, Leo, Amnesia
An Unexpected Discovery.. Sr. Cardelia
"Growing Up Catholic".. Company

ACT II

Robert to the Rescue.. Sr. Anne
"Growing Up Catholic" (Reprise) .... Srs. Anne, Leo, Hubert, Amnesia
"We've Got to Clean Out the Freezer"...................................... Company
A Minor Catastrophe... Company
"Just a Coupa Sisters".................................... Srs. Cardelia, Hubert
"Soup's On" (The Dying Nun Ballet) .... Sr. Leo
Baking With the BVM.................................... Sr. Julia, Child of God
"Playing Second Fiddle" (Reprise)....................................... Sr. Anne
"I Just Want To Be a Star" .... Sr. Anne
"The Drive In"... Srs. Anne, Amnesia, Leo
"A Home Movie"... Company
"I Could've Gone to Nashville"... Sr. Amnesia
"Gloria in Excelsis Deo"... Company
Closing Remarks....................................... Sr. Cardelia, Company
"Holier Than Thou" .... Sr. Hubert, Company
"Nunsense Is Habit-Forming" (Reprise) .... Company

NUNSENSE—Vicki Belmonte, Semina De Laurentis and
Marilyn Farina in a scene from the musical by Dan Goggin

To Whom It May Concern (106). Musical by Carol Hall. Produced by The Bedda Roses Company by arrangement with The Williamstown Theater Festival, Nikos Psacharopoulos artistic director, at St. Stephen's Church. Opened December 16, 1985. (Closed March 23, 1986)

Choir Master	Michael O'Flaherty	Frederika	Louise Edeiken
Child	Jennifer Naimo	Sister	Tamara Tunie
Priest	Dylan Baker	Celia	Becky Gelke
Grandad	William Hardy	Mike	Guy Stroman
Fay	Gretchen Cryer	Deloris	Kecia Lewis-Evans
Bob	Michael Hirsch	Elliott	Al DeCristo
Caroline	Carol Hall	Stranger	George Gerdes

Directed by Geraldine Fitzgerald; musical direction, staging, musical supervision, vocal arrangements, Michael O'Flaherty; lighting, Christina Giannelli; production stage manager, Noel Stern; press, Patt Dale Associates, Julianne Waldheim.

Churchgoers sing their thoughts during a service. Previously produced at the Williamstown, Mass. summer festival. The play was presented without intermission.

MUSICAL NUMBERS

"When I Consider the Heavens" .... Ensemble
"Truly My Soul" .... Ensemble
"Blessed Be God" .... Ensemble
"Holy God" .... Caroline, Sister, Elliott, Choir Master
"Miracles" .... Frederika, Company
"We Were Friends" .... Caroline, Mike
"Sandy" .... Celia
"Make a Joyful Noise" .... Women's Ensemble
"Ain't Nobody Got a Bed of Roses" .... Stranger, Company
"We Believe" .... Ensemble
"I Only Miss the Feeling" .... Deloris
"My Sort of Ex-Boyfriend" .... Celia
"Jenny Rebecca" .... Mike
"Skateboard Acrobats" .... Sister, Child, Company
"In the Mirror's Reflection" .... Stranger, Company
"In the Mirror's Reflection" (Reprise) .... Company
"Ain't Love Easy" .... Fay, Bob
"Walk in Love" .... Grandad, Company
"Who Will Dance
    with the Blind Dancing Bear" .... Choir Master, Company
"To Whom It May Concern" .... Priest, Stranger, Company
"Walk in Love" (Reprise) .... Ensemble

The Mirror Repertory Company. Schedule of three revivals. **The Time of Your Life** (17) by William Saroyan, opened December 18, 1985, in repertory with **Children of the Sun** (16) by Maxim Gorky, translated by Ariadne Nicolaeff, opened December 26, 1985. (Repertory closed January 19, 1986) **The Circle** (33). By W. Somerset Maugham. Opened February 20, 1986. (Closed March 23, 1986) Produced by The Mirror Repertory Company, Sabra Jones artistic director, at The Theater at Saint Peter's Church.

THE TIME OF YOUR LIFE

Joe	Mason Adams	Newsboy	Michael DiGioia
Nick	Charles Regan	Drunk	Phillip Pruneau
Arab	Clement Fowler	(Tom)	Francois de la Giroday, Tad Jones
Willie	Frank Faranda	(Kitty)	Tovah Feldshuh, Sabra Jones

Dudley	Rowan Joseph
Harry	Gabriel Barre
Wesley	Loni Berry
Lorene	Judith Cohen
Blick	Richard Leighton
Mary L.	Katharine Houghton
Krupp.	Richard Grusin
McCarthy.	Baxter Harris
Kit Carson	Tom Brennan
(1st Sailor) ...	Tad Jones, Gordon McConnell
Killer	Helen Wheels

2d Sailor.	Eric Eisenberg
Anna.	Erica Ferszt
Elsie	Nanette Werness
2d Whore.	Deirdre Madigan
Gentleman	Neil Vipond
Lady	Elizabeth Franz
1st Cop.	Don Gigliotti
2d Cop	Paul Serson

(Parentheses indicates roles in which the performers alternated.)

CHILDREN OF THE SUN

Protasov.	Michael Moriarty
Roman	Phillip Pruneau
Antonovna.	Susan Willis
Liza.	Denise Stephenson
Yegor.	Baxter Harris
Chepurnoy	Jess Osuna
(Melaniya)	Sabra Jones, Tovah Feldshuh
Fima.	Kelly Roman
Nazar	Clement Fowler
(Misha). ...	Tad Jones, Francois de la Giroday
Yelena.	Elizabeth Franz

Vaguin	Neil Vipond
Troshin.	Gabriel Barre
Avdotya	Katharine Houghton
Lusha	Judith Cohen
Doctor	Richard Leighton

(Parentheses indicate roles in which the performers alternated)

Rabble: Scott Bryant, Alexander D. Carney, Eric Eisenberg, Frank Faranda, Don Gigliotti, Omar Lotayef, Gordon McConnell, Paul Serson.

THE CIRCLE

Arnold Champion-Cheney,	
M.P.	Gordon McConnell
Footman.	Frank Faranda
Mrs. Shenstone	Ann Hillary
Elizabeth	Denise Stephenson
Edward Luton	Francois de la Giroday
Clive Champion-Cheney.	Bryan Clark
Butler	Charles Regan
Lady Catherine	
Champion-Cheney	Geraldine Page

Lord Porteous .... W.B. Brydon

Understudies: Mr. McConnell—Frank Faranda; Mr. de la Giroday—Don Gigliotti; Miss Hillary—Susan Willis; Miss Stephenson—Valerie Leonard; Mr. Clark—Charles Regan; Messrs. Faranda, Regan—Gabriel Barre; Miss Page—Ann Hillary.

ALL PLAYS: Scenery and lighting, James Tilton; costumes, Gail Cooper-Hecht; production stage manager, Nicholas Dunn; press, Shirley Herz Associates, David Roggensack.

THE TIME OF YOUR LIFE: Directed by Peter Mark Schifter; stage managers, Anne S. King, Kate Hancock.

Time: Afternoon and night of a day in October, 1939. Place: Nick's Pacific Street Saloon, Restaurant and Entertainment Palace at the foot of the Embarcadero in San Francisco and a suggestion of Room 21, New York Hotel, around the corner. The play was presented in three parts.

The last major New York revival of *The Time of Your Life* was by The Acting Company on Broadway 10/28/75 for 8 performances.

CHILDREN OF THE SUN: Directed by Tom Brennan; stage managers, Anne S. King, Kate Hancock.

Time: 1905. Place: Russia, the Protasov household. The play was presented in two parts.

Children of the Sun was presented on Broadway in the repertory of Vera F. Komisarzhevsky in March 1908. This is its first New York revival of record.

THE CIRCLE: Directed by Stephen Porter; sound, Rob Gorton; stage manager, Kate Hancock.

Place: The drawing room at Ashton-Adey, Arnold Champion-Cheney's house in Dorset. The play was presented in three parts.

The last major New York revival of *The Circle* was by The Roundabout Theater Company off Broadway 3/26/74 for 96 performances.

Lincoln Center Theater. Schedule of five programs. **Prairie du Chien** and **The Shawl** (48). Program of two one-act plays by David Mamet. Opened December 23, 1985. (Closed February 2, 1986) **The House of Blue Leaves** (38). Revival of the play by John Guare; with words and music by John Guare. Opened March 19, 1986. (Closed April 20, 1986 and transferred to the Vivian Beaumont Theater; see its entry in the Plays Produced on Broadway section of this volume) **Spalding Gray.** Series of three monologue programs written and performed by Spalding Gray. **Terrors of Pleasure** (15). Opened May 14, 1986. (Closed May 25, 1986) **Sex and Death to the Age 14** (7). Opened May 28, 1986. (Closed June 1, 1986). And *Swimming to Cambodia* scheduled to open June 3, 1986. Produced by Lincoln Center Theater, Gregory Mosher director, Bernard Gersten executive producer, at the Mitzi E. Newhouse Theater.

PRAIRIE DU CHIEN

Card Dealer	Tom Signorelli	Storyteller	Jerry Stiller
Gin Player	W.H. Macy	Listener	Brad Hall
Porter	Paul Butler	Listener's Son	Christopher Jennings

THE SHAWL

John	Mike Nussbaum	Charles	Calvin Leeds
Miss A.	Lindsay Crouse	Place: John's office.	

Understudy: Messrs. Macy, Hall, Leeds—Stephen Hamilton.

Directed by Gregory Mosher; scenery, Michael Merritt; costumes, Nan Cibula; lighting, Kevin Rigdon; production manager, Jeff Hamlin; stage manager, Kate Stewart; press, Merle Debuskey, Robert W. Larkin.

Self-described as "ghost stories," *Prairie du Chien* tells a murder tale and acts out a gin game aboard a railroad train (it was adapted by the author from his 1978 radio play); *The Shawl* is about a con man trying to cheat a widow (previously produced last season at the Goodman Theater in Chicago).

THE HOUSE OF BLUE LEAVES

Artie Shaughnessy	John Mahoney	2d Nun	Jane Cecil
Ronnie Shaughnessy	Ben Stiller	Little Nun	Ann Talman
Bunny Flingus	Stockard Channing	M.P.; El Dorado Bartender	Ian Blackman
Bananas Shaughnessy	Swoosie Kurtz	White Man; El Dorado	
Corrinna Stroller	Julie Hagerty	Bartender	Peter J. Dowling
Head Nun	Patricia Falkenhain	Billy Einhorn	Christopher Walken

Understudies: Mr. Stiller—Ian Blackman; Miss Falkenhain—Jane Cecil; Messrs. Mahoney, Walken—Brian Evers; Misses Kurtz, Talman—Kathleen McKiernan; Misses Channing, Hagerty—Melodie Somers.

Directed by Jerry Zaks; scenery, Tony Walton; costumes, Ann Roth; lighting, Paul Gallo; sound, Aural Fixation; stage manager, Kate Stewart.

Time: October 4, 1965. Place: The El Dorado Bar and Grill and an apartment in Sunnyside, Queens.

The House of Blue Leaves was first produced off Broadway 2/10/71 for 337 performances, was named a Best Play of its season and won the Critics Award for best American play. This is its first major New York revival and was presented in two parts.

SPALDING GRAY

One-man show with a minimum of theatrical trappings such as lighting and props, performed as a first-person, conversational autobiography. *Terrors of Pleasure* is about a city dweller's problems in buying a house in the country and trying to acclimatize himself to country living, plus the actor's problems in a Hollywood career. *Sex and Death to the Age 14* is about growing up in Barrington, R.I.

Sweet Will (9). Musical revue with music by Lance Mulcahy; lyrics from the works of William Shakespeare. Produced by David K. Drummond at the New Silver Lining Theater. Opened January 5, 1986. (Closed January 12, 1986)

Keith Amos	Stephanie Cotsirilos
Roslyn Burrough	Stephen Lehew

Musicians: Steve Postel, Scott Simpson.

Directed by John Olon; musical staging, Dennis Dennehy; musical direction, Michael Ward; design consultant, Desmond Heeley; lighting, John Michael Deegan; press, Jeffrey Richards Associates, C. George Willard, Susan Lee.

Sequel to *Shakespeare's Cabaret* (1981), with lyric excerpts from *Love's Labor's Lost, Twelfth Night, Much Ado About Nothing, As You Like It, A Midsummer Night's Dream* and the sonnets.

Be Happy for Me (1). By Jerry Sterner. Produced by David C. Gold at the Douglas Fairbanks Theater. Opened and closed at the evening performance January 7, 1986.

Directed by John Ferraro; scenery, David Potts; costumes, Abigail Murray; lighting, Greg MacPherson; music arrangements, Margaret R. Pine; production stage manager, William Hare; press, Bruce Cohen, Kathleen von Schmid. With David Groh, Philip Bosco, Priscilla Lopez, Russ Pennington.

Comedy, the romantic adventures of brothers vacationing in the Caribbean.

Gertrude Stein and a Companion (54). By Win Wells. Produced by Lucille Lortel at the Lucille Lortel Theater. Opened January 9, 1986. (Closed February 23, 1986)

Gertrude Stein	Jan Miner
Alice B. Toklas	Marian Seldes

Musician: Daniel Block.

Standby: Misses Miner, Seldes—Vera Lockwood.

Directed by Ira Cirker; scenery, Bob Phillips; costumes, Amanda J. Klein; lighting, Richard Dorfman; original music by Jason Cirker; additional music by Erik Satie and George and Ira Gershwin; production stage manager, Robert Bennett; press, Jeffrey Richards Associates, Ben Morse.

Time: Between 1907 and 1967. The play was presented in two parts.

Stein-Toklas conversation about their life and friends, much of it in the style of Miss Stein's writings. An American play previously produced at the 1984 Edinburgh Festival (best play award) and in Westport, Conn.

American Place Theater. Schedule of two programs. **Drinking in America** (94). One-man performance by and with Eric Bogosian. Opened January 19, 1986. (Closed April 27, 1986) **Williams & Walker** (77). Musical by Vincent D. Smith; with songs of the period; co-produced by New Federal Theater, Woodie King producer. Opened March 9, 1986. (Closed June 1, 1986). Produced by American Place Theater, Wynn Handman director, Julia Miles associate director at the American Place Theater.

DRINKING IN AMERICA

Directed by Wynn Handman; lighting, Marc Malamud; production stage manager, Rebecca Green; press, Fred Nathan, Philip Rinaldi.

Fourteen dramatic monologues enacted by the author, presented without intermission, personifying the cracks in the American dream caused by drugs, alcohol, distorted values, etc.

A Best Play; see page 227.

WILLIAMS & WALKER

Bert Williams................ Ben Harney Pianist...................... Ron Metcalf
George Walker .... Vondie Curtis-Hall Percussionist .... Joe Marshall

Directed by Shauneille Perry; choreography, Lenwood Sloan; musical direction, Ron Metcalf; scenery and lighting, Marc D. Malamud; costumes, Judy Dearing; stage manager, Lisa Blackwell.

Time: June 10, 1910. Place: Backstage dressing quarters of Bert Williams at the Majestic Theater in New York City. The play was presented without intermission.

Musical biography of *Ziegfeld Follies* and vaudeville comedy-singing-dancing team of Williams & Walker.

MUSICAL NUMBERS: "Magnetic Rag" (by Scott Joplin), "Constantly" (music by Bert Williams, words by Smith & Barris), "Bon Bon Buddy" (music by Will Marion Cook, words by Alex Rogers), "Somebody Stole My Gal" (by L. Wood), "Let It Alone" (music by Bert Williams, words by Alex Rogers), "Everybody Wants to See the Baby" (music by Bob Cole, words by James Weldon

GERTRUDE STEIN AND A COMPANION—Jan Miner as Gertrude Stein and Marian Seldes as Alice B. Toklas in the play by Win Wells

Johnson), "Save Your Money John" (by Les Copeland and Alex Rogers), "Nobody" (music by Bert Williams, words by Alex Rogers), "I'd Rather Have Nothin' All of the Time Than Somethin' for a Little While" (music by Bert Williams, words by John B. Lowitz), "I May be Crazy But I Ain't No Fool" (words and music by Alex Rogers), "I'm a Jonah Man" (by Alex Rogers), "Original Rag" (by Scott Joplin), "Chocolate Drop" (original Cake Walk, by Will Marion Cook).

El Grande de Coca-Cola (86). Revival of the musical revue by Ron House, Diz White, Alan Shearman and John Neville-Andrews. Produced by Ron Abbott, Susan Liederman and Michael Tucker at the Village Gate. Opened January 22, 1986. (Closed April 6, 1986)

Consuela Hernandez	Diz White	Senor Don Pepe Hernandez	Ron House
Juan Rodriguez	Rodger Bumpass	Maria Hernandez	Olga Merediz
Miguel Hernandez	Alan Shearman		

Understudies: Mr. House—Emilio Del Pozo; Messrs. Shearman, Bumpass—Don Stitt, Emilio Del Pozo; Misses White, Merediz—Cecilia Arana.

Directed by Ron House, Diz White and Alan Shearman; scenery, Elwin Charles Terrel II; lighting, Judy Rasmuson; sound, Paul Garrity; choreography, Anne Gunderson; production stage manager, Diane Mazey; stage manager, Robert Swanson; press, The Jacksina Company, Inc., Judy Jacksina, Jane Steinberg.

Somewhat revised version of the fractured Spanish musical originally produced in Europe and off Broadway 2/13/73 for 1,114 performances.

Halala! (Congratulations) (31). Musical by Welcome Msomi. Produced by Eric Krebs in the Izulu Dance Theater production at the Douglas Fairbanks Theater. Opened February 12, 1986. (Closed March 9, 1986)

Thuli Dumakude	Seth Sibanda
Lorraine Mahlangu	Linda Tshabalala
Mandla Msomi	Michael Xulu

Musicians: Stanley Bullock guitar, harmonica, shekere, percussion, flute; Zimbabwe Nkenya kalimba, percussion, flute, bass guitar, marimba; David Pleasant percussion, harmonica.

Directed by Welcome Msomi; choreography, Thuli Dumakude; lighting, Whitney Quesenbery; vocal arrangements, Thuli Dumakude; stage manager, Rachel Levine; press, Shirley Herz Associates, Peter Cromarty.

Zulu musical performed in English including traditional South African instruments in its score and dealing with political conflicts of the day. A foreign play having its world premiere in this production, presented without intermission.

MUSICAL NUMBERS

Scene 1: Drums communicate a warm welcome
  Introduction .... Mandla Msomi
Scene 2: Arrival at Kayelisha
  Personal Experiences .... Michael Xulu, Thuli Dumakude
  "Koze Kubenini" (Until When) .... Seth Sibanda, Lorraine Mahlangu
  "Sonqoba" (We Shall Conquer) .... Dumakude
Scene 3: At work; sivuk'ekuseni (a demonstration)
Scene 4: Arrest and solitary confinement
  Inside a Prison Cell .... Sibanda
Scene 5: Heroes and heroines remembered
  "Bayakhala" (They Mourn)... Dumakude
Scene 6: A family togetherness and friendship
  "The Halala Song"................ Xulu, Linda Tshabalala, Dumakude, Msomi, Mahlangu
Scene 7: Celebration; a boot dance

Scene 8: Izigubhu (drums speak)
Scene 9: Isangoma (the Diviner)
Scene 10: Zasho (a celebration)

Another Paradise (8). By Donna Spector. Produced by Shakespearewrights Players Theater in association with Donald H. Goldman at the Players Theater. Opened February 17, 1986. (Closed February 23, 1986)

Directed by Licia Colombi; scenery, Peter Harrison; costumes, Donna Zakowska; lighting, Jean Redmann; music, Carolyn Dutton; press, Patricia Krawitz. With Cass Morgan, Arleigh Richards, Tom Ligon, Meg Van Zyl, Mick Weber.

Appalachian father resents his daughter's daydreaming fantasies. Previously produced in another version off off Broadway at the Open Space Theater.

Anais Nin: The Paris Years (9). One-character play by and with Lee Kessler; adapted from the diary of Anais Nin. Produced by Brunnen Productions at the Actors' Playhouse. Opened March 2, 1986. (Closed March 9, 1986)

Directed by Spider Duncan Christopher; scenery, Keith Hein; costumes, Jean-Pierre Dorleae; lighting, Robert Googooian; associate producer, Didi Gough; production stage manager, Denise Yaney; press, Solters/Roskin/Friedman, Inc., Cindy Valk.

Literary friendships and other adventures in the Paris of the 1930s, in flashbacks from 1966, with Lee Kessler portraying Anais Nin. The play was presented without intermission.

Elisabeth Welch: Time to Start Living (22). One-woman musical entertainment performed by Elisabeth Welch. Produced by Arthur Cantor and Edwin W. Schloss by arrangement with Lucille Lortel at the Lucille Lortel Theater. Opened March 20, 1986. (Closed April 13, 1986)

Musicians: Peter Howard piano, Bruce Samuels bass, Tony Tedesco drums.

Musical direction, Peter Howard; scenic supervision, Leo Myer; sound, Tony Meola; production stage manager, William Castleman; press, Arthur Cantor Associates, Ken Mandelbaum.

Songs and highlights of her career on the international musical stage beginning in 1928, sung and narrated by Elisabeth Welch, presented without intermission.

The Eden Cinema (19). Revival of the play by Marguerite Duras; translated by Barbara Bray. Produced by UBU Repertory Theater, Francoise Kourilsky artistic director, at the Harold Clurman Theater. Opened March 23, 1986. (Closed April 6, 1986)

Mother	Marylouise Burke	Suzanne	Brooke Shields
Monsieur Jo	Ryan Cutrona	Corporal	Ching Yeh
Joseph	Josh Hamilton		

Directed by Francoise Kourilsky; music, Genji Ito; scenery, Beth Kuhn; costumes, Debra Stein; lighting, Curt Ostermann; sound, Phil Lee; production stage manager, Marilyn Dampf; press, Becky Flora.

Time: The early 1930s. Place: French Indochina.

Marguerite Duras's 1977 play about life on a Southeast Asia plantation told in children's reminiscences of their mother, foreshadowing things to come, presented without intermission.

The Alchemedians (44). Vaudeville revue conceived and performed by Bob Berky and Michael Moschen. Produced by Robert Cole and Michael Moschen at the Lamb's Theater. Opened March 27, 1986. (Closed May 4, 1986)

Directed by Ricardo Velez; choreography, Bob Berky and Michael Moschen; music, David Van Tieghem; artistic design and construction, John Kahn; costumes, Mei-Ling Louie; sound, Jan Nebozenko; production stage manager, Dave Feldman; press, Jeffrey Richards Associates, Bill Shuttleworth.

Act I: Laboratory—Sonics, Formula Formulae. Act II: Vital Principles—Light, Action, Fire.

The Messrs. Berky and Moschen juggling, clowning, etc. in a self-styled "collaborative work" of New Vauvedille. Previously produced at the Brooklyn Academy of Music.

*Beehive (73). Musical revue conceived and written by Larry Gallagher. Produced by Betmar and Charles Allen at Top of the Gate. Opened March 30, 1986.

Pattie Darcy	Adriane Lenox
Alison Fraser	Gina Taylor
Jasmine Guy	Laura Theodore

Musicians: Skip Brevis keyboards, Peter Grant drums, Peter Brown bass, John Putnam guitar, Benny Russell tenor sax, Chris Anderson trumpet.

Directed by Larry Gallagher; musical direction and arrangements, Skip Brevis; choreography, Leslie Dockery; scenery and lighting, John Hickey; costumes, David Dille; vocal adaptation, Claudia Brevis; sound, Lewis Mead; stage manager, Brian Kaufman; press, Betty Lee Hunt, Maria Cristina Pucci.

Understudies: Misses Darcy, Fraser, Theodore—Andre Petty; Misses Guy, Lenox, Taylor—Jenny Douglas.

Collection of songs remembering and celebrating singers of the 1960s like Petula Clark, Aretha Franklin, etc. Previously produced OOB at Sweetwaters.

MUSICAL NUMBERS, ACT I: "The Name Game"—Ensemble; "My Boyfriend's Back"—Alison Fraser; "Sweet Talkin' Guy"—Adriane Lenox; "One Fine Day"—Jasmine Guy; "I Sold My Heart to the Junkman"—Gina Taylor; "Academy Award"—Taylor; "Will You Still Love Me Tomorrow" —Laura Theodore; "Give Him a Great Big Kiss"—Pattie Darcy; "Remember (Walking in the Sand)" —Darcy; "I Can Never Go Home Again"—Darcy.

Also "Where Did Our Love Go?"—Guy; "Come See About Me"—Guy; "I Hear a Symphony" —Guy; "It's My Party"—Darcy; "I'm Sorry"—Fraser; "Rockin' Around the Christmas Tree"— Fraser; "I Dream About Frankie"—Guy; "She's a Fool"—Lenox; "You Don't Own Me"— Darcy; "Judy's Turn to Cry"—Darcy; "Where the Boys Are"—Fraser; "The Beehive Dance"— Ensemble; "The Beat Goes On"—Lenox; "Downtown"—Fraser; "To Sir With Love"—Theodore; "Wishin' and Hopin' "—Darcy; "Don't Sleep in the Subway"—Fraser; "You Don't Have to Say You Love Me"—Darcy.

ACT II: "A Fool in Love"—Taylor; "River Deep Mountain High"—Guy; "Proud Mary"— Taylor; "Society's Child"—Fraser; "Respect"—Taylor; "A Natural Woman"—Darcy; "Do Right Woman"—Taylor; "Piece of My Heart"—Theodore; "Try (Just a Little Bit Harder)"—Theodore; "Me and Bobby McGee"—Theodore; "Ball and Chain"—Theodore; "Make Your Own Kind of Music"—Ensemble.

Daughters (53). By John Morgan Evans. Produced by Margery Klain and Dan Fisher at the Westside Arts Theater. Opened April 3, 1986. (Closed May 18, 1986)

Tessie	Marcia Rodd	Grandma	Miriam Phillips
Mom	Bette Henritze	Cetta	Marisa Tomei
Patty Ann	Mary Testa		

Directed by John Henry Davis; scenery, Kevin Rupnik; costumes, Donna Zakowska; lighting, F. Mitchell Dana; sound, Tom Gould; production stage manager, Susan Whelan; press, Marilynn LeVine, Meg Gordean, Ken Sherber.

Time: The present. Place: Kitchen of the DiAngelo home in Brooklyn. Act I, Scene 1: An afternoon in early December. Scene 2: A Sunday afternoon in early January. Act II: Friday evening in late January.

DAUGHTERS—Marcia Rodd and Marisa Tomei in John Morgan Evans's play

Comedy, frictions within an Italian-American family living in Brooklyn. Previously produced in regional theater, including the Philadelphia Drama Guild.

*Goblin Market (57). Musical adapted by Peggy Harmon and Polly Pen from the poem by Christina Rossetti; music by Polly Pen. Produced by Ken Marsolais, Pat Daily and James Scott with Mark Beigelman, Lois Deutchman and Paulette Haupt-Nolan in the Vineyard Theater production, Douglas Aibel artistic director, Barbara Zinn Krieger executive director, Gary P. Steuer managing director, at Circle in the Square Downtown. Opened April 13, 1986.

Laura.. Terri Klausner
Lizzie.. Ann Morrison

Directed by Andre Ernotte; choreography, Ara Fitzgerald; musical direction, Lawrence Yurman; scenery, William Barclay; costumes, Muriel Stockdale, Kitty Leech; lighting, Phil Monat; orchestrations, James McElwaine; production stage manager, Laura Heller; press, Bruce Cohen, Kathleen von Schmid.

Transfer from off off Broadway of the "music erotica" adaptation of the 1862 poem about two sisters tempted by forest goblins, with Christina Rossetti's poem set as lyrics to Polly Pen's music, except as noted below. The play was presented without intermission.

A Best Play; see page 283.

MUSICAL NUMBERS: "Come Buy, Come Boy," "We Must Not Look," "Mouth So Charmful" (music by Antonio Lotti, lyrics by Theodore Baker), "Do You Not Remember Jeanie," "Sleep, Laura, Sleep" (lyrics by Christopher Morgenstern), "The Sisters" (music by Johannes Brahms), "Some There

Are Who Never Venture" (lyrics by John Gay, additional lyrics by Polly Pen and Peggy Harmon), "Mirage" (music by Charles Ives), "Passing Away," "Here They Come," "Like a Lily," "Lizzie, Lizzie, Have You Tasted," "The Sisters" (Reprise), "Two Doves."

*The Acting Company. Schedule of three programs. Orchards (18). Program of seven one-act plays adapted from stories by Anton Chekhov: *The Man in a Case* by Wendy Wasserstein, from a translation by Marian Fell; *Vint* by David Mamet, from a translation by Avrahm Yarmolinsky; *The Talking Dog* by John Guare, from *Joke*, translated by Marian Fell; *Drowning* by Maria Irene Fornes, from a translation by Avrahm Yarmolinsky; *A Dopey Fairy Tale* by Michael Weller, from *The Skit* translated by Avrahm Yarmolinsky; *Eve of the Trial* by Samm-Art Williams, from a translation by April FitzLyon and Kyril Zinovieff; *Rivkala's Ring* by Spalding Gray, from *The Witch* translated by Constance Garnett. Opened April 22, 1986. (Closed May 4, 1986)

Also *Ten by Tennessee. Two programs of short plays by Tennessee Williams. *Program A (8): *The Lady of Larkspur Lotion, Talk to Me Like the Rain and Let Me Listen, Portrait of a Madonna, The Unsatisfactory Supper, The Long Goodbye.* *Program B (8): *Auto-Da-Fe, The Strangest Kind of Romance, A Perfect Analysis Given by a Parrot, This Property Is Condemned, I Can't Imagine Tomorrow.* Opened May 18, 1986. Produced by The Acting Company, John Houseman producing artistic director, Margot Harley executive director, Michael Kahn artistic director, by special arrangement with Lucille Lortel, at the Lucille Lortel Theater.

ORCHARDS

The Man in a Case
Byelinkov . . . . Brian Reddy
Varinka . . . . Mariangela Pino
    Time: 1898. Place: A small garden in the village of Mironitski.
    An elderly classics teacher's romance with a 30-year-old.

Vint
Porter . . . . Craig Bryant
Commissioner
    Persolin . . . . Terrence Caza
Zvisdulin . . . . Joel Miller
Kulakevitch . . . . Phil Meyer
Nedkudov . . . . Kevin Jackson
Psiulin . . . . Aled Davies
    Time: Late at night. Place: The corridors of power.
    Workmen play a card game which makes fun of government functionaries.

The Talking Dog
F . . . . Susan Finch
M . . . . Michael McKenzie
F's Hang Glider . . . . Kevin Jackson
M's Hang Glider . . . . Phil Meyer
    Choreographer—Larry Hayden. Place: The Catskills.
    Man declares love for woman while joining her in the adventure of hang gliding.

Drowning
Pea . . . . Philip Goodwin
Roe . . . . Anthony Powell
Stephen . . . . Aled Davies
    Scene 1: A cafe, probably in Europe, late afternoon. Scene 2: ten minutes later. Scene 3: A month later.
    A man is paid to act out suicide.

A Dopey Fairy Tale
Smile . . . . Phil Meyer
Father Baker . . . . Terrence Caza
Mother Baker . . . . Susan Finch
Clarence . . . . Craig Bryant
Chatter (the dog) . . . . Joel Miller
Mayor . . . . Kevin Jackson
Magistrate . . . . Anthony Powell
Minister . . . . Philip Goodwin
Female Frog . . . . Wendy Brennan
Male Frog . . . . Brian Reddy
Sad Princess Gladys . . . . Laura Brutsman
    Another version of the frog-prince and princess fairy tale.

Eve of the Trial
Ma Lola . . . . Susan Finch
Lester Simmons . . . . Brian Reddy
Pearl Simmons . . . . Laura Brutsman
Tate . . . . Joel Miller
Lilly . . . . Mariangela Pino

Kitty.................... Wendy Brennan
Alex Buskin.............. Philip Goodwin
   Time: August 1919, midnight. Place: Ma
Lola's rooming house just outside of Baton
Rouge, La., just after the Bolshevik revolution in
Russia.
   A bigamist comes to judgment.

Rivkala's Ring
   With Aled Davies.
   Monologue of a lonely person describing the
events, emotions and philosophies of his life.

   Understudies for Various Roles: Laura Brutsman, Craig Bryant, Terrence Caza, Aled Davies,
Susan Finch, Philip Goodwin, Michael McKenzie, Phil Meyer, Mariangela Pino, Anthony Po-
well, Brian Reddy.
   Directed by Robert Falls; scenery, Adrianne Lobel; costumes, Laura Crow; lighting, Paul
Gallo; original music, Louis Rosen; dramaturg, Anne Cattaneo; staff repertory director, Rob
Bundy; production stage manager, Maureen F. Gibson; stage manager, Susan B. Feltman; press, The
Fred Nathan Company, Inc., Dennis Crowley, Marc Thibodeau.
   Previously produced in regional theater in Urbana-Champaign, Ill. The program was presented in
two parts with the intermission following *A Dopey Fairy Tale*.

TEN BY TENNESSEE: PROGRAM A

The Lady of Larkspur Lotion
Mrs. Hardwicke-Moore ... Mary Lou Rosato
Mrs. Wire.................... Lisa Banes
Writer...................... Randle Mell
   Place: A furnished room in the French Quar-
ter of New Orleans (written circa 1939).

Talk to Me Like the Rain and Let Me Listen
Man .... Derek D. Smith
Woman..................... Laura Hicks
   Place: A furnished room west of Eighth Ave-
nue in midtown Manhattan (written circa 1952).

Portrait of a Madonna
Miss Lucretia Collins .... Lisa Banes
Porter................. Anderson Matthews
Elevator Boy .... Richard Howard
Doctor .... Derek D. Smith
Nurse .... Mary Lou Rosato
Mr. Abrams................. Randle Mell
   Place: The living room of a moderate-priced
apartment (written circa 1944).

The Unsatisfactory Supper
Archie Lee............. Anderson Matthews
Baby Doll............. Mary Lou Rosato
Aunt Rose .... Laura Hicks
   Place: The porch and side yard of a shotgun
cottage in Blue Mountain, Miss. (written circa
1944).

The Long Goodbye
Joe......................... Randle Mell
Silva .... Derek D. Smith
Myra....................... Lisa Banes
Bill .... Richard Howard
Mother .... Laura Hicks
   Movers: Anderson Matthews, Richard How-
ard, David Manis, Tim White.
   Place: Apartment F, third floor south, in a
tenement apartment situated in the middle of a
large Midwestern American city (written circa
1940).

TEN BY TENNESSEE: PROGRAM B

Auto-Da-Fe
Mme. Duvenet................. Lisa Banes
Eloi .... Richard Howard
   Place: The front porch of an old frame cottage
in the Vieux Carre of New Orleans (written circa
1946).

The Strangest Kind of Romance
Landlady .... Mary Lou Rosato
Little Man .... Derek D. Smith
Old Man............... Anderson Matthews
Officer................... Richard Howard
Boxer .... Randle Mell

   Place: A furnished room in a small industrial
city of the Middle Western states (written circa
1942).

A Perfect Analysis Given by a Parrot
Bessie .... Mary Lou Rosato
Flora....................... Lisa Banes
Waiter............... Anderson Matthews
Sons of Mars ..... David Manis, Randle Mell
   Place: The interior of a St. Louis tavern (writ-
ten circa 1957).

This Property Is Condemned
Willie .... Laura Hicks

Tom .... Richard Howard
Place: A railroad embankment on the out-
skirts of a small Mississippi town (written circa
1940).

I Can't Imagine Tomorrow
One.................... Mary Lou Rosato
Two........................ Randle Mell
(Written circa 1957.)

BOTH PROGRAMS: Understudies for various roles—Lisa Banes, Laura Hicks, Richard Howard, David Manis, Anderson Matthews, Pamela Nyberg, Mary Lou Rosato, Derek D. Smith, Tim
White, Randle Mell.

Directed by Michael Kahn; scenery, Derek McLane; costumes, Ann Hould-Ward; lighting, Dennis
Parichy; original music, Lee Hoiby; sound, Aural Fixation; assistant director, Rob Bundy; animals,
William Berloni; connecting material compiled by Greg Leaming from writings by Tennessee
Williams; stage managers, Kathleen Boyette Bramlett, Michael S. Mantel.

Each program was presented in two parts, the intermission in Program A coming after *Portrait of
a Madonna*, in Program B coming after *The Strangest Kind of Romance*.

Smoking Newports and Eating French Fries (32). By Sebastian Stuart. Produced by RJ/JR
Enterprises (Robert J. McManus and Jodi Romanello) at the Actors' Playhouse. Opened
April 22, 1986. (Closed May 18, 1986)

Lucille Wimply .... Alexa Abercrombie
Bub Wimply................ William Swartz
Dana Lundy.............. David McCarthy
Tiffany-Dawn Lundy........ Holly Wilkinson
Judy Lahedje .... Jessica Gibson

George Dempsey........ Michael J. Mendola
Uncle Fester.............. Daniel Holmberg
Pauline Verplank........... Cameron Foord
Rodney Beemus................ John Finck

Directed by Jack Ross; scenery and lighting, David Raphel; associate producer, James J. Tom-
maney; production stage manager, Pamela Ross; press, Ken Cook.

Time: The present. Place: A trailer in West Saugerties, N.Y. The play was presented without
intermission.

Comedy about trailer people, previously produced off off Broadway at Theater for the New
City.

Mummenschanz (39). New version of the program of Swiss pantomime by and with
Andres Bossard, Floriana Frassetto and Bernie Schurch. Produced by ICM Artists at the
Joyce Theater. Opened April 24, 1986. (Closed May 25, 1986 and transferred to Broad-
way)

Production stage manager, Dino De Maio; press, Marilynn LeVine/P.R. Partners, Meg Gordean.

An entertainment of mime and masks, suggested by Swiss folk traditions and presented in two parts.
An earlier version of *Mummenschanz* was presented on a national U.S. tour beginning in 1973 and
on Broadway 3/30/77 for 1,326 performances.

*The Light Opera of Manhattan (LOOM) Repertory of one new operetta revival and 12
running operetta revivals. ***Sweethearts** (28). Book by Harry B. Smith and Fred De
Gresac; music by Victor Herbert; lyrics by Robert B. Smith. Opened May 7, 1986.
Produced by Light Opera of Manhattan, William Mount-Burke founder, Jean Dalrymple president, Raymond Allen and Jerry Gotham artistic directors, at the Eastside Playhouse and the Cherry Lane Theater.

Sylvia .... Susan Davis Holmes
Prince Franz .... Jon Brothers
Liane..................... Mary Setrakian
Mikel .... Tom Boyd
Paula.................. Ann J. Kirschner

Lt. Karl .... Mark Henderson
Hon. Percival Slingsby .... George H. Croom
Petrus Van Tromp .... David Green
Aristide Caniche ...... Donavon Armbruster
Capt. Lourent .... Bill Partlow

Jeannette.	Sally Jo Ries	Lizette.	Cindy Lee Fairfield
Clairette	Eileen Merle	Toinette	Andrea Calarco
Babette	Ruth Alison	Nanette.	Theresa Hudson

Ensemble: Shawn Davis, Martin J. Kugler, Robert Leary, Evan Matthews, Greg J. Witzany. Swings: Claudia Egli, William Marshall.

Directed by Raymond Allen and Jerry Gotham; choreography, Jerry Gotham; musical direction, Todd Ellison; scenery, Mina Albergo; costumes, Juliet Polcsa, George Vallo; lighting, Franklin Meissner Jr.; production stage manager, Michael Dean Smith; press, Gregory Tarmin.

Act I: Courtyard of the laundry of the White Geese, Bruges, Belgium. Act II: The royal hunting lodge, Zilania, a year later.

Sweethearts was first performed at the Academy of Music, Baltimore, 3/24/13 and arrived on Broadway 9/8/13 for 136 performances. Its last major New York revival of record was on Broadway 1/21/47 for 288 performances.

ACT I

Overture
"Iron! Iron! Iron!" . . . . Laundresses
"On Parade" . . . . Soldiers, Laundresses
"There Is Magic in a Smile" . . . . Liane, Laundresses
"Sweethearts" . . . . Sylvia, Chorus
"Every Lover Must Meet His Fate" . . . . Prince, Chorus
"Mother Goose" . . . . Sylvia, Laundresses
"Talk About This—Talk About That" . . . . Karl, Liane
"The Angelus" . . . . Sylvia, Prince
"Jeannette and Her Little Wooden Shoes" . . . . Liane, Slingsby, Van Tromp, Caniche
Finale. . . . . Company

ACT II

"Waiting for the Bride" . . . . Men
"Pretty as a Picture" . . . . Van Tromp, Chorus
"What She Wanted—and What She Got" . . . . Paula, Daughters
"In the Convent They Never Taught Me That" . . . . Sylvia, Chorus
"To the Land of My Own Romance" . . . . Sylvia, Prince
"The Game of Love" . . . . Karl, Chorus
"The Cricket on the Hearth" . . . . Sylvia, Prince
"Pilgrims of Love" . . . . Karl, Chorus
"When You're Away" . . . . Sylvia
Finale. . . . . Company

LOOM's 1985–86 repertory included 11 programs of 12 running revival productions mounted in previous seasons and presented on the following schedule (operettas have book and lyrics by W.S. Gilbert and music by Arthur Sullivan unless otherwise noted): *The Vagabond King* (28), lyrics by Brian Hooker, Russell Janney and W.H. Post, music by Rudolf Friml, 7/3/85–7/28/85; *The New Moon* (28), book and lyrics by Oscar Hammerstein II, Frank Mandel and Lawrence Schwab, music by Sigmund Romberg, 7/31/85–8/25/85; *H.M.S. Pinafore* (28), 9/4/85–9/15/85 and 4/9/86– 4/20/86; *The Merry Widow* (17), based on the book by Victor Leon and Leo Stein, music by Franz Lehar, English lyrics by Alice Hammerstein Mathias, 9/21/85–10/6/85; *The Gondoliers* (10), 10/12/85–10/20/85; *Rose Marie* (18), book and lyrics by Otto Harbach and Oscar Hammerstein II, music by Rudolf Friml and Herbert Stothart, 10/25/85–11/10/85; *Naughty Marietta* (21), book and lyrics by Rida Johnson Young, music by Victor Herbert, 11/15/85–11/24/85 and 1/3/86– 1/26/86; *Babes in Toyland* (34), book by William Mount-Burke and Alice Hammerstein Mathias, music by Victor Herbert, lyrics by Alice Hammerstein Mathias, 11/30/85–12/29/85; *The Mikado* (11), 1/17/86–1/26–86; *The Desert Song* (67), book and lyrics by Otto Harbach, Oscar Hammerstein II and Frank Mandel, music by Sigmund Romberg, 1/31/86–4/6/86; *Cox and Box*, book by F.C. Burnand, and *Trial by Jury* (14), 3/23/86–4/4/86.

Performers in LOOM repertory during the 1985–86 season included Raymond Allen, Ruth Alison, Sava Anthony, Elaine Bradbury, Sarah Brooks, Jon Brothers, Kevin Brunner, Susan Bo-

SWEETHEARTS—A number from LOOM's revival of the Victor Herbert operetta

rofsky, Ted Brackett, Sal Biagini, Christina Britton, Laura Berman, Francine Berman, John Bonk, Beth Cullinane, William Carter Corson, J. Kevin Coughlin, Leigh Chandler, Bob Cuccioli, Shane Culkin, Andrea Calarco, George Croom, Bruce Daniels, Joseph Donovan, Shawn Davis, Gigi Diekman, Lynne Dickey, Jackie Delval, Bill Daugherty, Brent Erdy, Claudia Egli, Dorene E. Falcetta, Cindy Lee Fairfield.

Also Cliff Goulet, Joe Guiffre, Barry Gallo, Helen Guilet, Susan Davis Holmes, Gary Harger, Joseph Michael Hume, Paul Hansen, David Thomas Hampson, Anne Jacobsen, Norma Joyce, Dana Jones, Renee Kramer, Martin J. Kugler, James Edward Kampf, Roger Keiper, Karl Lindevaldsen, Curtis LeFebvre, Michael Licata, Robert Leary, Brett Larson, Susan Marshall, Anthony Mellor, Bruce McKillip, Susan Murray, Eileen Merle, Evan Matthews, Susanna Organek, Terrence O'Brien, Dan O'Driscoll.

Also Pam Pardi, Millie Petroski, Bill Partlow, Barbara Rouse, Irma Rogers, Ruth Rome, Bruce Reizen, Edward J. Raarup, Sally Jo Reis, Sherrie Strange, Leslie Anne Skolnik, Rhanda Spotton, Douglas R. Steinbauer, Mary Setrakian, Scott Swagger, Irene Sameth, Lisa Jo Sagola, John Simmons, J.C. Sheets, Rebecca Spencer, Richard Skipper, Patricia Takala, Stephen Todar, Douglas Thom, Suzy Upton, John Uehlein, Darrell S. Williams, Christopher White, James Wilson, Christopher Zunner.

*National Lampoon's Class of '86 (14). Revue by Andrew Simmons (head writer), John Belushi, Chevy Chase, Stephen Collins, Lance Contrucci, Christopher Guest, Dave Hanson, Matty Simmons, Michael Simmons, Larry Sloman, plus Rodger Bumpass, Veanne Cox, Annie Golden, John Michael Higgins, Tommy Koenig and Brian Brucker O'Connor. Produced by Michael Simmons and Jonathan Weiss in a Matty Simmons–John Heyman production at the Village Gate Downstairs. Opened May 22, 1986.

Rodger Bumpass	John Michael Higgins
Veanne Cox	Tommy Koenig
Annie Golden	Brian Brucker O'Connor

Understudy—Amy Stiller.

The Band: Michael Sansonia keyboards, Robert Bond drums, Paul Guzzone bass, Stuart Ziff lead guitar.

Directed by Jerry Adler; musical staging, Nora Brennan; scenery, Daniel Proett, costumes, Nancy Konrardy; lighting, Robert Strohmeier; sound, Richard Dunning; neon design, Tony Hayes; associate producer, Jodi Sh. Doff; press, Jeffrey Richard Associates, L.G. Poppleton.

Satirical songs and sketches in a manner similar to *National Lampoon's Lemmings* which played this same off-Broadway cabaret 2/5/73 for 350 performances. The revue was presented in two parts.

SCENES: Paradise Lost, Eating Out, Honey I Have Something to Tell You, Five Minutes, Tasty Fresh, The Jumper, Living Well, Death & Apartment Rentals, Solid God, Publishing, Arrivederci Vito, Out of the Closet, Oval Office, The Psychiatrist.

MUSICAL NUMBERS: "Cocaine" (by Jim Mentel and Larry Sloman), "Yuppie Love" (music by Richard Levinson and Will Etra, words by Richard Levinson), "They Lost the Revolution" (music and words by Richard Levinson, reprise words by Michael Sansonia), "My Bod Is for God" (by Jeff Mandel and Phil Proctor), "I've Got It" (music and words by Michael Garin), "The President's Dream" (music and words by Michael Sansonia), "Don't Drop the Bomb" (music by Richard Levinson and Will Etra, words by Richard Levinson), "Apartheid Lover" (music by Michael Sansonia, Robert Bond, Paul Guzzone and Stuart Ziff, words by Jan Kirschner, Brian Brucker O'Conner and Michael Sansonia), "The Ticker" (words and music by Michael Sansonia).

A Place Called Heartbreak (6). By Robert S. Stokes. Produced by The Heartbreak Company and Victor Cannon at the Harold Clurman Theater. Opened May 22, 1986. (Closed May 25, 1986)

Lt. Cmdr. Ralph Connor . . . . Tom Felix	Marine Lt. Col. Cord
Lt. Cmdr. Rafferty . . . . Rony Clanton	Blass. . . . . Brian Patrick Clarke
Army 1st Lt. Chadd . . . . . . Patrick Kilpatrick	Cmdr. Richard Marquette . . . . Neil Bonin
Navy Capt. Tom Harrington . . . . Jason Heller	POWs . . . . Alexander Thomas,
Col. Nu . . . . Frank Michael Liu	Michael Raynor
Fowler . . . . Phil Harper	Vietnamese Guard. . . . . Ray Moy
Fidel . . . . Carlos Cestero	

Directed by Ellen Cannon; scenery and costumes, Michael Sharp; lighting, Howell Binkley; executive producer, Frank Scardino; production stage manager, Raymond Chandler; press, Howard Atlee.

Time: February 1973, 24 hours before the repatriation of the first group of U.S. prisoners of war in Indochina. Place: A large barracks room of the Hoa Lo Prison in Hanoi, the main prisoner-of-war camp in the Democratic Republic of Vietnam, and in a corridor outside the room. Act I, Scene 1: Dawn, Connor's cell. Scene 2: Evening. Act II, Scene 1: Same day, midnight, Connor's cell. Scene 2: Dawn, following day.

Vietnam prisoner-of-war drama by a journalist who covered the conflict for major news organizations.

*Professionally Speaking (21). Musical revue with music and lyrics by Peter Winkler, Ernst Muller and Frederic Block. Produced by Frederic Block and Irving Welzer in association with Kate Harper at St. Peter's Church. Opened May 22, 1986.

David Ardao	Hal Davis
Dennis Bailey	Kathy Morath
Meg Bussert	Marilyn Pasekoff

Understudies: Misses Bussert, Morath, Pasekoff—Joan Jaffe; Messrs. Ardao, Bailey, Davis—Sel Vitella.

Orchestra: Bruce W. Coyle piano 1, Robert Hirschhorn piano 2, Don Yallech percussion.

Directed by Tony Tanner; scenery, Robert Alan Harper; costumes, P. Chelsea Harriman; lighting, Barry Arnold; musical direction and additional arrangements, Bruce W. Coyle; production stage manager, Doug Fogel; press, Shirley Herz Associates, Glenna Freedman, Peter Cromarty.

Musical numbers satirizing the professions. The revue was presented in two parts.

MUSICAL NUMBERS, ACT I: "The Doctor's Out Today"—Marilyn Pasekoff; "Malpractice"
—Dennis Bailey; "Patient's Lament," Patient—Hal Davis, G.P.—Bailey, Orthopedic Doc—Meg
Bussert, Urologist—David Ardao; "Three Doctor's Wives"—Kathy Morath, Bussert, Pasekoff; "A
Doctor's Prayer," Doctor—Ardao, Patient—Morath; "Guadalajara," Doctor—Ardao, Wife—
Bussert; "Gastrointestinal Rag"—Bailey, Morath, Pasekoff; "Sibling Rivalry," Psychiatrist—
Ardao, Patient—Morath.

Also "The Lawyer's Out Today"—Pasekoff; "Malpractice II"—Davis; "Equitable Distribution
Waltz"—Bailey, Bussert; "Malpractice" (Reprise), Doctor—Ardao, Lawyer—Davis; "Portia's Plan"
—Pasekoff; "Lawyerman," Victim—Ardao, Victim's Wife—Bussert, Lawyerman—Bailey; "What
Price Have I Paid?"—Davis, Morath; "I Professionisti," Spokesman—Ardao, Plaintiff—Bussert,
Dentist—Davis, Dentist's Lawyer—Bailey, Plaintiff's Lawyer—Pasekoff, Judge—Ardao, Doctor—
Morath; "First, Let's Kill All the Lawyers"—Company.

ACT II: "The Teacher's Out Today"—Pasekoff, "The Best Part-Time Job in Town," Teacher—
Davis; "Emmy-Lou, Lafayette and the Football Team"—Davis; "Tamara, Queen of the Nile"—
Morath, Men; "Stupidly in Love"—Bailey, Bussert; "I Hate It"—Pasekoff; "Mathematical Quartet"
—Bussert, Pasekoff, Davis, Bailey; "Remember There Was Me"—Ardao; "Who the Hell Do These
Wise Guys Think They Are?", Gardener—Davis, Waitress—Pasekoff, Custodian—Bailey; "Over the
Hill"—Company; Finale—Company.

CAST REPLACEMENTS AND TOURING COMPANIES

Compiled by Stanley Green

The following is a list of the more important cast replacements in productions which opened in previous years, but were still playing in New York during a substantial part of the 1985–86 season; or were still on a first-class tour in 1985–86, or opened in New York in 1985–86 and went on tour during the season (casts of first-class touring companies of previous seasons which were no longer playing in 1985–86 appear in previous *Best Plays* volumes of appropriate years).

The name of each major role is listed in *italics* beneath the title of the play in the first column. In the second column directly opposite appears the name of the actor who created the role in the original New York production (whose opening date appears in *italics* at the top of the column). Indented immediately beneath the original actor's name are the names of subsequent New York replacements, together with the date of replacement when available.

The third column gives information about first-class touring companies, including London companies (produced under the auspices of their original New York managements). When there is more than one roadshow company, #1, #2, etc., appear before the name of the performer who created the role in each company (and the city and date of each company's first performance appears in *italics* at the top of the column). Their subsequent replacements are also listed beneath their names, with dates when available.

AREN'T WE ALL?

	New York 4/29/85	*San Francisco 9/24/85*
Lord Grenham	Rex Harrison	Rex Harrison
Lady Frinton	Claudette Colbert	Claudette Colbert
Rev. Ernest Lynton	George Rose	George Rose
Hon. Willie Tatham	Jeremy Brett	Simon Jones
Margot Tatham	Lynn Redgrave	Lise Hilboldt
Angela Lynton	Brenda Forbes	Joyce Worsley

ARMS AND THE MAN

	New York 5/30/85
Capt. Bluntschli	Kevin Kline
	John Malkovich 8/13/85

BIG RIVER

	New York 4/25/85	*Chicago 3/4/86*
Huckleberry Finn	Daniel Jenkins	Brian Lane Green
	Martin Moran 4/7/86	

Jim	Ron Richardson Larry Riley 2/21/86	Ron Richardson
The Duke	Rene Auberjonois Russell Leib 9/2/85 Brent Spiner 10/8/85 Ken Jenkins 1/7/86	Richard Levine
The King	Bob Gunton	Michael McCarty
Tom Sawyer	John Short Clint Allen 8/22/85	Roger Bart
Mary Jane Wilkes	Patti Cohenour Karla DeVito 7/9/85 Patti Cohenour 9/3/85 Marin Mazzie 10/15/85	Jessie J. Richards

BIG RIVER—Brian Lane Green as Huck and Ron Richardson as Jim in the touring company of the long-run Broadway musical

BILOXI BLUES

	New York 3/28/85	Ft. Lauderdale 2/24/86
Eugene Morris Jerome	Matthew Broderick Bruce Norris 8/26/85 William Ragsdale 12/24/85 Zach Galligan 1/27/86 Jonathan Silverman 4/8/86	William Ragsdale
Arnold Epstein	Barry Miller Mark Nelson 7/30/85	Andrew Polk

BRIGHTON BEACH MEMOIRS

	New York 3/27/83
Eugene Morris Jerome	Matthew Broderick Jonathan Silverman 7/9/85 Michael Strouse 7/21/85 Robert Leonard 3/4/86
Stanley Jerome	Zeljko Ivanek Peter Birkenhead 7/30/85
Nora	Jodi Thelen Lisa Waltz Louise Roberts
Laurie	Mandy Ingber Jennifer Blanc Kim Houser

Note: Only replacements during the 1985–1986 season are listed above under the names of the original cast members. For previous replacements and touring casts, see page 413 of *The Best Plays of 1984–1985.*

A CHORUS LINE

	N. Y. Off Bway 4/15/75 N. Y. Bway 7/25/75
Val	Pamela Blair Mitzi Hamilton
Mike	Wayne Cilento Danny Herman Charles McGowan
Larry	Clive Clerk J. Richard Hart
Maggie	Kay Cole Pam Klinger
Diana	Priscilla Lopez Gay Marshall Roxann Cabalero
Zack	Robert LuPone Robert LuPone 3/19/86
Greg	Michel Stuart Bradley Jones

Note: Only replacements during the 1985–1986 season are listed above under the names of the original cast members. For previous replacements, see page 437 of *The Best Plays of 1982–1983,* page 416 of

The Best Plays of 1983–1984, and page 414 of *The Best Plays of 1984–1985.* For touring casts, see page 472 of *The Best Plays of 1978–1979.*

DOUBLES

	New York 5/8/85
Guy	John Cullum Keir Dullea 7/23/85
Lennie	Ron Leibman Cliff Gorman 9/9/85
George	Tony Roberts Robert Reed 9/9/85
Arnie	Austin Pendleton Charles Repole 9/9/85

DREAMGIRLS

	New York 12/20/81	*Providence 10/8/85*
Effie Melody White	Jennifer Holliday	Sharon Brown
Lorrell Robinson	Loretta Devine	Arnetia Walker
C. C. White	Obba Babatunde	Lawrence Clayton
James Thunder Early	Cleavant Derricks Clinton Derricks-Carroll	Herbert L. Rawlings Jr.
Curtis Taylor Jr.	Ben Harney Weyman Thompson	Weyman Thompson
Deena Jones	Sheryl Lee Ralph Deborah Burrell	Deborah Burrell
Michelle Morris	Deborah Burrell	LueCinda RamSeur
Marty	Vondie Curtis-Hall	Larry Stewart

Note: Only replacements during the 1985–1986 season are listed above under the names of the original cast members. For previous replacements, see page 417 of *The Best Plays of 1983–1984* (also first touring cast) and page 415 of *The Best Plays of 1984–1985.*

THE FANTASTICKS

	New York 5/3/60
Luisa	Rita Gardner Virginia Gregory 11/12/85 Jennifer Lee 12/2/85

Note: As of May 31, 1986, 31 actors had played the role of El Gallo, 28 actresses had played Luisa, and 23 actors had played Matt. Only replacements during the 1985–1986 season are listed above under the name of the original cast member. For previous replacements, see page 442 of *The Best Plays of 1982–1983,* page 418 of *The Best Plays of 1983–1984,* and page 415 of *The Best Plays of 1984–1985.*

THE FOREIGNER

	New York 11/1/84
Charlie Baker	Anthony Heald Jack Gilpin 8/27/85

42nd STREET

	New York 8/25/80
Julian Marsh	Jerry Orbach
	Jamie Ross 10/29/85
Dorothy Brock	Tammy Grimes
	Louise Troy 12/17/85
Peggy Sawyer	Wanda Richert
	Clare Leach 9/17/85
Maggie Jones	Carole Cook
	Peggy Cass

Note: Only replacements during the 1985–1986 season are listed above under the names of the original cast members. For previous replacements, see page 418 of *The Best Plays of 1983–1984* (also touring casts), and page 417 of *The Best Plays of 1984–1985* (also London cast).

LA CAGE AUX FOLLES

	New York 8/21/83	London 5/7/86
Alban	George Hearn	George Hearn
	Keene Curtis 10/8/84	
	George Hearn 10/22/84	
	Walter Charles 8/19/85	
Georges	Gene Barry	Denis Quilley
	Jamie Ross 7/16/84	
	Keith Michell 8/13/84	
	Van Johnson 1/7/85	
	Steeve Arlen 11/12/85	

Note: For other replacements in New York and touring casts, see page 418 of *The Best Plays of 1984–1985*.

MY ONE AND ONLY

	New York 5/1/83	Washington, DC 3/8/85
Capt. Billy Buck Chandler	Tommy Tune	Tommy Tune
Edith Herbert	Twiggy	Sandy Duncan
		Lucie Arnaz 8/27/85

Note: For replacements in New York and touring cast, see page 418 of *The Best Plays of 1984–1985*.

THE NORMAL HEART

	New York 4/21/85	London 3/20/86
Ned Weeks	Brad Davis	Martin Sheen
	Stephen Rowe	Tom Hulce 5/13/86
	Joel Grey 9/6/85	

SUNDAY IN THE PARK WITH GEORGE

	New York 5/2/84
George	Mandy Patinkin
	Robert Westenberg 9/18/84

	Cris Groenendaal 1/15/85
	Robert Westenberg 1/22/85
	Harry Groener 4/23/85
	Mandy Patinkin 8/5/85
Dot	Bernadette Peters
	Joanna Glushak 8/27/84
	Bernadette Peters 9/10/84
	Betsy Joslyn 2/26/85
	Maryann Plunkett 3/12/85

THE TAP DANCE KID

	New York 12/21/83	*San Francisco 8/4/85*
Dipsey Bates	Hinton Battle	Hinton Battle
	Eugene Fleming 7/9/85	
Ginnie Sheridan	Hattie Winston	Monica Page
	Gail Nelson 6/84	
William Sheridan	Samuel E. Wright	Ben Harney
	Ira Hawkins 2/84	
Daddy Bates	Alan Weeks	Harold Nicholas
Willie Sheridan	Alfonso Ribeiro	Dule Hill
	Jimmy Tate 6/26/84	
	Savion Glover 11/84	
Emma Sheridan	Martine Allard	Martine Allard

TORCH SONG TRILOGY

	New York 6/10/82	*London 10/1/85*
Arnold Beckoff	Harvey Fierstein	Antony Sher
		Harvey Fierstein 3/31/86
Ed	Court Miller	Rupert Frazer

Note: For replacements in New York, see page 421 of *The Best Plays of 1983–1984* and page 420 of *The Best Plays of 1984–1985.*

ZORBA

	New York 10/16/83	*Schenectady 12/31/85*
Zorba	Anthony Quinn	Anthony Quinn
Mme. Hortense	Lila Kedrova	Lila Kedrova
The Woman	Debbie Shapiro	Donna Theodore
Niko	Robert Westenberg	Paul Harman
The Widow	Taro Meyer	Angelina Fiordellisi

THE SEASON
OFF OFF BROADWAY

OFF OFF BROADWAY

By Mel Gussow

OFF OFF Broadway remains the arena where theatrical artists can do almost anything, which is one reason why experimentalists such as Ping Chong, Martha Clarke and Charles Ludlam continue to flourish there. But there are severe economic problems, as in other areas of the theater. Companies have to fight for survival, and every year new ones are in jeopardy of losing a lease if not a financial base. As for the plays, they generally have a limited run; theatergoers have to be quick to catch them. A number, however, move off Broadway for extended engagements. Such was the case this season with Martha Clarke's *Vienna: Lusthaus* and the musical *Goblin Market*, among others. At the same time, individuals break through from underground into the mainstream—this year, both Eric Bogosian and Spalding Gray.

The most valuable work off off Broadway continues to occur in performance art, work that is experimental and often non-scripted and non-linear. It may be storyboarded or choreographed (dance is very much an allied medium). The author is often the director, a conceptual theater artist working within a company. Most of these works could not be done without the participation of that primary creative force. *Vienna: Lusthaus* is an outstanding example of the genre —a music-theater-dance piece that evokes the sight, sound, movement and memory of turn-of-the-century Vienna. Haunting stage pictures combine in living tableaux that stimulate the eye and mind. This was a breathtaking successor to Miss Clarke's *The Garden of Earthly Delights* of last year.

Tadeusz Kantor, the Polish innovater, returned to LaMama with *Let the Artists Die*, his contemplation of the contemporary history of his country as seen through his own autobiographical reminiscences. The art of mixed media was elevated by John Jesurun's *Deep Sleep*, in which actors on stage at LaMama played scenes with cinematic figures on large movie screens banked on either end of the room. *Deep Sleep* was a synchronicity of voice and picture and an entertaining crosscutting of imagery.

An ape played a leading role in *Kindness*, a Ping Chong theatrical variation on a high school movie. That is "Kind"ness as in species. The ape, Buzz, went about his adolescent habits, including prom-going, as if he were one of the boys after one of the girls. Chong continues to be a droll master of audio-visual-sculptural design.

Robert Wilson, whose productions are too expensive for most theaters to mount, appeared at New York University, directing a student company in a very professional version of Heiner Müller's *Hamletmachine*, a compelling deconstruction of Shakespeare into performance art. The Müller-Wilson piece filtered

379

Hamlet through turbulent political events of modern times; on one level it was an indictment of terrorism in all its forms. Over the bridge at the Brooklyn Academy of Music, there was this season's Next Wave Festival, with Wilson's *The Golden Windows* (the semblance of a children's tale), along with Chris Hardman's multimedia view of *Russia* (a letdown after Hardman's previous work) and *The Alchemedians*, a two-man evening of New Vaudeville from master juggler Michael Moschen and clown Bob Berky. *The Alchemedians* later moved off Broadway.

An award for improvement should go to the Squat Theater, a normally nihilistic European troupe whose latest work, *Dreamland Burns*, proved to be a creative synthesis of theater and film. Richard Foreman's *The Cure* was a return to his expressionistic roots as he took his prototypical heroine (played by Kate Manheim) on a search up a *cul de sac*. Ethyl Eichelberger did a clownish double-header of his hand-crafted *King Lear* (aptly called *Leer*) and *Casanova*, with, in the curtain-raiser, the author-director assuming all the roles.

Experienced writers returned with new work, Israel Horovitz with a trilogy of plays drawn from Morley Torgov's stories of his Canadian childhood in the city of Sault Ste. Marie. Presented by the American Jewish Theater, Horovitz's plays had ethnic flavor and family affection. The first two, the charming *Today I Am a Fountain Pen* and *A Rosen by Any Other Name*, were far more satisfying than the third, *The Chopin Playoffs*, but all three were blessed by the presence of Sol Frieder as Ardenshensky, a man of limitless disguises. As with other successful plays, the trilogy was scheduled to move onward.

Long an opera buff, Terrence McNally offered *The Lisbon Traviata*, about a man obsessed by the memory and the voice of Maria Callas—an amusing first act in a play that ascended into hysteria. Ronald Tavel was represented by the murky, but intriguing *Notorious Harik Will Kill the Pope*. Paul Foster, an off-off original, came back with a brace of plays in a projected cycle of comedy mysteries, *The Dark and Mr. Stone* (starring Kevin O'Connor as a transvestite sleuth).

Established companies had active, if not always rewarding, seasons. The WPA, in a new home, continued to stake out its territory as a haven for small, naturalistic plays, this year with Kevin Wade's *Cruise Control* (love on the rocks), Larry Ketron's *Fresh Horses* (confused youth) and Fred Gamel's *Wasted* (war). The Hudson Guild disappointed in its choice of new plays and took a sidestep into revivals with S. N. Behrman's *The Second Man*. The Second Stage prides itself, with justification, on its revivals from the recent past, as in a perceptive new production of Lanford Wilson's *Lemon Sky*. An early season guest in the Second Stage theater was Brenda Currin with a tender one-woman evening evocation of Eudora Welty, entitled *Sister and Miss Lexie*. John Guare was uptown with *The House of Blue Leaves* and off off with a revival of *Bosoms and Neglect*, starring Anne Meara as a mother ravaged by cancer.

The one-act is an honored form at the Ensemble Studio Theater, which annually presents its Marathon of short plays. Horton Foote's *Blind Date* highlighted this year's festival, and there was also good work by Alan Zweibel and Shirley Kaplan. Earlier in the season the E.S.T. offered James Ryan's *Dennis* (about the murder of Allard Lowenstein); Aishah Rahman's *The Tale of Madame Zora*, a musicalization of the life and work of Zora Neale Hurston; and Bill Boz-

Cited by Mel Gussow as Outstanding OOB Productions

Right, Amy Spencer in *Vienna: Lusthaus* conceived by Martha Clarke and produced by Music-Theater Group/Lenox Arts Center—"A music-theater-dance piece that evokes the sight, sound, movement and memory of turn-of-the-century Vienna"

Below, the ensemble in the finale of *Let the Artists Die* by Tadeusz Kantor produced by LaMama ETC—"Contemplation of the contemporary history of the author's country (Poland)"

zone's *Rose Cottages*. The last, a comedy sketch about residents of a seedy Florida motel, was the least ambitious and the most diverting. The City Stage Company tackled the lofty vision of Ibsen's *Brand*, with admirable results; presented a non–creature feature version of *Frankenstein*, and ended with *A Country Doctor*, Len Jenkin's anachronistic interpretation of Kafka. At the Ridiculous Theatrical Company, Charles Ludlam looked to Flaubert (briefly) for a beefcake romp, *Salammbó*. That British tranvestite troupe, Bloolips, delighted audiences with the vaudeville, *Living Leg-Ends*. In *Solo Voyages* the actress Robie Mac-Cauley reconsidered the fragmentary plays of Adrienne Kennedy, in a mono-drama directed by Joseph Chaikin.

The Music-Theater Group/Lenox Arts Center was responsible for *Vienna: Lusthaus* and also for *Africanis Instructus*, an anthropological musical by Richard Foreman and Stanley Silverman. The Pan Asian Repertory opened, cheerfully, with *Once Is Never Enough*, a lesser sequel to R.A. Shiomi's comedy caper *Yellow Fever*, then did a lavish production of the Indian epic *Ghashiram Kotwal*, followed by *Medea* and *The Man Who Turned Into a Stick*, an evening of short plays by Kobo Abe. Celebrating a quarter of a century of striking political theater, the San Francisco Mime Troupe revisited New York with the hard-hat *Steeltown*—less than their best. Something similar could be said about *La Chunga* by that extraordinary novelist, Mario Vargas Llosa, and *The Bone Ring*, an adaptation by Donald Hall of his lovely childhood memoir *String Too Short To Be Saved*. The Public Theater's Latino festival was brightened by Edward Gallardo's *Women Without Men*.

The musical season hit its stride with *Goblin Market*, a rarefied chamber musical—almost an opera—drawn from the Christina Rossetti poem, and brought breathlessly to the stage by the songwriting team of Polly Pen and Peggy Harmon, the director, Andre Ernotte, and the actresses, Terri Klausner and Ann Morrison (it later moved off Broadway and received a special Best Play citation). Otherwise the musical scene was impoverished. *Bingo*, a musical about black baseball, struck out. One of the most ambitious efforts was a musical version of *Moby Dick*, and, as one might expect, it suffered from overreach. Whale overboard. There was, however, an invigorating revival of *She Loves Me* at the Equity Library Theater.

The pursuit of the new can lead critics as well as theatergoers to the most unusual venues. A play called *A Midnight's Stripping* played a series of open-air, at-dusk performances in a dank alley deep in Soho; it dealt, unimaginatively, with mythical forces seething beneath the pavement of New York. *Living Cave Paintings* was an environmental expedition back to the world of Cro-Magnon man. In a series of living tableaux, punctuated by caveman dialogue, we caught a glimpse 20,000 years into the past, a record even for far-reaching off off Broadway.

PLAYS PRODUCED
OFF OFF BROADWAY

AND ADDITIONAL PRODUCTIONS

Here is a comprehensive sampling of off-off-Broadway and other experimental or peripheral 1985–86 productions in New York, compiled by Camille Croce. There is no definitive "off-off-Broadway" area or qualification. To try to define or regiment it would be untrue to its fluid, exploratory purpose. The listing below of hundreds of works produced by more than 80 OOB groups and others is as inclusive as reliable sources will allow, however, and takes in all leading Manhattan-based, new-play-producing, English-language organizations.

The more active and established producing groups are identified in **bold face type,** in alphabetical order, with artistic policies and the name of the managing director(s) given whenever these are a matter of record. Each group's 1985–86 schedule is listed with play titles in CAPITAL LETTERS. Often these are works-in-progress with changing scripts, casts and directors, sometimes without an engagement of record (but an opening or early performance date is included when available).

Many of these off-off-Broadway groups have long since outgrown a merely experimental status and are offering programs which are the equal in professionalism and quality (and in some cases the superior) of anything in the New York theater, with special contractual arrangements like the showcase code, letters of agreement (allowing for longer runs and higher admission prices than usual) and, closer to the edge of the commercial theater, a so-called "mini-contract." In the list below, all available data on opening dates, performance numbers and major production and acting credits (almost all of them Equity members) is included in the entries of these special-arrangement offerings.

A large selection of lesser-known groups and other shows that made appearances off off Broadway during the season appears under the "Miscellaneous" heading at the end of this listing.

Amas Repertory Theater. Dedicated to bringing all people, regardless of race, creed, color or economic background, together through the creative arts. Rosetta LeNoire, founder and artistic director.

16 performances each

BINGO! (musical) book by Ossie Davis and Hy Gilbert, based on William Brashler's *The Bingo Long Travelling All-Stars and Motor Kings*; music by George Fischoff; lyrics by Hy Gilbert. October 24, 1985. Director, Ossie Davis; choreographer, Henry LeTang; scenery, Tom Barnes; lighting, Jeffrey Schissler; costumes, Christina Giannini; musical director, Neal Tate. With Norman Matlock, James Randolph, Ron Bobb-Semple, David Winston Barge, Ethel S. Beatty, John R. McCurry, David King, Christian Holder.

LA BELLE HELENE (musical) book and directed by John Fearnley, adapted from A.P. Herbert's *Helen*; music, Jacques Offenbach; lyrics, David Baker. February 13, 1986. Choreographer, J. Randall Hugill; scenery, Donald L. Brooks; lighting, Deborah Matlack; costumes, How-

AMAS REPERTORY THEATER—David King and Christian Holder in *Bingo*

ard Behar; musical director, Patrick Holland. With Vanessa Shaw, Alexander Barton, Marcia Brushingham, Larry Campbell, Cliff Hicklen, Jozie Hill, Jay Aubrey Jones, Saundra McClain, Susan McDonnell, Kenneth McMullen, Steven Reidel, Alex Santoriello, Jeff Shonert, Ted Simmons Jr., Sunder, Marzetta Tate, Ivan Thomas.

SH-BOOM! (musical) book and lyrics by Eric V. Tait Jr.; music by Willex Brown Jr. and Eric V. Tait Jr. April 11, 1986. Director, Stuart Warmflash; choreographer, Audrey Tischler; scenery, Janice Davis; lighting, Eric Thomann; costumes, Candace Warner; musical director, Loni Berry. With Michael Accardo, Toni-Maria Chalmers, Sarah Clark, Barbara Warren-Cooke, Ruthann Curry, Reginald Hobbs, Michael Kostroff, Jill Kotler, Daniel Neusom, Peter J. Saputo, Crist Swann.

American Place Theater. In addition to the regular off-Broadway subscription season, cabaret and other special projects are presented. Wynn Handman, director, Julia Miles, associate director.

Women's Project:

BREAKING THE PRAIRIE WOLF CODE (26). By Lavonne Mueller. November 13, 1985. Director, Liz Diamond; scenery, Richard Hoover; lighting, Jane Reisman; costumes, Mimi Maxmen; original score, Alice Eve Cohen. With Keliher Walsh, Tenney Walsh.

WOMEN HEROES: IN PRAISE OF EXCEPTIONAL WOMEN (one-act plays): COLETTE IN LOVE by Lavonne Mueller, directed by Mirra Bank, with Shirley Knight, John Connelly; PERSONALITY by Gina Wendkos and Ellen Ratner, directed by Gina Wendkos and Richard Press; MILLIE by Susan Kander, directed by Carol Tanzman, with Louise Stubbs; PARALLAX (IN PRAISE OF DAISY BATES) written and directed by Denise Hamilton; HOW SHE PLAYED THE GAME by Cindy Cooper, directed by Bryna Wortman; EMMA

GOLDMAN written and performed by Jessica Litwak, directed by Anne Bogart. (24). March 21, 1986.

Venture play series:

TIMES AND APPETITES OF TOULOUSE LAUTREC (18). By Jeff Wanshel. November 29, 1985. Lyrics, Michael Feingold; director, John Ferraro; scenery, John Arnone; lighting, Stephen Strawbridge; costumes, Edi Giguere; musical director, Russel Walden. With Lonny Price, June Gable, Priscilla Lopez, Nicholas Kepros, Ron Faber, MacIntyre Dixon, Lezlie Dalton, Susanna Frazer, Judith Hoag, David Purdham, Rocco Sisto.

American Humorist Series:

DOINGS OF GOTHAM: THE WIT AND HUMOR OF EDGAR ALLEN POE (24+). June 17, 1985. With Conrad Pomerleau. (Reopened October 15, 1985.)

LAUGH-AT-LUNCH (12). May 20, 1986. With Roy Blount Jr.

DAMON RUNYON'S BROADWAY (16). June 2, 1986. With John Martello.

American Theater of Actors. Dedicated to providing a creative atmosphere for new American playwrights, actors and directors. James Jennings, artistic director.

16 performances each

DISTANT FRIENDS, ONE ROOM WITH BATH and APRES MIDI (one-act plays) by Donald Kvares. June 20, 1985. Director, Ted Mornel; scenery and lighting, Donald L. Brooks. With John Jiler, Cindy Keiter, William Maloney, Ann Saxman.

CH BD. Written and directed by Mark Druck. July 23, 1985. Scenery and lighting, Anton Evangelista. With James York, Will Buchanan.

ROMEO AND JULIET by William Shakespeare. August 14, 1985. Directed by James Jennings; with Thor Fields, Jane Culley, Robert Blue.

BROOMSTICKS. By Eleanor Harris Howard. November 27, 1985. Director, James Jennings; scenery and lighting, Shep Pamplin. With Seamus McNally, Joy Saylor, Julie Whitney, David Hummel.

MOTHER RUSSIA. By John Quinn. January 3, 1986, Director, James Jennings; scenery and lighting, Shep Pamplin. With Seamus McNally, James Lorinz, Katharine Van Loan.

THE GANDY DANCER. Written and directed by James Jennings. January 15, 1986. Scenery and lighting, Shep Pamplin. With Keith Barns, Ray Trail.

VISIONS OF KEROUAC. By Martin Duberman. February 5, 1986. Director, Bruce Kronenberg; scenery and lighting, Shep Pamplin. With Kevin O'Rourke, Steve Rapella, Scott Renderer, Susan Boehm, John Flynn, Helen Marcy, Donald Berman.

The Ark Theater Company. Exists to develop and produce new works in a wide variety of styles and forms, to stage plays of unusual interest from all nations and periods. Bruce Daniel and Donald Marcus, artistic directors.

EMERALD CITY (25). By Donald Marcus. April 16, 1986. Director, Rebecca Guy; scenery, Derek McLane; lighting, Betsy Adams; costumes, Gene Lakin. With Marcia Cross, Steven J. Gefroh, Christine Estabrook, John Jiler, Don Chastain.

Circle Repertory Projects in Progress. Developmental programs for new plays. Marshall W. Mason, artistic director.

4 performances each

PLAYING WITH LOVE by Arthur Schnitzler, translated by Trish Hawkins. October 28, 1985. Directed by June Stein; with Dennis Boutsikaris, Ben Siegler, Betsey Aidem, Deirdre O'Connell, Burke Pearson, Jayne Haynes, Michael Higgins, Elizabeth Werner.

A BIOGRAPHY by Berrilla Kerr. March 17, 1986. Directed by B. Rodney Marriott; with Edward Seamon, Lynn Milgrim, Arlene Nadel, Harrietta Bagley, Ching Valdes, Lisa Emery, Trish Hawkins, Marilyn Sue Morris, Lawrence Schulman, Abby Levin.

BEFORE I GOT MY EYE PUT OUT by Timothy Mason. March 31, 1986. Directed by B. Rodney Marriott; with Dana Bate, Caroline Kava, Ted Sod, Ken Kliban, D.W. Moffett, Karen Sederholm, James McDaniel.

WANDERING JEW by Ben Siegler. April 14, 1986. Directed by B. Rodney Marriott; with Zane Lasky, Danton Stone, David George, Anne DeSalvo, Cameron Johann, Peter Friedman, Bruce McCarty.

Extended readings:

THE EARLY GIRL by Caroline Kava. November 11, 1985. Directed by Munson Hicks; with Laura Hughes, J. Smith-Cameron, Roxanne Cabalero, Tonya Pinkins, Toni Reid, Lisa Emery, Susan Bruce.

THE RAPIDS by David Steven Rappoport. December 9, 1985. Directed by B. Rodney Marriott.

IN THIS FALLEN CITY by Bryan Williams. March 10, 1986. Directed by B. Rodney Marriott; with Ken Marshall, Michael Higgins.

MAGIC by N. Richard Nash. April 28, 1986. Directed by Daniel Irvine; with Armand Assante, Charles Harper, Richard Backus, Diane Venora, Robert Stattel, Roxann Cabalero, Richard Seff, Jesse Corti, Steven Gregan, Mark Meyers, Elise Thoron.

Ensemble Studio Theater. Membership organization of playwrights, actors, directors and designers dedicated to supporting individual theater artists and developing new works for the stage. Over 200 projects each season, initiated by E.S.T. members. Curt Dempster, artistic director.

OCTOBERFEST (festival of 74 plays). Schedule included: REMOTE CONFLICT by Kathleen Tolan; TERRY NEAL'S FUTURE by Roger Hedden; STRAY DOG by Shami Chaikin and Karen Ludwig; SORRY by Tim Mason; TEMPTING FATE by Louisa Jerauld; ROSE COTTAGES by Bill Bozzone; THE ADVENTURES OF LITTLE K by Avery Hart; THE BUTTERFLIES ARE LOVELY AND DEARLY SPLENDID TODAY by Howard M. Rice; ANOTHER BAD PLAY by Randy Lee Hartwig; INTIMACY by David Murray; SALT AIR by Mark Rosin; MEQUASSET BY THE SEA by Jolene Goldenthal; TANDEM by Fred Siraski; DAYS ON EARTH by Richard Caliban; SATIN ROUGE by Melodie Somers. September 30–October 20, 1985.

DENNIS (35). By James Ryan. November 20, 1985. Director, Dan Bonnell; scenery, James Wolk; lighting, Karl Haas; costumes, Deborah Shaw. With William Carden, Peter Freedman, Frank Girardeau, Sam Gray, Richmond Hoxie, Michael Alpert Mantel, Anne O'Sullivan, Myra Taylor, David Toney.

BEEN TAKEN (18). By Roger Hedden. December 3, 1985. Director, Billy Hopkins; scenery, Bob Barnett; lighting, Greg MacPherson; costumes, Isis C. Mussenden. With Perry Lang, Tim Ransom, Mary Stuart Masterson, Rick Martino, Helen Hunt, Lynn Goodwin.

THE TALE OF MADAME ZORA (musical) (14). Book and lyrics, Aishah Rahman; music, Olu Dara. February 18, 1986. Director, Glenda Dickerson; choreographer, Dianne McIntyre; scenery, Charles H. McClennahan; lighting, Marshall Williams; costumes, Sydney Inis. With Stephanie Berry, Keith David, Willie Barnes, Jean-Paul Bourelly, Deborah Malone.

MARATHON '86 (one-act play festival): SUNDAY MORNING VIVISECTION by Elise Caitlin, directed by Leslie Ayvazian; MINK ON A GOLD HOOK by James Ryan, directed by Jack Gelber; THE WORKER'S LIFE by Brandon Cole with John Turturro, directed by Aidan Quinn; BLIND DATE by Horton Foote, directed by Curt Dempster; THE WEST SIDE BOYS WILL ROCK YOU ANYTIME by Shirley Kaplan, directed by Billy Hopkins; TERRY NEAL'S FUTURE by Roger Hedden, directed by Billy Hopkins; COMIC DIALOGUE by Alan Zweibel, directed by Risa Bramon; VANISHING ACT by Richard Greenberg, directed by Jeff

Perry; DOLORES by Edward Allan Baker, directed by Risa Bramon; MA ROSE by Cassandra Medley, directed by Irving Vincent; LITTLE FEET by Shel Silverstein, directed by Art Wolff; MOONLIGHT KISSES by Stuart Spencer, directed by Barnet Kellman. May 7–June 16, 1986.

Equity Library Theater. Actors' Equity sponsors a series of revivals each season as showcases for the work of its actor-members. George Wojtasik, managing director.

A FLASH OF LIGHTNING by Augustin Daly. September 26, 1985. Directed by Stephen G. Hults; with Wendy Merritt, David Snizek, Susanna Frazer, Samme Johnston, Daniel Marcus, Kurt Ziskie.

SHE LOVES ME (musical) book by Joe Masteroff, based on Miklos Laszlo's play, music by Jerry Bock, lyrics by Sheldon Harnick. October 31, 1985. Directed by Robert Bridges; with Roxann Parker, Todd Thurston, Lee Chew, David Vogel, Carolyn DeLany.

ANOTHER PART OF THE FOREST by Lillian Hellman. December 5, 1985. Directed by Christian Angermann; with Juanita Walsh, Jack Mahoney, Nicola Sheara, Casper Roos, John Henry Cox.

THEY'RE PLAYING OUR SONG (musical) book by Neil Simon, music by Marvin Hamlisch, lyrics by Carole Bayer Sager. January 9, 1986. Directed by Philip Giberson; with Andrew Gorman, Lisa Meryll.

THE CONSTANT WIFE by W. Somerset Maugham. February 13, 1986. Directed by Howard Rossen; with Judy Frank, Susan Tabor, Tina Smith, Ray Collins, Bernard Kersal.

GIRL CRAZY (musical) book by Guy Bolton and Jack McGowan, music by George Gershwin, lyrics by Ira Gershwin. March 13, 1986. Directed by Stephen Bonnell; with Tom Hafner, Heidi Joyce, Mary Ann Kelleher, Michael Shane Rogers, Ciro Barbaro.

THREE SISTERS by Anton Chekhov, translated by Lanford Wilson. April 17, 1986. Directed by Rena Down; with Maura Vaughn, Arlene Lencioni, Sandra Laub, Sam Blackwell, James Goodwin Rice.

FUNNY GIRL (musical) book by Isobel Lennart, music by Jule Styne, lyrics by Bob Merrill. May 15, 1986. Directed by Alan Fox; with Carole Schweid, George McCulloch, Tracey Phelps, Frank Torren, Jeff Veazey.

Hudson Guild Theater. Presents plays in their New York, American, or world premieres. David Kerry Heefner, producing director, James Abar, associate director.

28 performances each

SEASCAPE WITH SHARKS AND DANCERS. By Don Nigro. October 16, 1985. Director, David Kerry Heefner; scenery, Daniel Conway; lighting, Phil Monat; costumes, Mary L. Hayes. With Susan Greenhill, Ivar Brogger.

AND THEY DANCE REAL SLOW IN JACKSON. By Jim Leonard Jr. December 4, 1985. Director, David Kerry Heefner; scenery and lighting, Paul Wonsek; costumes, Pamela Scofield; original music, Ivana Themmen. With Susan Wands, Dorothy Lancaster, J.R. Horne, David Manis, Mary Lou Rosato, Michael Countryman, Linda Kampley.

THE SECOND MAN by S.N. Behrman. February 5, 1986. Directed by Thomas Gruenewald; with Valerie von Volz, Daniel Gerroll, Ivar Brogger, Jane Fleiss.

WRESTLERS. By Bill C. Davis. April 2, 1986. Director, Geraldine Fitzgerald; scenery and lighting, Paul Wonsek; costumes, Mary L. Hayes. With Dan Butler, Elizabeth Berridge, Bill C. Davis.

WRITER'S CRAMP. By John Byrne. May 28, 1986. Director, David Kerry Heefner; scenery and lighting, Richard Harmon; costumes, Patricia Adshead. With Brooks Baldwin, Sullivan Brown, K.C. Kelly.

INTAR. Innovative cultural center for the Hispanic-American community of New York focusing on the art of theater. Dennis Ferguson-Acosta, managing director.

LA CHUNGA (35). By Mario Vargas Llosa, translated by Joanne Pottlitzer. February 5, 1986. Director, Max Ferra; scenery, Ricardo Morin; lighting, Beverly Emmons; costumes, David Navarro Velasquez. With Raul Aranas, Sheila Dabney, Pepe Douglas, Shawn Elliott, Ralph Marrero, Maritza Rivera.

LOVERS AND KEEPERS (28) (musical) book, lyrics and directed by Maria Irene Fornes; music, Tito Puente and Fernando Rivas. April 4, 1986. Scenery, Ricardo Morin; lighting, Anne E. Militello; costumes, Gabriel Berry. With Jesse Corti, Sheila Dabney, Jose Fong, Jossie de Guzman, Tomas Milian.

BURNING PATIENCE (28). By Antonio Skarmeta, translated by Marion Peter Holt. June 4, 1986. Director, Paul Zimet; scenery, Christopher Barreca; lighting, Arden Fingerhut; costumes, David Navarro Velasquez. With Monique Cintron, Angel David, Gregorio Rosenblum, Lola Pashalinski.

Interart Theater. Committed to producing innovative work by women theater artists and to introducing to New York audiences a bold range of theater that is non-traditional in form or theme. Margot Lewitin, artistic director.

WALKING THROUGH (18). By Bernett Belgraier. June 28, 1985. Director, Melody Brooks. With Connie Schulman, Maud Winchester, Kim Yancey.

ABOUT ANNE (47). Conceived and performed by Salome Jens, based on Anne Sexton's poetry; THE BEATRICE ROTH TRILOGY (24). Written and performed by Beatrice Roth; special direction, Valeria Wasilewski. July 1, 1985. (Performed in repertory).

SOLO VOYAGES: excerpts from Adrienne Kennedy's plays: *The Owl Answers, A Rat's Mass* and *A Movie Star Has to Star in Black and White* (37). September 11, 1985. Director, Joseph Chaikin; scenery, Jun Maeda; lighting, Beverly Emmons; costumes, Gwen Fabricant; music, Skip LaPlante and Edwina Lee Tyler. With Robbie McCauley.

THE HOUR BEFORE MY BROTHER DIES and ECHOES OF RUBY DARK (14). By Daniel Keene. January 8, 1986. Directed and performed by Lindzee Smith and Rhonda Wilson; production design, Robert Cooney, Jay Johnson, Lindzee Smith and Rhonda Wilson.

LATER (6). By Corinne Jacker. March 13, 1986. (Co-production of C&L Collective.)

LaMama Experimental Theater Club (ETC). A busy workshop for experimental theater of all kinds. Ellen Stewart, founder; Wesley Jensby, artistic director.

Schedule included:

SPIRIT RISING by Jawole Willa Jo Zollar; music by Carl Riley and Graig Harris. June 5, 1985.
MYTHOS OEDIPUS conceived and directed by Ellen Stewart; music by Elizabeth Swados. June 6, 1985.
TOKEN VISION: THE END OF THE PLAGUE CYCLE. By Rudolf Kocevar and Kip Peticolas; music, Janet Kerr. June 26, 1985. Director, Rudolf Kocevar; scenery, Paul Benney; choreographer, Harry Whittaker Sheppard.
MAX ROACH LIVE AT LA MAMA (multimedia collaboration with Kit Fitzgerald). October 2, 1985. Directed by George Ferencz.
GEOGRAPHY OF A HORSE DREAMER by Sam Shepard. October 2, 1985. Directed by Nicholas Swyrydenko.
LET THE ARTISTS DIE written and directed by Tadeusz Kantor. October 12, 1985. With The Theatru Cricot 2.
THE DARK AND MR. STONE. By Paul Foster. October 23, 1985. Director, Sylvain Lhermitte; scenery, Maurice McClelland; lighting, Howard Thies; costumes, Lou Zeldis; alligator costume, Gabriel Berry and Josefine Monter; music, Alkiviades Steriopoulos. With Kevin O'Connor, Vernon Morris, Kimberly Bruce, Paul Murray, Kit Latham, Ken Gold, Evelyn Tuths.

NOWHERE. By Reine Barteve. October 24, 1985. Director, Francoise Kourilsky; lighting, Blu; music, Genji Ito. With Yolanda Bavan, Genji Ito, Nicholas Kepros, Sims Wyeth.

MAGGIE SOBOIL (cabaret). Performed by Maggie Soboil; music by Eddie Reyes. November 1, 1985.

NORMA ALEANDRO (one-woman show) created and directed by Norma Aleandro. November 8, 1985.

HARM'S WAY. By Mac Wellman. November 14, 1985. Director, George Ferencz; scenery, Patrick Kennedy; lighting, Blu; costumes, Sally J. Lesser; music, Bob Jewett and Jack Maeby. With Tom Costello, Sheila Dabney, Stephen Mellor, Deirdre O'Connell, Zivia Flomenhaft, Gregg Daniel, Jeff Shoemaker, Tuwanda Coleman, Amy Sohn, Lute Ramblin.

SONGS FOR MY SISTERS by Abba Elethea; music by Grant Miller and Francis Thorpe. November 14, 1985. Directed by Tad Truesdale.

UNDER CONSTRUCTION by Pepon Osorio, Merian Soto and Patti Bradshaw; music by David Friedman. November 14, 1985. Directed by Pepon Osorio.

RETURN TO SENDER by Bill Obrecht and Perry Hoberman; music by Bill Obrecht. December 6, 1985.

COTTON CLUB GALA. December 26, 1985. Director, Ellen Stewart; choreographer, Larl Becham; scenery, Jun Maeda; lighting, David Adams; musical director, Aaron Bell. With Aaron Bell and the Ellingtonians, Andre De Shields, Ellia English, Chuck Green, Marilyn Amaral, Jeff Bates, Kendall Bean, Jacquelyn Bird, Sheila Dabney, Charles Douglass, Adrienne Eggleston, Joyce Griffen, Lance K. Hardy, Marcia McBroom, Jasper McGruder, George Morton III, Wayne Rhone, Valois and Nicole Worrell.

SCATTERING PINE NEEDLES conceived and composed by Ed Herbst and Beth Skinner. December 26, 1985. With Thunder Bay Ensemble.

THE SOCIAL ANIMAL written and directed by Carol Clements and David Wolpe; music by Sher Doruff. January 2, 1986.

THE DUEL. Based on Joseph Conrad stories. January 14, 1986. Director, Marika Lagercrantz; scenery and lighting, Chris Torch, Rainer Reitz; costumes, Cecilia Lovstrom; music, Nils Personne. With Chris Torch, Juan Rodriguez.

THE NORTH WIND. By Dave Hunsaker. January 31, 1986. Designed and directed by Ralph Lee; lighting, Paul Clay; costumes, Casey Compton; music, Barbara Pollitt. With Willie C. Barnes, Lenny Bart, Christine Campbell, Shelley Fine, Elliot Scott, Valois.

BRECHT'S BERLIN (cabaret) written and directed by Michael Ramach. January 31, 1986.

DEEP SLEEP written and directed by John Jesurun. February 1, 1986.

THE YELLOW HOUSE written and directed by Leonardo Shapiro. February 6, 1986.

THE MEDICIS HELD HOSTAGE written and directed by Richard S. Bach. February 26, 1986.

OFREI. Directed by Ellen Stewart; music by Genji Ito with Susann Diehm and Yukio Tsuji. March 6, 1986.

LA TROTA written and directed by Dario D'Ambrosi. March 7, 1986.

WORLD THEATER FESTIVAL OF THE ARTS. March 7–30, 1986.

TEMPTATION written and directed by Rudolf Kocevar; music by Janet Kerr. April 2, 1986.

ACTS FROM UNDER AND ABOVE and TURTLE DREAMS by Meredith Monk and Lanny Harrison; music by William Albright, Donald Ashwande, James Tenney and Meredith Monk. April 3, 1986.

THE CONCEPT written and directed by Lawrence Sacharow. April 30, 1986.

KINDNESS. Conceived and directed by Ping Chong; created by the Fiji Company. May 2, 1986. Scenery, Angus Moss; lighting, Blu; costumes, Mel Carpenter. With John Fleming, Louise Smith, Roger Babb, Louise Sunshine.

BERENICE by Edgar Allan Poe; music by Vito Ricci. May 2, 1986. Directed by Matthew Maguire.

ONCE UPON A DREAM COME TRUE written and directed by J.M. Mora. May 16, 1986.

THE BRIDE AND HER EXTRA-RAPID EXPOSURE based on Marcel Duchamp's "Large Glass" adapted and directed by Susan Mosakowski; music by Vito Ricci. May 29, 1986.

Little Theater at the Lambs. Committed to developing plays that encourage human dignity and values. Carolyn Rossi Copeland, executive director.

THE GIFTS OF THE MAGI (musical) book and lyrics by Mark St. Germain, based on the O. Henry story, music and lyrics by Randy Courts. November 27, 1985. Directed by Christopher Catt; with Glenn Mure, Lynne Wintersteller, Michael Kelly Boone, John David Westfall, Leslie Hicks, Bert Michaels.

BIG TIME (27). By Steven Braunstein. March 5, 1986. Director, Tony LoBianco; scenery, Bob Phillips; lighting, John McLain; costumes, Eiko Yamaguchi. With Brent Collins, Melinda Keel, Tony LoBianco.

THE ALCHEMEDIANS (40). Conceived, choreographed and performed by Bob Berky and Michael Moschen. March 20, 1986. Directors, Ricardo Velez and Joan Langue; music, David Van Tieghem; artistic design and construction, John Kahn; lighting, Jan Kroeze; costumes, Mei-Ling Louie; sound, Jan Nebozenko.

MAGGIE MAGALITA (41). By Wendy Kesselman. May 2, 1986. Director, Julianne Boyd; scenery, Michael C. Smith; lighting, James F. Ingalls; costumes, Nan Cibula; music, Tania Leon. With Trini Alvarado, Teresa Yenque, Blanca Camacho, Stephen Geoffreys. (Chiara Peacock replaced Trini Alvarado.)

Mabou Mines. Theater collaborative whose work is a synthesis of motivational acting, narrative acting and mixed-media performance. Collective artistic leadership.

STARCOCK (23). By Apple Vail. December 6, 1985. Director, Frederick Neumann; scenery and lighting, Sabrina Hamilton and Tom Andrews; image sequence design, Eric Cornwell; music, Richard Isen. With Honora Fergusson.

HELP WANTED (23). By Franz Xaver Kroetz, translated by Gitta Honegger. February 11, 1986. Director, JoAnne Akalaitis; lighting, Jennifer Tipton; sound, L.B. Dallas. With Ruth Maleczech, Ellen McElduff, Greg Mehrten, Terry O'Reilly, George Bartenieff, David Brisbin (co-production of Theater for the New City).

A PRELUDE TO DEATH IN VENICE written and directed by Lee Breuer; music, Bob Telson; scenery, Alison Yerxa; lighting, Julie Archer; puppet design, Linda Hartinian; sound, L.B. Dallas; with Bill Raymond, alternating with Greg Mehrten, Terry O'Reilly; HAJJ written and directed by Lee Breuer; scenery and lighting, Julie Archer; music, Chris Abajian; live mix, videography, Craig Jones; makeup and masks, Linda Hartinian; with Ruth Maleczech (11). May 7, 1986.

Manhattan Punch Line. New York's only theater company devoted to comedy. Steve Kaplan, artistic director; Mitch McGuire, executive director; Patricia Baldwin, managing director.

THE HIT PARADE (24). By Richard Dresser. July 12, 1985. Director, Don Scardino; scenery, Daniel Conway; lighting, Joshua Dachs; costumes, David C. Woolard; songs, Jim Wann. With Pamela Blair, Larry Block, Nada Despotovich, George Gerdes, James Lally, William Newman, Keith Reddin.

GOODBYE FREDDY (24). By Elizabeth Diggs. September 20, 1985. Director, Barbara Rosoff; scenery, Johniene Papandreas; lighting, Jackie Manassee; costumes, Martha Hally. With Walter Bobbie, Nicholas Cortland, Barbara eda-Young, Kit Flanagan, Carole Monferdini, Michael Murphy.

LOVE AS WE KNOW IT (24). By Gil Schwartz. October 24, 1985. Director, Josh Mostel; scenery, Randy Benjamin; lighting, Greg MacPherson; costumes, Mimi Maxmen. With Michael Countryman, Polly Draper, Marek Johnson, Karen Ludwig.

2d FESTIVAL OF ONE-ACT COMEDIES: ALONE AT LAST by Gina Barnett, directed by Melodie Somers; THE MIDDLE KINGDOM by Howard Korder, directed by Robert S Johnson; POWDER by Judy Engles, directed by Peter Glazer; SQUARE ONE by Richard Aellen, directed by Robert S. Johnson; LIP SERVICE by Howard Korder, directed by Robin Saex; SMOKE by Laurence Klavan, directed by Steve Kaplan; THE INTERROGATION by

Murphy Guyer, directed by Pamela Singer; THE JOB SEARCH by Brandon Toropov, directed by Jason Buzas; UNCLE LUMPY COMES TO VISIT by Laurence Klavan, directed by Steve Kaplan (36). November 30, 1985. Scenery, Brian Martin; lighting, Scott Pinkney; costumes, David C. Woolard, Marcy Grace Froehlich.

PRIME TIME PUNCH LINE (15). (Clown/comic festival). May 16–25, 1986.

Music-Theater Group/Lenox Arts Center. Working with a core of artists in the development of ideas flowing in all directions from the participants, based in Lenox, Mass. and showcasing productions in New York City, this season at St. Clement's. Lyn Austin, producer-director, Diane Wondisford, Mark Jones, associate producing directors.

AFRICANIS INSTRUCTUS (34). Written and directed by Richard Foreman; music, Stanley Silverman. January 14, 1986. Scenery, Richard Foreman and Nancy Winters; lighting, William Armstrong; costumes, Jim Buff; musical direction, David Oei. With Alan Scarfe, Eve Bennett-Gordon, David Sabin, Kate Dezina, Keith David, Tommy Hills, Susan Browning, Clark Brown, Gerald Gilmore, Charles Richardson, Peter Davis. (Co-production of Ontological-Hysteric Theater)

PAN ASIAN REPERTORY THEATER—Henry Yuk *(at top),* Ronald Nakahara and Glenn Kubota in R.A. Shiomi's *Once Is Never Enough,* sequel to his *Yellow Fever*

VIENNA: LUSTHAUS (30). Conceived and directed by Martha Clarke with members of the company; text, Charles Mee Jr.; music, Richard Peaslee with the aid of Johann Sebastian Bach, Eugene Friesen and Johann Strauss. April 8, 1986. Scenery and costumes, Robert Israel; lighting, Paul Gallo. With Robert Besserer, Marie Fourcaut, Richard Merrill, Paola Styron, Brenda Currin, Lotte Goslar, Gianfranco Paoluzi, Timothy Doyle, Robert Langdon-Lloyd, Amy Spencer, Lila York.

New Dramatists. An organization devoted to playwrights; member writers may use the facilities for anything from private cold readings of their material to public script-in-hand readings. Thomas G. Dunn, director, Chris Silva, program director, Lynn Holst, literary director.

Public readings

CHINA WARS by Robert Lord. September 3, 1985. Directed by Ethan Silverman; with Joyce Reehling, John Getz, Jerry Mayer, Concetta Tomei.

IN SEPTEMBER WOODS by David Hill. September 11, 1985. Directed by John Pynchon Holms; with Patty Mayer, David Jaffe, John Seitz, Anna Minot.

THE LAST GOOD MOMENT OF LILLY BAKER by Russell Davis. September 12, 1985. Directed by Susan Gregg; with Sam McMurray, Mary McDonnell, J.T. Walsh, Robin Groves.

THE TRAVELLING SQUIRREL by Robert Lord. September 17, 1985. With David Strathairn, Joanna Gleason, Nicholas Martin, Lisa Banes, James Secrest, Joyce Reehling, Tom Cashin.

THE WEDDING PARTY by Judith Herzberg. October 9, 1985. Directed by Rhea Gaisner; with Elizabeth Hart, Eric Booth, Marvin Einhorn, Tamara Daniel, Ron Faber, Ziska, Jim DeMarse, Ellin Rothstein, David Strathairn, Elzbieta Czyzewska, Olek Krupa, Deirdre O'Connell, Kathryn Petersen, Ann Timmons.

BETTER DAYS by Richard Dresser. October 15, 1985. With George Gerdes, Carole Schweid, Robert Alpert, Meg Kelly, Tony Rizzoli, Jude Ciccolella.

MY LIFE IN ART by Victor Steinbach. October 15, 1985. With Clarke Gordon, Werner Klemperer, Richard Schull, Jerry Matz, Robert Trebor.

KILLERS by John Olive. October 21, 1985. Directed by Robert Woodruff; with John Seitz, Christopher McCann, Holly Hunter, John Connolly, Carl Low.

NEW ORDER by Sheldon Rosen. October 23, 1985. Directed by John Pynchon Holms; with Mark Blum, Peter Zapp, Bruce Ornstein, Ellen Barber.

I LOVE YOU, TWO by Laura Cunningham. October 24, 1985. With Jeffrey De Munn, Natalia Nogulich, Tony Rizzoli, Pat McNamara, Pat Skipper, Mark Metcalf, Judith Granite.

IN PERPETUITY THROUGHOUT THE UNIVERSE by Eric Overmyer. October 25, 1985. With Tza Ma, Rocco Sisto, Tom Cayler, Deirdre O'Connell, Julia Newton, Laura Innes.

JAY by Anthony Giardina. October 28, 1985. Directed by Michael Bloom; with Nancy Mette, Florence Stanley, Natalija Nogulich, Mercedes Ruehl, Melissa Burk, Jill Holden, Marisa Zalabak, Stephen Jones.

MISS JULIE BODIFORD by James Nicholson. November 1, 1985. With Lisa Banes, Nora Chester, Maggie Low, Stephen Bradbury, Grant Shaud, Leo Finnie, John Connolly, Bruce Lecuru.

CRUISING CLOSE TO CRAZY by Laura Cunningham. November 4, 1985. Directed by Gloria Muzio; with Phyllis Somerville, Jayne Haynes, Raynor Schein, Lanny Flaherty, Mark Metcalf.

EAT ROCKS by Pedro Juan Pietri. November 14, 1985. Directed by Bob Holman; with Shawn Elliot, Pepe Douglas, Reno, Scott Robinson, Ginny Yang, Pamela Kirkpatrick, Marvin Einhorn, Dennis P. Huggins, Virginia White, Betty Laroe, Roma Maffia, Michelle Mais, Dee Martin.

NIGHTLUSTER by Laura Harrington. November 22, 1985. Directed by Alma Becker; with Deborah Hedwall, Chris McCann, Roma Maffia, Victor Slezak, Dennis Green.

RED LETTER DAYS by Dick D. Zigun. December 4, 1985. Directed by Costa Mantis; with Irving Burton, Virginia White, Tony Rizzoli, Roma Maffia, Bob Holman, Sturgis Warner, Paul

Venet, Jeffrey Hutchinson, Catherine Hayes, Jane Darby, Martha Braumfield, Lisa Barnes, Bob Alpert, Mark Stephen, Kelly Walker, Ryan Matthews, Nickie Feliciano, Ruth Ann Roberts, Camile Sautner, George Howard, Kim Delancy, Brooke Simpson, Corrie Safris.

ITALIAN-AMERICAN RECONCILIATION by John Patrick Shanley. December 10, 1985. With John Turturro, Matt Sussman, Mary Alice, Janice DeRosa, Jayne Haynes.

THE ORCHARD by John Nassivera. December 19, 1985. With Steve Coats, Tom Sleeth, Dion Anderson, Maggie Low, Nancy Heffner, Jim Fife, Helen-Jean Arthur.

FULFILLING KOCH'S POSTULATE by Joan Schenkar. January 15, 1986. With Marylouise Burke, Beverly Jacob, Irving Burton, Michael Morin.

POPS by Romulus Linney. January 16, 1986. Directed by Kent Thompson; with Kari Jenson, Greg Pake, Leon Russom, Robin Moseley, Kathleen Chalfant.

THE NAIN ROUGE and THE DISTANCE TO THE MOON by Mac Wellman; music by Melissa Shiftlett and Michael Roth. January 21, 1986. Directed by Rhea Gaisner; with Melissa Cooper, Cyndi Coyne, Maureen Born, Felicity La Fortune, Jimmy Occhino, Eugene Rohrer, Rusty Saylor.

SOUVENIRS by Sheldon Rosen. February 6, 1986. Directed by John Pynchon Holms; with Joe Morton, Alexandra Gersten, Charles Michael Wright, Helen Harrelson, Dion Anderson, John Connolly, Rudolf Shaw.

ELEEMOSYNARY by Lee Blessing. February 7, 1986. Directed by Gloria Muzio; with Shirley Vernard, Robin Bartlett, Katherine Hiller.

MR. AND MRS. COFFEE by William J. Sibley. February 12, 1986. Directed by Scott Rubsam; with James Gleason, Carlotta Schoch, Tom Matsusaka, Victor Slezak, Josh Pais, Yolande Bavan.

A CALL FROM THE COAST by David Hill. February 27, 1986. With Victor Slezak, Mark Metcalf, Erika Peterson, Beverly Jacob.

STOPS ALONG THE WAY by Jeffrey Sweet. March 13, 1986. Directed by John Pynchon Holms; with Fran Brill, John Monteith, Jeff Perry, Joseph Giardina.

DAKOTA'S BELLY, WYOMING by Erin Cressida Wilson. March 17, 1986. Directed by Paul Bernstein; with Paul Connell, Gail Dartez, Wendy Radford.

MONEY IN THE BANK by David Ives. March 25, 1986. With Joyce Reehling, Paul Collins, Anabelle Gurwitch, David Ives, Warren Keith, Tom Bade, Jerry Matz, Robert Trebor, Sturgis Warner.

BETTER DAYS by Richard Dresser. April 2, 1986. Directed by John Pynchon Holms; with Frank Girardeau, Bill Cwikowski, Paul Geier, Christine Jansen, Anne Pasquale.

COUNTRY COPS by Robert Lord. April 8, 1986. Directed by Ron Lagomarsino; with George Ede, Jeffrey Hutchinson, Joyce Reehling, Dan Desmond, Jon Polito.

AS WRITTEN by David Hill. April 9, 1986. With Anna Minot, Joe Warren.

MINSTREL BOYS by Martin Lynch. April 10, 1986. Directed by Jim Sheridan; with Pat McNamara, Mickey Kelly, Maurice C. Kehoe, Brian Mallon, Kevin Breslin, Noel Lawlor, D.J. O'Neil, Helen Harrelson, Carlotta Schoch, Aideen O'Kelly, Eddie Jones.

PRIMARY COLORS by Steve Carter. April 14, 1986. Directed by Alma Becker; with Beverly Jacob, Roma Maffia, Carol London, Rima Vetter, Steve Coats, Wayne Elbert, Mary Foskett, Ron O.J. Parson, Clarice Taylor, Graham Brown.

PELOPIA'S DOLL by Michel Marc Bouchard. April 15, 1986. Directed by Robert Moss; with Barton Heyman, Joan Grant, Catherine Marcroft, Connie Ventris.

FAMILY PRIDE IN THE 50'S by Joan Schenkar. April 16, 1986. Directed by Chris Silva; with Karen Lynn Dale, Jennifer East, Caroline Aaron, Jim DeMarse, Beverly Jacob, Bill Smitrovich, Chris Pace, Jason Pace.

THE GREENHOUSE KEEPER DIES OVER THE WEEKEND by Terri Wagener. April 30, 1986. Directed by Karen White; with Kevin O'Keefe, Katherine Hiler, Greg Germann, Nancy Mette.

ONCE REMOVED by Eduardo Machado. May 1, 1986. Directed by Gerald Chapman; with Diane Venora, Katherine Neuman, Joe Urla, Jesse Corti, Jossie de Guzman.

WAREHOUSE MOON by Adam Kraar. May 2, 1986. With Charles Michael Wright, Molly Noble, Peggy Ward, Karen Cristino.

HOW IT HANGS by Grace McKeaney. May 7, 1986. Directed by Jackson Phippin; with Veronica Castang, Debbie Monk, Peggity Price, Suzanna Hay, Robert Brock.

THE MEMORY THEATER OF GUILIO CAMILLO by Matthew Maguire. May 8, 1986. With Karla Barker, Constance Crawford, Rob Elk, Nadja Smith, Mic Woicek.

New Federal Theater. The Henry Street Settlement's training and showcase unit for playwrights, mostly black and Puerto Rican. Woodie King Jr., producer.

LONG TIME SINCE YESTERDAY by P.J. Gibson. October 10, 1985. Directed by Bette Howard; with Thelma Louise Carter, Loretta Devine, Sabrina DePina, Starletta DuPois, Petronia Paley, Denise Nicholas, Ayana Phillips, Emily Yancy.

ONCE UPON THE PRESENT TIME (12). Written and directed by Geri Lipschultz. October 10, 1985. Musical director and composer, Lawrence (Butch) Morris. With Geri Lipschultz, J.A. Deane, Wayne Horvitz, Lawrence (Butch) Morris.

NONSECTARIAN CONVERSATIONS WITH THE DEAD (12). By Laurie Carlos. November 13, 1985. Directors, Laurie Carlos and LaTanya Richardson; choreographer, Jawole Willa Jo Zollar; scenery, Erik Stephenson; lighting, Richard Leu; costumes, Amber Sunshower & Co.; music, Don Meissner and Lorenzo Laroche. With Laurie Carlos, Ruben S. Hudson, Jonathan Peck, LaTanya Richardson, Amber Villenueva, Marilyn Worrell.

THE SECOND HURRICANE (play opera) (12). Libretto, Edwin Denby; music, Aaron Copland. November 13, 1985. Director and choreographer, Tazewell Thompson; conductor, Charles Barker; scenery, Steve Saklad; special backdrops, Rudy Burckhardt, John Cage, Elaine De Kooning, Willem De Kooning, Red Grooms, Yvonne Jacquette, Alex Katz, Bill King, Larry Rivers, Pat Steir, Robert Wilson, Edwin Denby; lighting, Dan Kotlowitz; costumes, Laura Drawbaugh.

APPEAR AND SHOW CAUSE (24). By Stephen Taylor. December 3, 1985. Director, Woodie King Jr.; scenery, Richard Harmon; lighting, Leo Gambacorta; costumes, Judy Dearing. With David Bryant, Gilbert Lewis, Ronnie Newman, Cliff Frazier, Drew Eliot, Ken LaRon, Jack R. Marks, Terry Rabine, Robert Stephen Ryan, Warner Schreiner, David E. Weinberg.

IN THE HOUSE OF BLUES (24). By David Charles. December 5, 1985. Director, Buddy Butler; scenery, Llewellyn Harrison; lighting, Buddy Butler; costumes, Judy Dearing; choreographer, Hope Clarke; musical director, John McCallum. With Debra Byrd, David Connell, Crystal Lilly, Larry Marshall, Edna Chew, Earl Coleman, Katie Love, Andre Morgan, Leslie Reuben, Deborah Waller.

I HAVE A DREAM (24). Adapted by Josh Greenfeld from Dr. Martin Luther King's words. December 19, 1985. Director, Woodie King Jr.; scenery, Ina Mayhew; lighting, Richard Leu; costumes, Judy Dearing; musical director, Lee Coward. With James Curt Bergwall, Lee Coward, Chequita Jackson, Herman LeVern Jones, Bruce Strickland, Diane Weaver, Dwight Witherspoon.

DECEMBER SEVENTH (24). By George Rattner. January 8, 1986. Director, Gordon Edelstein; scenery, James Wolk; lighting, Leo Gambacorta; costumes, David C. Woolard. With Humbert Allen Astredo, Brian Backer, Scott Burkholder, Brett Goldstein, David Jaffe, Robin Morse.

WILLIAMS & WALKER (21). By Vincent D. Smith. February 5, 1986. Director, Shauneille Perry; choreographer, Lenwood Sloan; scenery and lighting, Marc D. Malamud; costumes, Judy Dearing; musical director, Neal Tate. With Ben Harney, Vondie Curtis-Hall. (Co-production of The American Place Theater.)

MA MA BLACKSHEEP (5). By Stafford Ashani in collaboration with Patrika Dallas. April 16, 1986. Designed and directed by Stafford Ashani; lighting, Edgar Gordon; video, Step Lively Production. With Patrika Dallas, Janice St. John.

New York Shakespeare Festival Public Theater. Schedule of workshop productions, in addition to its regular productions. Joseph Papp, producer.

THE SHOOTING OF DAN McGREW (3). Written and directed by Jacques d'Amboise, adapted from Robert Service's poem; music composed and conducted by Galt MacDermot. June 7, 1985.

Scenery, Charles Lagola; lighting, Don Abrams; costumes, Kenneth M. Yount. With Donlin Foreman, Charlotte d'Amboise, Bill Cratty, Norman Matlock.

THE TAMING OF THE SHREW by William Shakespeare. July 26, 1985. Director, Maureen Clarke; with Sonja Lanzener, David Adamson, Laurine Towler, Michael Preston, Paul Hebron, Joseph Reed, Vincent Niemann, Gene Santarelli, Andy Alsup, David Carlyon, Norma Fire. (Riverside Shakespeare Company).

FESTIVAL LATINO IN NEW YORK: THE DARK ROOT OF A SCREAM and SOLDADO RAZO by Luis Valdez, directed by Tony Curiel, with Ruben Garfias, Ricardo Salinas, Rosemary Ramos, T.G. Acosta; LA VERDADERA HISTORIA DE PEDRO NAVAJA written and directed by Pablo Cabrera, with Jose Felix Gomez, Jacqueline Ferrer; WOMEN WITHOUT MEN by Edward Gallardo, directed by Santiago Garcia, with Olga Merediz, Socorro Santiago, Shelly Colman; THE HOUSE OF BERNARDA ALBA by Federico Garcia Lorca, directed by Hugo Medrano, with Jewell Robinson; HIGH NOON . . . AL MEDIODIA by Pregones and Dolores Prida, directed by Ted Hannan, with Rosalba Rolon, Ted Hannan, Julio Santana, Alvan Colon Lespier, Sandra Rodriguez, Jose M. Melendez, Rosalba Rolon, Freddie De Arce; HOMAGE TO LUIS VALDEZ AND THE 20TH ANNIVERSARY OF TEATRO CAMPESINO; I AM CELSO by Leo Romero, adapted by Jorge A. Huerta and Ruben Sierra, directed by Jorge A. Huerta, with Ruben Sierra; MUFFET: INNA ALL A WI by The Sistren Theater Collective, directed by Eugene Williams, with Beverly Elliot, Lana Finikin, Lorna Burrell, Beverly Hanson, Lilian Foster; BOLIVAR by Jose-Antonio Rial, directed by Carlos Gimenez, with Roberto Moll, Pilar Romero, Carlos Ramirez, Francisco Alfaro; EL LOCO Y LA TRISTE by Juan Radrigan, directed by Raul Osorio, with Alex Zisis, Winzlia Sepulveda; IF YOU ALLOW ME TO SPEAK (writings of Latin American women), directed by Roberto D'Amico, with Susana Alexander; LA INCREIBLE Y TRISTE HISTORIA DE LA CANDIDA ERENDIRA Y DE SU ABUELA DESALMADA based on Gabriel Garcia's novel, adapted and directed by Miguel Torres, with Martha Suarez, Alberto Valdiri; FELIZ ANO VELHO by Alcides Noqueira, based on Marcelo Rubens Paiva's book, directed by Paulo Betti; SOLES by Marilina Ross and Susana Torres Molina, directed by Susana Torres Molina, with Marilina Ross; BASE OF SOUL IN HEAVEN'S CAFE written and directed by Tato Laviera, with Marie Torres, Steve Flores, Luis Ortiz, Evelyn Graxicirena, Efrain Nazario, Julia Lopez, Nilda Roldan, Gary Cruz; RENT A COFFIN written, performed and directed by Pedro Pietri; ORINOCO by Emilio Carballido, directed by Vicente Castro, with Ivonne Coll, Miriam Colon; EL JINETE DE LA DIVINA PROVIDENCIA written and directed by Oscar Liera; LOS COMPADRITOS by Roberto Cossa, directed by Villanueva and Roberto Castro, with Pepe Novoa, Marta Degracia, Alicia Zanca, Jorge Marrale, Leal Rey, Juan M. Tenuta; UNION CITY THANKSGIVING by Manuel Martin Jr., directed by Alba Oms, with Jeannette Mirabal, Beatriz Hernandez, Aracdio Ruiz Castellano, Graciela Mas, Cari Gorostiza, Tony Diaz, Eric Sabater, Puli Toro; STRAIGHT FROM THE GHETTO by Marvin Felix Camillo, Neil Harris, Miguel Pinero, Ringo Reyes, Christopher Currie and The Family Theater, directed by Marvin Felix Camillo; with The Family Theater. August 8–18, 1985.

MUCH ADO ABOUT NOTHING by William Shakespeare. September 3, 1985. Directed by Derek Goldby; with Elaine Bromka, Michael Mauldin, James McDonnell, Patricia Norcia, Victor Love, William Denis, Jon Matthews (part of the Celebrate Brooklyn annual festival).

Pan Asian Repertory Theater. Aims to present professional productions which employ Asian-American theater artists, to encourage new plays which explore Asian American themes and to combine traditional elements of Far Eastern theater with Western theatrical techniques. Tisa Chang, artistic director.

ONCE IS NEVER ENOUGH (26). By R.A. Shiomi, Marc Hayashi and Lane Kiyomi Nishikawa. October 8, 1985. Director, Raul Aranas; scenery, Christopher Stapleton; lighting, Victor En Yu Tan; costumes, Eiko Yamaguchi. With Henry Yuk, Carol A. Honda, Alkis, Papuchis, Glenn Kubota, Natsuko Ohama, Richard Voigts, Ronald Nakahara, Sam Howell.

GHASHIRAM KOTWAL (24). By Vijay Tendulkar, translated by Eleanor Zelliot and Jayant Karve. November 12, 1985. Director, Tisa Chang; choreographer and music recreated for dances, Rajika Puri; scenery, Atsushi Moriyasu; lighting, Victor En Yu Tan; costumes, Eiko

Yamaguchi; music, Bhaskar Chandavarkar; musical director, Daniel Paul Karp; special consultant, Satish Alekar. With Norris M. Shimabuku, Mel Duane Gionson, Jeffrey Akaka, Ismail Abou-el Kanater.

MEDEA (28). By Euripides, adapted by Claire Bush, translated by Claire Bush and Alkis Papoutsis. February 25, 1986. Director, Alkis Papoutsis; scenery, Alex Polner; lighting, Richard Dorfman; costumes, Eiko Yamaguchi. With Ching Valdez, Kati Kuroda, Norris M. Shimabuku, Roger Chang, Randy Chang, Christen Villamor, Lynette Chun, Mari Scott, Ismail Abou-el Kanater.

THE MAN WHO TURNED INTO A STICK, SUITCASE and THE CLIFF OF TIME (one-act plays) (24). By Kobo Abe. May 13, 1986. Director, Ron Nakahara; scenery, Bob Phillips; lighting, Tina Charney; costumes, Eiko Yamaguchi. With Donald Li, Mary Lee-Aranas, Ernest Abuba, Raul Aranas, Kati Kuroda.

The Puerto Rican Traveling Theater. Professional company presenting bilingual productions primarily of Puerto Rican and Hispanic playwrights, emphasizing subjects of relevance today. Miriam Colon Edgar, founder and producer.

A BEAT FOR FOUR LOSERS (24). Adapted from four short stories by Ana Lydia Vega and directed by Vicente Castro. August 6, 1985. Choreographer, Poli Rogers. With Carlos Carrasco, Bimbo Rivas, Jorge Luis Ramos, Soledad Romero (summer touring production).

BODEGA (30). By Federico Fraguada, Spanish translation by Freddy Valle. January 15, 1986. Director, Alba Oms; scenery, Carl Baldasso; lighting, Rachel Budin; costumes, Sue Ellen Rohrer. With Antonio Aponte, Olga Molina-Tobin, Donald Silva, Jaime Tirelli, Puli Toro, Millie Vega.

THE BITTER TEARS OF PETRA VAN KANT (30). By Rainer Werner Fassbinder; English translation by Denis Calandra; Spanish translation by Fernando Masllorens and Federico Gonzalez del Pino. March 5, 1986. Director, Andre Ernotte; scenery, Carl Baldasso; lighting, Rachel Budin; costumes, Betsy Gonzalez. With Monica Boyar, Alicia Kaplan, Caroline Kava, Jeannette Mirabal, Ilka Tanya Payan, Janne Peters, Arlene Roman, Barbara Wilder.

THE BIRDS FLY OUT WITH DEATH (30). By Edilio Pena, translated by Asa Zatz. April 23, 1986. Director, Vicente Castro; scenery and costumes, Rafael Mirabal; lighting, Craig Kennedy. With Lillian Hurst, Bertila Damas.

Playwrights Workshop staged readings

THE LAST PUERTO RICAN by Richard Irizarry. April 29, 1986. Directed by George C. Wolfe.
ABANDONED IN QUEENS by Laura Maria Censabella. May 5, 1986. Directed by Susan Gregg.
A SILENT THUNDER by Eduardo Lopez. May 6, 1986. Directed by Candido Tirado.
SILVERNOD by Russell McCollin. May 12, 1986.
IPHIGENIA IN TOMBSTONE by Sandra Torres. May 13, 1986.
DIVISIONS by Fred Crecca. May 19, 1986.
FIRST CLASS by Candido Tirado. May 20, 1986. Directed by Gloria Zelaya.
THE ROAD YOU LEAVE BEHIND by Gerald Ray Arrington. June 3, 1986.

Quaigh Theater. Primarily a playwrights' theater, devoted to the new playwright, the established contemporary playwright and the modern (post-1920) playwright. Will Lieberson, artistic director.

THE ERUDITE. By Spurgeon Crayton. September 7, 1985. Director, Don Durant; lighting, Eddie Baker. With Tammy Heyward, Saundra Marsh, Charles L. Norris, Eartha Frederick, Lee Story, Tyree Lewis Pope, Juanice Pryce, Michael de Lavallade.

BAD BAD JO-JO (8). By James Leo Herlihy. December 1, 1985. Director, Len Silver; lighting, Colletti Martin. With John Mudd, Tim Bass, Patrick Ferrara.

QUAIGH THEATER—Judith Thiergaard and Bob Jordan in a scene from the musical *To Feed Their Hopes* by Elaine Moe, Elaine Kendall and Dennis Poore

LIPPE. Written and directed by Ron Scott Stevens. December 18, 1985. Scenery, Don Jensen; lighting, Deborah Matlack. With William Hickey, Gary Warner, Barbara J. Fox, Dick Turmail, Bob Jordan, J.J. Johnson, Linda Roberts, Tom Hoover, Steve O'Brien, Bernard Feinerman, Herb Goldman.

DRAMATHON '85 (one-act plays in marathon). Schedule included: THE GREATEST MALE DANCER IN THE WORLD by Richard Garrick Bethell, directed by Carolyn Zatz; WEDDING BELL BLUES and BAR DREAMS by Steven Otfinoski, directed by Marion Brasch; DICKS by Jules Feiler, directed by Charles Gemmill; THE SWEETSHOPPE MYRIAM by Ivan Klima, directed by Alan Nicoll; FANTASY IMPROMPTU (musical) book by Hugh Dignon and Jonathan Littman, music and lyrics by Mark Bennett, directed by Jonathan Littman; THE BOX by Sheldon Rosen, directed by Karen E. White; THE BIG BANG by Sheila Walsh, directed by Leslie (Hoban) Blake; PRESENT COMPANY (musical comedy improvisation), directed by Robert Martin; THE SECRET DREAMS OF PROFESSOR ISAAC by John Minnigah, directed by Tara Tandlizh; THE WEDGE by Steve Shilo Felson, directed by Gary Walter; NO ONE LIVES ON THE MOON ANYMORE written and directed by Tony Martinetti; ROYAL FLUSH by Dan Bottstein, directed by David Scott Taylor; CHRISTIAN FOLLIES written and directed by Peter Manos; PRESCRIPTED by Pat Schneider, directed by Melissa Margolies; THEATER OF THE ABSURD written and directed by Mark Farnen; A LADY IN YELLOW BOUCLE by John W. Fiero, directed by Al Rees; THE ROCK by Roxanne Shafer, directed by Rebecca Kreinen; MUTULATION by Mark Troy, directed by Art Suskin; THE PUMPKIN CARVERS written and directed by Peter Hedges; TALKING WITH by Jane Martin, directed by Mildred Inez Lewis; ENCOUNTER WITH THE GODS by C. Dumas, directed by Francis Kane; CHATEAU FOIRELACOUR written and directed by Mark Robson; TIME MAKES EVERYTHING A MEMORY by Copper Cunningham, directed by Copper Cunningham and Charlise Harris; CONSENTING ADULTS by Ralph Hunt, directed by Andrea Odezynska; THE TIES THAT BIND by Matthew Witten, directed by Bryan Delatie; BEANSTOCK by David Shawn Klein, directed by Allan Michael Grosman;

LIARS by Joseph Yesutis, directed by Don Brenner; THE BREAK by Fred Saunders, directed by Lucian Vinci; THE NIGHT WE LOST WILLIE NIGHTINGALE by Dalene Young, directed by Solange Marsin; THE LOVEBIRDS by Pamela G. Bird, directed by Merriman Gatch; PLAYTIME written and directed by Gary Beck. December 31, 1985–January 1, 1986.

NECKTIES. By F.J. Hartland. January 15, 1986. Director, Peter M. Gordon; scenery, John Geurts; lighting, Nancy Blumstein; costumes, Claudia S. Anderson. With Jon Wool, Paul Zappala, Risa Brainin.

TO FEED THEIR HOPES (musical). Book, Elaine Kendall and Elaine Moe, adapted from John Sanford's book; music and musical direction, Dennis Poore; lyrics, Elaine Kendall. February 21, 1986. Director, Elaine Moe; choreographer, Karen Soroca; scenery and lighting, Aft, Inc.; costumes, Patric McWilliams. With Robert Boles, Mary Corcoran, Denise DeMirjian, Bob Jordan, Eleni Kelakos, Denise Morgan, Judith Thiergaard.

Lunchtime Series

EASY STREET by James DeMarse. November 11, 1985. Directed by Brian Calloway; with Patrick McNamara, Mary Tierney Kelly, Lawry Smith.
AFTER SCHOOL by Francine Storey. November 25, 1985. Directed by Jayne Wenger; with Brandon Epland, Kricker James, Susan Steffens, Laura vanMaanen.
THE HOROSCOPE DEPARTMENT (musical revue) music and lyrics by Adam Kraar and Karen Christino. December 2, 1985. Directed by John Margulis; with Deborah Unger, Karen Christino, Jeff Kalpak, Neil Schleifer, Michael Oppenheimer.
BARBI DON'T HAVE NAPPY HAIR by C. Dumas. December 16, 1985. Directed by Melissa Wyatt; with Lynnette Arthur, C. Dumas, Jeanette Freeman, Victoria Platt, Susan Strahon, Katherine Kendall.
SOMETHING UNSPOKEN by Tennessee Williams. January 6, 1986. With Betty Pelzer, Laura Castro.
THE NIGHT WE LOST WILLIE NIGHTINGALE by Dalene Young. January 20, 1986. Directed by Solange Marsin; with Laurel Keating, Doreen Kent, Sharon Spitz, Robert Tennenhouse.
LIARS by Joseph Yesutis. February 3, 1986. Directed by Don Brenner; with Sandy Kaufman, Steven Glick, Christopher Briante.
THE DICKS by Jules Feiler. February 17, 1986. Directed by Charles Gemmill; with Pat Freni, Louis Mustillo.
THE SWEETSHOPPE MYRIAM by Ivan Klima, translated by R. Willard. March 3, 1986. Directed by Barbara Nicoll; with Jerry Alan Cole, James Davies, Steff Gussin, Peter Johl, Michael Keresey, Anthony John Lizzuli, Jill Margolis, John Scocco, David Vosburgh, Betty Winsett.
THE BREAK by Fred Sanders. March 17, 1986. Directed by Lucian Vinci; with Mairzy Yost, Demetra Karras, Maggie Bilder.
THE BIG BANG by Sheila Walsh, directed by Leslie Blake. March 31, 1986. With Hoban Blake, Doug Barron, Susan Mitchell, Steven Viola.
GARAGE SALE by Bryan Patrick Harnetiaux. March 17, 1986. Directed by Charles Gemmill; with Barbara Bradish, Kelly Champion, Duncan Hoxworth, Nereida Ortiz, Gene A. Morra, Greg Spagna (also 2 evening performances).
TIME MAKES EVERYTHING A MEMORY by Copper Cunningham. April 14, 1986. Directed by Randy Frazier and Copper Cunningham; with Arthur French, Benny Russell, Willie Carpenter, Copper Cunningham, Dianne Kirksey, Sundra Jean Williams (also 2 evening performances).
THE TIES THAT BIND by Matthew Witten. April 28, 1986. Directed by Scott Kanoff; with Dani Klein, Ken Myles, Nancy Stewart Hill (also 2 evening performances).
THE FOURTH ONE by Mario Fratti. April 29, 1986. Directed by James Bormann; with Marie Costanza, Gayle Stahlhuth.
THE EARLY BIRD by John Jiler. May 12, 1986. Directed by Ted Mornel; with Alvin Moor, Erika Vaughn, Richard Dahlia, Ben R. Kelman.

The Ridiculous Theatrical Company. Charles Ludlam's camp-oriented group devoted to productions of his original scripts and broad adaptations of the classics. Charles Ludlam, artistic director.

Schedule included:

SALAMMBÔ. By Charles Ludlam, freely adapted from Gustave Flaubert's novel. November 7, 1985. Scenery, Edgar Franceschi; lighting, Richard Currie; costumes, Everett Quinton; music, Peter Golub. With Charles Ludlam, Everett Quinton, Philip Campanaro, Steven Samuels, John Heys, Katy Dierlam, Ethyl Eichelberger, Daniel Sambula, Deborah Petti, Arthur Brady, Arthur Kraft.

The Second Stage. Committed to producing plays of the last ten years believed to deserve another look, as well as new works. Robyn Goodman, Carole Rothman, artistic directors.

SISTER AND MISS LEXIE (48). Adapted from Eudora Welty's works, by David Kaplan and Brenda Currin. June 25, 1985. Director, David Kaplan; scenery and costumes, Susan Hilferty; lighting, Ken Tabachnick. With Brenda Currin, Karen Weingort, Kathy Zhukov.

LEMON SKY (49). By Lanford Wilson. November 25, 1985. Director, Mary B. Robinson; scenery, G.W. Mercier; lighting, Stephen Strawbridge; costumes, Connie Singer. With Jeff Daniels, Wayne Tippit, Jill Eikenberry, Laura White, Cynthia Nixon, Cameron Charles Johann, Patrick Koch.

BLACK GIRL by J.E. Franklin. February 3, 1986. Directed by Glenda Dickerson; with Ann Marie Cavener, Herbert L. Newsome III, Myra Taylor, Angela Bassett, Kimberly Russell, Ernestine Jackson, Arthur French, Yvonne Warden, Terry Alexander, Shawn Judge.

RICH RELATIONS (26). By David Henry Hwang. April 4, 1986. Director, Harry Kondoleon; scenery, Kevin Rupnik; lighting, Pat Collins; costumes, Candice Donnelly. With Joe Silver, Keith Szarabajka, Phoebe Cates, Susan Kellermann, Johann Carlo.

THE FURTHER ADVENTURES OF KATHY AND MO (35). By and with Mo Gaffney and Kathy Najimy. May 27, 1986. Director, Don Scardino; scenery, Andrew Jackness; lighting, Joshua Dachs; costumes, Gregg A. Barnes.

Shelter West. Aims to offer an atmosphere of trust and a place for unhurried and constructive work. Judith Joseph, artistic director.

DELTA LIVES by Steven Schwab, directed by Judith Joseph; MEMORIES (one-act play) by Brian Richard Mori, directed by Judith Joseph; VAMPIRE DREAMS (one-act play) by Steven Schwab, directed by Ray Hubener (12). August 8, 1985. Lighting, Laura Perlman; costumes, Marilena Gamble. With Bill Able, Rita Barnadas, John David Barone, David Allen Blackburn, Ryan Bowker, Christy Brotherton, Helena deCrespo, Don DeLorme, Nicholas Eastman, Rebecca Fay, Norma Jean Giffin, John Himmel, Ray Iannicelli, Susan Izatt, Constance Kane, Laurie Lathem, Sheila Linnette, Jane Manners, Rita McCaffrey, Bruce Mohat, Vivian Rothenberg, Marcia Swanger, Pamela Van Sant, Howard Wesson.

ZEPHYR (20). By Steven Schwab. January 24, 1986. Director, Judith Joseph; scenery and lighting, David Tasso; costumes, Marilena Gamble; music and sound, Kenn Dovel and Richard Harper. With Rita Barnadas, John David Barone, David Allen Blackburn, Christy Brotherton, Victor Castelli, Tom Dicillo, Cynthia Dillon, Dee Dee Friedman, Norma Jean Giffin, Raymond Iannicelli, Constance Kane, Neil Lyons, Pamela Van Sant, Howard Wesson.

PLAYERS by Brian Richard Mori, directed by Judith Joseph; THE SECRET DREAM OF PROFESSOR ISAAC by John Minigan, directed by Tara Tandlich (one-act plays) (13). March 12, 1986. Scenery, James Conway and Robert Tandlich; lighting, Shulemite Ziv. With Leland Gantt, William Lucas, Ryan Bowker, Christy Brotherton, Victor Castelli, Dee Dee Friedman.

Soho Rep. Infrequently or never-before-performed plays by the world's greatest authors, with emphasis on language and theatricality. Marlene Swartz, Jerry Engelbach, artistic directors.

16 performances each

THE TWO ORPHANS by Adolphe D'Ennery and Eugene Cormon, translated by John Oxenford, additional text adapted and direction by Julian Webber; music by Marshall Coid. February

14, 1986. With Richard Abernathy, Mimi Bensinger, Herbert Duval, Robert Hock, Ellen Mareneck, Laura Pierce, Michael Sexton, Victor Talmadge, Edward Trotta, Thomas G. Waites, Audrey Anderson, Avrom Berel, Suzanne Ford, Bill Jacob, Lois Markle, David Pursley, Kathryn Shield, Andrew Thain, Kimberly Van Dyke.

ONE FINE DAY. By Nicholas Wright. April 4, 1986. Director, Tazewell Thompson; scenery, Joseph A. Varga; lighting, David Noling; costumes, Laura Drawbaugh. With Gerald Gilmore, LaDonna Mabry, Evan O'Meara, Scott Whitehurst, Todd Jackson, Lex Monson, Jaison Walker.

THE GRUB STREET OPERA. By Henry Fielding; music and directed by Anthony Bowles. May 30, 1986. Scenery, Alison Ford; lighting, David Noling; costumes, Gabriel Berry; musical director, Robert Grusecki. With Richard T. Alpers, Fred Einhorn, Avril Gentiles, Nita Novy, Steve Steiner, Lee Winston, Ward Asquith, Colleen Fitzpatrick, Peter Jensen, David Pursley, Sharon Watroba, Helen Zelon.

Theater for the New City. Developmental theater and new American experimental works. George Bartenieff, Crystal Field, artistic directors.

Schedule included:

MAN OF WAX (musical). By Crystal Field, George Bartenieff and the company; music, Mark Hardwick. August 3–September 15, 1985. Director, Crystal Field; production and stage design, Anthony Angel; costumes, Edmond Felix; musical director, Christopher Cherney (touring production).

FABIOLA. By Eduardo Machado. August 29, 1985. Director, James Hammerstein; scenery and lighting, Donald Eastman; costumes, Deborah Shaw. With Adriana Sananes, Ivonne Coll, John Shepard, Bertila Damas, Leo Garcia, Eugenia Cross, James DeLorenzo, Wanda De Jesus.

ALEX AND JOANNA. By Herbert Liebman. September 19, 1985. Director, Christopher McCann; design, Mark Lutwak; costumes, Nancy Palmatier. With Christian Baskous, Wanda Bimson, Ed Cannan, Stephen Singer, Philip Levy.

LIVING LEG-ENDS. September 19, 1985. With Bloolips. CHAMPIONS OF THE AVERAGE JOE. By Peter Hedges. September 26, 1985. Director, Yury Belov. With Joe Mantello, Peter Hedges.

EROSION. September 26, 1985. With Theater Banlieue of Belgium.

LE LIVRE: LE DESERT. By Theater Banlieue. October 2, 1985. Director, A. Mebirouk. With Bernadette Feyereisen, Thierry Heynderickx, Phillippe Kesseler, A. Mebirouk, Eric Stone, Pierre-Michel Zaleski.

PUSHING THE D TRAIN BACK TO BROOKLYN. By Leah K. Friedman. October 10, 1985. Director, Bryna Wortman; scenery, John Paino; lighting, Craig Kennedy; costumes, David C. Woolard; music, Paul Schubert. With Martha Greenhouse, Marcy Kaplan.

I, WALT WHITMAN (one-man show). By and with Daniel Barshay. November 7, 1985.

ASPERSIONS CAST. By Daryl Chin. November 7, 1985. Directors, Daryl Chin and Larry Qualls; designer, Fred Wilson. With Marcus Alpert, Leigh Baxter, Seth Hawkins, Sheila Keenan, Charles Lahti, Francis Parkman, Erik Robertson, Leslye Wynn.

GET IT WHILE YOU CAN. By Larry Mitchell. November 29, 1985. Director, Bette Bourne; scenery, Paul Shaw. With William Castleman, Julia Dares, Daniel Holmberg, Sylvia Oshins, Bunny Pearlman, Bill Rice, Michael St. Clair, Joniruth White.

DAUGHTER OF VENUS. By Howard Zinn. November 29, 1985. Director, Jeff Zinn; scenery, Susan Bolles; lighting, Kathleen Herald. With Lee Beltzer, Candace Derra, Wallace K. Sheretz, Pamela Stewart, Michael Ornstein.

QUARTET. By Heiner Muller, translated by Carl Weber. December 12, 1985. Director and lighting, Gerald Thomas; scenery and costumes, Daniela Thomas. With George Bartenieff, Crystal Field.

4-LEAF CLOVER CABINS. By Sebastian Stuart. December 19, 1985. Director, Steve Lott; scenery, Michael Daughtry; lighting, Deborah Constantine; sound, Per-Ole Oftedal. With Daniel O'Shea, Cynthia Hoppenfeld, Charles Seals, Hal Haner.

DARK WATER CLOSING. Written, directed and performed by Steve Shill. January 9, 1986. Lighting, Paul Clay.

CRISIS OF IDENTITY. By Robert Heide. January 9, 1986. scenery, John Eric Broaddus; lighting, Michael Warren Powell. Regina David, Robert Frink, Daryl Marsh.

NOTORIOUS HARIK WILL KILL THE POPE. Written and directed by Ronald Tavel. January 16, 1986. Choreographer, David Semritc; scenery, Ronald Kajiwara and Warren Jorgenson; lighting, Craig Kennedy; music, Simeon Westbrooke. With Mark Diekmann, Lana Forrester, Crystal Field, George McGrath, Richard Briggs.

AND WHEN THE BOUGH BREAKS. Written and directed by Jamie Leo; music, David McGuire. February 1, 1986.

FULFILLING KOCH'S POSTULATE. Written and directed by Joan Schenkar. February 6, 1986. Scenery, Reagan Cook; lighting, Craig Kennedy; costumes, Tracy Oleinick; music, Christopher Drobny. With Marylouise Burke, Beverly Jacob, Irving Burton, Michael Morin.

NIETSCHE. Written and directed by Larry Myers. February 20, 1986. Scenery, Mark Marcante; lighting, Mike Grimes. With Kevin Gardiner, Brooke Myers.

HAMLETTO. Based on Giovanni Testori's L'Ambleto, adapted and directed by Antonio Abujamra. February 27, 1986. Scenery and translation, Daniela Thomas; lighting, Craig Kennedy. With Joan Wilder.

A MATTER OF FAITH. Written and directed by Maria Irene Fornes. March 6, 1986. Scenery, Donald Eastman; lighting, Anne E. Militello; costumes, Tavio Ito. With Sheila Dabney, George Bartenieff, Bennes Mardenn.

NAILS: PART ONE. Written and directed by Patricia Cobey. March 13, 1986. Scenery, Jody Pinto; lighting, David Edwardson; costumes, Natalie Walker. With Bill Castle, Aileen McCormack, Craig Richman.

THE PLATE. By Ray Dobbins. March 20, 1986. Director, Bette Bourne; scenery, Mark Marcante and Jiri Schubert; lighting, Janette Kennedy and Nancy Swartz. With Bette Bourne, Bill Rice, Debra Granieri, Roy Nathanson, Scott Caywood, Frank O'Looney.

FROM THE POINT OF VIEW OF THE SALT. By Liza Lorwin. April 3, 1986. Director, Lee Breuer; scenery and lighting, Julie Archer; costumes and film, Ghretta Hynd. With Vickie Rabb, Kevin Davis, Cristobal Carambo.

A MATTER OF LIFE AND DEATH. By Rosalyn Drexler. April 3, 1986. Director, John Vaccaro; scenery, Abe Lubelski; lighting, Jeff Nash; costumes, Gabriel Berry; music, John Braden. With Bill Evans, Alexa Hunter, Tom Cayler, Tony Zanetta, Jeremiah Bosgang, George Bartenieff.

3 UP, 3 DOWN. By Spiderwoman Theater Ensemble. April 10, 1986. Director, Muriel Miguel; lighting, Craig Kennedy. With Lisa Mayo, Gloria Miguel, Muriel Miguel.

IN THE TRAFFIC OF A TARGETED CITY. By Marc Kaminsky. May 15, 1986. Director, Arthur Strimling; scenery, Alan Glovsky; lighting, Robert Strohmeier; costumes, C. Ann Pelletier; music, Steve Browman. With Steve Browman, Diane Dowling, Arthur Strimling.

THE CASTING OF KEVIN CHRISTIAN. By Stephen Holt. June 4, 1986. Director, John Margulis; scenery, Cecil B. Songco and Phyllis Wilson; lighting, Jeffrey Nash; costumes, Natalie Walker. With Andrew Myler, Wanda-Gayle Logan, Stephen Holt.

COOKING WITH THE ELEMENTS. Conceived and directed by Theodora Skipitares. June 4, 1986. Music and associate director, Virgil Moorefield; lighting, Craig Kennedy; technical design, Michael Cummings.

SOLITAIRE. By Ward Oberman. June 4, 1986. Director, Mary Ann Hestand; scenery, John Paino; lighting, David Edwardson; costumes, David Nelson. With Alicia Gold, James Lish, Jackie McNally, Susan Varon.

Theater of the Open Eye. Total theater involving actors, dancers, musicians and designers working together, each bringing his own talents into a single project. Jean Erdman, founding director, Amie Brockway, artistic director.

THE LEGEND OF SLEEPY HOLLOW (16). By Washington Irving, adapted by Alice Hale. October 31, 1985. Director, Amie Brockway; scenery and lighting, Adrienne J. Brockway; costumes, David Kay Mickelsen. With Bruce Anthony, Kathy Barry, Harry Bennett, Frank Deal, William Ellis, Elizabeth Gee, Elizabeth Geraghty, Chris Gifford, Hugh Hodgen, Ebba James, John Moser, Mark Peters.

A CRICKET ON THE HEARTH by Charles Dickens, adapted and directed by Amie Brockway. December 14, 1985. With Deirdre Maris, Cordelia Richards, Ed Riner, Grace Ellen Poole, Alicia Gold, Leslie Mason, Phil Kaufmann, Robert Kilgore, Stephanie Martini, Arthur Lundquist, Mark McCracken, Molly O'Neil, Sharon Rosner.

THE BONE RING (20). By Donald Hall. February 1, 1986. Director, Kent Paul; scenery, Jennifer Gallagher; lighting, Karl E. Haas; music, Michael Bacon. With Ian Blackman, Michael Kelly Boone, George Hall, John Leighton, Lenka Peterson.

THE OPEN EYE-ON DIRECTORS: EQUALS by Patricia Ryan, directed by John Genke; THE RAVEN by Richard Atkins, directed by Rawleigh Moreland; SPURTS AND HIS DESIRE by Liz Sedlack, directed by Cynthia S. Stokes; SPHERE OF HEAVEN by Owen M. McGehee, directed by James H. Sweeney; LANDSCAPE WITH WAITRESS by Robert Pine, directed by Gary Pollard; PROPERTY OF WANDA PAYNE by Lucas Walker, directed by Neil Larson; GILGAMESH, adapted and directed by Tina Landau; JOHNNY STAR ON THE CORNER by William Robert Nave, directed by Joe Ferrell; THE SIXTEEN APPROPRIATE STEPS FOR VIEWING YOUR GRANDFATHER IN AN OPEN COFFIN by Billy Aronson, directed by Carol Elliott; THE HOBBIT by J.R.R. Tolkien, adapted by Patricia Gray, directed by Laurie Eliscu; ARMISTICE by Ed Musto, directed by Richard Galgano; LAST RITES by John Rawlins, directed by Rose Bonczek. March 29–April 8, 1986.

THE ALCHEMIST by Ben Jonson. June 7, 1986. Adapted and directed by Amie Brockway; with Loren Bass, Richard Clodfelter, Charles Derbyshire, Elizabeth Gee, Elizabeth Geraghty, Chris Gifford, Adam Grupper, Daniel Larkin, Sharon Rosner, Robert L. Rowe, Don Stroud, Pamela Wiggins.

WPA Theater. Produces neglected American classics and new American plays in the realistic idiom. Kyle Renick, artistic director, Edward T. Gianfrancesco, resident designer, Darlene Kaplan, literary advisor.

28 performances each

CRUISE CONTROL. By Kevin Wade. November 12, 1985. Director, Norman René; scenery, Edward T. Gianfrancesco; lighting, Debra J. Kletter. With John Getz, Patricia Richardson, Derek D. Smith, Elizabeth Berridge.

FRESH HORSES. By Larry Ketron. February 4, 1986. Director, Dann Florek; scenery, Edward T. Gianfrancesco; lighting, Phil Monat; costumes, Don Newcomb. With Suzy Amis, Craig Sheffer, Mark Benninghofen, John Bowman, Alice Haining, Haviland Morris, Marissa Chibas.

WASTED. By Fred Gamel. April 1, 1986. Director, Clinton Turner Davis; scenery, Charles H. McClennahan; lighting, Craig Evans; costumes, Don Newcomb. With Matt Mulhern, Walter Allen Bennett Jr., Eriq LaSalle, Jace Alexander, Ramon Franco, Emil Herrera, Alvin Alexis, Erik King, Burke Moses.

THEATER OF THE OPEN EYE—William Ellis and Mark Peters *(at top)* with Hugh Hogden and John Moser in *The Legend of Sleepy Hollow*

TRINITY SITE. By Janeice Scarbrough. June 3, 1986. Director, William Ludel; scenery, Edward T. Gianfrancesco; lighting, Phil Monat; costumes, Don Newcomb. With Royana Black, Christopher Curry, Mark Metcalf, Patricia Richardson.

York Theater Company. Each season, productions of classic and contemporary plays are mounted with professional casts, providing neighborhood residents with professional theater. Janet Hayes Walker, producing director.

ON THE TWENTIETH CENTURY (musical) Book and lyrics by Betty Comden and Adolph Green, based on plays by Ben Hecht, Charles MacArthur and Bruce Millholland, music by Cy Coleman. October 25, 1985. Directed by Dennis Rosa; with Margaret Benczak, Mimi Bessette, John Blair, Ron Bohmer, Victoria Brasser, Leonard John Crofoot, Steve Fickinger, Tom Galantich, Scott Harlan, Tim Hunt, Jeff McCarthy, Barbara McCulloh, Robin Taylor, Deanna Wells, Lance Brodie.

THE TIME OF THE CUCKOO by Arthur Laurents. January 17, 1986. Directed by Stuart Howard; with Michael Learned, George Guidall, Brent Barrett, Robert Cicchini, Nickie Feliciano, Alexandra Gersten, Lois Markle, Wyman Pendleton, Judith Roberts, Debra Jo Rupp.

MOBY DICK (16) (musical) book and lyrics by Mark St. Germain, adapted from Herman Melville's novel; music by Doug Katsaros. February 12, 1986. Director, Thomas Gardner; scenery, James Morgan; lighting, Mary Jo Dondlinger; costumes, Sheila Kehoe. With Ed Dixon, Victor Cook, Michael Ingram, Dennis Parlato, Buddy Rudolph, Gordon Stanley, John Timmons, Louis Tucker, Steven Blanchard.

MACBETH by William Shakespeare. March 21, 1986. Directed by Porter Van Zandt; with J. Kenneth Campbell, Francesca James, Maureen Clarke, Jude Ciccolella, Gus Demos, Norma Fire, Buck Hobbs, Chet London, Richard Marshall, Kam Metcalf, Bob J. Mitchell, Vincent Nieman, Matt Penn, Noni Pratt, Jim Pratzon, Jay O. Sanders, Elizabeth Soukup, Jim Stubbs, John Tillotson, Carl Tyson, Ralph David Westfall.

TALLEY'S FOLLY by Lanford Wilson. May 15, 1986. Directed by David Feldshuh; with Katie Grant, Eugene Troobnick.

Miscellaneous

In the additional listing of 1985–86 off-off-Broadway productions below, the names of the producing groups or theaters appear in CAPITAL LETTERS and the titles of the works in *italics*. This list consists largely of new or reconstituted works and excludes most revivals, especially of classics. It includes a few productions staged by groups which rented space from the more established organizations listed previously.

ACTOR'S OUTLET. *Crown Cork Cafeteria* by William Wise. January 31, 1986. Directed by Robert Owens Scott; with Jack Schmidt, Ron Stetson, Bill Mitchell, Robin Polk. *Olympus on My Mind* (musical) based on *Amphitryon* by Heinrich Von Kleist, book, lyrics and directed by Barry Harman, music by Grant Sturiale. May, 1986. With Ron Raines, Jason Graae, Peggy Hewett, Faith Prince, Lewis J. Stadlen, Emily Zacharias.

ACTORS PLAYHOUSE. *Anais Nin: The Paris Years* adapted from the diaries and performed by Lee Kessler. February 28, 1986.

AMERICAN FOLK THEATER. *3d Annual Playwrights Festival: Sly Old Bag* by Roland P. Meinholtz, directed by Hanay Geiogamah; *Coon Cons Coyote* written and directed by Hanay Geiogamah; *Red-Bwai* by Christopher Cornibert, directed by Oscar Lumley-Watson. July 24, 1985. *Surfacing* by C. Dumas. May 4, 1986.

AMERICAN JEWISH THEATER. *A Broadcast Baby* by Isaiah Sheffer. June 18, 1985. Directed by Dan Held; with Marilyn Sokol, Henderson Forsythe, Stan Free, Mart Hulswit. *Green Fields* by Peretz Hirshbein, translated by Joseph Landis. September 29, 1985. Directed by Stanley Brechner; with Michael Cerveris, Robin Moore. *Today I Am a Fountain Pen* by Israel Horovitz, based on Morley Torgov's stories. January 2, 1986. Directed by Stephen Zuckerman; with Grant Shaud, Melissa Leo, Josh Blake, Sol Frieder. *A Rosen by Any Other Name* by Israel Horovitz, based on Morley Torgov's novel *A Good Place to Come From*. March 1, 1986. Directed by Stephen Zuckerman; with Peter Riegert, Barbara eda-Young, Sol Frieder. *The Chopin Playoffs* by Israel Horovitz, based on Morley Torgov's stories. May 3, 1986. Directed by Stephen Zuckerman; with Nicholas Strouse, Jonathan Marc Sherman, Maddie Corman, Sam Schacht, Marcia Jean Kurtz, Karen Ludwig, Richard Portnow.

APPLE CORPS. *Murder at the Vicarage* by Agatha Christie, dramatized by Moie Charles and Barbara Toy. August 23, 1985. Directed by John Raymond; with Martha Farrar, William Van Hunter, Anne Newhall, Peter Bubriski, Anne Barrett. *Black Coffee* by Agatha Christie. May 14, 1986. Directed by John Raymond.

ART & WORK ENSEMBLE. *We Bombed in New Haven* by Joseph Heller. March 13, 1986. Directed by Anthony Di Pietro.

BILLIE HOLIDAY THEATER. *Mark VIII: XXXVI* by John H. Redwood. October 17, 1985. Directed by Lillie Marie Redwood; with Jack Aaron, Renetta Neal, Barbara Christie, Joy Moss, Dylan Ross. *Blues for a Gospel Queen* (musical) book and lyrics by Don Evans, music by John Lewis. May 1, 1986.

THE BOTTOM LINE. *Just Once* (musical) Conceived and written by Melanie Mintz; songs by Barry Mann and Cynthia Weil. April 17, 1986. Directed by Sam Ellis; choreography, Wayne Cilento; with Vivian Cherry, Ula Hedwig, Bobby Jay, Curtis King Jr., Eleanor McCoy, Peter Neptune, Earl Scooter, Kaz Silver, Doug Suvall, Beth Taylor, Tanya Willoughby.

BREAD AND PUPPET THEATER. *Bach Cantata*. March 23, 1986.

BROOKLYN ACADEMY OF MUSIC (BAM). *The Golden Windows* written and directed by Robert Wilson. October 22, 1985. With David Warrilow, Jane Hoffman, Gaby Rodgers, John Bowman, Charles Whiteside, Kimberly Farr, Cynthia Babak. *Russia* conceived, written and directed by Chris Hardman. November 19, 1985. With Jess Curtis, Annie Hallatt, Ed Holmes, Brenda Munnell. *The Alchemedians* by and with Bob Berky and Michael Moschen. November 20, 1985. Directed by Ricardo E. Velez. *The Birth of the Poet* libretto by Kathy Acker, music by Peter Gordon. December 3, 1985. Directed by Richard Foreman. (All productions listed were part of the Next Wave Festival.)

DON'T TELL MAMA. *Insert Foot* (musical) music by Jerry Sternbach, lyrics by Faye Greenberg. September 18, 1985. Directed by Catherine Cox; with John Hillner, Christina Saffran, Susan Terry. *Living Color, a Twisted Mnemonic Entertainment* (musical) by Scott Warrender. March 18, 1986. Directed by Susan Stroman; with Davis Gaines, Jason Graae, Nancy Johnston, Faith Prince.

DOUBLE IMAGE THEATER. *Savage in Limbo* by John Patrick Shanley. September 17, 1985. Directed by Mark Linn-Baker; with Jayne Haynes, Deborah Hedwall, Larry Joshua, Mary McDonnell, Randel Mell. *Filthy Rich* by George F. Walker. September 24, 1985. Directed by Max D. Mayer; with John P. Connolly, Reed Birney, Caris Corfman, Dan Moran, Joseph Siravo.

THE DUPLEX. *Miss Gulch Returns* (musical revue) by and with Fred Barton. August 12, 1985.

ECCENTRIC CIRCLES THEATER. *Natural Causes* by Lilian Lieblich. September 27, 1985. Directed by Rosemary Hopkins; with Judy Cole, Maria Robb, Karl Schroeder, Gerald Simon, Pat Squire. *Love Games* by Elaine Denholtz. October 18, 1985. Directed by Paula Kay Pierce; with Aurelia DeFelice, Paula Ewin, Martha Greenhouse, Eric Himes, Johnnie Mae, Muriel Mason.

FLEET THEATER COMPANY. *The Merchant of Venice, or Paper Promises: 1933* based on Shakespeare's play. August 16, 1985. With Rudy Caringi.

FREE THEATER PRODUCTIONS. Great Artist Theater Series, featuring a reading by Lynn Redgrave. June 13, 1985.

HAROLD CLURMAN THEATER. *Crime and Punishment* by Fyodor Dostoyevsky, adapted by L.A. Sheldon. November 9, 1985. Directed by Maria Mazer and John Van Ness Philip; with Shan Sullivan, Caroline Arnold, Barbara Sinclair, Diane Tarleton, Sully Boyar.

JEAN COCTEAU REPERTORY. *Lunin: Theater of Death* by Edvard Radzinsky, translated by Alma H. Law. September 5, 1985. Directed by Eve Adamson; with Craig Smith, Craig Cook, William Dante.

JEWISH REPERTORY THEATER. *Pearls* (musical) book, music and lyrics by Nathan Gross. June 29, 1985. Directed by Ran Avni; with Rosalind Elias, Richard Frisch, Gloria Hodes, Judy Kuhn. *The Special* (musical) book and lyrics by Mike Gutwillig, music by Galt MacDermot. October 19, 1985. Directed by Ran Avni; with Adam Heller, Patricia Ben Peterson, Mina Bern. *The Shop on Main Street* (musical) book and lyrics by Bernard Spiro, based on Ladislav Grosman's novel, music by Saul Honigman. January 2, 1986. Directed by Fran Soeder; with Gregg Edelman, Nancy Callman, Olga Talyn, Lilia Skala. *I, Shaw* (one-act plays): *The Shy and Lonely* by Irwin Shaw and *Sailor Off the Bremen* by William Kramer. February 19, 1986. Directed by Edward M. Cohen; with

YORK THEATER COMPANY—Dennis Parlato (Starbuck), Ed Dixon (Capt. Ahab) and Buddy Rudolph (Ishmael) in musical adaptation of *Moby Dick*

Rob Morrow, Tracey Thorne, Scott Miller. *Light Up the Sky* by Moss Hart. April 4, 1986. With Grace Roberts, William Gleason, Ilene Kristen. *Lies My Father Told Me* by Ted Allan, music by Margaret Rachlin Pine. May 31, 1986. Directed by Lynn Polan; with Chris Ceraso, Braden Danner, Sophie Hayden, Bill Nelson, Angela Pietropinto, Gary Richards, Stephen Singer, Mark Zeller.

JUDITH ANDERSON THEATER. *A Life Like the Rest* by Kevin Arkadie. January 1986. Directed by Dean Irby; with Jonathan Earl Peck, Melissa Fonts, Willie C. Carpenter, Brel Barbara Clarke, Gabrielle Platt. *Dry Land* by Cyndi Coyne. May 18, 1986. Directed by Kay Matschullat; with Marylouise Burke, Caris Corfman, Olivia Laurel Mates, Christian Slater.

LION THEATER COMPANY. *The Flatbush Faithful* written and directed by Gene Nye. September 9, 1985. With Christopher McCann, Michael Guido, Jim Ricketts, Alvin Alexis. *The Cabbagehead* by Oliver Goldstick. October 7, 1985. Directed by John Guerrasio; with Phyllis Somerville, Jim Abele.

LOUIS ABRONS ARTS FOR LIVING CENTER. *Stories about the Old Days* by Bill Harris. May 14, 1986. Directed by LaTanya Richardson; with Abbey Lincoln, Clebert Ford.

MANHATTAN REPERTORY. *Something Red* by Thomas Walmsley. October 2, 1985. Directed by Richard Schiff; with Agatha Balek, David Bottrell, Lisa Mozer, Steve Rapella.

METAWEE RIVER COMPANY. *North Wind* by Dave Hunsaker with Ralph Lee. September 6, 1985.

MORSE MIME REPERTORY THEATER. *Dracula*, adapted from Bram Stoker's novel. November 1, 1985. Directed by Anastasia Nicole; with Richard Morse, Robert Maiorano, Noreen Bartlin.

MUSICAL THEATER WORKS. *A Midsummer Night's Dream* by William Shakespeare. July 16, 1985. Directed by Stephen Zuckerman; with Mark Metcalf, Kristin Griffith. *Tales of Tinseltown* (musical) by Michael Colby and Paul Katz. August 8, 1985. Directed by Rick Lombardo; with Olga Talyn, Nora Mae Lyng, Elizabeth Austin, Alison Fraser, Bob Arnold, Greg Mowry, Jason Graae, Nat Chandler. *Tropicana* (musical) book and directed by George Abbott, music by Robert Nassif, lyrics by Peter Napolitano. May 29, 1986. With Roxann Cabalero, Constance Carpenter, Edmund Lyndeck, Lara Teeter.

NEW AMSTERDAM THEATER COMPANY. *George White's Scandals* (musical). October 20, 1985. With Obba Babatunde, Paula Laurence, Peggy Cass, Patrice Munsel. *Jubilee* (musical) book by Moss Hart, music and lyrics by Cole Porter. March 2, 1986. Directed by James Brennan; with Carole Shelley, Alyson Reed, Paula Laurence, Rebecca Luker, Reed Jones, John Remme, Robert Cook. *I Married an Angel* (musical) book by Richard Rodgers and Lorenz Hart, based on John Vaszary's play, music by Richard Rodgers, lyrics by Lorenz Hart. May 17, 1986. With William Cain, Lee Lobenhofer, Phyllis Newman, Kurt Peterson, Virginia Seidel, Maggie Task, David Wasson, Karen Ziemba.

NEW THEATER OF BROOKLYN. *The Double Bass* by Patrick Suskind, translated by Eric Overmyer and Harry Newman. November 6, 1985. Directed by Kent Paul; with Boyd Gaines.

NEW YORK ART THEATER INSTITUTE. *Gods and Goddesses*, adapted from Greek mythology. March 18, 1986. Directed by Donald Sanders; with Guy Custis, Kate Farrell, Janet Scurria.

NEW YORK GILBERT AND SULLIVAN PLAYERS. *Iolanthe*. December 29, 1985. Directed by Albert Bergeret; with Keith Jurasko, Heidi Merritt, John Reed, John Colin Wilson, Nancy Evers. *The Pirates of Penzance*. March 7, 1986. With Keith Jurasko, Del-Bourree Bach, Kristen Garver.

NEW YORK THEATER WORKSHOP. *Sore Throats* by Howard Benton. November 27, 1985. Directed by Rosey Hay. *1951* conceived and directed by Anne Bogart, text adapted by Anne Bogart and Mac Wellman, music by Michael S. Roth. May 20, 1986. With Ryan Cutrona, Karen Evans-Kandel, Mark Austin, Karen Trott, Randolyn Zinn.

OFF-CENTER THEATER. *Biting the Apple* by Tony McGrath and Stanley Seidman. October 17, 1985. Directed by Tony McGrath; with Nick Dimitri, Derrick Eason, Sheila Hecht, Crawford Mills, Julia Santana, Kim Sykes.

PARK ROYAL THEATER. *A Small Matter of Sacrifice* by Tony Perez. May 1986. Directed by Nonon Padilla; with Susan Valdez, Maria Barredo, Rudy Hermano, Lily Gamboa.

PEARL THEATER COMPANY. *The Lady from the Sea* by Henrik Ibsen, translated by Frances E. Archer. May, 1986. Directed by Shepard Sobel; with Joanne Camp, Frank Geraci, Robin Westphal, James Nugent, Patrick Turner.

PENGUIN REPERTORY COMPANY. *Treats* by Christopher Hampton. April 3, 1986. Directed by Joe Brancato; with Anne Barrett, S. Sherrard Hicks, Bruce McDonnell.

PERFORMANCE THEATER CENTER. *Flood* by Gunter Grass. May 22, 1986. Directed by Charles Otte; with Steven Haworth, Kristin Moneagle, Robin Siemens, John Siemens, Tom Delling.

PERFORMING GARAGE. *Chekhov* conceived and directed by Stuart Sherman. July 1985. With Stuart Sherman, Scotty Snyder, George Ashley, Black-Eyed Susan. *The Prometheus Project* adapted from Aeschylus's *Prometheus* and directed by Richard Schechner. December, 1985. With Annie Sprinkle, Becke Wilenski, Mahmoud Karimi-Hakak, Mollie Glazer. *The Age of Invention* (multimedia plays and puppetry) by Theodora Skipitares, music by Virgil Moorefield and Scott Johnson. January, 1986. *The Housing Project* conceived and directed by Yoshiko Chuma. February 5, 1986. *Leer* written, directed and performed by Ethyl Eichelberger and *Casanova* written and directed by Ethyl Eichelberger. February 20, 1986. With Lola Pashalinski, Katy Dierlam, Barbara Wise, Ethyl Eichelberger. *Image of None* (performance piece) by and with Butch Morris. March, 1986. *The Cure* written, composed, directed and designed by Richard Foreman. May, 1986. With Kate Manheim, David Patrick Kelly, Jack Coulter.

PERRY STREET THEATER. *Rabboni* (musical) book, music and lyrics by Jeremiah Ginsberg. June 13, 1985. Directed by Alan Weeks; with Paul Clark, Ned York, Wilbur Archie. *Bosoms and Ne-*

glect by John Guare. April 8, 1986. Directed by Larry Arrick; with Anne Meara, Richard Kavanaugh, April Shawhan.

PLAYERS THEATER. *Inside Out* written and directed by James Van Lare. November 26, 1985. With John Kudan, Adam Oliensis, Jo Anna Rush. *Another Paradise* by Donna Spector. February 17, 1986. Directed by Licia Colombi; with Cass Morgan, Arleigh Richards, Tom Ligon, Meg Van Zyl, Mick Weber.

PROVINCETOWN PLAYHOUSE. *Times Square Angel* by Charles Busch. December, 1985. Directed by Kenneth Elliott; with Charles Busch, Robert Carey, Arnie Kolodner, Theresa Marlowe, Meghan Robinson.

RIVERWEST THEATER. *Carrier* and *The Box* written and directed by Paul Benjamin. July 29, 1985. With Paul Benjamin, Regina Taylor, Themba Ntinga, Minnie Gentry, Moketsi Bodibe. *The Camel Has His Nose Under the Tent* by Andre Ernotte and Elliot Tiber. January 20, 1986. Directed by Andre Ernotte and Elliot Tiber; with Burt Edwards, Drinda La Lumia, Richard Merrell, Katie C. Sparer. *Dead Wrong* by Nick Hall. March, 1986. Directed by Bill Gile; with David Groh, Anita Gillette, Michael Wilding, Lachlan Macleay.

SAMUEL BECKETT THEATER. *Short Change* by Geoffrey Gordon. September 15, 1985. Directed by Joshua Astrachan; with David Breitbarth, Lea Floden, Josh Pais, Raphael Sbarge.

SILVER LINING THEATER. *Sweet Will* (musical) by Lance Mulcahy. December 26, 1985. Directed by John Olon; with Stephanie Cotsirilos, Stephen Lehew, Roslyn Burrough, Keith Amos.

SOUTH STREET THEATER. *One Man Band* (musical) book by James Lecesne, music by Marc Elliot and Larry Hochman, lyrics by Marc Elliot. June 12, 1985. Directed by Jack Hofsiss; with James Lecesne, Kay Cole, Judy Gibson, Vanessa Williams. *The First Night of "Pygmalion"* by Richard Huggett. September 18, 1985. Directed by Freeman Parks; with William Shust, Arlene Stern, George C. Nestor. Four One-act Musicals: *Madonna* book and lyrics by Jim Morgan, music by Stewart Wallace; *Leo* libretto by Fernando Fonseca, based on Cal Massey's story *Leo Spat*, music by Michael Ching; *Three Complaints* libretto by Craig Lucas, music by Stewart Wallace; *Soapopera* book and lyrics by Jim Morgan, music by Stewart Wallace. October, 1985. Directed by Ricardo E. Velez; with Nancy Ringham, Darlene Bel Grayson, Alison Fraser.

THEATER OFF PARK. *The Lisbon Traviata* by Terrence McNally. June 16, 1985. Directed by John Tillinger; with Benjamin Hendrickson, Seth Allen, Steven Culp, Stephen Schnetzer.

T.O.M.I. THEATER. *You Belong to Me* by Stan Leonard. October 17, 1985. Directed by John Margulis; with Deborah Snyderman, Winship Cook, Leonard Stanger, Marion Brasch.

VINEYARD THEATER. *Somewheres Better* by William Wise. June 18, 1985. Directed by Jeff Martin; with Cameron Charles Johann, Tom Stechschulte, Shelley Rogers, Stacey Glick. *Goblin Market* (musical) by Peggy Harmon and Polly Pen, adapted from Christina Rossetti's poem, music by Polly Pen. October 17, 1985. Directed by Andre Ernotte; with Terri Klausner, Ann Morrison.

WESTBANK CAFE. *Next, Please* (cabaret revue) songs by Jerry Sternbach. July 9, 1985. Directed by Sheryl A. Kaller; with Stuart Bloom, Michael Brian, Alison Fraser, Peter Herber, Mary Testa, Jennifer Leigh Warren.

WESTBETH THEATER CENTER. *New York International Festival of Clown Theater*. June 11–30, 1985. With Fred Yockers, John Towsen, Cheryl Cashman, Nion, James Donlon, Judy Sloan, Hank Smith, Bob Berky. *The Phil Stein Vaudeville Show* conceived and performed by Phil Stein. October, 1985. Directed by Billy Hoffmann.

WESTSIDE ARTS THEATER. *21A* (one-man show) by and with Kevin Kling. May 15, 1986. Directed by Steven Dietz.

THE WRITERS THEATER. *Beef* by David Pownall. January 28, 1986. Directed by Byam Stevens; with K.C. Wilson, Marko Maglich, Anderson Matthews, Stephen J. Brackley, Juanin Clay.

THE SEASON
AROUND
THE UNITED STATES

OUTSTANDING NEW PLAYS CITED BY AMERICAN THEATER CRITICS ASSOCIATION

and

A DIRECTORY OF NEW-PLAY PRODUCTIONS

THE American Theater Critics Association (ATCA) is the organization of 250 leading drama critics in all media in all sections of the United States. One of this group's stated purposes is "To increase public awareness of the theater as a *national* resource" (italics ours). To this end, ATCA has cited three outstanding new plays produced this season around the country, to be represented in our coverage of The Season Around the United States by excerpts from each of their scripts demonstrating literary style and quality. And one of these—August Wilson's *Fences*—was designated the first-place play and received the first annual ATCA New Play Award of $1,000.

The process for the selection of these outstanding plays is as follows: any ATCA member critic may nominate a play if it has been given a production in a professional house. It must be a finished play given a full production (not a reading or an airing as a play-in-progress). Nominated scripts were studied and discussed by an ATCA play-reading committee chaired by Lawrence DeVine of the Detroit *Free Press* and comprising Jeffrey Borak of the Poughkeepsie *Journal*, Ann Holmes of the Houston *Chronicle*, Damien Jaques of the Milwaukee *Journal*, Tom McCulloh of *Drama-Logue*, Julius Novick of the *Village Voice* and

Bernard Weiner of the San Francisco *Chronicle,* with Dan Sullivan of the Los Angeles *Times* as an ex officio member. The committee members made their choices on the basis of script rather than production, thus placing very much the same emphasis as the editor of this volume in making his New York Best Play selections. There were no eligibility requirements except that a nominee be the first full professional production of a new work outside New York City within this volume's time frame of June 1, 1985 to May 31, 1986. If the timing of nominations and openings prevented some works from being considered this year, they will be eligible for consideration next year if they haven't since moved on to New York production. We offer our sincerest thanks and admiration to the ATCA members and their committee for the valuable insight into the 1985–86 theater season around the United States which their selections provide for this *Best Plays* record.

*Cited by American Theater Critics
as Outstanding New Plays
of 1985–86*

FENCES

A Play in Two Acts

BY AUGUST WILSON

Cast and credits appear on page 446

FENCES: Around the turn of the century, European immigrants brought their dreams to American cities and made them come true by means of hard work and persistence. *"The descendants of African slaves were offered no such welcome nor participation,"* a *Fences* program note observes. *"They came from places called the Carolinas and the Virginias, Georgia, Alabama, Mississippi and Tennessee. They came strong, eager, searching. The city rejected them, and they fled and settled along the riverbanks and under bridges in shallow, ramshackle houses made of sticks and tarpaper. They collected rags and wood. They sold the use of their muscles and their bodies. They cleaned houses and washed clothes, they shined shoes, and in quiet desperation and vengeful pride, they stole, and lived in pursuit of their own dream: that they could breathe free, finally, and stand to meet life with the force of dignity and whatever eloquence the heart could call upon."*

In the yard of the Maxson house in an urban neighborhood of a northern American industrial city in the fall of 1957, two men are talking: Troy (*"53 years old, a large man with thick, heavy hands"*) and Bono (*"obviously the follower"*). They are refuse workers, dressed accordingly and carrying lunch buckets. It is Friday night, payday.

BONO: Troy, you ought to stop that lying!
TROY: I ain't lying! The nigger had a watermelon this big. *(He indicates with*

his hands.) Talking about . . . "What watermelon, Mr. Rand?" I liked to fell out! "What watermelon, Mr. Rand?" . . . And it sitting there big as life.

BONO: What did Mr. Rand say?

TROY: Ain't said nothing. Figure if the nigger too dumb to know he carrying a watermelon, he wasn't gonna get much sense out of him. Trying to hide the great big old watermelon under his coat. Afraid to let the white man see him carry it home.

BONO: I'm like you . . . I ain't got no time for them kind of people.

TROY: Now what he look like getting mad cause he see the man from the union talking to Mr. Rand?

BONO: Well, as long as you got your complaint filed they can't fire you. That's what one of them white fellows tell me.

TROY: I ain't worried about them firing me. They gonna fire me cause I asked a question? That's all I did. I went to Mr. Rand and asked him, "Why?" Why you got the white mens driving and the colored lifting? Told him, what's the matter, don't I count? You think only white fellows got sense enough to drive a truck. That ain't no paper job! Hell, anybody can drive a truck. How come you got all whites driving and the colored lifting? He told me to take it to the union. Well, hell, that's what I done! Now they wanna come up with this pack of lies.

BONO: I told Brownie if the man come and ask me any questions . . . just tell the truth! It ain't nothing but something they done trumped up on you cause you filed a complaint on them.

TROY: Brownie don't understand nothing. All I want them to do is change the job description. Give everybody a chance to drive the truck. Brownie can't see that. He ain't got that much sense.

BONO: How you figure he may be making out with that gal be up at Taylor's all the time . . . that Alberta gal?

TROY: Same as you and me. Getting just as much as we is. Which is to say nothing.

BONO: It is, huh? I figure you doing a little better than me . . . and I ain't saying what I'm doing.

TROY: Aw, nigger, look here . . . I know you. If you had got anywhere near that gal, twenty minutes later you gonna be looking to tell somebody. And the first one you gonna tell . . . that you gonna want to brag to . . . is gonna be me.

BONO: I ain't saying that. I see where you be eyeing her.

TROY: I eye all women. I don't miss nothing. Don't ever let nobody tell you Troy Maxson don't eye the women.

BONO: You been doing more than eyeing her. You done bought her a drink or two.

TROY: Hell yeah, I bought her a drink! What that mean? I bought you one, too. What that mean cause I buy her a drink? I'm just being polite.

BONO: It's all right to buy her one drink. That's what you call being polite. But when you wanna be buying two or three . . . that's what you call eyeing her.

TROY: Look here, as long as you've known me . . . you ever known me to chase after women?

BONO: Hell, yeah! Long as I done known you. You forgetting I knew you when.

TROY: Naw, I'm talking about since I been married to Rose.

BONO: Not since you been married to Rose. That's the truth. I can say that.

TROY: All right then. Case closed!

BONO: I see you be walking up around Alberta's house.

TROY: What you watching where I'm walking for? I ain't watching after you.

BONO: I seen you walking around there more than once.

TROY: Hell, you liable to see me walking anywhere! That don't mean nothing cause you see me walking around there.

BONO: Where she come from anyway? She just kinda showed up one day.

TROY: Tallahassee. You can look at her and tell she one of them Florida gals. They got some big healthy women down there. Grow them right up out the ground. Got a little bit of Indian in her. Most of them niggers down in Florida got some Indian in them.

BONO: I don't know about that Indian part. But she damn sure big and healthy. Woman wear some big stockings. Hips as wide as the Mississippi River!

TROY: Legs don't mean nothing. You don't do nothing but push them out the way. But them hips cushion the ride!

BONO: Troy, you ain't got no sense.

TROY: It's the truth! Like you riding on Goodyears!

> *Rose enters from the house. Ten years younger than Troy, her devotion to him stems from her recognition of the possibilities of her life without him: a succession of abusive men and their babies, a life of partying and running the streets, the Church, or aloneness with its attendant pain and frustration. She recognizes Troy's spirit as a fine and illuminating one, and she either ignores or forgives his faults, only some of which she recognizes. Though she doesn't drink, her presence is an integral part of the Friday night rituals. She alternates between the porch and the kitchen where supper preparations are under way.*

ROSE: What you all out here getting into?

TROY: What you worried about what we getting into for? This is men talk, woman.

ROSE: What I care what you all talking about. Bono, you gonna stay for supper?

BONO: I thank you, Rose. But Lucille say she cooking up a pot of pigfeet.

TROY: Pigfeet! Hell, I'm going home with you! Might even stay the night if you got some pigfeet. You got something in there to top them pigfeet, Rose?

ROSE: I'm cooking up some chicken. I got some chicken and collard greens.

TROY: Well, go on back in the house and let me and Bono finish what we was talking about. This is man talk. I got some talk for you later. You know what kind of talk I mean. You go on and powder it up.

ROSE: Troy Maxson, don't you start that now!

TROY (*puts his arm around her*): Aw, woman . . . come here. Look here, Bono . . . when I met this woman . . . I got out that place, say, "Hitch up my pony, saddle up my mare . . . there's a woman out there for me somewhere." I looked here. Looked there. Saw Rose and latched on to her. I latched on to her and told her . . . I'm gonna tell you the truth . . . I told her, Baby, I don't wanna marry, I just wanna be your man. Rose told me . . . Tell him what you told me, Rose.

ROSE: I told him if he wasn't the marrying kind, then move out the way so the marrying kind could find me.

TROY: That's what she told me. Nigger, you in my way. You blocking the view!

Move out the way so I can find me a husband. I thought it over two or three days. Come back . . .

ROSE: Ain't no two or three days nothing. You was back the same night.

TROY: Come back, told her . . . O.K., baby . . . but I'm gonna buy me a banty rooster and put him out there in the back yard . . . and when he see a stranger come he'll flap his wings and crow . . . Look here, Bono, I could watch the front door by myself . . . it was the back door I was worried about.

ROSE: Troy, you ought not talk like that. Troy ain't doing nothing but telling a lie.

TROY: Only thing is . . . when we first got married . . . forget the rooster . . . we ain't had a yard!

BONO: I hear you tell it. Me and Lucille was staying down there on Logan

YALE REPERTORY THEATER, NEW HAVEN—James
Earl Jones as Troy Maxson in *Fences* by August Wilson

Street. Had two rooms with the outhouse in the back. I ain't mind the outhouse none . . . But when that goddamn wind blow through there in winter . . . that's what I'm talking about! To this day I wonder why in the hell I ever stayed down there for six long years. But see, I didn't know I could do no better. I thought only white folks had inside toilets and things.

ROSE: There's a lot of people don't know they can do no better than they doing now. That's just something you got to learn. A lot of folks still shop at Bella's.

TROY: Ain't nothing wrong with shopping at Bella's. She got fresh food.

ROSE: I ain't said nothing about if she got fresh food. I'm talking about what she charge. She charge ten cents more than the A & P.

TROY: The A & P ain't never done nothing for me. I spends my money where I'm treated right. I go down to Bella, say I need a loaf of bread, I'll pay you Friday, she give it to me. What sense that make when I got money to go and spend it somewhere else and ignore the person who done right by me? That ain't in the Bible.

ROSE: We ain't talking about what's in the Bible. What sense it make to shop there when she overcharge?

TROY: You shop where you want to. I'll do my shopping where the people been good to me.

ROSE: Well, I don't think it's right for her to overcharge. That's all I was saying.

BONO: Look here . . . I got to get on. Lucille going to be raising all kind of hell.

TROY: Where you going, nigger? We ain't finished this pint. Come on, finish this pint.

BONO: Well, hell, I am . . . if you ever turn the bottle loose.

TROY *(hands him the bottle):* The only thing I say about the A & P is I'm glad Cory got that job down there. Help him take care of his school clothes and things. Gabe done moved out and things getting tight around here. He got that job . . . he can start to look out for himself.

ROSE: Cory done went and got recruited by a college football team.

TROY: I told that boy about that football stuff. The white man ain't gonna let him get nowhere with that football. I told him when he first come to me with it. Now you come telling me he done went and got more tied up in it. He need to go and get recruited in how to fix cars or something where he can make a living.

ROSE: He ain't talking about making no living playing football. It's just something the boys in school do. They gonna send a recruiter by to talk to you. He'll tell you he ain't talking about making no living playing football. It's a honor to be recruited.

TROY: It ain't gonna get him nowhere. Bono'll tell you that.

BONO: If he be like you in the sports . . . he's gonna be all right. Ain't but two men ever played baseball as good as you. That's Babe Ruth and John Gibson. Them's the only two men hit a baseball further than you.

TROY: What it ever get me? Ain't got a pot to piss in or a window to throw it out of.

They discuss the black man's lack of a first-class opportunity in sports, and how times are changing. Troy reminisces about a three-day struggle and victory over a deadly disease back in 1941—since then, death has no fears for him. Lyons,

Troy's son by a previous marriage, joins them in the back yard. Lyons is 34 and *"sports a neatly trimmed goatee, sport coat, white shirt, tieless and buttoned at the collar."* He has come, on payday, to borrow $10 from his father.

LYONS: . . . . . Look here, Pop . . . let me have that ten dollars. I'll give it back to you. Bonnie got a job working at the hospital.

TROY: What I tell you, Bono? The only time I see this nigger is when he wants something. That's the only time I see him.

LYONS: Come on, Pop, Bono don't want to hear all that. Let me have the ten dollars. I told you Bonnie working.

TROY: What that mean to me? "Bonnie working." I don't care if she working. Go ask her for the ten dollars if she working. Talking about "Bonnie working." Why ain't you working?

LYONS: Aw, Pop, you know I can't find no decent job. Where am I gonna get a job at? You know I can't get no job.

TROY: I told you I know some people down there. Get you on the rubbish if you want to work. I told you that the last time you came by here asking me for something.

LYONS: Naw, Pop . . . thanks. That ain't for me. I don't wanna be carrying nobody's rubbish. I don't wanna be punching nobody's time clock.

TROY: What's the matter—you too good to carry rubbish? Where you think that ten dollars you talking about come from? I'm just supposed to haul people's rubbish and give my money to you cause you too lazy to work. You too lazy to work and wanna know why you ain't got what I got.

ROSE: What hospital Bonnie working at? Mercy?

LYONS: She's down at Passavant working in the laundry.

TROY: Ain't got nothing as it is. I give you that ten dollars and I got to eat beans the rest of the week. Naw . . . you ain't getting no ten dollars here.

LYONS: You ain't got to be eating no beans. I don't know why you wanna say that.

TROY: I ain't got no extra money. Gabe done moved over to Miss Pearl's, paying her the rent, and things done got tight around here. I can't afford to be giving you every payday.

LYONS: I ain't asked you to give me nothing. I asked you to loan me ten dollars. I know you got ten dollars.

TROY: Yeah, I got it. Why you think I got it? Cause I don't throw my money away out there in the streets. You living the fast life . . . wanna be a musician . . . running around in them clubs and things . . . then you learn to take care of yourself. You ain't gonna find me going and asking nobody for nothing. I done spent too many years without.

LYONS: You and me is two different people, Pop.

TROY: I done learned my mistakes and learned to do what's right by it. You still trying to get something for nothing. Life don't owe you nothing. You owe it to yourself. Ask Bono. He'll tell you I'm right.

LYONS: You got your way of dealing with the world . . . I got mine. The only thing that matters to me is the music.

TROY: Hell, I can see that! It don't matter how you gonna eat . . . where your next dollar is coming from. You telling the truth there.

LYONS: I know I got to eat. But I got to live too. I need something that gonna help me to get out of the bed in the morning. Make me feel like I belong in the world. I don't bother nobody. I just stay with my music cause that's the only way I can find to live in the world. Otherwise there ain't no telling what I might do. Now I don't come criticizing you and the way you live. I just come by to ask you for ten dollars. I don't wanna hear all that about how I live.

TROY: Boy, your mama did a hell of a job raising you.

LYONS: You can't change me, Pop. I'm thirty-four years old.

ROSE: Let the boy have ten dollars, Troy.

TROY (to *Lyons*): What the hell you looking at me for? I ain't got no ten dollars. You know what I do with my money. *(To Rose.)* Give him ten dollars if you want him to have it.

ROSE: I will. Just as soon as you turn it loose.

TROY *(handing Rose the money):* There it is. Seventy-six dollars and forty-two cents. You see this, Bono? Now I ain't gonna get but six of that back.

ROSE: You ought to stop telling that lie. Here, Lyons.

 She hands him the money.

LYONS: Thanks, Rose. Look . . . I got to run . . . I'll see you later.

TROY: Wait a minute. You gonna say "thanks Rose" and ain't gonna look to see where she got the ten.

LYONS: I know she got it from you, Pop. Thanks. I'll give it back to you.

TROY: There he go telling another lie. Time I see that ten dollars . . . he'll be owed me thirty more.

LYONS: See you, Mr. Bono. Thanks, Pop. I'll see you again.

 Lyons exits the yard.

TROY: I don't know why he don't go and get him a decent job and take care of that woman he got.

BONO: He'll be all right, Troy. He's still young.

TROY: The boy is thirty-four years old.

ROSE: Let's not get off into all that.

BONO: Look here . . . I got to be going. I got to be getting on. Lucille gonna be waiting.

TROY *(puts his arm around Rose):* See this woman, Bono? I love this woman, I love this woman so much it hurts. I love her so much . . . I done run out of ways to love her. So I got to go back to basics. Don't you come by my house Monday morning talking about time to go to work . . . cause I'm still gonna be stroking.

ROSE: Troy! Stop it now!

BONO: I ain't paying him no mind, Rose. That ain't nothing but gin-talk. Go on, Troy. I'll see you Monday.

TROY: Don't you come by my house, nigger! I done told you what I'm gonna be doing.

 The lights go to black.

FENCES *was produced by Yale Repertory Theater under the direction of Lloyd Richards on April 30, 1985, with James Earl Jones as Troy, Ray Aranha as Bono, Mary Alice as Rose and Charles Brown as Lyons.*

FUGUE

A Play in Two Acts

BY LEONORA THUNA

Cast and credits appear on page 446.

FUGUE: Mary, a patient in a psychiatric clinic, is *"a very interesting-looking woman—interesting because it is difficult to pinpoint anything about her."* She is thin, with an unlined face and hair with no gray in it—she could be anywhere between mid-30s and mid-40s. Zelda, graying and 45 or more, comes into Mary's room, calls her "Cele" and claims to be a lifelong friend, but Mary doesn't remember her at all.

Meanwhile, through the two-way mirror in Mary's room, two psychiatrists, Dr. John Oleander and Dr. Daniel Lucchesi are watching Mary (the mirror is now lit so that the doctors are visible). The clinic has given Mary the name "Mary Smith" because they don't know who she is or anything about her, and she remembers nothing about herself.

OLEANDER (*picks up the folder and reads*): What is most curious about the patient is her total lack of concern regarding her condition. She is in consistently good spirits and exhibits no anxiety about the future.

DANNY: Possibly because there is no future.

> *He turns his attention to the two-way mirror. Lights come up in Mary's room. Zelda is still there.*

MARY: Can I get you something to drink? What would you like?

ZELDA: Do you have no-caffeine diet soda?

MARY: What is that?

ZELDA: You don't know what no-caffeine diet soda is?

MARY: No. How about a glass of seltzer?

ZELDA: Salt-free seltzer?

MARY *(with a sigh):* Look. This isn't going to be easy. Why don't you go home?

ZELDA: Cele, Cele! Of course it will be easy. Just give yourself time! I'm here to help you! Remember me? When I saw your picture in the paper, I didn't hesitate a minute! I said that is my old friend Cele, and I am going right up to see her, and the minute she'll lay her eyes on me, it will all come rushing back to her! Now I'll admit, maybe it doesn't always work that way, you know, the way it does in movies, maybe it doesn't *all* come back in a *rush*—but at least something comes back, doesn't it?

MARY: I forgot your name.

ZELDA: Zelda!

MARY: Zelda. Zel-da. Zee. Zee. Last letter of the alphabet. F. Scott Fitzgerald. Zzzelda, Zzzelda. Zel-da!

ZELDA: We were best friends. Zelda Spearman and Cecilia Scarlick. From the time we were in first grade we sat behind each other. We stood in line together, we got our periods together . . .

MARY: Cecilia *Scarlick?*

ZELDA: We had our first dates together, we shaved our legs together, we let ourselves be felt up together.

MARY *(with a glance at the mirror):* Listen, Zelda, I don't think I can deal with this right now, Zelda. Why don't we call it a day, Zelda?

ZELDA: But I'm part of your background! . . .

MARY *(still memorizing):* Zelda.

ZELDA: This is important!

MARY: Yes, it is. It's very important. It's just too much for me. Too much, too fast. I can't absorb it all.

ZELDA: What are you absorbing? I haven't even told you any details . . .

MARY: Yes, yes, that's what I mean. I'm not ready for details. I have to take this a little at a time. I mean, a very little at a time. Like right now I have to absorb that my name is Cecilia Scarlick.

ZELDA *(shaking her head in wonder):* Didn't you even know that?

MARY: No, I didn't. So you see where I am. I can't get into being felt up when I just learned what my name is.

ZELDA *(getting up):* Well, all right, I can understand that. *(Going to the door.)* But I want you to know something, Cele. Sometimes people grow up and they go off in different directions. *(Turning to her.)* I don't feel that about us. I feel we're still as close as we ever were—and after a few more visits, we'll be sitting and having bull sessions just the way we always did.

MARY: Just one question . . .

ZELDA *(annoyed):* You're not going to ask what my name is again!

MARY: No, mine.

ZELDA *(opening the door):* Cecilia Scarlick. Goodbye for now.

MARY: Wait a minute. What is Scarlick? Is it Greek? Italian? Hindu?

ZELDA: I think it's Czechoslovakian.

MARY: O.K. Thanks. 'Bye.

She closes the door, turns back into the room.

Czechoslovakian. Sure. That tells me a lot. What is Czechoslovakian? I don't even know what they eat.

There is a knock at the door. Mary turns away from the door; walks to the couch. Door opens and Oleander enters, Danny behind him.

OLEANDER: Hello, Mary.

MARY: Hello.

OLEANDER: Do you remember who I am? I'm Doctor Oleander.

MARY: Of course I remember. You're Doctor Oleander.

OLEANDER: I want you to meet a colleague of mine. Dr. Lucchesi . . .

DANNY: Danny.

OLEANDER: Yes. Danny . . . *(The informality bothers him.)* . . . is writing a book on amnesia.

MARY: Really?

DANNY: Yes. It's called "Amnesiacs I Have Known But Can't Quite Recall."
He looks pleased at this little quip. But neither Oleander nor Mary crack a smile.

OLEANDER: Dr. Lucc . . .

DANNY: Danny.

OLEANDER: . . . he is very interested in your case. So much so that he has agreed to stay here and devote his full time to observing and in every way helping you.

DANNY: For two days.

OLEANDER: Yes, for a few days.

DANNY: Two.

OLEANDER: Two.

MARY *(she doesn't care):* Fine.

OLEANDER: So I'll leave you now to get acquainted. If you need me, Doctor, you know where I am.

DANNY: Yes sir. Thank you.
Oleander leaves. Danny pulls up a chair, straddles it and opens a file folder.

DANNY: I'd like to ask you some questions, Miss Smith.

MARY: Call me Mary.

DANNY *(immediately alert):* Then you recognize Mary as your real name?

MARY: No. But I don't recognize Miss Smith, either. *(Beat.)* Zelda says my real name is Cecilia Skolnick. Is it?

DANNY: Scarlick. Yes, that's what she says, but we've got to check that out. In the meantime, the chart lists you as Mary Smith. Do you live in Chicago, Miss Smith?

MARY: Chicago? *(Thinks.)* Yes. What's with the names?

DANNY *(looks up):* Pardon?

MARY: Why are you so carefully "Danny" and I "Miss Smith?"

DANNY *(smiles at this perception):* Bothers me. The doctor thing. Patient walks into a doctor's office and it's Doctor So-and-So. But no matter how old or young the patient is, or rich or poor or sick or well, it's always the condescending first name.

MARY: And you don't do that with your patients.

DANNY: I don't have patients.

MARY: But you're a doctor.

DANNY: I don't practice.

MARY: Ah, you've perfected it.

LONG WHARF THEATER, NEW HAVEN—Richard Backus as Danny, Barbara Barrie as Mary and Alexandra O'Karma as Liz in *Fugue* by Leonora Thuna

DANNY: Bad joke.

MARY: I've been sick.

DANNY: I don't do people any more. People are too unpredictable. They don't always behave the way they're supposed to, and it throws me off. I give them an aspirin, and when I come back and the fever's not down, I scream, "What's the matter with you, the fever's supposed to be down!" I can't deal with it.

MARY: What do you deal with?

DANNY: Machines. They're more reliable. Garbage in, garbage out. And they don't call you in the middle of the night. Were you raised in Chicago?

MARY: I suppose so.

DANNY: You don't have a Midwest accent.

MARY: No?

DANNY: You sound very much as if you came from New York City.

MARY: Well, I suppose that's a clue.

DANNY *(reading the notes):* You were found on the Loop, walking through the cars of the El train. Back and forth, back and forth. At each station, you paused and looked out of the car. Then remained in the train, to continue your walk back and forth through the cars. Do you recall any of this, Mary?

MARY: No.

DANNY: When the police asked you what you were looking for, you said, "125th Street."

MARY: There you are. That's probably where I live.

DANNY: There is no 125th Street Station in Chicago.

MARY: Ah.

DANNY: But there is one in New York City.

MARY: Well! Talk about being on the wrong train!

DANNY: What about your meeting today? With your childhood friend? (*Glancing at a sheet of paper.*) Zelda.

MARY: Zelda. She's a flake. I don't know if she's from my past or a room down the hall. She's furious with me because I can't remember her. Listen, did you know my name was Skolnick?

DANNY (*checking the file*): Not Skolnick. Scarlick.

MARY: Scarlick?

NURSE'S VOICE: All right, Mrs. Skolnick, open your eyes.

DANNY: That's right.

NURSE: It's all over. You can go home now.

MARY: How does she know my name? Zelda.

DANNY: When the story broke about finding you in the El, several people recognized you. Or claimed they did. Zelda was one of them.

MARY (*mildly curious*): Who were the others?

DANNY: Nothing too meaningful. Mostly families looking for long-lost daughters or wives or mothers.

MARY: How did you weed them out?

DANNY: Details didn't check. Some were foreign. Obviously, you're an American.

MARY: And a New Yorker.

DANNY: Ah! You remember that?

MARY: You told me.

DANNY: Oh.

MARY: Forget?

DANNY: I'm allowed to forget.

MARY: My, you're touchy. Listen, why don't you go home?

DANNY: Do you remember *anything*?

MARY: No.

DANNY: Nothing?

MARY: Nothing.

> *Mary's mother appears. Mother is a bit heavy, usually wearing bright, cheerful colors—pinks, blues, yellows—gray hair—probably in her 70s now, though in her 50s at other times. A strong, honest, appealing woman (but now she is rather weak).*

MOTHER: Cele . . . help me out . . .

MARY (*winces*): Ah . . .

DANNY (*immediately observant*): What is it?

> *And her mother is gone.*

MARY: Nothing. (*Pause. She turns to him.*) I don't know. It's gone.

DANNY: But you remembered, didn't you? You remembered *something*.

MARY: It's like a tiny bird. Comes whizzing into my head. Whizzes right out.

FUGUE *was first produced at Long Wharf Theater under the direction of Kenneth Frankel on March 28, 1986, with Barbara Barrie as Mary, Peggy Cosgrave as Zelda, Jess Osuna as Dr. Oleander, Richard Backus as Danny and Rebecca Schull as Mother.*

HUNTING COCKROACHES

A Play in Two Acts

BY JANUSZ GLOWACKI

TRANSLATED BY JADWIGA KOSICKA

Cast and credits appear on page 451.

HUNTING COCKROACHES: Anka and Jan Krupinski are Polish emigres living in *"a squalid, shabby room, a mildew spot on the ceiling in the corner"* on the Lower East Side of Manhattan. In their native land, she was an actress and he a writer, both successful. Here in America—honored by a huge map on the wall of the room—they are having trouble finding a niche, and both suffer from insomnia. In the wee small hours, she is seated in front of the map and he is lying in bed, sleeping or feigning sleep.

SHE: . . . . . I told him he'd never make it here because he doesn't have a sincere smile. Everybody here has a sincere smile. And he's got a nasty one. He took it very hard. In Eastern Europe nobody has a sincere smile, except drunks and informers. *(Smiles.)* Yesterday he sat in front of the map and practiced the art of the sincere smile, checking it every so often in the mirror. I told him he should write a play about Polish emigres, but he said the subject is boring, either you make it or you don't.

HE *(waking or pretending to wake up):* What time is it?

SHE: An hour later than usual. Lately you've been asking me what time it is at 3 in the morning—now it's 4 in the morning.

HE: You've been screaming again . . . Lately you scream in your sleep all the time.

SHE: Do I?

HE: You sit up in the bed and scream. *(Imitates her scream.)*

SHE: You'll wake up everybody in the building.

HE: Then you go back to sleep immediately.

SHE: Immediately.

HE: Immediately. But I can't fall asleep.

SHE: Yes, I know, in the morning you have your lecture at Staten Island Community College. Where they don't pay you anything, but instead help us with our application for a green card. And you hate your classes, because: "How can you teach Kafka to students who drive to school in sports cars?" . . . All right, let's go to sleep.

> *They pull the blanket over their heads. Moment of silence.*

Oh my God!

HE: What are you dreaming about?

SHE: I'm not dreaming about anything.

HE: You weren't dreaming about anything?

SHE: No. I wasn't even asleep.

HE: But why did you start screaming?

SHE: Because I felt like it.

HE: Maybe you were dreaming that we were back in Poland.

SHE: No.

HE: Or that somebody broke into the apartment through the window.

SHE: We have heavy iron bars on all the windows. No one can get in through those bars.

HE: No harm checking.

> *At the window, shakes the bars.*

No, with those bars there, it would be impossible for anyone to get through that window. Your dreams are absolutely moronic.

SHE *(a look of disgust on her face, whacks the floor hard with her shoe, then whacks it again):* It ran under the floorboard.

HE: Cut it out. That old bag under us will call the super. He's been waiting for a chance to get rid of us. Do you know how much he'd get for an apartment like this? Nowadays, in a neighborhood like this? On the Lower East Side?

SHE: Oh, it's a terrific neighborhood all right. Some apartment. Constantly broken into, fifth floor without an elevator, cold in winter, hot in summer, and you can't put an air conditioner in because the fuses will be blown . . .

HE: We can't afford an air conditioner.

SHE: Muggers, rapers . . .

HE: It's a neighborhood for artists.

SHE: For cockroaches.

HE: What do you have against cockroaches? New York is full of cockroaches. They're everywhere. Even in millionaires' houses.

SHE: How do you know? Have you ever been in a millionaire's house?

HE: Cockroaches don't spread infection and they eat only garbage. Remember Gregor?

SHE: Gregor who?

HE: The hero of Kafka's *Metamorphosis.* The one who was transformed into a cockroach. His sister used to bring him fresh rolls, cheese and milk . . . he wouldn't even spit on it. The only thing he'd touch was garbage.

SHE: I've seen them touch our caviar.

HE: Even if they did, how much food could a cockroach eat?

SHE: Then it's the rats who eat up our food.

HE: The mice.

SHE: The rats.

HE: They're big mice. Anyhow, the mice eat the cockroaches.

SHE: How do you know?

HE: I watched them.

SHE: I heard that rats eat children.

HE: We don't have any children.

SHE: Aha . . .

HE: For God's sake, don't start that about having a baby. That's all we'd need. A baby. I'd like to know where we'd put it?

SHE *(points):* Over there.

HE: And what about us?

SHE: Over here.

HE: And what about me? Where'd I do my writing?

SHE: You're not doing any writing.

HE: I have nothing to write about.

SHE: Have you ever thought about writing nursery rhymes?

RIVER ARTS REPERTORY, WOODSTOCK, N.Y.—Elzbieta Czyzewska as Anka and Olek Krupa as Jan in *Hunting Cockroaches* by Janusz Glowacki

HE: Leave the baby alone.

SHE: That would change everything. You'd start writing. You wouldn't have any other way out.

HE: I'd always have one way out. Through the window.

SHE: With those iron bars?

HE: Let's go to sleep.

SHE: Let's.

Blackout. They lie down and pull the blanket up. the phone rings.

HE: What time is it?

SHE: Ten past four.

HE: Who could be calling at this time of night?

SHE: I have no idea.

HE: Burglars? Maybe they're checking to see if we're in?

The phone keeps ringing.

SHE: Well, answer it if you're so curious.

HE: Maybe it's the super. I told you not to pound on the floor. Maybe it's . . . *(Starts to whistle.)*

SHE: Stop that whistling. *(He keeps on whistling.)* You always whistle when you're afraid of something. I can't stand it any longer. Maybe it's who?

HE: The KGB?

SHE: The KGB?

HE: To scare me.

SHE: But why would they want to scare you?

HE: Because they know I hate them. Because I'm a writer, an emigre writer, and I could write something.

SHE: But you're not writing anything.

HE: But I could start writing at any time.

SHE: Then start.

HE: But I don't have anything to write about.

SHE: Why would they want to scare you? You're already scared of them. Maybe it's the Immigration Office?

HE: What for?

SHE: I don't know. Maybe someone squealed on us.

HE: Squealed about what?

SHE: That our visa have expired.

HE: But they promised we'd get green cards.

SHE: But we didn't get them yet. We've still got to go for another interrogation.

HE: It's not an interrogation, it's an interview. The fact that we got the notice to go means that everything's fine. Millions of people in New York are just waiting for that.

SHE: To go for an interrogation?

HE: To go for an interview.

The phone keeps ringing.

SHE: Maybe someone's calling from Europe? The time's different there. What time is it in Europe now?

HE: What time is it here?

SHE: Quarter past four.

HE: Then in Europe, it must be . . .

SHE: In the morning?

HE: Yes.

SHE: Then it must be someone from Europe.

HE: Andrzej is in France. Maybe he's calling. But just what do you think he wants from us?

SHE: Why did that guy from the Immigration office ask me that question?

HE: Maybe we should answer the phone.

SHE: Maybe we should.

The phone stops.

HE: Damn it, why did you tell me not to answer it? Now it's too late.

The phone starts ringing again. Twice only. A typical immigration officer crawls from under the bed. He spreads his papers and leafs through them. He's a very nice little bureaucrat and smiles radiantly throughout the interview.

HE: Immigration asks everyone the same questions.

SHE: Absolutely everyone?

OFFICER: Do you intend to engage in prostitution while you're in the United States?

HE: Take it as a compliment.

OFFICER: You haven't answered my question yet.

SHE: No, of course not, I don't intend to. But if I may . . .

OFFICER: Thank you. *(To Him.)* Did you come to America with the intention of killing the President of the United States? *(He clears his throat.)*

SHE: Is that a standard question?

OFFICER: I'm waiting for your answer.

HE: No. To tell you the truth . . . I don't understand.

OFFICER: Thank you. *(Puts his papers away.)* No more questions. That's all we wanted to know. *(Takes a step toward the bed, then stops.)* One more question. Have you ever been treated for VD?

SHE: What kind of VD?

OFFICER: That's exactly what I'm asking you.

SHE: No, never.

OFFICER: And you?

HE: No, never.

OFFICER: Thank you. You'll be notified when to appear for the next interview.

SHE: Excuse me, sir.

OFFICER: Yes?

SHE: Is it possible to obtain a temporary work permit? You see, we're in some financial difficulties, nothing serious but . . .

OFFICER: Sorry, that's impossible. But I don't want you to worry. As long as you don't work without a permit, you can sleep in peace.

HE: Thank you very much.

SHE: Thank you very much.

OFFICER: Not at all. Good luck to you.

Officer starts folding papers. Disappears under bed.

SHE: What I'd really like to know is whether they think that if you'd come to kill the President you'd give them an honest answer.

HUNTING COCKROACHES *was produced by River Arts Repertory at the Byrdcliffe Theater, Woodstock, N.Y. under the direction of Lawrence Sacharow on August 20, 1985, with Elzbieta Czyzewska as Anka (She), Olek Krupa as Jan (He) and Ray Xifo as Immigration Officer.*

A DIRECTORY OF NEW-PLAY PRODUCTIONS

Compiled by Sheridan Sweet

Professional 1985–86 productions of new plays by leading companies around the United States which supplied information on casts and credits of first productions at Sheridan Sweet's request, plus a few reported by other reliable sources, are listed below in alphabetical order of the locations of the producing organizations. Date given is opening date, included whenever a record was obtainable from the producing management. All League of Regional Theaters (LORT) and other Equity groups were queried for this comprehensive Directory. Those not listed here either did not produce new or newly-revised scripts in 1985–86 or had not responded by press time. Most of the productions listed—but not all—are American or world premieres. Some are new revisions, second looks or scripts produced previously but not previously reported in *Best Plays*.

Albany: Capital Repertory Company

(Producing director, Bruce Bouchard)

DREAMING EMMETT. By Toni Morrison. January 4, 1986. Director, Gilbert Moses; scenery, Dale F. Jordan; lighting, Dale F. Jordan; costumes, Lloyd Waiwaiole; sound, Kevin Bartlett.

Emmett	Joseph C. Phillips
Princess	Peggy Cowles
Eustace	Mel Winkler
George	Herb Downer
Ma	Beatrice Winde
Major	Frank Stoeger
Buck	Larry Golden
Tamara	Lorraine Toussaint

One intermission.

NOVEMBER. By Don Nigro. March 15, 1986. Director, Gloria Muzio; scenery, Rick Dennis; lighting, Larry Opitz; costumes, Lloyd K. Waiwaiole.

Aunt Liz	Mary Fogarty
Aunt Dor	Jane Welch
Aunt Moll	Phyllis Gottung
Mrs. Prikosovits	Jen Jones
Becky	Nicola Sheara
Rooks	Christopher Wynkoop
Mr. Kafka	Sherman Lloyd
Nurse Jane	Kymberly Dakin
Ben	Thomas Schall

Time: About 1980. Place: A nursing home near Arkham, a small town in the hilly rural part of east Ohio. One intermission.

THE PHANTOM OF THE OPERA (musical). Book adapted from Gaston Leroux's novel; lyrics, Kathleen Masterson; music, David Bishop. April 19, 1986. Director, Peter H. Clough; musical director, Hank Levy; scenery, Dale F. Jordan; lighting, Dale F. Jordan; costumes, Lloyd K. Waiwaiole.

Christine Daae	Yvette De Botton
The Phantom	Al DeCristo
Vicomte Raoul de Chagny	Joseph Kolinski
Usbek	Patti Perkins
Giulietta Giannini	Malita Barron
Mame Giry	Jan Buttram
Firmin Richard	John Barone
Armand Moncharmin	Robert Ousley
Meg Giry	Tracy Daniels
Gabrielle	Dyann Arduini
Jammes	Nicole Stokes
Madeleine	Carlotta Chang
Carolus Fonta; Faust; Fireman	Spencer Cherashore
Stanislav Kotyza; Mephisto; Ratcatcher	Will McGarrahan
Fraulein Krauss; Valentin; Fireman	Helen Lesnick

Madame Valla; Marthe;
 Fireman.................. Michele Ortlip
 Time: 1907. Place: France, The sprawling
Paris Opera House and Perros-Guirec in Brittany.

Staged Readings May 20–25:
WHEN THE MUSIC'S OVER. By Robert
Meiksin. Director, Susan Chast.

THIN AIR: TALES FROM A REVOLUTION. By Lynne Alvarez. Director, Kay
Long.
FAULT LINE. By Jon Klein. Director, Michael
J. Hume.
JUPITER AND ELSEWHERE. By Gram
Slaton. Director, Tom Bloom.
RAPIDS. By David Steven Rappoport. Director, Peter H. Clough.

Albany: Empire State Institute for the Performing Arts

(Producing director, Patricia B. Snyder; literary manager, Barbara R. Maggio)

RAG DOLLY (musical). Book, William Gibson; music and lyrics, Joe Raposo. October 25,
1985. Director, Patricia Birch; musical director,
Gregg A. Barnes; choreographer, Patricia
Birch; orchestrations, Stan Applebaum; musical
supervision and dance arrangements, Louis St.
Louis; scenery, Gerry Hariton, Vicki Baral;
lighting, Marc B. Weiss; costumes, Carrie
Robbins; sound, Abe Jacob.
Marcella.................... Tricia Brooks
Poppa....................... Gibby Brand
Doctors......... Neal Ben-Ari, Joe Barrett,
                         Gary O. Aldrich
Raggedy Ann................. Ivy Austin
Raggedy Andy............... Scott Schafer
Baby Doll......... Carolyn Marble Valentis
Panda.................... Jeanne Vigliante
General D .... David Schramm
Bat .... Pamela Sousa
Wolf .... Tom Pletto
Camel With the
 Wrinkled Knees .... Joel Aroeste
Witch .... Elizabeth Austin
 Company: Michaela Hughes, Nina Hennessey, Laura Carusone, Scott Evans, Helena
Binder, John Thomas McGuire III, Betsy
Normile.
 One intermission.

AN IMAGINARY REPORT ON AN AMERICAN ROCK FESTIVAL (musical). Adapted
for the American stage by W.A. Frankonis;
based on the novel by Tibor Dery; music, Gabor
Presser; lyrics, Anna Adamis. March 14, 1986.
Director, Rose Deak; scenery, Loren Sherman; lighting, Victor En Yu Tan; costumes,
Karen Krammer; staging, Patricia Birch.
Ester..................... Jeanne Vigliante
Jozsef .... Joseph Larrabee-Quandt
Beverly .... Lynnie Godfrey
Boy....................... Daniel Baum
Bill .... C.E. Smith
Manuel................. Forest Dino Ray

Joshua...................... Joel Aroeste
Marianne .... Betsy Normile
Frantisek .... Leonard John Crofoot
Rene.................... Gary O. Aldrich
Marianne's Husband......... Steve Owsley
District Attorney.......... David Pendleton
Witness.................... Greg Mowry
Hell's Angel;
 Voice of Arrowcross Bird ..... John Romeo
Juana .... Reena Phillips
Lucy Sky .... Laura Carusone
Sister Peace .... Carole Edie Smith
Maryjane .... Terri Garcia
Siren .... Joie Gallo
Pennilane .... Tracy Silver
Bobby X.................. Gregory Butler
Pinball .... Kevin Chinn
Speed .... Christopher Lipari
 One intermission.

A CLASS "C" TRIAL IN YOKOHOMA. By
Roger Cornish. April 1, 1986. Director, Ed
Lange; scenery, Anne Gibson; lighting, Victor
En Yu Tan; costumes, Gregg A. Barnes.
Lt. George Pelham .... David Bunce
Cmdr. Art Brown .... Gerard Curran
Sgt. Perry Sato.............. Doug Yasuda
Mama-san; Miss Fukuda;
 Nurse Haga.............. Lauren Mitsuyo
Dr. Kinosada Abbe.............. Isao Sato
Bailiff .... George Rafferty
G.I...................... Paul Evans III
Court Reporter .... Tom Orr
Capt. William Johnson.......... Kurt Ziskie
Maj. Chester Goss.......... George Siletzky
Capt. Berry .... Joseph Larrabee-Quandt
Col. P.J. Flynn .... William Metzo
Michi-ko.................. Mariye Inouye
Dr. Yoshita .... Tom Matsusaka
Dr. Kase................ Keenan K. Shimizu
Nurse Yoshiko Fujino................. Ako
G.I. Patient .... Eric Gulotty
Capt. Jaeger...... John Thomas McGuire III

Time: 1948. Place: Yokohama. One intermission.

GREAT EXPECTATIONS. Adapted from the Charles Dickens novel by Barbara Field. May 3, 1986. Director, Terence Lamude; scenery, Wynn Thomas; lighting, Frances Aronson; costumes, Barbara Forbes; sound, Tom Gould.

Allentown: Pennsylvania Stage Company

(Artistic director, Gregory S. Hurst)

QUALITY TIME. By Barbara Field. February 14, 1986. Director, Gregory S. Hurst; scenery, Atkin Pace; costumes, Karen Gerson; lighting, Curtis Dretsch.

Cast: Barry Cullison, Joanne Camp, Roscoe Born.
One intermission.

Blue Lake, Calif.: Dell'Arte Players Company

(Artistic directors, Michael Fields, Donald Forrest, Joan Schirle)

THE ROAD NOT TAKEN. By Michael Fields, Donald Forrest, Joan Schirle, and Jael Weisman. Director, Jael Weisman; scenery, Ivan Hess; lighting, Ted Vukovich; costumes, Nancy Betts; music, Tony Heimer.
Howard Deck; Charles Carson; Rick Pringle;
  Forest Ranger............. Michael Fields
Sam; Mrs. Carson; Rhonda James;
  Georgia Fipps; Carson Timber
  Representative............... Joan Mankin
Leonard James; Woody ...... Donald Forrest
Scar Tissue................... Joan Schirle
Boy Scouts...... Tony Heimer, Joan Mankin,
                                 Joan Schirle
Leslie Banks............... Lezley Troxell
Security Agent; Musician...... Tony Heimer
  Time and Place: Just prior to the public discovery of the Gasquet-Orleans Road, a road in Northwestern California under construction to give timber companies access to valuable land. One intermission.

WHITEMAN MEETS BIGFOOT (musical). Based on the comic book by Robert Crumb; adapted by Michael Fields, Donald Forrest, Joan Schirle and Jael Weisman; music and lyrics, Tony Heimer. Director, Jane Hill; scenery, Alain Schons; lighting, Michael Foster; costumes, Nancy Betts.

Mrs. Mildred Binky; Louise Whiteman;
  The Old One; Dr. Greyface;
  Accordian Player .... Joan Schirle
Mr. Natural; Pop Bigfoot..... Michael Fields
Technician; Yeti .... Donald Forrest
Band Leader; Baby Bigfoot; Sax
  Player .... Tony Heimer
Tyrolean Boys .. Donald Forrest, Jael Weisman
The Swell Sisters......... Bernadette Sabath,
                                 Joan Schirle
Whiteman.................. Jael Weisman
Dick and Jane Whiteman.... Donald Forrest,
                                 Bernadette Sabath
Mama Bigfoot; Doctor's Assistant; Orderly;
  Mime................. Bernadette Sabath
Hunters.......... Todd Bruse, Joan Schirle,
                                 Bernadette Sabath

GOING TO WASTE. By Joan Schirle. Director, Ralph Hall; scenery, Eva Hedberg, Torbjorn Alstrom; costumes, Marguerite Hammersley.
Reynaldo Sanchez; Toto.... Torbjorn Alstrom
Buzz Tompkins .... Barrie Ryan
Hildur Tengbom;
  Karstina Blick............... Eva Hedberg
Julie Tompkins ..... Marguerite Hammersley
Edna Bower .... Beverly Crawford
Dick Mann; Nelson Barron..... Rod Gerber
  Place: Buzz Tompkins' house in the State Capitol. One intermission.

Buffalo, N.Y.: Studio Arena Theater

(Artistic director, David Frank; managing director, Raymond Bonnard)

ARSENALS. By Jeremy Lawrence. May 1, 1986. Director, Gwen Arner; scenery, D. Martyn Bookwalter; lighting, Brett Thomas; costumes, Bill Walker.

Frances Berman.......... Laurinda Barrett
Joanne Berman .... Tanny McDonald
Andrew Tobin .... Matthew Lewis
Mike Schwartz................ Mark Arnott

Larry Berman .... Richard Ryder
    Time: June 1982. Place: Frances Berman's apartment on the Upper West Side in New York City. Act I, Scene 1: Early morning. Scene 2: That evening. Act II, Scene 1: Saturday, June 12, 1982 late afternoon. Scene 2: Very late that night. Scene 3: The next morning. Scene 4: A night, two weeks later. One intermission.

Staged Readings:
FORTUNE. By Michael Paller. Director, Kathryn Long.
HIPPIES FROM HELL. By David Babcock. Director, Kathryn Long.

Chicago: The Organic Theater Company

(Artistic director, Thomas Riccio)

RUBBER CITY. By Thomas Riccio. September 17, 1985. Director, Thomas Riccio; scenery, Mary Margaret Bartley; lighting, Larry Schoeneman; costumes, Mary Margaret Bartley; original music, Keith Uchima.

Skippy; Jesus .... Paul Barrosse
Mama .... Alex Kerr
Betty .... Lolita Lorre
Little Anthony.............. Relioues Webb
Abe .... Andrew May
JFK .... Paul Raci
Chet .... Peter Van Wagner
    Time: Last day in the life of an Elvis impersonator. Place: Akron, Ohio. One intermission.

KISS IT GOODBYE. By Scott Jacobs and Michael Miner. Director, Thomas Riccio; scenery, Mary Margaret Bartley; lighting, Larry Schoeneman; costumes, Mary Margaret Bartley; sound, Keith Uchima.

Lila .... Julie Crisman
Bodenheim; McTwitters; Dr. Farkus;
    Soldier .... Frank Farrell
Dunne; McHugh; Bailiff; Insull; Hare;
    Judge .... Gary Houston
Maltby; Regan; Caruso.......... Alex Kerr
Vera; Mrs. Figello; Mrs. Palmer;
    Copyboy .... Lolita Lorre
Hecht .... Andrew May
Duffy;
    Duggan .... Tom Towles
MacArthur......... Brian Van den Broucke
Truman; Darrow .... Peter Van Wagner

Chicago: Victory Gardens Theater

(Artistic director, Dennis Zacek)

THE GOD OF ISAAC. By James Sherman. June 1985. Director, Dennis Zacek; scenery, Nels Anderson; lighting, Robert Shook; costumes, Nan Zabriskie.

    Cast: Isaac Adams—James Sherman; Mrs. Adams—Roslyn Alexander; Actress II (Shelly, Scarecrow, Eliza)—Petrea Burchard; Actor I (The Hasid, Steiger, The Tailor, Lion, Rabbi Blumstein, Pickering, Dad)—Bernie Landis; Actress I (Chaya, Dorothy, Isaac's Mother, Ma Joad)—Barbara Gaines; Actor II (Huck, The J.D.L. Member, Brando, Tin Man, Higgins, Tom Joad)—Dennis Cockrum.

    Time: Now and the past. Place: Here and various locales in Chicago and Skokie. One intermission.

YOUNG   PSYCHO-VIVISECTIONISTS MEET MARILYN MONROE. By Steven Ivcich. June 14, 1985. Directors, Sandy Shinner, Steven Ivcich; scenery, Paul Miller; lighting, Paul Miller; costumes, Sheila Myrcik.

Jack .... Steven Ivcich
Bobbie .... John Haskell
M2 .... Lauren Campedelli
Ann .... Holly Fulger
Simone .... Lisa Kaminir
    Time: The present. Place: Jack's studio.

WILD INDIAN. By Theodore Shank. September 25, 1985. Director, Dennis Zacek; scenery, Rick Paul; lighting, Chris Phillips; costumes, Patricia Hart; sound, Galen G. Ramsey.

Ishi .... Ramiro Carrillo
Alfred Kroeber .... Joe D. Lauck
Hilary Addison .... Dawn Arnemann
Wing Su .... Cheryl Hamada
    Time: 1911–1916. Place: The Yahi Indian exhibit in a gallery of the Museum of Anthropology, San Francisco. One intermission.

GENTRIFICATION. By Dean Corrin. January 22, 1986. Director, Sandy Shinner; scenery, Jeff Bauer; lighting, Rita Pietraszek; costumes, Ellen Gross.

Ralph Morales.................. Carlos Sanz
Jorge Fraga .... David Hernandez
John Wade................. Sephus Booker
Robert Behrend........... Scott McPherson

Place: A street in Chicago. Act I, Scene 1: The middle of the night. Scene 2: The next morning. Scene 3: That afternoon. Scene 4: Later, the same day. Act II: That night. One intermission.

MR. 80%. By James Sherman. May 28, 1986. Director, Dennis Zacek; scenery, Nels Anderson; lighting, Robert Shook; costumes, Nan Zabriskie; sound, Galen G. Ramsey.

Sharon .... Barbara Gaines
Patricia................... Petrea Burchard
Jan .... Dennis Cockrum
Leslie .... Frank Farrell
Sam....................... Fredric Stone
Ronnie .... Barbara A. Woods

Time: The present. Place: Upper West Side, New York City.

Studio Theater

SLUMMING. By Marisha Chamberlain. April 19, 1986. Director, Sandy Shinner.

Cast: Janice St. John, Chip Hess, Celeste Januszewski, Shira Pivan.

ASOLO STATE THEATER, SARASOTA—Barbara Dana and Tresa Hughes in a scene from *Forgive Me, Evelyn Bunns* by Janet Couch

Chicago: Wisdom Bridge Theater

(Artistic director, Robert Falls)

YOU CAN'T JUDGE A BOOK BY LOOK-ING AT THE COVER: SAYINGS FROM THE LIFE AND WRITINGS OF JUNEBUG JABBO JONES. By John O'Neal, Nayo-Barbara Malcolm Watkins and Steven Kent. June 27, 1985. Director, Steven Kent; lighting, Ken Bowen; original music, Michael Keck; sound, Michael Keck.

Junebug Jabbo Jones . . . . John O'Neal
    Time: The present. Place: Here. One intermission.

THE MIDDLE OF NOWHERE IN THE MIDDLE OF THE NIGHT. By Tracy Friedman.

Based on songs by Randy Newman. December 5, 1985. Director, Tracy Friedman; vocal arrangements, Nick Venden; orchestrations, Steve Rashid; choreographer, Tracy Friedman; scenery, Michael S. Philippi; lighting, Michael S. Philippi; costumes, Nanalee Raphael-Schirmer; sound, Rob Milburn.

Joe . . . . Roy Hytower
G.I. . . . . Don Franklin
Salesman . . . . Ron Orbach
Girl . . . . Hollis Resnik
Redneck . . . . Neil Flynn
    Time: 1969. Place: A run-down Louisiana bus depot.

Costa Mesa, Calif.: South Coast Repertory

(Producing artistic director, David Emmes; artistic director, Martin Benson)

BEFORE I GOT MY EYE PUT OUT. By Timothy Mason. October 22, 1985. Director, David Emmes; scenery, Cliff Faulkner; lighting, Cameron Harvey; costumes, Barbara Cox.

Alex . . . . James Olson
Louise . . . . Pamela Dunlap
Hector . . . . Rick Najera
Nick . . . . Richard Doyle
Michael . . . . Timothy Shelton
Brooke . . . . Jessica Drake
Hermann . . . . Mark Del Castillo-Morante
    Time: February 1981. Place: A Caribbean Island. Act I, Scene 1: Afternoon. Scene 2: Evening. Scene 3: Later that night. Act II, Scene 1: Noon of the following day. Scene 2: That evening. One intermission.

DRIVING AROUND THE HOUSE. By Patrick Smith. January 24, 1986. Director, Martin Benson; scenery, John Ivo Gilles; lighting, Brian Gale; costumes, Charles Tomlinson; sound, Stephen Shaffer.

Grown-up Paddy . . . . Timothy Donoghue
Mommy . . . . Jane Atkins
Daddy . . . . Michael Canavan
Paddy . . . . Joe Dahman

Grampa . . . . Tom Rosqui
Debbie . . . . Gabrielle Sinclair
Uncle Billy . . . . Richard Doyle
    Time: 1963. Place: Middletown, Ohio.

UNSUITABLE FOR ADULTS. By Terry Johnson. March 14, 1986. Director, David Emmes; scenery, Michael Devine; lighting, Cameron Harvey; costumes, Susan Denison.

Kate . . . . Karen Hensel
Harry . . . . Wayne Grace
Tish . . . . Sally Klein
Nick . . . . Richard Doyle
Keith . . . . Troy Evans
The Man . . . . John Napierala
    Time and Place: The upstairs room of a pub in North London, last winter, and a cottage on Dartmoor, spring.

Staged Readings:

BOYS' LIFE. By Howard Korder.
ELAINE'S DAUGHTER. By Mayo Simon.
KILLERS. By John Olive.
HIGHEST STANDARD OF LIVING. By Keith Reddin.

Dallas: Dallas Theater Center

(Artistic director, Adrian Hall)

THE UPS AND DOWNS OF THEOPHILUS MAITLAND (musical). Book, Vinnette Car-

roll; music and lyrics, Micki Grant. October 1, 1985. Director, Vinnette Carroll; choreography,

Stephen Semien; musical direction, arrangements and incidental music, George Broderick; costumes, Donna M. Kress.
Miss Hannah; Miss Effie;

The Obiah Woman	Maryce Carter
Dolphy	Stephen Semien
Percy	Martron Gales
Winsom	Cathy Msingi Jones
Theophilus Maitland	Sam Wright
Rosa	Freda Foh Shen
Preacher Morris	Paul Osborne

Dr. Elyot Carter-Victor; Greedy Cut;

Inspector Ondercase	Michael Cherkinian
Rhinestone	Benita Arterberry
The Rhinestone Dancers	Martron Gales, Stephen Semien
Policemen	Paul Osborne, Gilbert Pritchett

Vendors: Sondra Murphy, Donald Ray Jones, Michael Cherkinian, Carol Fujii, Ben Bell, Tamara Sibley, Kriscia Hudgen, Gilbert Pritchett, Paul Osborne, Benita Arterberry.

Musicians: John Tatum, Arnold Sykes, Janice Franklin, Buddy Mohmed, Brent Nance, Ed Smith, Shawn Brown, Benn Bell Jr.

Time: May to December 1985. Place: Jamaica, West Indies.

KITH AND KIN. By Oliver Hailey. March 29, 1986. Director, Adrian Hall; scenery, Eugene Lee; lighting, Linda Blase; costumes, Donna M. Kress.

Tommy Joe	Robert Black
Darryl	Bill Bolender
Sarah	Christia Ward
Charlene	Margo Skinner
Big Boots	James Fields

Time: The present. Place: Daingerfield, Texas. One intermission.

Denver: The Changing Scene

(Artistic directors, Maxine Munt, Alfred Brooks)

SHADOWS OF CANYONS and THE FLAME. By Danny Kerwick. July 11, 1985. Director, Christine MacDonald; scenery, Dan Reeverts; lighting, Mark Cole; costumes, Margaret Sjoberg.
Shadows of Canyons

Barb	Ilise Gordon
Mac	Joe Marshall
Ed	John Fortin

The Flame

Xavier	John Fortin
Elizabeth	Ilise Gordon
Man 1, 2, 3	Joe Marshall

One intermission.

ANY GUITAR. By Don Malmgren. August 8, 1985. Director, Jacob Clark.

Eleanor	Georgia Athearn
Christopher	Gus Malmgren

Time: A misty day in May. Place: A room of a patio in a private estate suburb of a large U.S. city. One intermission.

HOSTAGES. By Mary Guzzy. September 5, 1985. Director, David Quinn; scenery, Paul Sehnerts; lighting, Kevin Bartlett; costumes, Lisa Mumpton; sound, Arthur James.

Spike	Jacob Clark
Cat	Susan Stringer
Molly	Peggy Russell

One intermission.

ALEXANDER. By Michael Hulett. October 10, 1985. Director, Margaret Mancinelli; scenery, Van Emden Henson; lighting, Van Emden Henson; costumes, Jane Nelson Rud; music, Steve Stevens.

Olympias	Akanda
Philip	John Bennet
Eurydice	Cynthia Papendick
Hephaistion	Roy Reents
Aristotle	Thomas George Thomas
Alexander	Conor O'Farrell

One intermission.

A Series of One-Acts, November 7, 1985
SIAMESE TWINS FACE FIRING SQUAD. By Richard Dean. Director, Dennis Bontems.

Alfredo	Jeffrey W. Nickelson
Jose	Jack Sullivan
Mama	Gloria King
Rosita	Cynthia Davies

THE CITY. By J.P. Allen. Director, Dennis Bontems.

Bates	Karl Greenberg
Jack	Lance Gray

TORNADO ULTRA. By J.P. Allen. Director, Richard Dean.

Jake	Charlie Wright
Rachael	Mary Leydon
Leah	Laurel Hunter
Larry	Ralph Palasek

One intermission.

ROAD. By David Earl Jones. February 6, 1986. Director, Dan Hiester; scenery, Dennis Bontems; lighting, Dennis Bontems; sound, Steve Stevens.

Henry .... Joe McDonald
Ottis .... Bruce Godsman
Construction Worker; Victim;
    Security Guard .... Blaine Stephens
Construction Worker;
    Policeman .... David A. Dalton
Becki....................... Robbie Raye
The Reverend .... James V. Aerni
Dorothy; Hitchhiker .... Alice Vaughn
    One intermission.

PORTRAIT OF DORA. By Helene Cixous. March 20, 1986. Director, Dan Hiester; scenery, Eugene Lee; lighting, Randolph Orenelaz; costumes, Christa Malgieri, Penny Stames; choreography, Jonelle Pascoe; music, Alfred Brooks.

Dora .... Shellie Ruston
Freud .... Alain Ranwez
Mr. B.................... Dimitri Cocovinis
Mrs. K. .... Frieda Sanidas
Mr. K. .... Dennis Bontems
Voice of the Play........... Irene Sclavenitis
Dora's Essence.............. Jonelle Pascoe

Denver: Denver Center Theater Company

(Artistic director, Donovan Marley)

WHEN THE SUN SLIDES. By Stephen Davis Parks. November 19, 1985. Director, Donovan Marley; scenery, Catherine Poppe; lighting, Wendy Heffner; costumes, Janet S. Morris.

William..................... Jamie Horton
Lola .... Caitlin O'Connell
Ginger .... Beryl Jones
Larry .... Mark Harelik
    Time: Christmas day and the day after, 1985.
Place: San Francisco. One intermission.

PLEASURING GROUND. By Frank X. Hogan. January 14, 1986. Director, Peter Hackett; scenery, John Dexter; lighting, Michael W. Vennerstrom; costumes, Janet S. Morris.

Truman Everts............. Michael Winters
Louise Everts............ Caitlin O'Connell
Samuel Hauser.............. Wiley Harker
Nathaniel Langford....... Michael X. Martin
Lt. Gustavus Doane .... Jack Casperson
William Henry Jackson ..... James Newcomb

Dr. Ferdinand V. Hayden . Frank Georgianna
    Time: The fall of 1871. Place: The Yellowstone region, before it became a national park. One intermission.

Staged Readings April 7–12:

CAL AND SALLY. By Robert Clyman.
FAT MEN ON THIN ICE. By Roger Cornish.
GOODNIGHT, TEXAS. By Terry Dodd.
THE WORLD OF MIRTH. By Murphy Guyer.
WATCH YOUR BACK. By Gary Leon Hill.
RACHEL'S FATE. By Larry Ketron.
HEATHEN VALLEY. By Romulus Linney.
AMERICAN DREAMER. By Carol K. Mack.
THE BALLAD OF EL GIMPO CAFE. By Jeff Carey.

Hartford, Conn.: Hartford Stage Company

(Artistic director, Mark Lamos)

A SHAYNA MAIDEL. By Barbara Lebow. November 12, 1985. Director, Robert Kalfin; scenery, Wolfgang Roth; lighting, Curt Ostermann; costumes, Eduardo Sicangco; sound, David Budries.

Rose Weiss........... Lindsey Margo Smith
Mordechai Weiss............ Mark Margolis
Lusia Weiss Pechenik .... Gordana Rashovich
Duvid Pechenik.............. Ray Dooley
Hanna....................... Kate Fuglei
Mama..................... Maggie Burke
    Time: Spring 1946, before and during the Second World War; and in fantasy. One intermission.

DISTANT FIRES. By Kevin Heelan. March 11, 1986. Director, Mark Lamos; scenery, Marjorie Bradley Kellogg; lighting, Stephen Strawbridge; costumes, G.W. Mercier.

Raymond .... Ellis E. Williams
Angel .... Barry Lee
Foos .... Leo V.Finnie III
Thomas................. David Alan Grier
Beauty .... Scott Dimalante
General...................... Art Kempf
    Time: Early 1970s. Place: The 10th floor of a construction site in Ocean City, Maryland. One intermission.

Horse Cave, Ky.: Horse Cave Theater

(Director, Warren Hammack)

EAST OF NINEVEH. By Jim Peyton. July 19, 1985. Director, Michael Hankins; scenery, Jon Partyka; lighting, Jon Partyka; costumes, Rebecca Shouse; sound, Tim Speevack.

John Bumpus . . . . Warren Hammack
B.W. Bumpus . . . . William Groth
Francine Boatwright . . . . Breton Frazier
Presence . . . . Bill Parsons

Time: Summer of 1955. Place: John Bumpus's small sitting room in a small community in Western Kentucky. One intermission.

Staged Reading:
THE DARKNESS AND THE LIGHT. By Sallie Bingham.

Indianapolis: Indiana Repertory Theater

(Artistic director, Tom Haas)

GOODBYE, MR. CHIPS (musical). Adapted by Leslie Bricusse from James Hilton's novel.

December 13, 1985.

Kansas City: Missouri Repertory Theater

(Artistic director, George Keathley)

Three From Kansas City: An Evening of Original One-Acts August 22 and 23, 1985
A CANDLE FOR JIMMY DREAM. By Philip blue owl Hooser. Director, Paul Burns; scenery, Chester White; lighting, Sharon Finley; costumes, Gwen Walters; sound, Charlene Taylor.
Kim . . . . Gina Thompson
Cheri . . . . Laura Schaeffer
Chip . . . . Craig Bushman
  Time: Night, September 30, 1985. Place: A hillside cliff overlooking I-435 in Kansas City, Missouri.
MISS MILLAY WAS RIGHT. By Felicia Londre. Director, Carl Hippensteel; music, Gerald Kemner; choreographer, Jennifer Martin;

scenery, Chester White; lighting, Deidre J. Fudge; costumes, Gwen Walters; sound, Reid Woodbury.
Lottie . . . . Trina Lance
Tracy . . . . Shilind McCall
Grammie . . . . Dorothy L. Williams
  Time: The present. Place: Grammie's house.
GODS AND UNBELIEVERS. By Martin Coles. Director, Ray Smith; scenery, Chester White; lighting, Deidre J. Fudge; costumes, Gwen Walters; sound, Charlene Taylor.
Leonid Andreyev . . . . Martin Coles
Figure in Grey . . . . Michele Kellerman
Anna Andreyev . . . . Vikki Marshall
  Time: 1919. Place: Russia.

Los Angeles: L.A. Stage Company

(Artistic director, Susan Dietz)

DELIRIOUS. By J. Bunzel. Director, Ron Link; scenery, Gerry Hariton, Vicki Baral; lighting, Gerry Hariton, Vicki Baral; costumes, Carol Brolaski; sound, Jon Gottlieb.
Nick . . . . Cyril O'Reilly
Mr. Richfield . . . . Russell Johnson
Hart Stephens . . . . Antony Alda
Real Cool . . . . Stogie Harrison
Naomi . . . . Barbara Howard

Cliff . . . . Dan Gerrity
Scott . . . . Tegan West
Lenny . . . . John Bunzel
Didi . . . . Claudia Christian
  Time: Now. Place: In and around Mr. Richfield's house, high in the canyons above Beverly Hills, over the course of an evening. One intermission.

Los Angeles: Los Angeles Theater Center

(Artistic producing director, Bill Bushnell)

NANAWATAI. By William Mastrosimone. September 6, 1985. Director, Lamont Johnson; scenery, Timian Alsaker; lighting, Timian Alsaker; costumes, Timian Alsaker; sound, Jon Gottlieb; music and collages, Fredric Myrow.

Sherina	Gina Gershon
Georgi Daskal	Philip Baker Hall
Anton Golikov	Tommy Swerdlow
Nikolai Kaminski	Adam Arkin
Samad	Gerald Papasian
Koverchenko	Bill Pullman
Shahzaman	Edwin Gerard
Taj Mohamud	Steven Bauer
Akbar	Stefan Gierasch
Iskandar	Mark Petrakis
Moustafa	Rene Assa

Village Women: Ariana Delawari, Setara Begum, Rahila Delawari, Soraya Delawari, Yasmine Delawari, Royo Fahmy, Khorshied Machalle Nusratty, Zarmina Popal.

Time: Spring. Place: Between Kabul and Jalalabad, Afghanistan. One Intermission.

IT'S A MAN'S WORLD. By Greg Mehrten. September 19, 1985. Director, David Schweizer; scenery, Simon Doonan; lighting, Barbara Ling, Greg Sullivan; costumes, Michael Kaplan; sound, Jon Gottlieb.

Harry Atwater	William Glover
Joey Fontina	Greg Mehrten
Cheryl Spring	Rhonda Aldrich
Eileen Mandel	Ruth Maleczech
Roy Rivertree	Roger Guenveur Smith
Red	Bill Raymond
Peter	Evan MacKenzie
Jon Waterson	Christopher Pennock

Time: Days and nights in 1974. Place: Interiors and exteriors in Los Angeles and Palm Springs.

A RICH FULL LIFE. By Mayo Simon. November 14, 1985. Director, Alan Mandell; scenery, Russell Pyle; lighting, Russell Pyle; costumes, Nicole Morin; sound, Jon Gottlieb.

Doris	Lois Nettleton
Christine	Rhoda Gemignani
Neil	Frank McCarthy
Ted	Peter Haskell
Alice	Rebecca Patterson
Bob	Malcolm Danare

Time: Several recent years. Place: A California condominium development.

THE QUARTERED MAN. By Donald Freed. December 19, 1985. Director, Mark W. Travis; scenery, Russell Pyle; lighting, Lawrence Metzler; costumes, Armand Coutu; sound, Stephen Shaffer.

Father Carl Cruze	Brock Peters
George O'Connor	John Carter
Reporter	Patti Yasutake
Sister Mary Agnes Cassidy	Diane Turley Travis
Graham Jones	William Glover
Julio Ortez	Robert Beltran
Maria	Nora Ekserjan
Ernesto	Ricardo T. Lopez
Buddy Heubing	Charles Parks
Mai O'Connor	Nancy Kwan

Time: The present. Place: San Jose, Costa Rica. One intermission.

HELP WANTED. By Franz Xaver Kroetz. December 26, 1985. Director, Robert Harders; scenery, Nicole Morin; lighting, Kathy A. Perkins; costumes, Nicole Morin; sound, Jon Gottlieb.

PART I

Steps
Billy	Dennis Redfield
Martha	Elizabeth Ruscio

Conversation
Man	Hal Bokar
Woman	Elizabeth Ruscio

Christmas Death
Husband	Hal Bokar
Wife	Sasha von Schoeler

Negative Balance
Woman	Elizabeth Ruscio

Last Judgment
Old Woman	Sasha von Schoeler
Old Man	Hal Bokar

PART II

Poor Poet
Writer	Brent Jennings
Woman	Sasha von Schoeler

Promises
Willie	Dennis Redfield
Mary	Elizabeth Ruscio

Homecoming
Anne	Elizabeth Ruscio
Charlie	Dennis Redfield

English as a Second Language
American Woman	Elizabeth Ruscio
Haitian Man	Brent Jennings

Time Out
Man .... Hal Bokar
Woman................ Sasha von Scherler
One Intermission.

I DON'T HAVE TO SHOW YOU NO STINK-
ING BADGERS. By Luis Valdez. Director,
Luis Valdez; scenery, Russell Pyle; lighting, Rus-
sell Pyle; costumes, Nicole Morin; sound, Jon
Gottlieb.
Connie Villa............. Anne Betancourt
Buddy Villa .... James Victor
Sonny Villa .... Robert Beltran
Anita Sakai .... Patti Yasutake
Time: The present, early in the year. Place:
Monterey Park, a suburb of Greater Los An-
geles, on the distant fringe of Hollywood, U.S.A.
Act I, Scene 1: Early Morning. Scene 2: Early
evening, the same day. Act II, Scene 1: Two
weeks later. Night. Scene 2: Six months later.
One intermission.

TUMBLEWEED. By Adele Edling Shank.
March 14, 1986. Director, Theodore Shank; sce-
nery, Karl Eigsti; lighting, Karl Eigsti; costumes,
Nicole Morin; sound, Jon Gottlieb.
Chavo..................... Rudy Ramos
Fanny............... Michael De Lorenzo
Alice..................... Ruth Manning
Anemone .... Ann Hearn
Paul .... Gregory Wagrowski
Lynn................... Margaret Klenck
Jean...................... Bette Ford
Ray.................... Frank McCarthy
Time: Act I, Scene 1: A night in late Septem-
ber. Scene 2: An afternoon ten days later. Scene
3: The next day. Scene 4: Later that night. Act
II, Scene 1: Sunrise the next day. Scene 2: Late
afternoon a week later. Scene 3: Before dawn a
week later. Scene 4: Afternoon five days later.
Place: An agricultural valley in Southern Califor-
nia.

Los Angeles: Mark Taper Forum

(Artistic director, Gordon Davidson)

THE BEAUTIFUL LADY (musical). Book by
Elizabeth Swados and Paul Schmidt, music by
Elizabeth Swados, lyrics translated from Russian
poets by Paul Schmidt. August 29, 1985. Di-
rector, Elizabeth Swados; with Jo Anne
Worley.

GREEN CARD. By JoAnne Akalaitis. May 29,
1986. Directed by JoAnne Akalaitis.

In the Works 1985:
THE DREAM COAST. By John Steppling.
MRS. CALIFORNIA. By Doris Baizley. Octo-
ber 22, 1985.

AMERICAN CONSERVATORY THEATER, SAN FRANCISCO—William Pater-
son and Joan Stuart-Morris in a scene from Nagle Jackson's comedy *Opera Comique*

PLANET FIRES. By Thomas Babe. October 29, 1985.
LEGENDS. By Kendrew Lascelles. November 19, 1985.

THE WASH. By Philip Kan Gotanda. November 20, 1985.

Los Angeles: Victory Theater

(Artistic director, Maria Gobetti)

Editor's note: The world premiere of Beth Henley's *The Miss Firecracker Contest* took place at this theater in 1980 under the direction of Maria Gobetti. This was wrongly credited to another theater in a previous *Best Plays* volume. We regret the error and are glad to set the record straight.

Louisville, Ky.: Actors Theater of Louisville

(Producing director, Jon Jory; literary manager, Julie Crutcher)

1985 Shorts, 5 bills October 30-November 17
Bill #1 (2 performances):
CHICKS. By Grace McKeaney. Director, Steven D. Albrezzi; scenery, Paul Owen; lighting, Jeff Hill; costumes, Marcia Dixcy; sound, David Strang.
Miss Phallon .... Veronica Castang
    Place. Kindergarten classroom.
A NARROW BED. By Ellen McLaughlin. Director, Jon Jory; scenery, Paul Owen; lighting, Jeff Hill; costumes, Marcia Dixcy; sound, David Strang.
Willie .... Patrick Husted
Lucy .... Debra Monk
Megan....................... Beth Dixon
John .... Bram Lewis
Nurse .... Ann Hodapp
    Time: The present, late winter. Place: Alvington, a tiny, rural town in upstate New York.

Bill #2 (2 performances):
21A. By Kevin Kling. Director, Frazier Marsh; scenery, Paul Owen; lighting, Jeff Hill; costumes, Marcia Dixcy; sound, David Strang.
    Ron Huber; Gladys; Chairman Francis; Student; Not Dave; Captain Twelve Pack; Steve; Jim Shiply—Kevin Kling
    Time: An autumn morning, the present. Place: The 21A bus that runs between Minneapolis and St. Paul.
MEGS. By Stephen Metcalfe. Director, Stephen Metcalfe; scenery, Paul Owen; lighting, Jeff Hill; costumes, Marcia Dixcy; sound, David Strang.
Bucky .... Bram Lewis
Megs....................... Steve Rankin
    Time: November 1974. Place: A dorm room.

Bill #3 (2 performances):
BOAZ. By Randy Noojin. Director, Larry Deckel; scenery, Paul Owen; lighting, Jeff Hill; costumes, Marcia Dixcy; sound, David Strang.
Clayton..................... Andy Backer
Rich .... Robert Brock
    Place: A living room in Boaz, Alabama.
ISLE OF DOGS. By Larry Larson, Levi Lee and Rebecca Wackler. Directors, Jon Jory, Larry Deckel; scenery, Paul Owen; lighting, Jeff Hill; costumes, Marcia Dixcy; sound, David Strang.
Tom .... Frederic Major
Willy .... Patrick Husted
Cuthbert.............. Christine Kauffmann
Dame Buckbill........... Veronica Castang
Viola....................... Suzanna Hay
Emilia...................... Peggity Price
Nicholas.................... Steve Rankin
I.A. Gold .... Ann Hodapp
    Time: The 1950s. Place: The town of Stratford, England.

Bill #4 (3 performances):
GOODNIGHT FIREFLY RAVINE. By Raima Evan. Director, Richard A. Cunningham; scenery, Paul Owen; lighting, Jeff Hill; costumes, Marcia Dixcy; sound, David Strang.
Ruby........................ Beth Dixon
Frannie..................... Zoe Jackson
    Time: Twilight, the end of August 1964. Place: On the porch and in the back yard of a small house in a small town outside Boston.
HOW IT HANGS. By Grace McKeaney. Director, Rob Spera; scenery, Paul Owen; lighting, Jeff Hill; costumes, Marcia Dixcy; sound, David Strang.

Sister Mosey............. Veronica Castang
Girlene Gillespy............... Debra Monk
Rowdy Gapp................ Suzanna Hay
B. Moore .... Robert Brock
Doll Fox.................. Peggity Price
Time: Early Sunday morning. Place: Arts Parts, a filling station outside Lusk, Wyoming. HOW GERTRUDE STORMED THE PHILOSOPHER'S CLUB. By Martin Epstein. Director, Frazier Marsh; scenery, Paul Owen; lighting, Jeff Hill; costumes, Marcia Dixcy; sound, David Strang.
Edgar .... Dana Mills
Edward................... Frederic Major
Jason................. Christine Kauffmann
Gertrude.................... Peggity Price
Time: The present. Place: The Philosopher's Club.

Bill #5 (2 performances):
KILLERS. By John Olive. Director, Kay Matschullat; scenery, Paul Owen; lighting, Jeff Hill; costumes, Marcia Dixcy; sound, David Strang.
Charles Blackwell .... Frederic Major
Landlady .... Suzanna Hay
Husband...................... Dana Mills
Earl.......................... Bob Burrus
Lou........................ Kevin Kling
VOICES IN THE HEAD. By Neal Bell. Director, Frazier Marsh; scenery, Paul Owen; lighting, Jeff Hill; costumes, Marcia Dixcy; sound, David Strang.
Arthur .... Robert Brook
Wes........................ Andy Backer
Jean...................... Adale O'Brien
The Head............. Christine Kauffmann

Humana Festival of New American Plays, February 27-March 29, 1986
TO CULEBRA. By Jonathan Bolt. Director, Jon Jory; scenery, Paul Owen; lighting, Paul Owen; costumes, Marcia Dixcy; sound, David Strang.
Agnes .... Beth Dixon
Charles De Lesseps....... William Verderber
Amault Rau................ Patrick Husted
Henri Barboux............ William McNulty
Jules Dingler .... Ray Fry
Lieutenant Lucien Wyse....... Larry Larson
Louise...................... Peggity Price
Baron Jacques De Reinach........ Levi Lee
General Istvan Turr .... Andy Backer
Philippe Bunau-Varilla........ Bruce Kuhn
Ferdinand De Lesseps....... Frederic Major
Time: 1876–1890. Place: In or near Paris and on the Isthmus of Panama, 1876–1890. The trail

occurs during the winter of 1889–1890 in Paris. One intermission.

ASTRONAUTS. By Claudia Reilly. Director, Tom Bullard; scenery, Paul Owen; lighting, Geoff Korf; costumes, Ann Wallace; sound, David Strang.
Francis Xavier Hoffman.... Wayne S. Turney
Bernice Bertolis.............. Debra Monk
Mary "Red" Dern.......... Louise Freistadt
JoDean O'Malley............. Peggity Price
Harvey Sherman .... John Shepard
Place: An apartment building in Forest Hills, New York City. One intermission.

NO MERCY. By Constance Congdon. Director, Jackson Phippin; scenery, Paul Owen; lighting, Paul Owen; costumes, Ann Wallace; sound, David Strang.
Young Roy Layton........... Robert Brock
Gene....................... Bruce Kuhn
Robert Oppenheimer.......... Jonathan Bolt
Jane...................... Melody Combs
Adam .... Jeffrey Hutchinson
Roy Layton .... Bob Burrus
Ramona Layton............. Adale O'Brien
Justin .... Joshua Atkins
Jackie .... Beth Dixon
Time and Place: The Jornada del Muerto area of southwestern New Mexico in mid-July 1945 and in different locations in the present.

SOME THINGS YOU NEED TO KNOW BEFORE THE WORLD ENDS: A FINAL EVENING WITH THE ILLUMINATI. By Larry Larson and Levi Lee. Director, Jon Jory; scenery, Paul Owen; lighting, Paul Owen; costumes, Marcia Dixcy; sound, David Strang.
Brother Lawrence .... Larry Larson
Reverend Eddie.................. Levi Lee
Place: A church sanctuary. One intermission.

HOW TO SAY GOODBYE. By Mary Gallagher. Director, Mary Robinson; scenery, Paul Owen; lighting, Jeff Hill; costumes, Marcia Dixcy; sound, David Strang.
Casey Staiger .... Suzanna Hay
Conor Staiger................. Adam Routt
Jana Sklarr................... Janet Zarish
Phyllis Castellano .... Christine Jansen
Marty Staiger................ Steve Rankin
Time: The action in the present takes place in 1980. The action in the past begins in 1972 and moves forward to 1979. Place: Cleveland.

THE SHAPER. By John Steppling. Director, Bob Glaudini; scenery, Paul Owen; lighting, Jeff Hill; costumes, Marcia Dixcy; sound, David Strang.

Bud........................ Lee Kissman
Jill........................... Jane Ives
Sherry..................... Debra Monk
Reesa .... Elizabeth Ruscio
Felix .... Dana Mills
Del .... George Gerdes
    One intermission.

SMITTY'S NEWS. By Conrad Bishop and Elizabeth Fuller. Director, Conrad Bishop; scenery, Paul Owen; lighting, Jeff Hill; costumes, Marcia Dixcy; sound, David Strang.

DeeDee.................... Suzanna Hay
Rob..................... Richard Ortega
Kim .... Melody Combs
Michael.................. George Gerdes
Dessie .... Jane Ives
LaMarr Washington .... Basil Wallace
Archie.................. Jeffrey Hutchinson
Francine.................. Adale O'Brien
Ted .... Bob Burrus
    Time: 1983. Place: Camden, New Jersey. One intermission.

Malvern, Pa.: The People's Light and Theater Company

(Producing director, Danny S. Fruchter)

New Play Festival, July 31-September 22, 1985
THE TATTLER. By Terri Wagener. Director, Abigail Adams; scenery, Joe Ragey; lighting, Joe Ragey; costumes, Megan Fruchter; sound, Charles Cohen.
    Cast: Greg Alexander, Carla Belver, Jessie K. Jones, Sean McKinley, Stephen Novelli, Shaw Purnell.
    Time: The present.

THE DEFECTOR. By Louis Lippa. Director, Ken Marini; scenery, Joe Ragey; lighting, Joe Ragey; costumes, Megan Fruchter; sound, Charles Cohen.

    Cast: Gerald Richards, Douglas Wing.
    Time: A winter day. Place: A room in the free world.

WHAT LEONA FIGURED OUT. By David J. Hill. Director, Tom Teti; scenery, Joe Ragey; lighting, Joe Ragey; costumes, Megan Fruchter; sound, Charles Cohen.
Leona Sayres .... Alda Cortese Jarvis
    Tangueray .... Carla Belver
    Time: Sometime between the two World Wars. Place: Somewhere in Tennessee.

Minneapolis: Illusion Theater

(Producing directors, Michael Robins, Bonnie Morris)

THE EINSTEIN PROJECT. By Paul D'Andrea and Jon Klein. June 20, 1985. Director, David Feldshuh; music, Kim D. Sherman; scenery, Paul Krajniak; lighting, Hugh Graham; costumes, Janet Groenert.
Einstein................... Ben Kreilkamp
Edward.................. Alfred Harrison
Werner Heisenberg .... Walton Stanley
Max Von Laue .... Randy Fuhrmann
Walter Gerlach .... Michael Robins
Otto Hahn .... Terry Bellamy
Fritz Haber .... Scott Glasser
Clara Immerwahr .... Mary McDevitt
Lisa Meitner .... Marysue Moses
Aniela Besant.............. Bonnie Morris
Hannah Gebhard............. Nanci Olesen
    Time: Selected moments from 1913 to 1945. Place: Germany, England and America. One intermission.

WANDERLUST. By Steven Dietz. June, 1985. Director, Steven Dietz; scenery, Hugh Graham; lighting, David Johnson; costumes, Robb Gordon, Kristian Kraai; sound, Lawrence Fried.
    Cast: Zach McGill—Rod Pierce; Sally Chase —Lizanne Wilson; C.J. Lincoln—Randy Fuhrmann; Rusty, Waitresses, Al Capone, Muriel, Mona, Liz, An Old Woman, Voice of Momma—Nanci Olesen; Cherry, Red, Amelia Earhart, Society Woman, Darla Sue, Customer—Buffy Sedlachek; Ed, Mitch, Apple Seller, Al Jolson, Preacher, Tagalong, Alex, Mr. Stewart, Voice of Poppa—Jim Haun.
    Time: 1925, 1945, 1965, 1985. Place: Various American cities. One intermission.

Montclair, N.J.: The Whole Theater

(Artistic director, Olympia Dukakis; managing director, Laurence N. Feldman)

ELECTRA: THE LEGEND. By Michael Sayers. Director, Austin Pendleton; scenery, Michael Miller; lighting, Carol Rubinstein; costumes, Sigrid Insull; sound, Richard Reiter; choreography, Elise Lynch.

Agamemnon....... Humbert Allen Astredo
Clytemnestra .... Maria Tucci
Electra; Iphigenia .... Beth McDonald

Orestes .... William Schroeder
Calchas..................... Tom Klunis
Aegisthus .... Daniel Southern
Cassandra.................. Kate Collins
Helen of Troy .... Novella Nelson
Time: The 11th Century. Place: The Trojan War.

Montgomery: Alabama Shakespeare Festival

(Artistic director, Martin L. Platt, managing director, Jim Volz)

THE IMAGINARY HEIR. By Jean-Francois Regnard, adapted and translated by Thomas D'Arfey. May 3, 1986. Director, Martin L. Platt; scenery, Philipp Jung; lighting, Paul Ackerman; composer, Matthew Greenbaum.

Lisette................... Patricia Boyette
Crispin .... James Donadio
Eraste .... Tom Rolfing
Geronte .... Charles Antalosky

Madame Argante............. Fiona Stewart
Isabelle .... Denise Krueger
Clistorel .... Tom Brooks
The Notary .... Tad Ingram
Pierre .... Tom Brooks
Geronte's Lackey................ Ty Smith
Time and Place: 17th Century France. One intermission.

New Brunswick, N.J.: Crossroads Theater Company

(Executive director, Rick Khan; artistic director, Lee Richardson)

TAMER OF HORSES. By William Mastrosimone. November 6, 1985. Director, Lee Richardson; scenery, Dan Proett; lighting, Susan A. White; costumes, Nancy Konrardy; sound, Rob Gorton.

Ty Fletcher .... Joe Morton
Georgiane Fletcher .... Michele Shay
Hector .... Tony Moundroukas
Time: Now. Place: The countryside. Act I, Scene 1: A week before Christmas. Scene 2: The same evening. Scene 3: A few days later. Act II, Scene 1: A few days after New Year's. Scene 2: Three weeks later. One intermission.

ROADS OF THE MOUNTAINTOP. By Ron Milner. February 12, 1986. Director, Rick Khan; scenery, Dan Proett; lighting, Shirley Prendergast; costumes, Anita Ellis; sound, Rob Gorton.

Dr. Martin Luther King Jr.. James Pickens Jr.

Coretta Scott King ...... Elizabeth Van Dyke
Ray............. Helmar Augustus Cooper
Howard .... Tommy Hicks
Abe........................ Jeff Mooring
Josh..................... Marvin Jefferson
Aaron .... Michael Genet
Time: 1965–1968. Place: Selma, Chicago and Memphis. Act I: Selma, 1965–1968. Act II: Chicago, 1966–1967. Act III: Memphis. One intermission.

THE COLORED MUSEUM. By George C. Wolfe. March 26, 1986. Director, Lee Richardson; scenery, Brian Martin; lighting, William H. Grant III; costumes, Nancy Konrardy; sound, Rob Gorton; original music, Kysia Bostic.

Cast: Arnold Bankston, Olivia Virgil Harper, Robert Jason, Myra Taylor, Vickilyn, Natasha Durant.

New Haven, Conn.: Long Wharf Theater

(Artistic director, Arvin Brown; executive director, M. Edgar Rosenblum)

PRIDE AND PREJUDICE. Adapted from Jane Austen by David Pownall. November 22, 1985. Directed by Kenneth Frankel; with Richard

Kiley, Marge Redmond, Peter Gallagher, Jane Fleiss.

Stage II

CRYSTAL CLEAR. By Phil Young. December 13, 1985. With Jack Coulter, Sofia Landon, Jessica Harper.

FUGUE. By Leonora Thuna. March 28, 1986. Directed by Kenneth Frankel; scenery, David Jenkins; costumes, Jess Goldstein; lighting, Judy Rasmuson.
Mary..................... Barbara Barrie
Zelda.................... Peggy Cosgrave

Dr. Oleander .... Jess Osuna
Danny.................... Richard Backus
Mother .... Rebecca Schull
Noel .... John Bowman
Liz .... Alexandra O'Karma
Tammy .... Laura White
Time: A two-month period. Place: The psychiatric ward of a university teaching hospital in Chicago. One intermission. (An ATCA selection; see the introduction to this section.)

New Haven, Conn.: Yale Repertory Theater

(Artistic director, Lloyd Richards)

FENCES. By August Wilson. April 25, 1985. Directed by Lloyd Richards; scenery, James D. Sandefur; costumes, Candice Donnelly; lighting, Danianne Mizzy; musical direction, Dwight Andrews.
Troy Maxson............. James Earl Jones
Jim Bono .... Ray Aranha
Rose .... Charles Brown
Gabriel .... Russell Costen
Cory .... Courtney B. Vance
(Raynell). Cristal Coleman, LaJara Henderson
(Parentheses indicate role in which the performers alternated)
Act I: Fall 1957. Act II, Scene 1: Fall 1957. Act II, Scenes 2–4: Spring, 1958. Act II, Scene 5: Summer, 1965. (ATCA New Play Award winner; see the introduction to this section.)

JOE TURNER'S COME AND GONE. By August Wilson. May 2, 1986. Directed by Lloyd Richards; scenery, Scott Bradley; costumes, Pamela Peterson; lighting, Michael Giannitti; musical direction, Dwight Andrews.
Seth Holly .... Mel Winkler

Bertha Holly .... L. Scott Caldwell
Bynum Walker .... Ed Hall
Rutherford Selig .... Raynor Scheine
Jeremy Furlow................. Bo Rucker
Herald Loomis........... Charles S. Dutton
(Zonia Loomis) .... Cristal Coleman, LaJara Henderson
Mattie Campbell ..... Kimberleigh Burroughs
(Reuben Mercer)....... Casey Lydell Badger, LaMar James Fedrick
Molly Cunningham.......... Kimberly Scott
Martha Pentecost .... Angela Bassett
(Parentheses indicate roles in which the performers alternated)
One intermission.

Winterfest, January 9, 1986–February 8, 1986

STITCHERS AND STARLIGHT TALKERS. Kathleen Betsko.
UNION BOYS. James Yoshimura.
CRAZY FROM THE HEART. Edit Vilarreal.
A CHILD'S TALE. Carl Capotorto.

Norfolk: Virginia Stage Company

(Artistic director, Charles Towers; managing director, Dan J. Martin)

WETTER THAN WATER. By Deborah Pryor. January 8, 1986. Director, Charles Towers; scenery, Michael Miller; lighting, Dirk Kuyk III; costumes, Candice Cain.

Staged Readings:

HAUT GOUT. By Allan Havis.
THE BEASTLY BEATITUDES OF BALTHEZAR. By J.P. Donleavy.

Park Forest: Illinois Theater Center

HANGIN' ROUND (musical revue). Book, Steve S. Billig. April 18, 1986. Director, Steve S. Billig; musical direction, Jonathan Roark; choreography, Lorian Stein; scenery, Jonathan Roark.

Sara....................... Laura Collins
Bert....................... Steve S. Billig
Harold .... David Katz
Jean...................... Vivian O'Brien
Ruth .... Etel Billig

Marie . . . . Judy McLaughlin
Tim . . . . R. Scott Brigham
    Time: The present. Place: A representative

lounge in a senior citizen apartment building located near a large city. One intermission.

Portsmouth, N.H.: *Theater by the Sea*

(Artistic director, Tom Celli; managing director, Janet Wade)

I'LL BE BACK BEFORE MIDNIGHT. By Peter Colley. October 3, 1986. Director, Tom Celli; scenery, Gary English; lighting, David Lockner; costumes, Lisa Micheals.
Greg Sanderson . . . . John Hickok
Jan Sanderson . . . . Kate Phelan
George Willowby . . . . Frank T. Wells
Laura Sanderson . . . . . . Maxine Taylor-Morris
Robert Willowby . . . . Robert Spelvin
    Place: A farmhouse near the Vermont-New Hampshire border. Time: Act I, Scene 1: An evening in early spring. Scene 2: The next morning. Scene 3: That night. Act II, Scene 1: A few moments later. Scene 2: Evening, a week later. Scene 3: That night, just before midnight. One intermission.

The Foundary, New Play Readings:
PHYSICAL PURSUITS. By Kenneth Rich. October 21, 1985.
SANCTUARY. By Paul Mroczka. November 18, 1985.
CAN THIS MARRIAGE BE SAVED? By Robby Fried. December 16, 1985.
THE GREAT, GREAT BAY. By Wayne Williams. January 13, 1986.
CAL AND SALLY. By Robert Clyman. March 10, 1986.
I'M SORRY, I'M SORRY. By R.F. Foley. March 31, 1986.
THE MITZVAH. By Jo Weinstein. April 14, 1986.
THE GALES OF MARCH. By Lee Bollinger. May 12, 1986.

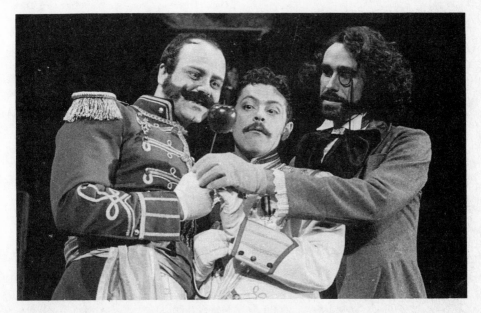

DELAWARE THEATER COMPANY, WILMINGTON—Allen Fitzpatrick, Mark Baker and Daryl Kroken in a new adaptation of *The Grand Duchess of Gerolstein*

Princeton, N.J.: McCarter Theater

(Artistic director, Nagle Jackson; managing director, Alison Harris)

CHRISTMAS GIFTS. By Robert Lanchester. December 19, 1985. Director, Robert Lanchester; scenery, Robert Little; lighting, Don Ehman; costumes, Barb Taylor; musical director, Richard M. Loatman.

Cast: Jerome Butler, Randy Lilly, Mary Martello, Cynthia Martells, Penelope Reed, Greg Thornton.

Staged Readings:

A SAINT BY ANY OTHER NAME. By Joseph Hart.

DOWN DEEP IN NEW ORLEANS. By Charles Wilbert.
BEFORE THE EVOLUTION OF THE SENSES. By John Reaves.
SOLO FLIGHT. By John Reaves.
GROTESQUE LOVESONGS. By Don Nigro.
FAT MEN ON THIN ICE. By Robert Cornish.
WAITER STATION and THE LOST COLONY. By Wendy MacLeod.

St. Paul: Actors Theater of St. Paul

(Artistic director, Michael Andrew Miner)

TRAKKER'S TEL. Created by Randall Davidson, Janie Geiser and D. Scott Glasser in collaboration with the Actors Theater Company. Director, D. Scott Glasser; scenery, Janie Geiser; lighting, Nayna Ramey; costumes, Janie Geiser.
The Tribe:

Olman	Paul Boesing
Belka	Charlotte Gibson
Trakker	Tim Goodwin
Sinda	Nanci Olesen
Xan	Mari Rovang
Timbul	John Seibert
Ratliff	Bart Tinapp
Libaron	Sally Wingert
The Weerdman	David Lenthall

The Troupe:

Zackajack	David M. Kwiat
Sonya	Dolores Noah
Col	Lizanne Wilson

Time: In the distant future after The Long Night. One intermission.

JOYOUS NOEL! A NOEL COWARD MUSIC HALL (musical). Words and music, Noel Coward. Director, David Ira Goldstein; musical director, Paul Boesing; choreographer, Randy

Winkler; scenery, James Guenther; lighting, Jean Montgomery; costumes, Karen Nelson.

The Company: Carole Jean Anderson, Paul Boesing, D. Scott Glasser, Tim Goodwin, Craig Johnson, Margit Moe, Dolores Noah, John Seibert.

MORE FUN THAN BOWLING. By Steven Dietz. Director, George C. White; scenery, Dick Leerhoff; lighting, Nayna Ramey; costumes, Chris Johnson.

Jake Tomlinson	James Cada
Molly Tomlinson	Annie Enneking
Lois	Terry Heck
Loretta	Nanci Olesen
Mister Dyson	John Seibert

Time: May of the present, and moments from the recent past. Place: A hill overlooking the small midwestern town of Turtle Rapids.

Staged Readings:

BLUE NIGHT. By Janie Geiser; music, Chip Epsten.
AMONG DREAMS. Stories, Barry Casselman; music, Randall Davidson.
PAINTING IT RED (musical). Book, Steven Dietz; music, Gary Rue; lyrics, Leslie Ball.

St. Petersburg, Fla.: The American Stage

(Artistic director, Victoria Holloway)

I LOVE ALICE. Based on *The Merry Wives of Windsor* by William Shakespeare; adapted by Peter Massey and Victoria Holloway; music, John Franceschina. November 29, 1985. Director, Victoria Holloway; musical treatment, Peter Massey; musical director, William Wade; choreographers, Karen Cardarella, Peter Massey; scenery, Sandy Eppling, Paul Eppling; lighting,

Peter Jay; costumes, Shari Kinney, Hugh Slack, Sandy Eppling, Joanne Johnson.

Jack Rugby .... Nevin De Turk
Alice Ford .... Ricci Mann
Meg Page............... Catherine Van Orr
Robin .... Joanne Johnson
Robert Shallow .... Robert Kelker Kelly
George Page............. Weston Blakesley

Dr. Caius .... Raymond Victorio
John Falstaff .... Patrick Nance
Frank Ford .... James Finnegan
Anne Page .... Karen Cardarella
Fenton .... Peter Massey
Beautician, Musician......... Susan Williams
Accompanist .... William Wade
   Time: 1950. Place: The suburbs of Windsor.

San Diego: Old Globe Theater

(Executive producer, Craig Noel; artistic director, Jack O'Brien)

BERT AND MAISY. By Robert Lord. November 30, 1985. Director, Robert Berlinger; scenery, Kent Dorsey; lighting, Kent Dorsey; costumes, Christina Haatainen; sound, Debby Van Poucke.

Bert.................... Ian Abercrombie
Tom .... David Harum
Maisy .... Anne Gee Byrd
Shona .... Laura Esterman
Grant .... Steven Peterman
   Place: The home of Bert and Maisy in a small town in New Zealand. Act I, Scene 1: An afternoon in early summer, not too long ago. Scene 2: A short while later. Scene 3: Later that night. Act

II, Scene 1: Saturday afternoon, a week later. Scene 2: Early afternoon, a few weeks later. One intermission.

Staged Readings:

NOCTURNE. By Brandley Rand Smith.
AMERICAN TATTOO. By Philip Kan Gotanda.
NATIVE AMERICAN. By Constance Congdon.
THE GENTLEMEN OF FIFTH AVENUE. By James Penzi.
THE DOLLMAKER. By Jose Rivera.

San Francisco: American Conservatory Theater

(Janice Hutchins, director)

THE MAJESTIC KID (musical). Book, Mark Medoff; music, Jan Scarborough; lyrics, Mark Medoff and Jan Scarborough. October 9, 1985. Director, Edward Hastings; scenery, Jesse Hollis; lighting, Derek Duarte; sound, Todd Barton, Douglas Faerber.

Judge William S. Hart
   Finlay .... Lawrence Hecht
Aaron Weiss .... Scot Bishop
Ava Jean Pollard............. Nike Doukas
Lisa Belmondo.............. Michelle Casey
The Laredo Kid .... Mark Murphey
   One intermission.

OPERA COMIQUE. By Nagle Jackson. November 6, 1985. Director, Nagle Jackson; scenery, Jesse Hollis; lighting, Derek Duarte; costumes, Fritha Knudsen; sound, Christopher Moore.

Odile......................... Joy Carlin
M. de la Corniche.......... Dakin Matthews
La Tartine .... Joan Stuart-Morris
Madame de la Corniche ..... Marrian Walters
Viviane..................... Marcia Pizzo
Georges Bizet.............. Henry Woronicz
Ernest Guiraud .... John Castellanos
M. Paul Vigneron .... Peter Donat
Hector Vigneron .... Daniel Zippi
Charles Gounod .... William Paterson
   Time: March 3, 1875. Place: A corridor in the lobby of the Opera Comique, Paris. One intermission.

San Francisco: Eureka Theater Company

BOOMER! GEOFF HOYLE MEETS GEOFF HOYLE. By Geoff Hoyle and Anthony Taccone. May 28, 1986. Director, Anthony Taccone.

Sarasota: Asolo State Theater

(Artistic director, John Ulmer)

FORGIVE ME, EVELYN BUNNS. By Janet Couch. April 18, 1986. Director, Alan Arkin; scenery, Bennet Averyt; lighting, Martin Petlock; original music, John Franceschina; sound, Bert Taylor.

Rose Leiberman.............. Tresa Hughes
Bertha Perry .... Dolores Sutton
Lonnie Batson .... Yvette Hawkins
Richard Fox................. Adam Arkin
Mitzi Fox................... Diane Kamp
Zachary Fox .... Anthony Arkin
Evelyn Bunns............... Barbara Dana

Voice of Rabbi Mander .... John Batiste
    Place: Rose Leiberman's Condominium Home, Westchester County, New York. Act I, Scene 1: A late Sunday afternoon, the first week in June. Scene 2: A Tuesday night, two weeks later, about 9 P.M. Act II, Scene 1: The following Sunday afternoon. Scene 2: Two weeks later, Sunday afternoon. Act III, Scene 1: That night, about 9:30. Scene 2: Sunday afternoon, two weeks later. Scene 3: A Saturday afternoon in late September. Two intermissions.

Sarasota: Florida Studio Theater

LEGAL TENDER. By Mark St. Germain. Director, Jeff Mousseau.
TENNESSEE JAR. By John Lewter. Director, Carolyn Michel.

BITTER BLOOD. By Griselda Gambaro; translator, Adam Verseyni. Director, Richard Hopkins.

Seattle: Seattle Repertory Theater

(Artistic director, Daniel Sullivan; producing director, Peter Donnelly)

CAT'S PAW. By William Mastrosimone. February 12, 1986. Director, Daniel Sullivan; scenery, Thomas Fichter; lighting, Rick Paulsen; costumes, Sally Richardson; sound, Michael Holten.
Victor .... John Procaccino

David Darling .... Mark Jenkins
Cathy .... Amy Caton-Ford
Jessica Lyons .... Kit Flanagan
    Time: The present. Place: Washington, D.C. One intermission.

Washington, D.C.: Arena Stage

(Producing director, Zelda Fichandler)

WOMEN AND WATER (revised version). By John Guare. November 29, 1985.

Waterford, Conn.: The O'Neill Theater Center

(Artistic director, Lloyd Richards)

National Playwrights Conference July 7–August 4, 1985

FUN. By James Bosley.
A CHILD'S TALE. By Carl Capotorto.
JAZZ WIVES JAZZ LIVES. By Laura Maria Censabella.
THAW: A RUSSIAN MELODRAMA. By Roger Cornish.

FUN IN THE PHYSICAL WORLD. By James D'Entremont.
DEUTSCHLAND. By Robert Kinerk.
OAK AND IVY. By Kathleen McGhee-Anderson.
JOSH WHITE—AN AMERICAN FOLKTALE. By OyamO.
JASS. By John Pielmeier.

ALL GOOD MEN. By George Rubino.
TRINITY SITE. By Janeice Scarbrough.
THE DREAMER EXAMINES HIS PIL-
LOW. By John Patrick Shanley.

BUTTERFLY. By Richard Wesley.
IN THIS FALLEN CITY. By Bryan Wil-
liams.
UNION BOYS. By James Yoshimura.

Wilmington: Delaware Theater Company

(Artistic director, Cleveland Morris; managing director, Dennis Luzak)

THE GRAND DUCHESS OF GEROL-
STEIN. New adaptation by Cleveland Morris
and Judy Brown; music, Jacques Offenbach; lyr-
ics, Ludovic Halevy. April 3, 1986. Director,
Cleveland Morris; musical director, Judy
Brown; scenery, Lewis Folden; lighting, Bruce
K. Morris; costumes, Catherine Adair.

Schwartz	Gary Newcomb
Schumacher	John Heffron
Schulz	Richard Coombs
Olga	Sarah Hills
Amelie	Deborah DeHart
Iza	Kristine Miller
Fritz	Scott Waara
Wanda	Lorraine Goodman
General Boum	Allen Fitzpatrick
Baron Puck	Daryl Kroken
The Grand Duchess of Gerolstein	Connie Coit
Pages	Stephen Lashbrook, David Wright
Prince Paul	Mark Baker
Baron Grog	David Van Der Veen

Time: Late 1860s. Place: The Grand Duchy of
Gerolstein. One intermission.

Woodstock, N.Y.: Byrdcliffe Theater, River Arts Repertory

(Artistic director, Lawrence Sacharow)

HUNTING COCKROACHES. By Janusz
Glowacki; translated by Jadwiga Kosicka. August 20, 1985. Directed by Lawrence Sacharow; scenery, Marek Dobrowolski; costumes,
Marianne Powell-Parker; lighting, Frances Aronson.

Anka Krupinski	Elzbieta Czyzewska
Jan Krupinski	Olek Krupa
Mr. Thompson; Rysio; Immigration Officer	Ray Xifo
Mrs. Thompson	Deirdre O'Connell
Czesio; Bum	Mark Margolis
Voice of TV Announcer	Sean O'Brien

Time and Place: One night in a Lower East
Side apartment in Manhattan. One intermission.
(An ATCA selection; see introduction to this
section.)

FACTS AND
FIGURES

LONG RUNS ON BROADWAY

The following shows have run 500 or more continuous performances in a single production, usually the first, not including previews or extra non-profit performances, allowing for vacation layoffs and special one-booking engagements, but not including return engagements after a show has gone on tour. In all cases the numbers were obtained directly from the shows' production offices. Where there are title similarities, the production is identified as follows: (p) straight play version, (m) musical version, (r) revival.

THROUGH MAY 31, 1986

(PLAYS MARKED WITH ASTERISK WERE STILL PLAYING JUNE 1, 1986)

Plays	Number Performances	Plays	Number Performances
*A Chorus Line	4,504	Mame (m)	1,508
*Oh! Calcutta! (r)	4,258	Same Time, Next Year	1,453
Grease	3,388	Arsenic and Old Lace	1,444
Fiddler on the Roof	3,242	The Sound of Music	1,443
Life With Father	3,224	How To Succeed in Business	
Tobacco Road	3,182	Without Really Trying	1,417
Hello, Dolly!	2,844	Hellzapoppin	1,404
My Fair Lady	2,717	The Music Man	1,375
*42nd Street	2,405	Funny Girl	1,348
Annie	2,377	Mummenschanz	1,326
Man of La Mancha	2,328	Angel Street	1,295
Abie's Irish Rose	2,327	Lightnin'	1,291
Oklahoma!	2,212	Promises, Promises	1,281
Pippin	1,944	The King and I	1,246
South Pacific	1,925	Cactus Flower	1,234
The Magic Show	1,920	Sleuth	1,222
Deathtrap	1,793	Torch Song Trilogy	1,222
Gemini	1,788	1776	1,217
Harvey	1,775	Equus	1,209
Dancin'	1,774	Sugar Babies	1,208
Hair	1,750	Guys and Dolls	1,200
The Wiz	1,672	Amadeus	1,181
Born Yesterday	1,642	Cabaret	1,165
The Best Little Whorehouse in		*La Cage aux Folles	1,161
Texas	1,639	Mister Roberts	1,157
Ain't Misbehavin'	1,604	Annie Get Your Gun	1,147
Mary, Mary	1,572	The Seven Year Itch	1,141
Evita	1,567	Butterflies Are Free	1,128
The Voice of the Turtle	1,557	Pins and Needles	1,108
Barefoot in the Park	1,530	Plaza Suite	1,097
Brighton Beach Memoirs	1,530	They're Playing Our Song	1,082
Dreamgirls	1,522	Kiss Me, Kate	1,070
*Cats	1,521	Don't Bother Me, I Can't Cope.	1,065

Plays	Number Performances	Plays	Number Performances
The Pajama Game	1,063	Oliver!	774
Shenandoah	1,050	The Pirates of Penzance (1980 r)	772
The Teahouse of the August		Woman of the Year	770
Moon	1,027	Sophisticated Ladies	767
Damn Yankees	1,019	My One and Only	767
Never Too Late	1,007	Bubbling Brown Sugar	766
Any Wednesday	982	State of the Union	765
A Funny Thing Happened on		The First Year	760
the Way to the Forum	964	You Know I Can't Hear You	
The Odd Couple	964	When the Water's Running	755
Anna Lucasta	957	Two for the Seesaw	750
Kiss and Tell	956	Joseph and the Amazing	
Dracula (r)	925	Technicolor Dreamcoat (r)	747
Bells Are Ringing	924	Death of a Salesman	742
The Moon Is Blue	924	For Colored Girls, etc.	742
Beatlemania	920	Sons o' Fun	742
The Elephant Man	916	Candide (mr)	740
Luv	901	Gentlemen Prefer Blondes	740
Chicago (m)	898	The Man Who Came to Dinner	739
Applause	896	Nine	739
Can-Can	892	Call Me Mister	734
Carousel	890	West Side Story	732
Hats Off to Ice	889	High Button Shoes	727
Fanny	888	Finian's Rainbow	725
Children of a Lesser God	887	Claudia	722
Follow the Girls	882	The Gold Diggers	720
Camelot	873	Jesus Christ Superstar	720
I Love My Wife	872	Carnival	719
The Bat	867	The Diary of Anne Frank	717
My Sister Eileen	864	I Remember Mama	714
No, No, Nanette (r)	861	Tea and Sympathy	712
Song of Norway	860	Junior Miss	710
Chapter Two	857	Last of the Red Hot Lovers	706
A Streetcar Named Desire	855	Company	705
Barnum	854	Seventh Heaven	704
Comedy in Music	849	Gypsy (m)	702
Raisin	847	The Miracle Worker	700
You Can't Take It With You	837	That Championship Season	700
La Plume de Ma Tante	835	Da	697
Three Men on a Horse	835	The King and I (r)	696
The Subject Was Roses	832	Cat on a Hot Tin Roof	694
Inherit the Wind	806	Li'l Abner	693
No Time for Sergeants	796	The Children's Hour	691
Fiorello!	795	Purlie	688
Where's Charley?	792	Dead End	687
The Ladder	789	The Lion and the Mouse	686
Forty Carats	780	White Cargo	686
The Prisoner of Second Avenue	780	Dear Ruth	683

Plays	Number Performances	Plays	Number Performances
East Is West	680	Wish You Were Here	598
Come Blow Your Horn	677	A Society Circus	596
The Most Happy Fella	676	Absurd Person Singular	592
The Doughgirls	671	A Day in Hollywood/A Night	
The Impossible Years	670	in the Ukraine	588
Irene	670	The Me Nobody Knows	586
Boy Meets Girl	669	The Two Mrs. Carrolls	585
The Tap Dance Kid	669	Kismet (m)	583
Beyond the Fringe	667	Detective Story	581
Who's Afraid of Virginia Woolf?	664	Brigadoon	581
Blithe Spirit	657	No Strings	580
A Trip to Chinatown	657	Brother Rat	577
The Women	657	Blossom Time	576
Bloomer Girl	654	Pump Boys and Dinettes	573
The Fifth Season	654	Show Boat	572
Rain	648	The Show-Off	571
Witness for the Prosecution	645	Sally	570
Call Me Madam	644	Golden Boy (m)	568
Janie	642	One Touch of Venus	567
The Green Pastures	640	The Real Thing	566
Auntie Mame (p)	639	Happy Birthday	564
A Man for All Seasons	637	Look Homeward, Angel	564
The Fourposter	632	Morning's at Seven (r)	564
The Music Master	627	The Glass Menagerie	561
Two Gentlemen of Verona (m)	627	I Do! I Do!	560
The Tenth Man	623	Wonderful Town	559
Is Zat So?	618	Rose Marie	557
Anniversary Waltz	615	Strictly Dishonorable	557
The Happy Time (p)	614	Sweeney Todd, the Demon	
Separate Rooms	613	Barber of Fleet Street	557
Affairs of State	610	A Majority of One	556
Oh! Calcutta!	610	The Great White Hope	556
Star and Garter	609	Toys in the Attic	556
The Student Prince	608	Sunrise at Campobello	556
Sweet Charity	608	Jamaica	555
Bye Bye Birdie	607	Stop the World—I Want to Get	
Irene (r)	604	Off	555
Sunday in the Park With		Florodora	553
George	604	Noises Off	553
Adonis	603	Ziegfeld Follies (1943)	553
Broadway	603	Dial "M" for Murder	552
Peg o' My Heart	603	Good News	551
Street Scene (p)	601	Peter Pan (r)	551
Kiki	600	Let's Face It	547
Flower Drum Song	600	Milk and Honey	543
A Little Night Music	600	Within the Law	541
Agnes of God	599	Pal Joey (r)	540
Don't Drink the Water	598	What Makes Sammy Run?	540

Plays	Number Performances	Plays	Number Performances
The Sunshine Boys	538	Fifth of July	511
What a Life	538	Half a Sixpence	511
Crimes of the Heart	535	The Vagabond King	511
The Unsinkable Molly Brown	532	The New Moon	509
The Red Mill (r)	531	The World of Suzie Wong	508
A Raisin in the Sun	530	The Rothschilds	507
Godspell	527	On Your Toes (r)	505
The Solid Gold Cadillac	526	Sugar	505
Irma La Douce	524	Shuffle Along	504
The Boomerang	522	Up in Central Park	504
Follies	521	Carmen Jones	503
Rosalinda	521	The Member of the Wedding	501
The Best Man	520	Panama Hattie	501
Chauve-Souris	520	Personal Appearance	501
Blackbirds of 1928	518	Bird in Hand	500
The Gin Game	517	Room Service	500
Sunny	517	Sailor, Beware!	500
Victoria Regina	517	Tomorrow the World	500

LONG RUNS OFF BROADWAY

Plays	Number Performances	Plays	Number Performances
*The Fantasticks	10,436	Cloud 9	971
The Threepenny Opera	2,611	Sister Mary Ignatius Explains It	
Godspell	2,124	All for You & The Actor's	
Jacques Brel	1,847	Nightmare	947
*Forbidden Broadway	1,816	Your Own Thing	933
Vanities	1,785	Curley McDimple	931
*Little Shop of Horrors	1,603	Leave It to Jane (r)	928
†You're a Good Man Charlie		The Mad Show	871
Brown	1,597	Scrambled Feet	831
The Blacks	1,408	The Effect of Gamma Rays on	
One Mo' Time	1,372	Man-in-the-Moon Marigolds	819
Let My People Come	1,327	A View From the Bridge (r)	780
The Hot 1 Baltimore	1,166	The Boy Friend (r)	763
I'm Getting My Act Together		True West	762
and Taking It on the Road	1,165	Dime a Dozen	728
Little Mary Sunshine	1,143	Isn't It Romantic	733
El Grande de Coca-Cola	1,114	The Pocket Watch	725
One Flew Over the Cuckoo's		The Connection	722
Nest (r)	1,025	The Passion of Dracula	714
The Boys in the Band	1,000	Adaptation & Next	707
Fool for Love	1,000	Oh! Calcutta!	704

†Erroneously listed as 1,547 in some previous volumes, owing to typographical error

Plays	Number Performances	Plays	Number Performances
Scuba Duba	692	Dames at Sea	575
The Knack	685	The Crucible (r)..............	571
*The Foreigner	678	The Iceman Cometh (r)	565
The Club.....................	674	The Hostage (r)	545
The Balcony..................	672	What's a Nice Country, etc.....	543
America Hurrah	634	Six Characters in Search of an	
Hogan's Goat.................	607	Author (r).................	529
The Trojan Women (r)........	600	The Dirtiest Show in Town	509
The Dining Room	583	Happy Ending & Day of	
Krapp's Last Tape & The Zoo		Absence...................	504
Story	582	Greater Tuna	501
The Dumbwaiter & The		The Boys From Syracuse (r) ...	500
Collection	578		

NEW YORK CRITICS AWARDS, 1935–36 to 1985–86

Listed below are the New York Drama Critics Circle Awards from 1935–36 through 1985–86 classified as follows: (1) Best American Play, (2) Best Foreign Play, (3) Best Musical, (4) Best, regardless of category (this category was established by new voting rules in 1962–63 and did not exist prior to that year).

1935–36—(1) Winterset
1936–37—(1) High Tor
1937–38—(1) Of Mice and Men, (2) Shadow and Substance
1938–39—(1) No award, (2) The White Steed
1939–40—(1) The Time of Your Life
1940–41—(1) Watch on the Rhine, (2) The Corn Is Green
1941–42—(1) No award, (2) Blithe Spirit
1942–43—(1) The Patriots
1943–44—(2) Jacobowsky and the Colonel
1944–45—(1) The Glass Menagerie
1945–46—(3) Carousel
1946–47—(1) All My Sons, (2) No Exit, (3) Brigadoon
1947–48—(1) A Streetcar Named Desire, (2) The Winslow Boy
1948–49—(1) Death of a Salesman, (2) The Madwoman of Chaillot, (3) South Pacific
1949–50—(1) The Member of the Wedding (2) The Cocktail Party, (3) The Consul
1950–51—(1) Darkness at Noon, (2) The Lady's Not for Burning, (3) Guys and Dolls
1951–52—(1) I Am a Camera, (2) Venus Observed, (3) Pal Joey (Special citation to Don Juan in Hell)
1952–53—(1) Picnic, (2) The Love of Four Colonels, (3) Wonderful Town

1953–54—(1) Teahouse of the August Moon, (2) Ondine, (3) The Golden Apple
1954–55—(1) Cat on a Hot Tin Roof, (2) Witness for the Prosecution, (3) The Saint of Bleecker Street
1955–56—(1) The Diary of Anne Frank, (2) Tiger at the Gates, (3) My Fair Lady
1956–57—(1) Long Day's Journey Into Night, (2) The Waltz of the Toreadors, (3) The Most Happy Fella
1957–58—(1) Look Homeward, Angel, (2) Look Back in Anger, (3) The Music Man
1958–59—(1) A Raisin in the Sun, (2) The Visit, (3) La Plume de Ma Tante
1959–60—(1) Toys in the Attic, (2) Five Finger Exercise, (3) Fiorello!
1960–61—(1) All the Way Home, (2) A Taste of Honey, (3) Carnival
1961–62—(1) The Night of the Iguana, (2) A Man for All Seasons, (3) How to Succeed in Business Without Really Trying
1962–63—(4) Who's Afraid of Virginia Woolf? (Special citation to Beyond the Fringe)
1963–64—(4) Luther, (3) Hello, Dolly! (Special citation to The Trojan Women)

1964–65—(4) The Subject Was Roses, (3) Fiddler on the Roof
1965–66—(4) The Persecution and Assassination of Marat as Performed by the Inmates of the Asylum of Charenton Under the Direction of the Marquis de Sade, (3) Man of La Mancha
1966–67—(4) The Homecoming, (3) Cabaret
1967–68—(4) Rosencrantz and Guildenstern Are Dead, (3) Your Own Thing
1968–69—(4) The Great White Hope, (3) 1776
1969–70—(4) Borstal Boy, (1) The Effect of Gamma Rays on Man-in-the-Moon Marigolds, (3) Company
1970–71—(4) Home, (1) The House of Blue Leaves, (3) Follies
1971–72—(4) That Championship Season, (2) The Screens, (3) Two Gentlemen of Verona (Special citations to Sticks and Bones and Old Times)
1972–73—(4) The Changing Room, (1) The Hot 1 Baltimore, (3) A Little Night Music
1973–74—(4) The Contractor, (1) Short Eyes, (3) Candide
1974–75—(4) Equus, (1) The Taking of Miss Janie, (3) A Chorus Line
1975–76—(4) Travesties, (1) Streamers, (3) Pacific Overtures
1976–77—(4) Otherwise Engaged, (1) American Buffalo, (3) Annie

1977–78—(4) Da, (3) Ain't Misbehavin'
1978–79—(4) The Elephant Man, (3) Sweeney Todd, the Demon Barber of Fleet Street
1979–80—(4) Talley's Folly, (2) Betrayal, (3) Evita (Special citation to Peter Brook's Le Centre International de Créations Théâtrales for its repertory)
1980–81—(4) A Lesson From Aloes, (1) Crimes of the Heart (Special citations to Lena Horne: The Lady and Her Music and the New York Shakespeare Festival production of The Pirates of Penzance)
1981–82—(4) The Life & Adventures of Nicholas Nickleby, (1) A Soldier's Play
1982–83—(4) Brighton Beach Memoirs, (2) Plenty, (3) Little Shop of Horrors (Special citation to Young Playwrights Festival)
1983–84—(4) The Real Thing, (1), Glengarry Glen Ross, (3) Sunday in the Park With George (Special citation to Samuel Beckett for the body of his work)
1984–85—(4) Ma Rainey's Black Bottom
1985–86—(4) A Lie of the Mind, (2) Benefactors (Special citation to Lily Tomlin and Jane Wagner for The Search for Signs of Intelligent Life in the Universe)

NEW YORK DRAMA CRITICS CIRCLE VOTING 1985–86

The New York Drama Critics Circle voted Sam Shepard's *A Lie of the Mind* the best play of the season on the first ballot by a majority of 11 of the 20 members present or voting by proxy, against 5 votes for *Benefactors* and 1 vote each for *The Perfect Party, Anteroom, Execution of Justice* and *Aunt Dan and Lemon.* The critics then named the British play *Benefactors* by Michael Frayn the best foreign play of the season, also on the first ballot, by a majority of 10 of 15 voting members, against 3 votes for *Let the Artists Die* and 1 vote each for *A Map of the World* and *Rat in the Skull.*

For the second season in a row, the critics decided to give no award for best musical, but they voted a special citation to Lily Tomlin and Jane Wagner for *The Search for Signs of Intelligent Life in the Universe.* Fifteen member critics were present and voting; five others voted by proxy in the best-play category; two others (Jack Kroll of *Newsweek* and John Simon of *New York*) were absent and not voting.

FIRST BALLOTS IN CRITICS VOTING

Critic	Best Play	Best Foreign Play
Clive Barnes Post	The Perfect Party	Let the Artists Die

John Beaufort *Monitor*	A Lie of the Mind	Benefactors
Michael Feingold *Village Voice*	Anteroom	Let the Artists Die
Brendan Gill *New Yorker*	A Lie of the Mind	Benefactors
Sylviane Gold *Wall St. Journal*	A Lie of the Mind	A Map of the World
Mel Gussow *Times*	A Lie of the Mind	Benefactors
William Henry III *Time*	A Lie of the Mind	Benefactors
Richard Hummler *Variety*	A Lie of the Mind	Rat in the Skull
Howard Kissel *Women's Wear*	Benefactors	Benefactors
Michael Kuchwara *Associated Press*	Benefactors	Benefactors
Don Nelsen *Daily News*	A Lie of the Mind	Let the Artists Die
Julius Novick *Village Voice*	Execution of Justice	Benefactors
Edith Oliver *New Yorker*	A Lie of the Mind	Benefactors
William Raidy *Newhouse Papers*	Benefactors	Benefactors
Frank Rich *Times*	A Lie of the Mind	Benefactors
Marilyn Stasio *Post*	A Lie of the Mind	
Allan Wallach *Newsday*	A Lie of the Mind	
Douglas Watt *Daily News*	Benefactors	
Edwin Wilson *Wall St. Journal*	Benefactors	
Linda Winer *USA Today*	Aunt Dan and Lemon	

CHOICES OF SOME OTHER CRITICS

Critic	Best Play	Best Musical
Judith Crist WOR-TV, *TV Guide*	The House of Blue Leaves	The Mystery of Edwin Drood
John Gambling *Broadcaster,* WOR-AM	I'm Not Rappaport	The Mystery of Edwin Drood
Alvin Klein WNYC Radio	A Lie of the Mind & The Search for Signs, etc.	Abstain
Jim Lowe WNEW Radio	The House of Blue Leaves	The Mystery of Edwin Drood
Richard Scholem Radio Long Island	I'm Not Rappaport	The Mystery of Edwin Drood & Tango Argentino
Leida Snow WNYW-TV	Benefactors	Abstain

PULITZER PRIZE WINNERS, 1916–17 to 1985–86

1916–17—No award

1917–18—Why Marry?, by Jesse Lynch Williams

1918–19—No award

1919–20—Beyond the Horizon, by Eugene O'Neill

1920–21—Miss Lulu Bett, by Zona Gale

1921–22—Anna Christie, by Eugene O'Neill

1922–23—Icebound, by Owen Davis

1923–24—Hell-Bent fer Heaven, by Hatcher Hughes

1924–25—They Knew What They Wanted, by Sidney Howard

1925–26—Craig's Wife, by George Kelly

1926–27—In Abraham's Bosom, by Paul Green

1927–28—Strange Interlude, by Eugene O'Neill

1928–29—Street Scene, by Elmer Rice

1929–30—The Green Pastures, by Marc Connelly

1930–31—Alison's House, by Susan Glaspell

1931–32—Of Thee I Sing, by George S. Kaufman, Morrie Ryskind, Ira and George Gershwin

1932–33—Both Your Houses, by Maxwell Anderson

1933–34—Men in White, by Sidney Kingsley

1934–35—The Old Maid, by Zoë Akins

1935–36—Idiot's Delight, by Robert E. Sherwood

1936–37—You Can't Take It With You, by Moss Hart and George S. Kaufman

1937–38—Our Town, by Thornton Wilder

1938–39—Abe Lincoln in Illinois, by Robert E. Sherwood

1939–40—The Time of Your Life, by William Saroyan

1940–41—There Shall Be No Night, by Robert E. Sherwood

1941–42—No award

1942–43—The Skin of Our Teeth, by Thornton Wilder

1943–44—No award

1944–45—Harvey, by Mary Chase

1945–46—State of the Union, by Howard Lindsay and Russel Crouse

1946–47—No award

1947–48—A Streetcar Named Desire, by Tennessee Williams

1948–49—Death of a Salesman, by Arthur Miller

1949–50—South Pacific, by Richard Rodgers, Oscar Hammerstein II and Joshua Logan

1950–51—No award

1951–52—The Shrike, by Joseph Kramm

1952–53—Picnic, by William Inge

1953–54—The Teahouse of the August Moon, by John Patrick

1954–55—Cat on a Hot Tin Roof, by Tennessee Williams

1955–56—The Diary of Anne Frank, by Frances Goodrich and Albert Hackett

1956–57—Long Day's Journey Into Night, by Eugene O'Neill

1957–58—Look Homeward, Angel, by Ketti Frings

1958–59—J.B., by Archibald MacLeish

1959–60—Fiorello!, by Jerome Weidman, George Abbott, Sheldon Harnick and Jerry Bock

1960–61—All the Way Home, by Tad Mosel

1961–62—How to Succeed in Business Without Really Trying, by Abe Burrows, Willie Gilbert, Jack Weinstock and Frank Loesser

1962–63—No award

1963–64—No award

1964–65—The Subject Was Roses, by Frank D. Gilroy

1965–66—No award

1966–67—A Delicate Balance, by Edward Albee

1967–68—No award

1968–69—The Great White Hope, by Howard Sackler

1969–70—No Place To Be Somebody, by Charles Gordone

1970–71—The Effect of Gamma Rays on Man-in-the-Moon Marigolds, by Paul Zindel

1971–72—No award

1972–73—That Championship Season, by Jason Miller

1973–74—No award

1974–75—Seascape, by Edward Albee

1975–76—A Chorus Line, by Michael Bennett, James Kirkwood, Nicholas Dante, Marvin Hamlisch and Edward Kleban

1976–77—The Shadow Box, by Michael Cristofer

1977–78—The Gin Game, by D.L. Coburn

1978–79—Buried Child, by Sam Shepard

1979–80—Talley's Folly, by Lanford Wilson

1980–81—Crimes of the Heart, by Beth Henley

1981–82—A Soldier's Play, by Charles Fuller

1982–83—'night, Mother, by Marsha Norman
1983–84—Glengarry Glen Ross, by David Mamet

1984–85—Sunday in the Park With George, by James Lapine and Stephen Sondheim
1985–86—No award

THE TONY AWARDS 1985–86

The American Theater Wing's Antoinette Perry (Tony) Awards are presented annually in recognition of distinguished artistic achievement in the Broadway theater. The awards are voted by members of the governing boards of the four theater artists organizations: Actors' Equity Association, the Dramatists Guild, the Society of Stage Directors and Choreographers and the United Scenic Artists, plus the members of the first and second night press, the board of directors of the American Theater Wing and the membership of the League of American Theaters and Producers, from a list of four nominees in each category.

The nominations (Broadway shows only) are made by a committee of theater professionals who are appointed by the Tony Award Administration Committee of the League of American Theaters and Producers. The 1985–86 Nomination Committee was composed of Jay P. Carr, critic, the Boston *Globe;* Schuyler Chapin, dean of the arts, Columbia University; Richard Coe, critic emeritus, the Washington *Post;* George Cuttingham, president and director of the American Academy of Dramatic Arts; Alfred Drake, actor; William Glover, former drama critic for the Associated Press; Leonard Harris, writer and critic; Dr. Mary Henderson, former curator of the Theater Collection of the Museum of the City of New York; Al Hirschfeld, caricaturist; Norris Houghton, author, producer and educator; David Oppenheim, dean of New York University's Tisch School of the Arts, and George White, president of the O'Neill Theater Center.

The Tony Administration Committee elected to change the category designation of "outstanding" to "best" and to add the word "leading" to actor/actress in both the play and musical categories. Thus, "outstanding actor in a play" is now "best leading actor in a play, etc."

The list of 1985–86 nominees follows, with winners in each category listed in **bold face type.**

BEST PLAY (award goes to both author and producer). *Benefactors* by Michael Frayn, produced by James M. Nederlander, Robert Fryer, Douglas Urbanski, Michael Codron, MTM Enterprises, Inc. and CBS Productions; *Blood Knot* by Athol Fugard, produced by James B. Freydberg, Max Weitzenhoffer, Lucille Lortel, Estrin Rose Berman Productions and F.W.M. Producing Group; *The House of Blue Leaves* by John Guare, produced by Lincoln Center Theater, Gregory Mosher and Bernard Gersten; **I'm Not Rappaport** by **Herb Gardner**, produced by **James Walsh, Lewis Allen** and **Martin Heinfling.**

BEST MUSICAL (award goes to producer). *Big Deal* produced by The Shubert Organization,

Roger Berlind, Jerome Minskoff and Jonathan Farkas; **The Mystery of Edwin Drood** produced by **Joseph Papp**; *Song & Dance* produced by Cameron Mackintosh, Inc., The Shubert Organization, F.W.M. Producing Group and The Really Useful Company, Inc.; *Tango Argentino* produced by Mel Howard and Donald K. Donald.

BEST BOOK OF A MUSICAL. *Big Deal* by Bob Fosse; **The Mystery of Edwin Drood** by **Rupert Holmes**; *Singin' in the Rain* by Betty Comden and Adolph Green; *Wind in the Willows* by Jane Iredale.

BEST ORIGINAL SCORE (music and lyrics) WRITTEN FOR THE THEATER. **The Mys-**

tery of Edwin Drood, music and lyrics by **Rupert Holmes**; *The News*, music and lyrics by Paul Schierhorn; *Song & Dance*, music by Andrew Lloyd Webber, lyrics by Don Black and Richard Maltby Jr.; *Wind in the Willows*, music by William Perry, lyrics by Roger McGough and William Perry.

BEST LEADING ACTOR IN A PLAY. Hume Cronyn in *The Petition*, Ed Harris in *Precious Sons*, **Judd Hirsch** in *I'm Not Rappaport*, Jack Lemmon in *Long Day's Journey Into Night.*

BEST LEADING ACTRESS IN A PLAY. Rosemary Harris in *Hay Fever*, Mary Beth Hurt in *Benefactors*, Jessica Tandy in *The Petition*, **Lily Tomlin** in *The Search for Signs of Intelligent Life in the Universe.*

BEST LEADING ACTOR IN A MUSICAL. Don Correia in *Singin' in the Rain*, Cleavant Derricks in *Big Deal*, Maurice Hines in *Uptown . . . It's Hot!*, **George Rose** in *The Mystery of Edwin Drood.*

BEST LEADING ACTRESS IN A MUSICAL. Debbie Allen in *Sweet Charity*, Cleo Laine in *The Mystery of Edwin Drood*, **Bernadette Peters** in *Song & Dance*, Chita Rivera in *Jerry's Girls.*

BEST FEATURED ACTOR IN A PLAY. Peter Gallagher in *Long Day's Journey Into Night*, Charles Keating in *Loot*, Joseph Maher in Loot, **John Mahoney** in *The House of Blue Leaves.*

BEST FEATURED ACTRESS IN A PLAY. Stockard Channing in *The House of Blue Leaves*, **Swoosie Kurtz** in *The House of Blue Leaves*, Bethel Leslie in *Long Day's Journey Into Night*, Zoe Wanamaker in *Loot.*

BEST FEATURED ACTOR IN A MUSICAL. Christopher d'Amboise in *Song & Dance*, John Herrera in *The Mystery of Edwin Drood*, Howard McGillin in *The Mystery of Edwin Drood*, **Michael Rupert** in *Sweet Charity.*

BEST FEATURED ACTRESS IN A MUSICAL. Patti Cohenour in *The Mystery of Edwin Drood*, **Bebe Neuwirth** in *Sweet Charity*, Jana Schneider in *The Mystery of Edwin Drood*, Eli-

sabeth Welch in *Jerome Kern Goes to Hollywood.*

BEST DIRECTION OF A PLAY. Jonathan Miller for *Long Day's Journey Into Night*, José Quintero for *The Iceman Cometh*, John Tillinger for *Loot*, **Jerry Zaks** for *The House of Blue Leaves.*

BEST DIRECTION OF A MUSICAL. Bob Fosse for *Big Deal*, **Wilford Leach** for *The Mystery of Edwin Drood*, Richard Maltby, Jr. for *Song & Dance*, Claudio Segovia and Hector Orezzoli for *Tango Argentino.*

BEST SCENIC DESIGN. Ben Edwards for *The Iceman Cometh*, David Mitchell for *The Boys of Winter*, Beni Montresor for *The Marriage of Figaro*, **Tony Walton** for *The House of Blue Leaves.*

BEST COSTUME DESIGN. Willa Kim for *Song & Dance*, Beni Montresor for *The Marriage of Figaro*, Ann Roth for *The House of Blue Leaves*, **Patricia Zipprodt** for *Sweet Charity.*

BEST LIGHTING DESIGN. **Pat Collins** for *I'm Not Rappaport*, Jules Fisher for *Song & Dance*, Paul Gallo for *The House of Blue Leaves*, Thomas R. Skelton for *The Iceman Cometh.*

BEST CHOREOGRAPHY. Graciela Daniele for *The Mystery of Edwin Drood*, **Bob Fosse** for *Big Deal*, Peter Martins for *Song & Dance*, The Tango Argentino Dancers for *Tango Argentino.*

BEST REPRODUCTION OF A PLAY OR MUSICAL. *Hay Fever* produced by Roger Peters and MBS Company; *The Iceman Cometh* produced by Lewis Allen, James M. Nederlander, Stephen Graham and Ben Edwards; *Loot* produced by David Merrick Arts Foundation, Charles P. Kopelman and Mark Simon; **Sweet Charity** produced by **Jerome Minskoff, James M. Nederlander, Arthur Rubin** and **Joseph Harris.**

SPECIAL TONY AWARD. **American Repertory Theater**, Cambridge, Mass.

TONY AWARD WINNERS, 1947–1986

Listed below are the Antoinette Perry (Tony) Award winners in the categories of Best Play and Best Musical from the time these awards were established (1947) until the present.

Bernadette Peters (winner of the Tony for best leading actress in a musical) with Victor Barbee in Andrew Lloyd Webber's *Song & Dance*

1958—Sunrise at Campobello; The Music Man
1959—J.B.; Redhead
1960—The Miracle Worker; Fiorello! and The Sound of Music (tie)
1961—Becket; Bye Bye Birdie
1962—A Man for All Seasons; How to Succeed in Business Without Really Trying
1963—Who's Afraid of Virginia Woolf?; A Funny Thing Happened on the Way to the Forum
1964—Luther; Hello, Dolly!
1965—The Subject Was Roses; Fiddler on the Roof
1966—The Persecution and Assassination of Marat as Performed by the Inmates of the Asylum of Charenton Under the Direction of the Marquis de Sade; Man of La Mancha
1967—The Homecoming; Cabaret
1968—Rosencrantz and Guildenstern Are Dead; Hallelujah, Baby!
1969—The Great White Hope; 1776
1970—Borstal Boy; Applause

1971—Sleuth; Company
1972—Sticks and Bones; Two Gentlemen of Verona
1973—That Championship Season; A Little Night Music
1974—The River Niger; Raisin
1975—Equus; The Wiz
1976—Travesties; A Chorus Line
1977—The Shadow Box; Annie
1978—Da; Ain't Misbehavin'
1979—The Elephant Man; Sweeney Todd, the Demon Barber of Fleet Street
1980—Children of a Lesser God; Evita
1981—Amadeus; 42nd Street
1982—The Life & Adventures of Nicholas Nickleby; Nine
1983—Torch Song Trilogy; Cats
1984—The Real Thing; La Cage aux Folles
1985—Biloxi Blues; Big River
1986—I'm Not Rappaport, The Mystery of Edwin Drood

THE OBIE AWARDS, 1985–86

The *Village Voice* Off-Broadway (Obie) Awards are given each year for excellence in various categories of off-Broadway (and frequently off-off-Broadway) shows, with close distinctions between these two areas ignored. The 31st annual 1985–86 Obies were voted by a panel of *Village Voice* critics (Eileen Blumenthal, Michael Feingold, Erika Munk, Julius Novick, Robert Massa and Gordon Rogoff with Ross Wetzsteon as chairman) plus Rosalyn Drexler and Gautam Dasgupta as guest judges.

DISTINGUISHED PLAYWRITING. **Wallace Shawn** for *Aunt Dan and Lemon.*

SUSTAINED ACHIEVEMENT. **Mabou Mines.**

BEST PERFORMANCE. **Swoosie Kurtz** in *The House of Blue Leaves.*

SUSTAINED EXCELLENCE IN PERFORMANCE. **Edward Herrmann, Kevin Kline.**

PERFORMANCE. **Elisabeth Welch** in *Time to Start Living,* **Tom Cayler** in *A Matter of Life and Death,* **Dylan Baker** in *Not About Heroes,* **Kathryn Pogson** in *Aunt Dan and Lemon,* **Jill Eikenberry** in *Lemon Sky* and *Life Under Water,* **Josef Sommer** in *Largo Desolato,* **Elizabeth Wilson** in *Anteroom,* **Farley Granger** and **Helen Stenborg** in *Talley & Son,* **Norma**

Aleandro in *About Love and Other Stories About Love.*

DIRECTION. **Richard Foreman** for *Largo Desolato.*

PLAYWRITING. **Eric Bogosian** for *Drinking in America,* **Martha Clarke** for *Vienna: Lusthaus,* **John Jesurun** for *Deep Sleep,* **Tadeusz Kantor** for *Let the Artists Die,* **Lee Nagrin** for *Bird/Bear.*

COSTUME DESIGN. **Rita Ryack.**

LIGHTING DESIGN. **Paul Gallo.**

SET DESIGN. **Edward T. Gianfrancesco.**

MUSIC. **Genji Ito.**

CASH GRANTS. **P.S. 122; Billie Holiday Theater; Mabou Mines.**

ADDITIONAL PRIZES AND AWARDS, 1985–86

The following is a list of major prizes and awards for achievement in the theater this season. In all cases the names of winners appear in bold face type.

1985 ELIZABETH HULL–KATE WARRINER AWARD. To the playwright whose work dealt with controversial subjects involving the fields of political, religious or social mores of the time, selected by the Dramatists Guild Council. **Christopher Durang** for *The Marriage of Bette and Boo.*

2d ANNUAL GEORGE AND ELIZABETH MARTON AWARD FOR PLAYWRITING. To recognize and encourage a new American playwright selected by a committee of the Foundation of the Dramatists Guild. **Larry Kramer** for *The Normal Heart.*

1ST ANNUAL ATCA NEW-PLAY AWARD. For an outstanding new play in cross-country theater, voted by a committee of the American Theater Critics Association. **Fences** by **August Wilson.**

OUTER CRITICS CIRCLE AWARDS. For distinguished achievement in the 1985–86 theater season, voted by critics of foreign and out-of-town periodicals. Broadway play: **I'm Not Rappaport.** Broadway musical: **The Mystery of Edwin Drood.** Off-Broadway play: **A Lie of the Mind.** Off-Broadway musical: **Nunsense.** Revival of a play or musical: **Loot.** Actor: **Judd Hirsch** in *I'm Not Rappaport.* Actress: **Lily Tomlin** in *The Search for Signs of Intelligent Life in the Universe.* Actor's debut: **Anthony Rapp** in *Precious Sons.* Actress's debut: **Semina de Laurentis** in *Nunsense.* Off-Broadway book and music: **Dan Goggin** for *Nunsense.* Off-Broadway lyrics: **David Crane, Seth Friedman** and **Marta Kauffman** for *Personals.* Director: **John Tillinger** for *Loot, The Perfect Party* and *Corpse!* Choreographer: **Bob Fosse** for *Big Deal* and *Sweet Charity.* Scenery: **Bob Shaw** for *The Mystery of Edwin Drood.* Costumes: **Lindsay W. Davis** for *The Mystery of Edwin Drood.* Lighting: **Paul Gallo** for *The Mystery of Edwin Drood.* John Gassner Award for the author of a new American play: **Herb Gardner.** Special awards: **Elisabeth Welch** for *Time to Start Living* and *Jerome Kern Goes to Hollywood.*

42d ANNUAL THEATER WORLD AWARDS. For outstanding new talent in Broadway and off-Broadway productions during the 1985–86 season, selected by a committee

comprising Clive Barnes, Douglas Watt and John Willis. **Suzy Amis** of *Fresh Horses,* **Alec Baldwin** of *Loot,* **Aled Davies** of *Orchards,* **Faye Grant** of *Singin' in the Rain,* **Julie Hagerty** of *The House of Blue Leaves,* **Ed Harris** of *Precious Sons,* **Mark Jacoby** of *Sweet Charity,* **Donna Kane** of *Dames at Sea,* **Cleo Laine** and **Howard McGillin** of *The Mystery of Edwin Drood,* **Marisa Tomei** of *Daughters,* **Joe Urla** of *Principia Scriptoriae.*

MARGO JONES AWARD. To the producer and producing organization whose continuing policy of producing new theater works has made an outstanding contribution to the encouragement of new playwrights. **John Lion** and the **Magic Theater of San Francisco.**

WILLIAM INGE AWARD. For lifetime achievement in playwriting, given by Independence, Kan. Community College. **John Patrick.**

ASCAP-RODGERS AWARD. For lifetime achievement in musical theater, voted by a committee comprising William O. Harbach, Richard Lewine and Hildy Parks. **Jay Gorney.**

1985 GEORGE OPPENHEIMER/NEWSDAY PLAYWRITING AWARD. To the best new American playwright whose work is produced in New York City or on Long Island. **Richard Greenberg** for *The Bloodletters.*

8th ANNUAL KENNEDY CENTER HONORS. For distinguished achievement by individuals who have made significant contributions to American culture through the arts. **Alan Jay Lerner, Frederick Loewe, Beverly Sills, Bob Hope, Irene Dunne, Merce Cunningham.**

THEATER HALL OF FAME. Annual election by members of the profession of nominees designated by the American Theater Critics Association. **Rosemary Harris, Raymond Massey, George C. Scott, Christopher Plummer, Roger L. Stevens, Geraldine Fitzgerald, Michael Bennett, Jerry Herman, Michael Redgrave.**

1986 JOSEPH MAHARAM AWARDS. For distinguished theatrical design for original American productions presented in New York, voted by a committee comprising Trish Dace, chairman, Henry Hewes, Edward F. Kook, Patricia MacKay and Julius Novick. Scenery: **Tony Walton** for *The House of Blue Leaves.* Costumes: **Everett Quinton** for *Salammbó.* Lighting: **Kevin Rigdon** for *Prairie du Chien* and *The Shawl.* Noteworthy unusual effects: **Eva Buchmuller** (scenery), **Theo Cremona** and **Rudi Stern** (special effects) for *Dreamland Burns.* Collaborative design: **Robert Israel** (scenery and costumes) and **Paul Gallo** (lighting) for *Vienna: Lusthaus.*

ASTAIRE AWARD. For distinguished achievement in the dance, given by the Anglo-American Contemporary Dance Foundation. 1985: **Jerome Robbins** (lifetime achievement). 1986: **Debbie Allen** (performance in *Sweet Charity*), **Gregg Burge** (performance in *Song & Dance*), **Bob Fosse** (choregraphy, *Big Deal*), **Peter Martins** (choreography, *Song & Dance*).

31st ANNUAL DRAMA DESK AWARDS. For outstanding achievement, voted by an association of New York drama reporters, editors and critics. Play: **A Lie of the Mind.** Director, play: **Jerry Zaks** for *The Marriage of Bette and Boo* and *The House of Blue Leaves.* Actor, play: **Ed Harris** in *Precious Sons.* Actress, play: **Lily Tomlin** in *The Search for Signs of Intelligent Life in the Universe.* Musical: **The Mystery of Edwin Drood.** Director, musical: **Wilford Leach** for *The Mystery of Edwin Drood.* Actor, musical: **George Rose** in *The Mystery of Edwin Drood.* Actress, musical: **Bernadette Peters** in *Song & Dance.* Featured actor, play: **Joseph Maher** in *Loot.* Featured actress, play: **Joanna Gleason** in *Social Security* and *It's Only a Play.* Featured actor, musical: **Michael Rupert** in *Sweet Charity.* Featured actress, musical: **Jana Schneider** in *The Mystery of Edwin Drood.* Score, book and orchestration: **Rupert Holmes** for *The Mystery of Edwin Drood.* Choreography: **Bob Fosse** for *Big Deal.* Revival: **The House of Blue Leaves.** One-person show: **Eric Bogosian** in **Drinking in America.** Unique theatrical experience: **The Search for Signs of Intelligent Life in the Universe.** Scenic design: **Tony Walton** for *Social Security* and *The House of Blue Leaves.* Costume design: **Lindsay W. Davis** for *The Mystery of Edwin Drood.* Lighting: **Pat Collins** for *Execution of Justice.* Special effects: **Showtech** for *Singin' in the Rain.* Sound design, music in a play: **Otts Munderloh** for *The Search for Signs of Intelligent Life in the Universe:* Musical direction: **Donald Pippin.** Lyrics: No award. Special awards: **Thomas Z. Shepard** for recordings of distinction; **Agnes de Mille** for her legacy of choreography; **Joyce Theater** for its American Theater Exchange program; the **New Amsterdam Theater Company** for concert productions of vintage American musicals; **Jessica Tandy** and **Hume Cronyn.**

JEAN DALRYMPLE AWARDS. For off-off-Broadway achievement. Best playwright, drama: **John Quinn** for *Mother Russia.* Best playwright, comedy: **David Lessoff** for *The Girl in My Fortune Cookie.* Best actors, drama: **Keith Burns** in *The Gandy Dancer,* **Seamus McNally** for *Mother Russia.* Best actor, dramatic classic: **Ted Zurkowski** in *Richard III.* Best actor, romantic classic: **Thor Fields** in *Romeo and Juliet.* Best actress, drama: **Joy Saylor** in *Broomsticks.* Best supporting actor: **Ray Trail** in *The Gandy Dancer.* Best supporting actress, **Katharine Van Loan** for *Mother Russia.*

GEORGE JEAN NATHAN AWARD. For dramatic criticism. **Jan Kott** for *The Theater of Essence.*

1986 MR. ABBOTT AWARD. For lifetime achievement in the theater, sponsored by the Stage Directors and Choreographers Workshop Foundation. **Bob Fosse.**

CLARENCE DERWENT AWARDS. For the most promising male and female actors on the metropolitan scene during the 1985–86 season. **Patti Cohenour** in *The Mystery of Edwin Drood,* **John Mahoney** in *The House of Blue Leaves.*

51st ANNUAL DRAMA LEAGUE AWARDS. **Bernadette Peters** for performance in *Song & Dance,* **Athol Fugard** for unique contribution to the theater, **Bob Fosse** for outstanding achievement in musical theater.

1986 PLAYWRIGHTS USA AWARDS. For outstanding works produced in American nonprofit theaters, sponsored by Theater Communications Group and Home Box Office. **Maria Irene Fornes** for her translation of Virgilio Pinera's *Cold Air,* **Allan Havis** for *Morocco,* **Emily Mann** for *Execution of Justice,* **Stephen Metcalfe** for *The Incredibly Famous Willy Rivers,* **Richard Nelson** for *Between East and West.*

NEW YORK STATE GOVERNOR'S ARTS AWARD. For contribution to the theater art. **Neil Simon.**

1985 COMMON WEALTH AWARD. For distinguished service in dramatic arts. **Zelda Fichandler** of Arena Stage.

EUGENE O'NEILL BIRTHDAY MEDAL. For enriching the understanding of that renowned playwright. **Colleen Dewhurst.**

1985 JUJAMCYN THEATERS AWARD. To a regional theater or organization that has made an outstanding contribution to the development of creative talent for the theater. **American Repertory Theater** and **Robert Brustein.**

4th ANNUAL ELLIOT NORTON PRIZE. To that person who, during the previous year, has made an outstanding contribution to theater in Boston, sponsored by the League of Boston Theaters. **Israel Horovitz** for his creative work as the founding artistic director of the Gloucester, Mass. Stage Company.

4th ANNUAL BOSTON THEATER CRITICS CIRCLE AWARDS. For distinguished achievement in Boston commercial theaters—Outstanding drama: **The Search for Signs of Intelligent Life in the Universe** by Jane Wagner. Actress in a drama: **Lily Tomlin** in *The Search for Signs of Intelligent Life in the Universe.* Actress in a musical: **Leslie Uggams** in *Jerry's Girls.* Actor in a drama: **Edward Duke** in *Jeeves Takes Charge.* Actor in a musical: **Anthony Quinn** in *Zorba.* Director of a drama: **Douglas Turner Ward** for *A Soldier's Play.* Director of a musical: **Gerard Alessandrini** for *Forbidden Broadway.* Scenery: **Bill Stabile** for *Torch Song Trilogy.* Costumes: **Dean Brown** for *Gigi.* Lighting: **Allen Lee Hughes.** For distinguished achievement in Boston non-profit Equity theaters—Outstanding drama: **The King Stag.** Outstanding musical: **A Little Night Music.** Actress: **Cherry Jones** in *Gillette.* Actor: **John Bottoms** in *Endgame* and *Gillette.* Scenery: **Richard M. Isackes** for *Uncle Vanya.* Costumes: **Julie Taymore** for *The King Stag.* Lighting: **Jennifer Tipton** for *Jacques and His Master.* Special awards: **Robert Wilson** and the **American Repertory Theater** for *The Civil Wars*; **J. Arnold Nickerson** for founding the Nickerson Theater.

2d ANNUAL HELEN HAYES AWARDS. In recognition of excellence in the Washington, D.C. professional theater. Resident shows—Best production of a play: **Arena Stage** for *Execution of Justice.* Best production of a musical: **Studio Theater** for *March of the Falsettos.* Best new play: **Ralph Hunt** for **Metamorphosis.** Outstanding lead actress, play: **Randy Danson** in *The Good Person of Setzuan.* Outstanding lead actor, play: **Thomas Schall** in *Fool for Love.* Outstanding actress, musical: **Janet Aldrich** in *Forbidden Broadway.* Outstanding actor, musical: **Romain Fruge** in *Baby.* Outstanding director: **Douglas Wager** for *Execution of Justice.* Touring or pre-New York shows—Outstanding production, touring: **La Cage aux Folles.** Outstanding pro-duction, pre–New York: **The Iceman Cometh.** Outstanding lead actor: **Jason Robards** in *The Iceman Cometh.* Outstanding lead actress: **Barbara Robertson** in *Kabuki Medea.* Outstanding supporting performer: **Barnard Hughes** in *The Iceman Cometh.*

13th ANNUAL JOSEPH JEFFERSON AWARDS. For outstanding work in Chicago theater during the 1984–85 season. Production of a play: **Wisdom Bridge** for *Hamlet* and **Steppenwolf** for *Orphans.* Best production of a musical: **Candlelight Dinner Playhouse** for *Nine.* Director of a play: **Gary Sinise** for *Orphans.* Director of a musical: **Rudy Hogenmiller** and **William Pullinsi** for *Evita.* Principal actor in a play: **Kevin Anderson** in *Orphans.* Principal actor in a musical: **Mark Jacoby** in *Nine.* Principal actress in a play: **Laurie Metcalf** in *Coyote Ugly.* Principal actress in a musical: **Hollis Resnik** in *Evita.* Supporting actor in a play: **Del Close** in *Hamlet.* Supporting actress in a play: **Glenne Headly** in *Coyote Ugly.* Supporting actress in a musical: **Kathy Santon** in *Carousel.* Ensemble: **Steppenwolf** for *Orphans.* Costume design: **Christa Scholtz** for *Candide.* Scenic design: **Michael S. Philippi** for *Terra Nova* and **John Lee Beatty** for *The Water Engine.* Lighting design: **Michael Merritt** for *Hamlet.* Choreography: **Rudy Hogenmiller** for *Evita.* Musical direction: **Rufus Hill** for *Po.*

1st ANNUAL DENVER DRAMA CRITICS CIRCLE AWARDS. For 1984–85's top theatrical achievements in the Denver area. Best production: **Denver Center Theater Company** for *Don Juan.* Best touring production: **Torch Song Trilogy.** Best production of a new play: **Denver Center Theater Company** for *Ringers* by Frank Hogan. Best season for a theater company: **Germinal Stage.** Best director: **Garland Wright** for *Don Juan.* Best season for an actor: **Ed Baierlein.** Best season for an actress: **Rachel Patterson.** Ensemble acting: **The Unvarnished Truth.** Best performance by an actor: **Dennis O'Farrell** in *P.J.* Best performance by an actress: **Sallie Diamond** in *The Philanderer.* Best supporting actor: **Mike Regan** in *Ringers.* Best supporting actress: **Ann Guilberg** in *The Immigrant.* Best scenery: **Douglas O. Stein** for *Don Juan.* Best costumes: **Ann Hould-Ward** for *Don Juan.* Best lighting: **Scott Pinkney** for *Don Juan.*

17th ANNUAL LOS ANGELES DRAMA CRITICS CIRCLE AWARDS. For distinguished achievement in Los Angeles Theater. Production: **Anna Giagni** and **Macheath Productions,** Zephyr Theater for *Berlin to Broadway* with Kurt Weill; **Martin Benson** and **David Emmes,** South Coast Repertory, for *Blue Window*; **Barry** and **Fran Weissler** in association with the **One and Only Joint Venture** and **Pace Theatrical Group,** Ahmanson Theater, for *My One and Only.* Writing: **Craig Lucas** for *Blue Window.* Direction: **Paul Hough** for *Berlin to Broadway with Kurt Weill,* **Norman René** for *Blue Window,* **Kristoffer Siegel-Tabori** for *Inadmissible Evidence.* Musical score: **Bob Telson** for *The Gospel at Colonus.* Concept: **Lee Breuer** and **Bob Telson** for *The Gospel at Colonus.* Lead performance: **Hume Cronyn** in *Foxfire,* **Ian McShane** in *Inadmissible Evidence,* **Dick Shawn** in *The 2d Greatest Entertainer in the Whole Wide World,* **Ray Stricklyn** in *Confessions of a Nightingale,* **Jessica Tandy** in *Foxfire.* Featured performance: **John Anderson** in *In the Sweet Bye and Bye,* **Bruce Davison** in *The Normal Heart.* Ensemble performance: **Andrea's Got 2 Boyfriends, Berlin to**

Broadway with Kurt Weill, Blue Window. Scenic design: **A. Clarke Duncan** for *Inadmissible Evidence,* **Ming Cho Lee** for *Traveler in the Dark,* **John Napier** for *Cats.* Lighting design: **Ken Billington** for *Foxfire,* **David Hersey** for *Cats.* Costume design, **Sam Kirkpatrick** for *Undiscovered Country,* **John Napier** for *Cats.* Sound design: **John Gottlieb** for *Nanawatai.* Musical direction: **Jack Elton** for *Berlin to Broadway with Kurt Weill.* Choreography: **Martha Clarke** for *Garden of Earthly Delights.* Fight staging: **John Robert Beardsley** and **David Boushey** for *Romeo and Juliet* Margaret Harford Award: **Mako** and **East West Players** for "releasing Asian-American actors from limitations of stereotyped roles and for enabling Asian-American playwrights to provide them more challenging opportunities." Special awards: **José Quintero** for "his vast career achievements as director in theater, television and films"; **Bill Bushnell** for "creation of Los Angeles Theater Center."

1985–86 PUBLICATION OF RECENTLY-PRODUCED PLAYS

Alone Together. Lawrence Roman. Samuel French (paperback).
As Is. William M. Hoffman. Random House. Vintage (paperback).
Aunt Dan and Lemon. Wallace Shawn. Grove (paperback).
Beethoven's Tenth. Peter Ustinov. Samuel French (paperback).
Better Times. Barrie Keeffe. Methuen (paperback).
Big River. William Hauptman. Grove (paperback).
Breaking the Silence. Stephen Poliakoff. Methuen (paperback).
Bubbling Brown Sugar. Lotften Mitchell. Broadway Play (paperback).
Chorus of Disapproval, A. Alan Ayckbourn. Faber & Faber (paperback).
Citizen Tom Paine. Howard Fast. Houghton Mifflin. (also paperback).
Entertaining Strangers. David Edgar. Methuen (paperback).
Fences. August Wilson. New American Library (paperback).
Grace of Mary Traverse, The. Timberlake Wertenbaker. Faber & Faber (paperback).
Les Liaisons Dangereuses. Christopher Hampton. Faber & Faber (paperback).
Life and Limb. Keith Reddin. Dramatists Play Service.
Murder Game. Tim Kelly. Broadway Play (paperback).
My Brother's Keeper. Nigel Williams. Faber & Faber (paperback).
Normal Heart, The. Larry Kramer. New American Library (paperback).
Pravda: A Fleet Street Comedy. Howard Brenton and David Hare. Methuen (paperback).
Quilters. Molly Newman and Barbara Damashek. Dramatists Play Service.
Red Noses. Peter Barnes. Faber & Faber (paperback).
Rough Crossing. Tom Stoppard. Faber & Faber (also paperback).
Sand Mountain. Romulus Linney. Dramatists Play Service (paperback).
Shawl, The/Prairie du Chien: Two Plays. David Mamet. Grove (also paperback).
Sunday in the Park with George: Libretto. James Lapine and Stephen Sondheim. Dodd, Mead.
Swimming to Cambodia. Spalding Gray. Theater Communications Group (paperback).
Tom and Viv. Michael Hastings. Penguin (paperback).

Tracers. John DiFusco. Hill & Wang (paperback).
Yellow Fever. R.A. Shiomi. Playwrights Canada (paperback).

A SELECTED LIST OF OTHER PLAYS PUBLISHED IN 1985–86

Ayckbourn, Alan. *Intimate Exchanges: Vol. 1.* Samuel French (paperback).
Benmussa, Simone and Helen Cixous. *Benmussa Directs.* Riverrun Press.
Bentley, Eric. *Monstrous Martyrdoms.* Prometheus.
Bond, Edward. *Plays: Two.* Methuen (paperback).
Brecht, Bertolt. *Fear and Misery of the Third Reich; In the Jungle of Cities; Life of Galileo* (translated by John Willet); *Man Equals Man & The Elephant Calf; A Respectable Wedding and Other One-Act Plays; The Rise and Fall of the City of Mahagonny/The Seven Deadly Sins.* Methuen (paperbacks).
Brenson, Ian and Eric Lane (editors). *Oberammergau Passion Play.* Hippocrene (paperback).
Bulgakov, Mikhail. *The White Guard.* Methuen (paperback).
Calderon de la Barca, Pedro. *Three Comedies by Calderon.* University Press of Kentucky (paperback).
Cao, Yu. *Peking Man.* Columbia University Press.
Churchill, Caryl. *Churchill: Plays—One.* Methuen (paperback).
Congreve, William. *The Comedies of William Congreve.* Penguin (paperback).
Delgado, Ramon. *The Best Short Plays—1985.* Chilton.
Euripides. *Euripedes' Helen.* University of Massachusetts Press (paperback).
Fassbinder, Rainer Werner. *Rainer Fassbinder: Plays.* PAJ Publications (paperback).
Ford, John. *John Ford: Three Plays.* Penguin (paperback).
Fornes, Maria Irene. *Maria Irene Fornes: Plays.* PAJ Publications (paperback).
Frayn, Michael. *Plays: One.* Methuen (paperback).
Fry, Christopher. *Selected Plays by Christopher Fry.* Oxford (paperback).
Gems, Pam. *Three Plays by Pam Gems.* Penguin (paperback).
Goethe, Johann Wolfgang. *Egmont: A Play.* F. Ungar (paperback); *Faust: Part I.* Banton (paperback).
Gogol, Nicolai. *The Government Inspector.* Methuen (paperback).
Ibsen, Henrik. *The Plays of Ibsen: Volumes 1 and 2.* Washington Square Press (paperback).
King, Woodie Jr. and Ron Milner. *Black Drama Anthology.* New American Library (paperback).
Machiavelli, Niccolo. *The Comedies of Machiavelli.* University Press of New England (paperback).
Mamet, David. *Goldberg Street.* Grove Press (paperback).
Middleton, Thomas. *Thomas Middleton: Three Plays.* Dutton/Dent (paperback).
Morton, Carlos. *The Many Deaths of Danny Rosales and Other Plays.* Arte Publico (paperback).
O'Casey, Sean. *Seven Plays by Sean O'Casey.* St. Martin's Press.
Offenbach, Jacques. *The Drum Major's Daughter.* Theodore Presser (paperback).
Picasso, Pablo. *Desire Caught by the Tail.* Riverrun Press.
Piñero, Miguel. *The Sun Always Shines for the Good.* Arte Publico (paperback).
Pirandello, Luigi. *Six Characters in Search of an Author; Henry IV.* Methuen (paperback).
Porter, Cole. *The Best of Cole Porter.* Warner Brothers (paperback).
Rand, Ayn and Nathaniel Edward Reid. *Night of January 16th: Director's Manuscript.* David McKay (paperback).
Rattigan, Terence. *Plays: Two.* Methuen (paperback).
Shepard, Sam. *The Unseen Hand and Other Plays.* Bantam (paperback).
Strindberg, August. *Plays: One; Plays: Two.* Methuen (paperback).
Webster, John. *The White Devil With Commentary & Notes Classical.* Methuen (paperback).
Wilson, Lanford. *Serenading Louie: Revised Edition.* Hill & Wang (paperback).
Wodehouse, P.G. *Four Plays by P.G. Wodehouse.* Methuen (paperback).
Wolfe, Thomas. *Welcome to Our City; Mannerhouse.* Louisiana State Press.
Woolf, Virginia. *Freshwater.* Harcourt Brace Jovanovich (paperback).

NECROLOGY

MAY 1985–MAY 1986

PERFORMERS

Ackerman, Mildred (65)—January 10, 1986
Aherne, Brian (83)—February 10, 1986
Albright, Arnita Wallace (71)—June 11, 1985
Alda, Robert (72)—May 3, 1986
Allan, Jacqueline (51)—December 24, 1985
Allen, Hilda (79)—March 3, 1986
Allison, John (46)—September 26, 1985
Alper, Leo (72)—February 18, 1986
Anden, Mathew (42)—July 19, 1985
Andrews, Ann (95)—January 23, 1986
Andrews, Kevin (29)—July 14, 1985
Ankers, Evelyn (67)—August 28, 1985
Atkind, Phyllis Davies Luce (95)—May 31, 1985
Atwater, Edith (74)—March 14, 1986
Baker, Hylda (78)—May 3, 1986
Baker, Kenny (72)—August 10, 1985
Bangert, Bernice G. (76)—November 14, 1985
Barner, Bill (62)—September 4, 1985
Barnett, Ron (47)—June 22, 1985
Barney, Jay (72)—May 19, 1985
Barr, Patrick (77)—August 29, 1985
Barton, Edward (43)—December 20, 1985
Bass, John (29)—September 24, 1985
Bate, Tom (85)—November 17, 1985
Baxter, Anne (62)—December 12, 1985
Beck, Julian (60)—September 14, 1985
Beldon, Eileen (83)—August 3, 1985
Bell, Marie (84)—August 15, 1985
Bergner, Elisabeth (85)—May 12, 1986
Bernardi, Herschel (62)—May 9, 1986
Best, Larry (68)—December 4, 1985
Blaxland, Audrey (67)—August 30, 1985
Boden, Herman (66)—June 28, 1985
Boleyn, Eleanor—November 25, 1985
Bonnell, Lee (67)—May 12, 1986
Boon, Dennis (27)—December 22, 1985
Bradley, Curley (74)—June 3, 1985
Brandt, Tolf (79)—January 30, 1986
Breen, Nellie (88)—April 26, 1986
Bremen, Leonard (71)—March 21, 1986
Briggs, Donald P. (75)—February 3, 1986
Britton, Aileen—April 19, 1986
Brooks, Louise (78)—August 8, 1985
Bruhn, Erik (57)—April 1, 1986
Bryan, Ken (32)—March 3, 1986
Brynner, Yul (65)—October 10, 1985

Bubbles, John W. (84)—May 18, 1986
Buckley, Hal (49)—March 17, 1986
Burge, James C. (41)—June 1, 1985
Burke, Georgia (107)—November 28, 1985
Burstein, Pesach (89)—April 6, 1986
Byron, Marion (73)—July 5, 1985
Cagney, James (86)—March 30, 1986
Caesar, Adolph (52)—March 6, 1986
Campbell, Kay (80)—May 27, 1985
Campos, Rafael (49)—July 9, 1985
Canutt, Yakima (90)—May 24, 1986
Capell, Peter (73)—March 3, 1986
Carlile, Robert (40)—May 4, 1986
Carr, Frankie (61)—March 20, 1986
Carroll, Doris L. (64)—August 17, 1985
Cassinelli, Claudio (47)—July 13, 1985
Cecil, Winifred (78)—September 13, 1985
Cehanovsky, George (94)—March 25, 1986
Celi, Adolfo (63)—February 19, 1986
Cevetillo, Louis (39)—July 16, 1985
Champagne, Joe (92)—September 17, 1985
Chandler, George L. (87)—June 10, 1985
Chase, Lucia (88)—January 9, 1986
Childress, Alvin (78)—April 19, 1986
Clancy, Dennis (62)—Spring 1985
Claridge, Norman (81)—June 11, 1985
Clarke, Philip Norman (81)—September 27, 1985
Clute, Sidney (69)—October 2, 1985
Cohen, Myron (83)—March 10, 1986
Connell, Polly (73)—January 14, 1986
Cook, Dick (58)—February 3, 1986
Copeland, Maurice (74)—October 3, 1985
Courtin, Robert Charles (36)—July 11, 1985
Courtney, Alex—December 2, 1985
Craig, James (73)—June 28, 1985
Crawford, Broderick (74)—April 26, 1986
Crompton, Colin (54)—August 24, 1985
Crothers, Joel (44)—November 6, 1985
Cunningham, Sarah (67)—March 24, 1986
Dahl, Edith (81)—November 17, 1985
da Silva, Howard (76)—February 16, 1986
Deering, Olive (67)—March 22, 1986
Deganith, Lea (82)—November 2, 1985
DeMarco, Tony (82)—November 4, 1985
Denney, Frank C. (91)—August 22, 1985
DeSapio, Rose—Winter 1985
Desmond, Johnny (65)—September 6, 1985
Dominique, Laurien (29)—March 23, 1986

Downey, Morton (83)—October 25, 1985
Draper, Stephan (79)—June 5, 1985
Dreano, Iva (91)—July 3, 1985
Duell, Joseph (29)—February 16, 1986
Dwyer, Ethel (86)—September 2, 1985
Dyall, Valentine (77)—June 24, 1985
Early, Stan (64)—September 3, 1985
Eccles, Donald (77)—Winter 1986
Eckstein, Robert L. (55)—May 27, 1985
Edwards, Guy (51)—May 2, 1986
Ellin, David (61)—May 27, 1986
Elliott, Russell (36)—June 30, 1985
Ellsworth, Stephen R. (77)—September 10, 1985
Engle, Morris (84)—January 22, 1986
Englund, Bryan (30)—February 25, 1986
Erickson, Leif (74)—January 29, 1986
Evans, Clifford (73)—June 9, 1985
Evans, Estelle—July 20, 1985
Farr, Derek (74)—March 22, 1986
Faylen, Frank (79)—August 2, 1985
Feury, Peggy—November 20, 1985
Fisher, James B.M. (82)—January 28, 1986
Fishof, Betty Green (mid-60s)—November 22, 1985
Ford, Jack (81)—March 2, 1986
Foster, Alan (80)—November 15, 1985
Foster, Phil (71)—July 8, 1985
Frank, Anne Ray—April 1, 1986
Frazee, Jane (67)—September 6, 1985
Freeman, Carrie E. (93)—May 4, 1986
Fuzak, Joan M. (31)—February 21, 1986
Gabel, Martin (73)—May 22, 1986
Gardner, John (44)—January 12, 1986
Garrow, William (91)—July 9, 1985
Gash, Salla Baumann (75)—February 5, 1986
Genna, Irene (53)—February 6, 1986
George, Don E. (75)—October 7, 1985
Geraghty, Tom (77)—July 25, 1985
Gibson, Walter B. (88)—December 6, 1985
Gilbert, Lorraine (59)—August 11, 1985
Gilbert, Mitchel (52)—March 4, 1986
Gillett, Betty (58)—August 13, 1985
Gilman, Pearl Fradlen (69)—August 22, 1985
Gilman, Sam (70)—December 3, 1985
Gilmore, Virginia (66)—March 28, 1986
Glade, Coe (85)—September 23, 1985
Godkin, Paul (70)—June 7, 1985
Gordon, Ruth (88)—August 28, 1985
Gordon, Scotty (33)—April 22, 1985
Gow, Miriam (95)—January 6, 1986
Granat, Rick (42)—March 22, 1986
Grandee, George (80s)—August 1, 1985
Greco, Peter—June 18, 1985
Greene, Richard (66)—June 1, 1986
Greenfield, Calvin (58)—July 10, 1985
Hall, Grayson (58)—August 7, 1985

Haller, Lelia (82)—May 15, 1986
Halliburton, Jeanne (91)—January 23, 1986
Haney, David (44)—October 19, 1985
Hanneford, Catherine (97)—October 22, 1985
Harris, Paul (67)—August 25, 1985
Harvey, Harry (84)—November 27, 1985
Hayden, Sterling (70)—May 23, 1986
Haynes, Hilda (72)—March 4, 1986
Heathcote, Thomas (68)—January 5, 1986
Henry, Alexander V. (42)—Fall 1985
Hickman, Bill (65)—February 24, 1986
Higbe, Mary Jane (70)—February 1, 1986
Hines, Patrick (55)—August 12, 1985
Holiday, Helen W. (90)—March 20, 1986
Holmes, Lois (86)—March 12, 1986
Hoskins, Fred (60)—June 29, 1985
Hudson, Rock (59)—October 2, 1985
Huse, Tom (29)—June 27, 1985
Irwin, Sally (74)—February 11, 1986
Isley, Kelly (48)—March 31, 1986
Izquierdo, Aldo (62)—September 6, 1985
James, Claire (65)—January 18, 1986
Jeans, Isabel (93)—September 4, 1985
Johnson, Johnny (73)—December 7, 1985
Jones, Tyrone (29)—September 19, 1985
Judson, Stanley—June 15, 1985
Justus, William (49)—April 1, 1986
Kelley, Paulette SanMarchi (61)—June 16, 1985
Kenin, Alexa (23)—September 10, 1985
Kimmelman, Jack (80)—February 8, 1986
Kullers, John (early 70s)—July 1985
Laffin, Dominque (33)—June 12, 1985
Lambert, Hugh (55)—August 18, 1985
Lang, Harold (64)—July 26, 1985
Lassanevitch, Boris (80)—October 20, 1985
Latchaw, Paul (38)—October 31, 1985
Lee, Carl (52)—April 17, 1986
Lemont, George W. (63)—October 12, 1985
Leonardos, Urylee (67)—April 25, 1986
Leone, Johnny (71)—May 15, 1986
LeRoy, Del (73)—October 6, 1985
Lewis, Jarma (54)—November 11, 1985
Linares, Marcelo Lopez (64)—January 10, 1986
Linton, Mark (28)—Summer 1985
Lodge, John (82)—October 29, 1985
Lopez, J. Victor (39)—March 28, 1986
Lormer, Jon (80)—March 19, 1986
Love, Bessie (87)—April 26, 1986
Lynd, Larry (28)—August 15, 1985
MacLaren, Mary (85)—November 9, 1985
MacKay, Bruce (65)—August 10, 1985
MacRae, Gordon (64)—January 24, 1986
Mahoney, Arthur (81)—August 2, 1985
Mallory, James (32)—Winter 1985
Maltagliati, Evi (77)—April 27, 1986

Taranto, Nino (79)—February 23, 1986
Teodorescu, Ion (51)—November 5, 1985
Terry, Sonny (74)—March 11, 1986
Thomson, Beatrix (85)—Winter 1986
Tiffany, Mary (69)—April 5, 1986
Tiny, Dave—May 10, 1986
Torres, Donald R. (49)—March 22, 1986
Trangas, Andreas Michael (79)—November 3, 1985
Tucker, Betty (71)—September 18, 1985
Tushar, Jim (56)—April 9, 1986
Tuttle, Lurene (79)—May 28, 1986
Usunov, Dimiter (63)—Winter 1985
Van Cleve, Edith (90)—October 10, 1985
Vincent, Alexandra (17)—February 24, 1986
Viola, Vicki—July 21, 1985
Warners, Robert (29)—April 17, 1986
Warning, Dennis (34)—September 2, 1985
Weissman, Lydia (71)—February 18, 1986
Welles, Orson (70)—October 10, 1985
Wermont, Irving (75)—June 25, 1985
West, Madge (93)—May 29, 1985
Whelan, Cyprienne (61)—October 10, 1985
Williams, Al (74)—May 3, 1985
Williams, Ernie (81)—January 27, 1986
Williams, Grant (54)—July 28, 1985
Williams, Tex (68)—October 12, 1985
Wilson, Margery (89)—January 21, 1986
Winter, Dale (92)—November 28, 1985
Worms, Robert A. III (52)—September 2, 1985
Wynn, Beatrice Pollock (72)—May 10, 1985
Ybarrondo, Luis (50s)—September 26, 1985

MUSICIANS

Bachmann, Edwin (95)—August 30, 1985
Banerjee, Nikhil (55)—January 27, 1986
Barnett, David (78)—December 7, 1985
Bender, Burton (82)—January 16, 1986
Bennett, Harold—September 17, 1985
Bernhardt, Clyde (80)—May 20, 1986
Best, Clifton (70)—May 28, 1985
Bockstein, Edna (74)—October 22, 1985
Bohl, Robert W. (59)—October 16, 1985
Brand, Percy (77)—August 8, 1985
Bridge, Danny (67)—August 13, 1985
Brigander, J. George (76)—May 2, 1986
Brown, Walter L. (81)—September 14, 1985
Ceroli, Nick (45)—August 11, 1985
Crayton, Pee Wee (70)—June 25, 1985
Cull, Joseph W. (77)—June 16, 1985
Davis, John Henry (71)—October 12, 1985
Davis, Stewart (67)—July 18, 1985
DeDroit, Johnny (93)—February 13, 1986
Del Negro, Ferdinand (89)—May 9, 1986

Dillon, Gordon (51)—June 12, 1985
Dixon, Reginald (80)—May 9, 1985
Duvivier, George (64)—July 11, 1985
Erb, Laura (73)—February 1, 1986
Fleischer, Louis (94)—November 16, 1985
Fletcher, Larry (41)—July 31, 1985
Fournier, Pierre (79)—January 8, 1986
Freeman, Ticker (74)—January 30, 1986
Garcia, Mike (57)—June 6, 1985
Gilels, Emil (68)—October 14, 1985
Gomberg, Harold (68)—September 7, 1985
Gorodnitzki, Sascha (81)—April 4, 1986
Hammer, Janice (55)—March 8, 1986
Healy, Albert (71)—April 24, 1986
Henkin, Milton (82)—September 13, 1985
Hillyer, Lonnie (45)—July 1, 1985
Holmes, Charles W. (75)—September 19, 1985
Holmes, Teddy (83)—January 1, 1986
Johnson, George (54)—December 29, 1985
Jones, Jonathan (73)—September 3, 1985
Jones, Philly Joe (62)—August 30, 1985
Kellet, Jack (40)—January 27, 1986
Keppard, Louis (98)—February 17, 1986
King, Gibner (80)—June 18, 1985
Kisco, Charles (89)—December 6, 1985
Kreigh, Charles S. (61)—October 18, 1985
Lalli, Luigi Nicola (53)—August 21, 1985
Lam, Maddy Kaululehuaohaili (74)—June 22, 1985
Lanagan, Peg (80)—April 3, 1986
Mansfield, Charlotte H. (72)—September 14, 1985
Manuel, Richard (41)—March 4, 1986
Martin, Al (63)—August 6, 1985
Massena, Martha Halbwachs (80)—January 14, 1986
McGraw, Warren R. (48)—December 26, 1985
Miska, Herbert (86)—January 25, 1986
Molnar, Ferenc (89)—May 10, 1985
Montgomery, Eurreal (78)—September 6, 1985
Morton, Henry Sterling (78)—December 28, 1985
Olevsky, Julian (59)—May 25, 1985
Pearlmutter, Ben (75)—March 13, 1986
Pennington, Lily May Ledford (68)—July 14, 1985
Perryman, Willie (73)—July 25, 1985
Principato, Guy (71)—August 31, 1985
Proto, Secondo (69)—February 11, 1986
Quinte, Michael S. (77)—September 22, 1985
Reynolds, Jimmy (69)—March 15, 1986
Rhodes, George (66)—December 25, 1985
Roland, Henry (71)—May 30, 1985
Rosenwald, Mary K. (79)—November 13, 1985
Ruggeri, Janet (45)—May 23, 1985

Salvo, Leonard (86)—July 23, 1985
Sandford, Richard (29)—December 8, 1985
Schlangen, Elsa (86)—December 1, 1985
Schneider, Mischa (81)—October 3, 1985
Sheiry, Kenneth (44)—June 24, 1985
Sims, Tommy (63)—May 6, 1986
Sorkin, Leonard (69)—June 7, 1985
Spitelera, Joseph T. (47)—September 17, 1985
Stewart, Ian (47)—December 12, 1985
Stoler, Barrett D. (78)—August 15, 1985
Sykes, James Andrew (78)—July 26, 1985
Upshaw, Bernard (47)—August 10, 1985
Val, Joe (58)—June 11, 1985
Valkenier, Willem A. (99)—April 23, 1986
Ventre, Humbert F.—January 10, 1986
Kemper, Ruth (83)—January 11, 1986
Wallace, Cedric (80)—August 19, 1985
Wells, William (78)—November 12, 1985
Williams, Charles R. (77)—September 15, 1985
Williams, Richard G. (54)—November 4, 1985
Wilson, Ralph M. (71)—April 12, 1986
Winer, Harold (81)—April 12, 1986
Wolfinsohn, Wolfe (86)—February 26, 1986
Woods, Chris (59)—July 4, 1985

PRODUCERS, DIRECTORS, CHOREOGRAPHERS

Aldrich, Richard (83)—March 31, 1986
Ashley, Ira (75)—November 18, 1985
Ask, Eli (52)—December 26, 1985
Awe, Jim (66)—December 11, 1985
Beckerman, Bernard (64)—October 7, 1985
Boulting, John (71)—June 17, 1985
Castellani, Renato (72)—December 28, 1985
Cherry, Wal (53)—March 7, 1986
Crampton, Esme—March 26, 1986
Cushingham, Jack (61)—July 5, 1985
Dollar, William Henry (78)—February 28, 1986
Eisenstadt, Gail (39)—February 9, 1986
Fletcher, Allen (63)—August 28, 1985
Gerasimov, Sergei (79)—November 28, 1985
Gnys, Charles (52)—March 13, 1986
Goldblatt, Larry (45)—February 15, 1986
Greene, Herbert (64)—September 25, 1985
Hewes, Margaret (87)—August 15, 1985
Hicks, David (48)—March 14, 1986
Hijikata, Tatsumi (57)—January 25, 1986
Hirschman, Herbert (71)—July 3, 1985
Kanter, David (76)—December 8, 1985
Kondolf, George (85)—December 25, 1985
Kosloff, Maurice (81)—January 22, 1986
Krokyn, Roberta Barrett (67)—December 18, 1985

Levine, Bill (74)—November 27, 1985
MacEwen, Walter (79)—April 15, 1986
Milton, Frank (66)—July 14, 1985
Moore, Charles (57)—January 23, 1986
Musgrove, Stanley E. (61)—March 15, 1986
Nixon-Browne, Jack (48)—March 14, 1986
Olney, Julian—November 7, 1985
Paris, Jerry (60)—March 31, 1986
Paylow, Clark L. (66)—September 25, 1985
Perry, Elaine (64)—January 30, 1986
Popplewell, Leslie (88)—May 1986
Preminger, Otto (79–80)—April 23, 1986
Schapiro, Phil (68)—December 7, 1985
Schenker, Joel W. (81)—August 3, 1985
Scherkenbach, Bobby Lee (47)—April 22, 1986
Skirball, Jack H. (89)—December 8, 1985
Spiegel, Sam (84)—December 31, 1985
Stevenson, Robert (81)—April 30, 1986
Victor, Lucia (74)—March 22, 1986
White, William H. (64)—July 14, 1985

CONDUCTORS

Almeida, Johnny Kameaaloha (83)—October 9, 1985
Bruno, Tony (82)—March 8, 1986
Callinicos, Constantine (60s)—January 17, 1986
Carner, Mosco (80)—August 3, 1985
Condie, Richard P. (87)—December 22, 1985
Dellicarri, Joseph (49)—August 20, 1985
Eisen, Sammy (82)—November 4, 1985
Fuchs, Harry L. (58)—April 4, 1986
Goss, John (43)—January 6, 1986
Hanscom, Isabelle D. (95)—April 6, 1986
Harrison, Guy Fraser (91)—February 20, 1986
Herrmann, Bud (60)—June 1, 1985
Hogan, Frank J. (77)—February 20, 1986
Hudkins, David (76)—August 6, 1985
Jenkins, Rae (81)—Spring 1985
Jiadosz, Joseph—September 7, 1985
Kalam, Endel (69)—December 11, 1985
King, Wayne (84)—July 16, 1985
Knight, Peter—July 30, 1985
Kroll, Bobby (early 70s)—October 30, 1985
Kutin, Alexander (87)—May 31, 1986
Kyser, Kay (79)—July 23, 1985
Miller, Frank (73)—January 6, 1986
Morris, Lawrence E. (83)—August 14, 1985
Murray, Max (70)—March 16, 1986
Oakley, Scott (36)—March 20, 1986
Ray, Floyd (76)—November 19, 1985
Robinson, Johnny (81)—January 28, 1986
Rosenstock, Joseph (90)—October 17, 1985
Staulcup, Jack Sr. (72)—May 10, 1985

Thal, Pierson (73)—September 20, 1985
Wooding, Sam (90)—August 1, 1985
Woolf, Sammy (78)—January 18, 1986

CRITICS

Blesh, Rudi (86)—August 25, 1985
Brennan, Barry (43)—July 27, 1985
Bruun, Paul M. (79)—October 25, 1985
Canaday, John (78)—July 19, 1985
Carberry, Edward H.—April 23, 1986
Crichton, Mamie—Fall 1985
Derobe, Jean (76)—September 1, 1985
Florquin, John (74)—September 11, 1985
Galey, Mathieu (51)—February 21, 1986
Gautier, Jean-Jacques (77)—April 20, 1986
Kalem, T.E. (65)—July 3, 1985
Keller, Hans (66)—November 6, 1985
Kennedy, James (72)—November 23, 1985
Kessell, Norman (82)—January 12, 1986
Kyrou, Adonis (62)—November 4, 1985
Leenhardt, Roger (83)—December 4, 1985
Martin, John—May 19, 1985
McKinnon, George (64)—November 19, 1985
Quinn, Frank P. (73)—May 23, 1986
Riccardi, Maria (26)—May 4, 1986
Saunders, Allen (86)—January 28, 1986
Schwartz, Edward P. (81)—March 21, 1985
Shocket, Dan (33)—May 4, 1985
Sobol, Louis (90)—February 9, 1986
Vigneron, Jean (57)—July 21, 1985
Zunser, Jesse (87)—November 27, 1985

COMPOSERS, LYRICISTS

Ahlert, Richard (63)—August 9, 1985
Alwyn, William (89)—September 12, 1985
Arlen, Harold (81)—April 23, 1986
Caussimon, Jean-Roger (67)—October 20, 1985
Chadwick, A.J. (63)—October 16, 1985
Cogane, Nelson (82)—July 12, 1985
Corday, Leo (83)—November 29, 1985
Creed, Linda (37)—April 10, 1986
Creston, Paul (78)—August 24, 1985
Elliott, William (41)—October 22, 1985
François, Carmille (84)—March 10, 1986
Greenfield, Howard (late 40s)—March 4, 1986
Heimo, Gustav H. (91)—January 29, 1986
Jackson, Calvin (66)—November 28, 1985
Lang, Philip J. (74)—February 22, 1986
Linke, Francesca Draper (37)—March 27, 1986
Lloyd, Alan (43)—March 30, 1986

Magidson, Herbert (79)—January 2, 1986
Maguire, Leo (80s)—December 17, 1985
Marks, Johnny (75)—September 3, 1985
Martinet, Henri (76)—November 27, 1985
May, Frederick (74)—September 10, 1985
McDowell, John Herbert (58)—September 3, 1985
Riddle, Nelson (64)—October 6, 1985
Rubbra, Edmund (84)—February 13, 1986
Rudhyar, Dane (90)—September 13, 1985
Schmidt-Boelcke, Werner (82)—November 6, 1985
Spoliansky, Mischa (86)—June 29, 1985
Stern, Jack (89)—August 16, 1985
Terry, George N. (79)—January 24, 1986
Velona, Anthony (65)—January 31, 1986
Warrack, Guy (86)—February 12, 1986
Watts, Grady (77)—January 8, 1986
Yardumian, Richard (68)—August 15, 1985

PLAYWRIGHTS

Aloma, René (38)—January 27, 1986
Arbuzov, Aleksei (77)—April 20, 1986
Baker-Bergen, Stuart (40)—May 9, 1986
Bernard-Luc, Jean (76)—May 18, 1985
Blount, Thom Patrick (42)—October 24, 1985
Boretz, Allen (85)—May 21, 1986
Craig, Robert Lewis (75)—December 12, 1985
Dobie, Laurence (58)—February 20, 1986
Dowell, Coleman (60)—August 3, 1985
Ehrlich, Ida (99)—February 22, 1986
Genet, Jean (75)—April 14, 1986
Howard, David Belasco (75)—February 9, 1986
Hanley, James (84)—November 11, 1985
Isherwood, Christopher (81)—January 4, 1986
Kamp, Irene Kittle (74)—June 15, 1985
Katayev, Valentin (89)—April 12, 1986
Keveson, Peter (70)—January 7, 1986
Koven, Stanley (54)—August 9, 1985
Lavery, Emmet (84)—January 1, 1986
Mackie, Philip (67)—December 23, 1985
Magdalany, Philip (49)—July 22, 1985
Nathan, Robert (91)—May 25, 1985
O'Donovan, John (64)—August 26, 1985
Ryskind, Morrie (89)—August 24, 1985
Sauvajon, Marc-Gilbert (75)—Spring 1985
Shue, Larry (38)—September 23, 1985
Whitney, Arthur O. (65)—April 5, 1986

DESIGNERS

Allison, Fred (42)—November 3, 1985
Colin, Paul (93)—June 18, 1985

Davis, Rick (71)—August 28, 1985
Elsen, Charles R. (39)—May 28, 1985
Kardos, Elizabeth (85)—April 29, 1985
Lovejoy, Robin (61)—December 14, 1985
Newton, Jim (45)—March 8, 1986
Pratt, John (74)—March 26, 1986
Rock, Norman (77)—November 14, 1985
Weintraub, Bruce (33)—December 14, 1985
Wilhelm, Kurt (41)—March 24, 1986

OTHERS

Akins, Virgil (46)—March 18, 1986
    Foundation for the Vital Arts
Baker, Robert (48)—September 14, 1985
    Talent agent
Billups, Kenneth Brown (67)—October 10, 1985
    National Association of Negro Musicians
Blair, E. Blake Jr. (82)—November 21, 1985
    Patron, Lyric Opera Company of Chicago
Blum, Stella (68)—July 31, 1985
    Costume Institute of Metropolitan
Brandon, Richard (80)—May 4, 1985
    Yale Puppeteers
Brandt, Bernard B. (75)—September 23, 1985
    Brandt Theaters chain
Brescia, Matthew Richard (76)—April 16, 1986
    Variety correspondent
Butrico, Tony (73)—October 19, 1985
    Maitre d'hotel
Chiantia, Salvatore (67)—September 13, 1985
    National Music Publisher's Association
Collingwood, Charles (68)—October 3, 1985
    CBS correspondent
Cote, Marie (78)—February 4, 1986
    Seven Gables actor's boarding house
Courtright, Hernando (81)—February 24, 1986
    Beverly Hills and Wilshire hotels
Cowles, Gardner Jr. (82)—July 8, 1985
    Cowles Communications
de Beauvoir, Simone (78)—April 14, 1986
    Author
de Gunzburg, Aileen Bronfman (60)—July 1, 1985
    Patron of arts
DiGiullo, Peter (81)—April 13, 1986
    Club 31, Buffalo
Dipson, William (69)—December 7, 1985
    Dipson Theaters
Dooley, John (57)—November 30, 1985
    Editor
Douglas, Torrington (84)—February 23, 1986
    London publicist

Efron, Morry (71)—March 18, 1985
    Company manager
Elliot, Nan (87)—February 1, 1986
    Vaudeville booker
Epstein, Carol (43)—November 20, 1985
    Margaret Herrick Library
Evans, R. Paul (42)—September 8, 1985
    Theatrical attorney
Ewen, David (78)—December 28, 1985
    Author
Felt, Elaine Edelman (72)—July 23, 1985
    NYC Ballet
Fenton, Robert J. Jr. (27)—July 11, 1985
    Shubert Organization
Fielding, Maisie J. (59)—November 23, 1985
    Theatrical costuming
Finocchio, Joseph (88)—January 13, 1986
    San Francisco female impersonation club
Francis, Muriel Bultman (77)—May 1, 1986
    Publicist
Garfield, Sid (72)—July 21, 1985
    Publicist
Gelb, Jimmy (79)—October 16, 1985
    Stage manager
Goodstein, Jacob I. (91)—February 3, 1986
    Actors Fund of America
Graham, Marian (84)—December 12, 1985
    Publicist
Grant, Harlan F.—May 26, 1985
    Weston, Vt. Playhouse
Graves, Robert (90)—December 7, 1985
    Poet
Grossman, Albert B. (59)—January 25, 1986
    Personal manager
Harris, Carson (72)—January 11, 1986
    Road manager
Hartke, Rev. Gilbert V. (79)—February 21, 1986
    Catholic University Drama Department
Haverlin, Carl (86)—August 27, 1985
    Broadcast Music, Inc.
Hedges, David (48)—December 25, 1985
    Company manager
Hedrick, A. Earl (89)—September 18, 1985
    Art Director's Guild
Herbert, Frank (65)—February 11, 1986
    Author
Highton, Hector (61)—September 28, 1985
    Stage manager
Hill, Robert (33)—August 26, 1985
    Herbert Barrett Management
Hobson, Laura Z. (85)—February 28, 1986
    Author
Holtzmann, Sondra (78)—January 16, 1986
    Melody Tent
Horowitz, Meyer (87)—July 22, 1985
    Nightclub owner

Hutner, Mike (71)—July 25, 1985
  Publicist
Jacobi, Henry N. (72)—July 9, 1985
  Voice teacher
Jaroff, Serge (89)—October 5, 1985
  Don Cossack Chorus
Jory, Margaret (48)—July 10, 1985
  ASCAP
Kamen, Stan (60)—February 20, 1986
  William Morris Agency
Kane, Murray (70)—January 31, 1986
  Personal manager
Kant, Bernard J. (43)—August 11, 1985
  Company manager
Kaselow, Joseph (73)—April 9, 1986
  Advertising columnist
Koeppel, Max E. (86)—September 24, 1985
  Brooklyn Philharmonic
Kramer, Maria (103)—March 12, 1986
  Big band bookings
Kusevitsky, David (74)—July 31, 1985
  Cantor
Kvapil, Otto A. (55)—November 17, 1985
  Xavier Theater Arts Dept.
Lawler, T. Newman (77)—July 13, 1985
  Attorney
Ledbetter, Les (44)—July 29, 1985
  Reporter
Lehman, John (79)—September 9, 1985
  Drama teacher
Lowinsky, Edward E. (77)—October 11,
  1985
  Musicologist
Malamud, Bernard (71)—March 18, 1986
  Author
Mamlin, Relba (67)—April 19, 1986
  Drama teacher
Maree, A. Morgan Jr. (85)—November 20,
  1985
  Business manager
McCaffrey, Bill (86)—August 28, 1985
  Talent agent
McKnight, Vincent (81)—September 22,
  1985
  Company manager
McQueeny, James R. (77)—March 8, 1986
  Publicist
Miller, Mabel R. (79)—July 30, 1985
  Shubert Organization
Miranda, Vincent (52)—June 2, 1985
  Pussycat Theaters chain
Nagel, William (32)—January 2, 1986
  Company manager
North, John Ringling (81)—June 4, 1985
  Ringling Bros. Circus
Norton, Kay—Winter 1985
  Publicist

Passantino, Charles V. (82)—September 14,
  1985
  Passantino Printing Co.
Perkes, William (80)—March 30, 1986
  Irish showman
Polan, Barron R. (72)—March 20, 1986
  Agent
Roberts, Renee (71)—January 26, 1986
  Publicist
Rubin, Milton (70s)—January 16, 1986
  Publicist
Safier, Gloria (63)—October 9, 1985
  Agent
Santy, Dr. Albert Christy (80)—August 10,
  1985
  Health care for performing artists
Sapper, Jerry (59)—March 22, 1986
  Artist
Scarne, John (82)—July 7, 1985
  International gambling authority
Schneider, Joseph (93)—March 24, 1986
  Steuben's Vienna Rooms
Schuller, William (72)—April 29, 1986
  Talent agent
Schwartz, Muriel (58)—March 6, 1986
  Publicist
Selby, Anne (51)—February 11, 1986
  Stratford (Ont.) Festival
Shaltz, Simon J. (74)—June 19, 1985
  Variety correspondent
Shanley, John P. (70)—November 28, 1985
  Editor
Shannon, Bernadette (35)—August 12, 1985
  Publicist
Shauer, Melville A. (90)—February 7, 1986
  Talent agent
Shonting, Rene Cummings (74)—February 14,
  1986
  Publicist
Shubert, Kerttu Helena (71)—July 12, 1985
  John Shubert's widow
Sindell, Bernard (72)—July 22, 1985
  Agent
Stellings, Ernest G. (85)—September 28, 1985
  Theater Owners of America
Stern, Jean Gordon (81)—October 22, 1985
  Dance Magazine
Stoller, Morris (74)—March 24, 1986
  William Morris Agency
Storer, Taylor (29)—July 18, 1985
  New Music Distribution Service
Stout, Leslie J. (89)—August 18, 1985
  Publicist
Strombel, Tom (65)—March 11, 1986
  Publicist
Tanner, Marion (94)—October 30, 1985
  Auntie Mame prototype

Terry, Carol (61)—April 8, 1986
  Psychotherapist
Thomason, A. Mims (74)—July 26, 1985
  UPI
Tillstrom, Burr (68)—December 6, 1985
  Kukla, Fran & Ollie
Tompkins, Elizabeth Vreeland (57)—August 3,
  1985
  Arts commentator
Tubens, Joe—April 25, 1986
  Hair designer
Van Dyke, Willard (79)—January 23, 1986
  Museum of Modern Art
Veeck, Bill (71)—January 2, 1985
  Baseball showman
Wallace, Maggie McDonald—June 17, 1985
  Publicist
Weichel, Daisy—June 7, 1985
  Publicist

Weisbord, Sam (74)—May 6, 1986
  William Morris Agency
Weiss, Benjamin (71)—February 14, 1986
  New Theater, Philadelphia
West, John K. (78)—October 14, 1985
  California Special Olympics
White, E.B. (86)—October 1, 1985
  Author
Wolfe, Bernard (70)—October 28, 1985
  Author
Wollock, Abe V. (65)—June 24, 1985
  UCLA Dept. of Theater Arts
Wood, Audrey (80)—December 27, 1985
  Agent
Zalken, William (82)—December 30, 1985
  St. Louis Symphony

THE BEST PLAYS, 1894–1985

Listed in alphabetical order below are all those works selected as Best Plays in previous volumes in the *Best Plays* series. Opposite each title is given the volume in which the play appears, its opening date and its total number of performances. Two separate opening-date and performance-number entries signify two separate engagements off Broadway and on Broadway when the original production was transferred from one area to the other, usually in an off-to-on direction. Those plays marked with an asterisk (*) were still playing on June 2, 1986 and their number of performances was figured through June 1, 1986. Adaptors and translators are indicated by (ad) and (tr), the symbols (b), (m) and (l) stand for the author of the book, music and lyrics in the cast of musicals and (c) signifies the credit for the show's conception.

NOTE: A season-by-season listing, rather than an alphabetical one, of the 500 Best Plays in the first 50 volumes, starting with the yearbook for the season of 1919–1920, appears in *The Best Plays of 1968–69.*

PLAY	VOLUME	OPENED	PERFS
ABE LINCOLN IN ILLINOIS—Robert E. Sherwood	38–39.	.Oct. 15, 1938.	. 472
ABRAHAM LINCOLN—John Drinkwater	19–20.	.Dec. 15, 1919.	. 193
ACCENT ON YOUTH—Samson Raphaelson	34–35.	.Dec. 25, 1934.	. 229
ADAM AND EVA—Guy Bolton, George Middleton	19–20.	.Sept. 13, 1919.	. 312
ADAPTATION—Elaine May; and NEXT—Terrence McNally	68–69.	.Feb. 10, 1969.	. 707
AFFAIRS OF STATE—Louis Verneuil	50–51.	.Sept. 25, 1950.	. 610
AFTER THE FALL—Arthur Miller	63–64.	.Jan. 23, 1964.	. 208
AFTER THE RAIN—John Bowen	67–68.	.Oct. 9, 1967.	. 64
AGNES OF GOD—John Pielmeier	81–82.	.Mar. 30, 1982.	. 486
AH, WILDERNESS!—Eugene O'Neill	33–34.	.Oct. 2, 1933.	. 289
AIN'T SUPPOSED TO DIE A NATURAL DEATH—(b, m, l) Melvin Van Peebles	71–72.	.Oct. 7, 1971.	. 325
ALIEN CORN—Sidney Howard	32–33.	.Feb. 20, 1933.	. 98
ALISON'S HOUSE—Susan Glaspell	30–31.	.Dec. 1, 1930.	. 41
ALL MY SONS—Arthur Miller	46–47.	.Jan. 29, 1947.	. 328
ALL OVER TOWN—Murray Schisgal	74–75.	.Dec. 12, 1974.	. 233
ALL THE WAY HOME—Tad Mosel, based on James Agee's novel *A Death in the Family*	60–61.	.Nov. 30, 1960.	. 333
ALLEGRO—(b,l) Oscar Hammerstein II, (m) Richard Rodgers.	47–48.	.Oct. 10, 1947.	. 315
AMADEUS—Peter Shaffer	80–81.	.Dec. 17, 1980.	. 1,181
AMBUSH—Arthur Richman	21–22.	.Oct. 10, 1921.	. 98
AMERICA HURRAH—Jean-Claude van Itallie	66–67.	.Nov. 6, 1966.	. 634
AMERICAN BUFFALO—David Mamet	76–77.	.Feb. 16, 1977.	. 135
AMERICAN WAY, THE—George S. Kaufman, Moss Hart	38–39.	.Jan. 21, 1939.	. 164
AMPHITRYON 38—Jean Giraudoux, (ad) S. N. Behrman	37–38.	.Nov. 1, 1937.	. 153
AND A NIGHTINGALE SANG—C.P. Taylor	83–84.	.Nov. 27, 1983.	. 177
ANDERSONVILLE TRIAL, THE—Saul Levitt	59–60.	.Dec. 29, 1959.	. 179
ANDORRA—Max Frisch, (ad) George Tabori	62–63.	.Feb. 9, 1963.	. 9
ANGEL STREET—Patrick Hamilton	41–42.	.Dec. 5, 1941.	. 1,295
ANGELS FALL—Lanford Wilson	82–83.	.Oct. 17, 1982.	. 65
ANIMAL KINGDOM, THE—Philip Barry	31–32.	.Jan. 12, 1932.	. 183
ANNA CHRISTIE—Eugene O'Neill	21–22.	.Nov. 2, 1921.	. 177
ANNA LUCASTA—Philip Yordan	44–45.	.Aug. 30, 1944.	. 957
ANNE OF THE THOUSAND DAYS—Maxwell Anderson	48–49.	.Dec. 8, 1948.	. 286

PLAY	VOLUME	OPENED	PERFS
ANNIE—(b) Thomas Meehan, (m) Charles Strouse, (l) Martin Charnin, based on Harold Gray's comic strip "Little Orphan Annie"	76–77.	.Apr. 21, 1977.	. 2,377
ANOTHER LANGUAGE—Rose Franken	31–32.	.Apr. 25, 1932.	. 344
ANOTHER PART OF THE FOREST—Lillian Hellman	46–47.	.Nov. 20, 1946.	. 182
ANTIGONE—Jean Anouilh, (ad) Lewis Galantiere	45–46.	.Feb. 18, 1946.	. 64
APPLAUSE—(b) Betty Comden and Adolph Green, (m) Charles Strouse, (l) Lee Adams, based on the film *All About Eve* and the original story by Mary Orr	69–70.	.Mar. 30, 1970.	. 896
APPLE TREE, THE—(b,l) Sheldon Harnick, (b, m) Jerry Bock, add'l (b) Jerome Coopersmith, based on stories by Mark Twain, Frank R. Stockton and Jules Feiffer	66–67.	.Oct. 18, 1966.	. 463
ARSENIC AND OLD LACE—Joseph Kesselring	40–41.	.Jan. 10, 1941.	. 1,444
AS HUSBANDS GO—Rachel Crothers	30–31.	.Mar. 5, 1931.	. 148
AS IS—William M. Hoffman	84–85.	.Mar. 10, 1985.	. 49
	84–85.	.May 1, 1985.	. 285
ASHES—David Rudkin	76–77.	.Jan. 25, 1977.	. 167
AUTUMN GARDEN, THE—Lillian Hellman	50–51.	.Mar. 7, 1951.	. 101
AWAKE AND SING—Clifford Odets	34–35.	.Feb. 19, 1935.	. 209
BAD MAN, THE—Porter Emerson Browne	20–21.	.Aug. 30, 1920.	. 350
BAD HABITS—Terrence McNally	73–74.	.Feb. 4, 1974.	. 273
BAD SEED—Maxwell Anderson, based on William March's novel	54–55.	.Dec. 8, 1954.	. 332
BARBARA FRIETCHIE—Clyde Fitch	99–09.	.Oct. 23, 1899.	. 83
BAREFOOT IN ATHENS—Maxwell Anderson	51–52.	.Oct. 31, 1951.	. 30
BAREFOOT IN THE PARK—Neil Simon	63–64.	.Oct. 23, 1963.	. 1,530
BARRETTS OF WIMPOLE STREET, THE—Rudolf Besier	30–31.	.Feb. 9, 1931.	. 370
BECKET—Jean Anouilh, (tr) Lucienne Hill	60–61.	.Oct. 5, 1960.	. 193
BEDROOM FARCE—Alan Ayckbourn	78–79.	.Mar. 29, 1979.	. 278
BEGGAR ON HORSEBACK—George S. Kaufman, Marc Connelly	23–24.	.Feb. 12, 1924.	. 224
BEHOLD THE BRIDEGROOM—George Kelly	27–28.	.Dec. 26, 1927.	. 88
BELL, BOOK AND CANDLE—John van Druten	50–51.	.Nov. 14, 1950.	. 233
BELL FOR ADANO, A—Paul Osborn, based on John Hersey's novel	44–45.	.Dec. 6, 1944.	. 304
BENT—Martin Sherman	79–80.	.Dec. 2, 1979.	. 240
BERKELEY SQUARE—John L. Balderston	29–30.	.Nov. 4, 1929.	. 229
BERNARDINE—Mary Chase	52–53.	.Oct. 16, 1952.	. 157
BEST LITTLE WHOREHOUSE IN TEXAS, THE—(b) Larry L. King, Peter Masterson, (m,l) Carol Hall	77–78.	.Apr. 17, 1978.	. 64
	78–79.	.June 19, 1978.	. 1,639
BEST MAN, THE—Gore Vidal	59–60.	.Mar. 31, 1960.	. 520
BETRAYAL—Harold Pinter	79–80.	.Jan. 5, 1980.	. 170
BEYOND THE HORIZON—Eugene O'Neill	19–20.	.Feb. 2, 1920.	. 160
BIG FISH, LITTLE FISH—Hugh Wheeler	60–61.	.Mar. 15, 1961.	. 101
BILL OF DIVORCEMENT, A—Clemence Dane	21–22.	.Oct. 10, 1921.	. 173
BILLY BUDD—Louis O. Coxe, Robert Chapman, based on Herman Melville's novel	50–51.	.Feb. 10, 1951.	. 105
*BILOXI BLUES—Neil Simon	84–85.	.Mar. 28, 1985.	. 492
BIOGRAPHY—S. N. Behrman	32–33.	.Dec. 12, 1932.	. 267
BLACK COMEDY—Peter Shaffer	66–67.	.Feb. 12, 1967.	. 337
BLITHE SPIRIT—Noel Coward	41–42.	.Nov. 5, 1941.	. 657
BOESMAN AND LENA—Athol Fugard	70–71.	.June 22, 1970.	. 205
BORN YESTERDAY—Garson Kanin	45–46.	.Feb. 4, 1946.	. 1,642
BOTH YOUR HOUSES—Maxwell Anderson	32–33.	.Mar. 6, 1933.	. 72
BOY MEETS GIRL—Bella and Samuel Spewack	35–36.	.Nov. 27, 1935.	. 669

PLAY	VOLUME	OPENED	PERFS
CLOUD 9—Caryl Churchill	80–81.	.May 18, 1981. .	971
CLUTTERBUCK—Benn W. Levy	49–50.	.Dec. 3, 1949. .	218
COCKTAIL PARTY, THE—T. S. Eliot	49–50.	.Jan. 21, 1950. .	409
COLD WIND AND THE WARM, THE—S. N. Behrman	58–59.	.Dec. 8, 1958. .	120
COLLECTION, THE—Harold Pinter	62–63.	.Nov. 26, 1962. .	578
COME BACK, LITTLE SHEBA—William Inge	49–50.	.Feb. 15, 1950. .	191
COMEDIANS—Trevor Griffiths	76–77.	.Nov. 28, 1976. .	145
COMMAND DECISION—William Wister Haines	47–48.	.Oct. 1, 1947. .	408
COMPANY—(b) George Furth, (m, l) Stephen Sondheim	69–70.	.Apr. 26, 1970. .	705
COMPLAISANT LOVER, THE—Graham Greene	61–62.	.Nov. 1, 1961. .	101
CONDUCT UNBECOMING—Barry England	70–71.	.Oct. 12, 1970. .	144
CONFIDENTIAL CLERK, THE—T. S. Eliot	53–54.	.Feb. 11, 1954. .	117
CONNECTION, THE—Jack Gelber (picked as a supplement to the Best Plays)	60–61.	.Feb. 22, 1961. .	722
CONSTANT WIFE, THE—W. Somerset Maugham	26–27.	.Nov. 20, 1926. .	295
CONTRACTOR, THE—David Storey	73–74.	.Oct. 17, 1973. .	72
COQUETTE—George Abbott, Ann Preston Bridgers	27–28.	.Nov. 8, 1927. .	366
CORN IS GREEN, THE—Emlyn Williams	40–41.	.Nov. 26, 1940. .	477
COUNTRY GIRL, THE—Clifford Odets	50–51.	.Nov. 10, 1950. .	235
COUNTY CHAIRMAN, THE—George Ade	99–09.	.Nov. 24, 1903. .	222
CRADLE SONG, THE—Gregorio & Maria Martinez Sierra, (tr) John Garrett Underhill	26–27.	.Jan. 24, 1927. .	57
CRAIG'S WIFE—George Kelly	25–26.	.Oct. 12, 1925. .	360
CREATION OF THE WORLD AND OTHER BUSINESS, THE— Arthur Miller	72–73.	.Nov. 30, 1972. .	20
CREEPS—David E. Freeman	73–74.	.Dec. 4, 1973. .	15
CRIMES OF THE HEART—Beth Henley	80–81.	.Dec. 9, 1980. .	35
	81–82.	.Nov. 4, 1981. .	535
CRIMINAL CODE, THE—Martin Flavin	29–30.	.Oct. 2, 1929. .	173
CRUCIBLE, THE—Arthur Miller	52–53.	.Jan. 22, 1953. .	197
CYNARA—H. M. Harwood, R. F. Gore-Browne	31–32.	.Nov. 2, 1931. .	210
DA—Hugh Leonard	77–78.	.May 1, 1978. .	697
DAISY MAYME—George Kelly	26–27.	.Oct. 25, 1926. .	112
DAMASK CHEEK, THE—John van Druten, Lloyd Morris	42–43.	.Oct. 22, 1942. .	93
DANCE AND THE RAILROAD, THE—David Henry Hwang	81–82.	.July 16, 1981. .	181
DANCING MOTHERS—Edgar Selwyn, Edmund Goulding	24–25.	.Aug. 11, 1924. .	312
DARK AT THE TOP OF THE STAIRS, THE—William Inge	57–58.	.Dec. 5, 1957. .	468
DARK IS LIGHT ENOUGH, THE—Christopher Fry	54–55.	.Feb. 23, 1955. .	69
DARKNESS AT NOON—Sidney Kingsley, based on Arthur Koestler's novel	50–51.	.Jan. 13, 1951. .	186
DARLING OF THE GODS, THE—David Belasco, John Luther Long	90–09.	.Dec. 3, 1902. .	182
DAUGHTERS OF ATREUS—Robert Turney	36–37.	.Oct. 14, 1936. .	13
DAY IN THE DEATH OF JOE EGG, A—Peter Nichols	67–68.	.Feb. 1, 1968. .	154
DEAD END—Sidney Kingsley	35–36.	.Oct. 28, 1935. .	687
DEADLY GAME, THE—James Yaffe, based on Friedrich Duerrenmatt's novel	59–60.	.Feb. 2, 1960. .	39
DEAR RUTH—Norman Krasna	44–45.	.Dec. 13, 1944. .	683
DEATH OF A SALESMAN—Arthur Miller	48–49.	.Feb. 10, 1949. .	742
DEATH TAKES A HOLIDAY—Alberto Casella, (ad) Walter Ferris	29–30.	.Dec. 26, 1929. .	180
DEATHTRAP—Ira Levin	77–78.	.Feb. 26, 1978. .	1,793
DEBURAU—Sacha Guitry, (ad) Harley Granville Barker	20–21.	.Dec. 23, 1920. .	189
DECISION—Edward Chodorov	43–44.	.Feb. 2, 1944. .	160
DECLASSEE—Zoë Akins	19–20.	.Oct. 6, 1919. .	257

PLAY	VOLUME	OPENED	PERFS
SEARCHING WIND, THE—Lillian Hellman	43–44.	.Apr. 12, 1944. .	318
SEASCAPE—Edward Albee	74–75.	.Jan. 26, 1975. .	65
SEASON IN THE SUN—Wolcott Gibbs	50–51.	.Sept. 28, 1950. .	367
SECOND THRESHOLD—Philip Barry	50–51.	.Jan. 2, 1951. .	126
SECRET SERVICE—William Gillette	94–99.	.Oct. 5, 1896. .	176
SEPARATE TABLES—Terence Rattigan	56–57.	.Oct. 25, 1956. .	332
SERENADING LOUIE—Lanford Wilson	75–76.	.May 2, 1976. .	33
SERPENT, THE—Jean-Claude van Itallie	69–70.	.May 29, 1970. .	3
SEVEN KEYS TO BALDPATE—(ad) George M. Cohan, from the novel by Earl Derr Biggers	09–19.	.Sept. 22, 1913. .	320
1776—(b) Peter Stone, (m, l) Sherman Edwards, based on a conception of Sherman Edwards	68–69.	.Mar. 16, 1969. .	1,217
SHADOW AND SUBSTANCE—Paul Vincent Carroll	37–38.	.Jan. 26, 1938. .	274
SHADOW BOX, THE—Michael Cristofer	76–77.	.Mar. 31, 1977. .	315
SHADOW OF HEROES—(see *Stone and Star*)	. .		. .
SHE LOVES ME—(b) Joe Masteroff, based on Miklos Laszlo's play *Parfumerie,* (l) Sheldon Harnick, (m) Jerry Bock	62–63.	.Apr. 23, 1963. .	301
SHINING HOUR, THE—Keith Winter	33–34.	.Feb. 13, 1934. .	121
SHORT EYES—Miguel Piñero	73–74.	.Feb. 28, 1974. .	54
	73–74.	.May 23, 1974. .	102
SHOW-OFF, THE—George Kelly	23–24.	.Feb. 5, 1924. .	571
SHRIKE, THE—Joseph Kramm	51–52.	.Jan. 15, 1952. .	161
SILVER CORD, THE—Sidney Howard	26–27.	.Dec. 20, 1926. .	112
SILVER WHISTLE, THE—Robert E. McEnroe	48–49.	.Nov. 24, 1948. .	219
SIX CYLINDER LOVE—William Anthony McGuire	21–22.	.Aug. 25, 1921. .	430
6 RMS RIV VU—Bob Randall	72–73.	.Oct. 17, 1972. .	247
SKIN GAME, THE—John Galsworthy	20–21.	.Oct. 20, 1920. .	176
SKIN OF OUR TEETH, THE—Thornton Wilder	42–43.	.Nov. 18, 1942. .	359
SKIPPER NEXT TO GOD—Jan de Hartog	47–48.	.Jan. 4, 1948. .	93
SKYLARK—Samson Raphaelson	39–40.	.Oct. 11, 1939. .	256
SLEUTH—Anthony Shaffer	70–71.	.Nov. 12, 1970. .	1,222
SLOW DANCE ON THE KILLING GROUND—William Hanley	64–65.	.Nov. 30, 1964. .	88
SLY FOX—Larry Gelbart, based on *Volpone* by Ben Jonson	76–77.	.Dec. 14, 1976. .	495
SMALL CRAFT WARNINGS—Tennessee Williams	71–72.	.Apr. 2, 1972. .	192
SOLDIER'S PLAY, A—Charles Fuller	81–82.	.Nov. 20, 1981. .	468
SOLDIER'S WIFE—Rose Franken	44–45.	.Oct. 4, 1944. .	253
SPLIT SECOND—Dennis McIntyre	84–85.	.June 7, 1984. .	147
SQUAW MAN, THE—Edwin Milton Royle	99–09.	.Oct. 23, 1905. .	222
STAGE DOOR—George S. Kaufman, Edna Ferber	36–37.	.Oct. 22, 1936. .	169
STAIRCASE—Charles Dyer	67–68.	.Jan. 10, 1968. .	61
STAR-WAGON, THE—Maxwell Anderson	37–38.	.Sept. 29, 1937. .	223
STATE OF THE UNION—Howard Lindsay, Russel Crouse	45–46.	.Nov. 14, 1945. .	765
STEAMBATH—Bruce Jay Friedman	70–71.	.June 30, 1970. .	128
STICKS AND BONES—David Rabe	71–72.	.Nov. 7, 1971. .	121
	71–72.	.Mar. 1, 1972. .	245
STONE AND STAR—Robert Ardrey (also called *Shadow of Heroes*)	61–62.	.Dec. 5, 1961. .	20
STOP THE WORLD—I WANT TO GET OFF—(b, l, m) Leslie Bricusse, Anthony Newley	62–63.	.Oct. 3, 1962. .	555
STORM OPERATION—Maxwell Anderson	43–44.	.Jan. 11, 1944. .	23
STORY OF MARY SURRATT, THE—John Patrick	46–47.	.Feb. 8, 1947. .	11
STRANGE INTERLUDE—Eugene O'Neill	27–28.	.Jan. 30, 1928. .	426
STREAMERS—David Rabe	75–76.	.Apr. 21, 1976. .	478
STREET SCENE—Elmer Rice	28–29.	.Jan. 10, 1929. .	601
STREETCAR NAMED DESIRE, A—Tennessee Williams	47–48.	.Dec. 3, 1947. .	855

INDEX

Play titles appear in **bold face**. *Bold face italic* page numbers refer to those pages where complete cast and credit listings for New York productions may be found.

499